TRANSNATIONAL

WOMEN'S RIGHTS AND
POLITICAL PARTICIPATION

Comparative
WOMEN'S
RIGHTS
and
POLITICAL
PARTICIPATION
IN EUROPE

Gisbert H. Flanz

 Transnational Publishers, Inc.
Dobbs Ferry, New York

Library of Congress Cataloging in Publication Data

Flanz, Gisbert H.
  Comparative women's rights and political participation in Europe.

  Bibliography: p.
  Includes Index.
  1. Women—Legal status, laws, etc.—Europe.
2. Women's rights—Europe. 3. Women in politics—
Europe. I. Title.
LAW   346.401′ 34   82-19317
ISBN 0-941320-02-2   344.06134

Manufactured in the United States of America

CONTENTS

iii

PART IV: WOMEN'S RIGHTS AND INTER-
NATIONAL ORGANIZATIONS

APPENDIX

Preface

This comparative study is primarily concerned with the contemporary status of women in all the thirty-four countries of Europe. It is an ambitious and complex undertaking not only because of its geographical scope but also because it requires research in several disciplines and languages. To date many important primary materials have not been readily available and after they were obtained were not easily translated.

Contrary to what is often said, women's studies are not for women only and this book is intended to accomplish more than to fill a gap in a rapidly expanding field of study. It also seeks to compensate for the unfortunate but persistent one-sidedness of the major textbooks on comparative politics. Although some of these books devote a few pages to "women in politics" in one or two countries of Europe, they fail to address themselves to the issues of inequality and inequity in various political systems. In many universities considerable progress has been made in developing genuinely interdisciplinary programs. The comparative study of women's rights and political participation in selected countries can contribute much to an innovative and productive program by linking historical studies of specific countries with analyses of their legal and political systems, their contemporary economic and social structures as well as their prevailing value systems. Broadly gauged studies of this kind show that cross-national studies must also take into account internal differences which are rooted in a variety of conditions and traditions.

Before embarking upon the study of women's rights and movements in each of the countries of Europe, it is necessary to clarify the various meanings which have been given to the terms "women's rights" and "political participation" over a period of nearly two centuries. This is done in the introductory chapter entitled: "Women's Rights and Political Participation: Historical and Ideological Trends."

As the Table of Contents shows, the comparative material has been arranged in three clearly defined periods. Within each period four area groups have been identified: (1) The Scandinavian, (2) The West European (3) The Southern and Mediterranean and (4) the East European. This grouping is not merely geographic but refers also to certain cultural, institutional and ideological affinities. The arrangement is continued in the Appendix, which contains relevant legislation from each area, as well as resolutions and directives from international and non-governmental organizations.

After the three time-periods, Part IV takes into consideration the important part played by international and non-governmental organizations. In the concluding chapter, an attempt is made to assess the achievements of the thirty-four European countries and these various international organizations. Finally, a comprehensive Bibliography is included for those who wish to study and put into broad perspective the struggle and relative gains women have made in Europe.

Acknowledgments

This ambitious undertaking could not have been accomplished without the collaboration of several specialists and scholars. I am indebted particularly to the following for their contributions to this book: Ilhan Arsel; Maria Leonor Beleza; Karen Shaw Kerpen; Blanka Kudej; Janine Mossuz-Lavau; Louis Pagonis; Mariette Sineau; Maria Regina Tavares da Silva. As Dr. Kudej's multilingual bibliography shows, there are considerable gaps in the literature, and I hope that this will be remedied in the near future. Hers is certainly the most comprehensive topical bibliography ever published, and she plans to update it periodically.

I also want to express my gratitude to several persons who have assisted me with my research in this country and on my annual trips in various parts of Europe during the past decade. A partial list includes the following: Hilde Albertini; Agnete Anderson; Claudette Apprill; Kaethi Belser; Anna Maria Stane Cervone; Marianne Dienes; Johanna Dohnal; Oskar Edlbacher; Felix Ermacora; Maeda Jones; Verena Laedruch-Feller; Inge Landberg; Elizabeth Lundberg; Walter Meinhart; Julie Mostov; Doris Muck; Edith Ostrovsky; C. Pichault; Kyra Sinkovsky; Katarina Sjoelander; Helga Stubianek; Margareta Wadstein; Friederike Zeitlhofer.

Finally, I want to thank several women who contributed greatly to the completion of this book. Heike Fenton, the publisher, Marjorie Moore, the editor, Barbara Moroch, who typed major parts of the manuscript, and my wife, Beth, who has always supported my efforts with patience and understanding.

The completion of the book was delayed about five months so that I could update the legislation of several countries. After completing my visiting professorship at the University of Vienna in May 1982, I was able to collect some material in several countries which had been published only a few days before my arrival. I apologize to those who ordered the book with the expectation that it would be ready in June and hope that they will conclude that it was worth waiting for.

HISTORICAL AND IDEOLOGICAL TRENDS IN WOMEN'S RIGHTS AND POLITICAL PARTICIPATION

Introductory Notes

What are "women's" rights? The name which is usually associated with this term is that of Mary Wollstonecraft whose "Vindication of the Rights of Women" was published in 1792. But she was not the first to use this term. Some three years earlier Olympe de Gouges, whose real name was Marie Aubry, had written "The Rights of the Woman" and addressed it to Queen Marie Antoinette. The format of her pamphlet was taken from the famous French "Declaration of the Rights of Man and Citizen" (1789). De Gouges' "Les Droits de la femme" was not "for women only." It was intended to defend the rights of all humans and to protect women from what she viewed as a "bizarre" blind principle of male domination. Like the earlier revolutionary document her "Les Droits de la femme" consists of a preamble and 17 articles. In addition, it has a "postambule."

Olympe de Gouges did not really formulate any distinctive or specific "women's rights". The rights of women were the rights of men extended to women. The underlying principles were equality and justice for all. There are a few references which might be interpreted as the basis for specific women's rights. For instance, in the original 1789 text Article XI, the free expression of thoughts and opinions is characterized as one of the most precious "human rights". Olympe de Gouges simply substituted "women's rights" for "human rights" but went on to state that "this freedom assures the legitimacy of fathers toward their children."

Critics may feel that this was a rather crude modification of the classical text, but there can be no doubt about the great need for such a principle because of the traditional right of fathers to disclaim paternity, which can still be found in many contemporary civil or "uncivil" codes. The author's intent becomes very clear in the subsequent sentence of her version of Article XI: "Every woman citizen can therefore say, I am the mother of the child which belongs to you and no barbaric prejudice should force the concealment of the truth." Olympe de Gouges amplified Article XVI, which in the original Declaration stated that the separation of powers and the guarantee of rights constituted the criterion of a real constitution, by adding that a constitution would be null and void "if the majority of the citizens who compose the nation did not 'cooperate' in its drafting." In a postscript to the "postambule" she noted that while the tract was being printed Talleyrand had expressed values which accorded with hers. She also added lavish praise for Lafayette. Olympe de Gouges did not have much chance to lead a movement for women's rights. She died on the guillotine, on March 11, 1793 not because of her advocacy of women's rights but because she had dared to condemn Robespierre for his cruel and unjust acts.

It is hardly necessary to characterize Mary Wollstonecraft's *Vindication of the Rights of Women* as a very influential work which laid the foundation for women's movements. It also contains certain elements from which a theory of women's rights could have been formulated. Although she wrote after Olympe de Gouges, it might be noted that as far back as 1787 she had written "Thoughts on the Education of Daughters" and in 1790 she had authored a "Vindication of the Rights of Men," which was directed against Burke. Her *Vindication of the Rights of Women* was dedicated to Talleyrand, who may or may not have been worthy of such a tribute. There is no evidence that he used his great influence to further the cause of women's rights. Much credit is due, however, to William Godwin, who married Mary Wollstonecraft in 1796 and who defended her cause after her premature and tragic death.

A few other names might be mentioned of those who used rational arguments in defense of gender equality and women's rights. In 1790 Condorcet wrote a most remarkable essay "On the Admission of Women to Civic Rights," in which he criticized "philosophers and legislators for having violated the principle of the equality of rights" in tangibly depriving one-half of the human race of the rights of taking part in the formation of laws by exclusion of women from the rights of citizenship. This essay may have influenced de Gouges' argument in Article XVI.

In 1792 T. G. von Hippel published an unusual treatise "On the Civic Amelioration of Women" (*Über die bürgerliche Verbesserung der Weiber*), which has recently been translated into English.

Jeremy Bentham also expressed some positive views on the rights of women. However, most of his followers failed to express similar values. Their silence has been interpreted as indicative of their essentially conservative orientation.

The period after the French Revolution was very unfavorable to the development of women's rights. This was a period in which some arch-conservatives called for the restoration of the pre-revolutionary order. The patriarchal principle, a fundamental part of that order, found its way into the codification of the French Civil Law in 1804 and the Austrian Civil Code of 1811. The liberal wave which set in around 1830 in most parts of Eastern Europe did relatively little for the cause of women's emancipation and women's rights, but some few individuals disagreed with the illiberalism of their liberal colleagues. Thus it may be noted that on April 22, 1832 two German radicals appealed to the Hambacher Fest to extend an invitation to German women (Frauen and Jungfrauen), whose political nonrecognition they characterized as a mistake and a blemish in the European order, "to grace and animate the gathering with their presence." Credit is also due to Saint-Simon and his followers who valued the emancipation of women as an essential element of progress. Some of them expressed ideas which seem to anticipate those of Karl Marx.

In the *Communist Manifesto* (1848) there are very few references to women, let alone women's rights. Marx and Engels charged that the bourgeois sees in his wife a mere instrument of production:

> He hears that the instruments of production are to be exploited in common, and, naturally, comes to no other conclusion, than that the lot of being common to all will likewise fall to the women. He has not even a suspicion that the real point aimed at is to do away with the status of women as mere instruments of production.

After 1848 women increasingly became instruments of production. As industrialization expanded in many parts of Western and Northern Europe women joined men to work in factories. They became part of the proletariat which Marx and his followers sought to organize into a class-conscious movement to do away with capitalism and "the exploitation of man by man." From the very beginning the Marxist socialists were preoccupied with the notions of class exploitation. They did not specifically address or analyze the exploitation of women. They were not interested in protective legislation for women because they were committed to a radical revolutionary change in the entire order—economic, political and social. This was the "spectre," as the *Communist Manifesto* stated at the very beginning, which was "haunting Europe". On June 20, 1848 across the Atlantic, another important "Manifesto" was issued at Seneca Falls. It was a clear and specific declaration which called for equal rights between men and women. Unlike the *Communist Manifesto*, which called for revolutions and a dictatorship of the proletariat, the women who met at Seneca Falls merely appealed for equality and equity. It was clear from the very beginning that the right to vote would have to be the centerpiece of any effective reform program. Although a few state constitutions were amended, all efforts to achieve the right to vote on the national level remained unsuccessful until 1920. What was accomplished were some changes in the law of property in a few states, but the overall progress was disappointing. Still these events in the United States, especially the women's movement from 1848 on, were very important for the development of the movement in several European countries. More specific references are made in the subsequent chapters to individual countries. What should be noted is the fact that these influences began before 1848, as has recently been documented.

The American influence on European feminists was less evident in the 1860s. The racial problem and the issue of slavery made it difficult for European liberals to present the United States as a model. However, they did know that many American feminists were also ardent abolitionists.

The word "emancipation" was widely used in Europe but mostly in connection with the issue of the abolition of slavery and serfdom. Unlike the American abolitionists, European advocates of the emancipation of serfs failed to make a connection with the issue of women's rights. Liberals did talk and write about the emancipation of women, but they usually meant little more than giving them access to higher education. Some of them favored legal reforms, especially in the field of family law, but they rarely touched on the basic issue of women's suffrage. The politicians, with very few exceptions, did not exert themselves on behalf of women's rights because they had to please only those who had the right to vote. Two events in the 1860s were of major importance for the development of women's rights and political participation. Both of them were the work of John Stuart Mill. In 1866, as a member of the House of Commons, he introduced a petition with 1,466 signatures which called for the grant of the right to vote to women who were heads of households. Florence Nightingale was among the last prominent individuals who had signed the petition. Mill failed, but he was encouraged that 75 members had voted for it.

The other important event came in 1869, when *The Subjection of Women* was published. To what an extent it was influenced or even written by his beloved wife Harriet Hardy Taylor has not been completely determined, but the basic arguments can readily be traced to John S. Mill's earlier writings and activities. *The Subjection of Women* has been widely regarded as the classical statement of liberal feminism as contrasted with the socialist ideology of women's emancipation.

From a comparative and historical point of view it is important to note that a most important socialist treatise, written by August Bebel, was not published until a decade later. During this intervening decade *The Subjection of Women* was translated into many European languages. Some of these translations are referred to in subsequent chapters. Judging by the references made to John S. Mill in the feminist literature of the 1870s he undoubtedly exerted great influence on the development of the feminist movement, but he did not really present a sufficiently specific-action program which could have served as the basis for legislation on women's rights. His arguments impressed many but not all proponents of bourgeois feminism. Hedwig Dohm (1833-1919), one of the foremost leaders of the feminist movement in Germany, was one of these independent thinkers. In her writings between 1874 and 1887 one can see certain changing attitudes as she sought to bridge the gap between liberal feminism and socialist emancipation. In 1887, after presenting an excellent summary of J. S. Mill's arguments, she provided an impressive list of counterarguments. Another remarkably independent writer and activist was Luise Otto-Peters (1819-1895), who is usually regarded as the founder of the German women's movement. Her views on the emancipation of women, like those of some of her Scandinavian contemporaries, were presented in the form of novels, but she also wrote about very specific women's rights and issues.

Before August Bebel's *Woman and Socialism* (*Die Frau und der Sozialismus*) there was no single work by a socialist writer which could be regarded as a counterpart to the *Subjection of Women*. Like John S. Mill's book, Bebel's *Die Frau und der Sozialismus* was translated into many languages. Most European Marxist-Socialists considered it the most authoritative statement of the "women's question". Another very influential theorist and activist of the socialist women's movement was Clara Zetkin (1857-1933). Like many of her predecessors, she studied to be a teacher but through her Russian-born husband came into contact with more revolutionary personalities. As indicated in the title of her first book, *Die Arbeiterinnen und die Frauenfrage* (1889), she was not concerned with feminism as such but with the condition of women laborers. Clara Zetkin's views were important because she established certain links between socialists and communists. In 1907, at the first International Socialist Congress held in Stuttgart, Clara Zetkin became acquainted with Lenin. This was the beginning of a long and important relationship.

In some of the chapters devoted to specific countries further light is thrown on the significance of these ideological contests for the development of the women's rights movements. As will be shown, they were not particularly useful to the formulation of a concrete-action program. Much more positive contributions were made by several international non-governmental organizations. Before the outbreak of World

War I the following organizations were active on behalf of women's rights: The International Council of Women (ICW), The International Alliance of Women, The World Union of Catholic Women's Organizations, and the World Young Women's Christian Association. For our purposes the work of the ICW may serve as an example of the kind of professional work by able and dedicated women which helped to achieve tangible progress in the face of all kinds of difficulties. It was one of the several non-governmental organizations which laid the foundations for the work of the United Nations.

The International Council of Women (Conseil International des femmes) (Internationaler Frauenrat) was founded in Zurich in 1888. It may seem ironic that Switzerland, which introduced women's suffrage only in 1971, should have played such a prominent role as a center of the international women's movement, but it should be pointed out that the University of Zurich was one of the important institutions which enabled foreign women students to qualify for advanced degrees at a time when many fields of study were not open to them in their native countries. Zurich was a particularly important center for Russian students. It was there that many of them became acquainted with feminists from Western European countries. As far as the activities of the ICW are concerned, there has always been a very close connection between the programmatic development of women's rights and the campaigns for greater political participation. The two were inseparably linked in the long and often frustrating struggle for woman's suffrage. At the first Congress which met in London in 1899, the main topic was "laws concerned with domestic relations." The individual national councils were urged to study the nature of such laws "in all civilized countries."

Five years later when the ICW met in Berlin the main subject was women's suffrage. The following resolution was passed:

> Inasmuch as all Governments equally affect the men and women living under them; therefore, be it resolved that under all Governments, whether nominally republican or monarchical, whatever political rights or privileges are accorded to men ought on corresponding terms to be accorded to women; and this Council advocates that strenuous efforts be made to enable women to obtain the power of voting in all countries where a representative Government exists.

When the ICW met in Toronto in 1909 it was decided "that each National Council be asked to prepare a digest of the laws concerning women and children in their respective countries." They were also asked to prepare bibliographical material "stating the sources of the information." Each national Council was also asked

> to prepare a Report of the existing unequal laws in their re-
> spective countries which deal with the relations of women in
> the home, the family, the municipality, and the State, and that
> the national reports should then be combined as an interna-
> tional report on the same lines as the newly published report
> on "Health of the Nations," special attention being paid to
> simple wording of the various reports, so that they may be
> easily intelligible to all classes of the people, and that on the
> further recommendation of the Executive the complete inter-
> national report be presented to the various Governments, ac-
> companied by a letter from the official Board of the ICW
> drawing the attention of the Governments to the need for bet-
> terment of many of these laws, and the desirability of women
> taking part in the deliberations equally with men on such laws,
> the ICW basing its support of Women's Suffrage on the facts
> shown in the reports submitted.

At the Toronto meeting the ICW reaffirmed "its earnest desire that the right of voting be given to women in all countries where representative governments exist." In addition it urged the national councils to make strenuous efforts

> to place women members on those public boards or bodies
> whose membership is already open to women, and to secure
> the inclusion of women on all other authorities or special
> commissions dealing with public work.

In 1914 the ICW was still able to meet in Rome before World War I was unleashed. It concerned itself with a variety of technical matters such as the "Civil Capacity of Married Women" especially "in relation to her personal rights and to her property." The Committee on Laws was renamed "Committee on the Legal Position of Women." Once again the importance of women's suffrage was reaffirmed. The ICW recommended that the national councils endeavor to secure greater protection in cases of desertion for "wives, mothers and children whether born in or out of wedlock." Finally it passed the following resolution:

> The ICW, protesting vehemently against the odious wrongs of
> which women are the victims in time of war, contrary to in-
> ternational law, desires to appeal to the next Hague Conference

to consider how a more effective international protection of women may be secured which will prevent the continuance of the horrible violation of womanhood that attends all wars.

Before the end of World War I there were only five countries in Western Europe in which women had been granted the right to vote. Four were Nordic or Scandinavian countries: Finland led the way in 1906. It was followed by Norway in 1913 and Denmark together with Iceland in 1915. Although Swedish feminists and women's organizations had contributed much to the movement for women's suffrage, national suffrage was not enacted until 1919.

The fifth country which proclaimed women's suffrage was Russia or more specifically, the three Soviet Socialist Republics of Byelorussia, the Ukraine, and the Union of Soviet Socialist Republics.

During the period from the end of World War I to the end of World War II there were major developments in Western Europe. Listed by groups and in chronological order, the following countries adopted women's suffrage: Great Britain and Ireland (1918), Luxembourg (1918), Austria (1918), Germany (1919), the Netherlands (1919), and finally France (1944) just before the end of World War II.

In Southern Europe and in the Mediterranean area three countries experimented with women's suffrage: The first was Greece (1929) and the second Spain (1931). Both experiments ended in failure. But the third, which was carried out in Turkey (1934), might be rated as a moderate success.

In Central and Eastern Europe there were three pioneering ventures after World War I: the first was tried in Poland with Pilsudski's strong support, but it succeeded only moderately. The second in the newly independent Czechoslovak Republic was a major success, the third in Hungary was a failure.

After World War II women's suffrage was introduced in all the remaining countries of Southern and Eastern Europe. In the west there were two long overdue actions: Belgium (1948) and Switzerland (1971). This leaves only the tiny Principality of Liechtenstein as a holdout. In the area of Southern Europe and the Mediterranean, a chronological listing would be as follows: Italy (1945), Portugal (1945), Greece (II) (1952), San Marino (1960), Cyprus (1960), Monaco (1962), Malta (1964), and Andorra (1971).

In Eastern Europe, women's suffrage was introduced for the first time in Albania (1946), followed by Romania (1946), Yugoslavia (1946), and Bulgaria (1947). It was reintroduced in Hungary in 1945. In order to provide a basis for a comparison of the development of women's rights and political participation in a cross-national and cross-cultural manner, it is deemed effective to treat all the 34 European countries in four groups. This is done most often in alphabetical order within each group. Departures from this arrangement occur when one country in the group stands out as a leader in women's rights. It is hardly necessary to justify placing the U.S.S.R. at the beginning of the Eastern European group, for example, because the Soviet Union was the pioneer in 1917. It sought to maintain this lead during the inter-war period and after World War II, as it was asserting its ideological and political primacy. Whether or not it was completely successful in this respect is left for the reader to decide.

Having provided this general overview, we begin by focusing on the developments before 1918 in the Scandinavian area. After the four pioneering Scandinavian ventures, we turn our attention to developments in other parts of Europe and to the efforts on the part of intergovernmental and nongovernmental organizations before 1918.

Part I

Women's Rights and Political Participation in Europe before 1918

CHAPTER 1

THE SCANDINAVIAN COUNTRIES BEFORE 1918

INTRODUCTION

There is little need for justifying the term "Scandinavian countries". This grouping has been quite common for many years. It is more than a geographical identification. If it were nothing more than that, it would be difficult to treat Iceland as part of this group. It is also more than an ethnic characterization, because the Finns belong to a different racial and linguistic group. So do other indigenous population elements, especially in the most northern areas. But there are many close historical and cultural connections between them. Scandinavian political and legal institutions have their roots in Germanic history, and this is important for the comparative study of women's rights and political participation.

There are enough historical records to prove that in the early Christian period the status of women was not unfavorable, but the gender roles were always sharply delineated. The men bore arms, the women bore children, and legitimate children were treated affectionately, irrespective of their gender.

There are also historical references to women who bore arms and fought bravely against invaders and would-be conquerors. But these were exceptional situations which did not leave a permanent imprint on the definition of gender roles. The patriarchal system was never seriously questioned until quite recently.

In our time many people think of the women of the Scandinavian countries as the most liberated or the most emancipated. This perception is based more on male fantasies than on social and sexual realities. There are no "Scandinavian women," if this designation is to mean more than a geographical area of origin. There are indeed widely differing attitudes among the women of individual Scandinavian countries and social classes. However, in certain respects the so-called Scandinavian women did achieve a better social and political status long before

3

the women of all the western industrial countries. But even this generalization requires more careful comparative analysis, because in all these countries the development of industry on a large scale was a threat to women and their status. And in all these countries women had to fight for their economic and social rights. As far as political rights were concerned they benefitted from two partly interrelated developments: One was the progressive democratization of their political systems and the other the impact of the struggle of American women for their rights. If one wants to understand these interrelated developments, one must have a basic understanding of the historical and political backgrounds of each of the five countries and one must also be somewhat familiar with the women's rights movements of the late 19th and early 20th Centuries. The comparative study of the political transformations in the individual countries of Scandinavia from absolute to constitutional monarchies and to parliamentary democracies is an essential part of the study of women's rights and political participation. It is necessary to have some basic understanding of the political and legal systems of each of the five countries in order to assess the advances that have been made and the work that remains to be done.

In a book of such vast scope it is hardly possible to convey such a basic understanding, but the following introductory comparative notes may help.

Denmark and Sweden are the oldest independent Scandinavian countries on the European continent. They have a very rich pre-Christian, Viking and medieval history. During the Sixteenth through the Eighteenth Centuries they shared the title of major power on the Continent. Danish dominance of the political scene began to decline with the reign of Sweden's Gustavus Adolphus beginning in 1611, and proud Denmark was no longer a significant power six decades later. In terms of the later democratic development of the Scandinavian countries, it is important to note that Denmark passed a law in 1792 which abolished the slave trade (effective in 1802). This was one of the earliest antislave laws to be passed in the world. Denmark sided with France during the Napoleonic Wars and lost Norway to Sweden as a compensation offer by Russia for its 1809 annexation of Finland. Norway had been part of Denmark since the Fourteenth Century. In 1450 the Norwegians accepted the formal act of union with Denmark which paved the way for the development of the political infrastructure of the kingdoms. The two kingdoms were supposed to be equal but coordinated. In reality, Denmark was the more powerful and dominant partner in the union. The Norwegian kings were selected by Danish nobles. Many Danes, therefore, considered their country to be Norway's overlord. Prior to the promulgation of the Constitution of 1849, Denmark was an absolute monarchy.

The new constitution came after a period of vocalized liberal and nationalist feelings, and reforms occurred which were inspired by the Paris Revolution of 1830. With the new constitution Denmark became a constitutional monarchy, and throughout the 19th Century the monarch continued to lose power to Parliament. In terms of its international standing, Denmark ceased to be politically important in Europe with its defeat by Prussia under the leadership of Bismarck in 1864, when it lost Schleswig, Holstein, and Lauenburg. This was also the period of extensive growth of the cooperative movement in Denmark, which is the foundation of the present liberal democratic society.

The neutrality which we associate with Sweden today became the nation's policy after the Napoleonic Age. From the period encompassing the years between the end of the American Civil War to the start of the Great European War in 1914, there was no major conflict in which Sweden chose to participate. When war did break out in Europe, Sweden remained neutral. Nazi Germany honoured Swedish neutrality during the Second World War.

Sweden allowed Norway to have its own constitution and an autonomous legislative and administrative system, but all under an executive and foreign policy controlled by Sweden. Sweden's Constitution of 1809 was until recently the second oldest functioning constitution in the world. It established a constitutionally limited monarchy, a system under which political power was divided between the parliament and the monarchy. Over the decades, more and more political power shifted into the hands of Parliament.

The roots of democracy in Norway are deep and strong. A comparative study of Norwegian social history shows that unlike all the other countries of Scandinavia, Norway did not attach much importance to social stratification. A remarkably equalitarian outlook was in evidence long before the French Revolution. But the ideals of the French Revolution did have a definite impact, as did the American Revolution and the Constitution of the United States. They found their clearest expression in the Constitution of 1814, which is still in force, and thus the oldest written Constitution of Europe and the second oldest in the world. Having acknowledged these foreign influences, we should note that the Constitution of Norway was in many ways a highly original document. Unfortunately, the national and democratic aspirations of the people of Norway were blocked by the union with Sweden, which had been created without any real popular support after Swedish and Russian troops invaded Norway on August 14, 1814. By incremental measures which increased local home rule, Norwegians moved toward independence, which was achieved in 1905 with the termination of the union with Sweden.

Finland was conquered by Sweden in 1152 and ruled from that time until 1809 by Swedish kings. Finland was a province of Sweden. As already mentioned, Finland was annexed by Russia in 1809, becoming a grand duchy within the Russian Empire, and enjoyed a considerable measure of autonomy, especially during the period from 1863 to 1890. The last decade of the 19th and the beginning of the 20th Century was one of attempted Russification and suppression of indigenous political life in Finland. The Russian Revolution of 1905 spilled over into Finland and made it possible for Finland to regain certain traditional constitutional rights, and in 1906 a major constitutional reform was carried out. The Finns drew up a new constitution, abolished the old four estates, and replaced representation (such as it was) by estate, with a unicameral legislature elected by popular vote. This vote was based on universal male and female suffrage. Thus, the Finns were the first to give women the right to vote in national elections. As a result of the granting of universal suffrage, the size of the electorate was increased by about ten times.

Finland was not yet independent from Russia. A new policy of Russification was introduced in 1909 and lasted until the Empire began to disintegrate as the Revolution spread across Russia. With the Bolsheviks in control of the Russian government, the Finnish Parliament declared Finland to be an independent republic on December 6, 1917.

Although Iceland is not part of the Nordic continental land mass of Europe, historically it has close connections with Denmark and Norway. In the opinions of nationalist Icelanders, these connections have been too close. They take particular pride in the fact that Iceland had a parliament before any other country in the world, the *Althing*, established in 930. It established Iceland as a republic at a time when feudal kingdoms fought each other in more or less futile wars. Like other early medieval parliaments, it was not only a legislative body but also a Supreme Court. It continued in this form for three hundred years, making the *Althing* the oldest legislative body in the world.

In many respects the system of government was remarkably democratic, but it did not afford women the opportunity to participate in political decision-making. The old Icelandic laws, like those of other Germanic countries, linked the capacity to bear arms with the right to participate in decision-making, which often centered on the issue of war and peace. But Icelanders were not sufficiently united to defend themselves against invaders. Internal dissension led to the recognition of the King of Norway as the head of Iceland in the Thirteenth Century. Along with Norway it became part of Denmark a century later. While under Norwegian control Iceland experienced a gradual erosion of self-government. In 1662 it accepted the absolute monarchy of Denmark in a marked departure from its democratic past. The *Althing* lost all of its powers in this period.

The struggle for independence began in the nineteenth century. And, in 1874, Iceland was given a constitution by Denmark which allowed for limited home rule in 1904. In the early part of the 20th Century the movement for independence gained momentum, and Denmark was compelled to make some concessions. Independence was granted in 1918, although Iceland was still united with Denmark through a common monarch.

SWEDEN

Sweden occupies an important place in the history of women's rights in Scandinavia because of the influence some of her pioneers of women's suffrage exerted on the advocates of women's rights in other countries.

Among the proponents of women's emancipation at the end of the 18th Century, along with Olympe de Gouges, Mary Wollstonecraft and von Hippel, the Swedish writer Thomas Thorild should be mentioned because of an essay he wrote in 1798 on "The Natural Dignity of the Female Sex." At that time the social system of Sweden was very stratified, and the patriarchal order was firmly established.

During the first half of the 19th Century, Sweden was a very conservative society. The liberal movements of the 1830s and 1840s which infected almost all European bourgeois strata had little impact in Sweden. However, those individuals interested in women's rights were familiar with developments in neighboring countries. One of them was Fredrika Bremer (1801-1865), who achieved literary fame at an early age. She not only wrote about the problems of women, but also became one of the founders of the Swedish women's rights movement. She had travelled extensively and was very familiar with the women's movements in England and in the United States. During a visit to the United States she met such leading feminists as Margaret Fuller, Lucretia Mott and Lucy Stone. Her feminist novel *Hertha* was published in 1856.

In some respects Sweden was ahead of the other Scandinavian countries, because as early as 1862 women had been given the right to vote in local elections. When the *Riksdag* was reformed in 1865 women were given the indirect vote for members of the Upper House on the same terms as men. But, of course, this equalization of rights was extended to only a small percentage of the population.

John S. Mill's *The Subjection of Women* reinforced the campaign for emancipation and improvements in the legal status of all women. However, the main preoccupation of liberal leaders was not the emancipation of women but rather the modernization of the political system. Various reforms undertaken in the 1860s by these individuals helped to create a condition of social and political change which benefitted the women's rights movement.

Louis DeGeer, who served as minister of justice until 1870, was the main architect of the newly designed parliamentary system. The old and outmoded four chamber system of representation (nobles, clergy, burghers and farmers) was replaced by a bicameral parliamentary system patterned on the British model. The most important constitutional document of this period is the *Riksdag* Act of June 22, 1866. The suffrage base was still very narrow, and only about 20 percent of those eligible to vote made use of their franchise. It was only in the last decade of the 19th Century that significant changes were taking place. Voters' participation doubled. As in several other Western European countries, notably England and France, the Socialists were then in alliance with the Liberals. Both parties demanded a broadening of the suffrage base.

Sweden lacked the presence of women's organizations on a level of development and political sophistication evident in Denmark. In World War I, Sweden remained neutral but not unconcerned about security matters. It was only in 1918 that another bill for universal male and female suffrage was introduced in the *Riksdag*. Finally, in 1919, the necessary legislation was passed to amend the Constitution and the *Riksdag* Act to give women the right to vote.

NORWAY

In many ways the development of the women's rights movement in Norway paralleled Sweden's. Its feminist movement had its beginnings in literature. The outstanding writer and pioneer of feminism was Camilla Collett, whose novel *The Governor's Daughter* (1855) had a similar influence as Fredrika Bremer's novel *Hertha*, which was published in Sweden a little later. Although a member of the upper class, Camilla Collett did not hesitate to break with it on the issue of women's emancipation. She and her followers criticized the social system, which deprived women of equal opportunities in acquiring higher education and in denying them access to economic and political activities. At the time Collett was writing, some reforms of the legal status of women had already been initiated. Thus, inheritance rights had been nearly equalized with those of men as early as 1854. However, with respect to inheritance of land, the male members of the family continued to have priority.

Norwegian society was not only less stratified, it was also less patriarchal. This can be seen particularly in the field of family law, especially in its provisions concerning parenthood and parental rights. Long before World War I the trend was toward equality. However, this generalization did not apply to illegitimate children, unless they were formally legitimized. Otherwise, illegitimate children were under the parental authority of their mother until the age of 18. In 1869 legislation was passed, which set the legal majority of unmarried women at the age of 21, the same as for men. But the condition of married women remained unchanged. The husband continued to have disproportionate rights not only with respect to property but also in other areas. Thus, the wife was compelled to live wherever the husband chose to reside. In the 1870s John S. Mill's *The Subjection of Women* became well known in Norway. It is believed to have stimulated interest in the problems faced by Norwegian women. Much more influential and controversial was Henrik Ibsen's play *A Doll's House*, first published in 1879.

The demands for women's suffrage may be traced back to about 1880. In 1884 appeared the first organization for women workers. A year later the Union for Women's Suffrage was founded.

In 1904, the last paragraph of Article 92 of the Constitution of 1814 was changed. The Article assumed that all officeholders would be men. The amended article stated:

> The extent to which *women*, who fulfill the conditions prescribed by the Constitution for men, may be appointed to state offices, shall be prescribed by law.

But there was no prompt action in enacting appropriate implementing legislation.

Although as early as 1901 women were granted conditional municipal suffrage, the conditions for eligibility were not the same for men and women. These inequalities were removed in 1910. A law of February 9, 1912 gave women access to public employment. Certain exceptions were maintained for a long time thereafter. These related to the ministry, as well as to military and diplomatic appointments. The most important change in the Constitution of 1814 was made in June and July 1913, when Article 50 was amended to give women the right to vote in parliamentary (*Storting*) elections.

The first elections in which women were allowed to vote came in 1915. Some concern was registered by feminists that women did not use their newly won suffrage as had been expected. While 70 percent of the eligible male voters cast their ballots, only slightly more than one half of the women participated. This differential was considerably reduced in subsequent elections.

The key provisions in the Norwegian Constitution of 1814, as amended in 1913, were Articles 50 and 61.[1] These articles were amended

[1] Article 61 concerns residency qualifications for those competing for the position of representative to the *Storting*. As amended, the Article dropped all reference to the sex of the candidate, using neuter phraseology and requiring ten year residence in the country prior to election.

several times thereafter. The original text had set the exclusive male voting age at 25. Now Norwegian men and women were qualified to vote, provided they had been domiciled in Norway for five years and were actually residing there. (Article 50)

These changes provided the basis for more dramatic changes in the post World War I decade.

DENMARK

We encounter a somewhat different situation in Denmark. The Danish movement for women's rights seems to have had a pronounced political character from the very beginning. It goes back to about 1850 when Mathilde Fibiger, under the pseudonym of Clara Raphael, wrote her *Twelve Letters* (*Tolv Breve*). Among the early proponents of women's suffrage were Mathilde Bajer and her husband. In 1886, Frederik Bajer introduced a motion in parliament which would have allowed women to vote in local elections. Although this effort failed, it led to the formation of women's organizations, which came to be highly effective in leading the campaign for women's suffrage. Initially, there were two such organizations, the *Dansk Kvindes Am Fund* (Danish Women's Association) and the *Kvindelig Fremskridts Forening* (The Women's Union for Progress), which date from 1887 and 1888. The Danish Council of Women was formed in 1899. It was later renamed the Danish National Council of Women and became the umbrella organization of several dozen smaller organizations.

In the early years of the twentieth century, Denmark continued to experience development of women's organizations. In 1904 another organization was formed: the *Kvindevalgrets - Foreningen* (Women's Suffrage Union), which was highly effective in setting up local organizations. It has been credited with spearheading the campaign that led to the achievement of women's suffrage in local affairs on April 20, 1908. Women's suffrage in national elections was introduced on June 5, 1915 as an amendment to the Constitution.

The constitutional reform of 1915 gave the right to vote, in elections to the *Folketing*, to all citizens over 25. It also abolished the property qualifications for candidates to the *Landsting*. Henceforth, all citizens over the age of 35 could vote for electors, who were qualified to elect the members of the *Landsting*. The old plurality system was replaced by proportional representation. However, the implementation of all these reforms was deferred until the end of World War I.

Overall, the Danish constitutional rights granted to women in the early years of the 20th Century were quite progressive, at least in terms of the pattern that emerges from the Swedish experience. Universal suffrage for men over 26 years of age was passed in 1901. The impact of this broadening of the electorate was manifested in the 1911 elections when the electorate doubled from what it had been in 1905. However, only half of the eligible voters actually cast their ballots.

FINLAND

In Finland the pattern was somewhat different in that all women were authorized to vote in the national elections (in 1906) before they could vote in local elections. Finnish women were the first in Europe to participate in national elections. Further extension of their right to vote did not occur until 1917. At that date, they were granted the right to participate in local elections. It should be noted, however, that as far back as 1865 some women were allowed to vote in rural elections, and by 1872 their local voting rights were the same as those of men. Thus, despite its association with Czarist Russia, Finland was quite progressive in terms of broadening the electorate.

In the parliamentary elections of 1907 women won 19 of the 200 seats in parliament (9.5 percent). In the following year they increased their membership to 25, which was the highest attained for more than forty years. From the very beginning, Finnish women voters have taken a fairly keen interest in parliamentary elections. On the basis of figures compiled by the Central Statistical Office in Helsinki in May 1980, the following comparisons may be made of male and female participation in parliamentary elections from 1908 to 1917.

	Female	Male
	voters in percent of eligible voters	
1908	60.3	68.9
1909	60.6	70.5
1910	55.8	64.9
1911	54.8	65.3
1913	46.7	55.9
1916	51.4	60.1
1917	65.7	73.1

13

Their membership in Parliament, as already indicated, did not increase after 1908. In 1909, it declined to 21 and continued to fall in 1910 (17) and 1911 (14). it rose again in 1913 (21) and 1916 (24), but dropped to 18 in 1917. During this entire period women constituted about 52.3 percent of the eligible voters. Thus, they remained under-represented, despite extension of the suffrage.

ICELAND

Iceland's development paralleled that of Denmark in that women over the age of 25 received the right to vote in the national Danish elections in 1915 on the same basis as Danish women. Icelandic women had to be 35 years of age in order to qualify for political office. But, as in Denmark, the implementation of these provisions was postponed until the end of World War I.

CHAPTER 2

THE WESTERN EUROPEAN COUNTRIES BEFORE 1918

INTRODUCTION

The reader may be somewhat baffled by this list of ten European countries defined here as constituting Western Europe. Should it not be subdivided? And why are such countries as Italy, Portugal, and Spain not treated as part of Western Europe? The answer is that these three countries are indeed part of Western Europe as far as geography and the history of civilization are concerned. But for purposes of this book, which seeks to develop a typology for the comparative study of women's rights, it is better to treat them as part of the Southern and Mediterranean group.

As for the possibility of subdividing the list of ten, it is feasible, especially if one focusses on the legal systems. If this is done, the following subgroups may be established:

Common Law countries: Great Britain
                        Iceland
French Civil Law Countries (1804): France
                                    Belgium
                                    Luxembourg
                                    Netherlands
Austrian Civil Law countries (1811): Austria
                                    Liechtenstein
German Civil Law countries (1900): Germany
Swiss Civil Law countries (1912): Switzerland

Such a subgrouping has to be considered as somewhat incomplete and in need of further qualifying statements. It is incomplete because every one of these five legal systems had much wider influence beyond the area of Western countries and because the "reception" of any of these systems was modified by certain indigenous as well as other, borrowed elements. It is hardly necessary to point out that the British

15

Common Law and the French Civil Code were spread throughout their former respective empires. The Austrian Code was applied in a more contiguous area which once constituted the Austro-Hungarian Empire. In 1918 the political system was largely dismantled in the succession states, but the Austrian Civil Code survived until after World War II, when Soviet–type law was introduced in such countries as Czechoslovakia, Hungary, Poland, Romania, and to a lesser extent in Yugoslavia. The German Code was extended to the geographical areas which were once part of the German Empire, but after World War II it was totally eliminated in what eventually became the German Democratic Republic and the western part of Poland. Finally the Swiss Civil Law exerted more than decisive influence in the area which was reconstituted as the Republic of Turkey, because Ataturk decreed that the old Islamic law was to be replaced with a modern Western legal code.

This introductory note is inserted here because it can facilitate the comparative study of women's rights in Western Europe as well as in other areas of the world. The point to be made is that all of these legal systems in various ways and degrees were based on patriarchal legal and social order. Anyone who wants to acquire a better understanding of the difficulties involved in transforming patriarchal systems into more equalitarian or parental ones, will have to become more familiar with this complex but interesting subject.

As a beginning to such an undertaking the history and the transformation of the Austrian patriarchal legal system is treated here in somewhat greater detail. It would be tempting to do the same with the other legal systems, but this would greatly increase the length of this book and add to its complexity.

In order to reasonably contain the size of this book I have not attempted to rewrite in great detail the history of women's rights and political participation in such countries as France, Germany, and Great Britain. As indicated in the bibliography, there are many excellent books in English, and there is no need at this time to refer at length to familiar historical details. The main purpose is to provide comparative perspective and supply relevant information which is not readily available.

AUSTRIA

The traditional patriarchal order in Austria was barely challenged before the 19th Century. It was particularly entrenched in the agricultural areas and reinforced by the immense influence of the Roman Catholic Church. In the more urbanized areas, the male oriented legal system, which was derived from the Roman law, was a tremendous obstacle to the achievement of gender equality or real equality before the law.

The *Codex Theresianus*, which was enacted by Empress Maria Theresia between 1753 and 1766, did not introduce any fundamental changes as far as the status of women was concerned. Her son, Joseph II, may be credited with having established in 1786 the first teaching institution for the education of female teachers and governesses, but this was an enlightened reform for the benefit of society rather than the advancement of women. Under the impact of the French Revolution, there was some agitation for the "rights of man," but as in France and elsewhere in Europe, the rights of females were not included in such slogans.

The Austrian Civil Code, which was promulgated on June 1, 1811, was one of the major codifications in modern legal history. Along with the French Civil Code of 1804, it was destined to survive many political and social upheavals. With relatively few modifications, it has remained in force to our own times. The Austrian Civil Code, like others which were derived from Roman law, identified the father as the head of the family. (Articles 91 and 147) The Code, usually referred to as the *Allgemeines Bürgerliches Gesetzbuch* (AGBG), was a masterpiece of draftsmanship and reflected the influence of enlightened jurists and philosophers. But such men as Zeiller, the chief architect of the code, were not very enlightened about the status and role of women. Equality before the law was not extended to them. It should be conceded, however, that the Austrian Civil Code of 1811 was in some respects less patriarchal than the earlier Napoleonic Code. Thus, Article 1237 provided for a separation of assets (Gütertrennung) between spouses, which may be contrasted with the property provisions of the French Civil Law.

During the first half of the 19th Century, the traditional notions of the role of women were reaffirmed by the influential Austrian writers of the era of Romanticism. Occasionally, the relationship between men and women was interpreted in a more rational manner as a necessary division of labor. But most of these writers viewed the family as an organic whole, of which the father was the undisputed head. In Austria, the women's movement began somewhat later than in Germany. While women's rights were being discussed in Germany during the 1848 revolutionary activities, the issue was hardly raised in Austria, where the ruling elements were preoccupied with nationality problems. The women loyally defended the traditional order.

In 1849 educated women who met certain property qualifications were given the right to vote in local elections. The same right was accorded to less affluent women in 1861.

The Austrian Constitution of 1867 provided for fundamental rights and equality before the law. This provision had no immediate effect on the rights of women. The Constitution did not do away with the discriminatory provisions of many laws and decrees which barred women from pursuing certain courses of study. A few women were able to study in foreign universities, but they were not able to make use of their advanced education.

A decree of April 7, 1869, concerning the admissibility of women to training and participation in the administration of the postal service, authorized female members of the families of male postal officials to exercise certain limited functions in an auxiliary capacity. Some three years later, this authorization was extended to women who were not members of such families.

Middle-class women regarded education as the prerequisite for advancement—not just the usual women's education but professional training as well. The regime responded to these aspirations on November 3, 1869 with a decree providing for the training of female teachers. This was viewed as a major step forward, and more women embarked upon careers as teachers. Their enthusiasm was somewhat dampened when they failed to be paid the same salaries as male teachers. And they resented the fact that they were not allowed to marry if they wanted to keep their jobs. It is important to be aware of these facts, because it explains why the Austrian women's rights movement started among the women teachers, and why teachers continued to play a prominent role in leadership for several decades.

A decree of August 17, 1871 provided the legal basis for the employment of unmarried women in the telegraph service. They were not eligible to become regular state employees, and no provision was made for any retirement benefits. Unlike the regular male employees, they could be dismissed with an advance notice of only fourteen days. Johanna Schrade and Emilie Meisel founded an association of female employees of postal and telegraph services (Reichsverein der Post- und Telegraphen-beamtinnen). The German title was somewhat misleading because they were not officials but rather temporary employees.

An important event took place in 1874, when the Austrian Workers Party met in Neudorf and adopted a nine-point program. The very first point called for the introduction of the general, equal and secret right to vote for "all citizens over twenty years of age." The German Socialists'

Eisenach program, which was similar in most respects, asked only for universal male suffrage. Only in 1878 were women allowed to take the qualifying examinations (Matura) required for admission to university study. But they still were not eligible to matriculate at universities to pursue academic and professional studies.

In 1883, with the nationalization of the railroads, a few women were given employment, but under circumstances inferior to that of men. These historical facts are mentioned here because events in Austria during this period were matched in many of the western European countries. A certain amount of historical perspective is necessary if one wants to understand the close interrelationship between the forms of economic, legal, and political discrimination. The struggle for the political rights of women began in Vienna, and women teachers played a prominent part in it. Two of them, Auguste Fickert and Marie Schwartz, organized the first political assembly of women, which met on October 3, 1890 and demanded full political rights on the basis of equality with men. In 1893, Auguste Fickert also established the general Austrian Women's Association (Allgemeiner Österreichischer Frauenverein), which came to concern itself not only with political and legal issues but also with economic and social problems. By this time, the Austrian women's movement tended toward a division along class and ideological lines. Auguste Fickert was one of the few who were able to provide some necessary links between these groups. There was enough agreement between them, and the government was forced to respond to reasonable demands.

In 1896, foreign doctorates of Austrian women were recognized by the State, and in the following year more women were allowed to matriculate at the Philosophical Faculty of the University of Vienna. Several more years were to pass before women were granted the right to study medicine and law. Because such study was the indispensable requirement for the higher civil service, the restriction was an insurmountable obstacle for women who wanted to pursue such careers.

Aside from the teaching profession, which was becoming an increasingly open field to middle-class single women, there were only low-paying clerical positions open to them. By the end of the century, though women represented more than one-quarter of the postal employees, their salaries were still considerably lower than those of male postal workers. They were not allowed to marry, a prohibition which was not lifted until the end of World War I.

Although women were given employment in several ministries, such as the Ministry of Agriculture (since 1899), the Ministry of Interior, and the Ministry of Commerce (since 1900), their status was generally inferior to that of men. This de facto situation was confirmed by a decree of July 19, 1902, concerning auxiliary personnel. Unlike men, women could still be dismissed upon notice ranging from three to six months.

In 1901, the so-called "Vienna program" of the Austrian Social Democratic Party restated as its first principle the introduction of a universal, equal, direct and secret right to vote for all citizens over 20, without regard to gender. It also called for the elimination of all laws which placed women at "disadvantage" in relationship to men.

In 1903, the attitude of the leadership of the Social Democrats was clearly stated by Victor Adler, who declared that while it was necessary to reaffirm at every possible opportunity that the Social Democrats favored women's suffrage, the main effort had to be concentrated on the achievement of universal suffrage.

With the founding in 1902 of the Bund Österreischer Frauenverreine (Federation of Austrian Women's Associations) by Marianne Hainisch, the struggle for women's rights, including women's suffrage, was more effectively coordinated. It should be noted, however, that women's suffrage continued to be more important to middle-class women than to the women who worked in factories. After 1902, the Social Democratic Women had their own organization: the Association of Social Democratic Women and Girls (Verein Sozialdemokratischer Frauen und Mädchen).

In 1904, the Austrian Women's Association joined the International Council of Women. This gave Austrian women leaders more opportunities to familiarize themselves with the struggles for women's rights in other countries. In Austria, the situation was not propitious for any significant advances. The leading politicians were preoccupied with demands being made by the numerous ethnic groups. It was only in 1906 that a viable coalition government could be put together. By the end of the year several parties agreed to support the introduction of universal male suffrage, and this major piece of legislation was passed by the Parliament on December 1, 1906. The emperor sanctioned it on January 26, 1907. The first elections based on the new system were held in May 1907.

In 1908, German women were accorded the same rights as men, with respect to membership in political organizations. This seems to have helped Austrian women leaders to obtain the repeal of the discriminatory provisions of the Law of Associations. Devout Catholic women in Austria had shown relatively little interest in politics. But this situation changed gradually, and in 1907 they formed their own organization—the Catholic Women's Organization (Katholische Frauenorganisation), which held its first Congress in 1910.

In 1911, paragraph 30 of the Law of Associations, which had prevented women from joining associations, was deleted. Austrian women became more active politically and tried to exert pressure on politicians to support their specific demands. As it turned out, they were not very successful because most politicians felt they could ignore them as long as they did not have the right to vote.

The outbreak of World War I brought setbacks in the Austrian women's struggle for equality. While they were called upon to take on many tasks usually performed by men, their compensation was almost always significantly lower. Many women were required to perform heavy and hazardous work without commensurate pay and benefits.

In 1918, women were allowed to matriculate at Faculties of Law. However, in spite of subsequent constitutional guarantees of equality (Art. 7), they were not eligible for appointments to civil service positions. They could only be practicing attorneys or work in legal departments of banks and business concerns. It was clear that without equal suffrage they could not achieve their professional goals.

BELGIUM

The Constitution of Belgium, which dates from 1831, is the second oldest in Europe. It was then a pioneering document of liberal constitutionalism, and for over a century and a half it has exerted great influence on the making of European and non-European constitutions. In view of this fact, one might reasonably expect that Belgium might have been in the forefront of the women's movement, and that its laws might long ago have made adequate provision for women's rights. But such was not the case. From the very beginning, the Belgian Constitution contained an admirably drafted catalogue of the "rights of Belgians." Unfortunately, although the Constitution did not specifically make this point, all the extensive political rights applied to men only. In 1831 that was to be expected, but in view of the fact that Luxembourg and the Netherlands had promulgated women's suffrage shortly after World War I, Belgium might have been a likely partner. As it turned out, Belgium adopted women's suffrage long after the end of World War II.

From the very beginning the Belgian Constitution ruled out any possibility of female succession to the throne. According to Article 60, the crown was to pass, according to primogeniture, in the male line only. Indeed, it has specifically provided for a "perpetual exclusion of women and their descendants." Generally speaking, the status of women in Belgium was very similar to that of French women under the French Civil Code, or "Code Civil Napoleon" of 1804, which was in effect in France and was not significantly changed during the subsequent century. As in France, it penalized married women by giving husbands extensive control over their property and lifestyle. Whereas the unmarried or widowed woman enjoyed full legal capacity, the married woman, according to Article 213 of the Civil Code, "owed obedience to her husband" in return for his "protection".

Around the turn of the century, some improvements did take place in the status of women. By a law of February 10, 1900, married women could have their own savings accounts. Working women could enter into contractual agreements on the basis of legislation of March 10, 1900. Some minor changes were made in the Civil Code, but the patriarchal principle was never seriously affected by them.

The Belgian Women's Movement started relatively late. A significant event took place in 1909 with the founding of the National Council of Belgian Women (Conseil National des Femmes Belges). Prior to that time, there were three women's organizations: the Belgian League for the Right of Women, the Society for the Amelioration of the Condition of Women and the Union of Women Against Alcoholism. However, it was a long time before the efforts of the National Council of Belgian Women achieved any major breakthrough. In 1909, the Belgian Women joined the International Women's Suffrage Alliance. In April and May of that year this Alliance sent delegates to the London Congress. Belgian women might have continued their campaign for women's suffrage had they not been needed to help in the relief of suffering that came with the German invasion of Belgium on August 3, 1914.

FRANCE

In the history of French politics, individual women have always had great influence. Women like Olympe de Gouges and Mme. de Staël probably expected France to lead the way in the struggle for equal rights. But as it turned out, France was among the last western European countries to introduce women's suffrage. After much political activism on the part of dedicated women during the French Revolution, they nearly withdrew from active politics during the Napoleonic period. It was only in the 1848 revolutionary period that they reentered the political battleground.

During the intervening period, the cause of women's rights was taken up by such prominent thinkers as Saint-Simon and Fourier, but their efforts had no practical significance. The Napoleonic Code remained in effect without relevant change. In the fields of family law and property law, the patriarchal principle remained unchallenged, with only a few concessions made from time to time. For instance, in 1881 women were allowed to open their own bank accounts and make withdrawals, but this concession benefitted only a very small number of unmarried upper-class women. Married women were under the "tutelage" of their husbands. It was only in 1907 that married women who worked were legally permitted to keep their salaries. Until 1908, married women were legally treated as minors. World War I obliged women to assume all kinds of unusual responsibilities, but these wartime experiences and experiments had no tangible effect on the traditional legal system.

Throughout this period there were prominent French feminists and women's organizations dedicated to the achievement of political and legal changes. Saint-Simon was a pioneer in France and was among the men who favored the emancipation of women prior to 1848. His views were endorsed by Fourier. Maria Deraisme was the founder of the periodical *Le Droit des Femmes* and the *Ligue française pour le Droit des femmes*. The *Conseil National des Femmes* (National Council for Women) was founded in 1901. Maria Deraisme, has been credited with reactivating the women's movement in France. The Conseil National des Femmes became a leading member of the International Council of Women.

It is generally recognized that French feminists failed in their efforts to effect the necessary legal and social reforms not because of poor leadership but because of the stubborn opposition in the Senate to enacting women's suffrage. Many senators were troubled by the strong pacifist orientation of French feminists. Those who wanted revenge for the French defeat in the Franco-Prussian War would not condone any pacifist agitations.

But the French women proved their patriotism in World War I, as they had in numerous previous wars. Many of them felt they had long ago earned their right to vote. But in 1918 French public opinion was not ready for women's suffrage.

GERMANY

At the time of the French Revolution, the roles of men and women were sharply delineated. Social stratification tended to be more important than regional differences, as far as the status of women was concerned. In the upper strata, there were a few women who exerted great influence in cultural affairs, but they were rarely concerned with politics. There is no evidence that Olympe de Gouges or Mary Wollstonecraft had any immediate or tangible influence in Germany. In 1792, Theodor G. von Hippel's treatise "On the Civil Amelioration of Women," was published, but it did not produce any excitement at the time.

During the Napoleonic period, German women were greatly preoccupied with national survival, and such feminists as Madame de Staël

23

did not find them greatly interested in the issue of equality for women. In 1814, after the final defeat of Napoleon, some liberal leaders in the southern and southwestern states wanted to replace the authoritarian regimes. They were moderately successful in Bavaria, Baden and Württemberg, but the charters which were promulgated in 1818 and 1819 did not provide for any fundamental rights. Men and women were treated as "subjects" by their more or less enlightened rulers. There were some liberal currents in such areas as Hanover during the 1830s, but liberal writers in most parts of Germany were severely hampered by the repressive press laws. In the 1840s, discontent and unrest gained momentum. At first, it was expressed in moderate language invoking "inalienable human rights" and calling for basic freedoms.

The German liberals of the pre-1848 period did not deal directly with "the women's question." It was only after the Socialists called for the "emancipation of women" that the German liberal politicians began to appeal to women; but as long as women did not have the right to vote, they could be ignored by the politicians. Politics was considered a male monopoly. Among the women who before 1848 were active in calling for their emancipation was Luise Otto-Peters, who was active as early as 1844. Some educated women were familiar with the ideas of Fourier and Saint-Simon, and early, pre-Marx champions of women's and workers' rights.

The *Communist Manifesto*, published in London on February 24, 1848, served as an impetus to women activists. Marx and Engels came to Cologne on April 11, with a document they had drafted earlier entitled "The Demands of the Communist Party in Germany." The German Constituent Assembly met in Frankfurt for the first time on May 18, 1848. Some five years after the *Communist Manifesto,* Luise Otto-Peters founded a newspaper for women. In 1865, she was the founder of the first German Women's Association, the "Allgemeine Deutsche Frauenverein," which, though illegal, became the chief organization for the German movement for women's rights.

The liberal feminists in Germany were influenced by the American women's rights movement and by John Stuart Mill's treatise on "The Subjection of Women," which was translated into German. A second German edition was published in Berlin in 1872. But the Liberals, like the Socialists, were being outmaneuvered by Bismarck, who had been named prime minister of Prussia in 1862. Shortly thereafter he declared that "Bavaria, Württemberg, [and] Baden may indulge in liberalism," but "Prussia must gather its power for the favorable moment, which had already been missed several times." He criticized the leaders of the 1848/49 period, and declared that it was not "through speeches and majority that the great questions of time were resolved . . . but through iron and blood."

German politics was increasingly Prussianized. The atmosphere was extremely unfavorable for any advancement of women's rights. Within the socialist movement there were some differences of opinion as to how to deal with the women's question. Ferdinand Lassalle, who in 1863 had founded the General German Workers Association, did not call for equality between men and women. Lassalle and his followers endorsed the traditional division of gender roles. The Social Democratic Workers' Party, after its founding in 1868, did not endorse this view, but leaned toward a gradual approach of equalization. In 1875 the two Socialist organizations met at Gotha and agreed on a compromise. One of the architects of the compromise was August Bebel, who had been elected two years earlier to the Constituent Parliament of the North German Federation. His *Woman and Socialism*, which was first published in 1879, was an immensely influential book. The only other German writer who approached Bebel's influence was Clara Zetkin. Whereas Bebel was still a late 19th Century Social Democrat, Zetkin provided the link with Communism and the 20th Century. By the time she started to write, Bismarck had already trimmed the sails of the Socialists.

Bismarck's social legislation of the 1880s was predicated on the notion that the husband or the father was the "breadwinner" of the entire family. All the social benefits were derived from his entitlement. Clara Zetkin's view was fundamentally different, as she had clearly shown in 1889 when her monograph on "the Women Workers and the Women Question" appeared in print. After the (Anti)Socialist Law was repealed in 1890, Zetkin became the leader of the German Socialist Women. Two years later, she became the founder and editor of the periodical, *Gleichheit* (Equality). Her extraordinary intellectual ability, coupled with tremendous energy, enabled her to exercise an important role in the Socialist International, as well as in the German Socialist movement. It was in Gotha, in 1896, when she was elected to the presidency of the German Socialist Party, that she presented a nine-point program, which included complete political and legal equality as well as equal pay for equal work. As a Marxist, she attached fundamental importance to the economic conditions of women's emancipation. At the same time, she emphasized the importance of women's suffrage. Clara Zetkin's *Zur Frage des Frauenwahlrechts*, published in Berlin in 1907, contains an interesting appendix on the history of women's suffrage.

But the women's prospects for political and legal equality were not good. This was apparent in the work of the German legal experts who had been engaged since the 1870s in codifying the German legal system. The task of producing a unified German Civil Code proved particularly difficult because of the disagreement of "Romanists" and "Germanists." Women had little to gain either way, because the Germanic legal tradition, with the Roman one, emphasized the notion of the father as the head of the family. A unified Civil Code was finally adopted in 1896 and put into effect on January 1, 1900. Its patriarchal features could readily be compared with those of legal codes that were derived from the Napoleonic Code (1804) and the Austrian Civil Code of 1811. Its fundamentals remained untouched until after World War II.

The German feminists were not discouraged by these developments. If anything, they became more keenly aware that more legal reforms would be insufficient, that it was necessary to understand the historical and cultural background which allowed such anachronisms to continue. They also understood very clearly that the education of women was one of the keys to their progress.

Helene Lange was the chief editor of the *Handbook of the Women's Movement* (*Handbuch der Frauenbewegung*), which was published in five volumes between 1901 and 1906. This monumental work was produced in collaboration with Gertrud Bäumer. Both women were teachers who believed that before women could expect to make progress in the area of politics, it would be necessary to open up more opportunities for them in the field of higher education. Among the scholarly women's literature of this period, mention should be made of Marianne Weber's treatise on the "Wife and Mother in Legal History," in which she related the dependency of the woman to her incapacity to bear arms.

Before 1908 women were not allowed to belong to political organizations. Therefore they concentrated their efforts on matters of educational and social policy. After 1908 several political parties attracted prominent women, and as a result, women's suffrage became part of their programs.

The previously mentioned Gertrud Bäumer was a prolific writer in German literature, but she was also a great political activist. From 1910 to 1919 she served as president of the League of German Women's Associations (Bund deutscher Frauenvereine), and she was co-founder with Friedrich Naumann of the German Democratic Party. She served in the German National Assembly and later in the *Reichstag*.

GREAT BRITAIN

In 1792, Mary Wollstonecraft attracted considerable attention with her "Vindication of the Rights of Women." After her death her cause was taken up by her husband, William Godwin, and others, but the time was not very propitious for equalitarian ideals. During the Napoleonic era, most Englishmen were preoccupied with problems of national security and economic issues.

In England, as in the United States, women suffered some setbacks in the first half of the 19th Century. The industrial revolution resulted in a large-scale movement of women who went to work in factories and were made to compete with men under most unfavorable conditions. The Reform Act of 1832 brought no improvement for women. On the contrary, in the legislation enacted during this period, male domination was reaffirmed. The Municipal Corporations Act of 1835 also restricted voting rights to "male persons". Although some of the Chartists took up the cause of women's suffrage, there seems to have been little determination to stick to women's rights as part of the "rights and liberties," which they wanted to have embodied in their Charter.

Little tangible progress was made in the middle period of the Century. It was John Stuart Mill who undertook an important effort to introduce women's suffrage in the House of Commons. In 1867, when new electoral legislation was under consideration in the House of Commons, he proposed a simple but important amendment to the Reform Act of 1832, which would have substituted the term "persons" for "men". If adopted, this would have established the basis for women's suffrage. The vote was 74 for and 194 against the amendment. Repeated efforts were made after that, but they could not succeed without the wholehearted support of such individuals as Prime Minister Gladstone. Gladstone and his supporters, however, were preoccupied with extending the suffrage in a way that would have perpetuated the Liberal Party in power. The key to doing so was increasing the electorate by extending the right to vote to the city people. On the other hand, Disraeli relied heavily on the conservative attitudes of the so-called "agricultural class".

To interpret this struggle in terms of a male conspiracy against women, as has occasionally been done in recent years, is to ignore the political realities of that period. It must be borne in mind that the male suffrage base was extremely small. Before the Reform Act of 1832, only about 1 percent of the population of England had the right to vote. The passing of the Reform Act did not greatly increase the size of the electorate. Only about 4 percent of the total population, or 7 percent of those over twenty years of age, had the right to vote. But it did pave the way for further modifications. In 1867, the extension of the vote to the boroughs doubled the electorate. About 8 percent of the total population, or about 16 percent of all males over 20, were now enfranchised. In 1884 the percentage was increased from about 10 to 18. Whereas in 1867 the male population of the cities had been given more strength, in 1884 it was the rural population which drew the main benefit of the Conservative Party.

Women's organizations for female suffrage had been active in various parts of England since the middle of the 19th Century. Such organizations had existed in Sheffield since 1850 and in Manchester since 1866. In 1867, the London Society for Obtaining Political Rights for Women was established in Kensington. It was subsequently renamed The London and National Society for Women's Suffrage. The National Council of Women was established in 1895. It became an important member of the International Council of Women (ICW). These and other organizations were also concerned with the improvement and equalization of women's working conditions.

After campaigning for several months, women were given the right to vote in local elections; but as far as voting rights in national elections were concerned, all efforts in the House of Commons came to naught. Gladstone's liberalism and liberal program did not include women's rights.

In the legal field, there were some improvements. The Married Women's Property Act of 1882 constituted an advance because women could now hold property separately rather than only jointly with their husbands. They also gained admission to some universities which had formerly been exclusive male domains.

In the field of social legislation, Britain was lagging behind Germany and several other countries, but Sir Charles Dilke was probably exaggerating when he complained in the House of Commons that British legislators "never paid the slightest attention to what took place in other countries." His criticism helped to make the House of Commons more concerned with the demands that were being made by organized labor, with respect to the Workmen's Compensation Bill. In its final version, its coverage broadened to apply to all persons engaged under contract in labor, clerical, and other activities. It thus benefitted women as well as men.

Comparisons were also made during the debates on the Old Age Pension Bill. A Royal Commission had been appointed in 1893 to study the problems of old-age assistance and had rendered a favorable report in 1895. A specific plan was presented in 1899 and largely endorsed in 1903 by a parliamentary committee. But the Conservative Government was in no hurry to enact old-age pension legislation. It was only after the Liberals returned to power that the proposals received favorable consideration. In March 1906, one of the M.P.'s declared that "on the question of old-age pensions, England was far behind her colonies and every country in Europe, with the exception of Russia."[1] Several speak-

[1]O'Grady, on March 14, 1906. *Parliamentary Debates House of Commons*, vol. 153, p. 1333.

ers recommended the Danish system as a model, and Herbert Asquith agreed with them. Charles Booth recommended another scheme, under which the state alone would pay pensions to all men and women. This plan had the endorsement of the trade unions. After further studies by the government, it was the New Zealand system, mentioned many times during the debates, which formed the basis for the Old-Age Pension Act of 1908. A comparison of the two shows that the British system remained behind in several important respects, as the labor leaders were quick to point out.[2]

The leaders of the women's suffrage movement were less concerned with questions of economic and social legislation than with their key objective: the right to vote. But the prospects had not improved. In fact, the public preoccupation with economic issues tended to undercut the demands for women's rights.

In the face of stubborn resistance by politicians in the House of Commons, the movement for women's rights became more militant. The Women's Social and Political Union was formed in 1903. The tactics of such suffragettes as Christabel Pankhurst aroused much animosity, but they succeeded in attracting unprecedented attention. The agitations and acts of violence came to an end as England entered World War I.

IRELAND

The history of women's rights and political participation is closely linked with Ireland's movement for independence, equality and equity. Irish feminism was always a group effort rather than an individual search for a different lifestyle. Although it was influenced by the French Revolution and contemporary developments in England, it grew out of its own cultural setting, tradition and values. In 1876, the Dublin Women's Suffrage Society, which later became the Irish Countrywomen's Association, was founded. Through a large number of rural local guilds, it carried on its work in the social and educational areas.

Women were qualified to vote in local elections. Section 1 of the Local Authorities (Ireland) (Qualification of Women) Act of 1911 provided:

A woman shall not be disqualified by sex or marriage from being elected or chosen or being a Councillor of the Council

[2]E. M. Burns, "State Pensions and Old Age Dependency in Great Britain." *Political Science Quarterly*, vol. 45 (1930), pp. 181-213.

Whereas, in New Zealand pensions were provided at the age of 65, the British system favored the less seldom attained age of 70, and the payments were smaller.

of any County or Borough or an Alderman of the Council of any Borough.

The Irish Suffrage Society was founded by Anna Haslam. She had been a signatory of the first Women's Suffrage Petition presented to the House of Commons by John Stuart Mill, and in 1881 she and her husband, Thomas Haslam, published a periodical called "The Women's Advocate." In the early part of the 20th Century several other women's organizations were formed. For a long time, with few exceptions, Irish women's organizations stayed away from confrontations and militant tactics. How they became increasingly radicalized is part of the unhappy history of the Irish political struggle before and after World War I.

In December 1918, Countess Markiewicz was the first Irish woman who was elected to sit in the House of Commons. This was the result of the British Representation of the People Act. However, because she was a member of *Sinn Fein* she was not allowed to take her seat. It was not until 1922 that women's suffrage was embodied in the second Constitution of Ireland.

LIECHTENSTEIN

The Principality of Liechtenstein is a very small country situated between Austria and Switzerland.

There have been some prominent women in Liechtenstein history but none of them, as far as is known, could be regarded a feminist. Unlike in Austria and Switzerland, no changes were made in the family law during this period. The Austrian Civil Code of 1811 remained in force in its original form.

LUXEMBOURG

Long before Luxembourg introduced women's suffrage in 1919, there were considerable, and often heated, debates on this issue. Many of the arguments advanced by its opponents were similar to the ones heard before in neighboring countries. Influential politicians of conservative persuasion insisted that women should not have a direct role in political decision-making. They were opposed to any significant changes in the Constitution which was promulgated on October 17, 1868. No changes were made for more than fifty years.

As it turned out, some women did play significant roles in Luxembourg politics. In 1907, Grand Duke William IV designated his eldest daughter, Marie Adelaide, as heir presumptive. When his health failed in 1908, he named his wife, Marie Ann, as regent. After the Grand Duke's death in 1912, the Grand Duchess acceded to the throne. Her pro-German orientation generated much controversy, especially after German troops invaded Luxembourg and occupied the country until 1918.

NETHERLANDS

A century ago, the constitutional and political system of the Netherlands was very similar to that of Belgium and Luxembourg. In view of the many historical links, this is hardly surprising. In the course of the second half of the 19th Century, the Kingdom of the Netherlands, like its two neighbors, was gradually transformed from a constitutional monarchy into a parliamentary system of government.

In 1887, the Constitution was extensively amended by means of eleven laws which resulted in a considerable liberalization of the electoral system. The electorate increased from about 100,000 to 300,000. There is no evidence that the constitutional commission, which had been appointed in 1883, ever gave serious consideration to the question of women's suffrage. But unlike the Constitution of Luxembourg it did not preclude female succession to the throne. In 1890, after the death of William III, Queen Emma became the regent for her ten-year-old daughter, Wilhelmina. The personal union with Luxembourg was terminated because the Succession Law of the neighboring state did not make allowance for female successors to the throne.

The Constitution of the Netherlands contained several articles which limited the right to vote and to be elected. (Articles 80, 84, 127, 143) The Communal Law, as amended in 1904, also precluded the election of a woman to be mayor. (Article 61) Other positions were also reserved to men. (Articles 96, 106, 107) Similarly, on the basis of Article 37 of the Provincial Law, as amended in 1905, all positions in the States General were reserved to men.

Women's organizations in the Netherlands had their beginnings in 1872. But there were considerable differences between them, and they tended to reflect the development of varying ideological currents: liberal, socialist, and Christian-democratic. In the late 19th Century, Dr. Aletta Jacobs was one of the chief organizers of the movement for women's suffrage. The first movement for women's suffrage may be traced to the early 20th Century. Male suffrage had been further extended after the passing of Van Houten's voting bill in 1896. The social legislation which followed was rather limited and had no significant effect on the status of women.

The National Women's Council of the Netherlands (Nationale Vrouwenraad Van Nederland) was established in 1898. From the very beginning it had close contacts with the ICW, and in 1899 it was formally affiliated with it. In 1907 and 1913, the Hague was the meeting place for the ICW Executive Committee. The National Women's Council was not only concerned with the issue of women's suffrage but also with other legal provisions which discriminated against women. Universal male suffrage was introduced in 1917, and it paved the way for women's suffrage. But it took another two years to pass the necessary legislation.

SWITZERLAND

Switzerland is a small country whose people have a distinctive historical and cultural heritage. But in spite of these common links and shared values, attitudes toward the issue of women's suffrage have differed sharply in the various cantons. Within many of the cantons one may trace distinctly progressive attitudes in the urban centers as contrasted with the conservative viewpoints in the rural communities.

As far back as 1868 Marie Goegg Pouchoulin (1826-99) founded the "Association internationale des femmes." In 1869 she started to publish the "Journal des femmes." Geneva was one of the centers of the feminist movement. The other center was the University of Zurich, which was the first university in Europe to admit women to various fields of study that were closed to them in their native countries. It is therefore surprising that it took over a century to achieve women's suffrage in Switzerland. Why should a country with such unquestioned democratic traditions be so opposed to an idea which was so widely regarded as an essential ingredient of a democratic society? One of the answers lies in the fact that the Swiss democratic tradition developed in the cantons. The Swiss Confederation could not interfere with the business of the Landgemeinden, the local assemblies, whose foundations go back to the Middle Ages.

The other answer is also linked with a paradox. Switzerland has an unbroken tradition of neutrality. It has not been involved in any wars, but it has the strictest enforcement of universal military service. Every male citizen has to undergo some military training and remains in the reserves. Women have never been allowed to serve in the military establishment. This principle goes back to old Germanic law which linked the capacity to bear arms with the right to participate in political decision making.[1] In a few of the cantons this view is still firmly entrenched. In others there was little opposition to allowing women to vote in local affairs.

The Council of Swiss Women's Organizations was formed in 1900 and became affiliated with the ICW in 1903. From the very outset the Council devoted particular attention to pending legislation, and from time to time women served on important federal commissions. In this way, although they could not vote on new federal laws, they were able to exert influence in the drafting process. This was particularly important in 1907 when work was under way on the drafting of the Swiss Civil Code which went into effect on January 1, 1912. During the interwar period this remarkable Code was generally recognized as being more progressive than the French Code of 1804, the Austrian Code of 1811, or the German Code of 1900. Women made important contributions to the codification effort, and they were successful in securing for women a better status as far as property law was concerned. In the field of family law they were less successful, because the notion of equal status of both parents was emphatically rejected.

---

[1] In German one might say that historically and legally "Wehrfähigkeit" (the capacity to defend) and "Wahlfähigkeit" (the capacity to vote) went hand in hand.

CHAPTER 3

THE SOUTHERN AND MEDITERRANEAN COUNTRIES BEFORE 1918

INTRODUCTION

In the decade immediately preceding World War I, the Southern and Mediterranean countries were not centers of activity for women's rights. In spite of San Marino's long republican tradition, women's political participation remained at a low level. Both San Marino and the ministate of Andorra were relatively isolated from the rest of Europe. Monaco was until 1911 an absolute monarchy. Turkey's bold modernization program under Ataturk did not take shape until the mid-twenties. Malta remained a part of the British Empire until 1964.

In Greece, Italy, Portugal and Spain there was activity; however, not all of it contributed to the advancement of women's rights.

GREECE

by Louis Pagonis

In the first Greek Constitution, the principle of equality for all citizens was incorporated as early as 1822. But, this did not include women, since women were not considered citizens.

During the 1820s, when the Greeks struggled for independence, some remarkable constitutions were drafted and promulgated, but they did not include any reference to women. Even though many women fought alongside their men for independence and gave their lives for their country, their status did not change significantly in this very patriarchal culture. Among the early feminists, Efrosyne Samaridou is often singled out because in 1842 she began publishing a magazine that favored women's suffrage. Ms. Samaridou had a very hard time getting her ideas across and finding support for her publication since women's rights was not a popular subject in any part of the world at that time.

In the elections of 1843 for the Constituent Assembly, 243 members were elected, but none was a woman. In 1875, a bill was introduced in Parliament asking for a clarification of the word "citizen;" however, the bill was never debated.

The first women's organization was founded as early as 1871. From 1884 to 1918, Calinhoe Perrea edited a women's publication: *Journal des Dames*. In this journal, many women expressed their ideas of the women's role in society. Attempts were made to publish a women's journal in the Greek language, but no publisher could be found for it. It was only toward the end of the century that the issue of women's rights was vigorously pursued. The National Council of Women of Greece was established in 1908 and became affiliated with the ICW in the same year.

A milestone was reached in 1911 in Athens at the first Panhellenic Women's Congress. It had limited support, but nevertheless it achieved its purpose by setting a precedent for similar congresses to follow in the future in Greece. The Greek Constitution of 1911, which was a revised version of the Constitution of 1864, was not very explicit on the right to vote. According to Article 66, members of the chambers of deputies were to be elected by citizens who had the right to vote. This not only confirmed the restricted male suffrage but seemed to leave the way open for further restrictive and discriminatory legislation.

ITALY

Of the three great leaders of the Italian independence, two, Garibaldi and Mazzini, were close to the feminist cause.[1] This can readily be shown on the basis of their correspondence.[2] But neither of the two ever explicitly stated that he favored women's suffrage. What they wanted to accomplish was a substantial change in the legal status of women—an emancipation from patriarchal bondage.

Count Cavour, the third great leader of the movement for independence and national unification, was not committed to any revolutionary changes, and it was his view which prevailed. In 1848 when universal male suffrage was introduced by the Second Republic, there was no inclination to do away with the rigid property qualifications which had been established in various parts of Italy as a precondition to the right to vote. After Italy was formally unified by the proclamation of the Kingdom of Italy in 1861, there were no significant changes. In the 1870s only a little more than 2 percent of the population had the right to vote. In the 1880s, literacy was accepted as a substitute for property. This resulted in some increases in the electorate. By 1900 it had grown to 7 percent, and in 1911 it was over 8 percent. In 1912 a major electoral reform was introduced which gave all literate males and illiterate former servicemen the right to vote.

At that time, compared with other countries, there was little feminist agitation in Italy. Women's organizations existed in various parts of Italy before the turn of the century, especially in the northern cities. In 1898 they formed the National Council of Italian Women (Consiglio Nazionale Delle Donne Italiane). Two years later it became affiliated with the ICW.

In 1908 the National Council held its first Congress, which was attended by the Queen and high-ranking state officials. In a lengthy report they presented a program for action which emphasized the need of women for more educational and professional opportunities. They also asked for specific changes in the legal system, especially in the areas of family law and property arrangements.

The legal status of women in Italy was very similar to that of French women. It was an emphatically patriarchal system which had its foun-

---

[1]Giuseppe Mazzini (1805-72) was one of the early champions of women's rights. He inspired several idealistic women including Maria Montessori, who became famous as a pioneer in new teaching methods. Judith Jeffrey Howard: "Patriot mothers in the Post-Risorgimento: Women after the Italian Revolution," in: *Women, War and Revolution*, ed., Carol R. Berkin and Clara M. Lovett, New York, H.M., 1980, p. 237f.

[2]In 1868 Mazzini wrote to Harriet Taylor (Mrs. John Stuart Mill) that the women must earn their emancipation. Translated from Anna Garofalo: *L'Italiana in Italia.* Bari: Laterza, 1956, p. 179.

dations in the Roman law. But in matters of family law, the Canon law had also exerted great influence. It could thus more readily be compared with Portugal and Spain than with France or Belgium, because in the latter two the process of legal secularization had advanced much further than in the three Mediterranean countries.

Although Italy was unified politically, there remained important differences between the north and the south. Cross-national comparisons can therefore be somewhat misleading, unless allowance is made for these cultural and sociological differences. The Italian women who were prominent in the national and international women's movement came mostly from the aristocratic and upper-middle class. Although the Socialists advocated the emancipation of women before the end of World War I, their influence was relatively slight. They made these demands within the context of a comprehensive economic and social change which was unacceptable to the defenders of capitalism. By 1914 this situation had changed somewhat, as was evident during the General Assembly of the ICW in Rome.

In one of the eight resolutions which were passed at that time it was recorded: "The ICW protesting vehemently against the odious wrongs of which women are the victims in time of war, contrary to international law" [and appealing] "to the next Hague Conference to consider how a more effective international protection of women may be secured which will prevent the continuance of the horrible violation of womanhood that attends all wars." The outbreak of World War I precluded any such consideration. The Italian women's organizations did their utmost to replace and support the men who went to war.[3] However, they did not demand the right to vote until after the war.

PORTUGAL

A short chronology—by Maria Regina Tavares da Silva

Although the Women's Rights Movement is usually associated with visible actions, demonstrations, speeches and banners, this has not been the case in Portugal. It was rather a slow, quiet process of affirmation and of participation of the Portuguese Women in the life of their country.

The situation of women in Portugal, influenced as it was by the

---

[3]The contributions made by Italian women in World War I are detailed in Donna Paola (Baronchelli-Grosson): *La Donna della Nuova Italia*, Milano: Dott. Riccardo Quintieri, 1917.

principle of Roman law and by Arabic culture, was always an inferior one, subject as they were to man, the all-powerful head of the family.

Some women became famous for their virtues or for their deeds, and a few literary works of the 17th and 18th Centuries record their names and their lives. But they were the exception, and the general situation of women was one of inferior status and unimportant social standing.

However, the defense of Women's Rights appeared very early on. In 1557 a very interesting book on the subject was published by Dr. Ruy Gonçalves, a professor of the old University of Coimbra. It is entitled *"Dos Priuilegios & Preaerogativas q̃ ho genero feminino tẽ por dereito comũ & ordenaçoens do Reyno, mais que ho genero masculino"*. (Of the Privileges and Prerogatives that Women have by common law & regulations of the Kingdom more than man) Dedicated to Queen Catherine, it was the first "feminist" book written in Portugal, a book in praise of women and their virtues, equal to those of men. It is also, in its second part, a compilation of women's legal privileges different from those of men.

Two centuries later, in 1785, this same work was reprinted by the Chaplain of Queen Maria I and presented to her in homage, "to show those to come that she was a defender of her sex against the slanders of the old-fashioned writers."

Recalling the ancient accusations against women, the author considered them false and unfair, as both men and women have good and bad qualities and neither of them depends on nature or sex but rather on education and customs. In order to accomplish what is required of them, women should—the book recommends—become more aware of the reality that exists beyond their domestic limitations.

Shortly following such defense, we find in 1790 an anonymous booklet—the author calls himself a friend of Reason—entitled *"Tractado sobre a Igualdade dos Sexos ou Elogio do Merecimento das Mulheres"* (Tract on Sex Equality or the Praise of Women's Merit). A short theoretical essay, it is, however, a most interesting one and strongly "feminist" in the sense of radical ideology conveyed before feminist times. According to its principles, although both sexes have different duties, some proper to woman and some proper to man, they are equivalent in dignity and social value. No one or nothing can deny "the equality of the sexes in the accomplishment of their duties." The time had now come for women to take up the defense of their own interests, to abandon forever the "eternal forgetfulness" of their own lives. If they have similar capacities, why should they not have equivalent responsibilities in public life?

The question was certainly relevant, particularly at a time of so little participation and social visibility of women.

The approaching 19th century was a time of political and social changes in Portugal. 1820 began a new political development; a new, liberal Constitution was approved in 1822, and political unrest followed the course of historical events. Whatever the changes, the general situation of women was still one of inferiority, domesticity, and rigid, stifling limitations.

But new signs started to appear:

In 1820 there was a proposal that the right to vote should be granted to a mother of six children, but it was rejected.

In 1822 the new Constitution established the law as equal for all, which meant that women were not legally disqualified from voting, although they never did so.

In 1867, the first Civil Code came into force, clearly stating that the law generally applied to both men and women, unless otherwise stated. However, following the principles of the Napoleonic Code, the woman had to obey her husband, while on the other hand, the mother could share parental power with the father.

In 1868 a feminist periodical began its publication, radical in tone and in purposes. Named *A Voz Feminina* (Feminine Voice), the collaboration was mainly feminine, and it adopted as its motto: "A free woman side by side with a free man."

Writings on women, first by men and then by women themselves, became frequent, and their impact increased in Portuguese society.

In 1872, Dr. Joaquim Lopes Praça, a university professor, published a book—*A Mulher e a Vida ou a Mulher considerada debaixo dos seus principais aspectos* (Women and Life or the main aspects of Women), in which he strongly defended the right of women to education at all levels and to full political participation, including their right to vote.

In 1892, a most important book appeared, written by D. António de Costa, a relevant figure in the educational sphere. *A Mulher em Portugal* (Woman in Portugal) is even nowadays a fundamental source for the study of the History of Women, and it certainly played an important role in the outbreak of the feminist movement which was soon to appear. Besides referring to the problem of women's education and professional training, he also defended their participation in public life, and the playing of a specific role in the "magnificent theatre" of their country.

The end of the 19th century was coming and with it the beginning of an organized movement in favor of women and by women. Maria Amalia Vaz de Carvalho, Caiel, Emilia de Sousa Costa, and Ana de Castro Osório were some of these women speaking of their own problems: the problem of education; of legal rights and responsibilities, and the problem of social and political participation. A large number of books and articles on women and specifically on feminist issues started to be published.

In 1905 Ana de Castro Osório published what could be considered the first feminist book of the movement and its manifesto, entitled Às mulheres Portuguesas (Address to Portuguese Women). In it she defined feminism and approached women's questions in a radical way. Women and politics, the legal status of women, women and work, and the education of women are some of the themes. And the fundamental aim to achieve, according to the author, was: "To educate the woman—that is the main problem to develop and implement. That is what we call feminism."

In 1909 the Republican League of Portuguese Women was created within the Republican Party, in order to help the establishment of the Republic, which took place in 1910. Its objectives, besides the political ones, were mainly along the lines of education and social participation of women, as well as equality before the law and the improvement of their whole situation.

In 1910, soon after the proclamation of the Republic, the League sent a petition to the Government concerning six specific points related to women: the divorce law, the revision of the Civil Code, the access of women to parental power on equal terms with men, the capacity for a woman to be a witness in all instances and member of a jury, the right to vote and to exercise civic and political rights, the access to some professions and careers closed to women, and the solution of the social problem of prostitution.

The right to vote, although recognized as a universal right to be established as soon as possible for all, was requested for only a small number of women—those with specific educational qualifications, writers and those having commercial or industrial careers or wealth and properties administered by themselves. Even so, it was not granted.

The Divorce Law was passed in November 1910, allowing it on equal terms for both sexes, and the new Family Law was approved in December 1910, with marriage being now based on the principle of equality between the spouses. Shortly afterwards, women were also allowed to enter new professions, namely to become civil servants. These were certainly important steps, but nothing was done concerning political rights.

In 1911, a new organization was formed, a clearly feminist one, that was going to help the debate on women's political rights and particularly the right to vote. The Association for Feminist Propaganda was led by Ana de Castro Osório. Its official organ, the periodical "A Mulher Portuguesa" (Portuguese Woman), though a short-lived one, echoed these concerns.

At the same time, women were getting into public life, into new careers, into the University. In the same year the first woman, Carolina Michaëlis de Vasconcellos, was appointed to a university chair, and in 1913 a woman graduated in law for the first time, although there were already some women doctors.

Following an interesting event in which a woman, Dr. Carolina Beatriz Ângelo, managed to vote for the first time in 1911, the law was changed in order to formally prevent women from voting.

In 1913, Law no. 3 stated that only "male citizens who can read and write" were allowed to vote. It thus legally created a new discrimination and aroused the anger of the feminist circles.

In 1914 the most important feminist organization, the *National Council of Portuguese Women*, was founded by Adelaide Cabete, a woman doctor and a leading feminist. Affiliated to the International Council of Women, it followed its trends: solidarity among women and women's associations, the improvement of women's legal status, the right to vote, the abolition of women's traffic, the education of women and the protection of women and children. The enthusiasm it aroused, the actions it developed, the network of women it managed to build, the international connections it achieved, the defense it made of women's rights—all these facts were extremely significant in the Women's Rights Movement in Portugal. The periodical *Alma Feminina* (Feminine Soul) echoed all the concerns and all the activities of the council.

The coming of the First World War, although not as important for the situation of women as in other countries, certainly had some impact.

In 1917, a new group appeared. Though not a feminist one, *The Crusade of Portuguese Women* was created to help the soldiers participating in the war and their families. It showed the growing intervention of women and the dynamism of women's associations.

Women's Rights, from a legal point of view, were also improving, and in 1917 legal discriminations in all fields but those of family law and political participation had been practically abolished.

CHAPTER 4

THE EASTERN EUROPEAN COUNTRIES BEFORE 1918

INTRODUCTION

In the period after World War II it has become quite common to look at the area of Eastern Europe as part of the Soviet orbit or the Russian sphere of influence. Communist writers have presented the historical developments of this area as decisively influenced by the Russian Revolution of October 1917. Whatever scholarly merit this view may have, it should be pointed out that before 1917 the various movements for women's rights were not significantly influenced by everything that was happening in Russia. This should not be very surprising to anyone who is familiar with comparative political and economic developments in Eastern Europe before World War I. Russia, or rather the Czarist Empire, was much more backward than the areas which are now part of Czechoslovakia, the German Democratic Republic, as well as much of Poland, and the northern part of Yugoslavia. The Russian influence was more important in Bulgaria, but even there it had little if anything to do with the women's rights movement. Ironically, Bulgaria had a constitution, and a remarkably liberal one, long before Russia did.

In addition there were other empires which exerted considerable influence in this part of the world. In the west there was the German Empire; in the southwest it was Austria-Hungary; and in the Balkans there was the Ottoman Empire.

Where and when can we speak of a women's rights movement in Eastern Europe?

If one includes the German Democratic Republic in the geographical area of Eastern Europe, one would have to begin with the German leaders. One would have to recall that there was not one unified women's movement but at least two: On the one hand there was a bourgeois-liberal feminist ideology, and on the other an increasingly more effective socialist women's movement. The latter derived much of its program from August Bebel, but toward the end of the 19th Century Clara Zetkin, who moved much further to the Left, came to exert considerable influ-

45

ence in Russia before and after the October Revolution.

In what is now Czechoslovakia, especially in the western part, there were some connections with the German and Austrian feminist movements, but there were also several indigenous developments.

RUSSIA

The first discussions of the "woman question" (*zhenskii vopros*) were influenced by such French writers as George Sand, Saint-Simon, Proudhon, Jules Michelet, and also by the English J. S. Mill. M. L. Mikhailov was one of the first Russian advocates of the emancipation of women.[1] In the 1860s, in the age of great reforms, the woman question was a topic discussed by early liberal feminists and some more radically oriented women students. But the issues were, initially at least, educational rather than political. As far as access to higher education was concerned, their successes compared favorably with those of women in many western countries.

Among the Russian intellectuals who exerted strong and lasting influence on Russian feminists of different backgrounds and orientations was N. G. Chernyshevsky. [His classic *What is to be done (Chto delat)?* was first published in 1867.] Russian feminists of the 1870s and 1880s were not interested in the efforts to secure women's suffrage through legal reforms and ultimately a written constitution. Actually, there was no reason why they should have supported the constitutionalists, because none of them advocated women's suffrage.

The percentage of women who participated in revolutionary activities had grown rapidly in the 1870s, and by 1880 women occupied key positions in the revolutionary movement.[2]

The Provisional Government headed by Kerensky, which was founded in March 1917, took the Fundamental Law of 1906 as the starting point for its reform program. In keeping with earlier pledges, the government directed that the electoral system be reformed along democratic lines. All men and women who had attained the age of twenty were to be eligible to vote. Equality before the law, irrespective of social position or any other criterion, was to be firmly established. After the Communists seized power on November 7, 1917, they reaffirmed the voting rights of women but they disenfranchised "class enemies".

[1] R. Stites: M. L. Mikhailov and the Emergence of the "Woman Question," *Canadian Slavic Studies*, vol. 3 (1969), p. 178.

[2] McNeal, Robert: Women in the Russian Radical Movement," *Journal of Social History*, vol. v (1971-72), p. 143.

ALBANIA

by Karen Shaw Kerpen

In the traditional Albanian society during the Ottoman rule the status of women was similar to that of other Moslem countries. In rural areas, feudalism reinforced patriarchy, and women were used as property to enhance family and clan wealth and alliances.[1] Foreign domination rested on ignorance, poverty, and oppression of the Albanians, with women being the most oppressed group.

In most instances:

> The girl was treated much like a market commodity rather than a human being; she was sold off for money and married when still a child, given to the highest bidder. The marriages transacted in this way made the girl a creature who had sold herself, her dignity, and her freedom . . . the wife's opinion carried no weight. She was considered to be preordained for manual labor, for sewing, treated as a beast of burden and obliged to wash the feet of the other members of the family.[2]
>
> Women were mute creatures who had no voice in household problems, and still less in social affairs. They were confined within the four walls of their house . . . not consulted about their personal affairs such as their marriages or betrothals which were arranged to suit private interests . . . Disdained at home by their fathers, husbands, and sons and outside the home by all society, the women had come to be regarded as ignorant creatures.[3]

Fathers and husbands could use violence to control wives and daughters. A preference for boy children was universal, and the high proportion of men to women (106 to 100) has been linked to the neglect infant girls experienced. Under Islamic law, polygamy was permitted. Women were economically dependent upon fathers and husbands and could not inherit property.

Customs further debased the position of women:

> The husband could ride while his wife had to follow on foot . . . at social gatherings the women danced and sang apart

---

[1] *An Outline of the People's Socialist Republic of Albania,* (Tirana; The "8 Nentori" Publishing House, 1978), p. 101.

[2] Z. Xholi, "Marxism and Leninism: The Fundamental Problems of Women," *Problems of the Struggle for the Complete Emancipation of Women,* (Tirana: Political Book Publishing House, 1973), p. 46.

[3] *Ibid.,* p. 58.

from men ... Women were assigned separate places apart from the menfolk, both in the church and the mosque. Even at home they had their separate places.[4]

Catholic and Moslem women wore veils. Religious leaders considered women unholy, and a folklore describing the wicked nature of women prevailed.[5]

The first women's organization was founded in 1910 in Korca, in part responding to the struggle for national independence. It was called "The Morning Star." Member activists participated in the drive for independence by sheltering partisans, organizing independence groups, and joining in front-line battles.

When the independence of Albania was declared on November 28, 1912, Albanian women began to organize other women's societies in several regions in the country. Women in these associations started schools for women and girls, helped those refugees who had fled areas of battle, and encouraged political participation in national plans. Independence was short-lived, however. The Great Powers met in 1913 to reset Albanian borders and send a German prince, Wilhelm Wied, to rule the country. During World War I, Albania was occupied by the Entente Powers, who wanted to eventually dismember it.

BULGARIA

Some Bulgarian legal historians of the inter-war period asserted that the status of women in their country was better in the 19th Century than in the 20th. They pointed to the fact that the patriarchal system was not as firmly established as in other areas of the Balkans. Women had responsibilities in domestic affairs, and they had impressive legal rights in matters involving family, property, and inheritance. The famous Constitution of 1878 did not refer to these rights, but it did not abridge them. But, at the turn of the century several decrees were enacted which were designed to restrict or weaken these rights. It was against these efforts that the first Bulgarian feminist organization was founded in 1901: The Bulgarian Women's Federation (Bulgarski Zenski Soyuz). Twice each month it published a paper called "Woman's Voice" (Zenski Glas).

---

[4]Zihni Sako, "Women in Albanian Society: Yesterday and Today," *Problems of the Struggle for the Complete Emancipation of Women*, p. 217.
[5]*Ibid.*, pp. 219-220.

CZECHOSLOVAKIA

The roots of the women's rights movement in the Czech-speaking part of the Austrian empire go back to the middle of the Nineteenth Century. Božena Němcová's novel *Babička* (The little grandmother) did much to reinforce the traditional respect for the role of women in society. While she may not be regarded as an ardent feminist, she did inspire others. In 1875, one of them, Eliška Krásnoharská, an excellent writer in her own right, became the editor of *Ženske Listy* (Women's Pages) and stayed on in that capacity until 1911, thus providing the much needed consistency and continuity of the women's movement. Some of the Czech women who came to assume leadership roles in independent Czechoslovakia received their apprenticeship working on the *Ženske Listy*. The pre-World War I women's rights movement included an important American-born woman, Charlotte Garrigue, who married Thomas G. Masaryk in 1878. At that time her husband was already known as a supporter of the movement. In 1918 when he became the first president of the Czechoslovak Republic he used his great prestige to press for a progressive women's rights policy. One of their daughters, Alice Masaryk, was very active in the women's rights movement before and after independence.

In the eastern part of what is now Czechoslovakia, there were relatively few activities as far as women's rights were concerned. Women were active along with men in the struggle for independence from Hungary, but their outlook was very traditional and in keeping with their strong adherence to the teachings of the Roman Catholic Church.

HUNGARY

Before World War I the question of women's rights was overshadowed by other forms of inequality. Hungary was one of the most feudal countries in the world, and at a time when neighboring countries were carrying on land reforms, no comparable steps were taken in Hungary. The legal system was not only feudal, it was emphatically patriarchal.

One exception to the strongly entrenched patriarchal principle was contained in the *Sanctio Pragmatica* (1722), which provided for female succession to the throne of Hungary. It must be remembered, of course, that this was a document designed to protect the dynastic interests of the Habsburgs.

In Hungary there was little organized feminist activity, but there were some highly energetic feminists. The name of Rosika Schwimmer is widely known in the United States because of the so-called Schwimmer case. What is less known is that Rosika Schwimmer was a very prominent feminist in Hungary as well as a pacifist of international renown. In 1913 she organized an International Congress in Budapest, which was devoted to the promotion of women's suffrage. Immediately after World War I she was the first Hungarian woman to serve as ambassador to Switzerland.

POLAND

Before World War I Poland's society was highly stratified, and the members of the nobility (Szlachta), with very few exceptions, were not receptive to progressive ideas. The middle class was very small compared with that of Austria, Bohemia, and Moravia.

There was a time at the end of the 18th Century when western ideas became widely known among intellectuals, and Poland had a written constitution before France. This was the famous Constitution of May 3, 1791. But like the French and all the other constitutions of that period, it was more concerned with the rights of men. One can speculate that it might have been a starting point for progressive changes, but this was not to be possible because Poland was divided at the end of the 18th Century.

The damage that these partitions caused to the political and economic development of Poland can hardly be overstated. There were virtually no opportunities in the Prussian– and Russian–controlled areas of Poland. Only in Galicia, the Austro-Hungarian part of what was formerly an independent Polish State, was some political participation possible. For a long time only the members of the nobility could exert any influence, provided they were willing to work within the framework of the Austro-Hungarian Monarchy. This began to change in the early part of the 20th Century. By 1912, most of the now legal political parties were committed to the reestablishment of an independent Polish State. Nationalistic men and women were unified toward the achievement of this goal.

Before the end of World War I, the condition of Polish women differed considerably in the various parts which were to become part of the Polish State. In the Austrian region the Austrian Civil Code (ABGB) of 1811 was in effect, while the German Civil Code (BGB) of 1900 was applied in the western part of the area. In the east, Russian legislation was in effect. Finally, in the small kingdom of Poland the

French Civil Code, which had been introduced in 1925, remained in force.

In some parts of Poland the beginnings of a women's movement may be traced to the middle of the 19th Century. But there were no significant further developments, and it was not until the first decade of the 20th Century that organizations for women's rights began to function. A few of the Polish Socialists favored women's suffrage, not as an end in itself but rather as part of their struggle against feudalism, capitalism, and imperialism. At the end of World War I Poland seemed an unlikely country for a more equalitarian social and political order. It came as a surprise when universal male and female suffrage was decreed on November 28, 1918, ten days after the establishment of an independent Polish government.

ROMANIA

It was not until 1878 that Romania emerged as an independent state; but a small feminist organization had existed in Bucharest since 1867. From the middle of the 19th Century women were active in several cities of Transylvania and the Bukovina, which were then provinces of Austria-Hungary. The early feminists were, for the most part, members of the rising bourgeoisie. They were concerned not only with the issue of emancipation but the improvement of educational opportunities and social services for women. In some respects the legal status of women was relatively favorable, but it was full of contradictions.

YUGOSLAVIA

Yugoslavia is a relatively recent name which identifies some very old political entities. Between 1918 and 1929, it was known as the Kingdom of Serbs, Croats and Slovenes. Prior to 1918, only Serbia and Montenegro were independent states. Slovenia was under Austrian rule and Croatia was controlled by Hungary. This suggests only part of the multiethnic, political, legal, religious, and cultural diversity of the people who now inhabit Yugoslavia.

The attitudes of women and of men toward women differed considerably in these various regions. In the Moslem areas there was virtually no interest in the feminist movement. But in Serbia, Slovenia and Croatia one can trace the beginnings of women's organizations long before independence. Vida Tomšič has called attention to the work of Svetozar Marković, who, a century ago, stated that "the question of the emancipation of women is indivisibly linked with the social transformation as a whole."[1] In 1906, a National Women's Union (Narodni Ženski Savez) was formed from a number of women's organizations. Soon after that a split developed between the bourgeois feminists and certain leaders of working women, who, like the Socialist women of western countries, believed that "the women's question" must be solved within the broader economic and social context. Tomšič refers to the 1910 International Conference of Social Democratic Women, held in Copenhagen, and to one of the leaders of the Serbian Social Democratic Party, who reported on a speech given by Clara Zetkin. At that time the Central Secretariat of Socialist Women was created. The first issue of a newspaper called *Jednakost* (Equality) was published on October 1, 1910. As cited by Tomšič it declared that working women cannot restrict their demands "to the programme of ladies from higher circles who would like greater rights for women, but on condition that the present day unjust social system be preserved . . ."[2] This marked the beginning of a more militant and class-conscious movement for women's rights in Belgrade and other localities.

[1]Vida Tomšič: *Woman in the Development of Socialist Self-Managing Yugoslavia.* Belgrade: Yugoslovenska Stvarnost, 1980, p. 20.

[2]Svetozar Marković emphasized this point in his introduction to the Serbo-Croatian translation of John Stuart Mill's book *The Subjection of Women,* in 1871. Here he stressed the importance of a woman's education and the effect a lack of education had on her role as a mother, in the economic sphere, and as a member of society at large. He encouraged readers of this book to seriously consider Mill's discussion of women's rights and to consider the question of women's emancipation as inseparable from the question of social transformation and "the emancipation of mankind from all forms of evil, vice, tyranny, and slavery." Svetozar Markovic, *Izabrani Spisi,* (Selected Works) Srpska Knjizevna Zadruga, Belgrade, 1937, pp. 46-50.

Part II

Comparative Trends in Europe between 1918 and 1945

CHAPTER 5

MAJOR TRENDS 1918-1945

As far as continental Europe is concerned, the so-called interwar period may be divided into two decades. The first, from 1918 to 1928, is quite different from the subsequent decade which began in 1929 and ended in 1939 with the Nazi invasion of Poland. During the first period impressive efforts were made, especially in central and eastern Europe, toward the development of parliamentary systems of government. By 1929, with a few notable exceptions, the future of these regimes appeared very much in doubt. After 1933 when Hitler came to power, authoritarianism was spreading rapidly, and with it women's rights, as other human rights, suffered great setbacks. Between 1918 and 1922 the principle of women's suffrage was incorporated into more than a dozen European National Constitutions. Included in this count are the Constitutions of Estonia (1920) and Latvia (1922). The specific provisions are, for the most part, very similar. In the constitutional conventions there appeared to be general agreement on the basic provisions concerning suffrage. Differences surfaced when it came to the debates on economic and social provisions. Some of the constitutions of this period reflect attempted compromises between liberal and socialist conceptions of women's rights. The drafters had no difficulty in agreeing on the principle of equality between men and women. But while the proponents of liberalism called for "equality before the law," socialists and communists were not satisfied with this conception because it did not go far enough and because the law appeared to them more of an obstacle than an avenue toward the development of a new society.

If one compares the basic trends in the four areas of Europe, the following may be noted:

1. By 1919 the constitutional and legal foundations for the advancement of women were firmly established in all the Scandinavian countries. But, contrary to what is usually assumed, no spectacular progress was made in any of the five countries between 1918 and 1945. The reasons given for this stagnation are largely economic, as will be further noted.

2. In some of the Western European countries, especially Austria, Germany and Great Britain, advances were made in the field of women's

rights and political participation. But efforts to introduce women's suffrage in France and Belgium ended in failure.

3. In the Southern and Mediterranean countries the first decade brought no encouragement to proponents of women's rights. One can speculate whether things could have been different if the fascists had not come to power in Italy. After 1922 the fascist ideologists set out to transform the fundamental goals of feminism by building on the traditional stereotype of motherhood. They discouraged women from seeking professional careers of their own. Mothers were told to take care of their children and provide happy homes.

4. In the Soviet Union the integration of women into the planned economy proceeded at a rapid rate. However, economic mobilization and political advancement did not go hand in hand. The percentage of women who moved into important decision-making positions was very small. Those who did had to demonstrate to the members of the Party that they were communists first and feminists only to the extent compatible with the goals set by the male leaders.

A much different atmosphere prevailed in Czechoslovakia. Women of different political persuasions had helped to build the new republic, and they were given a significant share in power once the state machinery was in place. However, this statement applies mainly to the western part of the state. In Slovakia the traditional political order was less conducive to women's participation. In the other parts of eastern Europe the initial gains were lost as more authoritarian regimes took over.

Many explanations and justifications for the enactment of emergency powers were given by the dictators or would-be dictators: the threat of foreign invasion, domestic unrest, political corruption. Dictatorships were established not only in Italy (1922) but also in Portugal (1929). About the same time King Alexander of Yugoslavia established himself as a royal dictator. In the Soviet Union, Stalin consolidated his power after he succeeded in eliminating Trotsky. As the first decade drew to a close there were ominous signs that the prospects for democracy and equal rights were becoming even more dismal.

Although parliamentary democracy was firmly established in Great Britain, the Scandinavian countries, Belgium, France, Luxembourg and the Netherlands, the women's movements either suffered setbacks or had to face formidable opposition. It is difficult to offer one specific explanation which would fit all these countries. But it is possible to point to one common factor: the deep and prolonged economic depression which in various degrees beset all these countries. There is ample evidence to show that many men and a large number of women were greatly worried that "the breadwinner" might lose his job. Competition from women seeking employment was viewed with alarm and resentment. Blunt slogans were directed particularly against married women. They were discouraged if not intimidated. "Double employment" of husband and wife was to be penalized. In some countries the beginnings of the legislation which discriminates against employed married women can be traced to this period.

In Italy the fascist regime had already turned the clock back in many areas of political, economic and social life. But it was left to the theorists and propagandists of national socialism to develop a total and totalitarian model of the new order. Many aspects of the new order were not new but an elaboration of old stereotypes. National Socialists agreed that women should stay at home and refrain from competing with men in the labor market. But church attendance was also frowned upon. There was only one loyalty: to Hitler and the New Order. As in Fascist Italy and the Soviet Union, there were rewards and benefits for families with several children. Women were no longer represented in the German Parliament, which had been reduced to an echo chamber of the Führer's statements.

In Portugal Salazar established a highly authoritarian regime which was supposedly built on traditional values. Whatever gains Spanish women had achieved during the short-lived republican regime were lost after the military victory of Franco's forces. For feminists there was only one more encouraging event. It took place in a rather unexpected place—Turkey. The first step toward women's suffrage had already been taken in December 1929, when women were authorized to vote in local elections. In December 1934 they were given equal rights with men in national elections. But what was done in Turkey was an isolated progressive reform. It was not followed by any further breakthroughs.

There was, of course, the Soviet Constitution of 1936, which was then known as the Stalin Constitution. It contained a remarkable catalogue of economic and social rights. But it was a document which was designed to improve the image of the Soviet regime. It did not drastically change domestic policy. The women of the area now defined as Eastern Europe continued to be subjected to discriminatory legislation. It is doubtful whether they benefitted from the so-called protective legislation. There is reason to believe that it was used against them on the ground that certain physical labor was either too hard or too dangerous for women. If one includes Czechoslovakia in the area of Eastern Europe, it might be seen as a remarkable exception to all these negative developments. In the second decade, as in the first, the women of Czechoslovakia continued to make progress, especially in the most western part of the country.

Having sketched these discouraging developments, we should make brief reference to the work of international and non-governmental organizations during this period.

With respect to the League of Nations, which came into being in 1919, relatively little needs to be said. Article 7 of the Covenant of the League of Nations had established the principle that women were to be eligible for appointments on equal terms with men. A relatively high percentage of women did find employment with the League, but the overwhelming number of jobs were secretarial or clerical.

In the International Labor Organization (ILO), which also started its work in 1919, the situation was similar. It is fair to say that the ILO did take a greater interest in the condition of women and laid some important groundwork for future international conventions. However from the very beginning the main concern was with the *protection* of women and children rather than equal opportunity. It was this concern with protective legislation pertaining to night work as well as heavy and dangerous work, which prompted member states to develop legislation of their own along these lines. In retrospect and on the basis of pertinent documentation one may conclude that it was largely the work of the non-governmental women's organizations which made systematic efforts in specific areas of major concern to women. The number of organizations increased greatly after World War I. As will be shown, almost every European country had some kind of women's organization. But they differed considerably in their objectives and methods of operating. Those affiliated with the ICW benefitted from the experiences of sister organizations in other member countries. But there were other, new international non-governmental organizations. The *International Federation of University Women* was founded in 1919. In addition to the *Union Mondiale des organisations catholiques*, which dates from 1910, there was the *Federation mondiale des jeunesses feminines catholiques* which grew rapidly after its founding in 1930. The *International Federation of Business and Professional Women*, which also dates from 1930, was relatively small, but it did important work on behalf of the women it represented. Similarly, after 1919 the *Medical Women's International Association* did important work in assisting women physicians and women workers in the field of public health.

All these and other organizations, national and international, deserve more recognition for their contributions. As far as civic and political activities are concerned the ICW continued its work immediately after the end of World War I. One of the issues which received systematic attention was that of the nationality of married women. A good beginning was made in Kristiania in 1920 and it was carried forward at executive meetings in The Hague (1922) and especially in Copenhagen (1924). When the ICW met in Washington in 1925 it was pleased to note that the League of Nations had appointed a Commission to study this problem with a view toward the codification of international law. They also recommended that women be added to the Commission. A new concern which was discussed at the Washington meeting was the role of women in political parties. The prevailing view was that in the countries where women had the right to vote, they should join political parties but organize their own sections within them so as to maximize their influence on the platforms and activities of political parties. The issue of the nationality of married women was again discussed at length in Vienna in 1930 and in Paris in 1934. It was considered a suitable topic for testing male attitudes toward gender or sex equality. It was for this reason that the delegates at the ICW meeting in Vienna urged that the principle of sex equality be incorporated into the Hague Convention on the Nationality of Women. This view was reaffirmed several times after 1934.

But gradually the principle of equality was brought out more directly. At the Executive meeting in Stockholm (1933) the ICW noted "with satisfaction the good results obtained by the collaboration of men and women in legislative and administrative bodies." In 1936 in Dubrovnik the ICW urged the national councils in countries in which women had achieved the right to vote to intensity their efforts before elections. In the countries in which women could not vote, national councils were asked to increase their efforts to achieve suffrage. The last meeting before World War II, held in Edinburgh in 1938, passed the following resolution:

> Whereas the ICW has affirmed its profound conviction that it is only by permitting and encouraging women to play a full and responsible part in the political, economic and intellectual life of their country that the civilisation and the prosperity of future generations may be developed on a sound basis of general understanding and enlightenment, the sanctity of the home preserved and moral standards be prevented from sinking; the ICW urges its member organisations to continue their work for the equality of rights between men and women in all fields.

CHAPTER 6

THE SCANDINAVIAN COUNTRIES
1918-1945

INTRODUCTION

In the period before 1918 the Scandinavian countries clearly led the way on the long road to women's rights and political participation. They continued to lead, but on several occasions the women of these countries might have been discouraged by obstacles and reverses. One of the impediments was the economic deterioration and large-scale unemployment. Another, which was not just temporary, was the deep-rooted conservatism and traditionalism, which now came to interact with the sporadic campaigns to get married women out of the workforce, to make room for the men who were unemployed or underemployed. A positive factor was the competition which was now provided by the Soviet Union, where it was said women had been completely emancipated and put on equal footing with men.

What needs to be analyzed on a comparative basis are the constitutional, legal, and political developments in the individual countries of Scandinavia. As will be shown, contrary to what is often assumed these developments do not reflect identical patterns, and there certainly were not continuous and steady advances in all these countries. There were impressive gains immediately after World War I, but the momentum did not last, and a decade later the situation looked rather discouraging in several of the Scandinavian countries. A look at the map of the area points up the strategic problems of at least three of these countries: Denmark, Finland, and Norway. Denmark and Norway were more troubled by the ambitions of Adolf Hitler than by the U.S.S.R. As it turned out these fears were entirely justified.

The situation in Finland was different but no less worrisome. In 1926 the first Socialist government was elected under the leadership of Vaino Tanner. Three years later Finnish fascists, known as the Lapua Movement, initiated a reign of terror in a bid for political power. They attacked Communist organizations and leaders. On November 11, 1930 bills were passed by the Finnish Parliament which destroyed the Finnish

Communist movement. Relations between the Soviet Union and Finland deteriorated, as Russia feared a German invasion of her territory by German forces coming across the Finnish border. The Soviets tried to pressure Finland into committing itself to a definite position in such a situation. Assurances were not enough for the Soviets, who also wanted to establish military bases on Finnish islands. The Finns refused. The situation worsened between the two countries, and on November 30, 1939 the Winter War began with the Soviet Union invading Finland. It was ended by the Treaty of Moscow on March 12, 1940. In this costly war the people of Finland had to fight against two enemies: the U.S.S.R. and Nazi Germany.

Peace was short-lived. The Finns entered into an alliance with Germany in an attempt to free themselves from Soviet control. Thus started the Second Finno-Russian War, also known as the Continuation War (1941-1944). This war established the nature of Finno-Soviet relations in the post-1945 period. The Friendship Treaty of 1948 greatly limited Finnish sovereignty and created a situation which came to be known as "Finlandization." While the country is technically independent and sovereign, it must seek Soviet approval on many issues and constantly reaffirm its friendship with the Soviet Union. This unique relationship is still operating today. However, Finland interacts with the rest of the Scandinavian countries by means of its membership in the Nordic Council.

It is against this background of economic depression and strategic insecurity that the development of women's rights and political participation should be studied. The Swedish situation was different in the sense that neutrality had been profitable economically and strategically. Sweden was not threatened by either Communism or Fascism.

SWEDEN

It may be recalled that Sweden was the only Scandinavian country where women did not achieve complete suffrage before the end of 1918. This came in 1919 when legislation was passed which amended the Constitution, and along with the *Riksdag* Act universal male and female suffrage became a reality.

In the general elections of 1921 all men and women over the age of 23 had the right to vote. But there was some controversy over why only 47 percent of the eligible women had cast their ballots, while 62 percent of the men had voted. Whatever may have been the explanation for this low turnout, it did not last because in subsequent elections women voted in large numbers, as did men. However, the number of women candidates and elected representatives remained small. Of the five women elected to the second chamber in 1921, two were members of the Liberal Party, two were Social Democrats, and one belonged to the Conservative Party.

On the basis of the official statistics of women's representation in the *Riksdag* (parliament), one may conclude that Sweden's record in the field of social legislation during the inter-war period was much more impressive than that of women's political participation. In 1921, after the first election in which women were allowed to vote, there were five women in the second chamber. In 1929, there were only three, in 1933 again five, and in 1937 their number had grown to ten out of 230 members. In the first chamber, which consisted of 150 members, there was only one woman in 1929 and 1933. Thereafter, no woman served in the first chamber until 1945.

Once again the statistical data indicate that women remained under-represented as a group. Enfranchisement gave them the right to participate in the political process, which they did in numbers smaller than male participation, but representation was still predominantly male. It is clear that women's participation in politics was not increasing significantly in this period. But it is necessary to look beyond mere quantitative data. One area which would have to be more closely studied is that of social legislation. The Marriage Code of 1920 was undoubtedly the first fundamental break with the patriarchal tradition. Women were no longer legally under the guardianship of their husbands but were equal partners at the age of 21. The constitutional change also paved the way for women's careers, or at least employment in the civil service. It should be noted, however, that the parliamentary legislation of 1923 did not provide access, let alone equal access, to all fields of public employment. An important law concerning equal entitlement to positions in government service was the Competence Act of 1925. The National Pension Act of 1935 established the principle that pensions were to be paid on an equal basis to men and women. By the end of the period, legislation was passed which prohibited dismissals of employees because of marriage. Still, the economic situation remained unsatisfactory.

The situation was, of course, much worse right after World War I and improved only slightly during the inter-war period. There were great wage differentials between men and women. Even more serious was the stereotyping of what was considered appropriate work for each gender. This is the reason why Swedish feminists have placed so much emphasis on the need for changes in the sex roles.

Thus, the actual gains achieved by women of Sweden up to the 1940s was very uneven to say the least.

DENMARK

In 1918, the historian Nina Bang was the first woman to become a member of Parliament, and in 1924 she was again a pioneer when she served as a member of the Danish government. The pertinent articles of the Danish Constitution, which provided the basis for further legislation and political action were the following:

Article 30:

All men and women natives of the Kingdom who have completed their 25th year, and have a fixed place of abode in the country are entitled to vote in the elections for the Folketing.

There were three legal grounds for disqualification: (1) if they had been found guilty in a judicial proceeding, (2) if they were recipients of public relief, and (3) if they had gone into bankruptcy.

Article 31:

Every person who satisfies the conditions required for the right to vote in the Folketing (See Article 30) is eligible for election to the Folketing.

Article 34:

> Every person qualified to vote for elections to the Folketing
> is also entitled to vote in elections to the Landsting, provided
> he has completed his 35th year, and has permanent residence
> in the electoral area in question.

Article 56 went further than most of the contemporary legislation
in other countries in that the principle of legal equality of both parents,
in relation to their children, was firmly established.

The only exclusive male right and duty refers to military service.
According to Article 88:

> Every man fit to bear arms is personally obliged to take part
> in defense of the fatherland, in accordance with the special
> rules prescribed by law.

Important legislation was passed during this period in the area of family
law; especially Act No. 277 of June 30, 1922, and Act No. 56 of March
18, 1925. While the constitutional and legal foundations for the equalization of rights between men and women was adequate, the traditional
attitudes toward the issue of women in politics had not changed.

Membership of women in the *Folketing*, during the entire inter-war
period, in the lower chamber, ranged from only 2.1 to 2.9 percent. Although women were supposed to have equal access to public office
since 1921, this process occurred very slowly, and in some areas, like
the diplomatic service, there was no change at all during the entire inter-
war period.

Until 1929, the *Landsting* remained a stronghold of conservatives
and conservatism. But attitudes began to change in that year when the
Social Democrats got together to form a coalition government. It was
this coalition which directed public policy until April 1940, when German troops invaded Denmark and Norway.

NORWAY

Developments in Norway during this period, unlike those in Denmark, were quite significant and dramatic. The 1913 constitutional
amendments which introduced women's suffrage were the foundations
upon which other advances were made. As far as the political field is
concerned, the advances were not spectacular. Indeed, during the first

decade after World War I, there was little tangible progress in political participation. In the field of family law the progress was more impressive. One of the most important pieces of legislation was the Marriage Act of 1927, which superseded that of 1888. The latter had codified the husband's right over property owned jointly by both spouses. In 1927 the wife was made an equal partner.

Shortly thereafter the women of Norway experienced a serious setback. Indeed, the advancement in the field of women's rights was almost completely hindered by the world economic crisis, which hit Norway very severely. In the face of rapidly mounting unemployment there was increasing pressure against the employment of married women. Fewer than 2 percent of married women were employed in 1930. Still there was bitter agitation to get these women out of the job market. The slogan was "Down with double earners." Of course, as the crisis deepened and spread, this was to become a widespread attitude in many European countries. Such attacks on women's right to work, however, acted as a stimulus to supporters of the feminist movement in the 1930s. Some progress was made in the later 1930s, but all further efforts were disrupted by the outbreak of World War II and Nazi Germany's invasion of Norway on April 9, 1940.

FINLAND

The Finnish Republic was established on February 17, 1919 with the promulgation of the Constitution Act of Finland. The Diet Act of July 20, 1906 remained in force. The principle of universal male and female suffrage was reaffirmed by the following articles, which are still in force. Article 4 of the Constitution provides:

> The rights of Finnish citizenship belong to every person born of Finnish parents and to every woman of foreign nationality who has married a Finnish citizen.
> A citizen of another country may be admitted to Finnish citizenship in accordance with the conditions and procedure laid down by law.

Article 5 declared that "all Finnish citizens shall be equal before the law." Thus, Finland maintained its progressive position toward suffrage in spite of the rather conservative nationalists in control of the government.

In Finland, the inter-war period was a time of considerable activity. The Diet Act of 1906 was superseded by the Parliament Act of January

13, 1928, which is officially regarded as part of the Constitution. Article 6, which concerns the right to vote, is included in the following passage. Its text was amended on November 24, 1944 to read as follows:

> Every Finnish citizen, man or woman, who has attained the age of 21 before the year in which the election takes place shall be an elector."

Article 7, as amended on November 24, 1944 states that

> Every elector shall be eligible to become a member of Parliament without regard to residence.
> Eligibility shall not, however, extend to those who are on active military service.

It should be noted that during the inter-war period the number of women in the unicameral Parliament, as compared with the most recent period, was relatively small. In 1919, there were 17 women in the Parliament. The figures for the subsequent years are as follows:

1922	20 out of a total of 200
1924	17
1927	17
1929	15
1930	11
1933	14
1936	16
1939	16
1945	17

Again we see the effects of the economic crisis. During the years of the world depression, women's representation declined but improved as the depression began to decline in severity and the world moved toward war. However, with more than 50 percent of the women participating in national elections since 1908, Finnish women were under-represented in terms of the parliamentary seats they held throughout this entire period.

While the political situation of women did not change significantly, there were important changes in their legal status. In 1926, legislation was enacted which was supposed to provide for equal access to the civil service in Finland. But in practice, equality was not achieved because most positions occupied by women were in the lower and middle echelons.

More important gains were made in legislation concerning the private area. The Marriage Law of June 13, 1929 broke new ground in safeguarding the rights of married women, as did the law for the protection of children of January 17, 1936.

From an economic point of view, the progress was less satisfactory as far as women were concerned. However, the lack of progress must be understood in the light of the economic crisis of the 1930s and the dangerous international situation. The Soviet Union invaded Finland on November 30, 1939. As with the other Scandinavian countries, not until the post-World War II years would there be a new movement to improve the status of women.

ICELAND

Iceland for reasons of geography and history followed a different course. During the first decades following the end of World War I, there were no major developments as far as women's rights were concerned. The Danish legislation was in effect, but the policy toward women tended to be somewhat more conservative than in Denmark. It might not have changed much had it not been for World War II.

On May 18, 1920 the Constitution of Iceland was promulgated. It did not alter the relationship with Denmark, but it provided the basis for further institution-building by establishing a Supreme Court. The sentiment for complete independence grew throughout the 1920s, and as early as 1928 the representatives of all political parties in the *Althing* (parliament) declared their intention to seek complete independence from Denmark.

In 1934, the Constitution was amended to reduce the voting age from 25 to 21. When German troops invaded Denmark on April 9, 1940 the link with Denmark was disrupted, and within hours the *Althing* acted to transfer the powers and functions vested in the Danish government to Iceland. Royal power was transferred to the Icelander cabinet.

On May 10, 1940 British military forces landed in Iceland to prevent the possibility of a German invasion. Iceland entered into a defense agreement with the United States on June 8, 1941. American troops replaced the British.

On June 16, 1941 the *Althing* elected a regent to assume the powers of the king of Denmark. On June 16, 1944 the *Althing* resolved to declare that the 1918 Act of the Union between Iceland and Denmark was no longer valid. The Constitution of the Republic of Iceland came into force on the following day, June 17, 1944. It is not a completely new document but rather a modified version of the 1920 text. Although it provides for a president, the basic features are that of a parliamentary cabinet system. Article 4 provides that:

> any person not less than thirty-five years of age who fulfills the qualifications necessary to vote for the Althing, with the exception of the residence qualification, is eligible for the Presidency.[1]

[1]This wording does not specify that the president has to be a male, but subsequent articles make references to "he" and "his" (articles 5, 7, 11, 12, 13, 15, 29). However, this did not prevent a woman from winning the presidency in 1980.

CHAPTER 7

THE WESTERN EUROPEAN COUNTRIES
1918-1945

INTRODUCTION

During World War I the women of Western Europe and their organizations had suspended their campaigns for equal rights and done whatever they could in backing up their men. With the end of the war the struggle for their rights was resumed. It was moderately successful in Great Britain, Iceland, Luxembourg, Austria, Germany, and the Netherlands, but it failed in Belgium, France, and Switzerland. The successes and failures in the ten Western European countries which have been grouped together are analyzed in the following pages.

AUSTRIA

On November 8, 1918, the Catholic Women's Organization joined the other women's groups in demanding women's suffrage. Four days later, the provisional National Assembly proclaimed universal suffrage for men and women as part of the Provisional Constitution. In February 1919, women participated for the first time in Austrian elections, but of a total of 170 there were only ten women in the Constituent National Assembly. Eight were Social Democrats, one a Christian Socialist, and one was identified as representing the "Grossdeutsche."

Several draft constitutions were produced by different political parties. The Christian Socialists completed their first draft constitution on May 14, 1919. According to Article 13, all citizens were obliged to participate in the defense, but it exempted women from "defense duty" (Wehrpflicht). Furthermore, service with weapons was to be limited to male citizens.

On April 28, 1920, the "Great German" Deputy Dr. Franz Donghofer presented another draft constitution on behalf of his party. According to Article 12, "all citizens are equal before the law, they have without gender distinction (Unterschied des Geschlechts) equal rights and duties. All privileges are abolished." It made no specific reference to military service.

The Social Democrats presented their draft constitution on July 7, 1920. Its Article 117 stated that "all citizens are equal before the law. Privileges, on the basis of nationality, confession, gender, estate or class, are forever abolished." In the original text of the Federal Constitution of October 1920, which was largely drafted by Prof. Hans Kelsen, the key article 7 stated:

> (1) All federal citizens are equal before the law. Privileges of birth, gender, social position, class and confession are excluded.
> (2) Public officials, including the members of the Federal Army, are guaranteed the undiminished exercise of their political rights.

On October 1, 1920, the Austrian National Assembly adopted a constitution which went into effect on November 10. All citizens, male and female, who had reached the age of 20 were given the right to vote. All who had reached the age of 24 were qualified to be candidates for election to the National Assembly, which was to consist of 165 deputies.

During the 1920s, the Social Democratic women deputies were the most persistent in demanding complete equality of rights between men and women. They pressed for the repeal of all legislation which discriminated against women and against illegitimate children. In 1926, the "Vienna Program" of the Austrian Social Democratic Party (1901) was replaced by the so-called Program of Linz (Linzer Programm), which not only updated the earlier one but was also regarded as a kind of codification of Austro-Marxism. A whole section (No 4) was devoted to the "women's question." It repeated the demand for the abolition of all laws which put women at a disadvantage and called for equal treatment in the public service.

The national elections of November 9 resulted in a realignment of political forces. The Social Democrats now emerged as the strongest party, with over 41 percent of the popular vote. However the Christian Socialists, who had won only 35.65 percent of the popular vote, were able to form a coalition government with two other parties and to exclude the Social Democrats from the cabinet, which was formed by Dr. Ender on December 4. It was Dr. Otto Ender who was entrusted by the Council of Ministers with the task of drafting a new constitution along more authoritarian-corporate lines. The wording of this document was as tricky as the manner in which this reactionary coalition had acquired power. The second part contained lengthy but often ambivalent provisions concerning the general rights of citizens. Article 16 was the one that referred to the status of women.

(1) All federal citizens are equal before the law. They may be treated unequally only insofar as real reasons (sachliche Gründe) justify. In particular, privileges of birth, social standing or class are excluded.

(2) Women have the same rights and duties as men, insofar as the law does not provide otherwise.

(3) Public offices are equally accessible to all patriotic federal citizens, who meet the prescribed requirements.

(4) Public officials are granted undiminished exercise of their political rights, insofar as the Constitution does not contain exceptions.

(5) For persons, who are serving in the Armed Forces, or are professionally serving it, furthermore, for State employees, who are active in the State Security Service, the law may introduce restrictions of political or otherwise constitutionally granted rights.

The final Article (182) of this document called for the promulgation of a special federal constitutional law which would provide the transition toward the establishment of a Corporate State. This was done a few days later, with the promulgation of the Federal Constitution Law of April 30, 1934 "concerning extraordinary measures in the area of the constitution," and the Constitution Transition Law of June, 1934. Through these manipulations the government was empowered to govern by decree. The highly authoritarian regime did not allow any real opposition. It did not dissolve the liberal and socialist women's organizations, but it did allow them to carry on their activities.

The status of women suffered a further deterioration after the German Nationalist Socialists annexed Austria to Germany. In the "Ostmark," as in National-Socialist Germany, there was no room for political pluralism. The Federation of Austrian Women's Associations was dissolved and incorporated into the National Socialist Women's Organization (Nationalsozialistische Frauenschaft).

BELGIUM

The Belgian Parliament met for the first time after World War I on November 22, 1918. It had not met since August 4, 1914, following the German invasion of Belgium. King Albert addressed the joint session of both houses and presented the program of the new government which had been formed on the previous day. A major part of this program was the proposed introduction of universal suffrage for all persons over the age of 21. At that time it was not clear whether the references to "persons," and "citizens" were to include women also. It became very clear on December 29, 1918 when the government introduced its proposal for electoral reform. It provided for universal suffrage for males over 21. The bill was passed on the same day. At that time there was no major movement for women's suffrage. However, some concessions were made to certain categories of women. A law of May 9, 1919 gave voting rights to war widows, if they had not remarried. On February 7, 1921 the principle of universal male suffrage was incorporated into the Constitution by amending its Article 47. On the same day, a temporary provision was adopted, which read as follows:

> The right of suffrage is granted on an equal basis to the citizen referred to in Article 47 of the Constitution, to those women who both fulfill the conditions specified in the said article and who come within one of the categories set forth in Article 2 of the Act of May 9, 1919.

This meant that a constitutional basis had now been provided not only for the voting right of war widows but also for patriotic women who had been imprisoned and widowed mothers of soldiers and civilians killed by the enemy in World War I. These women were qualified to vote in national elections. All the others were qualified to vote only in local elections. Article 47(3) stated that "a law may, under the same conditions, attribute voting rights to women. This law must secure at least two thirds of the votes cast." It was this two-thirds requirement which frustrated all efforts made during the inter-war period to extend the right to vote to all women.

During the 1920s, women did make some progress in certain fields of private law, i.e. family law, property, and inheritance law. Some of them also benefitted from the comprehensive nationality legislation of December 14, 1932. But there was no real change in the basic legal framework in which the patriarchal principle was firmly entrenched.

In the mid-thirties, when Belgium was severely affected by the economic crisis, there was much disagreement between political parties and mounting tension between national and ethnic groups. These differences were skillfully exploited by the supporters of totalitarian powers. In the face of these difficulties the issue of women's suffrage did not receive serious attention until Belgium was liberated at the end of World War II.

FRANCE

The inter-war period was one of great frustration for French feminists. In spite of excellent leadership and strong organizational efforts by the "Union française pour le suffrage des femmes" and other groups, very little progress was made either in legislative reform or in gaining access to political power. There was one short period when the prospects seemed brighter. That was during the Popular Front Government of Leon Blum. An important precedent was established in 1936 when two women, Mme. Leon Brunschwig and Mme. Suzanne Lacone, served as members of the Blum Government. A third woman held the post of undersecretary of state.

In World War II, as in World War I, women took over tasks usually performed by their husbands. They could be empowered to represent their husbands in legal matters.

Early in 1944, a decree was issued which provided that in times of war women could serve in special female military units. They could enlist or be drafted. This decree may have paved the way for the long overdue introduction of women's suffrage. The momentous step was taken by General de Gaulle on April 21, 1944. He issued an order from Algeria to the effect that a constituent assembly was to be convened within a year after liberation. It was to be elected by a single secret ballot "by all French men and French women with the exception of those judged incompetent under laws already in force. (*Journal Officiel*, 22 April 1944.) The signal was very clear, and in the fall of 1944 many working women in Paris were elected municipal councilors.

GERMANY

At the end of World War I, conditions in many parts of Germany were chaotic. In early November 1918, Kurt Eisner established a separate government and proclaimed "The Democratic and Social Republic of Bavaria," which was to be under the control of the Council of Workers, Soldiers and Peasants. It was short-lived, but it exacerbated the tensions between moderate socialist leaders and the radicals, who wanted to establish a Soviet Republic. Both failed in their effort to gain control over the armed forces. It was Field Marshal Hindenburg who decided the fate of the Weimar Republic by his support of the Social Democratic Government, headed by Friedrich Ebert. For a short period of time, there was a kind of alliance between the leaders of the Social Democratic Party (SPD), middle-class politicians, and moderate conservative elements, who were determined to prevent a Communist seizure of power.

In this atmosphere of tenuous tranquility, Hugo Preuss, an eminent legal scholar and secretary of the interior, undertook to draft a constitution for a German democratic republic. He completed most of his work around the end of the year 1918. On January 14, 1919, his first draft was presented to the government, which was then somewhat misleadingly called The Council of Commissars. This draft was very different from the final text, which came to be called the Weimar Constitution.

On January 19, elections were held for a Constituent National Assembly. Women were allowed to vote for the first time. There were no serious incidents, and more than 80 percent of the eligible voters cast their ballots. The Social Democrats had a plurality of 37.7 percent. The Center Party won 19.7 percent, the Democratic Party 18.6 percent and the Nationalist Party 10.3 percent. In the first Constituent National Assembly (*Reichstag*) 36 women were among the 469 deputies. It was a better beginning than many feminists had expected.

In order to assure the political participation of women, it was important and indeed imperative to anchor their newly won rights in the

Constitution. The final text was slowly being hammered out. A revised draft was presented by Preuss one day after the elections, and after long debates the task of revising was turned over to a constitutional committee of 28 members. Its work was disrupted by more revolutionary activities in various parts of Germany, especially in Bavaria, where it was deemed necessary to declare a state of war on April 19.

But the drafting and redrafting continued. Finally, on July 31, 1919, the revised text of the Constitution was adopted by a vote of 262 to 75. Hugo Preuss has often been called the father of this constitution. This would seem to be inaccurate because the final text consisting of 181 articles was, in many respects, quite different from his original draft. But the provisions concerning women's rights did not undergo significant changes. The most important provisions were incorporated in Part II, which was entitled "Basic Rights and Duties of Germans." Article 109 declared:

> All Germans are equal before the law. Men and women have fundamentally the same civic rights and duties.

The provisions against discrimination on the basis of gender were contained in Article 128:

> All citizens of the State without distinction, are eligible for public offices, as provided by law and in accordance with their qualifications and abilities.
> All exceptional provisions against women officials are annulled. The conditions of employment of officials shall be determined by the law of the Reich.

To be fully effective, as far as women's rights were concerned, Article 128 required further legislation to solidify its foothold in the Constitution. The civil service legislation failed to do that. It allowed a number of civil service positions to remain reserved to men.

The Constitution did not explicitly state whether or not women could serve in the armed forces. Article 133 merely stated that:

> All citizens are bound, according to the provisions of the laws, to undertake personal service for the State and the local authorities. Military service is organized in accordance with the terms of the Military Defence Law of the Reich.

Article 22 provided that deputies are to be elected "by the universal, equal, direct and secret suffrage of all men and women above the age of twenty" on the basis of a proportional representation, as determined by the Election Law.

In subsequent elections, women did not do very well. The fault was not attributable to the election but rather to the unsettled conditions and to the prevailing attitudes among voters. The majority not only of men but also of women believed that in such troublesome times the business of politics might better be conducted by men, who could govern and maintain order. These attitudes were clearly reflected on June 6, 1920, in the national election results. Whereas in 1919, the Social Democrats had obtained 37.9 percent of the votes, this time they received only 21.7 percent. The election result was followed by a massive defection.

The more nationalistic and authoritarian orientation in German public opinion was reinforced by the less than enlightened reparation policies of the Allied powers. On May 5, 1921, the Allies threatened to occupy the Ruhr industrial area unless Germany began to pay two billion marks annually of the total 132 billion marks of reparation payments.

The government headed by Fehrenbach collapsed, and from here on German cabinets had a very difficult time staying in office long enough to chart and implement major policies. Included among the casualties was the whole area of legal reforms which might have initiated the gradual transformation of the patriarchal legal system. No minister of justice could claim a mandate for such an undertaking. On June 6, 1921, the Socialists, who were the most likely supporters of such reforms, and the Zentrum Party saw their power base dwindle. More disturbing than the loss of popular support were the acts of violence. Matthias Erzberger, who had signed the Armistice at Compiègne, was assassinated by two extremists on August 26, 1921. Dr. Walther Rathenau, who had become foreign minister, was killed about a year later. Increasingly, the government found it necessary to invoke emergency powers and govern by decree.

In early 1923, five French and one Belgian division occupied the Ruhr. The British eventually declared the occupation illegal, but in the meantime the German economy collapsed. Germans experienced the most catastrophic inflation of all times. On August 31, 1923, the exchange rate for one dollar was ten million marks. On September 12, it was one hundred million marks, and it continued to climb.

It is necessary to have some basic understanding of these circumstances before passing judgment on the failure of the Weimar Republic. If one looks at the subsequent period, during which a certain amount of political and economic stabilization was achieved, there can be no doubt that the Reichstag failed to enact the necessary implementing legislation which would have transformed constitutional norms of gender equality into action programs on behalf of women's rights. This failure was not due to a betrayal by those politicians who had earlier expressed themselves in favor of gender equality. There was simply no consensus, even within the Social Democratic Party, that this was one of the most urgent issues. The overruling demand was the establishment of order and security, and this demand led to an excessive use or misuse of the emergency powers vested in the president under Article 48 of the Weimar Constitution. However it is erroneous to believe that excessive use of emergency powers was the chief cause of the demise of the German Republic. There were many causes, and they were not the same during the decade and a half before the National Socialists came to power. After Hindenburg assumed the presidency, the political system was transformed along more conservative lines. It might have survived the world economic crisis, which followed the collapse of the American stock market in 1929. But by that time, the enemies of democracy were unwilling to wait any longer.

The Weimar Republic was destroyed by the extremists of the left and the right. The Communists continued to reject "bourgeois feminism" and called for the emancipation or liberation of women. This was to be accomplished within the framework of the new "socialist society." The leaders of the right never left any doubt as to their views on the status of women. They wanted the men to be the "breadwinners" and the women to accept their traditional roles.

In the early 1930s as the economic depression worsened, many more women than men lost their jobs. Married women were often criticized for taking away jobs from men. Their arguments that they had to supplement their husbands' insufficient wages often brought angry reactions directed against the system and the "exploiters." Such reactions might have been expected from workers' wives who had been exposed to oversimplified leftist ideologies. But similar reactions could be heard from men and women who identified themselves as nationalists. They blamed the political and economic system of the Weimar Republic for their predicament. It is a well-known fact that women provided more votes for Hitler than men. Why this was so has not been sufficiently explained, and it may not be conclusively analyzed because it opens up too many old wounds. What is clear from the record is the fact that Nazi propagandists promised breadwinners that they could earn enough so that women would not have to take away work from men.

Increasingly, one could hear the old clichés about the role of women not only from men but especially from women. The share of women deputies had declined from a high of 9.6 percent (1919) in the National

Assembly to a low of 3.1 percent in 1933. Hitler's position on "the women question" was well known long before he seized power. His anti-feminism was consistent with his Weltanschauung and his notion of "pure" Germans as the Herrenvolk. Only men were qualified to govern. Herrschaft—or governing power—was to be reserved to men only. On September 8, 1934, he declared in Nürnberg that the plea for emancipation had emanated from Jewish intellectuals and was alien to German women.

Under the N.S. regime, a major effort was made to integrate women into the totalitarian state apparatus. The principal training and indoctrination took place in the Bund deutscher Mädchen (The Federation of German Girls). The active women were organized in the National-sozialistische Frauenschaft (National Socialist Womanhood). There were also professional organizations for women, such as the Bund deutscher Juristinnen (The Federation of German Women Jurists).

As Nazi Germany prepared for war, the women's organizations were mobilized for total war. Women had to assume all kinds of new responsibilities which were not part of the traditional pattern of division of labor between men and women.

GREAT BRITAIN

As early as 1917, some prominent members of Parliament had expressed their support of women's suffrage. But complete equality between men and women was in no way a reality. The Representation of the People Act imposed special requirements on women. Eligibility to vote was limited to women who had attained the age of 30. Ironically, it was the American born Viscountess Astor who became the first woman member of the House of Commons. In 1918, there had been 17 women candidates, but only one was elected. The proportion was about the same in 1922, when out of a total of 33 women candidates two were elected. The prospects seemed brighter in 1923, when seven were elected out of 34 women candidates. Among them were three Labor Party members and three Conservatives. But in 1924, the Conservatives won the elections, and only one Labor Party candidate was elected. Conservative women were successful in entering the House of Commons. But it was a bad year for women candidates because of a total of 41 only 4 were elected. In 1928, the voting age for women was lowered to 21, thus removing the discriminatory age-requirement of the previous decade.

The year 1929 brought economic disaster and a modest victory for the Labor Party. Of a record number of women candidates (69), 14 were elected. Nine of them belonged to the Labor Party.

The Conservative Party, which had won the elections in 1922 and 1924, returned to power in 1931. Of a total of 62 women candidates, 15 were elected, and 13 belonged to the Conservative Party. Not a single woman running on the Labor Party ticket was elected. The Conservative Party won again in 1935, but only 6 of its women candidates were elected. Out of a total of 67 women candidates, nine entered the House of Commons. This was to be the last election before World War II. The next election came in 1945, at the end of the war.

In comparing the attitudes of the leaders of the two major parties in Great Britain, we may conclude that the Labor Party has been more sympathetic to its female members. This view is particularly valid for the inter-war period. In 1923, for example, in the first Labor Party government, Margaret Bondfield was made parliamentary secretary to the Ministry of Labor, and in 1929, she was appointed Minister of Labor, thus becoming the first woman to serve in a British cabinet.

On the whole, the political advancement of women in Great Britain during the inter-war period was far from spectacular. Indeed, there were still legal and conventional obstacles which had to be overcome. Of the legal changes, the following may be noted:

The Sex Disqualification (Removal) Act of 1919 allowed women "to exercise any public function," including jury duty, but the judges were left with discretionary power to limit it to men only. As far as the civil service was concerned, the just-mentioned legislation did not mandate equal access for women, and it was still possible to issue administrative regulations which restricted certain positions to men. Thus, regulations were issued in 1921 stating that "(1) All female candidates for an established situation in any of His Majesty's Civil Establishments shall be unmarried or widows; (2) women appointed to or holding any established situation in any of His Majesty's Civil Establishments shall be required to resign their appointments on marriage . . ."[1]

The British Nationality Act of 1870, which had already been amended in 1914, was again amended in 1922 and 1933. It enabled British women to retain their nationality independently of their husbands.

It was only in 1928, with the passing of the "Equal Franchise Act," that genuine equal suffrage for men and women was instituted. In 1929 the Labor Party was the largest party, but it did not have a majority. The

---

[1]Quoted from Erna Reiss, "Changes in Law" in *Our Freedom and its Results*, ed. Ray Strachey (London: Hogarth Press, 1936), p. 83.

depression which developed shortly after that made the issue of unemployment the main concern. Political and legal equality once again became more or less academic issues. Prime Minister MacDonald was not really in control, and in 1935 he resigned and was replaced by Stanley Baldwin. The Conservatives were fully in control of the so-called National Government. In 1936, the country, and Stanley Baldwin in particular, were preoccupied with the affair of Edward VIII and Mrs. Wallis Simpson. Edward VIII resigned in December, but the national agony was not over.

New disasters and agonies awaited the people of Great Britain as Neville Chamberlain succeeded the unpopular Stanley Baldwin in May 1937. If Chamberlain's approach to domestic problems was inept, his initiatives in foreign affairs were unmitigated disasters. In February 1938 he sought an agreement with Mussolini and thus prompted Anthony Eden to resign as foreign secretary. In September 1938 he visited Hitler in Berchtesgaden. Hitler informed him that he was determined to annex the Sudetenland, and Chamberlain raised no objections. A few days later, on September 29, the infamous Munich conference was held. Chamberlain thought he had achieved "peace in our time," but in reality his blundering policy of appeasement encouraged Hitler to embark on further acts of aggression. These brief references to the blunders of the thirties are necessary to explaining the impasse of the women's rights movement. In retrospect one may conclude that there were no significant or positive achievements during the remaining part of the inter-war period, after the Equal Franchise Act of 1928.

Throughout the inter-war period, in the House of Commons, the number of women remained relatively small, but individually and collectively they exerted much greater influence than their numerical strength might suggest. This becomes apparent from reading not only the debates in the House of Commons but also the memoirs of leading members. As might be expected, their influence was mainly in the areas of social welfare, health and education, not as much by choice as because of the stereotyped notions of the leaders of both parties. They did speak out against appeasement and misguided foreign policy ventures. One can only speculate whether more women with equal access to the centers of power and decision-making could have prevented or lessened the disasters that led to World War II.

There is no doubt that such outstanding women as Beatrice Webb and Margaret Cole and their husbands contributed much constructive thought to what was to become known as the British Welfare State. Although neither they nor William Beveridge would be enthusiastic about the later bureaucratization of the original plan which was published in 1942, they would support the underlying principles. Out of a total of seven key legislative acts, the first two, the Education Act (1944) and the Family Allowance Act (1945), were implemented before the end of World War II. These, as well as the other five, will be analyzed in the period which concerns developments after World War II.

IRELAND

At the end of World War I, the Sinn Fein Party had emerged as the dominant political element in Ireland. In early 1919, all the delegates who were elected to the Dail Eireann (the Assembly of Ireland) were members of the Sinn Fein. In April 1919 Eamon de Valera was elected president of the Irish Free State, but he was prevented from assuming full control in the midst of continuing war and violence. The so-called "Anglo-Irish War" ended with the signing of the Anglo-Irish Treaty on December 6, 1921. This treaty recognized the partition of Ireland and compelled Eamon de Valera to resign after the Dail Eireann had ratified the treaty by a vote of 64 to 57. The Anglo-Irish Treaty called for the drafting of a constitution for the Irish Free State. (Saorstat Eireann). It was prepared by a select committee and approved by the Irish Parliament on October 25, 1922.

Article 3 of the Constitution of the Irish Free State (1922) stated that

> every person, without distinction of sex, domiciled in the area of the Irish Free State" shall enjoy the privileges of citizenship. All citizens, who had reached the age of 21, without distinction of sex were to have the right to vote for members of Dail Eireann and to take part in the Referendum and Initiative.
>
> All citizens, without distinction of sex, who were 25 years old, were eligible to vote for members of Seanad Eireann.

This provision was eliminated when the Senate was abolished by the 24th Amendment, which was introduced on March 22, 1934, passed by the Dail, and put into effect on May 29, 1936.

The Irish Federation of University Women was established in 1925. From the very beginning, it encouraged graduates of colleges and universities to participate in community activities. As early as 1925, it was established that women were qualified to enter the civil service on the same terms as men. However, they were not allowed to marry. If they did, they lost their positions. In practice, of course, this principle was not so important because the number of women in the civil service did not increase substantially.

After the general elections of 1932, de Valera returned to power. It was during this period that some legislation was enacted that concerned the rights of women, along with those of all citizens. The Irish Nationality and Citizenship Act of 1935 provided detailed provisions concerning the nationality of married women. The legal status of women in Ireland, in the economic field and especially in industry, was regulated by the Condition of Employment Act of 1936.

During the inter-war period, a considerable body of laws and regulations was enacted, which comes under the heading of "protective legislation." Aside from the usual prohibitions against employing women in mines, excessively burdensome work, or work with dangerous chemical substances, there were also legal injunctions against women's working on Sundays and holidays. Working hours were also regulated. Thus legislation was enacted in 1936 which stipulated that women working in industry were neither allowed to start before 8:00 a.m. nor to continue after 10:00 p.m. These laws have not yet been repealed and appear to be overprotective, if not discriminatory.

Between 1925 and 1937 the Constitution of 1922 was amended 26 times. Although most of the articles were amended, there were no significant changes as far as the status of women was concerned. As previously noted, the Senate was abolished in 1936, but of course this change affected men and women equally. Furthermore, a year and a half later when the new constitution went into effect, the legislature was again instituted as a bicameral body. In July 1937, the new constitution was adopted in a plebiscite. It won by a narrow margin and went into force on December 29, 1937. As far as women's rights are concerned, the provisions compared very favorably with any western constitution in force at that time. There are several articles, which provide a solid constitutional basis for equality and equal treatment.

Article 16.
1.° Every citizen, without distinction of sex, who has reached the age of twenty-one years, and who is not placed under disability or incapacity by this constitution by law, shall be eligible for membership of *Dail Eireann.*
2.° "Every citizen, without distinction of sex, who has reached the age of twenty-one years, who is not disqualified by law and complies with the provisions of the law relating to the election of members of *Dail Eireann,* shall have the right to vote at an election for members of the *Dail Eireann.*
3.° No law shall be enacted placing any citizen under disa-

87

bility or incapacity for membership of *Dail Eireann* on the ground of sex, or disqualifying any citizen from voting at an election for *Dail Eireann* on that ground."

According to Article 40. 1.:

All citizens shall, as human persons, be held equal before the law.

But this is followed by an interesting and important reservation:

This shall not be held to mean that the State shall not, in its enactments, have due regard to differences of capacity, physical and moral, and social function.

In many of its provisions, the Irish Constitution reflects an interesting synthesis of modern and traditional attitudes. The traditional attitude is clearly revealed in the article which is concerned with the family. Article 41 declares that:

1. 1° The State recognises the Family as the natural primary and fundamental unit group of Society, and as a moral institution possessing inalienable and imprescriptible rights, antecedent and superior to all positive law.
2° The State, therefore, guarantees to protect the family in its constitution and authority, as the necessary basis of social order and as indispensable to the welfare of the Nation and the State.
2. 1° In particular, the State recognises that by her life within the home, woman gives to the State a support without which the common good cannot be achieved.
2° The State shall, therefore, endeavour to ensure that mothers shall not be obliged by economic necessity to engage in labour to the neglect of their duties in the home.
3. 1° The State pledges itself to guard with special care the institution of Marriage, on which the Family is founded, and to protect it against attack.
2° No law shall be enacted providing for the grant of a dissolution of marriage.
3° No person whose marriage has been dissolved under the civil law of any other State but is a subsisting valid marriage under the law for the time being in force within the jurisdiction of the Government and Parliament established by

this Constitution shall be capable of contracting a valid marriage within that jurisdiction during the lifetime of the other party to the marriage so dissolved.

There were other traditional provisions which have since been repealed. For instance, Article 44 concerning religion. The 5th Amendment (1972) eliminated Sections 2 and 3 of this Article.

Aside from the guarantees the Constitution also contains certain directive principles. Article 5 (2) directs the state to treat "men and women equally."

LIECHTENSTEIN

A new constitution of the Principality of Liechtenstein was promulgated on October 5, 1921. Several of its articles were amended in 1938 and 1939, but the provisions restricting suffrage to males were never amended. Article 2 of the Act of August 31, 1922, concerning the exercise of political rights, stipulated as follows:

All male Liechtenstein citizens over twenty-one years of age, who are not legally disqualified, who have resided in the Principality for one month before the election or referendum and whose right to vote in elections or referenda has not been suspended, shall have the right to vote and to be elected . . .

LUXEMBOURG

At the end of World War I, Grand Duchess Marie Adelaide had become so unpopular that demands were made for her to resign. There were agitations for the abolition of the monarchy. The matter was put to a popular referendum in 1919. The monarchy survived, and the grand duchess eventually abdicated in favor of a grand duchess who was to reign for about forty-five years.

The Constitution was revised for the first time on May 15, 1919. Changes reflected the experiences of several decades and the popular demands for a more democratized political system. Article 32, which originally made the grand duke the source of all power, was amended to embody the principle of popular sovereignty. Another sentence was added, taken from the original Belgian Constitution (1831) stating that the grand duke "has no powers other than those formally vested in him by the Constitution and the special laws passed by virtue of the Constitution . . ." Although the Constitution continued to refer to the grand duke and employed the male gender to refer to "his" powers, the head of state was a woman. As previously noted, there were other limitations introduced on the powers of the head of the state, with regard to treaty-making and military command functions. (Article 37) As far as the status of women was concerned, the most important amendment was Article 52. It provided for universal suffrage for both sexes, along with proportional representation in the Chamber of Deputies.

During the inter-war period, Luxembourg was ahead of Belgium and France with respect to the political rights of women. Since 1924 women had been eligible to vote and be elected on the same terms as men. This improvement in the political status of women may be contrasted with the apparent stagnation in the field of civil law. Compared with the other countries in which the French Civil Code of 1804 had been introduced, this major piece of legislation remained nearly unaltered in Luxembourg during the entire inter-war period.

Among the changes, one should note the nationality provisions of the Civil Code, which were changed by a law of April 23, 1934. It introduced provisions which were essentially derived from the corresponding Belgian legislation.

NETHERLANDS

Women's suffrage was introduced in the Netherlands by a law passed on August 9, 1919. In the following year, a constitutional commission presented recommendations for amending the Constitution of 1887. The amended text, which was promulgated as the new Constitution on December 9, 1922, contained appropriate guarantees for "all persons." After 1922 Dutch women voted on equal terms with men, and they took their newly gained suffrage seriously. With respect to candidacy for political offices they were not very successful. Relatively few women were elected to Parliament. (The first woman, Suze Groeneweg, took her seat in 1918. In 1921, two women deputies were elected.) From 1922 to 1923, six seats were occupied by women. In 1924, there were seven. Between 1925 and 1928, the participation fell to six and rose again to 7 between 1929 to 1931. The membership continued to fluctuate throughout the inter-war period. In 1932, there were eight women, but women's participation declined after that. The ideological differences between the various women's groups became more pronounced.

The middle-class feminists had been the pioneers. They wanted to achieve complete legal, political, and social equality. To achieve these goals, they demanded better educational opportunities and access to the professions and to the civil service.

The Socialist women, like their counterparts in other western and northern European countries, called for emancipation as part of the restructuring of the capitalist society. They criticized the bourgeois feminists because they condoned the existing social order.

The Christian Democratic women, Protestant and Catholic, were closer to the Liberals than to the Socialists. But they were less individualistic and more concerned with the social fabric and socially oriented work based on Christian ethics. The *Nederlandsche Christen Vrouwenbond* (Netherlands Christian Women's Organization) was founded in 1919. These differences tended to have a negative effect on the advancement of women's rights in the Netherlands.

In the Netherlands, the inter-war period was one of consolidation of gains rather than new advances for women in the economic and social fields. The Civil Service Law of 1929 might have provided more opportunities for women, but the economic crisis tended to be a serious obstacle. The new legislation did not do away with the practice of discharging women from the civil service if they married. They could keep their jobs only if they were 45 years of age. This was the law from 1922 to 1971. In 1934, it was deemed necessary to enact legislation to protect Dutch workers against competition by foreigners. Women were discouraged from competing with men, and some of the protective laws did, in effect, block women's access to certain kinds of jobs.

While the Constitution guaranteed equality before the law, there remained many pieces of legislation which did discriminate against women. The patriarchal principle was firmly entrenched in the Civil Code, which remained very similar to its French model. As in the neighboring countries, married women remained in the tutelage of their husbands.

One tangible advance was made in 1936, when the Nationality Law was changed. With that change, a woman who married a foreigner could either acquire the nationality of her husband or keep her own. If the marriage was terminated by divorce, she could reclaim her Dutch citizenship. By that time the independence of the Netherlands was already threatened by Nazi Germany. On May 10, 1940, the German invasion began. Queen Wilhelmina and her cabinet left for England on May 13 to establish a government in exile.

SWITZERLAND

For the women and men of Switzerland who favored women's suffrage and the extension of women's rights the inter-war period was one of disappointments and considerable frustration.[1] The alliance of Swiss Women's Organizations continued to work closely with the International Council of Women, and Swiss Feminists were well informed about the activities of women's organizations in other countries. They were greatly interested in the work of the League of Nations and the International Labor Organization, but this was more evident in the major cities than in the rural cantons. Among the men, irrespective of social class and education there was no appreciable change in attitudes. The traditional "K K K" perception of the role of women remained deeply entrenched. Women were expected to bear children and to care for them. The idea that women might be called upon to bear arms was rejected by an overwhelming majority of men and women. "Wahlfähigkeit"—the right to vote—and "Wehrfähigkeit"—the capacity to bear arms—remained intricately linked.

In 1929 many major attempts were made in the cantons to introduce women's suffrage on the federal level by means of petitions.[2] Only in Ticino (231:208) did more men than women sign the petition. Almost everywhere else the women outnumbered men at least two to one.

In 1933 another effort was made to have the Federal Constitution amended so as to grant women the right to vote. It failed, as did all subsequent attempts for nearly four decades. The anti-feminist propagandists did not hesitate to use the not unsubstantiated charges that women had voted Hitler into power.

In 1938 a women's auxiliary (Frauenhilfdienst) was established, and two years later it was organizationally attached to the military establishment. However, the women's auxiliary remained an organization of volunteers. No attempt was made to give it a more formal or legal status. During World War II it was widely recognized that the women of Switzerland once again contributed much to the well-being of the mobilized men, but the men were slow to change their ways of expressing appreciation by according women equal political rights.

---

[1]In 1975, in her excellent book, Susanna Woodtli, characterized this period as one of stagnation (*Stillstand*). *Gleichberechtigung*, p. 138 f.

[2]The names of the Petition Zur Einführung des Frauenstimm-und Wahlrechts auf Bundesebene 1929 are reproduced by Woodtli, *op. cit.* p., 249.

CHAPTER 8

THE SOUTHERN AND MEDITERRANEAN COUNTRIES 1918-1945

INTRODUCTION

Of all of the ten countries which are grouped here under the heading "Southern and Mediterranean," only one country, Turkey, introduced and implemented women's suffrage before the end of World War II. In or around 1918 any well-informed person would not have singled out Turkey as the country most likely to enfranchise women. Indeed, it would probably have been said that not only alphabetically but also chronologically Turkey would be in the last place.

It was reasonable to expect that Italy, Portugal, and Spain would be the next countries. As previously noted, Greece tried to move in this direction in 1929. Spain took this giant step in 1931, but it ended in failure, as did the republican experiment. In Turkey the experiment succeeded, at least moderately and temporarily, because Ataturk made it a fundamental principle of his historic modernization effort.

TURKEY

by Ilhan Arsel

Although the Turkish Constitution of 1924 did not enfranchise women, it did provide a suitable basis on which important legal reforms could be carried out. But the Constitution was much less important than the remarkable leader of modern Turkey: Mustafa Kemal Ataturk. The emancipation of women was an essential element in his bold program for the modernization of Turkey. He provided much encouragement to what few Turkish feminists there were and supported them in every possible way.[1] The reform of the legal system was, in a real sense, another phase of the ongoing revolution. The Turkish Civil Code of 1926 was based on that of Switzerland. As a result, the legal position of Turkish women in family life changed drastically. Previously, under Islamic Law as laid down in the Koran and the Sayings of Mohammed, men were deemed to have been set above women by God. Women's alleged "deficiencies" were used as justification for a completely inequitable system. With the introduction of the new Civil Code, the principle of legal equality or near legal equality was established. However, conditions *de jure* and *de facto* continued to differ in various social strata and regions of Turkey. Ataturk had attached great importance to educational reforms and improvements. But in this respect he was less successful.[2] The main problem, then as now, was the fact that in the villages young girls were not encouraged to continue their education. Traditional attitudes rooted in Islamic teachings were widespread in the rural areas. Villagers would either defy the law altogether by not sending their daughters to school or withdraw them after a minimal amount of schooling. Few girls were given the opportunity to complete their primary education. Legislation was enacted in 1929 which gave Turkish women the right to participate in municipal elections. In 1934, Article 10 of the Constitution of 1924 was amended to give all men and women over 22 years of age the right to elect deputies to the Grand National Assembly. Women voted for the first time in national elections on February 25, 1935. Women were also given many more opportunities to enter government service. By 1938 there were 12,716 women in civil service positions. This constituted 9.5 percent of the total of civil service employees.

[1]In 1925 the first Turkish women's organization, The Turk Kadinlar Birgli, was founded in Istanbul.
[2]The total number of girls attending primary schools during the first year of the Republic was only 62,954.

From 1924 until his death in 1938, Ataturk dominated every segment of public policy. The emancipation of women remained a fundamental part of his program. But he was always much more successful among the urban middle-class people than in the villages. His successor as president of Turkey was Ismet Inonu who had been his close associate from the very beginning of the revolution and had served as prime minister from 1923 to 1937. He was able to maintain the basic direction of public policy, but the advancement of women did not maintain the initial momentum. Between 1935 and 1939 there were 18 women in the Grand National Assembly which then consisted of 399 members (4.51 percent). This was the highest share ever. Between 1939 and 1943, when the membership was enlarged to 424, there were 15 women (3.53 percent). During the subsequent period (1943-1946) the membership was again enlarged. Although women had only 16 seats (3.51 percent), this reduction was small compared with the sharp reversals which came after 1946.

ITALY

In Italy the prospects for women's suffrage were brightest right after World War I. Various attempts had been made in the late 19th and early 20th centuries to introduce women's suffrage, but there never was sufficient support in Parliament to embark on a major campaign. There seemed to be a chance in 1919 when Deputy Gasparotti introduced his bill. But the initial support faded quickly, and although the women's organizations exerted themselves on behalf of women's suffrage, the only concession that was made to them was the granting of access to public employment.

In May 1923, when the International Alliance of Women held its Congress in Rome, Mussolini agreed to serve as its patron. In his speech on May 12, he even promised to introduce legislation "to grant to several categories of women the right to vote, starting from the administrative vote."[1] An appropriate bill was actually introduced, but it failed.

Even before the Fascists came to power, the movement for women's suffrage in Italy was greatly weakened by ideological divisions and rivalries between women's organizations, and the Fascist organizers were quick to exploit this situation. Already in 1921 the *Fascio Femminile*

[1]Whittick, Arnold: *Woman into Citizen*. Santa Barbara, ABC-clio, 1979, p. 82.

had been created. It was to serve as a Fascist alternative to the existing women's organizations. In 1925 it appeared that Italian women were going to be able to vote in communal and provincial elections, but in the following year (Law of December 1926, No. 2962) this possibility was rendered ineffectual, because Mussolini did not allow the local bodies to become bases of political power. The Fascist regime's only contribution to women's rights legislation was concerned with their protection at places of work.

During the Fascist regime, a major effort was made to preclude the continued growth of a genuine feminist movement. Just as the 8-year-old boys were organized and regimented in the *Balilla*, the girls of the same age were incorporated into an organization called *Piccole Italiane* (the Little Italians). At the age of 14 they were promoted to the status of *Giovani Italiane* (Young Italians). Finally, in 1929 the girls who had reached the age of 18 were offered an opportunity to qualify for membership in the organization of *Giovani Fasciste* (Young Fascists). This organization was placed under the supervision of the *Fascio Femminile*.

In this respect the Fascists in Italy may have provided a basic blueprint for the Nazi system of coordination and total integration.[2] But this was not the only model, because the Communists had long ago established a comprehensive network of youth organizations (*Komsomol*).

The Fascist organizing efforts were largely successful in the 1930s when the National Council of Italian Women was unable to continue its work. Whatever skeletal organization still existed at the beginning of World War II was now replaced by war mobilization efforts. The total effect of the Fascist regime was to set the women's movement further back than it had been when World War I started. It is easier to make diachronic comparisons, i.e. to compare, as was just indicated, the situations faced by women in one country at the beginning of two major wars. It is more difficult to compare the status of women cross-nationally and ideologically. Many writers contend that Fascist Italy, like Stalin's regime and Nazi Germany, was a totalitarian system. But this is a dubious contention, because in several important respects Italy's Fascist regime was different. In practice, it was unable to achieve total integration and mobilization. During the Fascist regime, important parts of the legal system remained largely intact. The Civil Code of 1865 had remained practically unaltered. Fascism could not abolish the family and the patriarchal system. It did not even try. When Fascism collapsed at the end of World War II, there were some elements that were still intact.

[2] A few years ago Maria-Antonietta Macciocchi presented some interesting comparisons of Mussolini's and Hitler's policies toward women. *Jungfrauen, Mütter und ein Führer, Frauen im Faschismus*, Berlin: Wagenbach, 1976, p. 49.

The rebuilding and the transformation process could begin with a fair chance of success.

PORTUGAL

by Maria Regina Tavares da Silva

In 1918 the Republican League of Portuguese Women disappeared, and the action of the National Council of Portuguese Women became more and more important. The sense of becoming a movement and of belonging to an international network grew stronger and the Council's leader, Adelaide Cabete, participated in the International Feminist Conventions of Paris, Rome, and Washington.

In 1924 an important Feminist Convention was held in Portugal. Significantly called the First Feminist Convention on Education, it stressed the concern for education that characterizes Portuguese feminism. But other questions came up in the discussions held and the papers presented. Some of the themes discussed were: the general situation and rights of women, namely the question of women's suffrage; legal rights in marriage; nationality; and matrimonial regimes; women in local administration; abolitionism; health protection of women and children; sexual education, etc.

Aurora de Castro e Gouveia, the first woman holding the office of public notary, presented a paper on "Political demands of the Portuguese Woman" and strongly contended that: "The right to vote is an innate right of every human being, independent from sex."

The First Feminist Convention was a great success and had the open support of important political figures, including the president of the Republic and other outstanding politicians.

In 1926 an event occurred that was going to change the course of Women's Rights in Portugal. It was a military uprising which led to the establishment of a new regime called "The New State." Conservative in thought and policy, the models it proposed to women were completely different from the ones advocated by the Women's Rights Movement.

In 1928 a Second Feminist Convention was still held in Lisbon. Although it may be considered a successful event in itself, the situation was now completely different. The new political forces could hardly accept a group of women openly claiming social and political rights.

In the opening session, one young and influential feminist, the jurist

Elina Guimarães, defended the aspirations of Portuguese Women, saying: "the rights we demand, namely political rights, are not being demanded as a caprice. We demand them, first of all, out of a desire for justice. Belonging, just like men do, to a community interested, just as they are, in general prosperity, subject, just as they are, to the same laws, we must intervene, just as they do, in public questions."

In spite of the difficulties, the Council managed to continue its action, as the attitude of the "New State" was not one of open hostility but rather one of subtle indoctrination, defending and praising the traditional virtues, the role and status of women.

In 1931, the right to vote was recognized, although for a very limited number of women—those having university degrees or secondary school qualifications. (Decree-Law no. 19694)

In the new Constitution of 1933 the principle of equality for all before the law was contained but immediately restricted in regard to women—"except for women the differences resulting from their nature or from the interest of the family." It is a restriction that can be used to justify practically all kinds of discriminations.

In 1937 a new women's organization, conveying the official ideology, was created. It was the *Mothers' Organization for National Education*, and the name itself is meaningful. Motherhood is considered the highest value, and woman's life and role are oriented towards this aim.

In 1940 a new factor appeared that was going to influence women's lives. It was a Concordat between Portugal and the Holy See that changed the existing situation concerning divorce, as it established that people marrying in the Catholic Church cannot be allowed to divorce by the civil law.

As the new ideology was growing, the action of the feminist Council was fading. It still existed, but its impact and its dynamism were not the same. Facing a hostile opposition, the Women's Rights Movement in Portugal was now a pale and poor image of what it had been in the two decades following the Republic, mainly the twenties and the thirties.

GREECE

by Louis Pagonis

The work of the National Council of Women, which had been disrupted during the Balkan Wars and World War I was resumed shortly thereafter, and legislative proposals were introduced which sought to equalize the rights of men and women.

In 1920, the Greek League for Women's Rights was founded by Anna Theodoropoulos. The League set the stage for the development of women's rights in Greece.

The republican Constitution of June 3, 1927 did not sufficiently clarify the question of women's rights. According to Article 6 all Hellenes were equal before the law. On the other hand Article 36, like Article 66 of the 1911 Constitution, stated that the members of the Chamber of Deputies were to be elected by those who had the right to vote.

It was assumed that the Constitution of 1927 would pave the way for the admission of women into the civil service. But this did not happen. A presidential decree of February 5, 1930 granted women the right to vote in municipal and communal elections. In the communal elections of 1934, 12,000 women voted for the first time. This very small participation should not be interpreted as a lack of interest on the part of women. The government had discouraged women and, perhaps more importantly, the attitude of most men was clearly negative or even hostile. The atmosphere became even more unfavorable in 1936 as the Greek regime turned more authoritarian under General Metaxas.

In spite of its declaration of neutrality at the beginning of World War II, Greece was invaded first by Fascist Italy and later by Nazi Germany. During the resistance women once again played crucially important roles in the struggle for liberation from foreign domination.

CHAPTER 9

THE EASTERN EUROPEAN COUNTRIES 1918-1945

THE SOVIET UNION

The leading proponents of women's rights in the years before the Communist Revolution had divergent views and visions of the future roles of women in the new social order. These were the intellectual feminists of the upper-middle class who looked to the West as models. Their views were opposed by women who came from similar social backgrounds but whose orientation was much more radical. Most of them thought of themselves as Socialists, and some of them did not want any part of revisionist socialism. Clara Zetkin seems to have exercised considerable influence long before she took up residence in the Soviet Union. The best known woman was Nadezhda Krupskaia, the wife of Lenin, who in her later years rose to membership in the Central Committee. Alexandra Kollontai in her book *Communism and the Family*, which was published in English in 1918, wrote with great enthusiasm about the changed role of women in Soviet society.[1] But her ideas of "free union" as contrasted with "the conjugal slavery of the past" did not become the official doctrine of the Communist regime. For a few years she wielded considerable influence as the director of *Zhenotdel*, the women's section of the Central Committee of the Communist Party, but in 1922 she was replaced by a more conventional defender of women's interests: Sofia Smidovich, whose influence was in part due to the fact that she was married to the president of the Moscow Soviet. But she was a forceful person with a mind of her own, and during the 1920s, before its dissolution in 1930, she had increased the influence of the women's section, although it was never much more than a women's auxiliary of a powerful organization of ambitious and often ruthless male politicians. Lenin was certainly a strong supporter of the

---

[1]Beatrice Brodsky Farnsworth, *Aleksandra Kollontai: Communism, Feminists and the Bolshevik Revolution* (Stanford: St. Un. Press, 1979).

advancement of women, but Stalin was not, and the latter was probably closer to the prevailing point of view on women in many parts of the Soviet Union.

The Constitution of the Russian Socialist Federative Soviet Republic was adopted by the Fifth All-Russian Congress of Soviets on July 10, 1918. Article 64 stated that "the right to vote and to be elected to the Soviets belongs to all citizens of the Russian S. F. S. Republic without distinction of sex, religion or nationality," provided they met certain requirements which were spelled out in three categories.

But the subsequent Article 65 declared that "the following persons have neither the right to vote nor the right to be elected, even if they are included within one of the above-mentioned categories: (a) those who employ others for the sake of profit. (b) those who live on income not arising from their own labor, interest or capital, industrial enterprises, landed property, etc. (c) private businessmen, agents, middlemen, etc. (d) monks and priests of all religious denominations. (e) agents and employees of the former police, special corps of gendarmerie, and secret service; and also members of the late ruling dynasty of Russia. (f) persons legally recognized as mentally deranged or imbecile; together with those under wardship. (g) persons convicted of infamous or mercenary crimes, during a period fixed by law or by the sentence of the court."

Other than Article 64, the Constitution of July 10, 1918 did not contain specific provisions for women's rights. Neither did the constitutions that were promulgated in the union republics: the Byelorussian Soviet Socialist Republic of February 4, 1919; the Ukrainian Soviet Socialist Republic of March 10, 1919; the Azerbaidjan Soviet Socialist Republic of May 19, 1921; the Armenian Soviet Socialist Republic of February 2, 1921; and the Georgian Soviet Socialist Republic. Even the second Constitution of the Soviet Union of May 11, 1925 was quite barren as far as specific guarantees or rights for women were concerned.

Inasmuch as the three Baltic States of Estonia, Latvia, and Lithuania were annexed to the U.S.S.R. after World War II, it may be appropriate to note here that these countries during their short periods of independence did include women's suffrage in their constitutions.[2] There

[2]In Estonia the principle of gender equality was confirmed in 1918 with its declaration of independence. It was formally incorporated into the Constitution of June 15, 1920. In the first Estonian Parliament (1919/20) there were six women out of a total of 114 deputies.

With the proclamation of Lithuanian independence on February 16, 1918 the principle of gender equality became part of the legal framework. §98 of the Constitution of October 5, 1921 proclaimed the principle of equality of both parents.

Latvia achieved its independence on November 18, 1918. The Provisional Constitution of May 5, 1920 and the Constitution of February 15, 1922, incorporated the principle of gender equality, but in actuality it was not as real as in Estonia.

were active women's organizations in all the three Baltic states which united into national councils. The Estonian National Council was founded in 1921 and became affiliated with the International Council of Women in the same year. The Latvian National Council, which was founded during World War I, became affiliated in 1922. The first Lithuanian Women's Congress was held in Kaunas as early as 1907, but a national council was not formed until 1929. In the following year it became affiliated with the International Council of Women.

As far as political participation was concerned, the women of Estonia were probably the most successful in achieving appointments to some of the higher positions in the ministries and in their legislative activities. As will be shown in the detailed analysis of political participation in the U.S.S.R. in recent years, the women from the Baltic states have been able to maintain an impressive record.

If one were to compare the developments in the Baltic states and such countries as Czechoslovakia with those of the U.S.S.R. during the inter-war period, one might conclude that the women with a more western orientation made more impressive progress than those of the U.S.S.R. Communist writers would dismiss this kind of feminism as part of the bourgeois ideology which had no place in the new society. Official Soviet statistics show that in the city councils the women's share was about 10 percent in 1922, rising to 13 percent in the following year. Then it climbed rapidly to 18.6 percent between 1924 and 1925, and to 19.7 percent between 1925 and 1926. It continued to grow after that. These figures should be compared with the participation of women on the national level and in the higher echelons of the party hierarchy.

Before the promulgation of the Soviet Constitution of 1936 the legal status of women was not a matter of major concern. Women had been emancipated politically since 1917 and from that time on the main concern was to integrate womanpower into the work force "in the building of socialism." The attitude toward women as far as legislation was concerned was essentially protective. This may be seen in the text of a Resolution of RSFSR People's Commissariat of Labor of March 4, which was extended in 1923 by the Decision of U.S.S.R. People's Commissariat of Labor to the whole territory of the U.S.S.R. It specified "the maximum permissible loads to be moved by adolescents" and decreed that "female adolescents under 18 shall not be allowed to move weights in wheelbarrows at all." Different specifications were established for moving weights in two-wheeled handcarts and three-and-four-wheeled carts.[3]

[3]English translations of extracts of this Resolution may be found in *Soviet Legislation on Women's Rights*. (Moscow: Progress Publishers 1978), pp. 115-116.

When tractors came to be used very extensively, the U.S.S.R. People's Commissariat of Labor deemed it necessary to enact provisions "on the working conditions of Women Tractor- and Lorry-Drivers." In a Decision No. 110 of May 9, 1931, it was stated as follows: "In view of the extensive use of tractors and lorries in the socialist sector of agriculture, in transport and other branches of the national economy, there are now more opportunities for the mass employment of women as tractor- and lorry-drivers. Noting the exceptional importance of the employment of women on these jobs and taking account of the peculiarities of the female organism, which require special working conditions for women, the U.S.S.R. People's Commissariat has decreed:"[4] The decree consisted of five specific regulations which were to be applied to women. All women entering training were required to undergo medical examinations in accordance with other regulations. Those with physical defects or diseases were not to be admitted. They also had to have monthly medical examinations. The decree provided other regulations as to the permissible work for women during their menstruation periods and similar details.[5] According to a Decision of the Central Executive Committee and the Council of the People's Commissars of the U.S.S.R., dated March 7, 1933, No. 307, "Pregnant mothers, nursing mothers and minors of 14 to 16 years of age" were to be "permitted only light work" as specified by the U.S.S.R. People's Commissariat of Labor.[6] Article 122 of the Constitution of the U.S.S.R. of December 5, 1936 also contained specific protective provisions. It read as follows: "Women in the U.S.S.R. are accorded all rights on an equal footing with men in all spheres of economic, government, cultural, political and other social activity." The possibility of exercising these rights is ensured by women being accorded the same rights as men to work, payment for work, rest and leisure, social insurance and education, and also by State protection of the interests of mother and child, State aid to mothers of large families and to unmarried mothers, maternity leave with full pay, and provision of a wide network of maternity homes, nurseries and kindergartens.

During World War II State assistance to pregnant mothers and mothers of several children was increased. Provisions were also made for assistance to unmarried mothers and their children. The following extract of a Decree of the Presidium of the Supreme Soviet of the U.S.S.R. of July 8, 1944, as amended, speaks for itself: "A further decree of the Presidium of the Supreme Soviet of the U.S.S.R. of August 18, 1944

[4]*Soviet Legislation*, p. 98.
[5]*op. cit.*, p. 99.
[6]*op. cit.*, p. 107.

provided regulations on conferring the honorary title of 'mother-heroine,' the order of maternal glory and the maternity medal."[7]

[7]This decree was amended on May 28, 1973. See Appendix.

ALBANIA

by Karen Shaw Kerpen

Albania's sovereignty was still in question after the end of World War I. The victorious powers could not decide on Albania's future after the occupation ceased, so that Albanian nationalists had to resume their quest for independence. By 1920, Albanians had set up their own congress to create their own government, free of outside forces. Various political parties vied for supremacy until 1924, when Ahmet Zog became ruler. He later was proclaimed King Zog I and ruled for fifteen years. He encouraged foreign penetration of Albania, colluded openly with fascists, and eventually submitted to Italian occupation in 1936.

Once Ahmet Zog came to power, the democratic and egalitarian aspirations of men and women plummeted. Although Albanian women had fought against occupation troops in World War I and had joined the drive for independence, the Zog regime refused to grant them any status. Few jobs were open to them; no schools would admit them; they were denied political rights and suffrage; and they were excluded from positions in state and public institutions. Women were expected, sometimes forced to be housewives, economically dependent upon men.[1]

Not all women succumbed to this fate. Over the years, activists began to join trade associations, enter the market place, and participate in the opposition forces like the Albanian Communist Party, which was founded in 1929. The outbreak of World War II created a national resistance, which coalesced in 1942 as the Albanian National Liberation Front. The Front was headed by Enver Hoxha, the leader of the Albanian Communist Party. The Front had more than 6,000 women members,

[1]Mediha Shuteriqi, "Albanian Women Fighting for National Liberation," *Problems of the Struggle for the Complete Emancipation of Women* (Tirana: The Political Book Publishing House, 1973), pp. 116-130.

who became soldiers, commanders, propagandists, nurses, couriers, and rear-guard supporters. The women were represented by Nexhmije Xhuglini, who later married Hoxha. The Union of Anti-fascist Women grew out of the resistance activities of the Front and the Albanian Communist Party, and carried out coordinated actions from 1943 until the War was over.

BULGARIA

During the inter-war period the women of Bulgaria appeared to be making some progress toward the achievement of equal rights. The National Council of Women, which had become affiliated with the ICW in 1908, grew to include some 126 associations by the end of the inter-war period. The *Woman's Voice* (*Zhenski Glas*) continued to be published on a regular basis until the beginning of World War II. Perhaps the most tangible achievement was a law enacted in November 1937, which enfranchised married women. However, it was of little consequence, as the authoritarian regime hardened in the subsequent period. There was no room for a women's movement to function freely and effectively.

CZECHOSLOVAKIA

During the inter-war period the people of Czechoslovakia thought of their country as the "Heart of Europe." Except for the most eastern part of Carpathia, it was neither geographically nor culturally part of eastern Europe. The Czechoslovakian women's rights movement was firmly rooted long before 1918 when Czechoslovakia became independent. It was never significantly affected by the radical feminists of the West. Czech women had to become more keenly aware of the need for partnership between women and men, if the outmoded and oppressive laws and customs of the past were to be eradicated.

This was particularly important in the work of the National Assembly and its key committees. Another favorable factor was the relatively large area of common interest in matters of women's rights among the Czechoslovakian political parties. On the other hand, there were considerable difficulties in developing unified legislation for the entire territory of the republic. This was due to the fact that there was a great difference in legal norms, as well as social and cultural patterns between the western and the eastern halves of the territory. Traditionally, Slovakia had maintained a much more patriarchal system and orientation. The Ministry of National Unification encountered considerable difficulties in carrying out its task of achieving legal unification. The so-called Bohemian Crownlands had been under Austrian rule since 1620, while Slovakia had been a part of Hungary for about one thousand years. Different cultural and political traditions resulted from this fact. In the 19th Century a persistent struggle was urged in the Crownlands for political, economic and social emancipation. The family structure was never as patriarchal as in Austria, and women played prominent roles in the arts and in the nationalist movement. Almost all the leading women writers were feminists.

Professor Thomas G. Masaryk, who became the first president of the republic, and his American-born wife were strong supporters of the women's rights movement. In Slovakia the attitudes were different in many ways, because agriculture was the dominant occupation and the Catholic Church was much more conservative than in the western part of the country. Before and after independence was achieved, Czech and Slovak leaders had important disagreements, but there was never any major disagreement on the kind of democratic regime that was to be established. Equal rights for men and women was one of the foundations on which the system was to be built.

A firm constitutional foundation was established on February 20, 1920. Even before that the principle of equality between men and women was in the electoral legislation of January 31, 1919. The most important provisions of the Constitution of the Czechoslovakian Republic of February 20, 1920 were the following:

Article 9:   The right to vote for the Chamber of Deputies may be exercised by all citizens of the Czechoslovakian Republic, without distinction of gender, who are past 21 years of age and who comply with the other provisions of the electoral law relating to the Chamber.

Article 10:   All citizens of the Czechoslovakian Republic who are 30 years of age and who comply with the provisions of the electoral law relating to the Chamber may be elected as Deputies to the Chamber.

Article 14:   The right to vote for the Senate may be exercised by all citizens of the Czechoslovakian Republic, without distinction of gender, who are past 26 years of age and who comply with the other provisions of the law relating to the Constitution and the rights and powers of the Senate.

107

Article 15: All citizens of the Czechoslovakian Republic, without distinction of gender, who are 45 years of age and who comply with the conditions of the law relating to the Constitution and the powers of the Senate may be elected to the Senate.

Article 56: Any citizen of the Czechoslovakian Republic, who is eligible for the Chamber of Deputies, and has reached the age of 35 years, may be elected as President.

All other elective or appointive offices were covered by Article 106.

In terms of numbers there were relatively few women members in the Chamber of Deputies and in the Senate. But women served on key committees and were highly respected by their male colleagues. Senator Františka Plaminková was also the president of the National Women's Council. At the very beginning, more than a dozen political parties established special women's sections. The political parties were competing with each other for the women's vote, and this tended to advance legislation which protected the interests of women.

HUNGARY

At the end of World War I, activities on behalf of the women's rights movement were resumed. But progress was slow, and it was not until the mid 20s that some tangible advances could be recorded.

Article 2(1) of Law XXVI/1925 stipulated certain conditions for women's suffrage. Women were qualified to vote for deputies in the Chamber of Deputies if they were 30 years old, had been citizens of Hungary for at least 10 years, and had been domiciled in the same community for two years. They also had to meet certain educational requirements. School attendance was required at six years of age. But women who had given birth to three children were also eligible to vote, even if they had lost some in war because legally these children were still alive. The age requirement of 30 did apply to women who had completed their studies at a university or institution of higher learning. The right of women to vote in municipal elections was regulated by Law XXX/1929, which required only a six-months' residence in the municipality.

According to Article 9 of Law XXVI/1925 women were eligible to be candidates for the Chamber of Deputies provided they were 30 years of age and met certain other requirements. However, at the end of the inter-war period there were only two women in the Chamber of Deputies.

The laws just mentioned did not establish complete equality between men and women, because men were eligible to vote at the age of 24 and with only four years of primary education.

The first Hungarian woman to become a delegate to the League of Nations was Augusta Rosenberg. This was in 1928, and subsequently, until 1933, she also served as a delegate to the ILO. Countess Apponyi first became a delegate to the League in 1928, and served several times thereafter.

The campaigns for universal suffrage, which succeeded in 1905, were always for men only. The Electoral Reform Law of 1913 (GA XIV) did not alter this fact. When Hungary was proclaimed a republic on November 16, 1918, legislation was enacted which was to include universal suffrage, but this could not be implemented because of the unsettled conditions.

In 1920 Law No I, concerning The Reestablishment of the Constitutional Order and the Provisional Exercise of Sovereign Power in Hungary, gave women the right to vote in all elections. Men were eligible to vote at the age of 21, but women had to be 24 years old. The electoral reform of January 27, 1922 did not abolish this discriminatory requirement. It was also not abolished in August 1925 by Law No 26, which increased the voting age for men to 24, and for women to 30. An exception was made for women who were university graduates. They were eligible to vote at the age of 24. But by that time the ruling classes of Hungary were already combining feudalism with fascism. A formal treaty with Fascist Italy was signed on April 5, 1927. In 1938, new discriminatory provisions against women were enacted. Only those who were university graduates or professional women were authorized to vote at the age of 24 on equal terms with men. Women who had graduated from secondary schools could vote at 26. Literary and other requirements had to be met by all others.

POLAND

The election decree mentioned earlier, which was issued by General Pilsudski on November 28, 1918, gave women the right to vote for the Constituent Assembly. It was this body which promulgated the so-called "Little Constitution" on February 20, 1919. The first regular constitution was the ' March Constitution" of March 27, 1921. It embodied a system of government largely patterned on that of the French Republic, which at that time did not have a completely codified constitution but had evolved certain characteristic features, such as legislative supremacy and a relatively weak presidency. But, as may be recalled, the democratization of the French parliamentary system did not include women's suffrage. In this respect, the Polish Constitution was a more democratic document than the Constitution of the Third Republic of France.

Article 12 of the Polish Constitution of 1921 established equal suffrage for all citizens over the age of 21. Women and men, who had affirmed the age of 25, were qualified to be candidates for legislative office. There was a strange discrepancy in that soldiers on active service were not entitled to vote but were eligible for membership in the Diet. The provisions were as follows:

Article 12:

The right of taking part in the elections belongs to every Polish citizen, without distinction of sex, who has reached the age of 21 years on the date when the elections are announced, and who is in full enjoyment of civic rights, and has been domiciled in the electoral area since the day before the announcement of the elections in the Journal of Laws. The right to vote must be exercised in person. Soldiers on active service are not entitled to vote.

Article 13:

Every citizen is eligible for membership of the Diet, who has reached the age of 25 years and is qualified to take part in the elections thereto, including soldiers on active service and without regard to domicile.

The explanation for this discrepancy could be found in the importance which was attached to the military establishment. Soldiers on active duty were to be kept out of politics, but they were not to be disqualified from political office. Women continued to have the right to vote, but at that time (1921) they were not effectively organized for concerted political activities.

The National Council of Women of Poland was established in 1924, and it became affiliated with the ICW at that time. The 12 constituent organizations had been largely concerned with social welfare work, and this, along with the problems of public health and education, remained the main activities. Since most of the women deputies and senators were also members of the NCW of Poland, the relationship between governmental and non-governmental organization was fairly constructive.

But the democratization of the Polish political system was not proceeding smoothly. Pilsudski had relinquished the presidency in 1922 to a civilian who was murdered two days later. On May 10, 1926 Pilsudski carried out a coup d'état but declined the presidency. Ignacy Moscicki, the newly elected civilian president, was given more power on the basis of amendments to the Constitution, which were adopted in August, 1926. There were to be further amendments, along more authoritarian lines, but these were vigorously opposed by the deputies of the left. The result was almost perpetual paralysis. In March 1930 Pilsudski outlined his own ideas about constitutional reform, which centered around the concept of a strong presidency. Stanislaw Car, a former minister of justice and key member of the Constitutional Committee, elaborated Pilsudski's constitutional design in a still more authoritarian manner. There were long debates in the *Sejm* (parliament), and on March 28, 1933 an Enabling Law was passed, which authorized the president to legislate by decree.

In Poland, as in many neighboring countries, the growing international tensions increased the influence of the military and the militarists. Under these conditions the women's rights movement did not have much chance for further advancement.

The Constitution of April 23, 1935 was a much more authoritarian instrument of government than the Constitution of 1921. It was greatly preoccupied with the cult of the state and the authority of the president. It did not specifically proclaim the principle of equality before the law. Instead, Article 7(1) declared that "the rights of a citizen to influence public affairs will be estimated according to the value of his efforts and services for the common good." The second paragraph of this article was more encouraging by declaring that "these rights cannot be restricted by origin, religion, sex, or nationality." The Constitution of 1935 raised the minimum age for voting to 25, and the age of eligibility for elective office to 30. (Article 33)

The government tried to transform the NCW into a kind of auxiliary organization, but it was not completely successful in these efforts. The membership of the NCW of Poland continued to grow impressively. When Germany invaded Poland on September 1, 1939, the NCW consisted of more than two dozen constituent organizations with a total membership in excess of 100,000. The occupation by German and Russian forces did irreparable damage to the NCW of Poland, and many of its members were subjected to cruel treatment.

ROMANIA

In 1917. Elena Meissner, one of the leading feminists in Romania, founded the "Association for the Civil and Political Emancipation of the Roumanian Women" (A.E.C.P.F.R.). Women, mostly of middle-class origin, were very active in the immediate postwar period, but they failed in their efforts to obtain the right to vote. The Romanian Constitution of 1923 was a remarkably liberal document, which contains a long section devoted to the "Rights of Romanians," but the right to vote and to hold public office was reserved to men. This did not mean that women were without political influence. Mme. Lupescu, the mistress of King Carol who later became his wife had some influence, but she was not a feminist.

Toward the end of the inter-war period the women of Romania seemed to be moving toward political equality. In 1938 they were given the right to vote in what was in every respect a more authoritarian constitution than its 1923 predecessor. The Constitution of 1938 and the women's right to vote were of little practical significance, because King Carol was forced to abdicate in September 1940, and the new dictator, Marshal Antonescu, suspended the Constitution and became a collaborator of Nazi Germany.

YUGOSLAVIA

In Yugoslavia, or the kingdom of the Serbs, Croats and Slovenes, as it was officially called during the early post-World War I period, the problem of legal unification was even more complex than in the other succession states. While Serbia and Montenegro had indigenous legal codes, the Vojvodina retained Hungarian civil law. In Slovenia and Dalmatia the Austrian Civil Code of 1811, as amended in 1915, 1916 and 1917 remained in effect. The Austrian Civil Code was also in force in Croatia, but the amendments had not been introduced there. In Bosnia-Hercegovina some Ottoman laws were applied along with customary law. No attempt was made to bring about a speedy unification. This would have greatly reinforced the separatist tendencies, which were in existence in several areas of this succession state.

The legal differences were only part of the cultural diversity. There were profound contrasts in social attitudes along ethnic and denominational lines. The middle-class people of Slovenia took very similar positions to those of their fellow Catholics across the border in Austria.

A totally different outlook was evident in the predominantly Moslem areas of Bosnia and Hercegovina.

The Constituent Assembly, which was convened on October 28, 1920, never gave serious consideration to the possibility of introducing women's suffrage immediately. There was enough disagreement already. Six different drafts for a constitution had been introduced. The key problem in all of them was the territorial organization of powers. Several of the drafters thought only a federal system would facilitate a gradual national integration. But this was not the view that prevailed. The Constitution of June 28, 1921 carried over many of the authoritarian features of the Serbian Constitution of 1888. The Kingdom of Serbs, Croats and Slovenes was established as a centralized unitary system, and the Serbian politicians played the dominant role.

Article 70 of the Constitution of 1921 limited the right to vote to "every male citizen by birth or naturalization, who has completed his twenty-first year." Military personnel, active or on reserve, could "neither vote, nor be eligible for elections." The same article also provided that "women's suffrage shall be the subject of legislation." However, such a law was never enacted. Although women did not have the right to vote, they were eligible for appointment in some parts of the public service. This was provided for in specific legislation in 1923 and 1931. They were not eligible to serve in the armed forces in time of peace.

There were no wars, but there were serious internal conflicts. King Alexander found it very difficult to govern the newly independent state in the manner prescribed by the Constitution. In 1926, his powers were increased by the Constitutional Amendment of June 28, but he found them to be insufficient and turned increasingly to the army. He sought to legitimize his authoritarian regime on January 6, 1929 by enacting a charter which provided for the replacement of the difficult legislature by what was called the Supreme Legislative Council.

On September 3, 1931 a new and much more authoritarian constitution was promulgated. Although it did restrict fundamental rights, it did not completely rule out the possibility of giving women the right to vote. Indeed, Article 55 of the Constitution of 1931 carried over the text of Article 70 of the Constitution of 1921. But again, no further action was taken.

No attempt was made to work out a more equitable system of representation. The electoral laws enacted a few days after the promulgation of the 1931 Constitution copied provisions from Italian Fascist electoral legislation, which entitled a party to two-thirds of the seats in the Lower House, if it had won a plurality of votes in the elections. Vida Tomšič has emphasized that "the Communist Party of Yugoslavia was the sole party, that from the very beginning championed equal rights for women."[1] But it must be remembered that, unlike in Czechoslovakia, the Communist Party was outlawed and many of its leaders were in prison. It was only after the outbreak of World War II that the liberation of Yugoslavia and women's liberation were effectively joined in a common cause.

[1]Tomšič: *Woman* (1980) p. 21.

Part III

Achievements and Advances after World War II

CHAPTER 10

THE SCANDINAVIAN COUNTRIES AFTER WORLD WAR II

DENMARK

Since the end of World War II, the Danish women's movement and the Danish National Council of Women in particular, have been in the forefront of efforts to advance women's rights at home and in other parts of the world. In 1946, Mrs. Bodil Begtrup, who was then president of the Danish National Council of Women, chaired the meetings of the U.N. Commission on Women, which laid the foundations of the U.N. program on behalf of women's rights. She has also remained active in the Danish National Council during the subsequent three and a half decades.

The Danish Government has enacted a considerable amount of legislation to rid its legal structure of sexual bias. Prior to 1953, succession to the throne of Denmark was limited to male heirs. The Succession of the Throne Act of March 27, 1953 reduced male exclusiveness to mere precedence. Henceforth, men and women were eligible. This was confirmed in the Constitution of June 5, 1953. Section 2 states that:

> The form of government shall be that of a constitutional monarchy. The Royal Power shall be inherited by men and women in accordance with the provisions of the Succession to the Throne Act, 27th of March, 1953.

The unfinished business of constitutional reform was taken up as early as February, 1946 when the prime minister appointed a constitutional commission. Some of the issues which had been debated in 1939 were raised again. Among these was that of unicameralism versus bicameralism, and the lowering of the voting age. In a referendum on May 28, 1953 the voters approved the new Constitution which set 23 as the minimum age for voting. They also opted for unicameralism. The *Folketing* was not to exceed 179 members. Proportional representation was retained. The existing parliamentary system was made an integral part of the Constitution. Section 15 (1) provides that:

> A minister shall not remain in office after the Folketing has passed a vote of no confidence in him.

The voting age was not specified in the Constitution. Section 29 (2) specified that this should be done by referendum. This was set at 23 in a national referendum on May 28, 1953, in which the Constitution was approved. Section 30 (1) stipulated that:

> any person, who has the right to vote at Folketing elections shall be eligible for membership of the Folketing.

Members of the *Folketing* are elected for four years. In a 1961 referendum the voting age was lowered from 23 to 21. Section 81 limits military service to men:

> Every male person able to carry arms shall be liable with his person to contribute to the defense of his country under such rules as are laid down by statute.

In 1969, an attempt was made to have the voting age lowered to 18. However, this was overwhelmingly rejected in a national referendum.

King Frederik IX, who had succeeded the very popular Christian in 1947, died on January 14, 1972. In accordance with the Succession to the Throne Act of 1953, Queen Margrethe became the head of state. She has taken a personal interest in the question of women's rights, which she further demonstrated when she delivered the inaugural address to the World Conference of the U.N. Decade for Women in July, 1980. There had not been a Danish Queen since the late 14th Century (Queen Margaret).

These changes were not isolated phenomena in the advance of women's rights. Between 1945 and 1970 the membership of women in the *Folketing* rose from 5.4 percent to 11.8 percent. During the following decade it climbed to 23 percent. In the 1979 elections 21.8 percent of the candidates were women and 23 percent of the seats were occupied by women.

One of the anomalies in Denmark is the fact that there are fewer women (only about 16 percent) in local governmental bodies than in the *Folketing*. As in many other countries, attitudes toward greater participation by women are not the same in various regions and strata of society. There are some rural areas in which rather conservative attitudes have continued to prevail. Many interesting facts came to light in connection with a comprehensive study by the "Commission on the Position of Women in Society."[1] This Commission was appointed in 1965 by the prime minister, who noted in his mandate that technological and economic developments had brought about "a definite shift in the traditional perceptions of the position of women and men in the family and in society, and such shifts have been reflected in changes in legislation during the past half century." He went on to observe that "in spite of the fact that the two sexes legally have become equal in almost all areas the women's actual position in society does not correspond to such equality."

The Commission appointed seven committees in such matters as training and education, work conditions, conditions of family and children, social conditions, health, participation in public life and women civil servants, and issues on which the Commission had disagreed with the testimony of various ministries. In summarizing the report of the Committee on Equality, the final report concluded that:

> in several areas of Danish Society there are overall differences between the position of women and men. Many of these differences are experienced by the women involved—and often also by men—as an unjustified discrimination against women, whereas other(s) apparently are accepted or at least do not provide occasion for active protest.[2]

The Committee on Equality proposed that a "Permanent Equality Agency" be established, and two other countries also proposed a permanent agency. The Commission endorsed the establishment of a "council on equality" on March 29, 1974.[3] The majority of the Commission suggested that the council should consist of a chairman and 12 members. The council was to be an agency, as well as "an organ of advice and cooperation for authorities, organizations and the public."[4] The council was also expected to deal with concrete cases "on request or on its own initiative."

In November, 1975, the prime minister acted on the recommendation and established the Equal Status Council. Another important step toward equal treatment came a few weeks later with the passing of The

---

[1]"The Position of Women in Society," Final Report of the Commission appointed by the Prime Minister. Copenhagen, 1974.
[2]*op. cit.*, p. 91.
[3]*op. cit.*, p. 97.
[4]*op. cit.*, p. 98.

Equal Remuneration (Men and Women) Act of Feb. 4, 1976. Comprehensive legislation was passed by the *Folketing* in 1978. It is entitled Law on Equal Treatment for Men and Women as Regards Employment and Related Matters. (Statute No 161 of April 12, 1978)[5] This law meets all the standards set out in the EEC Directives. In certain respects it goes further than the Council Directive 76/207 in that it extends the concept of discrimination on the basis of sex to include "pregnancy and maternity." (Art. 1 (2)) It is very clear in stating in Article 2 that "employers shall treat men and women equally for the purposes of access to employment, transfer and promotion." It recognizes the distinction between direct and indirect discrimination and prohibits both. (Art. 1 (1))

According to Article 7 "any provisions in agreements, company rules, etc., which conflict with Articles 2 and 5 of this law, are hereby declared null and void." No specific mention is made of legislation, but several laws concerning employees in agriculture and other fields were amended to conform with Law No 161/1978.

As in most other Community member states specific provision was made for exceptions or "derogations." This is clearly stated in Article 11:

> In so far as the sex of the worker constitutes a determining factor, for certain occupational activities the Minister within whose sphere of competence the activity in question lies, may, after obtaining the opinion of the Minister of Labor and the Equal Treatment Commission, authorize a derogation from the provisions of Articles 2 to 6.

Such derogations would apply to male actors and singers, as well as to fashion models and fitters. In Denmark, the clergy is reserved for males. But certain activities in the army and navy may now be performed by women. As far as the police forces are concerned, the derogations allow different criteria for admission, such as height requirements. This is considered to be an equitable form of discrimination or "positive discrimination."

Danish women are still "banned" from certain types of work. These exclusions are not regarded as discrimination but considered "protective legislation." Compared with other member states of the Community, there are very few such exclusions left. Among them are jobs which

---

[5]Extensive portions of both the Equal Remuneration Act and the Equal Treatment Act can be found in the Appendix.

involve the use of lead compounds or lead processing and certain bronzing processes. In Denmark women are not barred from night work.

Persons who feel they have been denied equal treatment may bring actions in an ordinary court. Article 9 of Act No 161/1978 sets the compensation which is due to workers who were dismissed because they demanded equal treatment.

FINLAND

In 1947, the Soviet Union added insult to injury by imposing heavy territorial losses and war reparations on Finland. During the difficult postwar decade the men and women of Finland continued to work together in rebuilding the country's economy. Political participation, which had been fairly high in the prewar period, increased substantially. In the parliamentary elections of 1939 the total voters' participation was 66.6 percent. In 1945, it jumped to 74.9 percent. Male participation was 77.5 percent and female participation was 72.7 percent. The total votes and distribution of voters between males and females remained about the same in the subsequent elections of 1948, 1951, 1954, and 1958. But in 1962, total participation jumped to 85.1 percent. The difference between male and female voters' participation narrowed as 86.1 percent of the male and 84.2 percent of the female voters cast their ballots. This voting pattern continued through the elections of 1966, 1970, 1972. It changed somewhat in 1975 and 1979, after the voting age was lowered from 20 years to 18. While the overall vote dropped to 73.8 percent in 1975 and 75.3 percent in 1979, the general distribution between male and female votes was roughly the same. During these years there has been an impressive increase in the number of female candidates in parliamentary elections. Between 1948 and 1970 the percentage of women candidates rose from 12.1 to 17.3. In 1945, there were only 17 women deputies. By 1970, there were 43.

In 1970, a government committee was appointed to study the need for a comprehensive revision of the 1919 Constitution Act. On July 28, 1972 the Constitution was amended to establish an obligation on the part of the state to find employment for its citizens. Article 6, Part 2 now states:

The labor of the citizens shall be under the special protection of the State.
The State is thus very much involved in the labor situation and it must be particularly careful to avoid any action which

121

might be deemed discriminatory.

The Council for Equality was established by decree on June 8, 1972.[1] Its organization and functions are very similar to that of the Danish council, but its importance is perhaps even greater because during the past two decades Finland has consistently had the largest percentage of women in its labor force. In 1977, it was up to 46.6 percent as compared to 43.7 percent in Sweden, 42.2 percent in Denmark, and 39.6 percent in Norway.

On April 29, 1980, in connection with the second half of the U.N. Decade for Women 1980-1985, the government of Finland adopted a National Program for Promoting Equality between Women and Men.[2]

ICELAND

In the period after World War II Iceland not only ceased to be isolated but became very involved in European and Atlantic affairs. It became a member of the U.N. in 1946 and joined Denmark, Norway, and Sweden in what came to be known as the Organization for Economic Cooperation and Development. Although Iceland does not have a military establishment, it has been a member of NATO since 1949. As previously noted, Iceland was a country in which the old Germanic tradition of male exclusiveness in military matters was strongly supported. However, the Constitution does not affirm this principle. As stated in Article 75, "every person able to carry arms shall be obliged to take part in the defense of the country." The ability to bear arms is subject to legal definition.

Article 33 of the original 1944 text of the Constitution declared that:

Every person, man or woman, who has attained his or her twenty-first year of age at the time of the election and who is an Icelandic citizen and has been domiciled in the country for five years prior to the election, shall have the right to vote. No person shall have the right to vote unless he or she is of unblemished character and financially solvent.

[1]See Appendix.
[2]See Appendix.

This article was amended on April 5, 1968 and the voting age was lowered from 21 to 20. Article 34 remained unchanged. It reads:

> Every citizen qualified to vote is eligible for the Althing. Judges who do not hold administrative office are, however, not eligible for the Althing.

In the early 1970s the women's movement in Iceland was also gaining strength with respect to greater equality in the economic field. An Equality of Wages Board was created by Law No 37 of April 24, 1973. In 1975, the government decided to establish a Commission of Women. On October 24, 1975, the majority of Icelandic women stopped work and staged demonstrations for women's rights and equality. It was a highly effective campaign and expedited the passage of the Law No 78 on the Equality of Women and Men on May 31, 1976. This law is remarkable for its brevity and clarity. As stated in Article 1, its purpose is "to promote the equality and equal position of women and men." It stipulates that both "shall receive equal wages for performing comparable work of equal value" (Article 2). The law emphasizes the importance of education, the media and responsibility on the part of advertisers (Articles 7 and 8). Provision is made for an Equality of Treatment Board (Article 9), whose functions are detailed in Article 10. (An English translation of the entire Law appears in the Appendix.)

Since 1952, Iceland has been a member of the Nordic Council, along with Denmark.

Prior to 1959, the *Althing* consisted of 52 members. Since that time there have been 60 members who are elected for four year terms. (Article 31) Like the Norwegian *Storting* it is divided into an Upper and a Lower House: One third sit in the Upper House and two thirds in the Lower House. (Article 32)

Women's participation in local and national elections has not been as high as in the other Scandinavian countries. In 1974 and 1978 it was slightly more than 49 percent. The percentage of women elected to local offices was 3.7 in 1974, but rose to 6.2 in 1978. Women elected to the *Althing* constituted 5 percent of the total both in 1974 and 1978. To date, women have not held important positions in the judicial or executive branches of the government, but on June 29, 1980 Vigdis Finnbogadottir was elected president of the Republic of Iceland. She thus became the first woman in Europe to be elected to the position of head of state.

NORWAY

Norway's experience in World War II was unique for the Scandinavian countries. After the Nazi invasion of Norway on April 9, 1940, the *Storting* met promptly, in accordance with the Constitution, to authorize emergency measures and to vote on the establishment of a government in exile. King Haakon took up residence in England and stayed in touch with the national coalition government headed by J. Nygaørdsvold.

The struggle for the liberation of Norway ended on May 8, 1945. Elections were held on October 27th. The Labor Party won an absolute majority, and the first woman entered the government. On June 28, 1946, Article 50 of the Constitution was amended to lower the voting age to 21. In 1948, Norway joined the Marshall Plan and in 1949 signed the North Atlantic Treaty.

After the general elections on October 10, 1949, the Labor Party increased its majority in the *Storting*.

Although the Labor Party suffered a setback in the 1953 elections, it did much better four years later. Sweden and Denmark had entered into a common-market agreement as early as 1945. Norway and Finland accepted an invitation to join in 1954. This opened up new opportunities for Norwegians, especially men. Women were expected to benefit from the fact that, in 1959, Norway signed the ILO Convention No. 100. While the acceptance of the principle, "equal pay for equal work" was of fundamental importance, it did not satisfy the leaders of the women's organizations because they felt then, as they still do, that the main issue is equal opportunity. The Council on Equal Pay was established in 1959 to examine wage disparities.

In 1962, the *Storting* voted to apply for full membership in the European Common Market. Article 50 of the Constitution was amended in 1967. The voting age was lowered from 21 to 20. It now reads:

> Those entitled to vote are Norwegian citizens, men and women, who have completed their 20th year at the latest, during the polling year.

During the 1970s, Norwegian women made considerable gains. In 1969, women in the *Storting* accounted for 9.3 percent of the total. In 1975, there were 25 women out of a total of 155 or 16.1 percent. The percentage grew to 23.9 when 37 women took their seats. Of these, 20 were socialists and 12 conservatives.

The percentage of women in municipal councils had remained relatively low, especially in the more rural areas. In 1963, women accounted for only 6.3 percent. The percentage increased to 9.5 in 1967 and to 14.8 in 1971. These overall figures may be somewhat misleading because in the larger municipalities women scored very impressive gains. The women of Oslo did particularly well in 1971, when 46 of the 85 members of the Oslo City Council, or 54 percent, were women.

The Equal Status Council was established in 1972. It took over the functions formerly vested in the Council on Equal Pay. It consisted of 12 permanent members and a chairman.

Women had gained in the economic sector. In the political field, especially on the national level and in the rural local units of government, however, relatively little progress had been made.

After the 1975 elections, there were 25 women in the *Storting*. This came to 16.1 percent of the total 155 members. It may be compared with 9.3 percent in 1969. Women were numerous in the clerical positions and in the lower administrative echelons. After the 1975 Mexico City meeting improvements began to be apparent.

Shortly after the 1975 U.N. Women's Conference, the Equal Status Council conducted a detailed study on the status of women in the social, economic, political and cultural life of Norway. It concluded in its Report to the U.N. that many important tasks remained "to be tackled." One important aspect of this task was a reevaluation of existing legislation and major bills on which there had been much debate but no definite action. Among these was the Bill Concerning Equality between the sexes. In April 1976, it was returned to the government with a request to draft a new bill. The government was more successful with the amendments it had proposed to the government pension system. In the spring of 1976 new regulations were adopted which equalized the requirements for men and women. Equalization was also proposed by the Ministry of Finance in tax legislation as it relates to spouses. In the field of education greater emphasis was placed on vocational and adult education for women. Progress was reported on the matter of equal remuneration. The differentials between the pay for men and women had been reduced. In some areas, the pay of women constituted as much as 85 percent of that of men.

But in the political arena Norway led all other European countries in the number of women cabinet members: Inger Louise Valle, who served as minister of justice, Ruth Ryste, minister of social affairs, Gro Harlem Brundtland, minister of environment, and Kristen Myklevoll, minister of consumer affairs. In 1981, Gro Harlem Brundtland served for eight and a half months as the first female prime minister of Norway. However, after 10 years in power, the Socialists were defeated in the general elections of September 14, and a conservative government headed by Kare Willoch took over in October.

One of the most important pieces of Norwegian legislation has been the Act relating to Equal Status between Sexes of June 9, 1978. An English translation may be found in the Appendix.

The Equal Status Act is a very comprehensive document. It concerns itself with every aspect of the women's rights struggle and addresses the areas in which women have made advances over the last century: suffrage, legal equality, employment, family life, and so on. The document declares, "Discrimination between women and men is not permitted." Thus, the gains of the Norwegian women's rights movement have been codified.

SWEDEN

Sweden, in postwar years, demonstrated a very similar pattern of social and political advances for women. During the first three decades after World War II the number of women members in the Second Chamber increased steadily. In 1945, as in 1941, there were 18 women out of a total of 230. This number rose to 22 in 1949 and 28 in 1953. In 1953 and 1957, when the total membership increased to 231, there were 29 (1953) and 31 women (1957). In 1961, there were 32 women out of a total of 232. The membership of the Second Chamber increased again to 233. Out of this total there were 31 women in 1965, 33 in 1966, 34 in 1967 and 35 in 1968. In 1971, women accounted for 14 percent; in 1974 for 21 percent. In 1976, out of a total of 349 members, there were 79 women in the Riksdag (22.6 percent). By 1977, the percentage was up to 23. In the local elective bodies the percentage of women has been much higher in the larger cities (about 20 percent) than in rural communities.

Before 1968, the amended text of the Riksdag Act read as follows:

Article 9:

> A man or a woman shall not be entitled to be elected a member of the First Chamber unless he or she has attained the age of 23 years and is entitled to vote on public matters in the commune.

Article 16:

> Every Swedish citizen, irrespective of sex, shall have the right to vote provided that he (or she) attained the age of 20 years during or before the preceding calendar year.

Article 19:

> A man or a woman shall not be entitled to be elected a member
> of the Second Chamber, unless he or she has attained the age
> of 23 years and is entitled to vote in a constituency, or, in the
> case of a city consisting of more than one constituency, in one
> of several constituencies.

In 1968, the *Riksdag* approved the constitutional amendments, which lowered the voting age from 23 to 20. In the 1970s, work was progressing on a new constitution.

In 1972, the Social Democratic Party appointed a delegation or advisory council to the prime minister to concern itself exclusively with matters relating to the policy of equality between men and women. A government commission charged with the task of making recommendations toward the revision of family legislation helped to bring about changes in the law in 1973. Maternity allowances were increased in 1974; and measures were proposed which would support one-parent and two-parent families with small children.

In 1973, new marriage legislation was enacted. It did not drastically alter the Marriage Code of 1920. The main changes involved simplification in matters involving divorce.

The progress that had been made toward the democratization of the Swedish political system and the equalization of the rights of women was confirmed in the very first article of the new "Instrument of Government." Article 1 of Chapter 1 states:

> All public power in Sweden emanates from the people. The
> Swedish democracy is founded on freedom of opinion and on
> universal and equal suffrage and shall be realized through a
> representative and parliamentary polity and through local self-
> government. Public power shall be exercised under the laws.

The other important provisions of the Constitution are contained in the following articles:

Chapter 1, Article 8:

> In the exercise of their functions the courts and administra-
> tive authorities shall maintain objectivity and impartiality.
> They may not, without legal grounds, treat persons differently
> by reason of their personal conditions, such as faith, opinions,

race, skin-color, origin, sex, age, nationality, language, social status, or financial circumstances.

Chapter 3, Article 2:

The right to vote in elections for the Riksdag is granted to every Swedish national who is a resident of Sweden. Provisions regarding the suffrage of Swedish nationals not having their residence in Sweden shall be laid down by law. A person who has not reached the age of 18 years on or before the day of the elections or who has been declared by court order to be under legal disability shall not have the right to vote.

Any question of whether there is a right to vote under the preceding paragraph shall be determined on the basis of an electoral register established before the elections.

Chapter 8, Article 1 makes provision for legislation:

relating to the personal status of private subjects or to their personal and economic interrelationships.

Included, by way of example, are:

provisions concerning 1) Swedish citizenship, 2) the right to a family name, marriage and parenthood, heritage and testaments, or other family affairs. Also, 3) the right to real estate and movable property, concerning contracts, companies, associations, communities and foundations.

This article provided the constitutional basis, if not the mandate, for extensive legislation that was enacted in the subsequent six years to implement and strengthen the equality between genders in Sweden.

Of all this legislation the most important one, at least from an economic point of view, is the Act on Equality Between Women and Men at Work, which entered into force on July 1, 1980.

The Act on Equality between Women and Men at Work which entered into force on 1 July 1980, aims to promote equal rights for women and men in respect of employment, conditions of employment and opportunities for development in employment.

The Act applies to all kinds of employment, in both the public and the private sectors. Many of its rules also relate to job applicants. The Act is targeted at the employers. An Equal Opportunities Ombudsman is responsible for ensuring compliance with the Act.

The Act has two main parts: One contains rules on the prohibition of discrimination on the ground of sex and the other deals with active measures to promote equality. The Act also contains provisions regarding an Equal Opportunities Ombudsman and an Equal Opportunities Commission as well as rules governing sanctions and procedures.

The *ban on discrimination* means that an employer may not disfavour an employee or job applicant on the ground of her/his sex. The ban applies from recruitment until the termination of employment. Discrimination on the ground of sex is thus forbidden at recruitment, as regards promotion or training for promotion, as well as in the application of terms of employment (e.g. remuneration) in the management and distribution of work and as regards dismissals, transfers etc.

Exceptions are made for what is known as the favourable treatment of the under-represented sex. This means that an employer can give preference to a person of the under-represented sex with merits of lower standard than those of a person of the opposite sex, on condition that this is part of a conscious effort to promote equality. Exceptions can also be made for the furtherance of ideological or other special interests.

The prohibition of discrimination is mandatory. An employer who contravenes the ban can be sentenced to *payment of compensation*. Disputes on discrimination on the ground of sex will normally be tried by the Labor Court.

The obligation of an employer to take *active measures to promote equality* implies that the employer shall consciously pursue action to further equality at the place of activity and in proportion to resources. Work places, i.e. both work environment and the organization at work, are to be adapted so that both women and men can work there. The employer is to try to ensure that vacancies are sought by members of both sexes. By means of training and other appropriate measures, the employer shall also promote an even distribution between the sexes (at least 40 percent of each sex) in different types of work and in various categories of employees. When recruiting, the employer must make special efforts to get applicants from the under-represented sex.

Rules on active measures to promote equality can be replaced or supplemented through collective agreements. An employer who is not bound by agreements of this kind and who does not observe the rules on active measures can be ordered to fulfil his obligations under penalty of a fine. Such orders are issued by the Equality Opportunities Commission. If an employer does not observe the provisions contained in a collective agreement, the ordinary rules on sanctions for breach of collective agreements are applicable.

The Equal Opportunities Ombudsman's main task is to ensure that the Act is observed. The Ombudsman shall in the first place try to

129

persuade employers to comply voluntarily with the rules of the Act, by means of advisory services and information and negotiation, etc. Not until it is found that such reminders have no effect does the Ombudsman take other measures. The Ombudsman may appear on behalf of an individual employee or job applicant in a discrimination dispute before the Labor Court. If the person in question is a member of a trade union, however, it is the trade union which shall appear on behalf of the plaintiff. An action can also be brought by an employee or a job applicant in person. In the case of active measures to promote equality, the Ombudsman can make representations to the Equal Opportunities Commission regarding fines.

The Ombudsman is also responsible for information to the general public and for taking other appropriate action to contribute towards the promotion of equality. The Ombudsman thus has an important role to play in the mobilization of public opinion. This means, for instance, that the Ombudsman must keep in constant touch with the organisations on the labor market and with institutions and public bodies on the labor market, as well as with other organisations concerned with equality.

The Government has appointed District Judge Inga-Britt Törnell Equal Opportunities Ombudsman. Ms. Lena Svenaeus, attorney-at-law, has been appointed to deputize for the Ombudsman.

The Equal Opportunities Commission is appointed by the Government and has the task of imposing fines concerning active measures to promote equality after representations by the Ombudsman. The Commission is chaired by an experienced court lawyer and consists of persons with a good knowledge of conditions on the labor market and experience of work to further equality, together with representatives of the main organisations on the labor market.

CHAPTER 11

THE WESTERN EUROPEAN COUNTRIES AFTER WORLD WAR II

INTRODUCTION

At the end of World War II it was not difficult to predict that the great majority of those European countries which had not yet introduced women's suffrage would not be able to postpone it much longer. In the West this was long overdue. France, or more exactly de Gaulle, had already taken the necessary steps to give women the right to vote before the war ended. Belgium followed in 1948. In 1971, at long last, the male voters of Switzerland finally decided to amend their Constitution so that women could vote in federal elections on equal terms with men. Only one country, a very small one, remains which does not seem inclined to take the final inevitable step of allowing women to vote not only in communal elections but in "national" elections as well.

In the other western states which had introduced women's suffrage during the inter-war period there were important new developments, which are analyzed here in a comparative manner. As in the earlier period we have arranged all the ten western countries in alphabetical order: Austria, Belgium, France, Germany, Great Britain, Ireland, Liechtenstein, Luxembourg, Netherlands, and Switzerland.

AUSTRIA

The rebuilding of Austria since the end of World War II is undoubtedly one of the great success stories of our time. In 1945 even the most optimistic Austrians could not imagine such a rapid recovery and steady development of their country. How much have the Austrian women benefitted from these remarkable achievements? Most of them would probably say that they have not gained as much as men have. From an economic point of view this is certainly true because of the continuing differentials in pay. If one looks at the record of women's political participation, it is clear that women have not achieved political equality in every respect. Still, their progress in both fields has been noteworthy. Even more significant have been the changes that have taken place in the legal system. The legal relationships between men and women have definitely been altered from a rather rigid patriarchal system to one of growing partnership. How and why did this happen? There are no easy answers to this question, but it becomes easier if one traces the historical development of women's rights and political participation since 1945. In doing this, one must also recall that the women's organizations of Austria had achieved major gains by the turn of the century and obtained the right to vote right after World War I. But then they were victimized by the reactionary politics of the 1930s.

After World War II the various political parties of Austria started to attach more importance to the role of women in the political process. In 1945, more than 35 percent of the members of the Social Democratic Party (SPO) were women, and the other parties could not ignore this fact. They, too, would have to recruit more women and get them interested in the political process. As early as August 4, 1945, the Allied Central Council had allowed political parties to operate, provided that they were committed to the reconstruction of a free and independent Austrian State. The amended text of the Constitution of 1920 had already been reinstated on April 28. It was deemed to provide a good basis for a progressive policy toward an equalization of rights between men and women. The most important constitutional provisions toward this goal were Articles 7, 26(1), and Article 95(1).

Article 7, it may be recalled, laid down the principle of gender equality within the legal and political framework.

Article 26(1) stated that:

> the National Council is elected by the people of the Federation on the basis of equal, direct, secret, and personal suffrage by men and women.

The voting age was reduced to 20 and the minimum age for eligibility was lowered to 26.

Article 95(1) concerns elections in the Länder, which are also to be carried out

> on the basis of equal, direct, secret proportional representation, in accordance with the electoral regulations of the Land legislatures by all eligible male and female Federal citizens, who have their regular domicile in the Land.

The first electoral legislation was enacted on October 19, 1945, and the first general elections were held on November 25. In the *Nationalrat*, the Austrian People's Party (OVP) had 85 seats. The Socialist Party (SPO) won 76 seats. In the *Bundesrat*, the OVP occupied 27, and the SPO 23.

On December 20, the Federal Assembly (Bundesversammlung), in a joint meeting of both houses, elected Dr. Karl Renner to be the first President of Austria. He received 204 out of 205 ballots, which constituted a clear mandate: A progressive policy of democratization. This development of democracy required a restoration of basic constitutional rights. Toward this end, freedom of the press had already been reestablished on October 1, 1945. However, the Allied Council had stipulated that the press must adhere to democratic principles and refrain from publishing any material which might endanger the military security of the Allied occupation forces.

A progressive policy of the equalization of rights between men and women required that discriminatory practices be identified and eliminated. In 1945, women lawyers were finally allowed to enter the Austrian Civil Service. But the policy of providing access to government service proceeded very slowly, and the appointments that were made were, for the most part, in the lower echelons.

In the private sector, there were great differences in the pay of men and women. The Salary Law (Gehaltsüberleitungs Gesetz), which went into effect on February 5, 1947 was among the early legislative measures intended to equalize the rights of men and women. Since that time, it has repeatedly been amended.

New electoral legislation for the Federal Council was enacted on May 18, 1949. Article 22 specified that:

> All men and women who are Austrian citizens, who have completed their twentieth year of age before the first January of the year in which the elections are held and who are not excluded from the right to vote, are entitled to vote.

Article 47 provided that:

> All men and women who are Austrian citizens, who are not excluded from the right to vote and who have completed their twenty-sixth year of age before the first January of the year in which the elections are held, may stand for election.

The Citizenship Law was amended in 1949, so that Austrian women who married foreigners could retain their Austrian citizenship. However, this amendment and subsequent amendments in 1973 and 1978, did not achieve a complete equalization of rights of the sexes with respect to nationality. At the present time, more than two decades later, efforts are still being made to achieve full equality.

All of these legislative changes were important as elements of a comprehensive program of legal reform. But it was widely realized that, if such a program were to be effective, a reform of the Civil Code of 1811, as partially amended in 1914, would have to be undertaken. In 1949, Otto Tschadek, the minister of justice, took an important initiative toward a comprehensive review and reform of the Austrian Civil Code. A commission, appointed by him, drew up a 48-point program, which set forth the basic principles for this undertaking. The main objectives were to strengthen the position of the woman within the family, and to improve her property rights. Little progress was made during the subsequent years. As will be noted, it took about a quarter of a century to achieve the desired "enshrinement of the principle of partnership between men and women." As far as the political system was concerned, democratization did move forward. One of the important changes came in early 1951, when a new presidential election law was passed. Only the Communists opposed the change of having the president elected by the people, instead of the indirect election by the Federal Assembly. The first elections of a president by popular vote took place on May 6, 1951.

In the early 1950s, the main issue was the negotiation of the Austrian treaty, which came into force on July 27, 1955. On April 5, 1956, Austria joined the Council of Europe. The government made it clear that this membership was consistent with Austria's policy of neutrality. In the subsequent years, Austria joined other international organizations. Occasionally, some of the new legislation was considered contrary to the basic policy of the equalization of rights between men and women. An example of this was the Pay Act for Civil Servants (Gehalts Gesetz) of 1956, providing for household allowances which made the distinctions between men and women. At the time, this was deemed to be discriminatory, and possibly unconstitutional. More than two decades later, the Constitutional Court held unconstitutional those sections which differentiated civil servants on the basis of gender.

Important legislation for the protection of mothers went into effect on May 1, 1957. (BGBL No 76/1957) It was intended to afford employed mothers a paid leave of absence (Karenzurlaub) to take care of newly born children. This leave was originally set at six months, but was subsequently increased to one year. (BGBL No 459/1974) Some improvements were made in 1959 in the legislation concerning divorced women and single mothers.

Major pension legislation, concerning federal employees, was promulgated on November 18. (BGBL 340/1965) It was subsequently amended several times, especially in 1974. (BGBL 393/1974) A women's section was established in 1966, in the Federal Ministry of Social Affairs. This marked an important step in the development of machinery for an effective implementation of the new legislation.

Significant changes were made in 1967 in the guardianship system (Vormundschaftswesen), which concerned Articles 93, 98, and 211 of the Civil Code. In the original version, the mother was disqualified from exercising the powers of guardianship. Aside from passing a large number of legislative acts, the Austrian Federal Council was also engaged in incorporating some of the major U.N. Conventions concerning the status of women into its own legislation. In 1968, the U.N. Convention concerning the nationality of married women, which had been signed in New York, on February 20, 1957, was published in the Official Gazette of Austria. (BGBL No 238/1968) In 1969, the U.N. Covenant concerning the political rights of women was published in the Official Gazette of Austria. (BGBL No 256/1969) Not only U.N. documents but also the European Conventions and Charters were included in the Austrian Official Gazette. Thus, the European Social Charter of October 18, 1961 was published in the Austrian Official Gazette in 1969. (BGBL 460/1969)

In the 1966 elections, the Socialists had suffered a considerable setback, but in 1970 they scored a victory over the People's Party. Dr. Bruno Kreisky became Chancellor on April 21, 1970. This marked a new phase not only in Austrian politics but also in the struggle for women's rights and political participation. In the course of the 1970s, the Socialists extended their lead, and Chancellor Kreisky was able to push vigorously, not only for needed legal reforms but also for effective enforcement of the new women's rights.

In 1971, legislation was passed which changed the legal status of illegitimate children. The mother could now request to be appointed guardian under the general guardianship of the state.

On January 18, 1972, the government presented a bill which was designed to bring about a basic modification of certain inheritance provisions of the Civil Code. (Articles 757, 758, 762, 765, 769, 781, 785, 789, and 796) The Civil Service Law of 1914 was amended on January 25, 1972, so as to eliminate any differential provisions pertaining to men and women. (BGBL No 213/1972)

A Federal Law of May 30, 1972 (BGBL 234/1972) was to provide additional safeguards to protect the life, health, and morality of workers. This law, known as the "Arbeitnehmerschutzgesetz" was further amended in 1974. (BGBL No 144/1974)

A bill was presented on July 3, 1973, which sought to modify Article 89-96 of the Civil Code in accordance with the principle of equality between men and women. The Council of Ministers endorsed a constitutional amendment on October 29, 1973, which gave voting rights to everyone who in the electoral year would attain the age of 19. Also those who would reach the age of 25 could be elected to office.

Important protection against arbitrary dismissals of men and women was provided by the Federal Act concerning the Labor Constitution (Arbeitsverfassung) of December 14, 1973. (BGBL No 22/1974) It provided for legal challenges before a Conciliation Board. The new *Gewerbe Ordnung*, which went into effect on August 1, 1974, removed all discriminatory provisions in such fields as masonry, carpentry, stone work, and well-digging.

Income tax legislation was passed which abolished the distinction between married and unmarried persons. It went into effect on January 1, 1975.

On January 1, the new criminal code came into effect. The highly controversial provisions concerning abortion or termination of pregnancy had been passed by a narrow vote of 93 to 90, after a vigorous campaign, by the Social Democrats over the opposition of the Austrian People's Party and the Austrian Freedom Party. The new Penal Code abolished the penalties previously applicable in cases of induced abortions performed by physicians during the first three months of pregnancy, and in response to certain conditions, such as physical or mental harm to the mother, or the likelihood of a physically or mentally defective baby. If the prospective mother was a minor at the time of conception, abortions were also legally permissible.

The Federal Act of July 31, 1975 (BGBL No 412/1975) concerning the reform of the personal legal effect of marriage (Bundes-Gesetz über die Neuordnung der persönlichen Rechtswirkungen der Ehe) went into effect in 1976. On October 7, 1977, the Constitutional Court declared unconstitutional a part (Section 4, part II) of the 1956 Civil Servants' Pay Act on the grounds that it contained different provisions for men and women concerning the suspension of household allowances. The Federal Act concerning the Reform of the Law on Child-Parent Relations (Neuordnung des Kindschaft-Rechts) of June 30, 1977, went into effect on January 1, 1978. The concept of paternal authority, as formerly entrenched in Articles 91 and 176 of the Austrian Civil Code, was now replaced by parental authority. (Federal Law Gazette (BGBL) No 403/1977) In the summer of 1978, further changes were made in the Austrian Civil Code, especially in the field of inheritance law, which marked the end of a long process of bringing the traditional family law in harmony with changed circumstances and values. The new divorce law went into effect on July 1, 1978.

One of the most important pieces of legislation during the entire period under review is the Federal Law on the Equal Treatment of Women and Men (Gleichbehandlung von Frau und Mann bei Festsetzung des Entgelts), which was promulgated on February 23, 1979. (BGBL No 108/1979, pp. 683-687) Because of its importance, an English translation especially prepared for this book is included in the Appendix. The Law on Equal Treatment is considered to be the beginning of a comprehensive policy of equalization. It is anticipated that before the end of the U.N. Decade for Women, legislation will be enacted which will extend the principle and practice of equal treatment into the areas of equal access to work and working conditions.

On December 18, 1979, Austria, along with 129 member states of the United Nations, voted for Resolution 34/180, in favor of the Convention on the elimination of all forms of discrimination against women. As far as the record of legislation is concerned, there can be no doubt that the Austrian achievement during the past decade is most impressive. Few countries have promulgated as many and as innovative measures. But Austrian feminists contend that there remain profound differences between legal norms and actual conditions. Popular attitudes have not changed as drastically as the laws might suggest. There remain significant differences among different strata and regions of Austrian society. Substantial progress has been made to reduce discrimination in salaries and wages, but it has by no means been eliminated. The 1979 Law on Equal Treatment (Gleichbehandlungsgesetz) may accelerate the process of equalization. But even if and when "equal pay for equal work" becomes a reality, much will remain to be done to foster the principle of equality of opportunity. (Chancengleichheit.) In the final analysis, further progress will depend very largely on much greater political participation by women. The percentage of women in the National Council (Nationalrat) has not yet reached 10. In the Federal Council (Bundesrat), the percentage of women has been close to 20 in recent years. This compares favorably with other Western European countries, but Austrian feminists think they should be able to do much better.

Relatively little progress was made between 1975 and 1979 with respect to the participation of women in the legislatures of the *Länder*. The biggest increase was in Carinthia, where the women's share rose from 2.8 percent to 5.6 percent. Increases were also recorded in the Burgenland (9.1 percent to 13.9 percent) and Voralberg (5.6 percent to 8.3 percent). In Tyrol, where there had been no women in the 1975 legislature, the percentage was 3.0 in 1979. It was still the lowest, but it showed a significant breakthrough. The representation in Lower Austria and Upper Austria remained unchanged (5.4 percent). It dropped in Styria from 5.4 percent to 3.6 percent, and in Vienna from 18 percent to 17 percent.

In the late 1970s, the participation of women in public life did not increase much over what it had been in the mid 70s. The percentage of women in elected public offices had risen from about 6.5 to over 8. It was much smaller, and always constant, in the higher echelons of the civil service. Depending on where one draws the line on what constitutes the higher echelons, it was not more than 4 percent. In the judiciary, there have been very few women, none in the higher positions. In the most recent period (1975-1980), the highest percentage of women in the higher grades of the Austrian Civil Service has been in the Federal Chancellery and Ministry of Social Affairs (7-8 percent).

Somewhat fewer than one-third of all state employees are women. In some of the lower echelons of the administrative and educational hierarchies they outnumber men. But in the higher ranks, the percentages are much smaller. Although a few women have risen to the rank of "State Secretary," and a very small number have been members of cabinets, the general outlook for advancement has remained rather unfavorable.

The major political parties have continued to make considerable efforts to persuade women to vote for their candidates. Their leaders often profess their commitment to the principle of equality between men and women. It may, therefore, come as a surprise that within their own organizations they have not adhered to this principle. Between 1974 and 1978, all chairmen were men. The percentage of female deputy chairmen of the Socialist Party rose from 14.3 to 20. But, in the Austrian People's Party, the number dropped from 25 to 16.7 percent. The Austrian Liberal Party has had no women occupying positions as deputy leaders. In the Central Committee of the Austrian Communist Party, the percentage of women has dropped from 8.2 to 7.9. The situation is somewhat better in the *Länder*. Although the Socialist Party has no chairman in the *Länder*, over 20 percent of the deputy "Chairpersons" were women. The Communist Party showed an increase in participation by women in the *Länder* Party management, from 12.9 to 15.5 percent. In the Austrian People's Party, all *Länder* chairmen were men, but in 1974, 8.2 percent of the members of the *Länder* Executive Committees were men. The percentage increased to 10.4 in 1978. There were no women in leadership positions in the *Länder* organizations of the Austrian Liberal Party, and the percentage of women in the management dropped from 9.8 to 5.3.

BELGIUM

After Belgium was liberated, the country was preoccupied with problems of reconstruction. In addition to the enormous economic tasks, there were serious controversies of a decidedly political nature. The conduct of King Leopold III ever since his unconstitutional surrender to the German Army on May 28, 1940 seemed to preclude any possibility of his resumption of the throne. On September 20, 1944 the Belgian Parliament elected Prince Charles, the brother of King Leopold, to serve as Regent. The "royal question" occupied many Belgians until the summer of 1950, when Leopold abdicated and Prince Baudoin took his oath as the new king of Belgium.

After the end of World War II, the struggle for equal rights was resumed. Some modest inroads were made, such as the admission of women to the required examinations for the diplomatic and consular service. This was done in the fall of 1945 and in the following year the first female attache was posted abroad. In 1946, based on a Law of February 21, qualified women were admitted to the judicial service. The right to vote in national elections was finally granted to Belgian women on March 27, 1948. But it was not entrenched in the constitution by means of an amendment. It was done by amending the Electoral Code of August 12, 1928. On March 27th the amendment was passed and the number of eligible voters increased by 66 percent. The key article of the amended Electoral Code is number 2, which states that "women are entitled to vote under the same conditions (as men) with respect to age, nationality and domicile. These conditions are stated in Article 1:

In order to qualify as an elector in parliamentary elections a person must: (1) be a Belgian citizen by birth or be naturalized with full political rights: la grande naturalisation; (2) have attained the age of 21 years; (3) have been domiciled in the same commune for not less than six months. Each elector is entitled to one vote only.

The other pertinent conditions are Articles 223 and 224.

Article 223:

In order to be eligible for election to the Chamber of Representatives a person must: (1) be Belgian by birth or naturalized
with full political rights: la grande naturalisation; (2) be in
possession of his civil and political rights; (3) have attained
the age of 25 years: (4) be domiciled in Belgium.

Article 224:

In order to be eligible for election as a senator, a person must:
(1) be Belgian by birth or naturalized with full political rights:
la grande naturalisation; (2) be in possession of his civil and
political rights; (3) be domiciled in Belgium; (4) have attained
the age of 40 years.

Compared with the other European countries in which the Napoleonic Code of 1804 formed the basis of civil law, the changes in Belgium
after World War II proceeded very slowly. It was not until April 30,
1958 that the Belgian Civil Code was modified so as to improve the legal
status of the married woman. This was done by amending Articles 212
through 218 of the Belgian Civil Code. Legally, the principle of equality
between married partners had been established. Further legislation was
enacted in 1974, guaranteeing equal rights and duties of both parents
in relationship to their children. The new Law on Marriage of July 14,
1976 permits a married woman to use her maiden name if she so chooses.
On July 14, 1978 additional legislation was passed which equalizes the
legal rights of fathers and mothers in family relations. There have clearly
been major changes in the fundamental features of the Belgian Code.
But many Belgians still feel that these changes are not as apparent in
actual family relations.

In recent years, the *Commission Consultative de la Condition de
la femme* has sought to bring about a change in the Belgian nationality
legislation, which still provides that a Belgian woman who marries a
foreigner automatically loses her Belgian citizenship.

Many Belgians believe that the most troublesome problem for them
continues to be the inequality of wages and salaries between men and

women. To date, the most important legislation is the Law of August 4, 1978 on equal treatment between men and women. An English translation has been prepared for this work, as it appears in the Appendix. A few notes and comments are in order so as to facilitate a comparative analysis of the various countries of western Europe, especially the ones who are members of the European community. What was done in this law must also be measured against the standards and requirements set forth in the Council Directive 76/207, whose main objectives have already been discussed.

How does the Belgian Equal Treatment Law compare with that of the Community? On the whole, it represents an important achievement, and it is apparent that a major effort was made to harmonize the Belgian legislation with the new conceptions of equality and equal treatment. Belgium, along with Denmark, Ireland, and Italy met the deadline of August 12, 1978, set by the Commission for the development of appropriate legislation on equal treatment. On the negative side, it must be noted that to date Belgium has failed to enact a comprehensive implementing decree.

As far as the language and technical terminology is concerned, Title V of the Belgian Law of August 4, 1978 follows the Standards of the Directive very closely. It also states clearly that any "provisions contrary to the principle of equal treatment, as defined in Title V of this law, are void." However, the problem is not only one of identifying and repealing earlier legislation which is contrary to the new law but also one of reducing the number of so-called "derogations." These are exceptions claimed for certain positions in the public and private sectors, which have been identified as exclusively linked to one or the other gender. They are entirely legal, but they may not be very equitable or reasonable.

General references may be found in Article 153 of the Transitory Provisions. They include certain positions in the Ministry of Finance, the Prime Minister's Office, the Ministry of Justice and several other central offices. All of them were established by a number of royal decrees between 1967 and 1975. They are now supposed to be without legal basis because Article 153 states that they shall all be terminated within one year from the date of publication of the law. This would mean August 17, 1979. But there seem to be some questions as to whether this has actually happened in all the categories enumerated in Article 153.

In one such category are the security forces. The Gendarmerie continues to be an exclusively male domain on the basis of a law enacted on July 13, 1976. In the navy, formerly another such male domain, some training facilities have recently been opened to women. Some army positions are also open to women, but women are still excluded from becoming customs officials. Most of the remaining derogations are not deemed to be violations of the principles of equal treatment and non-discrimination, as defined in Article 2(2) of the EEC Directive. In the Belgian law, as in the Directive, one finds references to several kinds of discrimination, such as explicit, implicit, direct, indirect, and *de acto*. The latter usually is used to refer to discriminatory "practices." Indirect discrimination is not defined in the law, but situations and practices considered to fall under this heading are identified. Thus, Article 121(1) states:

> It is specifically forbidden: (1) to make reference to the gender of the worker in the offers of employment and to professional promotion, or to use in such offers or advertisements which, though not referring explicitly indicate or suggest the gender of the worker.

The term "positive discrimination" does not seem to be defined in Belgian legislation, but it is being used in the way laid down in the Directive (Article 24). This is evident also in Article 119 of the Belgian Equal Treatment Law, where it is stated that the provisions of Title V "shall not impede the measures seeking to promote the equality of opportunities between men and women, in particular by removing actual inequalities, which affect the opportunities of women . . ." The king is to determine in which cases such measures are to be taken. This is now largely a matter of opening up certain fields of vocational education to girls and women. The implementation of this policy appears to be well under way. The law also seeks to protect job security for women and to provide protection against dismissals. (Article 136) A considerable effort was made to inform workers of their rights under the Equal Treatment Law and the new opportunities which have been made available to them.

The wage differentials between men and women has narrowed in recent years. Unfortunately, at the same time the economic situation has deteriorated. There are few job openings, and women often continue to lose out when competing with men. Vocational training patterns have not changed greatly, and there are few qualified women for such openings as develop from time to time.

By 1980, the unemployment situation in Belgium had grown alarmingly, and the government drew up an "economic and social recovery plan," calling for an amendment which would have reduced unemployment benefits to individuals who are not heads of families. Since about 90 percent of the unemployed women did not qualify as heads of families, the effect of such a provision would have been very serious in many instances.

143

In response to protests from women's organizations and women deputies, the lower house passed a motion by a vote of 106 to 1, with 12 abstentions, "regretting the absence of women from the Council of Ministers and demanding special attention to be given to any measures that the government may decide to take to alleviate female unemployment."

In 1977 there were 15 women in the Belgian Chamber of Deputies, which consists of 212 members (7.1 percent). In 1980, the participation rose to 7.5 percent, when 16 women served in the lower house. Percentagewise, there have been more women in the Senate. In 1977, there were 16 out of 181 (8.8 percent) and in 1980 there were 20 (11.1 percent).

For reasons that have not been sufficiently explained, Belgian women candidates did poorly in June 1979 in the first direct elections to the European Parliament. Ironically, they had the highest percentage of candidates but the lowest representation. There were 62 Belgian women candidates out of a total of 246, or 25.2 percent. Out of the total of 24 who were elected, only two were women. This still gave them an 8.3 percentage, but considering that the women of Luxembourg won 33.3 percent of their country's seats, Belgian women suffered a major setback. Some think it was a mistake to put together a feminine list on what was called the United Feminist Party (Parti Feministe Unifié). Since it did not win a single seat, this seems a plausible explanation. The two successful candidates: Anne-Marie Lizin and Antoinette Spaak were well known, but they were not given choice committee assignments because they did not have sufficiently strong support in their own political parties.

The percentage of women in the civil service of Belgium has also increased. But in the higher echelon, progress has been very slow. During the 1970s, women's employment in the civil service rose from about 4 percent to about 8 percent. In 1980, there were four women who had cabinet status, but without the title of minister.

In the diplomatic service women were until recently at a distinct disadvantage. They were not given opportunities to rise to the top positions. Furthermore, Belgian women diplomats were not allowed to marry. This prohibition was not abolished until 1973 by a royal decree of April 13.

Prime Minister Wilfried Martens was generally regarded as a strong supporter of women's rights and especially of their political participation. Due to his initiative and continuing interest in the advancement of women a new ministerial committee for the status of women was set up in September 1980. The Comité ministeriel pour le statut de la femme is chaired by the prime minister. Although Wilfried Martens is no longer prime minister, it is believed that this work will go forward on such

144

issues as maternity leaves, which are to be extended. The minister of justice was asked to draft a bill which would bring Belgian law in line with U.N. recommendations, i.e. that marriage should not result in loss of nationality.

A Commission on the Condition of Women (Commission de la Femme) was established in 1975.

FRANCE

On October 21, 1945, French women voted in the national referendum to decide whether the new National Assembly was to be a constituent one, i.e. to decide whether there should be a new constitution or a reinstatement of the Constitution of the Third Republic. The result was a clear-cut mandate for change: 96.4 percent of the voters, as against 3.6 percent, voted for a Constituent Assembly. But the voters (66.3 percent to 33.7 percent) wanted a Constituent Assembly with limited powers. On November 6, the newly elected Constituent Assembly met for the first time.

General de Gaulle became the head of the government on November 13, 1945, but he resigned on January 20, 1946 because he did not approve of some of the basic features of the emerging Draft Constitution. Now the left became the dominant element in the Constituent Assembly. The final text of the Draft Constitution, which was prepared under the chairmanship of Pierre Cot, consisted of 125 articles. It contained a long list of economic and social rights, but no new provisions concerning the rights of women. The introductory 39 articles were still entitled "The Rights of Man." This text was adopted by the Constituent Assembly on April 19, by a vote of 309 to 249. It was narrowly rejected on May 5 in a national referendum. On June 2, a new Constituent Assembly was elected, and after four months it produced the document which was to become the Constitution of the Fourth Republic.

In the initial period of the Fourth Republic, women were active in the municipal councils. They also played prominent roles in the National Assembly, but, as in other western legislative bodies, they were usually assigned to committees concerned with social policy. In 1946, in the first National Assembly elected on the basis of proportional representation, there were 40 women out of a total of 630 deputies. More than half of them belonged to the Communist Party. The first woman to serve in a French Cabinet was Madame Poinsot-Chapois (MRP), who in 1947 became minister of health.

The Draft Constitution of April 19, 1946 did not contain very detailed provisions to guarantee the rights of the newly enfranchised women. Article 28 for instance, stated that

> men and women have the right to a just remuneration according to the quality and quantity of their work.

This qualification was not very helpful because such a provision might have been used to justify discriminatory practices. The Constitution of the Fourth Republic of October 27, 1946 was in some respects more satisfactory. In the Preamble, a clear statement was inserted that

> the law guarantees to the woman, in all domains, equal rights with those of the man.

There were no specific provisions designed to protect the rights of women. There were also more serious deficiencies in that constitution. The main defects were in the provisions which contributed to instability. Cabinets under the Fourth Republic, as the Third, were notoriously unstable. The advancement of women's rights depended on a greater degree of stability. Well-intentioned cabinet members simply could not implement their policies if they were to be replaced in six months or less.

The need for constitutional reform was widely recognized. There were many prolonged political crises and cabinet changes, but no new directions. On May 27, 1953, Paul Reynaud, the prospective prime minister, declared that France had become the sick man of Europe and that constitutional reforms were essential. The National Assembly rejected his proposals. On May 29, 1958, President Rene Coty asked General de Gaulle to form a new government. He told the National Assembly that he would resign if they refused to confirm the new premier.

The National Assembly not only confirmed de Gaulle on June 1 but on the following day, and by an even greater majority, granted him emergency powers for six months. During this period major decisions were made and the foundation was laid for a new constitutional and political system.

The Constitution of the Fifth Republic of October 4, 1958 contains only one basic provision concerning women's rights. Article 3 reads as follows:

> National sovereignty belongs to the people, which shall exercise this sovereignty through its representatives and by means of referendum . . .

Suffrage may be direct or indirect under the conditions stipulated by the Constitution. It shall always be universal, equal and secret.

All French citizens of both sexes who have reached their majority and who enjoy civil and political rights may vote under the conditions to be determined by law."

This article was implemented by Order No. 58,998 of 24 October 1958 Enacting An Organic Law Concerning The Conditions Of Eligibility And Grounds Of Disqualification For Election to Parliament:

Article 1

Any citizen who is a qualified elector may be elected to the National Assembly and to the Senate under the conditions and subject only to the reservations set forth in the following articles.

Article 2

No one may be elected to the National Assembly unless he has completed his twenty-third year.

No one may be elected to the Senate unless he has completed his twenty-fifth year.

Article 3

No one may be elected to Parliament unless he has fully satisfied the statutory requirements in respect of active military service.

It will be noted that although Article 3 of the Constitution refers to "all French citizens of both sexes," the Organic Law reads as if only men were to be elected to the National Assembly and to the Senate. This was certainly not the intent, but the percentage of women during the past decade and a half has usually been under 5 in the National Assembly, and under 3 in the Senate. Of the western European countries, only Great Britain and Ireland have fewer women in their legislatures. The status of women has changed rather slowly because the gender inequality was so deeply entrenched in the legal, political, and economic system.

The Napoleonic Code was probably the biggest obstacle. The patriarchal principle was still firmly established at the time that the Fifth

Republic was institutionalized. Before 1866, husbands could dispose of joint property and even some of the wife's property without her consent. These anachronistic powers have gradually been reduced, and by 1970 the wife's legally subordinate status had been replaced by one of shared rights and responsibilities. In the field of family law, this principle of legal equality meant the substitution of parental authority for the traditional patriarchal one.

The changes in the fields of family law and property law were not easily made, but they were not as controversial as the issue of abortion. In the 1960s, most politicians still tried to avoid commenting on it. This changed after the establishment of the *Conseil National Superieur de L'Information Sexuelle*. It now became one of the major issues in the politics of women's rights. In the mid-seventies, it was the highly articulate and respected Mme. Simone Weil who, as minister of health, brought about the passage of a liberal abortion law. The legislation, which was enacted on January 17, 1975, was to be in force for five years on a trial basis. Modifications were made on December 31, 1979 to the effect that abortions by a physician before the fourth month would continue to be legal. It was left to the individual physician to decide whether a pregnant woman was "in distress." The costs have not been reimbursable under the national social security plan.

Progress has been made in increasing maternity benefits. In 1974, maternity leaves were extended to fourteen weeks. Law No 75-6 of January 3, 1975 specified the manner of payment of prenatal allowances for pregnant women. It also spelled out the procedure to be followed in seeking postnatal allowances. Most of this legislation is, of course, more family-oriented than directed toward the achievement of individual women's rights. It is briefly referred to because it is intrinsically linked with the aspirations of women to achieve genuine economic and political equality. If a woman is denied control over her own body, she cannot play her legitimate role in the body politic. And she cannot be politically active unless she is secure economically and socially.

France has developed a very comprehensive government family policy which involves family allowances, tax exemptions, maternity allowances, housing and educational assistance, and other social programs. The sharply differing payments are determined by the size of the family and income levels. The principle of equal pay for equal work was reaffirmed in 1952, when France ratified the ILO Convention No. 100 of June 29, 1951. However, considerable wage differentials between men and women continued for at least a decade and a half.

On December 22, 1972, initial legislation was passed which was to provide the basis for an equalization of wages between men and women. (Law no 72-1143) (J.O. Dec., 1972) There is no doubt that in the 1970s

148

progress was made in this direction. In 1960, the differential between the salaries of men and women was much greater than it was twenty years later. According to a study by the State Secretariat for Women, the salaries of men in 1960 were 35 percent higher. By 1974, the difference had dropped to about 11 percent.

Discrimination on the basis of sex was by no means totally eliminated by the mid-seventies. It persisted because it was economically profitable for employers and not always illegal. A study of legal provisions in a variety of fields disclosed that several legal codes would have to be amended. Much of this effort was undertaken in 1975. It started in the field of civil service, with the Law concerning Civil Servants. Law No 75-599 of July, 1975 modified an earlier Ordinance (No 59-244) of February 4, 1959. It was to provide the basis for equal treatment of men and women in the civil service.

The Labor Code was amended by Law No 75-625 of July 11, 1975. The same law also amended Article 298 of the Social Security Code, and Articles 187(1) and 416 of the Penal Code. Article 187(1) of the Penal Code was amended to prohibit any discrimination in public employment. Penalties included imprisonment from two months to one year.

Similar penalties were provided for in the amended Article 416 of the Penal Code with respect to job offers. Allowance was made for exemptions in cases where a "legitimate motive" could be established. To date, there has been no further definition of what might be considered legitimate motives. The amended Article L-122-25 of the Labor Code ruled out pregnancy as a legitimate ground for refusing employment in the private sector to a woman applicant. It prohibited inquiries about pregnancy and freed women from any obligation to disclose such facts.

These laws were intended to bring French legislation in harmony with the earlier Directives of the Commission of the European Communities. With respect to Council Directive 76/207 EEC of February 9, 1976, the Commission found in 1981 that France had not gone far enough in implementing the principle of equal treatment.

In France, men have had about ten times as many career possibilities as women. In recent years, the government has made an effort to allow women access to jobs formerly reserved to men. A new list would open up such occupations as auto mechanics, carpenters, construction workers, electricians, truck drivers, and several others that have long been considered distinctly male occupations. In a cabinet meeting of September 6, 1978, it was decided to make these occupations accessible to women. How successful these efforts will be remains to be seen, but it should be possible to let women become party chiefs, horticulturists, or bus conductors, and to work at many more occupations previously considered exclusively for males. The French legislation did not use the specific phrases of the Commission as frequently as some of the other member states. It made no reference to "indirect discrimination." While it outlawed any discrimination on the grounds of gender or family situation, the last paragraph of Article 11 (Law No 75-625) left the way open for dismissal for a "legitimate motive." But the main objections on the part of the Commission concerned the large number of "derogations."

At this time, it would probably be impossible to state with certainty what positions are or are not open to women. For instance, there appears to be no comprehensive listing anywhere as to what army positions may be occupied by women. Women are also excluded from many positions in the police, the gendarmerie, customs and postal service. One of the "derogations" is identified in Annexes printed in *The Journal Officièl de la République Française* on April 10, 1977 (p. 2135).

The following positions in the Ministry of Interior were restricted to males only: police commissioners, inspectors and "enqueteurs" of the National Police. Distinctive conditions for access have continued to exist in the Ministry of Posts and Telecommunications.

In France, it was recognized long ago that legal reforms in favor of women's rights are of little practical significance without effective enforcement machinery. A Committee on Feminine Labor (Le Comité du Travail Féminin) was set up in 1965, but it was a mere consultative body, whose main function was to carry on research on the working conditions and to make recommendations. More effective measures were taken during the presidency of Valery Giscard d'Estaing. In 1974, the State Secretariat on the Condition of Women (Secretariat d'État à la Condition Féminin) was created, and two years later the administrative machinery was strengthened.

A state secretary was appointed in March, 1978 to assist the minister of labor in matters pertaining to the work of women. An important further step was taken in September 1978, when the president appointed a minister on the status of women. (Ministre delegue auprès du Premier Ministre chargé de la Condition Féminin.) This minister had the support of the prime minister and was empowered to request the cooperation of other ministers. The minister was to be consulted by other ministers in all matters concerning the status of women. There was also an Interministerial Committee (Comité Interministerièl de l'Action pour les Femmes) which was presided over by the minister on the status of women. In addition to this highly placed central organization, regional offices were to implement policies concerning women. The importance of this office was further enhanced in July 1979, when the president charged the minister with the task of coordinating governmental policy concerning family matters.

WOMEN AND POLITICS IN FRANCE TODAY

By Janine Mossuz-Lavau and Mariette Sineau

Center for the Study of Contemporary French Political Life

Translated by: Patricia K. Lane

Kept out of political life for a long time, French women are more seriously concerned with public affairs today. This is one of the new features of the French political scene which must be emphasized from the start. Its scope, however, should not be overrated: the recent changes ought not to conceal the persistence of continuing political inequality between the male and female populations.

I—Women enter politics

1. *As citizens and militants*:

Women who used to abstain more frequently than men from participating in general elections now vote as much as men do: this is a recent phenomenon, observed in 1977 in Paris during the municipal elections, happening again in 1978 (during the parliamentary elections) and once more in 1981 (during the presidential and parliamentary elections).[1] It has taken more than three decades, since French women were emancipated in 1944, for them to get used to going to the polls.

But is it a sign of greater "politicization"? In any case, a larger number of women take an interest in politics: in 1953, 60 percent stated that politics did not interest them at all; in 1969, only 47 percent of them felt this way, and in 1977, only 23 percent.[2] Moreover, while they formed the bulk of the conservative troops under the Fourth Republic

---

[1] MOSSUZ-LAVAU (Janine), SINEAU (Mariette)—"L'abstentionisme électoral à Paris" ("Electoral abstention in Paris") *Revue Française de Science Politique*, n° 1, February 1978, pp. 73-100; MOSSUZ-LAVAU (Janine), SINEAU (Mariette), *Les Femmes françaises en 1978, Insertion sociale, insertion politique*, (French women in 1978. Social insertion, Political insertion), Paris, National Foundation of Political Science/CORDES, March 1980, 400 p.; the 1981 results come from two polls conducted by SOFRES after the presidential election of May 1981 and the parliamentary elections of June 1981 for the *Nouvel Observateur*.

[2] At SOFRES, L'opinion française en 1977 (*French Opinion in 1977*), Paris, published by The National Foundation of Political Science, p. 221.

151

as well as at the beginning of the Fifth, supporting in force the Popular Republican Movement (Christian Democratic Party) and the Gaullist groups, they no longer fear to venture to the left. In 1965, at the time of the first presidential election by universal suffrage, less than 40 percent of them had voted (at the second ballot) in favor of François Mitterand. In 1973, 41 percent voted for the left at the parliamentary elections. Since 1976, however, one out of two supported left-wing candidates. The gulf which separated their choices from the men's, originally very great, seems to be narrowing now. Even their traditional anticommunism tends to soften; the evolution of the French Communist Party electorate's compositions bears witness to it: in the 1950s, it included 60 percent men and 40 percent women; in 1978, 54 percent men and 46 percent women; in 1981, the ratio was more equitable: 52 percent men versus 48 percent women.

In general, women are also becoming more active. They join organizations with more determination. In 25 years, the proportion of women among members of the FCP doubled; it quadrupled among members of the Socialist Party and quadrupled also (but between 1974 and 1979 according to the party concerned) in the UDR, which has become the RPR.[3] More women are also found in the unions.[4] In addition, they protest in organizations, in firms, in the streets.

In the 1970s, long strikes during which work places were taken over occurred in establishments where the personnel was composed essentially of women.[5] In the left-wing parties, women have begun to protest against their underrepresentation at the managerial level and, more widely, against the fact that women's problems (issues) were not sufficiently taken into account: for example, in the spring of 1979, women created in the Socialist Party a new "wave" called "Women's Wave" (Courant Femmes) which presented (during the congress held by this party in the same year) a motion competing with the text to be voted on presented by MM. Mitterand, Mauroy, Rocard and Chevenement.[6]

---

[3]The Gaullist group changed its acronym several times in the course of its history. From UDR = Union pour la Défense de la République (Union for the Preservation of the Republic), it has become RPR = Rassemblement pour la Republique (Mustering for the Republic).

[4]Margaret Maruani remarks: "In 1900, 6.3 percent of the unions members and 34.5 percent of the active population were women; in 1975, the percentage of women had gone up to 30 percent in the unions and 38 percent in the active population." Les Syndicats à l'épreuve du féminisme, Paris, Syros, 1979, 271 p.

[5]Ibid.

[6]This motion got less than 5 percent of the votes but it cannot be branded as a total failure, because all the other factions felt compelled to include in their own platforms a feminist paragraph in order to win the votes of the women in the Socialist Party.

In the Communist Party, the "rebellion" began in June 1978 after the failure sustained by the left in the parliamentary elections: some women published a paper deploring the FCP's lack of support for the women's struggle; then, after being blamed by the party, they founded a newspaper—*They See Red*.

Finally, women joined the feminist movement which became visible to the general public in France in August 1970.[7] The different groups making up this movement (Psychanalyse et Politique, MLAC, Choisir, etc.) have led a violent campaign to obtain the legalization of abortion, some of them organizing, for example, publicly supported abortions in several large cities. On a broader basis, these groups contributed to the popularization of women's aspirations to be treated in a more egalitarian manner and to the breaking down of barriers between a private domain, which they would be supposed to take care of, and a public domain reserved to men. The movement has not touched the great masses, but it has aroused educated women and those occupying important positions, as well as many left-wing militants. Besides, in October 1979, in order to put pressure on the deputies voting on the law authorizing abortion, feminist militants, militant unionists, and political militants jointly organized a large public demonstration in Paris.

Women, thus, are becoming more important on the political scene even if, as we shall see later, they are far from being integrated. This evolution reflects, of course, their socio-economic evolution and particularly their higher level of schooling and their massive entry into the working world. In 1980, 40.7 percent of the working population were women versus 34.9 percent in 1968 and 34.5 percent at the start of the century; 77.6 percent of these women are salaried workers; 68.8 percent are employed in the service sector, whereas most of the female population at the turn of the century was employed in agriculture or industry. Moreover, during the last 20 years, they acceded in a non-negligible manner to the high strata of the socio-professional hierarchy: in 1954, they represented only 13.8 percent of those employed in "upper management and the liberal professions" and 36.7 percent of those in middle management, compared to 23.2 percent and 45.2 percent respectively in 1975.[8] Finally, what denotes a very real break with traditional women's roles and behavior is that fewer of these "new" women inter-

[7]At that time, feminists placed a bouquet under the Arch of Triumph (the monument consecrated to the unknown soldier) in homage to this soldier's wife, "even more unknown than he is." During this occasion, the acronym MLF was used for the first time by the media in connection with French feminists.

[8]THEVENOT (Laurent), "Les catégories sociales en 1975: L'extension du salariat," (Social divisions in 1975: the widening of the wage-earners), *Economie et statistique*, n° 91, July/August 1977, p. 7.

rupt their professional activity when they have one or even two young children.[9] Consequently, as more and more women join the working world, they are confronted more and more with the problems of the people and, therefore, take public affairs more to heart.

In the context of the confrontation between the left and the right that has characterized French political life since 1974, the evolution of women results from the fact that they have become a real political target aimed at by both the right, which does not want to see its traditional supporters slip away, and the left, which expects to win new recruits.

2. *Women as political stake:*

Since women constitute 53 percent of the electorate, political forces have very quickly grasped the importance of their appearance on the political scene and most of them have tried to capture their attention, first, by giving them, in their different bodies, a little more room than they have had for the past ten years. As early as 1974, the Socialist Party decided that, at every level of the organization, 10 percent of all positions would be reserved for women and that this number will ultimately be brought up to 15 percent and by 1979 to 20 percent. During its 12th and 13th Congresses (1976 and 1979), the Communist Party also introduced in one of its supreme organs—the Central Committee—not only women and young people, but even young women. One third of the (pro-Giscard) Republican Party's nominations to its National Council were women. The small far-left parties went even further by having women as their leaders: Huguette Bouchardeau at the "PSU" (United Socialist Party) and Arlette Laguillier at the "Lutte Ouvriere" (Worker's Struggle). Moreover, both of them, along with a third woman, Marie-France Garraud, were candidates for the presidency of the Republic in 1981 (Arlette Laguillier had already been a candidate in 1974, but at that time she was the first and only woman to aspire to that position).

The parties also tried to show their good will by having more women on their tickets in the general elections. This very recent development had happened only rarely before the 1978 elections: 15.9 percent of the candidates were women versus 3.3 percent in 1968 and 6.7 percent in 1973. However, the 1978 percentage was mainly due to marginal groups (far-left, environmentalists, feminists) presenting 22.6 percent women. The large parties did not show much audacity until 1979 when the

---

[9]Thus, the activity rate went, between 1968 and 1975, from 50.5 percent to 66.6 percent among 25-29 years old women with one infant; from 31.2 to 47.9 percent among 30-34 years old women with 2 children (one an infant). DEVILLE (Jean-Claude), "Feminine activity and fecundity," *Economie et statistique*, n° 93, October 1977, p. 52.

elections to the European Parliament took place, but the advances became rather spectacular with women representing 27.2 percent of the Communist ticket, 25.9 percent of the Socialist and Radical Left tickets, 25.6 percent of the Giscardian ticket (headed by a woman, Madame Simone Weil), and 16 percent of the "RPR" (Mustering for the Republic) ticket, the only party which refused to take sex into consideration when allocating responsibilities. But in 1981, during the parliamentary elections, this progress slowed down considerably. Not only did the various political groups nominate fewer women than in 1979 but the right guaranteed the promotion of women less than at the 1978 elections: the "UDF" (Union for French Democracy) reduced it from 5 percent to 3.2 percent, the "RPR" from 2.9 percent to 2 percent. The Communist Party maintained the same number as in 1978 (the proportion of women went from 13.3 percent to 13.5 percent). The Socialist Party alone increased it slightly, from 5.9 percent to 8 percent.

Just as these attempts to promote a few women were being made, a simultaneous growth in systematically taking into account women's problems in political as well as union programs could be noticed; this was particularly due to the fact that, as early as 1974, the new president of the Republic, Valery Giscard d'Estaing, asserted that under his government women's conditions would improve.

As soon as he took office, he worked toward this goal. He first created a State Secretariat for Women's Conditions (which became the Acting Ministry devoted to Women's Conditions in 1978) and brought four women into the government (by 1978 there were six). Under the Fourth and Fifth Republics of General de Gaulle and Georges Pompidou, there was never more than one woman in the government,[10] and from 1949 to 1959—ten years—there was none. In addition, since 1975, an important series of laws was passed aimed at giving equal rights to working men and women (forbidding sex discrimination in hiring), fathers and mothers (mothers now have the same rights as fathers concerning decisions of routine management), husbands and wives (wives now have the same rights as their husbands in choosing the family home). Divorce procedures are also being reformed.[11] But the most important law—voted in for five years in 1974 and permanently in 1979—gives women the right to have an abortion before the tenth week of their pregnancy.[12]

[10]The only exception concerns the Messmer government (April 3, 1973-February 24, 1974) which included *two* women as secretaries of state.

[11]Occasionally adultery is given the same definition for women as it is for men. Up to now, feminine adultery was subject to severe sanctions, including incarceration, while male adultery was practically given penal immunity.

[12]Under certain conditions, naturally, *i.e.* in private or public medical establishments and after submitting to a special procedure.

155

Laws on the following were passed in 1980: re-definition of rape and its sanctions; elaboration of a statute for wives of farmers working on the family property; setting up of a widow's insurance for women left without any means of support after their husbands' deaths.[13]

Finally, let us mention a project directly aimed at the political promotion of women: a bill filed with the National Assembly by the Ministry for Women's Conditions providing for 20 percent representation by women among the candidates running in municipal elections in cities of 9,000 or more. But this bill, adopted at its first reading at the National Assembly on November 19, 1980, entitled "Bill relating to mixed tickets for municipal elections," has never been presented to the order of the day at the Senate, and unless the government decides to submit it to the Senate's vote, this project has every chance of being short-lived. During 1979 and 1980, however, the simple fact that it was introduced to the National Assembly has given a certain notoriety to the question of women's admission to political responsibilities.

After their 1981 victory, François Mitterand and all the Socialists reaffirmed, of course, the need to strengthen women's rights; in this, they were not only true to their pledges of recent years and campaign promises but also to Leon Blum who had had the idea of including three women (under-secretaries of state) in the United Popular Front government in 1936, at a time when women did not even have the right to vote. There are six women in Pierre Mauroy's government (First Ministry), and one of them is secretary of agriculture, a true innovation.[14] The Ministry for Women's Rights was created with, for the first time, an autonomous budget, and its program was approved by the Council of Ministers as early as 1981. This program has three main objectives: 1. To render women's professional life easier: for example, it was proposed, that at least 60 percent of the young people attending training courses designed to facilitate their integration into the working world be young women; a new bill on part-time work aims at giving women who wish to reduce their working time (but also men—they are mentioned in the bill) new guarantees. 2. To fight sexism: measures to be

[13]The law of July 17, 1980 instituted a new allowance (*i.e.* a degressive annuity paid over a period of 3 years) to be paid to widows under 55 years and who, raising or having raised children, do not have a professional activity capable of assuring them of financial autonomy.

[14]These six women are Nicole Questiaux, Minister of the National Solidarity; Yvette Roudy, women's rights minister (minister assigned to the prime minister); Edwidge Avice, minister assigned to the minister of recreation, in charge of youth and sports; Catherine Lalumiere, minister of consumption; Edith Cresson, minister of agriculture; Georgina Dufoix, state secretary to the National Solidarity Ministry. Moreover, there are more women than before in the ministerial cabinets: out of 360 members 71 are women, *i.e.* 19.7 percent against 20 out of 234 members in Raymond Barre's government.

taken to eliminate sexism from professional life, information and education. The associations concerned will be able to start judicial proceedings in case of sex discrimination or even violence against women.
3. To grant freedom of procreation: an information campaign on contraception to be organized, including television information, and instructions to be given in order to actually enforce the law legalizing abortion.[15]

A general design is hence taking shape, leading to the achievement of an equality and freedom which until very recently existed much more on paper than in fact. For the present time, these projects seem to convince even the feminists: while they were refusing, until now, to choose between the plague of the right and the cholera of the left, they have assured François Mitterand of their support even before the first ballot and "Choisir's" president—Gisele Halimi—has even been elected as a representative with the support of the Socialist Party.

Women have therefore advanced and, in the political realm, have been attended to. But not all of them have yet attained the "political age" to feel concerned by their country's political life.

II—But they remain marginal.

1. Compared to men, women still lag behind in their access to the political and electoral fields. Recent opinion polls bear witness to this fact.[16] French women are less interested in politics than French men: while a rather large number (22 percent in 1981)[17] still consider it a domain strictly reserved to men, they admit more often than men their incompetence at handling political and economic problems (high percentage of unanswered questions in poll), but they speak up now when questioned on everyday problems. In fact, a fairly large number of them espouse the traditional idea of the division of labor between the sexes: public sector for the men, private sector for the women.

Their lack of political knowledge and background can be seen in their inability to position themselves on the political chessboard. They also do not understand the elementary and fundamental forms of po-

[15]Indeed, clandestine abortion has not disappeared in France, since the hospitals are not in a position to handle all the operations requested by women.
About the details of the governmental program, refer to *Le Monde*, June 19, 1981 and the information bulletin of the Ministry of Women's Rights, "*Citoyennes à part entière*," n° 1, September 1981.
[16]Refer to MOSSUZ-LAVAU (Janine), SINEAU (Mariette), *Les femmes françaises en 1978 (French women in 1978), op. cit.*
"Les Femmes face à la politique" ("Women facing politics"), *Le Matin de Paris*, December 7, 1977, polls Louis Harris-France.
[17]SOFRES poll—*Le Figaro-Madame*, March 28, 1981.

litical life: they do not quite see, as men do, the implications of any suppression of political parties and the right to strike. This lack of political education is to be attributed mainly to their lack of interest in seeking information.[18] They devote less time than men to making inquiries, attending political meetings, reading newspapers, and listening to political news on the radio and television.

They have fewer political conversations than men with their close friends and associates and are less eager to take part in political meetings; when they work, they are not as willing as men are to participate in a strike and are less often unionized (19 percent of women versus 30 percent of men according to a December 1979 poll).[19] Even their participation in associations not directly related to politics, such as sport clubs, parent-teacher and consumer associations, etc. is more limited: 61 percent of the men, but only 43 percent of the women, belonged to one or more such associations in 1977.[20]

CHART I—VOTES LISTED BY SEX IN THE FIRST BALLOT FOR THE PRESIDENTIAL ELECTION (April 26, 1981)

	G. Marchais (PC)	A. Laguillier (LO)	H. Bouchardeau (PSU)	F. Mitterand (PS)	M. Crépeau (MRG)	B. Lalonde (Ecologist)	V. Giscard d'Estaing (PR)	J. Chirac (RPR)	M. Debré and M. F. Garraud (RPR)
MEN (100%)	17	2	1	29	2	4	23	19	3
WOMEN (100%)	14	2	1	24	2	4	32	18	3

[18]Les practiques culturell es des Français (Cultural practices of the French people), December 1974, study by the State Secretary of Culture: quoted in Donnees Sociales, 1978 edition, INSEE, p. 310.

[19]"Syndicats ? Non merci" ("Unions ? No thank you"), La Vie, December 6-12, 1979.

[20]"Les français et la vie collective" ("French people and collective life"), poll carried out by SOFRES for Le Nouvel Observateur, September 1977.

Less involved, women remain politically and culturally somewhat more conservative. In the first round of the May 1981 presidential election, only 43 percent of the women—versus 51 percent of the men—voted for one of the five left-wing candidates (G. Marchais, A. Laguillier, H. Bouchardeau, F. Mitterand, or M. Crepeau). (Chart I)

The 8-point difference stems from the shortage of women's votes for the CP candidate (3 points) as well as for the SP candidate (5 points). The structural analysis of the electorate in the first round of the presidential election shows clearly that Georges Marchais and François Mitterand had a more male electorate (52 percent and 53 percent respectively), while on the contrary Valery Giscard d'Estaing had a very female electorate (59 percent women).

In the same way, in the second round of the presidential election, a majority (56 percent) of French men voted for François Mitterand while a majority (51 percent) of French women had wished to re-elect V. Giscard d'Estaing.

It is fair to state that French women kept their conservative tendencies quiet during the parliamentary elections of June 1981 (which followed the presidential election). More than half of them (54 percent) opted for a left-wing candidate in the first round, as did 58 percent of the men. The gap between men and women in the left-wing vote was only 4 points.[21]

Can this definite reversal to the left, from May to June, be ascribed to a certain "legitimism" on the part of the women: that from the time a socialist president is elected, he should be given a majority of deputies in order to govern? This is a hypothesis which would need to be verified. . . .

Slightly more to the right politically, women are also more religious. They assert their link with the Catholic Community more often than men do and make up the main core of the regularly practicing Catholics who go to Mass every week or every month (21 percent of women versus 13 percent of the men).[22] As far as morals are concerned, women are often more repressed, and this makes them quicker to censor premarital sex, abortion and homosexuality,[23] practices which are, in any case, still

[21]SOFRES post-electoral survey, Le Nouvel Observateur, June 1-7, 1981. The five candidates were nominated, respectively and in the order indicated, by the Communist Party, the Workers' Struggle, the Unified Socialist Party, the Socialist Party and the Left-wing Radicals' Party.
[22]SOFRES survey made in October 1977 for the newspaper La Croix.
[23]Concerning cultural attitudes, refer to a series of polls taken by SOFRES: "L'opinion des Français à l'egard de l'avortement" ("French opinion on abortion"), Le Figaro, October-November 1979.
"L'opinion des Français à l'egard des moeurs" ("French opinion on morals"), Le Nouvel Observateur, June 1980.

strongly condemned by the church. Moreover, a large number of women adhere to a double standard: what is reprehensible on the part of a woman is not necessarily so on the part of a man. Thus, in 1980, 20 percent of the women (against 13 percent of the men) did not find it normal for women to have as much sexual freedom and independence as men.

It is understandable that, under these conditions, fewer women (63 percent) than men (70 percent) should be in favor of the feminist movement which fights for, among other things, role equality in society.

2. Under-representation of French women in politics.

Above all, the very large absence of women in positions of political responsibility deserves to be stressed. Among European countries, France has one of the smallest numbers of women in parliament: women represent only 5.3 percent of the deputies and 2.3 percent of the senators (26 out of 491, and 7 out of 295 respectively). The general councils (regional assemblies) number only—since the 1979 elections—120 women out of 3,650 members, i.e. 3.2 percent. Locally, the situation is less unfavorable: 38,859 women (out of 400,000 or 8.4 percent) have held seats in the municipal councils since 1977. But the proportion of municipal councilwomen varies according to the size of the town: it reaches 20 percent in districts numbering more than 30,000 people, 17.4 percent in towns of 9,000 to 35,000 people, but only 12.8 percent in small towns (2,500 to 9,000 people). Finally, out of a total of 36,352 mayors, 1,061 are women (i.e. 2.9 percent), and there are about 8,430 women deputy mayors (6 percent). It must be stressed, however, that most women mayors are to be found in small rural districts. In large urban districts, where political problems take precedence over administrative problems, women's representation is low. Only 23 women are mayors of towns with more than 10,000 people and 6 of towns with more than 30,000 people.

Hence, only a minority of women can be found in elected bodies. This is so because women get the meagre share in the political parties. Small in number among party supporters, even fewer among the active militants, women become scarce among the governing bodies. (Chart II)

More pronounced in the RPR than in the SP, men's predominance is evident at every level of the responsible bodies. This disparity is increased by the specialization of military duties, so that responsible women look after the private sectors, such as the family, education, and

"Les Française et le mouvement feministe" ("The French people and the feminist movement"), Le Figaro-Madame, March 1980, and Louis-Harris poll, Le Matin de Paris, already mentioned.

"feminine questions," which do not prepare them to defend the whole range of community problems for their party and which maintain, in the eyes of the public, women as caretakers of others' needs.

CHART II—PERCENTAGE OF WOMEN IN THE DIFFERENT BRANCHES OF THE FOUR LARGE FRENCH POLITICAL PARTIES
(The number of supporters is the one claimed by the parties themselves. Very likely it is inflated and rather unreliable).

	Principal political parties	Supporters	Legislative branches	Executive branches
Majority	Republican Party (PR)	37% (out of 170,000 supporters)	National Council 32%	Political Bureau 20%
	Mustering for the Republic (RPR)	41% (out of 760,000 supporters)	Central Committee 8%	Political Council 14%
Opposition	Socialist Party (PS)	22% (out of 180,000 supporters)	Managing Committee 19%	Executive Bureau 19%
	Communist Party (PFC)	33% (out of 700,000 supporters)	Central Committee 21%	Political Bureau 19%

II—Profoundly unequal economic conditions.

How can the still considerable exclusion of women from political power be explained? Without any doubt, *cultural and ideological causes* exist. In France, a Latin and Catholic country, public opinion on the assumption of political responsibilities by women is, in spite of a manifest evolution, still reserved. In the spring of 1981, 20 percent of those polled were opposed to having a woman as president of the French Republic in the near future (19 percent men and 22 percent women). Women cannot rely on women to make their political promotion easier. French women are at least as sexist as French men.[24]

However, the mere misogyny of public opinion in general and of the political class in particular, is not reason enough to explain why

[24]SOFRES survey, *Le Figaro-Madame*, March 28, 1981.

women have been kept out of politics. It is mainly due to a different reason: in France, in order to belong to the political elite, one first has to belong to the socio-economic elite.

1. A privileged political class.

In political parties, as in elected assemblies, the political class springs fundamentally from the most favored social strata—with the exception of the Communist Party whose structure obeys other rules and has to be analyzed separately. Here are some examples: 62 percent of the members of the National Assembly elected in 1978 were members of the "liberal professions" or "upper management." It is true that the make-up of the new assembly elected in June 1981 has somewhat changed: if there is a decrease in the categories of "upper management" and "liberal professions," it is in favor of the teaching profession (which forms 30 percent of the new assembly versus 20 percent of the previous one) and not in favor of the white and blue collar workers who are in the minority. The candidates' sociological approach to the parliamentary elections makes us draw almost the same conclusions. The right-wing parties naturally presented more "bourgeois" candidates than the left-wing parties: 64.4 percent of the RPR candidates, 59 percent of the UDF candidates—versus 30.5 percent of the SP and 5.1 percent of the CP—belonged to the most well-to-do levels of society (upper management, business executives, upper government employees, and members of the liberal professions). However, even the CP and the SP underrepresent the less privileged classes (39.6 percent of the white- and blue-collar workers in the CP and 3.6 percent in the SP) in favor of the teaching profession and middle management (47.7 percent in the CP and 57.7 percent in the SP).[25] We should mention that, on the whole, the "proletarians" listed as such in the candidates' list are, in a number of cases, permanent members of the CP, coming from a working-class background, who have generally left labor to work full time in one of the branches of the party—an "elitism" all the greater as one goes up in the hierarchy. In the SP, to give this example only, there is a real "preponderance of the intelligentsia, teachers, technicians, and managers."[26] In short, it is remarkable that, even in the feminist movements, the public promotion of women is the promotion of "bourgeoises": nearly all of the 43 candidates presented in 1978 by the movement "CHOISIR" (headed by attorney Gisele Halini) belonged to a privileged social strata.

[25]FABRE-ROSANE (Gilles), GUEDE (Alain), "Les partis politiques à travers leurs candidats" ("The political parties as seen through their candidates"), Le Monde, September 27, 1981.
[26]HARDOUIN (Patrick), Revue Française de Science Politique, April 1978, p. 252.

The question is to find out how many women figure in the economic elite which constitutes the privileged reservoir of the political personnel?

2. *Women, absent from the economic elite.*

There are no or few women at the tip of the pyramid of responsibility. Who are, in fact, the upper government employees, the majority of whom graduated from the National School of Administration? Almost all of them are men. What is the proportion of women in business, the liberal professions, engineering and upper management? Once again, it is very small: 13.5 percent, 22 percent, 4.4 percent and 17.1 percent respectively in 1975, while their share among white-collar workers (63.9 percent) and public service employees (77.9 percent) is very large. As blue-collar workers, women hold the least qualified jobs; even when they hold a graduate degree, they seldom find jobs in the liberal professions; in education, they are the majority among elementary and vocational school teachers (67 percent) and the minority among university professors (35 percent). Women's salaries are, on the average, 31 percent lower than men's. Finally, female employees face a greater chance of being unemployed nowadays: in 1980, women represented 60 percent of the unemployed. Women's unfavorable situation in the job market is explained mainly by their lack of professional training. Women hold diplomas less sought after by employers.

This situation still exists at the present time: in 1980, during their last year of high school (lycée), 75 percent of the students in the "philosophy sections" were girls, as compared to only 35 percent in the sections devoted to the sciences. At the university level, approximately 66 percent of the students pursuing degrees in literature or the liberal arts are young women, but only 14 percent of them are studying law and economics and 20 percent of them the so-called exact sciences. All women are far from practicing a profession, hence far from opening themselves to the outside world, from taking charge of the problems of the public world, and far, a fortiore, from entering the ranks of supporters of partisan training. In order to assume responsibilities, as minimal as they may be, or simply to attend meetings, distribute pamphlets, follow a training course, one must devote at least lunchtime and often some evenings and weekends to militant action. Which woman has all this time at her disposal if she has children, no help at home or no adequate facilities; or in the event that she works, does not practice one of the professions at the top of the social hierarchy that allow her to have time, independence, security and a variety of possibilities; or if, finally, she is not lucky enough to have a husband who shares household and child-raising tasks with her and approves of women having political activities? All told, it would be surprising to find among the militants some blue- and white-collar women who have a taste for dabbling in politics in spite of their professional and familial duties.

Noting that a large number of women still remain outside the professional world, that they are weakly represented among the socio-economic elite and that, on the contrary, they are overrepresented among the elderly who are affected by loneliness and poverty,[27] we emphasize the obstacles slowing down not only their access to active politics and political professionalism but also their entry into the political field as simple citizens.

This is the reason why, when they work and hold positions which place them among the privileged social strata, women are attracted—as men are—by politics, and consequently they may be led to accept responsibilities. We can support this fact in presenting some results of our 1978 post-electoral investigation.[28]

3. Social and political insertions: French women in 1978.

When they practice—or have practiced momentarily—a profession, women often assert their political ability—as men do—and claim a part of the political power for the female population (Chart III); this is far from being the case for the women we have called, as compared to the formerly active women (i.e., homemakers who have worked at one time or another), the "real" non-professional women, i.e., the ones who have never held a job and who went directly from parental tutelage to marital dependence. These women are indeed the least "politicized" and the most unwilling to participate in politics, with the exception of casting their ballots at election time.

These "truly" non-professional women stay away from politics because they have no knowledge of the working world, and also because they are, more often than the other women, practicing Catholics from rural and conservative environments—a background which also explains why they have not been prepared to exercise a professional activity. The seclusion of a home constitutes therefore an important element in the understanding of women's political "marginalization".

[27]The French population numbers about 3 million widows over 65 years, a consequence of the difference in average life expectancy of the sexes: women's life expectancy is actually 77 years and men's 71 years.

[28]MOSSUZ-LAVAU (Janine), SINEAU (Mariette), Les femmes françaises en 1978. insertion sociale, insertion politique. (French women in 1978, Social insertion, political insertion), op. cit.

An analysis of the composition of the municipal councils points out that socio-professional activity favors political commitment, since 67 percent of the women elected to the councils work.

CHART III—INTEREST AND POLITICAL PARTICIPATION ACCORDING TO SEX AND EXERCISE OF A PROFESSIONAL ACTIVITY (% per category)

	Active men N = 602	Active women N = 640	Ex-active women N = 384	Real non-professional women N = 133
Politics: Should be men's rather than women's concern totally agree + somewhat agree	22	24	23	40
Politics: too complicated totally agree + somewhat agree	44	45	42	54
Often discuss politics with their entourage	21	15	12	10
Find absolutely normal for a woman to become President of the Republic	41	56	55	37
Voted in the 1st ballot of the 1978 parliamentary elections	94	92	94	92
Took part in a political meeting (in the past 2 years)	22	12	6	2
Would participate in an action for the creation of a day-care center	30	47	42	35

One should not, however, mythicize work and think that women will become whole political beings once they have (or have had) a professional activity. After all, let us not forget that the most politically active women, i.e. the ones who discuss politics, take part in demonstrations and in strikes as much as men, and those who show a real ability, are either in upper management, in the liberal professions, or in middle management (Chart IV). Therefore, in order for a woman to have the same choices as men in acceding to the political field, she has to belong to the economic elite, hold cultural privileges, or have a relatively large income. In short, our investigation proves that a woman is all the more "politicized" as she is active and in addition is situated at the apex of the social hierarchy because of her job.

The obstacles to women's access to political responsibilities must be searched for very far, beyond even party membership, because the vast majority of the female population finds it impossible to give a political dimension to their daily lives, to consider politics as a domain in which they have a place and a voice. At this time, politics remains a luxury of the privileged woman.

CHART IV—INTEREST AND POLITICAL PARTICIPATION ACCORDING TO SEX AND SOCIAL CLASS (% per category)

INTEREST & PARTICIPATION		POLITICS SHOULD BE MEN's CONCERN: totally agree + somewhat agree	OFTEN DISCUSS POLITICS WITH THEIR ENTOURAGE	TOOK PART IN A MANIFES- TATION	VOTED IN THE FIRST BALLOT IN 1978
Socio- profes- sional group	Sex				
Upper Management/ Liberal professions	AM [+] N = 81	11	32	20	97
	AW N = 61	8	33	18	93
Middle Management	AM N = 104	14	26	18	89
	AW N = 106	12	25	15	96
White collars	AM N = 67	24	18	5	93
	AW N = 140	17	15	3	95
Artisans/ Tradespeople	AM N = 104	23	16	18	97
	AW N = 116	32	13	3	˙97
Farmers	AM N = 91	28	18	15	95
	AW N = 89	34	1	13	93
Blue collars	AM N = 128	23	20	29	97
	AW N = 80	33	14	16	85

[+] AM = Active Men
    AW = Active Women

166

THE FEDERAL REPUBLIC OF GERMANY

The constitutional and political foundations for greater women's participation in what was to become the Federal Republic were laid as far back as June 30, 1946, when elections were held in the American zone of occupation to elect delegates to the constituent assemblies of the *Länder* (States). Before the end of the year, constitutions were promulgated in Würtemberg-Baden, Hessen, and Bavaria. All of them contained basic provisions designed to guarantee equal rights to women. Thus, Article 53 of the Bremen Constitution of October 12, 1947, stated that

> for equal work women and young people have a claim to the same wages as men. Women whose abilities are equal to those of men have a claim to the same type of work.

While seeking to provide access to work usually reserved to men, the Constitution also contained provisions of a more conventional and protective nature. Article 54 stipulated that:

> institutions for the protection of mothers and children shall be created by law, in order that women may be safeguarded in their professional and civic tasks as well as in their duties as women and mothers.

A draft Constitution, or rather a Basic Law of 149 articles for the future Federal Republic, was completed in August 1948. A revised text of 146 articles was adopted by the Parliamentary Council on May 8, 1949 and promulgated on May 23. Unlike many of the recent constitutions which contain several articles devoted to the safeguarding of women's rights the Basic Law has only one such article.

The English translation of Article 3 (Basic Rights) reads as follows:

(1) All persons shall be equal before the law.
(2) Men and women shall have equal rights.
(3) No one may be prejudiced or favored because of sex, his parentage, his race, his language, his homeland origin, his faith, or his religious or political opinions.

The translation is that of the Press and Information Office of the Government of the Federal Republic of Germany. It was edited by the Linguistic Section of the Foreign Office of the Federal Republic of Germany.

The German official text of Article 3(3) uses the word "Geschlecht" or "gender" rather than sex. But the drafters may be criticized for having used the term "everyone" which requires the adjective "his," rather than "they" (men and women) and "their."

Article 117(1), which was inserted as part of the Transitional and Concluding Provisions of the Basic Law stipulated:

> Law which conflicts with paragraph (2) of Article 3 shall remain in force until adapted to that provision of this Basic Law, but not beyond 31 March 1953.

In the early 1950s, the people of the Federal Republic of Germany laid the foundations for what has come to be known as "the economic miracle" by rebuilding the shattered German industry. No comparable miracle was achieved in the legal field. It was generally recognized that there were many discriminatory provisions in German legislation and that it would be difficult to eradicate these remnants from the authoritative past. If only the legislation enacted during the Nazi period had been involved, the task would have been relatively simple. But the patriarchal principle was firmly rooted in many laws which antedated the Nazi period. The deadline of March 31, 1953, as set in Article 117, was simply unrealistic. As it turned out, it took very much longer to make significant progress toward this goal. Indeed, the legislative efforts proceeded very slowly. Had it not been for the German Constitutional Court, which did not hesitate to declare specific older legal provisions unconstitutional, the legislative advances would have taken even longer.

On June 24, 1968, a new Article 12a was inserted into the Basic Law. It concerned the obligation to render military or substitute services. The relevant part, Article 12 (1) reads as follows:

> Men who have attained the age of eighteen years may be required to serve in the Armed Forces, in the Federal Border Guard, or in a Civil Defense organization.

The appropriateness and constitutionality of this provision was a matter of considerable parliamentary debate in December 1962, and long after that it was contested by German feminists, who argued that it violated Article 3 of the Basic Law and represented sexist discrimination. Some of them pointed to the example of Israel, which required equal military service of men and women.

The defenders of the traditional roles system argued that no discrimination existed because Article 12a(4) did provide an opportunity for women, who may be assigned to perform specific services if a "state of defence" were declared. Article 12a(4) reads as follows:

> If, while a state of defence exists, civilian service require-
> ments in the civilian public health and medical system or in
> the stationary military hospital organization cannot be met on
> a voluntary basis, women between eighteen and fifty-five years
> of age may be assigned to such services by or pursuant to law.
> They may on no account render service involving the use of
> arms.

There is no doubt that the last sentence is clearly discriminatory. From time to time, the issue has been raised by feminists, but nowadays it is more likely to be brought up by young men of pacifist persuasion.

By way of comparison with the German Democratic Republic, it may be noted that Article 23(1) of their Constitution declares that:

> the protection of peace and the socialist fatherland and its
> achievements is the right and the honorable duty of the citizens
> of the German Democratic Republic. Every citizen is obligated
> to serve and to contribute to the defense of the German Dem-
> ocratic Republic in accordance with the laws.

The German Democratic Republic has put much greater emphasis on participation. It is a right and duty of all citizens. Leaving aside ideological differences as to the nature of participation, it is clear that the record of the German Democratic Republic is much more impressive. In 1950, the percentage of women in the *Volkskammer* of the German Democratic Republic was three times larger than that of women deputies in the *Bundestag* (23.0:7.1). By 1954, the percentage in the *Volkskammer* was still the same; in the *Bundestag*, it had risen to 8.8. By 1958, the difference was further reduced (23.8:9.2 percent). But after that, the percentage of women in the *Volkskammer* continued to rise, whereas in the *Bundestag* it began to decline. In 1963, it was 26.5:8.3. By 1966, the difference was greatly increased, 30.2:6.9.

General elections were held on September 28, 1969. The Christian Democrats and the Christian Socialists won 242 seats, one more seat than in 1965. The Social Democrats gained 22 more seats for a total of 224. The Free Democrats suffered a setback. They now had only 30 seats, as compared with 49 in 1965. On October 21, Willy Brandt, the leader of the Social Democrats, was elected chancellor by a vote of 251 to 233, with 5 abstentions. He thus became the first Social Democrat to head a government since the days of the Weimar Republic. One of his priorities was to improve relations with the GDR. The voting age was lowered from 21 to 18, on July 31, 1970. This was done by amending Article 38(2) of the Basic Law (27th Amendment).

In recognition of his efforts to improve relations between East and West, Chancellor Brandt was awarded the Nobel Peace Prize on October 20, 1971. About a year later, he staged an interesting political maneuver, which resulted in the dissolution of the *Bundestag* and a call for new elections. They were held on November 19, 1972, and achieved more than the desired goal. With a record participation of 91 percent of the qualified voters, the SPD received 45.8 percent of the popular vote, as compared with 42.7 in 1969. The CDU-CSU, which won 46.1 percent in 1969, now received 44.9 percent. Substantial gains were achieved by the Free Democratic Party, which obtained 8.4 percent, as compared with 5.8 percent in 1969. The SPD was now able to enter into a coalition with the FDP, which turned out to be more viable than the so-called Grand Coalition. While the SPD had reason to rejoice, the election results were not favorable from the women's point of view. Their percentage was down to an all time low of 5.8.

On December 14, 1972, Chancellor Brandt was reelected. In view of their electoral disappointments, women were elated when Annemarie Renger became the first woman in history to serve as president of the *Bundestag*. The enlarged Ministry of Health, now called the Ministry for Family, Youth and Health was occupied by Katherina Focke, from 1972 to 1976. During her term of office the *Bundestag* lowered the legal age of majority from 21 to 18. The law which was passed on March 22, 1974, went into effect on June 1, 1975.

Walter Scheel was elected president of the Federal Republic on May 15, 1974. Helmut Schmidt became chancellor on the following day to succeed Willy Brandt, who had resigned a few days earlier. In December 1976, Antje Huber was put in charge of the Ministry for Family, Youth and Health. She emphasized the importance of information services to acquaint women with their rights, the modification of the traditional roles of men and women, and a more flexible division of tasks in the family, the professions and in society. She also sought to encourage more political and social activism on the part of women. A very large number of women are civil service employees, but only about 5 percent can be found in the higher echelons of the administrative hierarchy. Until recently, there was usually one state secretary. In most of the *Länder*, there are only male state secretaries.

The designation by the U.N. of 1975 as the International Year of the Woman seems to have had a positive effect on the advancement of women in the Federal Republic. Whether it was a matter of conviction or political expediency is difficult to determine, but there definitely was more activity by women and on behalf of women than there had been in the previous decade. One of the tangible results was a reversal of the decline of women's representation in the *Bundestag*. In the 8th *Bundestag*, which was elected in 1976, the percentage of women rose from 5.8 to 7.5. The political parties also seemed to make greater efforts to recognize their women members and the contributions they had made. In the Social Democratic Party, the women members constituted 19 percent in 1975. The figure rose to 22.5 percent by 1978. Women in the FPD represented 18 percent of the members. By 1978, their number had risen to 22 percent. But there were only slight increases in the number of women who were elected delegates to party congresses. At the 1977 Party Congress of the SPD, only 8.3 percent of the delegates were women.

From time to time, proposals have been made for fixed quotas for women. A minimum of 25 percent has been suggested, but the idea has never appealed to women party activists, who look at it as a kind of discriminatory formula. Their real objective is to achieve access to the higher echelons of the party organization, and to have greater influence on public policy.

Compared with the German Democratic Republic, the women's organizations are not effectively coordinated. The German Women's Council is merely an organization. Its officers can urge and try to persuade, but they cannot do much more than that.

Women have been quite active in municipal councils. In the larger cities, about 14 percent of the members have been women. In most of the *Länder*, there were some increases in the number of women who were elected to their legislatures. In 1980, the highest percentages could be found in Bremen, Hamburg, and Hessen. In Bremen, there were actually more women in the 1975 legislature than in 1980. The overall increase was not spectacular. It rose from 7.2 percent in 1975, to 8.2 percent in 1980. If one considers the *Länder* legislatures to be the training grounds for the *Bundestag*, then the situation is hardly encouraging.

Women who wanted to make careers in the judiciary have encountered considerable difficulties. Advancement has been very slow. The participation of women in the higher echelons has remained under 6 percent, and even in the lower instances, there have not been significant increases. As has already been noted, this is a phenomenon paralleled in other western and southern European countries. To date, no good explanation, let alone justification, has been offered for this fact. The judiciary is of considerable importance to women because it is left to the judges to decide what constitutes equality and equity.

In the European Parliament, the percentage of women among the German members is below the average, which in 1980 was 16.8. The

171

German members number 81, the same as France, Great Britain, and Italy. While France was represented by 18 women (22.2 percent), there were only 12 women (14.8 percent) in the German delegation. In France, 25 percent of the candidates were women. In the Federal Republic, only 19.6 percent of the candidates were women. There are obviously important opportunities for German and other women to contribute to the building of the European Community.

The problem of greater political participation is closely linked with issues of legal reform. It is true that from a technical point of view, the redrafting and interpretation of law is a task best left to jurists. Presumably, it has nothing to do with gender bias; but how valid is this presumption? Unless women and their male supporters exert themselves more than they have, legal change will proceed very slowly. And as long as the German Federal Labor Court is dominated by men, equal pay for equal work, and equal value decisions, are likely to be based on narrow juridical technicalities.

How far has legal reform progressed during the past decade toward providing a more effective basis for the protection of the equal rights of women? One might begin with the law concerning the organization of enterprises, of January 15, 1972. (Betriebs-Verfassungs-Gesetz v. 15.1.1972) The most important provisions concerning equal treatment are contained in Article 75(1). As far as equal access and equal treatment in the civil service are concerned, it may be noted that the pertinent paragraphs of Article 33, of the Basic Law, did not make any specific reference to gender. Article 33(2) reads:

> Every German shall be equally eligible for any public office according to his aptitude, qualifications, and professional achievements.

It is ironic that an article which was intended to safeguard the principle of equality contains this all too common type of male-oriented linguistic discrimination. Surely, the drafters did not mean to exclude women from access to the civil service, but one would not know that judging by the references to "his" (seiner) aptitude.

This defect is aggravated by the wording of the subsequent paragraph, Article 33(3):

> Enjoyment of civil and political rights, eligibility for public office, and rights acquired in the public service shall be independent of religious denomination. No one may suffer any disadvantage by reason of his adherence or non-adherence to a denomination or ideology.

f one thought that reference to "his" in the previous paragraph was a matter of careless drafting, then one will probably dismiss the second "his" in Article 33(3) as much of the same. But in this paragraph, there is another problem. It mentions religious denomination (religiöse Bekenntnisse) and ideology (Weltanschauung), which was very much in order, considering the notorious discrimination during the Nazi regime. But why did they stop there? By the time the Basic Law was being drafted, the U.N. Declaration of Human Rights was well known, and the other forms of discrimination could also have been included in Article 33(3). One of the leading commentaries on the Basic Law refers to this paragraph as guaranteeing "religious neutrality."

The Basic Law did not provide for what may be called "gender neutrality." Although this term is not specifically used, it has now been established by Article 67(1) of the Law of March 15, 1974, concerning representation for federal employees. Some of the other codes, like the German Civil Code and the German Labor Code of August 13, 1980 were also amended to bring them in harmony with the standards and directives of the European Economic Community.

Occasionally, German government officials and academicians express some impatience and irritation over the Directives of the Community. They argue that the EEC should not try to prescribe specific ways of combating or eliminating discrimination. They look to the German Constitutional Court in Karlsruhe to provide authoritative judgments and opinions in matters of discrimination. Neither the new legislation nor the Constitutional Court has recognized the concepts of "indirect discrimination" and "positive discrimination." There is also considerable reluctance to repeal all the "protective legislation." As a matter of fact, the essentially negative concept of discrimination is used much less frequently than the positive terms: "equal entitlement" (Gleichberechtigung) and "equal treatment" (Gleichbehandlung).

In 1980, there was considerable controversy as to whether there was real need for a comprehensive antidiscrimination law, as had been urged by the FDP. A special commission (Enquete-Kommission) concluded that this was unnecessary or superfluous because the Basic Law provided a very strong mandate. It was thought that it would be sufficient to review all the pertinent legislation and to adapt it to conform to the 1976 Directive of the Community. Law No 48/80 of August 20, 1980 is considered to be the appropriate legal instrument for the purpose of "assimilation." (See English translation in the Appendix.)

The Equal Treatment Law (Anpassungsgesetz) is supposed to be primarily concerned with labor law, but many more provisions concern the Civil Code, which had been amended as recently as July 24, 1979 What was done now, on August 13, 1980, was to insert two new para graphs after 611. The new paragraph 611a prohibits any discriminatior on the basis of sex (gender) in the hiring, promotion and firing of em ployees. However, the same paragraph allows for exceptions or dero gations, if the nature of the job in question requires it to be filled by one particular gender (*Unverzichtbare Voraussetzung*). If an employee makes an allegation that such discrimination did take place, the burder of proof now rests with the employer. The broad basis for derogation; would seem to leave too much discretionary power to a judicial authority as to whether a certain job can be filled only by a man or a woman Conventional notions, rather than objective determinations, may influ ence a judge's decision. Furthermore, the assimilation law is much les; comprehensive than the EEC Council Directive of February 10, 197! (75/117/EEC), because it does not include equal treatment in vocationa training.

Recent official statistics concerning apprenticeship training in var ious vocational programs show that there has been no significant change in what are considered male and female jobs. In the fields of engineering and mechanics, the percentage of women trainees is less than 1.

On January 1, 1980 two laws concerning family relations came into force: the Law on Parental Duties, of July 18, 1979 (No 20/1979) and the Law on the Maintenance of Children of Single Parents. Some of the legislation pertaining to pregnancy and maternity has been amended so as to provide for additional maternity leaves. A mother can now reques a leave up to a maximum of six months from the date of the birth of he child.

Compared with other member states of the Community, there are relatively few jobs in the German Federal Republic which are not oper to women. They are still barred from working in mines and quarries (Their exclusion is based on a law that was enacted on April 30, 1938. Some jobs in the building and construction industry are closed to them as are certain operations in foundries, iron and steel works. Manua work by women, at night, is also legally prohibited. However, nurse: are not included in this category. From time to time, feminists have demanded that all these exclusions be abolished, but the main effort or the part of the government has been to reduce the wage differential between men and women. Herbert Ehrenberg, Minister of Labor, reaf firmed this policy in a recent address to German Women's Organiza tions. (*Presse-und Informations-Dienst der Bundesregierung Sozialpolitische Umschau* No 78, 1981-May 29, 1981) He noted that ir 1950, women were receiving 60 percent of the wages paid to men fo equal work. In 1979, the differential had been reduced to 79 percent

He conceded that the situation was still less favorable than in many other states.

The slogan, of course, remains "equal pay for equal work," but nowadays one also hears the phrase "equal worth." There is a legal basis for it now because the previously mentioned Law No 48/1980, which amended the Civil Code, refers to it. A new subparagraph 3 was inserted into Article 612, which states that "in a work relationship no smaller compensation, on the basis of gender, may be paid to an employee for equal work or work of equal worth." But no precise definition or explanation has been presented as to what constitutes "equal worth."

GREAT BRITAIN

On July 26, 1945, in the first general elections after World War II, the Labor Party won by a landslide. A Labor Party victory had been predicted by some of the experts, but not on this scale. The Labor Party took 393 seats, the Conservatives retained 212, and the Liberal Party was down to 12. There was wide agreement that it was "time for a change." But, what this was to mean in terms of women's rights and political participation was not so clear. Some of the more optimistic feminists hoped that it could mean the achievement of equality and the end of discrimination. To achieve these goals, there would have to be comprehensive legislation and effective enforcement machinery. There would have to be more women in the House of Commons and in the civil service; not just in the lower level positions of the official hierarchy but also with unobstructed access to the echelons exclusively occupied by men. It started promisingly on July 26, 1945. Out of the 87 women candidates, 24 were elected to the House of Commons. This was a record in at least two respects: It was the highest number of women candidates and the highest success ratio. For the Labor Party, it was an unprecedented triumph as 21 women took their seats.

During the immediate post-World War II period, the House of Commons was busily engaged in developing the implementing legislation for the Beveridge Plan: the Education Act of 1944 and the Family Allowance Act of 1945. These were followed in 1946 by the National Insurance Act and the National Health Service Act. The Town and Country Planning Act was completed in 1947. In 1948, the National Assistance Act and the Children Act completed the legislative program.

Of course, none of these Acts was a specific piece of women's rights legislation. But the Labor Party theorists viewed them as essential foundations on which a more equitable order could be built. There were many critics of conservative persuasion whose criticism was not as much concerned with the substantive parts of the legislation as with the manner in which they were carried out. Many criticized what they considered to be too much haste. Others really did not agree that the country was obligated to provide such an extensive and expensive framework of services in the fields of education, health, housing, unemployment, retirement benefits, and similar forms of public assistance. Most of the benefits were equally important for men and women. Others, like the prenatal and maternity care, as provided for in the National Insurance Act of 1946, concerned women more than men, although the whole approach was family oriented.

The principle of equal pay for equal work was endorsed by a royal commission in November, 1946. In the same month, the British National Health Act was promulgated. Its express purpose was to promote the establishment "of a comprehensive health service designed to secure improvement in the physical and mental health of the people of England and Wales and the prevention, diagnosis and treatment of illness . . ." Similar legislation was enacted in Scotland in 1947, and a year later in Northern Ireland. All these legislative measures went into effect simultaneously on July 5, 1948. They were frequently amended in subsequent years, and many of them remained subjects of considerable controversy. Housing was something of an exception. The rebuilding of the country under the Labor Government, and since 1951 under the Conservatives, was an outstanding achievement.

No less impressive, has been the expansion and reform of the British educational system. It has been particularly important for women because in the past there was neither equality nor equity. The higher civil service positions were largely reserved for graduates of Oxford and Cambridge. The admission of women to these exclusive educational institutions, along with the establishment of many new institutions of higher learning, was an important new policy of equalizing educational opportunities and abolishing discrimination on the basis of social origin as well as sex.

In the political field, the most important legislation in support of the principle of equality was the Representation of the People Act of 1949. According to Section 1

(1) The persons entitled to vote as electors at a parliamentary election in any constituency shall be those resident there on the qualifying date who, on that date and on the date of the poll, are of full age and not subject to any legal incapacity to vote and either British subjects or citizens of the Republic of Ireland.

There were many debates over the function and the future of the House of Lords and its compatibility with the equalitarian aspirations of a large part of the electorate. When it became clear that the House of Lords was here to stay, it was deemed appropriate to end its discrimination against women.

Section 1(2) of the Life Peerages Act of 1958 provided that

> persons on whom life peerages were conferred, were entitled to receive writs of summons to attend the House of Lords and sit and vote therein accordingly.

The Act also provided that "a life peerage may be conferred under this section on a woman." In this way, a new kind of discrimination was introduced because hereditary peeresses, unlike newly created ones, continued to be ineligible to sit in the House of Lords. This anomaly was removed some five years later with the Peerage Act of 1963. According to Section 6

> A Woman who is the holder of a hereditary peerage in the peerage of England, Scotland, Great Britain or the United Kingdom shall (whatever the term of the letters patent or other instrument, if any, creating that peerage) have the same right to receive writs of summons to attend the House of Lords, and to sit and vote in that House, and shall be subject to the same disqualifications in respect of membership of the House of Commons and elections to that House, as a man holding that peerage.

In 1980, there were 41 life peeresses in the House of Lords. The life peers and peeresses are completely outnumbered in this body, but many of them have contributed to the quality of the debates and deliberations.

Representation of women in the House of Commons has not changed significantly since the end of World War II. Out of a total membership of 635, there were usually about 20 women. As already noted, there were 24 in 1945; but the participation of women dropped to 21 in 1950, and to 17 in 1951 when the Conservatives returned to power. It rose to 24 in 1955 and to 25 in 1959. The Labor Party won the elections in 1964, and 29 women took their seats in the House of Commons. Their number fell to 26, and remained at 26 in 1970 when the Conservatives returned to power. In 1975, it was still only 28 or 4.4 percent of the total membership of the House of Commons. In 1980, it was down to 19 or 3 percent.

177

Beverly Parker Stobaugh has compiled some interesting statistics on successful and unsuccessful women candidates for Parliament.[1] She has also compared men and women elected to Parliament in 1929, 1945 and 1970.[2] She found that "members of Parliament elected in 1945 did not have a great deal of local political experience, but, as in 1929, the women (46 percent) were better prepared than the men (34 percent)." She also established that 96 percent of the women had been party workers, as compared with 15 percent of the men. In her view, "this indicates that women were continuing to use party activity to gain access to political office, whereas male candidates could depend on accomplishments in other areas."[3] Unfortunately, among the "key variables" she did not include military service, which was a major consideration after World War II. Many of the women candidates had made significant contributions to Britain's war effort, but male candidates in or out of uniform obviously had more appeal to voters.

In the European Parliament, the proportion of British women is also small. Out of a total of 81, there are 11 women (13.6 percent). However, considering that there were only 25 women candidates out of a total of 270, they did fairly well. It is important for British women to compare their progress since the end of World War II with what has happened in other countries of the European Community. There are some specific areas in which further progress can be made in spite of unfavorable economic conditions, because the desired legal changes do not involve tremendous expenditures. For the most part, they involve equalization of pay, working conditions and pensions of men and women. Married women are often complaining about unequal and inequitable treatment in matters of taxation. Some of them want to have nationality and citizenship law reformed to equalize the rights of men and women.

The process of legal equalization has been going on for more than three decades, and much has been accomplished by about a dozen major acts, such as the Marriage Act (1949) and the Matrimonial Causes Act (1965), the Abortion Act (1967), the Family Law Reform Act (1969), the Divorce Reform Act (1969), the Equal Pay Acts (1970 and 1975), the Sex Discrimination Act (1975), the Social Security Pension Act (1975), the Unemployment Protection Act (1975), the Social Security Act (1980), and several more. While all of them have been important in contributing to a foundation on which a more equitable order can be developed, we shall be mostly concerned with the legislation of the past decade, beginning with the Equal Pay Act of 1970.

[1]Beverly Parker Stobaugh, *Women and Parliament 1918-1970*. Hicksville Exposition Press, 1978, p. 77ff. Also provides interesting details concerning the Duchess of Atholl, Ellen Wilkinson and Eleanor Florence Rathbone.

[2]Stobaugh, *op. cit.*, pp. 97ff.

[3]Stobaugh, *op. cit.*, p. 104.

Equal Pay Act 1970:

Its stated Purpose:

is to eliminate discrimination on grounds of sex in remuneration and other terms and conditions of employment.

Part I:

provides for equal treatment with regard to terms and conditions of employment of men and women. This applies if and only if work is of the same or "broadly similar" nature. This applies conversely to treatment of men relative to women.

As specified in Part II:

In order to register a complaint, an employee must be employed at least six months prior to complaint. The burden of proof is on the employer to show that the difference in pay is the result of a material difference between the jobs. The industrial tribunal hears the complaint, as established under section 12 of the Industrial Training Act of 1964.

Part III:

A pay structure is defined as "any arrangements adopted by an employer (with or without any associated employer) which fix common terms and conditions of employment for his employees or any class of his employees, and of which provisions are generally known or open to be known by the employee concerned."
Specific discrimination between men and women in a collective agreement is removed.

Part IV:

If wages regulation orders contain any provisions to men only, or to women only, the Secretary of State may refer them to the Industrial Court for necessary amendments.

Part V:

The same procedure applies to agricultural wages.

Part VI:

lists "exclusions."

Part VII:

contains specific provisions for the Armed Services (including women's services) and regulates Armed Services.

The Sex Discrimination Act of 1975 broke new ground in combating discrimination on the basis of sex. It seeks to protect both genders and covers discrimination not only in fields of employment but also in education and other areas. It has been an important piece of legislation not only from the British point of view, but it has also exerted considerable influence on women's rights legislation in several European and non-European countries. But critics feel it is not always precise enough and allows for too many exceptions.

In Part I discriminatory behavior is described rather than defined. No clear or explicit distinction is made between direct and indirect discrimination. Several examples are given, which might be viewed as cases of indirect discrimination. What seems to differentiate indirect from direct discrimination is the fact that in the former the act of discrimination centers on individuals of either gender. In the latter, the discriminatory act involves certain conditions which favor one gender against the other. The discrimination need not be gender-centered. It could favor an unmarried person of either gender over a married one. (Section 3(1))

Part II deals in great detail with "Discrimination in the Employment Field." It rules out certain situations "where being a man is a genuine occupational qualification for the job" (Section 7), and it provides examples and criteria, such as physical strength, the nature of the establishment, and location, including assignments overseas. It also deals with what are referred to as "special cases," which include certain provisions not considered discriminatory. They refer to police and prison officers, ministers, and mineworkers. Originally, midwives were also listed among these cases. But that was changed on January 1, 1976. Men are no longer barred from becoming midwives. Some of these provisions are of dubious compatibility with the present standards and criteria of the EEC. An example is Section 18(1), which states that "nothing in this Part renders unlawful any discrimination between male and female prison officers as to requirements relating to height."

Part III deals with discrimination in the field of education, as well as with discriminatory provisions involving "goods, facilities, services and premises." In addition to the general provisions against discrimination in educational establishments, there are others which refer to training courses organized by employers (Section 6) and other training courses in vocational education (Section 14). Denial of "facilities for education" is listed in Section 29 as an example of discrimination against women. Discriminatory training is also referred to in Sections 47 and 48, which deal with exceptions.

"Other Unlawful Acts" are detailed in Part IV. Included are such acts as "discriminatory advertisements." According to Section 38(3) "use of a job description with a sexual connotation (such as 'waiter,' 'salesgirl,' 'postman,' or 'stewardess') shall be taken to indicate an intention to discriminate, unless the advertisement contains an indication to the contrary."

More problems are the "General Exceptions" from provisions of Parts II and III, which are enumerated, or at least exemplified, in Part V. They cover a great deal of ground ranging from charities to national security. Important powers are vested in the Equal Opportunities Commission (Part VI). Aside from its general duties set forth in Sections 53 to 56, the EOC is empowered to conduct investigations (Sections 57-61), and it has broad enforcement powers (Sections 71-74). Section 75 specifies the forms of assistance which the EOC may render to victims of discrimination. They range from giving advice to seeking a settlement, arranging for the assistance by a solicitor or counsel.

Part VII of the Sex Discrimination Act deals with enforcement in cases of alleged discrimination in employment. Section 63 provides that "a complaint by any person that another person has committed an act of discrimination against another person . . . may be presented to an industrial tribunal." Section 64 spells out the conciliation procedure to be followed in the event the tribunal finds a complaint is "wellfounded." According to the EEC Commission Report, p. 199, 821 applications were brought between 1976 and 1979. It also notes that two-thirds of the disputes were settled by conciliation. In other cases of discrimination not involving employment, complaints may be brought before the county courts. (Section 74) There is some disagreement as to where the burden of proof of discrimination should rest. Under the SDA the claimant must prove that he or she was the victim of discrimination. Only in cases of dismissal does the burden of proof rest with the employer, who must show that no discrimination was involved.

The Sex Discrimination Act (1975) did not repeal all the earlier laws and regulations which were designed to protect women from exposing themselves to exceptionally strenuous and hazardous conditions. Because the Act antedated Directive 76/207/EE, the European Commission could not expect the British Parliament to embark immediately upon a comprehensive review and revision of the earlier protective legislation. Some of this legislation goes back to the early 20th Century. The prohibition against employing women in the manufacture of paints and colorants dates from 1907; that against tin-plating work dates from 1909. Other regulations of this type go back to the inter-war period, when the International Labor Office was very active in this area. During the post-World War II period, the Factories Act of 1961 contained many prohibitions against the manufacture and use by women of certain lead products, as well as regulations of working hours. In recent years, the Equal Opportunities Commission has studied the existing health and safety legislation and made some preliminary recommendations. It is expected to make recommendations for new legislation, but no specific date has been set for such initiatives.

The Social Security Pensions Act 1975 lists five specific objectives:

1) to relate rates of social security retirement pensions and other benefits to the earnings on which contribution has been made
2) to enable employed earners to be contracted out of full social security contributions and benefits where requisite benefits are provided by occupational scheme
3) to make sure men and women are afforded equal access to occupational pension schemes
4) to make other provisions about occupational pensions
5) to make other amendments in law relating to social security

This act amends and supplements Social Security Act 1975, to give effect to proposals set out in the White Paper, "Better Pensions." It aims toward improving benefits payable under social security pension schemes and introduces a "measure of partnership" between social security pension schemes and occupational pension schemes to which many employers belong. Attention may be called to the following provisions:

Part I:

#3
Abolishes reduced contribution rates in respect to married women and widows.

Part II:

#18
Repeals provision of the Social Security Act of 1975 which imposed lower rate of sickness and unemployment benefits on married women.

Part II:

#19
Permits years in which a contributor was absorbed by responsibilities at home to count towards satisfaction of contribution conditions.
It also abolishes the "half-test," whereby a married woman was precluded from category A retirement pension unless she had had the necessary earning for at least half of the years between marriage and pension age.

#20
Replaces the Social Security Act of 1975 provision for a widow to use spouse's contributions to satisfy contributions for category A with a similar but extended provision applying to spouse of either sex whose marriage has terminated for any reason.

#24
Widowers, like widows at present, become entitled to half the graduated retirement benefit earned by late spouse.

Part III:

#28
Reviews and alters contracted-out rates of contribution without distinction on grounds of age or sex.

Part IV:

In occupational pension schemes, men and women shall be treated equally. It is incumbent upon the employer to see that regulations conform to equal access requirements.

The Employment Protection Act 1978 seeks to improve industrial

relations, amend workers' rights, and establish maternity pay fund.
In *Part II* the following principles are established:

> With certain exceptions, dismissal on grounds of pregnancy
> constitutes unfair dismissal. A woman is also entitled to six
> weeks maternity pay, with the right to return to work before
> the end of twenty-nine weeks.
> A maternity pay fund is established under the control of the
> Secretary of State. This spreads the financial burden equally
> among employers and avoids discrimination which might re-
> sult from fear of having to pay maternity pay.
> An employee failing to receive her benefits has recourse to an
> industrial tribunal, which Part V describes in more detail.

The Social Security Act 1980 was drafted with particular attention
to Directive 79/7/EEC requiring all member states to undertake a "progressive implementation of the principle of equal treatment for men and
women in matters of social security." The Equal Opportunities Commission has made major contributions toward the goals of eliminating
discrimination on the basis of sex. It has made good use of its powers
and made numerous recommendations to the House secretary and the
secretary of state for employment. It has conducted investigations and
sought settlements. Its influence is reflected in the recent legislation.
The principle of equal pay has been enforced with all the means at the
disposal of the EOC. However, it should be noted that in the British
legislation the principle of equal pay for work of equal value has not
yet been incorporated, and the Equal Opportunities Commission has
asked the home secretary to support some amendments to the Equal Pay
Act and the Sex Discrimination Act, which would assimilate British law
to that of the European Community.

The lifting of the prohibition of night work for women has been a
matter of disagreement between the Equal Opportunities Commission,
which favors it, and the Trade Union Congress, which opposes it on the
ground that it might lead to new abuses. This may or may not be the
real reason. Some male union members have been concerned that
women are going to take over more and more jobs and that there should
be legislation to protect them as well as women.

It is perhaps unnecessary to note that in Great Britain, as in most
western European countries, the recession has had a more adverse effect
on women than on men. Women have found it increasingly more difficult to get jobs in fields where they are competing with men. Some
women with small children have found it difficult to continue in their

jobs because many day nurseries have been closed. Those who are employed are still often underpaid in spite of legislation against discrimination and effective support from the Equal Opportunities Commission. In 1980, in its Fourth Annual Report, the Equal Opportunities Commission noted the wage differentials between men and women were not narrowing but actually widening. They were at their narrowest in 1977 when women received 75.5 percent of the average rates paid to men. In 1978 they fell to 73.9 percent, and in 1979 they were down to 73 percent.

There are women in some categories who feel they have special problems which require urgent action. One of these groups is made up of widows. It is estimated that there are about three million widows in Great Britain. In 1971 their special needs led to the formation of the National Association of Widows. In 1980 it produced a "Widows Charter" which called for tax exemption of widows' benefits. Copies of this publication were sent to all members of Parliament. (The National Association has 95 branches and a dozen advisory centers.)

The continuing inflation has made many of the formerly adequate benefits very inadequate. Baroness Lockwood, who has chaired the Equal Opportunity Commission since 1975,[4] has called for a comprehensive review of the maternity benefits which are considered to be the lowest in the European Community. They have not been adjusted since 1969, and they are considered to be completely insufficient at this time. The fact that Great Britain or the United Kingdom, as it is now officially called, is a member of the European Community, is likely to benefit women. The British women members have many opportunities to compare their situation with the status of women in other member states. Four of its members serve on the Committee on Women's Rights, which has a total membership of 35. They and the other seven elected women members serve on other committees affording them excellent opportunities to assess the progress that has been made in their country.

The EEC is not unduly constrained by diplomatic niceties. Thus, the Commission of the European Communities in Brussels, in its Report from the Commission to the Council (COM(80) 832 final) dated February 11, 1981, found certain deficiencies in the current British legislation, and some further positive action is expected in such matters as retirement benefits, taxation as it relates to married women, as well as nationality and citizenship law.

---

[4] In 1980 she was reappointed by the Home Secretary to serve until November 1982.

IRELAND

The Republic of Ireland Act was passed in 1948, and the independence of Ireland was proclaimed on April 18, 1949. The Constitution of 1937 has remained in force, but there have been some efforts to replace it with a new one. In 1966, Prime Minister Lemass initiated a comprehensive review by a Constitution Revision Committee which reported in 1967. The Committee proposed one basic change in the form of government by abolishing the presidency and by transferring the powers of the president to the prime minister. The Committee also believed that in times of emergency the two houses should have the power to suspend certain constitutional guarantees. The categorical prohibition of divorce should be modified, and the privileged status of the Roman Catholic Church should be abolished. Except for the proposals concerning divorce, none of the other recommendations for constitutional reform had anything to do with the status of women. Some of the recommendations were subsequently enacted as amendments to the Constitution. Article 29 had to be amended in 1972, so that Ireland could join the European Coal and Steel Community and other international organizations. Although it was not fully realized at the time, this was to have an important impact on the status of women because Ireland would be expected to comply with the principles of non-discrimination.

As has already been noted, the Constitution, from the very beginning, had some very clear and impressive provisions concerning women's rights and non-discrimination. The problem was not the Constitution but rather antiquated laws and, of course, deeply rooted social attitudes. A careful reading of this document shows that the Constitution of Ireland, like most constitutions of the world, continues to show a distinctly male-oriented attitude when it comes to the chief offices in the state.

Article 9(3) provides that:

> no person shall be excluded from Irish nationality and citizenship by reason of the sex of such person.

This implies that sex is no consideration in running for any public office. But Article 12.4 1° states:

> Every citizen, who has reached his thirty-fifth year of age is eligible for election to the office of President.

Why not "all citizens who have reached their thirty-fifth year of age are eligible for election to the Office of the President?" It seems necessary to dwell on this point, because it is clearly not just misleading language but basic orientation. This becomes obvious if one starts to count all the other references to "he" and "his" in this otherwise very well drafted document.

There are other features in the Constitution and the political system of Ireland which favor men over women. One of these is the nominating system for the president, as specified in Article 12. A presidential candidate has to be nominated either by:

1. not less than twenty persons, each of whom is at the time a member of one of the Houses of the *Oireachtas*, (National Parliament), or
2. by the Councils of not less than four administrative counties (including County Boroughs) as defined by law.

The political parties of Ireland, like those of other countries, are male oligarchies which are not likely to give up control over the election process. In the Constitution no specific reference is made to political parties, but their extra-constitutional national status does not prevent them from being the prime movers in the political process. According to Article 40.6:

Laws regulating the manner in which the right of forming associations and unions and the right of free assembly may be exercised shall contain no political, religious or class discrimination.

It does not refer to *de facto* parties and other associations. Article 16 of the Constitution does state very clearly that:

1° Every citizen without distinction of sex who has reached the age of twenty-one years, and who is not placed under disability or incapacity by this Constitution or by law, shall be eligible for membership of Dail Eireann.
2° Every citizen, without distinction of sex, who has reached the age of twenty-one years who is not disqualified by law and complies with the provisions of the law relating to the election of members of Dail Eireann shall have the right to vote at an election for members of Dail Eireann.

187

The provisions were amended in 1972 by the Fourth Amendment, which lowered the voting age to 18.

Article 16.1.3° adds:

> No law shall be enacted placing any citizen under disability or incapacity for membership in the Dail Eireann on the ground of sex or disqualifying any citizen from voting at an election for members of Dail Eireann on that ground.

This provision may be of particular interest to proponents of the ERA (Equal Rights Amendment to the U.S. Constitution) because it shows that prohibitions of legislation are not enough to achieve equality—let alone equity.

The Electoral Act of 1963 spelled out specific conditions for voting:

Section 5 (1):

> A person shall be entitled to be registered as a Dail elector in a constituency if he has reached the age of 21 years and he was, on the qualifying date—
> (a) A citizen of Ireland and
> (b) Ordinarily resident in that constituency.
>   2 (a) A person shall be entitled to be registered as a local government elector in a local electoral area if he has reached the age of 21 years and—
>   (i) He was, on the qualifying date, ordinarily resident in that area, or
>   (ii) He has, during the whole of the period of six months ending on the qualifying date, occupied, as owner or tenant, any land or premises in that area.

Subsequently, in accordance with the Fourth Amendment of 1972, the age requirement was lowered to 18.

The Senate (*Seanad Eireann*) has continued to be a body to which some of its members are still nominated. According to Article 18.1:

> (the) Seanad Eireann shall be composed of sixty members, of whom eleven shall be nominated members and forty-nine shall be elected members.

To be eligible for membership in the *Seanad Eireann*, a person must be eligible for membership in the *Dail Eireann*. (Article 18.2)

Nominations are made by the prime minister (Taoiseach), who is by custom, head of the majority political party. The system which governs the process of electing senators is also highly structured. Three members are elected by the National University of Ireland, three by the University of Dublin and forty-three are elected from five "panels of candidates."

Article 18.7 states that the candidates whose names appear on these panels shall have "knowledge and practical experience of the following interests and services, namely:

1. National language and culture, literature, art, education and such professional interests as may be defined by law for the purpose of this panel;
2. Agriculture and allied interests, and fisheries;
3. Labour, whether organised or unorganised;
4. Industry and commerce, including banking, finance, accountancy, engineering and architecture;
5. Public Administration and social services, including voluntary social activities.

It is clear that this quasi-corporate system of representation tends to support the status quo and the patriarchal system, since relatively few women can expect to succeed to key positions in any of these interest groups. Even if they do, the process of selection of panel candidates is likely to put them at a disadvantage. It is constitutionally possible that a certain imbalance of representation may arise because Article 18.7.2 allows as many as eleven to be elected from one panel. But it also stipulates that "not less than five members of the *Seanad Eireann* shall be elected from any one panel."

What have the women of Ireland done in recent years to have a larger share in the political process? Until recently, they have done relatively little toward this end. They seem to have been willing to accept the traditional political order without protest, and even now there is little tendency toward radicalism. The changes in the late 1960s were due to economic factors. As the process toward industrialization accelerated, more women entered the labor market. The majority of them were classified as unskilled or semiskilled workers working for much lower pay than men doing comparable work. In 1975, on a comparative basis, the participation of Irish women in the economy was still relatively small. According to an OECD study, the labor force participation in Ireland was 92.1 percent for men and 33.5 percent for women. This may be contrasted with Great Britain, where 91.5 percent of men and 55.3 percent of women participated in the labor force. Ireland's relatively low participation on the part of women may be compared with Greece's (30.8 percent), Italy's (30.7 percent), Portugal's (32 percent), and Spain's (32.5 percent).

The Government of Ireland had given recognition to the changing conditions when it established the Commission on the Status of Women in 1970. It was charged with undertaking a broad-gauged study on the status of women in Ireland, and to make recommendations which would ensure their:

> participation on equal terms with men in the political, social, cultural and economic life of the country.

The Commission Report, published in May 1973, provided an important blueprint for constructive change.

In 1971, Gemma Hussey was one of the founder-members of the Women's Political Association, a non-partisan or all-party organization which seeks to encourage women to be more active in the public and political life of Ireland. The Women's Representative Committee was established in 1974 in the Department of Labour and served as an advisory committee to the minister in matters involving equal pay and equal treatment. However, this committee was abolished in 1979 on the grounds that the Employment Equality Agency had effectively taken over its original task. The Council for the Status of Women, which started out as a coordinating body for 10 women's organizations, was chiefly responsible for the establishment of the Government Commission on the Status of Women. The 1974 Report of the Commission was an important blueprint for subsequent government activities on behalf of women.

On January 1, 1976, the Anti-Discrimination Act (Pay Act) of 1974 came into effect. The term employed was not "equal work" but "like work." It thus did not require that the work be the same but similar, if not of equal value. It was to apply to men and women employed by the same employer. The Employment Equality Act was passed on June 1, 1977. Section 2 forbids direct and indirect discrimination on the basis of sex or marital status. Provision is made for the establishment of the Employment Equality Agency, whose functions are defined in Section 35 of the Act. The agency commenced its work on October 1, 1977. However, until recently the funding arrangements had not been satisfactorily worked out. It was only after Senator Mary T. W. Robinson submitted a motion in the Senate in October of 1979 that slight increases were made. Some occupational categories and activities have been excluded from coverage by the provisions of the Employment Equality Act. Questions did arise in connection with these exceptions or derogations, and on July 29, 1980 the Commission of the European Communities "gave the Irish Government notice to review the exceptions that conflict with Article 2(2) of the Directive." The principle of equal treatment does not apply to employment abroad under the existing law.

There are also questions about the conditions under which women might serve in the army and in the police. The commission has called attention to the fact that while women may enter the police force, the minimum height requirements are different for men and women, implying reverse discrimination.

Equal access to vocational education in Ireland appears to be a matter of concern to the Commission of the European Communities. In the 1981 Report there is a statistical table which shows the "number of boys and girls receiving technical and vocational education on 30 June, 1980."[1] Most of the percentages are quite comparable to those of other West European countries. However, it is surprising to find that 514 male but only 21 female students are taking courses in interior decorating. Also surprising is the fact that 355 female but only 17 male students are being trained in tailoring.

One of the problems with the Equal Employment Act, like many similar pieces of legislation in other European countries, is that it does not make provisions for mandatory information services, as required by Article 8 of the Council Directive 76/207/EEC of February 9, 1976. In view of the complexity of the sections of the Act dealing with the procedure to be followed in cases of disputes, this appeared to be a serious shortcoming which has been partly corrected by booklets issued by the Ministry of Labour. These have been distributed to all ministries as well as to trade unions. The Employment Equality Agency also prepared a number of pamphlets, which were widely distributed. In addition, it prepared posters, organized seminars, and made effective use of radio and television to disseminate essential information about the Act to employees and employers.

A Law Reform Commission was established by the government in 1975. As its name suggests, it is to study existing laws and to make recommendations for reform. The commission's task is difficult from a technical point of view and very complex in terms of contemporary Irish politics, because it involves such controversial and constitutional issues as divorce law, abortion, illegitimate children, as well as tax reform, and several others. Some aspects of these issues have already been decided by the High Court and the Supreme Court. As far as tax reform is concerned, this is a matter of particular interest to feminists

---

[1]"Commission of the European Communities." Report to the Council. Brussels, 11 February 1981.

as well as to married women. The feminists are opposed to income-splitting for tax purposes, because they think that this undercuts the married women's financial independence while not making the husband accountable for the way he spends his half of the income. This controversial and divisive matter is of special concern to the Married Persons' Tax Reform Association in Dublin. (See Appendix)

The Divorce Law reform is difficult because Article 41.3.2 states that:

> no law shall be enacted providing for the grant of a dissolution of marriage.

In 1980, Minister of Justice Gerry Collins announced that the government had no intention to allow Article 41 to be amended. However, it has been increasingly recognized that a wide gap exists between the constitutional norm prohibiting divorce and the actual practice. Senator Mary Robinson, who is an authority on Irish Constitutional Law, has lent her support to the Divorce Action Group in Dublin.

The question of illegitimacy has also become a political issue, because the youth section of the opposition party has proposed legislation which would abolish the distinction between legitimate children in matters of inheritance.

Difficult as these matters are to resolve, it can nevertheless be expected that major changes will take place in the near future. This is due to the fact that Ireland is no longer as isolated from the European continent as it was until a few years ago. One of the major factors has been Ireland's participation in the Council of Europe; especially since 1973, when Ireland joined the European Economic Community along with Great Britain and Denmark. After the 1979 direct elections to the European Parliament, two Irish women and 13 men were elected, thus constituting 13.3 percent of the total. In the Lower House of the Irish Parliament their representation is much smaller: 6 out of 148 or 4 percent.

Women occupy less than 7 percent of senior positions in the Civil Service and Local Authorities. There are conflicting statistics on the number of women in the civil service, especially in the higher echelons. To date, the highest appointed position is held by Mrs. Maire Geoghegan-Quinn, minister for the *Gaeltacht* (the Irish-Speaking Areas). Before her appointment in December 1979, she served as minister of state at the Department of Industry, Commerce and Energy.

The 1981 general elections resulted in an increase in the number of women elected to the *Dail*. Now there were 11 women out of 166 members or 6.8 percent. However, seven of these women were new and several prominent women candidates were defeated in their bids for reelection: Dr. Mary Robinson, Gemma Hussey, for example.

Eileen Desmond was appointed minister of health in the new government headed by Dr. Janet Fitzgerald.

It is premature to speculate whether the recent change in government should be viewed as good news for the advancement of women.

LIECHTENSTEIN

The Principality of Liechtenstein is a very small country situated between Austria and Switzerland. According to the Statistical Yearbook of Liechtenstein, the total population in late 1979 was 25,808, of which 7,656 were men and 8,527 were women.

In 1982, the Principality of Liechtenstein remains the only country in Europe in which women do not have the right to vote in "national" elections. Although Article 29 of the Constitution states that

> all citizens of the Principality shall be entitled to civic rights
> in conformity with the provisions of the present Constitution

the right to vote has been limited to communal elections. Until 1976 the women of Liechtenstein did not even have that right. But in early 1976, 288 women from Vaduz exercised the right of initiative to present a petition to the Diet (*Landtag*), asking for the right to vote in communal elections. The Diet took the necessary action on July 7, 1976, by enacting the Enabling Law (Ermächtigungsgesetz zum Frauenstimmrecht). It authorized the eleven communes to hold referenda to that end. Elections on this issue were held during September 1976 in Vaduz. The results were 315 for and 265 against, granting women the right to vote in communal elections. The women of Vaduz voted for the first time on April 15, 1977.

The issue of women's suffrage has been the subject of three popular referenda. The first was held in 1968, the second in 1971, and the third in 1973. On July 4, 1968 it was narrowly rejected, 2,152 to 2,582. According to official electoral statistics, 1,341 men voted against and 887 for it; but women voted for it by a slim margin, 1,265 to 1,241. On February 26/28, 1971, it was rejected 1,897 to 1,816. On February 9/11, 1973, it was again rejected 2,156 to 1,675.

There appear to be no official figures on how the women voted in 1971 and 1973, but there is reason to believe that more women now favor a constitutional amendment giving women the right to vote in national elections. A decade later, the main issue for women seems to be more economic than political or legal. As the economic development has continued, women have been more and more concerned with equal pay for equal work. Women feel that they have better opportunities in private enterprise than in government service.

In late 1979 only 297 men and 131 women were employed in public administration. Whether or not there are now significant differentials in pay is not known, but there is no legal basis for it. Article 31 of the Constitution of the Principality of Liechtenstein states that:

> all citizens shall be equal in the eyes of the law. The public offices shall be equally open to them, subject to observance of the legal regulations.

It is unlikely that drastic or rapid changes will take place in the legal system of Liechtenstein. The social system and its underlying values have remained highly traditional. The economic development has necessitated changes in the commercial and corporation law, as Liechtenstein has been very successful in attracting foreign investors. One of the most recent major pieces of legislation is the Law of June 14, 1980 concerning commercial enterprises. However, these legal modernization efforts are not expected to have any significant impact on the family law, which is based on the Austrian Civil Code of 1811 in its original form.

LUXEMBOURG

Although after World War II Luxembourg was confronted with major problems of economic reconstruction, constitutional and legal issues were not ignored. By 1948, the Chamber was ready to act on several proposed amendments. A large number of articles was amended on April 28. Additional amendments were passed on May 6, May 15, and May 21. As far as voting rights were concerned, the most important change was made on May 15 (1958) by the amendment of Article 52. It now set four conditions for eligibility to vote:

Electors must:
1) be Luxembourg nationals
2) enjoy civil and political rights
3) have completed their twenty-first year
4) be domiciled in the Grand Duchy.

Other conditions could be added by law, but it was specifically stated that "no property qualification may be imposed."

Article 52 further provided that "in order to qualify for election, a person must have completed his twenty-fifth year and fulfill the other three conditions enumerated above. No other qualifications shall be required."

The amendments which were passed on May 21 are also relevant. The amended Article 11(1) reaffirms the principle of equality before the law, but then constricts this statement by proving that "only Luxembourgers are admissible to civil and military functions, subject to the exceptions that may be established for particular cases by the law." Women have, of course, been able to enter the civil service in spite of this seemingly discriminatory provision.

Article 11(4) guarantees "the right to work." Article 11(5) states: "The law organizes the social security, health protection and rest for workers and guarantees the liberties of the trade unions."

On July 27, 1956 Article 56 was amended to provide that "deputies are elected for five years."

The Benelux Economic Union was formed in 1958 and became effective in 1960. In November 1964 Grand Duchess Charlotte abdicated in favor of her son, Grand Duke Jean. In 1967 the first woman, a member of the Christian Socialist People's Party, became a member of Cabinet. Women have come to occupy important positions in local governments. There were three women in the Chamber of Deputies, which consists of 59 members, in 1975.

A survey conducted in 1978 in the then nine Community countries, questioned men and women whether conditions would be better if there were more women in Parliament. They were also asked: "In what way would things be better?" About one half of the Luxembourg men thought "there would be less playing politics for its own sake." Sixty percent of the women thought "the problems of women would get more serious consideration."

The progressive political and social transformations which had been carried out during the two decades after World War II were not matched by fundamental changes in the legal system. Generally speaking the patriarchal principle remained firmly entrenched. The legal provisions concerning divorce were not significantly liberalized. Thus, until 1963, Article 295 of the Civil Code prohibited remarriages of divorced spouses. Women in Luxembourg feel there are some outmoded and inequitable features in the property and tax law.

Although Luxembourg ratified ILO Convention No 89, which prohibits restrictions on night work by women, the situation has not changed significantly since 1932, when the Grand Ducal Decree of

March 30 prohibited night work (from 1:00 p.m. to 5:00 a.m.) in private industrial establishments. The same prohibition has been applied to public employment, with a few exceptions in the field of transportation.

Luxembourg has proceeded somewhat slowly and very cautiously to comply with the directives of the Council of the European Communities. The first implementing measures were the laws of February 21, 1976 and May 21, 1979, which applied the equal treatment principles in the areas of public employment and education. However, the European Commission does not feel that Luxembourg has gone far enough in implementing all its directives, especially Council Directive 76/207/EEC of February 9, 1976.

On March 14, 1980 the Ministry of Labor and Social Security transmitted a Draft Law on Equal Treatment, along with an *Exposé des Motifs*. It would appear that the Draft Law seeks to incorporate most, if not all, the criteria set forth in the Council Directive of February 9, 1976 on the implementation of the principle of equal treatment for men and women (76/207/EEC). In most of the articles the language and terminology are very similar to that of the Council Directive. Such terms as indirect discrimination, implicit discrimination, and positive discrimination are being used in Luxembourg, but the Draft Law has not undertaken to define them. The Commission of European Communities has suggested the Draft Law should also define what is meant by "working conditions."

On the positive side it should be noted that Luxembourg is one of the countries which has enacted legislation designed to protect the children of divorced mothers whose former husbands have reneged on their obligations. In July 1980, appropriate legislation was passed to establish a special fund from which payments can be made in such situations. The state will seek repayment from the delinquent father.

Some changes have been made in the "Draft Law relating to the equality of treatment between men and women" of March 14, 1980, and there may be further changes due to the pressure from the women's groups in Luxembourg and the Commission of the European Communities. (An English translation of the text of the Draft Law is appended.) Some of the articles of the Draft Law seem unnecessarily complex and legalistic. For example, the provisions contained in Article 8, even if one disregards unnecessary repetition and the somewhat tortured style, do not state clearly what the workers' rights are. Workers may be awarded damages, but there is no guarantee that they can insist on being rehired if they had been dismissed for "extraneous motives." The language used in Article 2(2) is somewhat awkward. It states that this law shall not constitute an "obstacle" to existing laws and regulations concerning maternity, industrial night work by women, and employment in the mines. What it really means is that it shall have no effect on the laws and regulations concerning the above mentioned conditions and situations. In other words, these are specifically mentioned as exceptions or derogations. Except for the reference to maternity, they would appear to be in conflict with Article 3(2) of 76/207/EEC, which states clearly that "member states shall take the measures necessary to ensure that: a) any laws, regulations and administrative provisions contrary to the principle of equal treatment shall be abolished."

NETHERLANDS

In June 1945, the first cabinet was again functioning in the Hague. There were many urgent tasks of physical reconstruction, but efforts were also made to develop policies which would benefit women. Thus, an advisory committee for the work of women and girls was set up as early as 1946. Major constitutional and legal changes were not undertaken until 1948. The changes in the Constitution were so extensive that it was decided to publish a consolidated text and refer to it as a new constitution. On September 4, 1948 Queen Wilhelmina abdicated in favor of her daughter, Juliana.

A new Electoral Law was passed on July 13, 1951. It stated that "the Second Chamber of the States General shall be elected by persons who are residents in the Realm on the day of nominations, provided they are Netherlands citizens and have attained the age of twenty-one years."

About the same time, the State Commission, appointed in April 1950, presented its first report on proposed amendments to the Constitution; more amendments were proposed after that. It took about a dozen years before final action was taken on all of these proposed amendments. In the meantime other important legislation was passed. In 1952, the Social Insurance Act was passed, and the Unemployment Insurance Act came into force. The State Commission presented its final report on proposed constitutional changes in January 1954. On the basis of amendments passed on September 10, 1956, the number of seats in the Lower House was increased from 100 to 150. (Article 91) The First Chamber of the States General was to consist of 75 members. (Article 92) In the same year, Dr. Marga Klompe became the first woman cabinet member. The Old Pension System went into effect on January 1, 1957. On October 1, it was followed by the Widows and Orphans Benefit Act. The amended text of the Constitution went into force on December 19, 1963. Article 90 set the voting age at 21. Articles 94 and 100 stipulated a minimum age of 25 for eligibility to the second and first chamber.

A crisis developed in February 1964, because Princess Irene had failed to ask for the consent of the States General before announcing her engagement to Spanish Prince Carlos-Hugo of Bourbon-Parma. As a result she forfeited her rights to the throne. The first crisis involving a Dutch Princess was followed in 1965 by another one. Although Princess Beatrix asked and received approval for her marriage to a German nobleman, public opinion did not support this action. Serious disturbances erupted after her marriage in 1966. Princess Margriet Francisca married a Dutch commoner in 1967.

In the 1960s the Dutch women's rights movement was gaining momentum. Some experts have called it the second wave, which came some six decades after the first. While the first was centered on the issue of women's suffrage, the second wave was more concerned with economic and social issues. Perhaps one should say societal issues, because the moving spirits were much more radically oriented. One of the action-oriented groups, founded in 1968, called itself *Man-Vrouw-Maatschappij* ("Men-Women-Society") and resembled Danish and Swedish groups in that it called for an equal division of labor in the home and at work. Other groups have been preoccupied with the abortion issue. But the main drive was for greater equity in wages and job opportunities. In 1969, when the Wages Act was passed by Parliament, it was by a vote of 82 to 59. Since that time a much better situation has emerged, but not entirely as a result of drastic changes of attitudes. The European Economic Community has undoubtedly been a significant factor, because it is understood that a member must comply with the directives of the EEC. There have been some other changes. The minimum voting age was lowered from 21 to 18. This was done by amending Articles 90(1), 137 and 152 on March 11, 1972.

In the Lower House of Parliament, participation of women increased slightly during the 1970s. It was 13.3 percent in 1973 and 1974. In 1979, it increased to 14 percent (21 women out of a total of 150.) In the Upper House it rose more sharply: 5.3 percent in 1973, 6.7 percent in 1976 and 9.3 percent in 1979.

There has been little change in the women's share of top level political and administrative positions. In 1973, the cabinet was composed of 16 members. Only one woman held the rank of minister. All the 15 state secretaries were men. In 1974 out of 16 cabinet members only one was a woman. There were 17 state secretaries but not a single woman. By 1979 there was still only one woman in the cabinet of 16. Progress had been made on the level of state secretaries: 4 out of 16, or 25 percent, were women.

When Prime Minister Adreas van Agt formed a new government in

September 1981, he appointed Mrs. Mathilda Gardeniers-Berendsen (Christian Democratic Appeal–CDA) to serve as minister of health and environment. She had served as minister for culture, recreation and social services in the previous government. Thus the only woman member remained in one of the cabinet posts frequently assigned to women.

The diplomatic corps has remained an exclusive male domain. In 1974 there were no women above the lower levels. From the ambassadors down to the assistant vice consuls, all positions were held by men. There has been a slight increase in recent years but only in the lower positions. By way of contrast, it should be noted that 5 out of the 20 Dutch members in the European Parliament were women.

Some gains were recorded on the local levels of government between 1966 and 1974. The percentage of women in the provincial councils had increased from 6.5 to 11.8. In the municipal council, the percentage of women had also doubled (4.8 percent to 9.9 percent). By 1978, 16.5 percent of the members of the provincial councils were women. In the municipal councils 12.5 percent of the councillors were women in 1978.

There has been some criticism on the part of women's organizations that the government has not done enough to promote women's rights and political participation, and that it has failed to develop a clear plan for action on behalf of women. Late in 1973, the Social and Cultural Planning Office was set up to assist the government in the development of what was called a coherent government policy of "emancipation." In the same year, the government supported Netherland's Association for Women's Concerns (Nederlandse Vereniging voor Vrouwenbelangeu), in cooperation with eight other women's organizations, and embarked on new activities in the field of political education and training with a view to increasing the number of women in elected positions. Two basic courses were organized. One focused on the national government and the political system. The other was concerned with international affairs, the role of the United Nations, the Council of Europe, the European Parliament and related matters.

In late 1977, the government appointed a woman to serve as state secretary for emancipation policy in the Ministry of Cultural Affairs, Recreation and Social Welfare. More expeditious and decisive government action has also been due to the activities of the United Nations. The Emancipation Commission, which was to advise the government on policy matters involving women, was created in December 1974, just before the Proclamation of the International Women's Year. Its main task has been to coordinate the activities on behalf of women in the various ministries and to work closely with the special committee on emancipation policy of the Lower House.

In recent years a major effort has been made to identify all existing laws, decrees and regulations which discriminate or are deemed to discriminate against women. A list of such provisions was compiled by the Ministry of Social Affairs during 1975 and 1976. In August 1977, a' review was made of provisions which had not been amended. This was followed by annual reviews in 1978 and 1979. According to the EEC, the problem was more a matter of terminology than of substance. One of the terms questioned was that of "breadwinner," because it appeared to favor men.

Compared with the other Western European countries, the participation of women in the labor market of the Netherlands has remained relatively low. In 1975, it was 27 percent, and by 1980 it was still below 30 percent. As unemployment has been increasing in recent months, it is likely that the percentage of women will drop again. Those who do stay employed will benefit from the legal requirement of equal pay for equal work. The differential is relatively small at this time. It has become less a matter of equal pay as of equal opportunities in economics and in politics.

In response to the EEC Council Directive 76/207 of February 9, 1976 on the Implementation of the Principle of Equal Treatment for Men and Women as Regards Access to Employment, Vocational Training and Promotion, and Working Conditions, the Government of the Netherlands has undertaken a number of measures which seek to comply with this mandate. The legislative action came in the form of Law No 86/1980 on the Equality of Treatment Between Men and Women of March 1, 1980. This brief law of 6 articles was transmitted to the EEC by the permanent representative of the Kingdom of the Netherlands to the European Communities on April 8, 1980, with the explanation that Law No 86/1980 constituted "a partial application" to Directive No 207/76.

Further and more comprehensive legislative action was taken in the form of Law No 384 of July 2, 1980 Pertaining to the Adaptation of the Netherland Legislation Concerning the Personnel of the Public Services, (in response to) the Directive of the Council of the European Communities of February 10, 1975 Relating to Equal Pay Between Male and Female Workers and the Council Directive (No 76/207/EEC) of February 9, 1976, Relating to the Equality of Treatment Between Men and Women. It is clear that this law of 9 articles was carefully drafted to comply with all the requirements of Directive No 76/207/EEC. With respect to personnel in the public service, the first article essentially restates the language employed in Article 2(1). "The competent authority shall make no discrimination between men and women, neither directly, nor indirectly, for instance, by referring to the matrimonial or family status . . ."

As in the legislation of several other EEC countries, there are still some problems in regard to the specifics of professions in which exceptions (derogations) may be made on the ground that "gender constitutes a determining factor." In the public sector, exceptions or "derogations" include some but not all activities in the armed forces. Among the trade unions are some doubts about the provisions calling for "positive discrimination" or affirmative action, stated in Article 1 of Law No 86/1980 and Article 4(4c) of Law No 384/1980. The Ministry of Education and several other ministries have embarked upon a policy of affirmative action deemed to be corrective rather than discriminatory. (See Appendix)

SWITZERLAND

In Switzerland women's suffrage was not introduced until 1971. One can speculate as to whether it might have been achieved earlier if Switzerland had chosen to apply for membership in the United Nations. As has been noted, the United Nations contributed much to the support of women's rights movements in other European and non-European countries. In any case, Switzerland decided on April 2, 1946 not to seek membership in the United Nations. Some qualified observers believe that such membership would not have made any difference because many cantons of Switzerland were not ready to grant women political as well as legal equality. In the field of private law some further progress was made, but it is necessary to remember that the Swiss Civil Code was in several respects more progressive than the earlier major codes of France, Austria and Germany. Still, there was good reason for discontent among women with respect to marriage and family law.

Another area in which action was needed was in the laws dealing with the nationality of married women. Women and men were not endowed with equal powers as far as citizenship was concerned. A Swiss man who married a foreigner could readily help her to obtain Swiss citizenship if she desired. This was not so with respect to a Swiss woman marrying a foreigner, and the situation is still unresolved.[1]

Only after a decade and a half since the end of World War II was tangible progress made in some of the cantons. In 1959 the cantons of Waadt, Geneva and Neuchâtel granted women the right to vote in cantonal elections. The cantons of Basel (city) followed in 1966 and Basel (land) in 1968.

Ever since the end of World War I attempts have been made in various cantons to amend Article 74 of the Swiss Federal Constitution

[1]Since January 1, 1978 children of a Swiss mother and a non-Swiss father can acquire Swiss citizenship.

so as to give women the right to vote in federal elections. More than half a century had to elapse before this goal could be achieved. The decisive event came on February 7, 1971, when Article 74 was amended so as to give women the right to vote. The original Article 74 read:

> Every Swiss who has completed the age of twenty and who is not excluded from the right of active citizenship by the legislation of the Canton in which he is domiciled has the right to take part in elections and referenda.

The amended Article 74 consists of four paragraphs and reads as follows:

(1) In federal referenda and elections all male and female Swiss citizens (Schweizer und Schweizerinnen) have the same rights and duties.
(2) Entitled to vote are all male and female Swiss citizens who have completed their twentieth year and are not excluded from active citizenship by the law of the Confederation or the canton of their domicile.

On October 30, 1971 women voted for the first time in a Swiss national election. A total of 1,696 candidates competed for the 200 seats in the *Nationalrat*. Among the candidates were 268 women (15.8 percent). Ten women (5 percent) were elected. Of these, nine were sponsored by the three major parties: the Christian Democrats, the Social Democrats, and the *Freisinn*. Each succeeded in placing three representatives in the *Nationalrat*. The tenth elected representative was sponsored by the Communist party.

Switzerland ratified ILO Convention No. 100, and since October 25, 1973 the principle of equal pay for equal work has been in effect. However, at the present time it applies only to federal administration and not to cantonal and private employees. In 1971 the Federal government confined itself merely to recommending that this principle be observed. In the 1975 elections there were 1,947 candidates seeking election to the *Nationalrat*. This represented a 14.8 percent increase in candidates over 1971. There were 329 women candidates as compared with 268 in 1971 (16.9 percent in 1975; 15.8 percent in 1971). In 1975 the overall membership of women in the *Nationalrat* was 7.5 percent as compared with 5 percent in the first national elections. But the progress was very uneven. It came as no surprise that the little cantons of Appenzell–Inner Rhodes and Appenzell–Outer Rhodes had not elected any women. After all, they were entitled to only one and two seats respectively. The sit-

202

lation was similar in some of the other small cantons (Glarus, Nidwalden, Obwalden, Schaffhausen, Uri and Zug). What was difficult to comprehend was the fact that the Canton of Bern, which has the largest number of representatives in the *Nationalrat* (31) failed to elect a single woman. The surrounding area of Basel, which is entitled to seven seats, did not elect a woman. Progress was recorded in the canton of St. Gallen where three out of twelve representatives were women. In Geneva the ratio of men to women representatives was 11 to 3. It was 5 to 2 in Neuchâtel and 35 to 5 in Zurich.

There have been further impressive increases in the participation of women in the federal parliament. It was 5 percent in 1971, 7.5 percent in 1975, and 10.5 percent in 1979. The political parties have discovered that women candidates have been successful, and they have increased the number of women on the party tickets. In 1971 women represented 15.8 percent of the candidates, in 1975 the percentage increased to 16.8 and in 1979 it was 18.4.

On the other hand, as in most countries Swiss women have not been able to move up into the higher positions in the various political parties. Professional politicians contend that women draw fewer votes than men, but this may no longer be true in the urban centers. They also point out that fewer women bother to vote than men. It is true that in the 1979 national elections about 16 percent fewer women voted than men. There are various interpretations of this discrepancy. In the absence of an in-depth study of this phenomenon no single explanation is convincing. One view repeatedly mentioned in interviews is that politics in Switzerland has not greatly changed since women were given the right to vote. Politics, many women contend, is still a male domain. The rules of the game are still determined by men.

On June 14, 1981 the voters approved an amendment to Article 4 of the Constitution. As a result a second paragraph was added which reads:

> Men and women are equal before the law. The law provides for their equality, particularly in the domains of the family, education and work. Men and women are entitled to equal wages for work of equal value.[2]

The present Article 4 may be compared with Article 9 of the Draft Constitution which was presented to the Federal Council by a commis-

[2]Translation by Jürg K. Siegenthaler in *Constitutions of the Countries of the World* Oceana Publications, Inc., Dobbs Ferry, NY, 1982).

sion of experts on November 11, 1977. As translated by Dr. Siegenthaler, it reads:

1. All men and women are equal before the law.
2. No one must be impaired or given advantage on grounds of origin, sex, race, language, social position, or philosophical or political convictions or opinions.
3. Men and women have equal rights. The law provides for their equal status, particularly in the realms of the family, of education, and of work. Men and women are entitled to equal pay for work of equal value.

On the local level also, significant advances have been made recently in many parts of Switzerland. But in some of the cantons male attitudes have not changed. The most recent example was provided by the small canton of Appenzell–Inner Rhodes, which has a population of about 13,000. On April 25, 1982 the male voters voted by a show of hands in the traditional assembly (*Landsgemeinde*) to deny women the right to vote in local elections. The vote was reported to have been 4 to 1. The only surprise was the margin. Perhaps it would have been smaller if it had been a secret vote, but for the time being the men of Appenzell–Inner Rhodes want to keep things as they have always been

CHAPTER 12

THE SOUTHERN AND MEDITERRANEAN COUNTRIES AFTER WORLD WAR II

INTRODUCTION

Since the end of World War II, the ministates of Andorra and San Marino have become more a part of mainstream Europe. Malta has gained independence. Monaco has promulgated a new constitution. Gender equality has been discussed and dealt with in a variety of ways, not all of which have achieved equal rights for women.

In Italy women gained the right to vote in 1945. In the same year women's suffrage was promulgated in Portugal, but women were not entitled to vote on completely equal terms with men. In 1952 Greece put women's suffrage on a firmer basis than it had been in 1929.

Cyprus established the principle of gender equality and non-discrimination with its Constitution of 1960, Article 28 of which reads:

1. All persons are equal before the law, the administration of justice and are entitled to equal protection thereof and treatment thereby.

2. Every person shall enjoy all the rights and liberties provided for in this Constitution without any direct or indirect discrimination against any person on the ground of his community, race, religion, language, sex, political or other convictions, national or social descent, birth, color, wealth, social class, or any ground whatsoever, unless there is express provision to the contrary in this Constitution.

Constitutional approval of exceptions to the equality and non-discrimination provisions, as stated in Article 28, strongly suggests that in Cyprus, as in the other southern and Mediterranean countries, tradition and social custom will continue as dominant factors in women's rights and political participation.

ANDORRA

Although Andorra is situated between France and Spain, and although the president of France is by law and tradition the "co-prince" of this ministate, the cultural links have been much closer with Catalonia. The official language is Catalan, and the Bishop of Urgel in northern Spain, the other co-prince, has been an influential figure.

Andorra has been rather isolated from the rest of Europe, as far as political development is concerned. But in recent years, the women's rights movement has had somewhat greater influence than in the other ministates of Europe. In assessing recent developments in Andorra, it should be kept in mind that the democratization of the highly traditional regime had proceeded rather slowly. Prior to 1868, voting rights were restricted to the heads of important households (caps grossos). As a result of the 1868 electoral reform, all heads of households (caps de casa) acquired the right to vote. Universal male suffrage was not introduced until 1933, but it was abolished by decree in 1941, by Marshall Petain, in his capacity as co-prince of Andorra. It was reestablished by a decree of August 23, 1947.

After the introduction of female suffrage in France (1944), some women in Andorra felt their time had come, but it was not until 1970 that decisive action was taken. The first step came in the related field of nationality legislation. In this instance, property considerations were probably more important than women's rights, when it was stated in a decree of April 7, 1970 that children born in Andorra of a foreign father and an Andorran mother would be given a right of option, at the age of 21, to choose their nationality. The principle of equality between genders was most explicitly formulated in Article VII of this decree, which stated that "a foreign woman married to a first generation Andorran will have the right, if she requests it, to an Andorran passport, by the same right as her husband." More directly relevant was a subsequent decree, issued on April 14, 1970. This document, consisting of a single Article, contains an "Explanation of the Reasons for the Decree on the Political Rights of Andorran Women." In the opening paragraph, it is stated that "the co-princes, attentive to the needs and the legitimate aspirations of the Andorran people, consider that the moment has come to grant political rights to Andorran women, given that the constantly increasing role that women play in the Valls' (Andorra) social and economic life seems unfitted to their exclusion from public affairs." In the "Explanation" it was also noted that "the greater part of modern nations have granted the same political rights to citizens of both sexes, although in some cases access to public affairs has been accomplished in stages (etapes), in order to prepare the women progressively for their new mission." These decrees were followed by others in 1971 and 1973. English translations of relevant parts are included in the Appendix.

GREECE

by Louis Pagonis

From the end of World War II until 1949, Greece was faced with civil war. Women were not qualified to participate in the first national elections held on March 31, 1946.

The New Constitution was promulgated on January 1, 1952. It embodied what was called a "crowned democracy," but its democratic features did not satisfy the aspiration of more progressive individuals and groups. It failed to establish complete gender equality. The patriarchal system remained firmly entrenched. A further implementation of the constitutional provisions concerning the right of women to vote in national elections was provided by Act No. 2159 of June 1952, granting women the right to vote and to be elected in parliamentary elections. It stated:

Article 1

1. The right to vote in parliamentary elections shall be exercised also by women who have completed their twenty-first year of age. The restrictions on the exercise of the voting provided for in the legislation on parliamentary elections shall also apply to women. 2. Women registered on the electoral rolls or the lists of electors' identity cards of their municipality or regional administrative unit shall be entitled to exercise the aforementioned right. 3. The registration of women voters on electoral rolls or lists of electors' identity cards shall be compulsory. 4. The exercise of the voting right shall be compulsory also for women. The penalties provided for men in the act concerning parliamentary elections shall apply also to women who fail to comply with this obligation.

Article 2

Women who have completed their twenty-fifth year of age shall also have the right to be elected in parliamentary elections and shall also be subject to the relevant provisions of the legislation concerning parliamentary elections.

The first four woman deputies were elected in 1952. In 1954 women were made eligible to serve on juries. They were also qualified for judicial careers and authorized to serve as notaries as stated in Article 1 of Law no. 3192 of 21 April 1955 Concerning Public Offices exercised by women and their appointment to government posts:

Women may exercise all public functions, except ecclesiastical ones and be appointed to all posts of civil servants of the State or Public Law Legal Entities (Public Corporations) on equal terms with men.

The other articles provide as follows:

Article 2

In the armed forces of the land, sea and air forces, the Gendarmerie, City Police, Harbours' Corps, Fire Brigade, Forest Service and Coast Guard, women may occupy auxiliary posts, as determined through Royal Decrees to be issued on the proposal of the competent Ministers.

Article 3

1. The regulations in force concerning qualifications for occupying a State post or one with a public corporation apply also to women, except the one relative to military service. 2. The citizenship of women is established through certificate of the competent Mayor or Community President relative to their entry in the General Register (of citizens) and their age ascer-

tained under the terms of Law 1811/1951 Concerning Code of status of Administrative Civil Servants.

Article 4

1. The Clauses of Legislative Decree 3075/1954 (Concerning Amendment and Supplementing of Law 5026 concerning 'Court of Assizes') are maintained in force. 2. Any other general or special clause conflicting with the present law is abrogated.

The first woman mayor was elected in Corfu in 1955. The first woman cabinet member was appointed in 1956. Lina Tsaldaris became minister of health and social welfare. But there was no steady progress and no clear indication that women would have greater political influence from here on. The record was actually rather discouraging. In 1956 there was only one woman in the parliament, and although the number increased to four in 1958 it fell again to two in 1961. In 1963 only one woman was elected and in 1964 there was none. Part of the explanation for these setbacks would require a detailed analysis of the new electoral law of September 4, 1963 which distorted the principle of proportional representation.

The situation became catastrophic after Colonel Papadopoulos and his co-conspirators launched their successful coup d'état on April 27, 1967. The only positive development, which benefited only a few women, was the opening of certain careers which were formerly reserved to men. Thus, beginning in 1969 women could enter the diplomatic service. In November 1973 General Ioannides overthrew the Papadopoulos regime but was crushed in July 1974 after an ill-fated attempt to oust President Makarios of Cyprus.

A new and more promising phase began a few days later with the return of Constantin Karamanlis. The Constitution of 1952 was reinstated on an interim basis. This was followed by other legislative measures which were to pave the way for a new and more democratic regime. Parliamentary elections were held on November 17, 1974, and four women were elected.

The new Constitution went into effect on June 11, 1975. Article 4 declares that:

1. All Greeks are equal before the law.

2. Greek men and women have equal rights and equal obligations.

The latter provision is contradicted by Paragraph 6 of the same article which states that "every Greek capable of bearing arms is obliged to contribute to the defense of the Fatherland as provided by law." The military service legislation does not provide for equal rights and obligations between men and women. An important legislative measure was Law no. 133/1975 which affirmed the principle of equality between men and women and called for the equalization of wages by the end of June 1978. This objective was not reached and has yet to be attained.

In the rural areas of Greece the recent legal enactments concerning the status of women have had little effect and it will take time before the traditional patterns begin to change. But in the cities, changes are proceeding at a more accelerated rate. Educational reforms, especially the extension of compulsory education from six to nine years, which was introduced in 1977, are expected to help girls gain access to better jobs. In the field of higher education there have been impressive increases in the percentages of women attending colleges and universities. In the 1970s in some fields the number of women students attending universities doubled and even tripled. The study of law and political science is still the main avenue to civil service careers and therefore the increases in the number of female students are believed to constitute the foundation for their greater political participation. In 1978 some positions in the Greek Merchant Marine were opened to women, but the number of applicants has remained small. In 1979 women were admitted to police academies. However very few have achieved positions comparable to those of their male counterparts.

The population of Greece, according to the 1980 census, was comprized of 49.5 percent males and 51.5 percent females. Yet even though there was a higher percentage of women than men, women constituted a much smaller percentage of the work force and the number of persons completing higher education. Out of 4,809,000 females, 905,400 work at jobs outside the home. About fifty percent of these women are employed in agriculture, livestock, forestry and fishing.

Eight hundred thousand women are illiterate; 1,650,000 completed only primary education; 371,604 completed secondary education; 60,000 completed higher education; 1,454,492 women did not finish grammar school.

In 1980 the teaching staff at the University of Athens was made up of 32 percent females; the University of Thessalonica has 30 percent, Thrace 29 percent, Ioannina 36 percent, Patra 24 percent, Polytechnic Institute 26 percent, Pandios (Political Science) 43 percent, Fine Arts 10 percent, Medicine 32 percent, Law 30 percent. Of all the graduates who received post-graduate certificates, 10 percent were female. Among the graduates who received doctorate degrees, 19 percent were women.

On January 1, 1981 Greece became the tenth member of the European Economic Community, and it was expected that there would now be more effective pressure exerted from the outside to implement the equal rights provisions of the Greek Constitution of 1975.

The domestic political constitution of forces changed in the fall of 1981 as a result of the elections, which, on October 18, resulted in a victory of Andreas Papandreou and his Panhellenic Socialist Movement (*Pasok*).

A preview of things to come was provided during the election campaign in which more than 10 percent of the candidates were women. There were 250 women candidates as compared with 103 in 1977. Out of a total of 300 members, 12 women were elected. Of these, eight were Socialists. Before the elections, there were few women members. The moving spirit behind the campaign and after the election was the American-born wife of the new prime minister, Margaret Papandreou. In the new government a well known woman has become minister of culture. She is Melina Mercouri, the actress, a member of the Communist Party. In the ministry of health and welfare, there are two women undersecretaries: Anna Simodinou and Roula Kaklamanaiki.

ITALY

In Italy, as in France, many women had been prominent in the resistance. Although the deeply entrenched social attitudes, especially in the southern part of Italy, had not changed significantly, it was expected that women would be given equal rights in political affairs. The great interest which Italian women took in the politics of the early postwar period can readily be documented by statistics. In 1945, in the first municipal elections, about 81 percent of all eligible women voted. Ever since June 1944 much attention had been centered on the development of a new constitution. But it was overshadowed by the question of the form of government. The two issues were linked in 1946 in Legislative Decree No. 48 which set the date for the election of a constituent assembly as June 2, 1946. A referendum was to be held on the same day to allow the people to choose between a monarchy or a republic. The vote was 54.3 percent in favor of a republican system, with the pro-republican sentiment being much stronger in the north than in the south. Some well-informed people also believed that a majority of women, especially of middle-class backgrounds, favored the retention of the monarchy because they feared its abolition would usher in a period of great instability. The composition of the elected Constituent Assembly was very heterogeneous. There were 207 Christian Democrats, 115 Socialists, 104 Communists, 23 Republicans and 19 Liberals. Of the total 556 members, 21 were women.

The heterogeneity of this body explains in part why it took about a year and a half to produce the final text of the Constitution. It was approved by a vote of 453 to 62 on December 22, 1947 and became effective on January 1, 1948. What emerged was an outstanding document in terms of draftsmanship as well as political compromise.

The Records of the Constituent Assembly show that the women members were particularly concerned with the formulation of Articles 3 and 37 of the Constitution. The first paragraph of Article 3 states:

All citizens are invested with equal social status and are equal before the law, without distinction as to sex, race, language, religion, political opinions and personal and social conditions.

The second paragraph reflects what was later called an "opening to the left.":

It is the responsibility of the Republic to remove all obstacles of an economic and social nature which, by limiting the freedom and equality of citizens, prevent the full development of the individual and the participation of all workers in the political, economic and social organization of the country.

Article 37 stipulates that:

Female labor enjoys equal rights and the same wages for the same work as male labor. Conditions of work must make it possible for them to fulfill their essential family duties and provide for the adequate protection of mothers and children. The law prescribes the minimum age for paid labor.

The Republic prescribes special measures for safeguarding juvenile labor and guarantees equal pay for equal work.

Article 48 granted voting rights to all citizens over 21. Article 51 (1) explicitly states that "all citizens of either sex are eligible for public office and for elective positions on conditions of equality, according to the requisites established by law." Article 56 states that all "persons who have reached the age of twenty-five years are eligible for membership in the Chamber of Deputies."

Most of the relevant articles deserve attention not only from a substantive but also from a technical point of view. The wording usually avoids the common complexities that result from the use of the term "everyone," which is followed by "his." The Italian Constitution uses the plural form.

But there are a few contradictions. Article 84 states that "any citizen of fifty years of age enjoying civil and political rights is eligible for election as President of the Republic." This would appear to mean that the possibility of a female President is not ruled out.[1]

Important legislation was enacted in 1950 to protect working women's pay and employment rights during periods of pregnancy and leave after delivery. The law was amended in 1971 so as to guarantee eight weeks before and 12 weeks after delivery. During this period, women are entitled to 80 percent of their regular pay. This period can actually be extended up to six months. However, in such cases they would be entitled to only 30 percent of their pay.

In 1957, Italy was one of the founding members of the European Common Market.[2] The close links which Italy has had with the Western bloc countries has had a beneficial effect on the status of women.

From a strictly legal point of view, what has been done in Italy during the postwar period compares quite favorably with the achievements of other member states in the European Community.

The legislation which was enacted in response to the various directives has been comprehensive and has conformed in almost all respects to the standards and criteria of the Commission of the European Communities. Some of the legislation of the early 1970s has already been significantly amended in order to put the principle of equality of opportunity on a firmer basis.

Article 19 of Law No. 903/1977 provided the basis for repealing a

[1] This impression may be misleading because Article 87 which spells out important powers of the President begins every sentence with "He." There are a few other "he" references in this Constitution, but they are more in the nature of "linguistic" rather than "gender" discrimination.

[2] The Treaty of Rome was signed on March 25, 1957.

number of earlier laws concerning women and minors. This article states very clearly that "all legislative provisions at variance with the rules of this law are repealed." Also included are conflicting internal rules and administrative acts concerning individual and collective employment.

Circular No. 92/78 of December 28, 1978 identified the earlier legislative provisions which were repealed by Law No. 903/1977. Among them were certain provisions of protective laws for women of the Fascist era: Article 4 of Law No. 370/34 which provided for specified rest times for adult women. It repealed in its entirety Law No. 653/34 on the protection of women in employment. The recent trend appears to break away from the earlier philosophy that women and children are in need of special protective legislation. The key concept in the new legislation is equality even if it means a surrender of the earlier protective measures. This may also be seen in the repeal of protective measures of the post-Fascist era. Thus, in the name of equality, women are no longer banned from working on suspension bridges in the construction industry.[3]

In 1956 Article 33 of Presidential Decree No. 321/56 prohibited the employment of women for work in pneumatic caissons and decompression chambers. This article has now been repealed. If women want this kind of work, they are legally qualified to apply for it under the same terms as men, except, of course, with the understanding that they are entitled to maternity leaves, as confirmed in Articles 5 and 6 of Law No. 903/77.[4] The principle of equality was also applied to girls and boys. All previous distinctions have been repealed. Boys and girls are qualified at the age of sixteen to "do whatever" kind of work the law permits.

Law No. 903/77—The Equal Treatment Law.

To date, as already indicated, the most important piece of legislation has been Law No. 903/1977, the Equal Treatment Law. A complete English translation is included in the Appendix. Therefore it will suffice to point out a few major features and compare them with those of Council Directive 76/207.

This law was promulgated on December 9, 1977, nine months before the deadline set by the commission for the implementation of Council Directive 76/207.[5]

Article 1 reaffirms that "no discrimination of this Law shall be permitted on grounds of sex as regards employment . . . hierarchy." It went beyond the language of the Constitution and Law No. 300 of May

[3]The ban was enacted by Article 48 of Presidential Decree No. 164/54.
[4]The Commission has emphasized the need for protective legislation with regard to pregnancy and maternity.
[5]August 12, 1978.

215

1970 (Concerning the Status of Workers) in specifying what shall be deemed to constitute discrimination including "indirect" discrimination, as referred to in Article 2(1) of the Directive. It did not define indirect discrimination but listed some examples, such as "selection criteria or advertisements which imply one particular sex." (Art. 1(2)) As for direct discrimination, it referred to marital or family status as well as pregnancy. (Art. 1(1))

With respect to the principle of "equal treatment," Law No. 903/76 went beyond the scope defined in Law No. 300/1970. Article 13 of Law 903 also amended Article 15 of Law No. 300/1970. Equal treatment now covers access to employment and promotion, access to vocational guidance and training as well as conditions of employment. The directive excluded certain occupational activities in which "by reason of their nature or the context in which they are carried out, the sex of the worker constitutes a determining factor." (Article 2(2)) Law 903 is not very specific in this respect. The only reference may be found in the last paragraph of Article 1 to "fashion, art or spectacle."

The Mandate called upon the member states to carry out periodic reviews in order to determine whether a continuation of certain exclusions is justified. The commission was to be informed of the results of such assessments (Article 9(2)). Law No. 903 was not very specific in this respect, and it appears that the commission was not entirely satisfied with the reply which the Italian government sent concerning the implementation of equal treatment. On May 12, 1980, the Italian government stated that, except for the armed forces, there are no other exclusions. Women were being admitted to the police force on the basis of Law No. 1083/59 of April 7, 1959. The issue is not so much exclusion as promotion. This generalization would probably also apply to several other services; for example, customs, fire and prison personnel.

There are many areas in which social attitudes reflect more traditional values. Conversations with Italians, male and female, readily confirm this statement. Among men, especially in the lower classes, one continues to encounter a strongly expressed view that there are many jobs which most women cannot do and should not do. Aside from the requirement of physical strength, it is often stated that women have a higher record of absenteeism for one or more reasons. This absenteeism may not be a matter of one or two days. They point to interruptions due to pregnancies and maternity leaves.

Articles 1, 5 and 6 of Law No. 903/77 deal with cases of pregnancy. Article 1 prohibits discrimination in recruitment. It prohibits any inquiries prior to employment. Pregnancies which occur during employment are covered by earlier labor legislation. As previously noted, under

216

existing law mothers are entitled to leaves of up to six months. Article 7 of Law No. 1203/77 also provides for similar leaves for a father, but only if he is in fact replacing his wife in taking care of the child. There are other protective provisions in Law No. 903/77 which are not considered to constitute discrimination, such as the prohibition laid down in Article 5 which states that "in manufacturing establishments, including small workshops, the employment of women shall not be permitted between midnight and six o'clock in the morning, with the exception of those engaged in management or employed in the establishment's medical services."

One area in which Italian legislation has not gone as far as most of the other Community member states is that of legal remedies in cases of presumed discrimination. The procedure as laid down in Article 15 of Law No. 903/77 calls for an appeal by the worker or by a delegate to the *pretore*, who, in such cases, acts as labor judge.

How successful have Italian women been in gaining a greater share in political power? In 1975, the percentage of women in the Italian Chamber of Deputies was 7.8. By 1979 it had risen to 8.1. Out of a total of 630 members, there were 52 women. By far, the greatest contingent of women belonged to the Italian Communist Party (Partito Comunista Italiano) which was represented by 35 women out of a total of 191. The Christian Democrats (Democrazia Christiana) had a delegation of 261, of which only 9 were women. On a percentage basis, the largest contingent of women within a party delegation was provided by the Radical Party (Partito Radicale). Out of a total of 18 deputies, 5 were women. The other parties, including the Socialists, have hardly made a real effort to run women candidates.

In the European Parliament, the percentage of women among the Italian delegation was 13.6. Out of a total of 81 members, there were 11 women. This was the same ratio as that of Great Britain and slightly higher than Ireland. But France was represented by a delegation of which 22.2 percent were women. The poor showing is probably due to the fact that Italy had the smallest number of women candidates. Out of a total of 968 candidates, there were only 74 women (7.6 percent). By way of comparison or contrast, France had 225 women candidates out of a total of 891 (25 percent). This raises some interesting questions: why have Italian women attached less importance to the Parliament of Europe? Or have the men in the political parties possibly not been willing to share power with women?

The number of women in the civil service has grown steadily, but there has been little change in the general pattern. Very few higher positions are held by women.[6] For the most part, they are still engaged in secretarial and clerical work. There are few women who have risen to the ministerial and subministerial level. Tina Anselini served as minister of health and Franca Falcucci has had many years of experience as state secretary in the Ministry of Education.[7] In 1980 and 1981 there were no women in the Forlani and Spadolini Cabinets.

Recently, one woman observer noted that there remains a wide gap between appearances and realities as far as the political roles of women are concerned. She failed to be impressed by the number of women senators, deputies, mayors and local councillors because the decisions in matters of economics, work and foreign policy are still made by men.[8]

MALTA

From 1814 until 1964, Malta was part of the British Empire. Some partial concessions toward self-government were made as early as 1887, but they were of little practical significance. After World War I and during the inter-war period, several constitutions were granted and revoked. Representative government and male suffrage were restored in February, 1939.

In World War II, the men and women of Malta demonstrated great heroism, which was recognized in 1942 when King George VI awarded the George Cross to "the Island Fortress of Malta." It was expected that after the war the constitutional status of Malta within the Commonwealth would be upgraded, and there was some speculation that it might even become an independent state within the Commonwealth. But this development proceeded very slowly and uncertainly. In 1947, women were granted suffrage on equal terms with men.

From 1955 on, there were several formal and informal discussions in London on the future constitutional status of Malta. In 1960, the British government appointed a constitutional commission to make recommendations for a constitution for Malta. On the basis of the proposals, the Constitution was drafted and was promulgated on October 24, 1961.

In 1962, the prime minister of Malta took the necessary steps to achieve independence. In 1964, the British Parliament passed the Independence Constitution for Malta, which went into effect on September

[6]The first woman ambassador, Signora Graziella Simbolotti, was appointed in 1980 to represent Italy in seven Central American countries.

[7]There have never been more than two women State Secretaries out of a total of 56

[8]Olga Patanc: "Le femme italienne et la politique," In: Femmes et politiques autour de la mediterrannee, Ed., Christiane Souriau, Paris: L'Harmattan, 1980, p. 64.

21, 1964. On December 1, 1964, Malta joined the United Nations, and the problem of women's rights in Malta became a matter of international interest, compared with other constitutions of newly independent states. The provisions of the Maltese Constitution of 1964 were less emphatic in asserting the legal equality of men and women. Indeed, the wording then, as now, is rather unsatisfactory because it associates the term person with the male gender, and it also contains some contradictory provisions. It rules out discrimination on the basis of sex, but goes on to refer to members of the House of Representatives as if they were expected to be males only. The most pertinent sections of the Constitution are the following: 15, 33, 54, 55, 58 and 59.

Section 15 states that:

the State shall aim at ensuring that women workers enjoy equal rights and the same wages for the same work as males.

It does not mandate equal pay for equal work.

The Constitution refers to women in several articles, but it is in connection with economics rather than politics. The only references relating to politics concern the citizenship or nationality of women. (Sections 24 and 27 were amended in 1974.) There is a lengthy chapter (IV) entitled "Fundamental Rights and Freedoms of the Individual," but it contains only one short prohibition, in Section 33, on the basis of "race, place origin, political opinions, colour, creed or sex." The fundamental rights and freedoms, which are specifically listed in this section are:

a) life, liberty, security of the person, the enjoyment of property and the protection of the law;
b) freedom of conscience or expression, and of peaceful assembly and association;
c) respect for his (a person's) private and family life.

The main antidiscrimination provisions are in Section 46, which prohibits the enactment of any law "that is discriminatory either of itself or in its effect." Subsection 3 defines discriminatory as

affording different treatment to different persons attributable wholly or mainly to their respective descriptions by race, place of origin, political opinions, colour or creed whereby persons of one such description are subjected to disabilities or restrictions to which persons of another such description are not made subject or are accorded privileges or advantages which are not accorded to persons of another such description.

It is strange that in the listing of the categories of discriminatory treatment, which is the same as stated in Section 33, the term sex is omitted. Whether this was an oversight or a deliberate omission is not known.

Section 54, which deals with the qualifications for membership of the House of Representatives provides that "a person" shall be qualified if "he" meets the qualifications for registration as a voter, as specified in Section 58. In its original form that section stated, in somewhat complex language, that a "person" shall not be qualified to be so registered unless:

a) he is a citizen of Malta
b) he has attained the age of eighteen years and
c) he is a resident of Malta and has during the immediately preceding his registration been a resident for a continuous period of one year or periods amounting in the aggregate to one year.

The use of the plural form would have avoided all these misleading suggestions of male exclusiveness not only in these two sections but in many others where only males appear to be persons.

Major changes were made in the text of the Constitution on December 13, 1974, when Malta became an independent republic. It would have been a good time to eliminate these male-oriented references. In fact, there is evidence that the drafters of the amended document were insensitive to these deficiencies. An example may be found in the provisions concerning the newly established Employment Commission, which was intended to guard against discrimination in employment. To accomplish this, two new sections (122A and 123) were added to the Constitution.

Section 122 (A)1 provides that "there shall be an employment Commission for Malta, which shall consist of a chairman and four other members."

After referring to members in the plural, there follow many sentences which suggest that the possibility of a woman serving as a member of this important commission hardly entered the minds of the drafters.

According to Section 122 A(2) the president is to appoint the members of the commission. He is expected to consult the prime minister and the leader of the opposition prior to making such appointments. Aside from all the references to the commission members as of male gender, there is another unfortunate deficiency. It may be found in Section 122 A(8), which reads:

> It shall be the function of the Employment Commission to ensure that, in respect of employment, no distinction, exclusion or preference that is not justifiable in a democratic society is made or given in favour or against any person by reason of his political opinion.

This would have been a very good place to insert a specific prohibition of discrimination on the grounds of gender, along with other unconstitutional forms of discrimination. It may be argued, of course, that the equal rights of women in matters of employment are fully protected in Section 7, which provides that "the State recognises the right of all citizens to work and shall promote such conditions as will make this right effective."

Section 13 may also be cited, because it imposes an obligation upon the State "to protect work" and to "provide for the professional or vocational training and advancement of workers." This is a very important provision, because it is a precondition for the professional advancement of women. Progress has been made toward providing more educational and vocational opportunities for females, but the Constitution could help to accelerate the process by the inclusion of more explicit obligations toward the provision of equal opportunities and equal access.

It appears the drafters of the Constitution of Malta assumed that the key offices of the newly independent state would be occupied by men. As long as Malta remained in the Commonwealth, the head of the state would be a woman, Queen Elizabeth II. But in 1974, Malta became a republic, and the queen was replaced by a president. It obviously did not occur to the drafters of the necessary constitutional amendment that within less than a decade a woman might occupy the office of the president.

Section 49, of the Constitution, as amended in 1974, states that there shall be a President: "who shall be appointed by Resolution of the House of Representatives."

Instead of listing the required qualifications for any person seeking the appointment to the Office of President, Section 49(2) of the Constitution starts out with a negative statement:

A person shall not be qualified to be appointed to the office of President, if—a) he is not a citizen of Malta, or . . .

This is followed by two more unnecessary references to "he."

Chapter VI, which deals with the Executive, has several more references to the president, followed by provisions concerning the prime minister and other ministers. All of them seem to be offices "for men only."

As it turned out, a few women have been able to move into these constitutionally male domains. One woman has stood out over a long period of time, Agatha Barbara. She had been a member of the Malta Labour Party Executive since 1947, and has chaired the women's section of the MLP. In 1971, following the elections, Agatha Barbara was first appointed minister of education and culture. In 1974, she was appointed minister of labour, employment and welfare. The culmination of her career came on February 16, 1982 when the House of Representatives elected her president of Malta.

MONACO

Until 1911, Monaco was an absolute monarchy. By a decree of January 5, 1914 Prince Albert I granted a Constitution which paved the way for certain institutional transformations and the elevation of subjects to citizens. This process was repeatedly interrupted but proceeded more consistently after World War II. When the Constitution of the Principality was amended on November 18, 1917, a legislative assembly and a national council were established. The right to vote for these bodies was given to men only. They alone were qualified for election.

In 1945, women were granted the right to vote in municipal elections. Full legal equality was achieved on December 17, 1962, when the new and current Constitution was promulgated. Article 17, of this short, but carefully drafted, document states that all "Monegasque citizens are equal before the law." This principle is restated and elaborated in Articles 53, 54 and 79.

Article 53 made provisions for a National Council consisting of eighteen members. They are elected for five years "by universal direct suffrage and by list vote." All citizens "of both sexes of at least twenty one years of age who have possessed Monegasque nationality for at least five years have the right to vote." Article 54 provides that "all Monegasque citizens who are at least twenty-five years of age are qualified for election to the National Council," but the same Article contains a list of offices which are incompatible with the Mandate of National Councillor.

The territory of the Principality is considered to be a single commune (Article 78) administered by a mayor and associates who are appointed by a communal council (Article 79) consisting of 15 members. (Article 80) "All citizens of both sexes of at least twenty-one years of age have the right to vote" (Article 79) for members of the Communal Council. There is no incompatibility between membership in the Communal Council and the National Council. (Article 80) The Communal Council meets every three months for not more than fifteen days. (Article 81)

On February 24, 1963, women voted for the first time in the elections for the National Council. Since that time, there have been no significant changes in the status of women. The legal system, which is of French origin, has been only slightly modified.

During the French occupation, from 1792 to 1815, French legislation was introduced in the Principality of Monaco. The family code, derived from the French Civil Code of 1804, was revised in 1880 and reissued in 1958. There have been a few supplements since that time. As far as property rights of women are concerned, these revisions have had little effect. Essentially, Monegasque married women cannot engage in commercial transactions without the consent of their husbands. This applies also to foreign women who marry Monegasque men. On the basis of a law of June 26, 1900, a Monegasque woman who has lost her Monegasque nationality by having married a foreigner can, if she should become widowed, recover her original nationality, provided she plans to reside in Monaco.

PORTUGAL

by Maria Regina Tavares da Silva

The Second World War, with all the changes it brought about, was also bound to affect women in Portugal, although in a different and less visible way than in other European countries.

The end of the War and the following years were going to witness a new though short revival of the National Council of Portuguese

Women. Maria Lamas, a feminist writer, became its new president. She said: "The war gave to women, especially young women, a new sense of life and a new self-trust, it made them realize how unfair their situation was." The Council was opened to new women, not an elite anymore but women of all social spheres.

In 1946, a new project of law proposed that married women should not have the right to vote. The Council protested, and the existing law was changed in the opposite sense. It extended the right to vote to a new category of women, those paying a certain amount of tax. But, the different requirements for men and women remained. (Law no. 2015)

In 1948, following another successful action by the Council—a large exhibition of books written by women, accompanied by lectures and discussions—the ·Council was closed by the government and its organized action came to an end. From now on, only individual women and individual voices would keep conveying feminist ideals. Maria Lamas was one of them. In the same year, she published an interesting study on the situation of Portuguese Women, "As Mulheres do meu País" (The Women of my Country), and later on, in 1952, a learned history of women, A Mulher no Mundo (Woman in the World). The jurist Elina Guimarães was another feminist who constantly wrote about women and for women—as she still says nowadays—to keep the flame burning in the middle of a dark period.

By the end of the sixties, the following changes were being made:

In 1966 Convention no. 100 of the International Labour Office, concerning equal pay for both sexes, was ratified by the National Assembly.

In 1967, a new Civil Code came into force. According to its principles, the family was again headed by the husband, who is meant to decide on all matters concerning marital life. On the other hand, new rights concerning their working capabilities were granted women.

In 1968, Law no. 2137 proclaimed equality of political rights for men and women, with the exception of local elections, where the principle of the head-of-the-family still prevails.

In 1970, a working group for the participation of women in economic and social life was created within the Public Administration. As it made the first survey of legal discriminations against women, it also proposed alterations, mainly in regard to family law.

In 1971 the Constitution was amended, keeping, in what concerns women, "the differences justified by nature" but dropping "the interest of the family."

A controversial feminist book was published in 1972. It shattered the traditional view of woman and her role. "Novas Cartas Portuguesas" (New Portuguese Letters), was written by the "three Marias." Maria

Teresa Horta, Maria Velho da Costa, and Maria Isabel Barreno. Forbidden and confiscated, it still remains an important factor for reflection and change.

In 1973 the Commission for Social Policy Concerning Women was created following the action and the mandate of the previous working group.

The Revolution of 1974 was going to change everything, including lives of women. First measures concerning women were access to the magistracy (Decree-Law 492/74), to the diplomatic service (Decree-Law 308/74), and to all posts of local administration (Decree-Law 251/74).

In 1975 some dispositions of the Concordat between the Church and the State were changed to allow civil divorce to be granted to people married in the Catholic Church.

In 1976 a new Constitution was approved and put into force. It openly recognized equality between men and women in all spheres. Family and work, equal pay and education, maternity and family planning, all these areas are fairly treated in regard to equality and women's rights.

Other laws were passed dealing with sectorial but significant matters. Maternity leave of ninety days was approved (Decree-Law 112/76); Family planning consultations were created within the health structures (Secretary of State for Health Order of the 16th March); etc.

In 1977, the Commission on the Status of Women was institutionalized under the prime-minister (Decree-Law 485/77), thus recognizing its importance as a vital instrument to implement policies concerning the Status of Women.

In 1978 new dispositions of the Civil Code, that was thoroughly revised, came into force (Decree-Law 496/77). Equality between the spouses came back into family law, and the figure of the head-of-the-family died out again.

Another important legal provision was approved in 1979. It deals with equality between men and women in work and employment, including equal pay, equal treatment and equal opportunities (Decree-Law 392/79).

1979 was also the year in which a woman—Maria de Lourdes Pintasilgo—became prime minister for the first and only time.

In 1980, a legal instrument on advertising included some provisions concerning the image of women (Decree-Law 421/80). It was now possible to say that the most important legislative steps had been taken. (See Appendix for legislation and anaylsis) This situation opened the possibility for an early ratification of the United Nations Convention on the Elimination of All Forms of Discrimination against Women, which Portugal was the fifth country to ratify. Still there is much to be done in informing and educating women and in influencing public opinion on women's rights and responsibilities.

Social and political participation are still very low. According to information supplied by political parties in 1980, the percentage of women within the parties varies from 20.5 to 40.1, with no woman leaders and very small representation in leading posts.

There are only 22 women in Parliament in a total of 250 deputies. And in the VIII Constitutional Government, which took office in September 1981, only 4 women hold governmental posts in a total number of 60.

In all these years women's groups—although there are not many in Portugal—together with the Commission on the Status of Women have helped to make this development process go further. From the first survey and identification of existing discriminations, to the proposal and implementation of actions to change the situation, and finally to the information of women, and the launching of research on women, much ground has been covered. Full implementation of Women's Rights in Portugal, however, still has a long way to go.

SAN MARINO

San Marino is the smallest of the European ministates, but no European country can claim an older and more continuous republican tradition. Its traditional institutions have been based not only on the patriarchal principle but on a system of representation by the heads of families. In 1797, after Napoleon had conquered northern Italy, he decided that San Marino was a small republican gem which should be preserved. The Congress of Vienna confirmed its independent status. During the turbulent 1840s, San Marino served as a refuge for nationalists and republicans. The most prominent personality was Garibaldi, who is still remembered with much respect and affection. In 1900 a compilation of the laws and decrees of the Republic of San Marino was published.[1] It was done at the behest of the *Capitani Reggenti* by Torquato C. Giannini and M. Bonelli. Drastic constitutional reforms were undertaken by means of electoral legislation in 1906, 1909, and 1920.

During the Fascist era in Italy, San Marino's electoral system of 1920 was replaced by Italian Fascist regulations.

In 1943, an earlier electoral law of 1906 was reinstated. In 1945, liberalizing legislation was passed. The medieval *Arengo* which used

[1]*Raccolta delle Leggi Decreti della Republica di San Marino.* Prima Edizione Ufficiale. Citta di Castello, 1900.

to be composed of the heads of all families was made much less patriarchal by including all males over the age of twenty-one. Some changes were also made in the ancient legal system. Law No. 35/1953 of September 22, 1953 gave women a measure of legal authority in business transactions, and Law No. 37/1953 of the same date introduced the institution of civil marriages without touching the traditional ecclesiastical provisions, as stated in the *Codex Juris Canonici* of May 27, 1917. On the basis of this new legislation, males were permitted to marry upon completion of their 16th year. Females were allowed to marry at the age of 14. Civil marriages were performed by the state secretary of the interior (Segretario di Stato per gli affair interni) with the assistance of an "Ufficiale dello Stato Civile." No changes were made in the traditional patriarchal system as far as children were concerned. The "patria potestas" was affirmed in the new legislation.

General elections were held on August 15, 1955, and the Communists and left-wing Socialists scored a major electoral victory. Together they occupied 35 out of the 60 seats in the Grand and General Council. This body elected two *Capitani Reggenti*. One was a Communist and the other a left-wing Socialist. A prolonged crisis followed. It was eventually resolved by a new electoral law of December 23, 1958. This law established women's suffrage in San Marino. The pertinent provisions are the following:

ELECTORAL LAW OF 23 DECEMBER 1958

Article 1
All citizens of San Marino of full age, including naturalized citizens, are entitled to vote, provided that they are not disqualified in accordance with the provisions of article 2.

Article 2
The following persons shall be disqualified from voting: (a) persons placed under legal disabilities or incapacitated by reason of infirmity of mind; (b) persons permanently or temporarily deprived of full legal capacity by sentence of a court or sentenced to criminal penalties for corrupt electoral practices or offences; (c) persons permanently or temporarily deprived of political rights by sentence of a court.

Article 4
The electoral lists, of which there shall be one for each section, shall be compiled officially, in duplicate, men and women being listed separately in alphabetical order and the following particulars being given for each voter: (a) name and surname and, in the case of married

women or widows, husband's surname; (b) names of mother and father; (c) place and date of birth; (d) academic qualifications; (e) profession or trade; (f) place where the voter is living and, if the voter resides abroad, State and place of residence and address abroad; . . .

. . . .

Article 5

. . . .

those persons who are registered in the lists that have been definitively approved and who have completed 21 years of age on the day of the elections shall be entitled to vote.

. . . .

Article 18

In addition to the general qualifications for voters set out in articles 1 and 2, all persons seeking election must: (a) be able to read and write; (b) have completed 25 years of age on the day of the elections; (c) not hold church office; (d) be domiciled in the Republic; (e) be of the male sex.

. . . .

Article 59

The commencement of the active electoral rights for women shall be fixed by a forthcoming legislative provision which shall be promulgated by 30 April 1959.

The required additional legislative provision was enacted by Law of April 29, 1959, No. 17, Extension to Women of the Right to Vote, which read: "Under article 59 of the electoral law of 23 December 1958, No. 36, the commencement of electoral rights of women will be effective as from 1 January 1960."

Women voted for the first time in the general elections of September 13, 1964. The participation of women resulted in a change of the party alignment. A coalition of Christian Democrats and Social Democrats now dominated the Grand and General Council. Together they held 39 out of the 60 seats. In the 1970s further progress was made toward the equalization of rights between men and women. On September 10, 1973, Law No. 10 was passed providing for the "equalization of the rights of women." It went into effect on October 1, 1973.[2]

On December 20, 1973, Law No. 56, published on December 27, 1973, modified Article 22 of the Electoral Law No. 36 of December 23, 1958. On July 8, 1974, the Council passed Law No. 59 entitled "Dichiarazione dei diritti dei cittadini e dei principi fondamentali dell'

[2]*Bolletino Ufficiale della Republica di San Marino*. San Marino, December 28, 1973.

ordinamento sammarinese." This brief law of 16 articles is, constitutionally, of fundamental importance.

General elections were held for the Grand and General Council. This was the first time that women were eligible to run as candidates. Out of a total of 22, three women were elected: two Communists and one Christian Democrat. The latter was subsequently named minister of public works.

In March 1981 two new Captains-Regent were elected by the Grand and General Council to serve for six months. For the first time a woman was elected to this post. Signora Maria Lea Pedini Angelini, who is a member of the Socialist Party, was elected to the highest position in the government of San Marino.

SPAIN

The highly authoritarian regime, which Franco had established in the summer of 1936, was somewhat modified in March 1943 when the Cortes were convened for the first time. Franco wanted to involve them in some of the institutional transformations which he deemed necessary for its stabilization and orderly development. They were to share with him and at his discretion the power to make laws. Two major laws were promulgated in 1945: the Statute Law of the Spaniards (*Fuero de los Españoles*) of July 17 and the National Referendum Law of October 22. They may be regarded as milestones in the process of institutional change, but they did not have an immediate effect on the status of women. Indeed the word "women" does not appear in the *Fuero de los Españoles*. Neither do the terms "gender" or "sex". Article 3 stated, "The law protects in equal measure the right of every Spaniard, without preference in respect of classes and without favor in respect of persons." In the very brief Law on the National Referendum of October 22, 1945 there is a reference to both genders in Article 2: "The referendum shall be extended to all men and women of the nation over the age of twenty-one years." In the *Fuero* much emphasis was put on family and family honor. Article 22 declared that: "The State recognizes and protects the family as a natural institution and the foundation of society, with rights and duties anterior and superior to every positive human law. Matrimony shall be indissoluble. The state shall give special assistance to large families."

The patriarchal principle was, of course, taken for granted, but reference was made to the possibility of suspending it. This may be seen in the text of Article 23: "Parents are obliged to feed, educate and instruct

229

their children. The State shall suspend the exercise of the *patria potestas* or withhold such privilege from those who do not exercise it honorably, and shall transfer the guardianship and education of minors to those qualified by law to undertake this duty."

As far as political rights and participation are concerned, reference was made to them in Articles 10 and 11. Article 10 declared that

All Spaniards have the right to participate in public functions of a representative nature, through the family, the municipality and the trade union, without prejudice to other forms of representation as established by law.

According to Article 11 "All Spaniards shall be eligible for public office in accordance with their merit and capacity."

A similar statement may be found in Principle VIII of The Law on the Principles of the National Movement of May 17, 1958. But it was more emphatic in stating, "Any political organization whatever outside this representative system shall be deemed illegal." Women's organizations were not deemed to be political and thus not illegal. But they were controlled by very conservative females who shared traditional views about the status of women.

Although under Franco women retained the right to vote and were eligible to run for public office, they made few if any gains. The regime emphasized traditional values and traditional ways of life. As stated in Principle V of the Law on the Principles of the National Movement:

The National Community is founded on man, the bearer of eternal values, and on the family, the basis of society; but individual and collective interests must be always subordinate to the common good of the Nation, constituted by generations past, present and future. The Law upholds in equal measure the rights of every Spaniard.

While the political status of women remained unchanged, it should be noted that some efforts were made toward the equalization of the rights of women in the field of private law. Work on amending the Civil Code began in 1958 and subsequently changes were made in the legislation concerning education and access to various professions. But side by side with these efforts measures were taken which show that the traditional attitudes toward the role of women in society and politics remained strongly entrenched. Women were to be protected rather than enabled to compete with men. Thus legislation was enacted in 1952 establishing the *Patronato de Proteccion de la Mujer* in the ministry of justice. As the name suggested, its function was to protect women and to ensure public morality.

The Constitutive Law of the Cortes of July 17, 1942 was frequently amended in the 1950s and 1960s but only one amendment specifically referred to women's rights: The State Organic Act No. 1 of January 10, 1967, which stated that the purpose of the amendment was "to admit to the Cortes a new group of members representing the family and elected by heads of families and married women, in accordance with the principle of equal political rights for women." But this provision did not change the political system. Politics for all practical purposes remained a male monopoly. In the field of labor law, however, some changes brought improvements to working conditions of women workers. These changes were made in the late 1960s in response to widespread strikes and disturbances. In 1971 a *Comision Nacional de Trabajo Femenino* was created by an order of the ministry of labor.

In 1975 important changes were made in the Spanish Civil Code by a law of May 2, 1975 which removed certain highly distasteful anti-feminist features. As in the Napoleonic Code women had been expected to "obey their husbands" (Article 57) and follow them to their place of residence (Article 58). According to the previous version of Article 60 "The husband was the representative of his wife and she could not enter into legal obligations without her husband's consent." The new Article 62 moved definitely toward legal equality of married men and women by stating that the capacity to work of either was not affected by marriage.

The *Subdireccion General de la Mujer*, was created on August 27, 1977 in the ministry of culture. It started its work with only 29 persons to focus on the media so as to change the traditional image of and attitude toward women, but the scope of its work was subsequently expanded and it has become the most important body for the protection of women's rights. The *Comision Nacional de Trabajo Femenino* was abolished in 1978. With the promulgation of the Spanish Constitution on December 26, 1978 a solid foundation was laid for the advancement of women. The most pertinent articles are Articles 14 and 23. Article 14 declares that:

> Spaniards are equal before the law, without any discrimination for reasons of birth, race, sex, religion, opinion or any other personal or social condition or circumstance.

Article 23 links the principle of gender equality with political participation:

1. Citizens have the right to participate in public affairs, directly or through representatives freely elected in the periodic elections by universal suffrage. 2. They also have the right to accede, under conditions of equality to public functions and positions, in accordance with the requirements established by law.

Article 32 establishes the principle of gender equality with respect to marriage legislation:

1. Man and woman have the right to contract matrimony with full juridical equality. 2. The law shall regulate the forms of matrimony, the age and capacity for contracting it, the rights and duties of the spouses, causes for separation and dissolution and their effects.

The economic aspects are dealt with in Article 35 (1):

All Spaniards have the duty to work and the right to work, to the free selection of profession or office career, to advancement through work and to a sufficient remuneration to satisfy their needs and those of their family, while in no case can there be discrimination for reasons for sex.

Chapter IV (Articles 53 and 54) concerns the "guarantees of liberties and fundamental rights." Article 53 (2) authorizes any citizen to make a claim before the regular courts, and Article 54 makes provision for the establishment of a *Defensor del Pueblo*. An organic law is to provide the details. The Defender of the People is to function as the High Commissioner of the Cortes. He/she is to be appointed by them and report to them. On December 26, 1978 these provisions were implemented by Law 62/1978 concerning The judicial protection of fundamental rights. The Organic Law 2/1979 concerning the Constitutional Tribunal (*Ley Organica del Tribunal Constitucional*) was another important step against discrimination.

A further strengthening in the economic position of women was achieved with the promulgation on March 10, 1980 of the new Statute of Workers (*Estatuto de los Trabajadores*). Article 28 imposes upon employers an obligation to pay equal wages for equal work.[1]

[1]"El empresario está obligado a pagar, por la prestación de un trabajo igual, el mismo salario, tanto por salario base como por los complementos salariales, sin distinción alguna por razón de sexo."

232

The legal foundations for gender equality have been established. When it comes to political participation the progress has been less impressive. Out of a total of 350 members in Parliament, 21 are women. There have been no major advances on the part of women into the higher echelon of state administration. But there is one woman in the cabinet, and she has attracted considerable attention. The new minister of culture is Soledad Becerril de Atienza. She has emphasized the importance of increasing educational opportunities for girls, and in this respect Spain has made great advances.

TURKEY

by Ilhan Arsel

President Ismet Inonu lacked the charisma of Ataturk but was a very able statesman who steered a careful course in foreign and domestic affairs. He kept Turkey out of World War II and laid the foundations for improved relations with the West. As has already been suggested, the period after World War II was not a good one for the political advancement of women. Between 1946 and 1950, the percentage of women in the Grand National Assembly dropped to 1.93.[1]

According to political scientists specializing in Turkish affairs, the reason for the decline in the number of women representatives in Parliament was twofold: the transition to a multiparty system and the adoption of universal suffrage, both of which occurred in 1946 and altered the preferential system of choice for women in elections. Following the 1950 elections, which brought in a majority with a growing dislike for a liberal policy and social revolution, the Democratic Party Government began flirting with the traditionalists and banked heavily on the religious feelings of the rural population. This policy resulted "in the encouragement of conservative and reactionary views, mainly in the newly emerging larger towns and ports, where a return to the wearing of the black veil, and a decrease of girls' registration in the vocational schools was partly encouraged by social pressure."[2] With the adoption of a new electoral law in 1961 which favored the primaries, those who were eliminated in the primaries had very little chance of being elected. Since women—especially in the provinces—were regarded as unqualified in matters of politics, the participation of women in the primaries became practically nil.

Between 1950 and 1954, the percentage of women in the Parliament

[1] Out of 465 members, there were only 9 women.
[2] N. Abadan, op. cit., p. 9.

dropped to an all-time low of 0.6. It rose to 0.73 between 1954 and 1957, and to 1.31 between 1957 and 1960.[3]

The regime headed by Adnan Menderes had become increasingly repressive and lost much of its earlier popularity. Vigorous student demonstrations were held in the latter part of April 1960. On May 25, there were fistfights in the Turkish Parliament. During the night of May 26, a bloodless revolution or coup by 38 military officers was carried out. The Grand National Assembly was dissolved. The president of the republic was arrested along with Prime Minister Menderes and his cabinet. Pro-Menderes members of the Grand National Assembly were also taken into custody. All kinds of controversial acts followed, but eventually the National Union Committee which ran the government promulgated a law which called for the creation of a constituent assembly. This body commenced its work on January 6, 1961.[4] It benefitted greatly from the preparatory work which had been undertaken by a group of qualified jurists and political scientists from the universities of Ankara and Istanbul. The final text of the new Constitution was adopted on May 27 and promulgated on May 31, 1961. It was approved in a popular vote on July 9, 1961 by 62 percent of the voters. The Constitution puts great emphasis on fundamental rights. It contains many provisions which were intended to assure equality before the law and thus serve the interests of women.

Article 12 declares that "All individuals are equal before the law irrespective of language, race, sex, political opinion, philosophical views, religion or religious sect. No privileges shall be granted to any individual, family, group or class."

Great emphasis has been placed on what are called "social and economic rights and duties." An entire chapter (III) consisting of 19 articles is devoted to these rights and duties. Article 42 states that "it is the right and duty of every individual to work." The State is to protect workers and promote employment. But some provisions may be overprotective and deemed to be discriminatory. According to Article 43, "No individual can be employed at a job that does not suit his age, capacity and sex. Children, young people and women shall be accorded special protection in terms of conditions of work."

Article 45 seeks to assure equity in wages, but it does not guarantee equity in employment or access to employment. Article 43 could indeed be used to keep women out of fields of employment on the grounds that they are unsuited for certain kinds of work.

[3]The size of the Grand National Assembly had been expanded or overexpanded to 610 members. There were only 8 women between 1957 and 1960.

[4]The Constituent Assembly consisted of 274 members of whom 3 (1.09 %) were women.

The relative lack of opportunities for women is closely related to the problem of providing easier access to education beyond the primary grades. Education is characterized in Article 50 as "one of the foremost duties of the State." According to this article, "primary education is compulsory for all citizens, male and female, and shall be provided free of charge in state schools." Although the number of girls attending primary schools has expanded tremendously, the results have been far from satisfactory. Despite all the constitutional and legislative measures, little real progress has been made in the educational field as far as the female population is concerned. Today, after fifty years of the Republic, 63.7 percent of the women of Turkey are still illiterate, and only 6.4 percent have some knowledge of the alphabet. In other words, seven out of ten women do not know how to read and write. Education in the higher grades is another problem. Even today there are very few who can afford to continue their study. In 1974, 52 percent of elementary school graduates were economically unable to go to the higher schools; of those attending the universities, 53.6 percent were from middle-class families (civil servant or military), 16.1 percent were from families with business or professional income, 15.5 percent from families of land-owners or farmers, 15.7 percent were from families of workers, and only 15 percent of them were girls.

The right to elect and be elected is defined in Article 55 of the Constitution. "All citizens are entitled to elect and be elected, pursuant to the conditions provided in the law. Elections shall be free and secret and shall be conducted on the basis of equality, direct suffrage, open counting and classification." The Constitution does not stipulate the voting age. This is determined by the laws on elections. There are three statutes dealing with the elections of the Parliament (the Grand National Assembly) which consists of two Houses: National Assembly and Senate of the Republic. These statutes are: Law No. 298, April 26, 1961 on "General Principles of the Elections"; Law No. 298, April 26, 1961 on "The Elections of the Members of the Senate of the Republic"; Law No. 306, May 25, 1961 on "Elections of the Deputies". According to these statutes, every Turkish man and woman over 21 years of age has the right to vote for the election of the members of both Houses. The qualifications for membership in both Houses are the same for both sexes: every Turkish man and woman over 30 years of age who is able to read and write may be elected to the National Assembly for a term of 4 years. (Art. 68) The membership of this assembly is 450, as fixed in the Constitution (Art. 67) and subject to change only by constitutional amendment. All of its members are elected by direct ballot.

The qualifications for Senate membership are higher, but again the same for both sexes: every Turk who has completed his or her fortieth year, and received a university education may be elected to the Senate of the Republic for a term of 6 years. (Art. 72) There are 150 elected senators. There are also 15 senators appointed by the president of the Republic. (They do not have to satisfy the condition of higher education, but must be distinguished in their field; Art. 72/2)

Currently, activities by political parties have been banned by the military regime. It is therefore interesting to read what the drafters of the Constitution of 1961 declared in Article 56: "Whether in power or in opposition political parties are indispensable entities of democratic political life." The same article states that "citizens are entitled to found political parties and to join in or withdraw from them pursuant to pertinent rules and procedures." No prior authorization was to be required. The role of women in political parties can easily be overrated. Some observers have noted that the small parties often include the names of several women on their lists of candidates. To understand this political phenomenon, it is necessary to point out that the electoral laws stipulate that the parties must present an equal number of candidates in each district. In some of them, the chances for election are very slim and male candidates do not want to risk defeat. Apparently, women are considered politically more expendable, and so the small parties offer women candidates. The large parties do not afford many opportunities to their women members. They are rarely entered as candidates. Between 1961 and 1977, there were only 351 women candidates out of a total of 135,000 (2.6 percent). Only 25 were elected to the Grand National Assembly. Twenty-one of these were chosen from the lists of the big parties: the Justice Party and the Republican Party.[5]

Years	JP	RPP	RSPDP	NP	NMP	NSP	TUP	TLP	NTP	Ind.	Total
1961	9 (2)	6	——	—	10 (1)	—	—	—	8	4	37
1965	7 (3)	14 (3)	—	8	12	—	—	15 (1)	17 (1)	2	76
1969	6 (2)	12 (2)	11—	13 (1)	6	—	8	7	22	3	88
1973	5 (2)	6 (3)	1312 (1)	12	15	1	2	—	—	9	75
1977	8 (2)		4 (2) 3011	—	14	—	1	4	—	2	75
Total	35	42	23 54	33	57	1	11	26	47	22	351

[5]Percentage of women candidates in relation to the total number of candidates (Between 1961-1977). Chart.

236

According to the latest figures, the female population of Turkey in 1975 was 19,603,000, about 48.6 percent of the total population (40,348,000). Generally speaking, women are less interested in politics than men and they participate less in political activities. However, studies have shown that working women are much more active in political life than nonworking women; especially women industrial workers and lower-middle-class women participate more actively at the polls than women agricultural workers and upper-middle-class women. The percentage is 96.5 and 89, respectively, as opposed to 82.9 for the last two categories combined. These figures suggest a relationship between voting participation and certain categories of economic life. It has been established that the participation of married women at the polls is higher than that of nonmarried or divorced women. As to married couples, 83.8 percent of the wives and husbands vote together, and in a majority of cases women vote the same way as their husbands.

Of the 116 women who were elected to Parliament between 1935 and 1977, 68 percent were university graduates. Although the female population is less well-educated than men, women representatives in Parliament had had much more education than their male colleagues. The percentage of women representatives during the entire postwar period has never risen above 1.93. This was at the very beginning of the period, and it was a drastic decline from the previous decade. Between 1946 and 1950, participation remained at the 1.93 level. It dropped sharply in 1950 to 0.6. In 1954 it rose to 0.73, and in 1957 to 1.31. In the Constituent Assembly 1.09 percent of the members were women. Between 1961 and 1965, the percentage of women in the National Assembly dropped to 0.7, rose to 1.7 between 1965 and 1969 and fell again between 1969 and 1973 to 1.1. Between 1973 and 1977, the percentage was 1.3. After that it was 0.9. The number of seats in the National Assembly remained the same after 1961: 450 seats. There were never more than 8 women members. In the Senate, out of a total of 150 members, there were usually 3 women (2 percent). Between 1961 and 1965 there were only 2 (1.3 percent). The first woman to serve in a Turkish cabinet was Dr. Turkan Akyol who became minister of health in March 1971. But she served only a few months until the end of the year. Two years later, Neftçi Neftei was made Deputy Speaker of the National Assembly.

Turning to the situation of women in public employment, it should be noted that according to Article 58 "every Turk is entitled to enter public service. In hiring personnel, no discrimination shall be made other than job qualifications." As noted earlier, the percentage of women in public service was relatively large before World War II. It continued to grow after the war. By 1977, 244,305 women (25.3 percent) were public employees. However, the percentage of women in the higher echelon was very small. The greatest number were employed by the Ministry of Education, the Ministry of Health, and the Post Office.

Military service has remained an exclusive male obligation, but the Constitution makes provisions for alternate services. As stated in Article 60, "Every Turk has the right and obligation of patriotic service. The method of accomplishment of this obligation to serve in the armed forces or in public services shall be regulated by law."

In the legal system, the great advances that were made during the Ataturk regime have not continued. Indeed, one might go so far as to say that much of the system has remained stagnant and in some areas there has even been retrogression.

In 1961, a British scholar wrote that "in spite of the legal emancipation and the suppression of the Sharia, the villages are still quite backward in this respect. The modern urban Turk would have foreigners believe that all Turkish women are as free as in Europe. In theory they are, but old customs die hard, and even in the villages quite near to big centers one only rarely sees a woman's face. Here veils are still common, and there is no such thing as a village function or dance in the People's House at which women and girls attend. In the remoter parts of Anatolia Plateau, the old custom of the seclusion of women is as strong as it has ever been."[6]

G. Lewis noted more than a dozen years later that "although the law recognizes only civil marriages and civil divorce, in country districts, particularly in the east, marriages are still contracted in front of the *imam* in accordance with Islamic practice which allows a man up to four wives at a time, while divorce is still in the old Islamic form of repudiation."[7]

To what extent the gap between legal norms and actual conditions has been narrowed is difficult to assess unless one undertakes a much broader study and examines in depth prevailing practices in various parts of the country. As far as legal norms are concerned under the Civil Code, which, as previously noted, is based very largely on the Swiss Civil Code, the married woman has equal rights in specifically defined family matters. The appreciation of the principle of equality begins with the engagement. As stated in Article 82 of the Turkish Civil Code, mutual

---

[6]M. P. Price, *A History of Turkey, From Empire to Republic*, Humanities Press, Inc., New York, 1961, pp. 188-89.

[7]*Modern Turkey*, New York, Praeger, 1974, p. 236. Several important studies have been undertaken especially by Deniz Kandiyoti, who has also written in English.

agreement and promises by the fiances are essential conditions for marriage. Proxies may not be used and neither parents nor guardians have the right to enter into an engagement on behalf of persons to be married. The minimum age is 17 for the groom and 15 for the bride. (Articles 88, 90) The legal age of majority is 18. For persons under 18, parental consent is required. An engagement can be ended by mutual agreement or by unilateral breach of one of the fiances. The marriage ceremony must be celebrated by an authorized person (in general, the mayor) and it is a punishable offense for any member of the clergy to celebrate a marriage before the civil ceremony has been performed. (C.C. Art. 108; Criminal Code, Art. 237) The spouses owe each other fidelity, support, assistance and the duty of cohabitation on an equal basis. (C.C. Art. 151-153) Parental authority over children is exercised jointly by the father and mother, but in cases of disagreement in such matters as the choice of names for children, schooling, property rights and other legal issues, the opinion of the father prevails. (C.C. Art. 262-264, 268, 273, 283) However, upon the divorce, the judge has discretionary power to give the parental authority over the children to one of the spouses. The husband is still the head of the family. He has the legal right to represent it in all matters. Although the wife can act on behalf of the family unit for certain domestic needs, the husband has the right to put restrictions on her even in that field. Without the specific consent of her husband, the wife cannot exercise her right to work or to take employment in the public or private sector; she cannot go into business, or participate in an established one without the permission of her husband. To overcome the refusal of the husband, she may go to the court, but in a male-dominated society like Turkey, very few women would take this risk.

By entering into a contract, the spouses are at liberty to arrange their property rights during the marriage in such manner as they choose within the limits prescribed by the Civil Code. The spouses are free to adopt either the system of separation of property or the system of "joint" or "common" property. In the absence of such a marriage contract between the spouses, the system of separation of property shall apply. (C.C. Art. 170-1, 186-210) In practice, separation of property is the rule.[8]

Under the Islamic system, preference was given to males in matters of inheritance. Women were allowed to inherit only one-half of the husband's estate. The Civil Code now regulates the law of succession without distinction of sex. (C.C. Art. 439-617) Male and female successors in the same degree of closeness to the deceased participate in the

---

[8]Y. Gurbuz, "Family Law," in *Introduction to Turkish Law*, Ed. by T. Ansay and D. Wallace, Jr., 1966, pp. 114-129.

estate on an equal basis. The only difference between man and woman in inheritance matters relates to agricultural land. If it is to be partitioned and distributed among the heirs, male children are preferred to females. (C.C. Art. 581, 583, 588, 611)

The right to ask for divorce, which was the privilege of the husband under the Islamic law, was extended by the Civil Code to the wife. Either spouse can bring an action for divorce on any ground recognized by the law: adultery, plot against life, grave assaults and insults, crime or dishonorable life, desertion, mental infirmity, incompatibility. (C.C. Art. 129-134) The only difference is that on the ground of adultery, the husband can bring an action if his wife has been involved only once with another man, whereas several involvements of the husband with the same woman are necessary for a divorce action to be initiated by the wife.

As a legal consequence of divorce, the wife chooses a new and independent domicile; she has the right to resume her maiden name; she may keep the nationality she has acquired by marriage (C.C. Art. 141); she can get an allowance after the divorce or during the action for divorce. (C.C. Art. 137, 144-5, 149)

So much for the legal dispositions. Sociologists who studied actual conditions found considerable variances not only in rural areas but also in the cities. It is still quite common practice on the part of the bride's father to ask for a bride price from the prospective husband. Polygamy has not been completely abolished. Many marriages are still arranged.[9]

The emigration of peasants to the cities has brought old traditions into the urban culture. Ever since the Menderes era, political considerations have often prompted those in authority to ignore illegal practices. There are many new voters whose support is needed by politicians. Aside from the differences between *de jure* and *de facto* conditions, there are others that are part of the legal system. A few examples may suffice: If a woman is appointed as a guardian by a judge she may refuse the guardianship, whereas a man may not. (C.C. Art. 366) In the law of succession, as previously noted, male children are preferred to females in the distribution of agricultural land. The domicile of the husband becomes the domicile of the wife; she bears the family name of her husband; in cases of disputes in family matters, the views of the husband may prevail. (C.C. Art. 21, 152, 153, 159, 263) Foreign women acquire Turkish nationality at the time of marriage to a Turkish man, if they

[9]O. Erten, *Woman and Our Women in Our Time* (in Turkish), Ankara, 1978, pp 109-121; L. A. Fallers, *The Social Anthropology of the Nation State*, Aldine Publishing Co., Chicago, 1974, pp. 97-8; G. Lewis, *Modern Turkey*, Praeger, New York, 1974, pp 235-6; M. P. Price, *A History of Turkey, From Empire to Republic*, Humanities Press Inc., New York, 1961, pp. 188-9.

make a declaration of intention to this effect to the marriage officer. (Art. 5 and 42 of Nationality Act. See: T. Ansay, "Law of Persons," in *Introduction to Turkish Law*, Ankara, 1966, pp. 87-88)

From a more sociological point of view, several excellent monographs have recently been published, especially by Nermin Abadan-Unat, and Deniz Kandiyoti. Munise Aren has compiled an extensive bibliography.

CHAPTER 13

THE EASTERN EUROPEAN COUNTRIES AFTER WORLD WAR II

THE SOVIET UNION

At the end of World War II the U.S.S.R. faced enormous problems of reconstruction. Women had performed vital services in support of the armed forces, and a considerable number of them had participated directly in the total war effort. It was clear that without them the healing and rebuilding could not proceed effectively and expeditiously. They did not disappoint the Soviet leaders in carrying out these tasks. It is reasonable to ask whether they have been adequately rewarded for all that they have done and whether new doors have been opened for them which were previously shut or very hard to open. Many doors have indeed been opened, but they lead into the fields of economic and professional activities rather than political participation. This was hardly a new development because the groundwork had already been laid by the requirements of a total war. Now additional measures were taken toward the mobilization of womanpower in times of peace. It should also be emphasized that the progress made by women in the U.S.S.R., as in other parts of the world, was greatly stimulated by the work of the United Nations and other international organizations. A key document in this respect was the Universal Declaration of Human Rights, adopted and proclaimed by the General Assembly of the United Nations on December 10, 1948. By a decree dated March 18, 1954 the Presidium of the Supreme Soviet ratified the Convention on the Political Rights of Women of December 20, 1952 but reaffirmed reservations it had made two years earlier.

The ILO Convention No. 100 of June 29, 1951 concerning equal remuneration for men and women workers for work of equal value was ratified some years later by a decree of the Presidium of the Supreme Soviet dated April 4, 1956. On September 6, 1957 the Soviet representative signed the Convention on the Nationality of Married Women, and the Presidium of the Supreme Soviet ratified it on August 28, 1958.

But, as is well known, there have been many cases in which the government of the U.S.S.R. has refused exit to Russian women who married foreigners. Article 3 of the Convention may provide a basis for such action, as it allows for "limitations as may be imposed in the interests of national security or public policy."

The economic and social rights which were already firmly established in the 1936 Constitution have undoubtedly been strengthened in the 1977 Constitution. Women in the U.S.S.R. have had increased opportunities to enter all kinds of professional fields. However, when it comes to advancement toward the higher positions in the professional and bureaucratic establishments women have been confirmed to be at a disadvantage. One factor, which is often cited as an explanation, if not a justification, is the familiar argument that most women want to have children and this, inevitably, delays their careers. It is also pointed out that in professional and political careers a high degree of mobility is required and women with family responsibilities are confronted with very difficult choices. These factors tend to direct women toward more local concerns.

When it comes to the legal safeguards and the enforcement of equal rights between men and women there are ample provisions on labor legislation which guarantee women equal rights with respect to remuneration, leisure and social security. Thus legislation enacted on July 15, 1970 prohibits "direct or indirect limitation of rights or direct or indirect preference shown in granting jobs because of sex, race, nationality or religious beliefs."[1] There is no comparable provision in the new constitution or other legislation, which could be invoked by women in cases of discrimination in situations involving alleged political or administrative advancement.

Impressive advances have been made in doing away with traditional stereotypes of "women's work." The Soviet statistics are impressive but not entirely convincing. Thus one may read that in 1960, 76 percent of the doctors were women. None of the Eastern European countries comes anywhere near this percentage. However, women doctors in these countries do not hesitate to question this figure. They also say that from what they have been able to see in the U.S.S.R., Soviet women doctors are not as thoroughly trained as male doctors, are not allowed to perform surgery, and are generally assigned to routine activities. If these statements are valid, they confirm that in the professional fields, as in politics, women are numerous but have less access to important positions and fewer opportunities for advancement.[2]

---

[1]*Soviet Legislation* ed. Belyakova p. 75

[2]According to Soviet statistics the percentage of women doctors has been declining significantly and consistently during the past two decades.

Soviet statistics continue to be somewhat unrevealing in that they lump together figures concerning women's participation on all levels of government, and they are often considerably out of date. Thus one may read in a 1980 publication that in 1969 women deputies in the territories, cities and local Soviets constituted 45 percent of the total. No comparable figure is given for 1979. The percentage of women in the Supreme Soviet is given as 31 in 1970 and 1974. In 1979 membership was reported as 32 percent. The significance of this slight increase must be evaluated in terms of what importance has been attached to the Supreme Soviet under the 1977 Constitution, as compared with the Constitution of 1936.

According to Article 108 the Supreme Soviet of the U.S.S.R. is "the highest body of state authority." The same article states that the Supreme Soviet is empowered to adopt and amend the constitution, endorse the formation of new autonomous Republics and Autonomous Regions, approve state plans for economic and social developments, as well as the budget of the U.S.S.R.

From the language, it should be clear that the Supreme Soviet is the highest endorsing and ratifying body. It is not really a policy-initiating body. Before the new constitution was promulgated L. G. Churchward wrote, "The Supreme Soviet is not and has never been the main legislative body of the U.S.S.R."[3] This appraisal is still valid, as can readily be seen by studying Chapter 15 of the new constitution. Article 112 provides that "Sessions of the Supreme Soviet of the U.S.S.R. shall be convened twice a year." The Presidium of the Supreme Soviet is empowered to call special sessions. According to Article 113, the Presidium is also authorized to initiate legislation in the Supreme Soviet along with the Soviet of the Union, the Soviet of Nationalities, the Council of Ministers, the Supreme Court, the Procurator General and a few others.

Thus, even if the Supreme Soviet were more of a policy-making body than it has been, the role of women in it would be difficult to assess without analyzing the role of women in all the organizations which have exerted great influence over it. The position of deputy to the Supreme Soviet has remained a part-time job. Deputies are relieved from regular duties during the sessions of the Supreme Soviet. Even the most conscientious deputies cannot be expected to prepare themselves sufficiently to participate effectively in the debates, as called for in Article 114. The principle of gender equality was restated on July 6, 1978 in Article 3 of the Law on Elections to the Supreme Soviet of the U.S.S.R.:

[3]Contemporary Soviet Government. N. Y. American Elsevier Pbl. 1975 p. 117.

245

Elections of deputies of the Supreme Soviet of the U.S.S.R. shall be equal; each citizen shall have one vote; all voters shall exercise the franchise on an equal footing. Women and men shall have equal rights . . .

The real power, now as before, is exercised by the leadership of the Communist Party. Article 6 of the new constitution declares:

The leading and guiding force of Soviet society and the nucleus of its political system, of all state organizations and public organizations, is the Communist Party of the Soviet Union.

It goes on to state that the CPSU exists for the people and serves the people.

What has been the role of women in the Communist Party of the Soviet Union since the end of World War II? If one begins by comparing the growth in membership during the inter-war and post-World War II period, it becomes apparent that the rate of increase in women members has slowed considerably. Whereas the membership doubled between 1917 and 1941 (7.4 percent to 14.9 percent), the increase from 1946 (18.7 percent) to 1980 (25.1 percent) has been much smaller. Indeed it dropped under the 20 percent level between 1950 and 1961 and passed 20 percent only in 1966. Women in the U.S.S.R. have always been politically much more active on the local than on the national level, a fact reflected in the statistics of the Communist Party of the Soviet Union. At the end of the inter-war period women members in the local Soviets constituted about one-third of the total membership. After the war this percentage grew gradually, especially during the Khrushchev era (1958-1964). By 1979 membership of women in local Soviets had risen to 40 percent. Significant changes have taken place in the composition of the Soviets of the Republics. By 1959 the percentage in the fifteen Republics averaged 32.1. The republics in whose Soviets women accounted for less than 30 percent of the membership were Azerbaidjan (27.7), Georgia (28.8), Lithuania (27.7) and Uzbekistan (29.0). There have been some impressive increases in all of these republics. In 1980 the following percentages were reported: 39.7 in Azerbaidjan, 35.9 in Georgia, 35.7 in Lithuania, and 34.9 in Uzbekistan.

There is no general agreement as to how these increases should be evaluated. Some would suggest that they represent further evidence that traditional attitudes toward the role of women have continued to decline and that the Moslem heritage is more cultural than religious or political. This may be valid in Azerbaidjan and Uzbekistan, but it does not explain the substantial increase in Lithuania. Perhaps it is significant to compare Lithuania with the two other Baltic Republics: Estonia and Latvia. In 1959, 32.8 percent of the members of the Soviet of Estonia were women, and in Latvia 31 percent were women. As was pointed out before, in these two formerly independent Baltic states women had taken a very active interest in politics. Lithuanian women were somewhat less active, and perhaps recent developments should be regarded as a successful drive to catch up with the neighboring republics.

Some scholars have sought to establish a connection between economic development and increased political activism on the part of women. The level of economic development of each individual republic seems to have a noticeable effect on the level of political participation. The percentage of women among candidates to the Communist Party increases in proportion to the increase in the number of women in the labor force. For example, in Uzbekistan the percentage of women among Communist Party candidates rose from 15.9 in 1959 to 29.6 in 1971, while the percentage of women in the labor force in 1959 was 43.8 to 47.8 in 1970. In all the republics each increase in the ratio of women in the labor force was paralleled by an increase in women political candidates. The four republics with the highest level of economic development (Estonia, Latvia, Lithuania and RSFSR) have also the greatest number of women members in the Communist Party and Tadzhikistan , with the lowest level of economic development, has the smallest number of women party members. While the relationship between economic development and political activity is not always corresponding (as in the case of Uzbekistan which has a low level of economic development with the highest percentage of women in local soviets), there are enough examples to suggest such a relationship.

In all of the republics the Communist Party and the government perform complementary functions. The Communist Party of the Soviet Union performs the vital political functions of socialization, recruitment and goal specification. The governments of the Soviet republics perform the actual goal attainment functions under the direction of the Communist Party of the Soviet Union.

The importance of the Communist Party of the Soviet Union has increased, as reflected in the 1977 Constitution. In the report concerning the draft constitution, Leonid Brezhnev explained the role of the Party as that body which "implemented its decisions through the Soviet bodies, within the framework of the Soviet Constitution." Brezhnev quoted this resolution from the Eighth Congress of the Communist Party of the

Soviet Union and maintained that this principle would be reflected in the new Constitution. As stated in Article 6 of the new Constitution, the Communist Party, "armed with Marxism-Leninism, determines the general perspectives of the development of society and the course of the home and foreign policy of the U.S.S.R., directs the great constructive work . . . and imparts a planned, systematic and theoretically substantiated character to their struggle."

Political careers are formed exclusively within the Party and promotion is achieved through the Party. The Party is the only source of political legitimacy, reward and opportunity. The Communist Party of the Soviet Union alternates its recruitment policy between a pattern of selectivity and a broadening of the membership bases. Women's political participation in the U.S.S.R. must be understood in this context.

In the period following the Russian Revolution we see that female membership in the Communist Party of the Soviet Union increased, reflecting the Party commitment to full political equality of all members of society. In the early years of the soviet state, *Zhenotdel*, a women's organization, was formed by the Communist Party of the Soviet Union to increase female political activity. *Zhenotdel* served as an organ of propaganda and agitation with a strong emphasis on women's emancipation. It was dissolved in 1930 because it became incompatible with a unified Communist Party of the Soviet Union and because it was argued that it in fact alienated women from the mainstream of political activity by segregating them into a group which had different priorities from the rest of the workers' revolution. This line of reasoning has resulted in an apparent lack of self-awareness of women in Soviet society. An increased preoccupation with the abstractions of Communist ideology and an emphasis on unity have in turn placed the issue of women's liberation in the background. Since 1917 female membership in the Communist Party of the Soviet Union has increased steadily except for a decline during the purges in 1934 and a slight drop in 1952, after Stalin's death. In the past sixty-three years the percentage of women has risen from 7.4 to 25.1. Since the end of World War II there has been a steady increase in the responsibility level of women members of the Communist Party of the Soviet Union.

At the lower echelons of the party structure, women make up a high percentage. In the Komsomol, women constitute more than 50 percent of the membership. Studies also indicate that within the Komsomol women tend to be more active than their male counterparts. The high rate of activity at this level has been explained in terms of the age group of Komsomol members, who as a rule are young and not married and thus have more time to devote to studies of party history and attend lectures and meetings concerning the party. Several researchers have found that women in the Soviet Union become involved in politics at a later age than men. The overall average age of women involved in politics is 45-53 years.

The number of women delegates has increased substantially, especially since the Khrushchev era. In 1956, 14.2 percent of the delegates were women. This was still relatively low in view of the fact that at that time women made up 19.7 percent of the Communist Party membership. In 1961, 22.3 percent of the delegates to the Party Congress were women. This was a substantial increase if one notes that the percentage of women members had actually dropped to 19.5. A comparison of the official statistics of women party members with those of women delegates attending party congresses shows that from 1961 to 1981 the percentage of women delegates exceeded that of party membership:

	Women Party Members	Women Delegates to Party Congress
1961	19.5%	22.3%
1966	20.6%	23.3%
1971	22.2%	24.3%
1976	24.7% (1977)	25.1%
1981	25.1% (1980	26.6%

The situation of women in the Central Committee has been quite different and quite disappointing for those women aspiring to key positions in the Communist Party. If one recalls that at the time of the 1917 revolution women members in the Central Committee represented 9.7 percent of the total membership, the subsequent history has been an almost continuous failure. At the beginning of World War II the membership had stagnated at 2.2 percent. By 1952 it was up to 3.1 percent. It peaked in 1966 at 4.2 percent and has been going down ever since. In 1981 it was down to 2.8 percent, about the same low level which was recorded during the Stalin era.

As is generally understood, the core of the tremendous power of the Communist Party is the Politburo. It is also widely known that in the entire history of the Politburo there has been only one woman member: Ekaterina Furtseva. Next to the Politburo, the Council of Ministers has always been a crucially important body in Soviet government and politics. In the new Constitution its powers and functions are defined in Chapter 16 (Articles 128-136):

The Council of Ministers of the U.S.S.R., i.e. the Government of the U.S.S.R., is the highest executive and administrative body of state authority of the U.S.S.R.

The Council of Ministers has continued to be an almost exclusively male domain. Most of its members have achieved recognition in the highest echelons of the Communist Party over a long period of time.

Compared with the Scandinavian countries and most of the Western European countries, the U.S.S.R. and most of the Eastern European countries have not shown any readiness to allow women to occupy key positions in their governments. This is true not only of the Union ministries but also of the top administrative positions in the republics.

Although Article 70 of the Constitution defines the U.S.S.R. as a federal state composed of 15 socialist republics and Article 72 states that "each Union Republic shall retain the right freely to secede from the U.S.S.R.," the political realities are clearly quite different. Some of the contradictions are usually explained by pointing to the principle of democratic centralism. As defined in Article 3:

> The Soviet State is organized and functions on the principle of democratic centralism, namely the electiveness of all bodies of state authority, from the lowest to the highest, their accountability to the people, and the obligation of lower bodies to observe the decisions of higher ones. Democratic centralism combines central leadership with the local initiative and creative activity and with the responsibility of each state body and official for the work entrusted to them.

This notion of democratic centralism is clearly more centralistic than democratic. It does not support the principles of the equality of multiple sovereignties but legitimizes the hierarchic relationships between the "bodies of state authority." The central bodies, as has been noted, are controlled by a male gerontocracy and the chances for women to advance to key positions are not particularly favorable. The hierarchic nature of the system is underscored in Article 131 which states:

> the Council of Ministers of the U.S.S.R. is empowered to deal with all matters of state administration within the jurisdiction of the Union of Soviet Socialist Republics insofar as, under the Constitution, they do not come within the competence of the Supreme Soviet of the U.S.S.R. or the Presidium of the Supreme Soviet of the U.S.S.R.

If women in the republics were to advance politically as they have economically, it would not necessarily make a great deal of difference in their power. There has been no indication that power is becoming more decentralized or diffused. Power continues to be held by a relatively small number of seasoned male politicians whose outlook on the political role of women is not very different from prevailing attitudes among their counterparts in more traditional societies.

ALBANIA

by Karen Shaw Kerpen

The People's Republic of Albania was founded in 1944 after the Fascists had been routed. The Albanian National Liberation Front, the major resistance group, assumed control of the government; and the leader of the Front, Enver Hoxha, became head of state. Hoxha, and the Albanian Labor Party (the new name for the Communist Party) instituted a Socialist government in Albania.

The problems of women were addressed early by the Socialists, and the Albanian government had taken a series of impressive steps to improve the social, legal, political, and economic status of women. Initiatives have arisen from different sources. Legal and constitutional protections for women have been incorporated into the laws since 1946. Enver Hoxha, as head of state and party, has made several major speeches on the emancipation of women. The Party has instituted policies designed to enhance the advancement of women. Along with the Party, the Albanian Women's Union (AWU) has addressed the role of women consistently. The AWU is a descendant of the Union of Anti-fascist Women. It is a mass organization set up to determine working conditions for women, protect women's rights, agitate against regressive social customs, inform women about opportunities in education and work, and urge promotion of women to higher posts. The Union has district branches and special research committees on specific problems related to women. It has a national congress every five years to plan activities to carry out state and Party programs that are important to women. Nexhmije Hoxha, president of the AWU from 1946 to 1955, was also a member of the Central Committee of the Party and a deputy to the People's Assembly until 1955. Her respective high positions helped foster greater coordination with governmental policies and broader mobilization of women members. She was succeeded by Vito Kapo as president; Ms. Kapo is married to an influential Party leader.

The need for legal statutes and special consideration of the woman issue was imperative, since women's plight was so desperate after the end of the war. Eighty percent of the total population was illiterate, but ninety four percent of the women could not read or write.[1] Of the small industrialized working class in Albania, fewer than 200 were women. These worked at the most menial tasks and were denied any education or training in a skill or trade. They worked 12-15-hour shifts but received

[1]Nicholas Pano, *The People's Republic of Albania*, (Baltimore: Johns Hopkins Press, 1968), p. 15.

251

35-60 percent less pay than males.[2] One researcher found:

> the number of women having any special training and profession could be counted on one's fingers . . . Throughout Albania, there were only 21 women teachers, two or three doctors, and not a single woman engineer, agronomist, or chemist. No woman took part in parliament or in the state apparatus. In the secondary schools, girls made up only 2.4 percent of the students.[3]

In rural areas, opportunities for women were severely restricted. Most labored in their homes, or on farms, as drudges.

Enver Hoxha's 1946 address to the Second Congress of the AWU set the tone for the government's work on behalf of women.: "Our country will not be able to advance, Albania will not be built as it should without the participation of the woman, because the woman, not only by her physical forces, but also with her intellectual and spiritual strength must contribute to the reconstruction of the country."

This view has been expressed in constitutional documents from 1946 on. The first statement came from the Declaration of the Rights of Citizens, which was issued by the Anti-fascist Council of Liberation in 1944. In appreciation of the vital contribution women had made to the war effort, the Declaration recognized the total equality of men and women. The wording of the Declaration of the Rights of Citizens was incorporated into the first Constitution of March 14, 1946, and women were given equal rights with men "in all the domains of private, political and social life." Article 16 of this Constitution declared that "every citizen, without distinction as to sex, nationality, race, creed, degree of education or residence, who has attained the age of 18 years shall be entitled to vote and may be elected to any organ of the state." According to Article 26, all citizens were to have "equal access to government office under the conditions prescribed by law."

Revisions of the 1946 Constitution were promulgated on July 4, 1950, but the major provisions pertaining to women were kept intact. Article 16 of this revision was directed to eliminating discrimination against women and establishing equality. Article 17 stated "Women

[2]Eleni Pashko, "The Role Women Play in the Socialist Industry of the People's Republic of Albania," *Problems in the Struggle for Complete Emancipation of Women*, (Tirana: Political Book Publishing House, 1973), p. 72.

[3]*An Outline of the People's Socialist Republic of Albania*, (Tirana: The "8 Nentori" Publishing House, 1978), p. 101.

enjoy equal rights with men in all spheres of private, political and social life. Women enjoy the rights of equal pay with men for the same work. They enjoy the same right in social insurances." The state gives special protection to the interest of mother and child by securing the right for a paid leave before and after childbirth and by setting up residences for pregnant women and homes for bringing up and sheltering children. Article 19 provided the constitutional basis for a new family code which was promulgated some 15 years later. Religious marriages were not recognized, and the state courts were given exclusive jurisdiction in all matters connected with marriage. Children born outside marriage had the same rights as legitimate children.

The Women's Union pressed for more improvements in women's opportunities. In 1954, the Fourth Congress of the AWU emphasized the need for more educational opportunities for women and better technical and professional training. These opportunities were necessary to upgrade women who heretofore had been prepared only for work at home.

One of the major legal changes was effected with the promulgation of a new family code on June 23, 1965. Marriage was declared to create the family as the "basic cell of society," and to be based on "communist morality." The principles of equality, mutual aid, and respect were affirmed in Article 2. Article 4 stated that parents are to respect their children and to educate them to become responsible citizens. Adult children had to care for aged and disabled parents. Divorce was permitted. Adultery by the male—including polygamy—became grounds for divorce, as did lack of financial support and incompatibility. As women found new employment opportunities available, they sued for divorce in great numbers to escape arranged or violent marriages. Marriages based upon love or consent result in lower divorce rates, and Albania's divorce rate is quite low compared to the industrialized west.[4]

The Family Code marked a further improvement in the social status of women, since it outlawed old traditions and practices that denigrated and reduced women to chattel.

As early as 1971, Enver Hoxha had stated that the Constitution no longer reflected the social reality of Albania and that it ought to be completely revised. But another four years elapsed before decisive action was taken toward this goal. Hoxha assumed the chairmanship of a committee of 51 members whose task was to prepare a draft constitution.

[4]Ismet Elezi, "Penal Legislation of the People's Republic of Albania in Defense of Socialist Matrimonial Relations," *Problems in the Struggle for Complete Emancipation of Women, op. cit.,* 258-267.

It was published on January 21, 1976, and approved, after numerous textual changes, by the People's Assembly on December 28, 1976. The provisions concerning women's rights remained unaltered.

The sum of all these guarantees presents a broad array of protections for women. In addition to those already mentioned, suffrage is universal, education for all is free, no "restriction or privilege" based on sex is permitted,[5] and women have equal rights in the family as well as society. A married woman can keep her own name.[6] Contract marriages are forbidden, and the practices of bride price and dowries have diminished markedly. Equality before the law and equal pay for equal work were reaffirmed in the 1976 Constitution. Like Article 36 of the 1946 Constitution, Article 62 of the present Constitution states that "the defense of the socialist homeland is the supreme duty and greatest honor for all citizens."[7] A new Article 63 specifies that "military service and the constant training for the defense of the socialist homeland are duties for all the citizens."

As head of state, Enver Hoxha has said that socialist development will not succeed unless women are fully emancipated and equal to men. In major speeches during 1967, 1972, and 1978 Hoxha outlined the means the State and the Labor Party use to eliminate discrimination and suppression of women. For example, in a 1967 address to the Central Committee Plenum, Hoxha insisted that the principles of equality before the law and equal consideration be carried out in real life.[8] Political participation by women was an area that sorely needed change; although the membership of the AWU was then 250,000, only 40 women had been elected as deputies to the People's Assemblies, the main representative mass body in the country.

Hoxha urged that women be more actively involved in production, the national economy, affairs of state, culture and learning. By engaging actively in these areas, women would be encouraged to change the habits and practices that had governed their behavior in the past. Women were hired for jobs they had previously been excluded from, brought from the farms into the factories and towns, and urged to register for educational classes from basic literacy to scientific and technical training.

By 1969, impressive gains had been made. Women represented 42 percent of the work force in general, 80 percent of machine-shop and metal workers, 82 percent of textile workers, 62 percent of food pro-

---

[5]*The Constitution of the People's Socialist Republic of Albania*, (Tirana: The "8 Nentori" Publishing House, 1977), Article 40.

[6]Ismet Elezi, *op. cit.*

[7]*The Constitution of the People's Socialist Republic of Albania, op. cit.*

[8]Enver Hoxha, "On Some Aspects of the Problems of the Albanian Woman," *Speeches: 1967-1968*, (Tirana: The "8 Nentori" Publishing House, 1969), pp. 140-168.

cessors, 50 percent of agricultural workers, 12 percent of transport and communications workers, and 10 percent of construction workers.[9] By 1975, women made up 47 percent of the work force and dominated the light industries, food processing, health, and educational professions.[10] Forty-two percent of the students in secondary school in 1970 were women, and this figure has continued to mount. Women professionals included 700 teachers, 230 engineers, 335 physicians and dentists, and 215 economists in 1970—a dramatic increase over the postwar figures but still lower than male rates.[11]

In 1979, the government reported that women were 46 percent of the work force, and the majority of agricultural workers as well. Females were 51 percent of the student body in lower and middle schools and nearly 45 percent of enrollees in higher education.[12] Registration of women in the rural areas jumped twelve times from 1973 to 1978, reflecting the intense efforts made by cadres there.

A high percentage of women workers attend secondary or vocational courses related to their jobs or aspirations. Curricula had to be designed expressly for women who were unaccustomed to learning or who had no skills. Part-time and special classes are trying to make up this deficit, but it has been slow going. Twelve thousand women were attending part-time workers' schools or vocationally related classes in 1979.

Participation in production has brought new social changes for women. Leaving farms and their families, young women are becoming independent of parents and developing their own circle of friends. Work, school, and political activities enhance the opportunities to meet a mate of one's choosing. Women are no longer confined to the home and no longer respond to patriarchal domination. Contradictions between generations have arisen due to this factor. The pace of change has been gradual since 76 percent of the population still resides in rural areas where old practices still have influence.[13]

To facilitate the participation of women in production, the state has created supportive services to socialize tasks formerly done by women. Special regulations for working women have been promulgated. Women retain salaries and posts during confinement and for three months after delivery. Creches and day care centers are set up in factories and in neighborhoods. Nursing mothers have work breaks to feed their infants. Vitamins for pregnant women and infants are free as are most medical

[9]Eleni Pashko, "The Role Women Play . . .", op. cit. p. 75.
[10]An Outline of the People's Republic of Albania, op. cit., p. 103.
[11]Eleni Pashko, "The Role Women Play . . .", op. cit., p. 77.
[12]Zeri I Popullit March 6, 1979, p. 1.
[13]Secretary General of the United Nations, "Status of Women in Education and in the Economic and Social Fields," May 23, 1980, (N.Y.: UNESCO, 1980).

services. Locales have maternity centers, midwives, and physicians in attendance. Working mothers have one month paid sick leave to care for sick children. Electrification, household appliances, factory canteens, and catering services have been introduced by the state to lighten the burden normally carried by women.[14]

The political progress women have made is limited in comparison to their potential. Although females make up nearly half the labor force, they are underrepresented in the political structures of Albania. The 1970 elections resulted in substantial increases in the positions held by women in various people's councils. On the local level, the percentages were all above 40. In the People's Assembly, the highest organ of the state, women's participation was only 33 percent. One of the three vice presidents was a woman, but only two women members were in the Presidium of the People's Assembly, of a total of fifteen members.[15] In 1975, women held one-third of the seats in the People's Assemblies, 41 percent of the leadership positions in mass organizations, but only 35 percent of Party memberships.[16] By 1979, the figures had not altered radically. Women still held one-third of the Assembly seats, slightly more than 41 percent of mass organization leadership posts and 42 percent of the state employee jobs. Nearly 44 percent were chosen to serve on the People's Councils, the local governing bodies. However, membership in the Party had increased only to 27 percent.[17] Both Enver Hoxha and Vito Kapo, the head of the AWU, have faulted the Party for its poor record in recruiting women. By 1980, one-third of the People's Assembly seats were held by women.

Concrete advances had to be coupled with ideological changes, and Hoxha has said that the Labor Party members and cadres in every enterprise, state institution, council, or industry have to take a leading role in educating men and women to accept the new status of women.

Hoxha has also criticized males who stand in the way of women's progress toward equality.[18] Older men in particular have resented the change in family relationships and sex roles. Although women work outside the home, these men do not share in the housework but expect everything to be done for them. Women who do not work still are isolated by men who refuse to share their experiences and the news of social and political life in the neighborhood and nation. Hoxha wanted

[14]An Outline of the People's Socialist Republic of Albania, op. cit., pp. 82-99.
[15]Annick Miske, Des Albanaises (Paris: Editiones des Femmes, 1976), p. 254.
[16]An Outline of the People's Socialist Republic of Albania, op. cit. p. 103.
[17]"Zeri I Popullit," March 8, 1979.
[18]Enver Hoxha, "On Promoting Socialist Development in the Family," Speeches, 1971-1973, (Tirana: The "8 Nentori" Publishing House, 1974) pp. 201-222.

the Party to educate these men, so that "relations between husband and wife should be characterized by mutual and equal obligation and rights, by mutual respect, confidence, and love." Fathers should share relationships with daughters that are based on equality and respect.

Others have accused men of deliberately resisting advancement for women. A 1978 study of two districts, Lezhe and Kruje, found that although women were half the labor force and were nearly equally represented in the major political bodies, they held only a tiny fraction of executive positions in any of the organizations.[19] An even smaller number held posts in the military. A near-majority of the women surveyed had completed middle school, and others had finished advanced training, so ignorance was not a reason for exclusion. The author concluded that men opposed promotion of women because "placing a woman in a high position means removing a man from it."[20] Men deny or underestimate the competency of women in order to keep their jobs and their compensations. Due to past influences and beliefs, men still want to dominate women, and to think them slow or incompetent.

In other ways, men keep their positions by neglecting the situation of women. The Women's Union found that male heads of cooperatives, industries, and councils did not allocate sufficient funds to creches, child care, health facilities, and other services that would free both parents for productive labor.[21] Instead of tackling such problems as problems for the whole community, males foist them off on the Women's Union for solution, and the Union can only educate and agitate, not finance projects. Also, men assigned women workers to tedious, minor chores which diminished their interest in work. Ultimately, these methods have a negative impact on society, since disinterested or inhibited workers do not produce consistently.

Occasionally, women have been faulted for low ambitions. Women aged 45 to 65 may prefer to remain in the home, not only because they are more accustomed to this idea but also because their living standard is higher, housework is easier, and it is more comfortable at home.[22]

The socialist government in Albania has shown itself to be sensitive to the needs of women, and it has implemented many changes to erode male supremacy and inequality. As women move into new roles and opportunities, progress will increase. One observer, Lavide Leka, has written, "The 35-year experience of socialist Albania has fully vindi-

[19]Arshin Xheze, "It is not only a Question of Mistrusting," *Zeri I Popullit*, January 12, 1978, p. 1.

[20]*Ibid.*

[21]Vito Kapo, "Women's Rights as a Great Problem of the Party," *Zeri I Popullit*, April 7, 1978, p. 2.

[22]Jet Meta, "Increasing Participation of Women in Agriculture Urged," *Shqiptarja E Re* February 1979, pp. 3-4.

cated, first, the absolute necessity of linking the problem of the complete emancipation of the woman with the problem of the national liberation and the socialist revolution, and, second, that this revolution cannot be carried out with success without the broad participation of women in it, without their emancipation."[23]

BULGARIA

The chief model for the Bulgarian Constitution of December 4, 1947, was the Constitution of the U.S.S.R. (1936). It was reported that the Yugoslav Constitution of 1946 was also consulted. But there can be no doubt that the Soviet Constitution was favored by George Dimitrov, the undisputed leader of the Bulgarian Communist Party. The fact that the Constitution was promulgated on the 11th Anniversary of the Stalin Constitution was hardly a coincidence.

Article 3 of the Bulgarian Constitution provided that "all citizens of the People's Republic who are 18 years of age irrespective of sex, national origin, race, religion, education, profession, social status or material situation, with the exception of those who are under judicial disability or deprived of their civil and political rights, are eligible to vote and to be elected." The equality of men and women was affirmed in Act 72.

The role of women was much increased after Todor Zhivkov became first secretary of the Bulgarian Communist Party in 1954. In 1962 he was made prime minister and was reelected in 1966. For several years he combined the two powerful positions at a time when this was no longer done in the other Communist states of Eastern Europe. One of the important changes in the status of women was achieved by the promulgation of a new family code which went into effect on May 22, 1968.

Elena Lagadinova, the president of the Committee of Bulgarian Women, wrote a few years ago that the role and position of women in society are indicative of the nature of a social system. They indicate how progressive, humane and democratic it is. In the 1970s Bulgarian women have made much progress not only in the economic field but also with respect to political participation.

---

[23]Laudie Leka, "The Revolutionary Road of Emancipation of the Woman in Albania," *Albania Today*, No. 4(53), 1980, pp. 22-27.

A new Draft Constitution was presented to the National Assembly and was adopted on May 1, 1971. Following a national referendum, it was promulgated on May 18. The basic rights and obligations of the citizens are set forth in Chapter III. Articles 35 to 38 provide detailed principles concerning the equality of men and women before the law.

Article 35

(1) All citizens of the People's Republic of Bulgaria are equal before the law.

(2) No privileges or limitations of rights based on nationality, origin, creed, sex, race, education, social and material status are allowed.

(3) The state secures the equality of the citizens by creating conditions and opportunities for the exercise of their rights and the fulfillment of their obligations.

(4) The propagation of hate or humiliation of man because of race, national or religious affiliation is forbidden and shall be punishable.

Article 36

Women and men enjoy equal rights in the People's Republic of Bulgaria.

Article 37

Mothers enjoy special protection and care on behalf of the state, the economic and public organizations, including paid leave-of-absence before and after childbirth, free obstetric and medical care, maternity homes, alleviation in her work, extension of the network of children's establishments, or the enterprises for communal services and public catering.

Article 38

(1) Marriage and the family are protected by the state.

(2) Civil marriage alone is legal.

(3) The spouses have equal rights and obligations in marriage and in the family. Parents have the right and obligation to attend to the upbringing of their children and to their communist education.

(4) Children born out of wedlock enjoy equal rights with those born in wedlock.

Bulgarian legislation established that a woman, after giving birth to her first child, is entitled to four months of fully paid maternity leave.

For the following six months she may receive compensation based on minimal wages. Maternity leaves are even longer after the birth of a second or third child.

In the economic and educational fields the participation of women during the past quarter century has about tripled. In the political field women account for more than one-third of the local legislative and judicial positions. Although most of the top positions in the administration as well as the party are still controlled by men, about 20 percent of the members of the National Assembly are women. In 1979 Todor Zhivkov's daughter, Ludmila Zhivkova, was appointed to membership in the Politburo. Another woman who achieved greater prominence was Drazha Vulcheva, who had been minister of education since 1977, and was made deputy prime minister.

Among the twelve full members of the Bulgarian Communist Party Politburo who were confirmed on April 4, 1981, at the 12th Party Congress were two women: Mrs. Ludmila Zhivkova and Mrs. Tsola Drazoicheva. In the Cabinet approved by the National Assembly on June 17, Mrs. Zhivkova was confirmed as chairman of the Committee for Culture and Mrs. Svetla Daskalova as minister of justice.

CZECHOSLOVAKIA

Under the Nazi occupation the leadership of the women's movement in the so-called Protectorate of Bohemia and Moravia was almost completely eliminated. After Czechoslovakia was liberated a new network of women's organizations was created, which followed the Soviet pattern.

After February 1948, the basic official conception and ideology of women's rights in Czechoslovakia differed sharply from the one of the inter-war period. Bourgeois notions of emancipation were replaced by Marxist-Leninist ideas and strategies. The Constitution which was promulgated in May 1948 put more emphasis on economic and social rights. The family code was redraped to reflect this ideological change.

In late 1947, in the first Gotwald Cabinet, Ludmila Jankovcová, a registered Socialist, became minister of industry. She was the first woman ever to serve in a Czechoslovakian Cabinet, but her tenure lasted only about eight weeks. It ended with the February 1948 coup, which gave the Communists complete control. She was reappointed in June of the same year as minister of food. In this capacity she served about six months. In late 1954 she was made deputy prime minister, a post she held about one and a half years. After that no woman held any cabinet position.

If we compare the membership of the Central Committee of the Czechoslovakian Communist Party during the inter-war period with the postwar period, it becomes apparent that the percentage of women was not as high after World War II as it had been during the "bourgeois" period, in which the Communist party was free to function legally and openly. In the 1930s the percentage of women was always above 15, and before the dismemberment of Czechoslovakia and the liquidation of the Communist Party it was above 25. By contrast it may be noted that the percentage of women in the Central Committee of the Czechoslovakian Republic rose to about 15 only in the early post-World War II period, and it dropped after 1948 to about 13. During the 1950s, until 1968, the percentage was around 10. Then it fell sharply and remained at about 5 during the 1970s.

According to Otto Ulč:

> between 1948 and 1968 the Czechoslovakian Central Committee also suffered a decline in membership among women. Although females accounted for a full third of the membership in 1949, this dropped to 27.4 percent in 1966. An even greater decrease in women's participation in political roles was evident.

The Constitution of July 11, 1960 marked a further step toward Marxism and Leninism. Article 20 declared that "all citizens shall have equal rights and equal duties" and that "men and women shall have equal status in the family, at work and in public activity." Article 27 provided that "the equal status of women in the family shall be secured by special adjustment of working conditions and special health care during pregnancy and maternity, as well as by the development of facilities and services which will enable women fully to participate in the life of society."

In 1963 a new family code was promulgated, which was closer to the Soviet model because it went beyond the earlier ideas of partnership and responsibility of both parents and made the state the guardian of collective interests. As women were increasingly integrated into the work force, it became necessary to provide greatly expanded crèches and day care centers.

All of these measures have helped to reduce the unequal status of women. However, there are some basic obstacles which have not been completely overcome. During the 1970s further legislation was enacted to implement the principle of equality in various fields of employment. Further progress has been made, but difficulties and differentials have remained in the quest for equalization. This has been recognized by scholars in Czechoslovakia, who have cited official statistics to show that women are usually paid less for the same kind of work. Furthermore, most women still have a disproportionate amount of work in the home after their regular employment hours.

Much progress has been made toward implementing the principle of equal pay for equal work. But equal opportunities usually depend on whether a woman raises a family. If she does, she can benefit from a highly developed system of medical and social services, and child allowances. Her service record is considered uninterrupted if she returns to her work after her child's second birthday. A mother who decides to resume her work while her children are still very small may place them in day care centers. As one Czechoslovakian study group concluded in 1971, women continue to perform multiple duties as citizens, workers, wives, mothers and widows. Legislation can help to create more equitable conditions, but complete equality or equalization is elusive.

A resolution was passed at the 14th Congress of the Communist Party of Czechoslovakia, which expressed "high appreciation of the contributions of the mothers and working women" to socialist society. It stated that the Party "will encourage the continued growth of women's involvement in political and economic affairs." All government and economic bodies were admonished to show initiative in tackling problems of living and working conditions and to "create the prerequisites for enhancing their public activity." The resulting participation has been more impressive in the economy than in the political field. Whereas in some fields of the economy it has increased by as much as 66 percent during the past three decades, this has not been so in the political arena. In the Federal Assembly women have accounted for about 28 percent of the membership in recent years. In the local national committees it has been somewhat higher. Women have continued to be very active in the trade unions, and in some of the committees they constitute more than 40 percent.

The number of women who are employed in the various sectors of the national economy is very high. The latest figures (1979), according to the official statistics of 1980, show that in such fields as internal commerce women account for 73.9 percent. In external commerce they represent 63.1 percent of the total. In social welfare 86.7 percent of the work is done by women. In the field of health 78.3 percent, and in education 72.4 percent of the employees are women. In view of this high level of participation by women, it may come as a surprise that a disproportionate number of decorations was awarded to men during the past three decades. All 26 gold stars to heroes of the Czechoslovak Socialist Republic went to men. Of the 119 gold stars to heroes of socialist labor, only 13 went to women. The Order of the Republic was awarded to 529 men, but to only 33 women. The Order of the Victorious February was awarded to 277 men, but only to 13 women. The Order of Work was given to 4,237 men, but only to 338 women.

An interesting difference still exists between men and women as to the age at which they become eligible for pensions. Men qualify at the age of 60. The qualifying age for women depends on the number of children. A woman without any children may retire at 57. A mother of one may retire at 56. If she had two children at 55, if she had three or four at 54. Finally, if she raised five or more children, she becomes eligible for a pension at 53.

The Politburo currently consists of 12 members and has remained almost the same since 1976. There are no women among the full members and the candidate members. In April 1981, Mrs. Marie Kabrhelova was reappointed to the Secretariat. In the large federal cabinet, headed again by Lubomir Strougal, which was sworn in by President Husak on June 7, 1981, there were no women members. There are also no women members in the current cabinets of the Czech and the Slovak Socialist Republics.

GERMAN DEMOCRATIC REPUBLIC

Up to the end of World War II the area which is now the German Democratic Republic was treated, along with the rest of Germany, as part of Western Europe. But after the Red Army of the U.S.S.R. completed its occupation, it was referred to by most Germans as the "Eastern Zone." In the summer of 1945, the principle of equality of all citizens was written into the Potsdam Agreement by the Allied Powers.

Eastern Germany, as it had come to be referred to, was transformed into the "German Democratic Republic" by the Constitution of October 7, 1949. This document, like the Bonn Basic Law, was considered to be a transitional document. It was not patterned on the Soviet Constitution of 1936. On the contrary, it contained many features which are found in liberal and democratic constitutions. Students of German politics did not fail to see certain similarities between the Basic Law of the Federal Republic and the Constitution of the German Democratic Republic. Article 7 (1) of the Constitution of the German Democratic Republic stated that "men and women are equal before the law."

The drafters of the Constitution of the German Democratic Republic found a more direct way toward the legal equalization of the women in East Germany by declaring in Article 7(2) that all laws and provisions which are in conflict with the principle of equality were null and void.

263

In West Germany allowance was made for a transitional period of about four years, in which to repeal or amend such laws and regulations which were in conflict with Article 3 of the Basic Law. Another positive feature of the Constitution of the German Democratic Republic could be found in Article 18, which stated simply that "men and women, adults and youths are entitled to equal pay for equal work." This was not an original feature but was carried over from the Constitution of 1919.

As was pointed out before, in the Federal Republic of Germany, the problem of legal constituency and continuity was an extremely difficult one which could not be completely resolved within the period originally stipulated in the Basic Law. No such requirement existed in the German Democratic Republic because there, as in the other Communist states, the concept of legality simply meant that whatever changes were to be effected had to be made by appropriate legal enactments. Thus, by their kind of due process of law "a radically different order could be established in a short period of time." The key principle was "democratic centralism" and its directing force was the central committee of the Socialist Unity Party (SED), which had been created in April 1946 through the merger or submerger of the Social Democratic Party (SPD) and the Communist Party (KPD). About a year later, on March 8, 1947, the Democratic Federation of Women (DFD) was created by the SED to function as its auxiliary representing the interests of women.

However, this process of power coordination and consolidation seemed to favor a small oligarchy of men. Even the most dedicated Communist women were hardly ever allowed to participate in the decision-making process. In July 1950 Walter Ulbricht became secretary general of the SED, and from that time until his death in 1973 he was the undisputed ruler of East Germany, whom some observers called "The Stalin of the GDR." During this long period all kinds of transformations took place in the GDR and its relations with other countries. Ulbricht had proved himself a loyal Stalinist, and on September 29, 1950 the German Democratic Republic was admitted to membership in the Council for Mutual Economic Aid, which is usually called COMECON in the West. The planned economy of the GDR was thus to be coordinated with that of the U.S.S.R. and the other COMECON members. For that purpose the first five-year plan was inaugurated on January 1, 1951. In 1952 power was increasingly centralized and without any constitutional amendment. The federal structure was scrapped by abolishing the States (Länder) and a unitary system put into operation. The judicial system was also drastically altered on October 2nd with a new law on judicial organization. But all of this institutional engineering failed to provide the basis for the desired economic development, and in 1953 German workers protested against increased work quotas. Their protests were silenced by the armed forces of the GDR and the U.S.S.R. At a time when capitalism, revitalized by the Marshall Plan, was beginning to show results in the West, the planned economy of the GDR appeared to be in great difficulty. But this did not stop Walter Ulbricht from declaring in July 1955 that the transitional period between capitalism and socialism had come to an end.

What did women achieve during this period? In 1949, in the provisional People's Chamber, women constituted 16.1 percent of the total membership. In 1950, in the first People's Chamber, this percentage rose to 23, but it did not increase significantly during the next decade. According to the official Statistical Yearbook of the GDR, it was still 23 percent in 1954, 23.8 percent in 1958, but it rose to 26.5 percent in 1963 in the 4th People's Chamber. During the most recent decade and a half the women's numerical representation has increased impressively. In 1967, it rose to 30.2 percent. In 1971, in the 6th People's Chamber it was still 30.2 percent, but in 1976 it increased to 33.6 percent, and it seems to have stabilized at that level. Of all the Communist states, only Bulgaria has a higher representation of women.

There appears to have been a correlation between the increasing share of women in the work force of the GDR and their greater political participation. If one uses the latest available statistics, as compiled by the Council of Mutual Economic Assistance in Moscow, the following comparisons can be made.[1]

	1960	1970	1975	1978
Percentage of Women in				
Total Population	54.9	53.9	53.5	53.3
Women in labor force	44.4	48.6	50.2	50.5
Women Deputies	16.4	30.4	33.5	33.5
Women People's Judges	30.4	35.5	40.9	47.2

It is very difficult to compile reliable statistics on the number of women in top political and administrative positions. With respect to the number of deputies, it must be remembered that, as in the other Communist statistics, no details are provided as to the level at which women occupy certain positions.

[1]"La Mujer En La Sociedad Socialista." Moscow 1980. For an interesting comparison, see Harry G. Shaffer, Women in the Two Germanies. A Comparative Study of a Socialist and Non-Socialist Society. Pergamon Press, 1981.

The constitutional and legal foundations of women's rights have also been strengthened during this period. The new constitution which came into effect on April 9, 1968 characterized the GDR as a "socialist state of German nationhood." Although it emphasizes the "foundations of the Socialist Social and State Order," it also elaborates the provisions concerning women's rights, and the two are closely and even inextricably interrelated. The primacy of the socialist order is immediately apparent in that the pertinent provisions are Part I of the documents. "Citizens and Organizations in the Socialist Society" constitute Part II. Article 19(3) states that "every citizen has equal rights and manifold opportunities to develop his abilities to the full extent and to unfold his own powers, upon free decision unhindered in the socialist society, for the welfare of society and for his own benefit." The wording is interesting, not only because it illustrates the primacy of the "welfare of society," but because the wording refers to "his" rather than "theirs." The apparent male bias could easily have been avoided by simply using the plural form. "All citizens have equal rights to develop their abilities." If this were done, one might not have the impression that the opportunities are more "manifold" for men than for women. But this may only be clumsiness on the part of the drafters of the Constitution. In any case Article 20(2) is worded much more satisfactorily: "Men and women have equal rights and have the same legal status in all spheres of societal, state, and personal life. The advancement of women, particularly with regard to vocational qualification, is a task of society and the state."

The right of participation "in shaping the political, economic, social, and cultural life of the socialist community and the socialist state" is set forth in Article 21(1).

Article 21(2) states that "the right to codetermination and participation is safeguarded in that the citizens elect democratically all organs of power, and participate in their activities in planning, management and shaping of societal life." According to the same article, they can demand an accounting on the part of officials, express "their demands with the authority of their societal organizations," and can manifest their will through plebiscites.

Article 21(3) notes that "the realization of this right to codetermination and participation is at the same time a highly moral obligation for every citizen."

In addition to these somewhat unusual provisions, there are the more standard definitions of what criteria were required for voting (18 years) and elective offices (21 years). Article 22(2) was amended in 1974 to read: "Every citizen can be elected to the People's Chamber and to the local people's representative bodies if he has reached the age of 18

266

on election day." In the GDR, as in other countries, many people think there is no relationship between biological and political maturity, but they are not worried that the amendment of this article will bring about a drastic change in the composition of these bodies.

Much more interesting is Article 23(1), which states: "The protection of peace and the socialist fatherland and its achievements is the right and the honorable duty of the citizens of the GDR. Every citizen is obligated to serve and to contribute to the defense of the GDR in accordance with the laws." This broadly stated civic obligation has been interpreted by some West German scholars to mean that women serving in the armed forces could be called to participate in military operations. But to date this has not been the case, either in Czechoslovakia (in 1968) or anywhere else. Women serving in the armed forces have not been given the same opportunities as men. Most of them have performed clerical or technical duties in health and communication services.

The principle of "equal pay for equal work" was reaffirmed in Article 24(1). Legal equality in family relations is "safeguarded" in Article 38, but no new principles or guidelines were added in the amended text of 1974.

HUNGARY

In Hungary the war came to an end on April 4, 1945, and the Provisional National Assembly as well as the Provisional Government moved from Debrecin to Budapest. Women participated in the municipal elections that were held in Budapest in the fall of 1945 on the basis of the new election Law No VIII/1945. The non-Marxist Smallholders Party achieved an absolute majority with 57.5 percent of the votes cast. At that time the fusion ticket of the Communist Party and the Social Democratic Party could muster only 17 percent of the votes, but Matyas Rakósi, the leading Communist, was given some key posts in the coalition government. The Communist Party led the campaign to transform Hungary into a republic, or more specifically "a people's republic." This was accomplished by Law No I /1946. Law XX/1946, which came into effect on October 21, 1946, proclaimed women's equal rights to higher education. Law XLIII/1948 forbade discrimination against women in public employment as well as other fields. During this period the Communist Party sought to achieve complete control, and Rakósi was able to eliminate the chief opposition elements. In early 1949 Cardinal Mindszenty was charged with conspiracy against the state and sentenced to life imprisonment. Rakósi also eliminated the chief ideologist and potential rival, Laszlo Rajk.

Law XI/1949 provided for the participation of working people in judicial proceedings. Rakósi was now ready to have a constitution drafted. The Soviet (Stalin) Constitution of 1936 was to be the main model, but the drafting committee was also to take into account the recent constitutions of other Communist states, namely the Bulgarian Constitution of December 4, 1947, the Romanian Constitution of May 1, 1948, and the Constitution of Czechoslovakia of May 9, 1948. The Constitution of the Hungarian People's Republic was promulgated by Law XX/1949 on August 20th. Article 50 declared: "In the Hungarian People's Republic, women enjoy equal rights with men." Article 63(1) provided that "All Citizens of the Hungarian People's Republic, who are of age, have the right to vote." However, the next paragraph qualified this statement: "Enemies of the working people and those who are unsound of mind are excluded from suffrage by law." All others who have the right to vote were "eligible for election." (Art. 65)

In 1953, the election laws of 1945 (VIII), 1947 (XXII), and 1949 (IX) were amended by Law II/1953. The voting age was lowered to 18 (Art 2). A National Election Commission was established for the supervision of elections. Article 7 of this same law provided for the nomination of candidates by mass organizations, local industrial and agricultural organizations, through administrative offices and the organs of the armed forces.

During the subsequent period the Constitution was frequently amended. Thus, the seventh amendment of September 25, 1954 (Law VIII/1954) provided the basis for changes concerning election to local councils. The implementing legislation was provided by Law IX/1954 and Law X/1954.

These technical changes were overshadowed by demands for more fundamental changes and democratization. In July 1956, Rakósi was dismissed from his post as the leader of the Party. Power struggles ensued, which were based on personal as well as ideological differences. The momentous events which led to the Hungarian Revolution cannot and need not be detailed here, but they explain some of the changes that were made in the constitutional and legal system in the subsequent period. The term of the Parliament, which had been elected in May 1953, was extended three more years by Law I/1957. The election law was modified by Law III/1958. The legal equality of women was reaffirmed in the new Civil Code, which was promulgated by Law IV/1959.

The new military service law (Law IV/1960) established the principle that all citizens between the ages of 18 and 50 were subject to the draft. However, women were not obliged to serve in the armed forces except in time of war.

Law III/1961 introduced comprehensive legislation for the educational system. Schooling was made compulsory for all between the ages of six and 16. The number of teachers expanded substantially and the percentages of women teachers rose impressively.

The third Five-Year Plan, which was enacted by Law II/1966 also resulted in bringing more women into various sectors of the economy. In the following year, Law II/1967, a new Labor Code, was promulgated. Part III of this comprehensive document confirmed special provisions concerning the rights of working women and the rights of children.

Law III/1970 once again amended the election law. All citizens who had reached the age of 18 were entitled to vote unless they had been deprived of this right by a criminal sentence, or were considered to be mentally ill. On November 28, 1970, at the Tenth Party Congress, James Kadar, who had been a highly controversial figure in 1956, was unanimously reelected first secretary of the Party. The long delayed revision of the Constitution of 1949 got under way. But the final text was not published until March 19, 1972. (Law I/1972) Hungary was not defined as a Socialist State.

The provisions which concern the fundamental rights and duties of citizens were not greatly changed, but the constitutional and legal status of women were strengthened. Article 61, which corresponds to Article 50 of the 1949 Constitution, is much more explicit. After declaring that "the citizens of the Hungarian People's Republic are equal before the law and enjoy equal rights," a second paragraph warns that "the law severely punishes any prejudicial discrimination of the citizen by sex, religious affiliation or nationality."

In 1972 it was repeated that "women enjoy equal rights with men." This is amplified in the second subparagraph, "The equality of rights of women is served by the guarantee of opportunity of employment and conditions of employment in the appropriate manner; by paid leave in the event of pregnancy and childbirth, increased legal protection of maternity and children, and by a system of institutions for maternity and children's welfare."

There are several other paragraphs which deal with the rights and duties of citizens. (Paragraphs 63-70) But they do not specifically refer to the equality of the rights of women. They are rights and duties of all citizens. Article 70, which deals with the duty to defend the country, does not specify what functions women are expected to perform. The electoral rights are grouped in a separate chapter. (VIII)

Between 1960 and 1976 women's employment rose from 32.5 to 44 percent. The increase was not so great as far as political participation was concerned. In 1958 women constituted 12.6 percent of the deputies. The percentage rose to 18 in 1967 and to 25.1 in 1973. The increase in the number of women among the people's judges is startling. In 1958 women constituted 12 percent. This percentage rose to 15 in 1964, 30 in 1977, and 44 in 1978. Elections were held on June 8, 1950 for 352 seats in Parliament and for some sixty thousand seats of local councils. Ninety-seven percent of all eligible voters participated. The latest official percentage of women in local councils is 31, as compared with 25.1 in 1973. As of December 1981 there were 104 women in the National Assembly. They constitute 29.5 percent, up from 24 percent in 1971, and 18 percent in 1949. In July 1981 there were no women in the cabinet, but two served as deputy ministers. In the Presidential Council there are four women out of a total of 21. Several women occupy prominent positions on the Staff of the National Assembly. Mrs. L. Erdes is the speaker, and Mrs. S. Horvath is one of the three deputy speakers. Mrs. Erdes is also president of the National Council of Hungarian Women and is thus in an excellent position to exert influence on legislative activity. It was reported that the National Council held a conference in October 1980 to examine the adequacy of the Family Act of 1952, as amended in 1974. It concluded that it should be further revised so as to "promote the development of a better socialist family pattern."

POLAND

The fate of Poland was settled by the leaders of the Great Powers when they met at Yalta in February 1945. Roosevelt and Churchill accepted Stalin's demand that a part of Eastern Poland be ceded to the U.S.S.R. As a compensation for this loss of territory Poland was to be allowed to extend its sovereignty over a large area of eastern and northern Germany.

In the early summer of 1945 a coalition government was formed which included members of the former London-based government in exile. A national referendum was held a year later on a number of important issues: the abolition of the Senate, the nationalization of key industries, as well as the new frontiers. This referendum, as well as elections of January 17, 1947, which resulted in a Communist victory were widely believed to have involved serious irregularities.

The so-called "Little Constitution," which was promulgated on February 19, 1947, was essentially a modified version of the old Constitution of 1921, except that it provided for one chamber only and that it did not incorporate the chapter on fundamental rights and duties. This was remedied, however, a few days later, on February 27, when a "Declaration of Rights and Liberties" was adopted by the Sejm.

A new instrumentality of power was the State Council, which was set up in April 1947. It was given power to legislate by decree during interim periods when the *Sejm* was not in session.

Tito's break with Stalin had serious repercussions in Poland. Gomulka, the secretary general of the Communist Party, was dismissed from this key position in September 1948. A year later he was expelled from the Party.

From early 1949 on, the real power was in the hands of the Soviet Marshall Rokossovsky, who was made defense minister and commander of the Polish Armed Forces. The Constitution was amended to legitimize his participation in the meetings of the State Council. In 1950, it was reported that he had been elected to membership in the Politburo of the Polish Communist Party. A process of power consolidation was coming to an end, and in 1952 the stage had been reached for a new constitution which would reflect the new realities.

The Polish Constitution of July 22, 1952, like its counterparts in other Eastern European countries, was patterned on the Soviet or "Stalin Constitution" of 1936. The pertinent articles concerning women's rights were put in Chapter 7 (Fundamental Rights and Duties of Citizens). As stated in Article 57: "The Polish People's Republic, by consolidating and multiplying the gains of the working people, strengthens and extends the rights and liberties of the citizens." The most specific provisions may be found in Articles 66, 81, 82 and 83.

Article 66:

> Women in the Polish People's Republic have equal rights with men in all fields of public, political, economic, social and cultural life.

Article 81:

> Every citizen, who has reached the age of eighteen, irrespective of sex, nationality and race, religion, education, length of residence, social origin, profession and property, has the right to vote.

Article 82:

> Every citizen, who has reached the age of eighteen, is eligible to be elected to the People's Councils, and every citizen who has reached the age of twenty-one is eligible to be elected to the Sejm.

Article 83:

> Women have all electoral rights on equal terms with men.

In April, 1956 Gomulka was released from prison and once again elected first secretary of the Party. A new electoral law was promulgated by the *Sejm* on October 24, 1956.

According to Article 1(1):

> Elections are universal: every Polish citizen who has reached the age of eighteen on the day of elections has the right to vote, irrespective of sex, nationality, race, religion, education, length of residence, social origin, profession and property.

Article 3:

> Everyone who has the right to vote is eligible for elections if he has reached the age of twenty-one.

A new Electoral Law for the People's Council was promulgated on October 31, 1957. Article 1(1) was unchanged.

Article 3 stated:

> Everyone who has the right to vote is eligible for elections.

In 1963, by means of a constitutional amendment of Article 34(2), the terms of office of the elected members of people's councils were extended from three to four years. In 1964, the Civil Code was published, which came into effect on January 1, 1965.

A new defense law was passed on November 21, 1967, which obliged men and women who had not been called to regular military service to serve in the home defense service.

From 1972 to 1976 the Constitution of 1952 was extensively amended several times. The tenth amendment, which was passed on February 10, 1976, was the most comprehensive one. About one-third of the original 91 articles were amended. Twelve new articles were added and one was deleted. It was now deemed necessary to publish a completely amended text. Many of the changes were extremely controversial.

The original wording of Article 78, which affirms the duty of every citizen to defend the country and to perform military service, was left unchanged but renumbered Article 92.

As for voting rights, the pertinent articles are numbered 95, 96, and 97. They correspond to the original, already cited Articles 81, 82 and 83.

What about participation of women? According to a Polish scholar, the participation of women from 1958 to 1968 increased from 5.8 percent to 15.4 percent. In the 1970s the participation of women in the various sectors of economic life continued to be much greater than in politics. Women accounted for more than 40 percent of the labor force. In 1970 women members of the Sejm constituted 13.5 percent of the total membership. The percentage was much larger than in the people's councils (18.9). In 1978 there were 95 women deputies in the Sejm, as compared with 73 in 1974. This represents an increase from 16 percent to 21 percent. In 1980, according to the Central Statistical Office, women deputies in the Parliament constituted 23 percent of the total. The increase was consistently larger in the people's councils. In 1958, the percentage was only about 6, but fifteen years later it had grown to 23. In the district people's councils they now represent about 28 percent of the total membership. Women have been very active in the Solidarity movement. But they seem to have made little progress in gaining more participation in the governmental apparatus. In 1980 there were several Cabinet reorganizations. In the fourth, which was approved by the Sejm on November 21, Mrs. Maria Milczarek, the minister of labor, was replaced by her male deputy, Jerzy Ozdowski. Among the 15 members of the Politburo, who were confirmed July 18, 1981 by the Congress of the Polish United Workers Party, there was only one woman, Mrs. Grzyb.

ROMANIA

On April 13, 1948 the National Assembly approved a new constitution, officially known as the Constitution of the Romanian People's Republic. Western commentators, for the most part, referred to it as a copy of the Soviet Constitution of 1936. This was not entirely correct because this constitution was not designed for a state in which Marxism-Leninism was already firmly rooted. It was intended as a transitional document and, therefore, contained provisions which acknowledged some remnants of a bourgeois-capitalist institution. Thus, Article 9 referred to private property but stated that it could be nationalized in the interest of society. The provisions concerning fundamental rights and duties showed closer resemblance to the Yugoslav Constitution of 1946 than to the Stalin Constitution.

With respect to women's rights, the following articles may be noted: Article 16:

> All citizens of the People's Republic of Romania, irrespective of sex, nationality, race, religion or educational qualifications, are equal before the law.

Article 18:

> All citizens, irrespective of sex, nationality, religion, educational qualifications, profession, including servicemen, magistrates and civil servants, have the right of electing and being elected to all the organs of the State.

> All citizens, who have reached the age of 18 have the right to vote, and all citizens who have reached the age of 23 have the right to be elected.

Article 21:

> Women are accorded equal rights with men in all spheres of public, economic, social, cultural, private law and political life. ·
> For equal work women have the right to equal pay as men.

Between 1948 and 1952 important institutional transformations were carried out to implement the Marxist-Leninist principles of the unity of governmental power and democratic centralism. The collectivization of agriculture and the nationalization of private enterprises were rapidly implemented. In 1950, the National Assembly enacted a new election law, which paved the way for a victory by the People's Democratic Front.

In the spring of 1952 the National Assembly decided that the time had come for the drafting of a new constitution, which would reflect the economic, political and social transformations which had taken place. It was this constitution, adopted by the National Assembly on September 24, 1952, which showed much greater resemblance to the

Soviet Constitution of 1936. Indeed, several articles were completely taken from the Soviet model.

The articles which concern the equality of men and women were placed in Chapter VII rather than Chapter III, as in the Constitution of 1948. This was not a technicality but rather an expression of the changed political system and its ideological orientation. As stated in the Introductory Chapter: "The present Constitution of the Romanian People's Republic consolidates the results so far obtained by the working people, headed by the working class in the task of building socialist society in our country."

The Introductory Chapter is followed by Chapter I entitled Social System; Chapter 2, The State System; Chapter 3, The Supreme Organ of State Power of the Romanian People's Republic; Chapter 4, The Organs of the State Administration of the Romanian People's Republic; Chapter 5, The Organs of Local State Power; Chapter 6, The Judicial Institutions and the Procurator's Office. Only after all of these predominantly state-centered Articles, Chapter 7 dealt with "The Fundamental Rights and Duties of Citizens." The very first article (77) of this chapter reads: "The citizens of the Romanian People's Republic are ensured the right to work, that is the right to obtain guaranteed work paid according to its quantity and quality."

But the constitutional provisions concerning women's rights are not always entirely clear.

Article 81:

> The working people, citizens of the Romanian People's Republic without regard to their nationality or race, are guaranteed full legal equality in all areas of economic, political and cultural life.

Sex, or gender, is not mentioned, as far as can be determined. The second subparagraph, which declares that any direct or indirect restrictions are punishable by law, does not mention sex.
There is no problem with Article 83:

> Women in the Romanian People's Republic have equal rights with men in all areas of economic, political, governmental and cultural life. The women have equal rights with the men to work, pay, rest, social insurance and education.

The last paragraph places marriage and the family under the protection of the state and provides for state grants to mothers with many children, paid vacations for pregnant women, maternity homes, and nurseries.

Article 91 provides for compulsory military service, but it does not specify whether women are included. An interesting discrepancy may be found in the translations of Article 92. One reads: "To defend the motherland is the sacred duty of every citizen of the Romanian People's Republic." Other translations refer to the fatherland.

The articles concerning elections are much clearer: Article 94 states that the right to participate in the election of deputies belongs to all who have reached the age of 18 "without regard to race, nationality, sex, religion, educational level, profession or length of residency." Excepted are those who are insane, those who have been deprived of the right to vote or have been declared "unworthy" by law. The same article states that any citizen, aged 23, who has the right to vote, may be elected a deputy of the Great National Assembly. Although it may appear redundant, Article 96 states that women have the right to elect and be elected on equal terms with men.

At first, the participation of women was less than spectacular, but they did participate, especially in local affairs. Of the 423 deputies elected on November 30, 1952, 63 were women.

Up to 1952, one of the most powerful women in the Communist world was the Romanian-born, Ana Pauker. At the age of 28, in 1922, she had come to be the leading figure in the Romanian Communist Party. She returned from the Soviet Union with the Red Army in 1944 and became secretary general of the Communist Party. Subsequently, she served as Romania's foreign minister. But she fell out of favor, and in 1952 she was denounced as a "Moscovite" and removed by Gheorghin-Dej, who had risen to the top position in the Politburo. He had been the ideological archivist of the 1952 Constitution and had charted the new course toward a more national communism. After his death in March 1965, Nicolae Ceausescu succeeded him as leader of the party and as president of the Constitution Commission which had been elected in 1961 to draft a new constitution. New Party Statutes were approved by the Ninth Party Congress in July 1965, and the new Constitution was approved by the National Assembly on August 21, 1965. Not unexpectedly, it was in many respects quite different from the Soviet model, and there were no more references to the Soviet Union. It contained an impressive Catalogue of Fundamental Rights and Duties.

Articles 17-41, which were contained in Chapter II, were not changed when the Constitution was amended on April 20, 1972 by Law No. 1/1972. They are very clear and explicit in emphasizing the constitutional and legal equality of men and women.

Article 17:

Citizens of the Socialist Republic of Romania, without distinction as to nationality, race, sex or religion, shall have equal rights in all fields of economic, political, legal, social and cultural activity.

The State shall guarantee the equal rights of citizens. No restrictions of these rights and no discrimination in the exercise thereof on grounds of nationality, race, sex or religion shall be permitted.

Any manifestation aimed at establishing such restrictions, nationalist-chauvinist propaganda and incitement to racial or national hatred shall be punishable by law.

Article 18 stipulated:

For equal work there is equal remuneration.

The same article recognized the need for special measures to protect women as well as young persons:

The law establishes the measures for the protection and safety of labor, as well as special measures for the protection of the work of women and young people.

Article 23 declared:

In the Socialist Republic of Romania women shall have equal rights with men. The state shall protect marriage and the family and shall defend the interests of mothers and children.

The provisions for assuring "material security" are specified in Article 20, which also states that "paid maternity leave is guaranteed."

Article 25 deals with electoral rights:

Citizens of the Socialist Republic of Romania shall have the right to elect and to be elected to the People's Councils.

The vote shall be universal, equal, direct and secret. All citizens who have reached the age of eighteen years shall have the right to vote.

Citizens who have the right to vote and who have reached the age of twenty-three years can be elected as deputies to the Grand National Assembly and to the People's Councils.

The same article identifies the organizations which are entitled to nominate candidates:

The Organizations of the Romanian Communist Party, the Trade Unions, the Cooperatives, the Youth and Women's Organizations, and other Mass and Public Organizations.

It is stated that "the Electors have the right to recall their deputy at any time, according to the same procedure under which he has been nominated or elected." Stated in the English translation there appears to be a suggestion here that the deputies will be men. This unwarranted suggestion of male exclusiveness could readily have been avoided by using the plural form: "recall their deputies."

With respect to freedom of association, Article 27 states that:

Citizens of the Socialist Republic of Romania shall have the right to associate in trade unions, co-operative, young people's, women's, social and cultural organizations, unions of creative artists, scientific, technical and sports associations and other public organizations . . .

Article 28 deals with freedom of assembly:

Citizens of the Socialist Republic of Romania shall be guaranteed freedom of speech, of the Press, of assembly, of meeting and of demonstration.

In 1966, a new election law, No 28/1966 was promulgated, which contains detailed regulations for the implementation of Articles 25, 44, 45, and 81 of the Constitution, concerning the election of deputies to the Grand National Assembly and the People's Councils. Of the 94 articles of this comprehensive law, the most relevant ones are: Articles 1, 10, 16 and 17. Some of these articles, including Article 1, restate specific articles of the Constitution. Thus, Article 3 repeats the provisions of Article 25 of the Constitution, concerning the recall of deputies. Article 4 specifies that deputies are to be elected for four years. Article 5 provides for the creation of 465 constituencies.

Law No 28/1966, on the Election of Deputies to the Grand National Assembly and to the People's Councils is a well drafted document, but some of the articles could be revised so as to eliminate misleading references to the implied male gender of the voter. Thus, Article 16 might read "all voters" rather than "every voter."

English translation of Articles 1, 10, 16 and 17 follow:

Article 1:

Under article 25 of the Constitution of the Socialist Republic of Romania, citizens of the Socialist Republic of Romania shall have the right to elect and to be elected to the Grand National Assembly and the People's Councils.

The vote shall be universal, equal, direct and secret. All citizens who have reached the age of eighteen years shall have the right to vote.

Citizens who have the right to vote and who have reached the age of twenty-three years can be elected as deputies to the Grand National Assembly and to the People's Councils.

The following shall not have the right to elect and to be elected: the insane, the mentally deficient and persons deprived of these rights for a period fixed by the sentence of a court. The interdiction order of the court shall constitute proof of the state of insanity or mental deficiency.

Article 10:

The names of all citizens of the Socialist Republic of Romania who have the right to vote shall be entered on the electoral rolls for the communes, towns or urban districts in which they are resident.

The names of all citizens who acquire the right to vote up to and including the date of the elections shall also be entered on the electoral rolls.

The name of a voter shall not be entered on more than one electoral roll.

Article 16:

Every voter shall have the right to verify whether his name has been entered on the electoral rolls and to lodge a complaint with the Executive Committee of the People's Council which prepared the rolls if his name has been omitted from, or incorrectly entered on, the rolls, or if the rolls contain errors of other kinds.

The Executive Committee of the People's Council shall be obliged to settle the complaint and publish a notice of its decision within three days from the date on which the complaint is registered.

The complainant shall have the right to appeal against a decision by the Executive Committee of the People's Council, within three days from the date on which notice of the decision is published, to the People's Court of the constituency in which the electoral roll has been placed on display.

The appeal may also be deposited with the Executive Committee of the People's Council, which shall be obliged to forward it immediately to the People's Court.

The People's Court shall be obliged to deliver its judgement within three days from the date on which the appeal is registered and to inform the complainant and the Executive Committee of the People's Council of its decision within twenty-four hours after it delivers its judgment, in order that the electoral rolls may be corrected accordingly.

The decision of the People's Court shall be final.

Article 17:

If the voter changes his domicile after the closing of the electoral rolls or is absent from his place of domicile on the date of the elections, a "certificate concerning the exercise of the right to vote" shall be handed to the voter by the Executive Committee of the People's Council which prepared the electoral rolls, and this circumstance shall be noted on the electoral rolls.

At his new place of domicile or at the place where he is temporarily on the date of the elections, the voter shall be entered on a separate electoral roll by the electoral commission for the polling station upon presentation of the "certificate concerning the exercise of the right to vote" and of his identity papers.

The Electoral Law, which was enacted in 1974 (Law No 67/1974) did not alter the basic provisions of the just cited Law No 28/1966. But it contains several articles (95-102), which spell out the procedure to be followed in the recall of deputies.

The basic constitutional and legal framework concerning women's rights was not changed when the constitution was amended in 1972, 1974, and 1975. But there have been new laws, which seek to implement certain constitutional provisions. Law No 3/1977 provided new regulations concerning eligibility for pensions and social assistance for men and women.

Decree No 197/1977 established detailed regulations for financial aid to mothers with many children. Two hundred lei was due to mothers with 5 to 6 children, 350 lei to mothers with 7 to 9 children, and 500 lei to mothers with 10 or more children.

Law No 28/1978, the Law on Education, is an interesting and comprehensive piece of legislation. Article 2 states that the citizens of the Socialist Republic of Romania have the right to education, without any distinction on grounds of national origin, race, sex or religion, and without any other restriction which could represent a discrimination.

As stated in Article 120:

> The teaching personnel in the field of social sciences shall have the duty to continuously raise the level of political-ideological training, to ensure the teaching of political-ideological disciplines in close connection with socio-political realities, the questions our party and state are concerned in, the problems of international life and the evolution of contemporary society; they shall have the duty to participate in the practical and socio-political activity, in the propagation of the party, ideology and policy in the ranks of the working people.

The ideological guidelines in all fields, including the advancement of women have been clear and consistent. But Ceausescu has not relied too much on ideological firmness. He has put great emphasis on organization control arrangements. Like seven other Communist leaders, he has not hesitated to bring in members of his family to direct and supervise major policy efforts. As early as 1967, Ceausescu had come to be recognized as one of the most astute Communist leaders in the world. He had successfully extended Romania's independence in the field of foreign policy, and he seemed prepared to allow further liberalizations in domestic affairs. However, he made it clear that whatever liberalizations were to be carried out would have to be undertaken through the instrumentality of the Communist Party. The women's movement has been encouraged but also directed by the Communist Party, and more particularly by his wife, Elena.

In November 1979, at the 12th Party Congress, Ceausescu, in his capacity as secretary general, presented some statistical data on the membership of the CPR. Women were reported to constitute 28 percent of the membership. Ceausescu's wife, Elena, was firmly in control of the National Council of Women. A few weeks before the Congress, her prestige was further enhanced when she was appointed president of the National Council of Science and Technology. In 1980, Elena Ceausescu was made one of the eight deputy prime ministers. Another woman, who was made deputy prime minister, was Cornelia Filipas, the vice-chairperson of the National Council of Women.

YUGOSLAVIA

At the end of World War II, the situation in Yugoslavia was very different from that of all the other countries of Eastern Europe. Yugoslavia did not owe its liberation to the Red Army of the Soviet Union. The people of Yugoslavia were able to free themselves, but at a heavy cost. More than a million men and more than half a million women were killed. An independent Yugoslav government was established as early as March 5, 1945. A new National Assembly was elected to draft a new Constitution. It met as a Constituent Assembly from November 29, 1945 until the end of January 1946. The first Constitution, which was promulgated on January 31, 1946, showed close resemblance to the Soviet Constitution of 1936, but it also had many original features. With respect to women's rights, some of the key provisions were contained in Article 24:

> Women shall have equal rights as men in all spheres of state, economic and socio-political life. Women shall have equal pay for the same work as men and shall enjoy special protection at work. The State shall in particular protect the interests of mother and child by establishing maternity wards, children's homes and day nurseries, and by granting mothers the right to a paid leave before and after childbirth.

The first Constitution also contained very comprehensive provisions guaranteeing the equality of political rights. After Tito's break with Stalin in 1948, Yugoslavia embarked upon a remarkably original and creative approach which gradually came to center on the principle of self-management. The Constitution of 1953, Yugoslavia's second fundamental law, incorporated this idea, but it was in the nature of a transitional framework, which was to facilitate further transformations. These came on April 7, 1963, when the third Constitution was adopted by the Federal Assembly. Article 33 reaffirmed that "citizens are equal in their rights and duties, regardless of differences in nationality, race, religion, sex, language, education and social position. All are equal before the law."

Article 35 confirmed the rights of all citizens who had reached the age of eighteen:

> In exercising these rights, citizens shall nominate candidates for election and elect delegates to representative bodies and organs of social self-government, and may stand for election to these bodies and organs.

> Every member of a work community shall have the right to elect and to stand for election to the bodies of management and his work organization.

It should be noted that in this article, as in many others, some technical terms are used which are distinctly part of the Yugoslav system of self-management or self-government, as it was called before the promulgation of the Constitution of 1974, i.e. the current Constitution.

This system, linked as it was with a policy of decentralization and debureaucratization, facilitated the political participation of women, because they were able to be more active in their local communities. Article 156 of the Constitution of 1974 provides that "all citizens who have reached the age of eighteen shall have the right to elect and be elected members of delegations in basic self-managing organizations and communities, and to elect and be elected delegates to the assemblies of the socio-political communities."

Article 154 reaffirms that "citizens shall be equal in their rights and duties regardless of nationality, race, sex, language, religion, education and social status. All shall be equal before the law." This principle is so well established that relatively few articles refer to women in particular. They are all encompassed under the designation "citizens." There are several provisions, such as Article 188, dealing with the protection of mothers and children.

The Associated Labor Act of 1976, which is a long and complex piece of legislation, is the most important implementing Act of the Constitution of 1974.[1]

Like the Constitution, which has been called "the Self-Management Charter" of Yugoslavia, the Associated Labor Act is not concerned with

---

[1]An English translation and a commentary by Gisbert H. Flanz was published in December 1979 as a special supplement to *Constitutions of the Countries of the World.* Oceana Publications, Dobbs Ferry, N.Y.

the status of women. It is, as its title suggests, primarily concerned with labor relations. The constitutional principle of gender equality is now sufficiently established, but it is recognized that the patriarchal family order has not entirely disappeared in all parts of Yugoslavia. In order to make gender equality more than a constitutional principle, a considerable body of legislation has been passed by republican and provincial assemblies which deal specifically with family relations and related matters, such as child welfare, education, health protection, retirement and disability insurance.

Vida Tomšič has provided us with detailed information on the participation of women in the economic and noneconomic activities in Yugoslavia as a whole as well as in various parts of the country. By noneconomic activities are meant a) cultural and welfare activities, and b) public services and public administration. The comparative percentages for the years 1954 to 1976 in all of Yugoslavia are as follows:[2]

Noneconomic Activities	1954	1964	1974	1976
a) Cultural and welfare activities	51.8	56.3	59.6	60.5
b) Public Services and public administration	27.3	42.0	48.3	50.3

These cumulative percentages may not be generally accepted as sufficiently meaningful. But they do show that the increases in women's participation in public services and public administration have been much larger than in cultural and welfare activities. While in the latter field the participation was very high from the beginning, participation in public services and public administration had a long way to go. Tomšič also provides us with more recent (1979) statistics on the SFRY and on the "percentage of employed women by Socialist Republics and Autonomous Provinces." For Yugoslavia as a whole (SFRY), the percentages are:

In economic activities	30.5
In noneconomic activities	58.3

This would mean that in the course of 25 years the participation of women in public services and public administration has doubled. The breakdown by republic and autonomous provinces is even more inter-

[2]Tomsic, *op. cit.*, p. 194.

esting in the sense that it confirms what was said in the very beginning of this section on Yugoslavia. Overall national comparisons tend to be superficial, if not misleading. There are regional and other differences which scholars should not ignore. Here are the percentages as of 1979 of the participation of women:

	In economic activities %	In noneconomic activities %
Bosnia and Hercegovina	25.9	55.5
Croatia	34.0	64.7
Macedonia	26.0	49.1
Montenegro	26.3	49.2
Serbia	27.8	54.3
Serbia proper	28.0	55.7
Kosovo	16.3	32.1
Vojvodina	30.2	61.0
Slovenia	39.2	70.6

To those who know Yugoslavia well, it will come as no surprise that the women of Slovenia, Croatia, and the Vojvodina lead in the "noneconomic activities." What is surprising is that the participation of Serbian women is now only slightly greater than in Bosnia and Hercegovina. Montenegro and Macedonia are now nearly tied. It also shows that the ethnic Albanians in Kosovo are much less active.

The delegate system has been very important in implementing women's rights and in increasing the participation of women. Recent amendments to the 1974 Constitution disclose that this process is continuing.

According to a recent statistical study, there are over 3 million working people and citizens participating in self-management decision-making today. One out of every 8 workers in 1979 carried out some self-management function in an organization of associated labor (OAL) with a workers' council (with over 30 members), while only 1 out of every 15 did so in 1952.[3]

In 1952, only 13 percent of the members of workers' councils were women, while in 1979, the number of women delegates had more than doubled.

[3]All the following data is from *Trideset Godina Samoupravnog Razvoja Jugoslavije* [Thirty Years of Self-Management Development of Yugoslavia] Federal Bureau of Statistics (Savezni Zavod Za Statistiku), Belgrade 1981

The participation of women in management organs after the constitutional changes has significantly increased. In 1972, women made up 17 percent of the members of workers' councils and in 1979 29 percent. The greatest number of women is in workers' councils in work communities (communities that perform accounting and other such services for firms), then in work organizations without basic organizations of associated labor (BOAL), and the smallest in workers' councils of complex organizations of associated labor. Women are most highly represented in workers' councils in basic forms of organization; where self-management organization is more complex, there are fewer women.

In organizations of associated labor and work communities in which there are no workers' councils (under 30 members) the participation of women is greater, as all the women employed are included, and more than half the workers employed in these organizations are women.

The number of women in executive organs of the workers' councils in OAL and work communities with workers' councils is somewhat smaller than in the workers' councils themselves. However, in executive organs of organizations without councils, the percentage of women members is greater than the percentage of women employed in these organizations. The highest number of women among members of delegations is in delegations of work communities, 46 percent; then in work organizations without BOAL, 43 percent; while in delegations with BOAL, the number is only 28 percent.

The participation of women in delegations for the selection of delegates to the assemblies of Self-Managing Communities of Interest (SCI) is approximately the same as their participation in delegations to elect delegates to the assemblies of Socio-Political Communities (organs of government).

The percentage of women in the assemblies of SCI is 19. Participation differs according to the activities concerned and the chambers considered. Greatest participation is in the chambers made up of working people providing services, 26 percent, and the least, in one-chamber assemblies, 17 percent. The greatest participation is in SCI for childcare and social welfare, 40 percent, and education, 32 percent; and the least in those SCI concerned with water power and traffic, 5 percent. Women make up approximately one-fourth of the members of the executive organs of the communities.

In the professional services of the SCI, about 35,000 workers are employed, of which women make up 60 percent. Forty-eight percent of them have high school education, 19 percent have associate degrees, and 15 percent, university degrees or higher.

The participation of women in assemblies of local communities is increasing, from 3 percent in 1974 to 10 percent in 1978. It has reached 20 percent in urban locations, while only 3 percent in village areas.

In 1974, 22 percent and in 1978 26 percent of the total number of members of delegations were women. The greatest number of women was in delegations of work communities from government organs and socio-political organizations, 38 percent; then in delegations from BOAL, 34 percent; and the smallest in delegations of working people who work in the private sector in agriculture, crafts, restaurants and hotels, etc., 9 percent.

Women had higher representation in the assemblies of the Autonomous Regions, 23 percent, than in the assemblies of the Republics, 18 percent. Women comprised 18 percent of the members of the assemblies of the communes and the Federal Assembly of the SFRJ.

Part IV

Women's Rights and International Organizations

CHAPTER 14

THE ROLE OF THE UNITED NATIONS AND OTHER INTERNATIONAL ORGANIZATIONS

Now that developments in individual countries have been analyzed it is necessary to refer to the important role of the United Nations and other international organizations. Without them much less would have been accomplished during this postwar period. As had been done in Article 7 of the Covenant of the League of Nations, the principle of equality and equal access to all the positions was written into the Charter of the United Nations. (Article 8)

The Commission on the Status of Women (CSW) was established by the Economic and Social Council (ECOSOC) in 1946. Its function has been to make recommendations to ECOSOC on urgent matters in the field of women's rights. It was to become a very important body as the principal international advocate and guardian of women's rights. The Commission lost no time in embarking on a study of the contemporary political rights of women. On the basis of a report by the Commission, ECOSOC requested on March 3, 1948 that the Secretary-General

> bring up to date, [information on] action taken by govern-
> ments since the signing of the Charter ... on the political
> rights of women and their eligibility for public office. . . . [1]

In 1948 the principle of equality was anchored into the Universal Declaration of Human Rights.[2] Article 2 states that

> everyone is entitled to all the rights and freedoms set forth
> in this Declaration, without distinction of any kind, such as
> race, color, sex, language, religion, political or other opinion,
> national or social origin, property, birth or other status. ·

The General Assembly of the United Nations adopted and promulgated the Universal Declaration on December 10, 1948.[3]

---

[1] ECOSOC Resolution 120 E (VI) 1948.
[2] ECOSOC Resolution 445 B (IX).
[3] General Assembly Resolution 2200 (XXI).

The Universal Declaration is, of course, a great historic document, and the principles embodied in it were intended to be standards for all mankind. From the point of view of draftsmanship, it is, unfortunately, somewhat defective in that the many articles which begin with the word "everyone" are always used with the male gender. This emphasis could easily have been avoided by referring to "all humans" or "all persons." Unfortunately, this deficiency in the official English text has been carried over into many of the other languages into which it has been translated.

In the early 1950s the Commission on the Status of Women concentrated its efforts on the development of a Draft Convention on Political Rights of Women. A short document consisting of three articles was adopted by ECOSOC on May 26, 1952. The "contracting parties" were invited to sign and ratify a Convention which stated that

(1) women shall be entitled to vote in all elections on equal terms with men. (2) women shall be eligible for election to all publicly elected bodies, established by national law, on equal terms with men. (3) women shall be entitled to hold public office and exercise all public functions, established by national law, on equal terms with men.

The complete final text consists of eleven articles. It was approved by General Assembly Resolution 640(VII) on December 20, 1952, and came into force on July 7, 1954, in accordance with Article VI of the Convention, which states that it will come into effect "on the ninetieth day following the date of deposit of the sixth instrument of ratification or accession."

Aside from the fact that such a low percentage of ratifications can hardly suffice to make it a convincingly general expression of consensus, there were so many reservations by the governments which ratified the Convention after "it came into force" that its effectiveness was very much in doubt.

The main disputes centered on two articles of the Convention; namely, the last sentence of Article VII and Article IX. Article VII provides that "in the event that any state submits a reservation to any of the articles in this Convention, at the time of signature, ratification or accession, the Secretary-General shall communicate the text to all States which are or may become parties to this Convention." Any state which objects to a reservation may notify the Secretary-General within ninety days "that it does not accept it." The disputed last sentence reads as follows: "In such case, the Convention shall not enter into force as between such state and the state making the reservation." The U.S.S.R. objected to this last sentence stating that

> the juridical effect of a reservation is to make the Convention operative as between the state making the reservation and all other states parties to the Convention, with the exception only of that part thereof to which the reservation relates.

The representatives of the Communist governments of Eastern Europe: Albania, Bulgaria, the Byelorussian Soviet Socialist Republics, Czechoslovakia, the German Democratic Republic, Hungary, Poland, Romania and the Ukranian Soviet Socialist Republic made identical declarations. Objections to the reservations made by the governments just mentioned were offered by Canada, the Republic of China, Denmark, the Dominican Republic, Ethiopia, Israel, Norway, Pakistan, the Philippines and Sweden.

Not unexpectedly, the Communist governments raised strong objections in the form of reservations to Article IX of the Convention which states that

> any dispute which may arise between any two or more contracting states concerning the interpretation or application of this Convention which is not settled by negotiation, shall at the request of any one of the parties to the dispute be referred to the International Court of Justice for decision, unless they agree to another mode of settlement.

The U.S.S.R. took exception to this article, stating, that "the agreement of all the parties to the dispute shall be necessary in each individual case." Identical language was used by all the previously mentioned communist states. It should be noted, however, that Yugoslavia maintained its independent position.

There is no evidence that the Convention on the Political Rights of Women had much influence on the actual participation of women in any part of the world, including Europe. Progress was very slow in most European countries in spite of energetic efforts by women's organizations. The United Nations was not in a very good position to urge member states to move more quickly toward the implementation of General Assembly Resolution 640(VII) because it had not set a good example in advancing capable women within the Secretariat.

Indeed, within a decade after its creation, the United Nations had developed into a kind of international patriarchy. While the percentage of women in the Secretariat was relatively high, the overwhelming majority of women worked in secretarial and clerical positions. As the organization became more and more inundated in the paper it generated, one of the major roles of women was to file away enormous quantities of all kinds of documents. In the mid-1950s women held barely one-fifth of the higher posts and, as in their own countries, occupied jobs mainly concerned with social welfare and humanitarian programs. As far as the main political activities were concerned, very few women were seen in important positions.

Among the achievements of the U.N. with respect to women's rights was the Convention on the Nationality of Married Women. Considering the previously mentioned efforts by such organizations as the ICW, this Convention is a very modest accomplishment.

The Convention was opened for signature on January 29, 1957 and entered into force on August 11, 1958. The ratification process took a long time. Some ten years after it was opened for signature, only 21 European countries had ratified it.[4] But there were relatively few reservations. Of the European countries, only the GDR declared that it "does not consider itself bound by the provisions of Article 10, according to which a dispute between the State parties to the Convention in respect of the interpretation and application of the present Convention which has not been settled through negotiation is to be submitted to the International Court of Justice for decision at the request of one of the parties to the dispute, unless the parties have agreed on another way of adjustment."[5] The GDR declared that the International Court of Justice had no competence in matters arising from the Convention unless all parties agree "to submit a particular dispute to the International Court for decision."

As far as most European nationality laws are concerned, the Convention does not break any new ground. The three basic articles are concerned with situations in which the husband's nationality is the issue. They seek to protect the wife's rights to the husband's nationality if she so chooses. They do not resolve the basic inequality and inequity arising from situations in which the husband, who is a foreigner, cannot readily acquire the nationality of his wife. This has long been a problem in Switzerland where the foreign wife of a Swiss citizen can readily acquire Swiss citizenship, but a Swiss woman cannot do much to fa

<hr />

[4]Commission on the Status of Women: Constitutions, Electoral Laws and Other Legal Instruments relating to the Political Rights of Women, 1968. Twenty years later this number had increased to 23.

[5]United Nations Treaty Series, vol. 309, p. 65.

cilitate the acquisition of Swiss citizenship for her foreign-born hus-band.[6]

In the early 1960s closer cooperation was established between the U.N. Commission on Human Rights and the Commission on the Status of Women (CSW). In 1961, in its seventeenth session, the Commission on Human Rights asked the Secretary-General to transmit reports re-ceived for the years 1957 to 1959 to the Commission on the Status of Women. Some doubts were expressed about the value of this informa-tion, and it did not seem to produce any specific actions.

In 1966 the CSW expressed its appreciation to the Commission on Human Rights but thought that "the information supplied by Govern-ments in these reports on matters affecting the status of women could be more comprehensive" and noted that few countries had reported "significant progress in the implementation of Article 16 of the Uni-versal Declaration." The same observation was made concerning Arti-cles 21, 23 and 26, especially with respect to "the access of women to public service." But in the following year (1967) the CSW seemed more pleased with the progress that had been made. In its Periodic Report on Human Rights 2(XX), it noted "with satisfaction" that between January 1963 and June 1966 several governments had taken "legislative or ad-ministrative steps to promote the civil and political rights of women, in particular as regards electoral rights, jury service, marriage and the guardianship of children." The Commission did not specify which gov-ernments had taken these steps.

An important achievement of the mid-1960s was the International Covenant on Civil and Political Rights, a document which had taken about a decade to hammer out. It was finally adopted by the General Assembly on December 16, 1966 and opened for signature three days later. It entered into force on March 23, 1976.

The International Covenant on Civil and Political Rights consists of 53 articles and covers many subjects. Relatively few of the provisions are directly related to women's rights. Article 2 obligates "each State party to the present Covenant" to respect

> the rights recognized in the present Covenant, without dis-tinction of any kind, such as race, color, sex, language, religion, political or other opinion, national or social origin, property, birth or other status.

Article 3 states that

> the State parties to the present Covenant undertake to ensure

[6]Switzerland, which is not a member of the United Nations, is currently seeking to resolve this anomaly in an equitable manner.

the equal right of men and women to the enjoyment of all civil and political rights set forth in the present Covenant.

Article 25 provides that

every citizen shall have the right and the opportunity without any of the distinctions mentioned in Article 2 and without unreasonable restrictions:
(a) to take part in the conduct of public affairs, directly or freely chosen representatives;
(b) to vote and to be elected at genuine periodic elections which shall be by universal and equal suffrage and shall be held by secret ballot, guaranteeing the free expression of the will of the electors;
(c) to have access, on general terms of equality, to public service in his [sic] country.

Article 26 reaffirms that "all persons are equal before the law and are entitled without any discrimination to the equal protection of the law."

Provision is made in Article 28 for a Human Rights Committee which is to consist of 18 members. They, as stated in Article 29, are to be selected by secret ballot by the "State parties" for four years. (Art. 32) It is stipulated in Article 31 that "the Committee shall not include more than one national of the same state." But no provision is made anywhere to provide for equal representation of men and women. As it has turned out, there have been no women on this Committee.

The other important international instrument which was the result of a decade of labor pains is the International Covenant on Economic, Social and Cultural Rights which was also adopted on December 16, 1966 but did not enter into force until January 3, 1976. It contains several provisions which are identical with those of the International Covenant on Civil and Political Rights. Often, as is done in Article 3, it merely substitutes the phrase "economic, social and cultural rights" for "civil and political rights."

A different though not original set of provisions may be found in Article 7(i) which calls for

fair wages and equal remuneration for work of equal value without distinction of any kind, in particular women being guaranteed conditions of work not inferior to those enjoyed by men, with equal pay for equal work.

In 1968 the Commission on the Status of Women produced an important and comprehensive report entitled Constitutions, Electoral Laws and Other Legal Instruments relating to the Political Rights of Women. It contains information concerning the legal status of women in 129 member states.[7] The material is arranged in alphabetical order and annexed to it are six informative tables identifying, as of 1968, the countries in which women had the right to vote on equal terms with men; countries which imposed some limitations that were not applied to men; and countries in which women did not have the right to vote.

The report tabulates the dates on which women were granted the right to vote. There follows another table of states which have taken such action since 1945 and a listing of countries which had ratified the Convention on the Political Rights of Women as of August 15, 1968. Finally, an appendix contains declarations and reservations to this Convention as well as objections to the reservations.

Although the information is now very much out of date, it is one of the most informative documents the U.N. ever produced.

The work of the United Nations has been referred to first in this section because national and international developments have been very closely intertwined during this postwar period, in sharp contrast to what was done and not done during the inter-war period by the League of Nations.

It is also necessary to note that there have been several other international or intergovernmental organizations which have been very positively involved in promoting the rights of women. More specifically, reference should be made to the International Labor Organization, the Council of Europe, and the European Community.

The ILO had already made a good start during the inter-war period on behalf of women's rights. Initially, the ILO was still primarily concerned with protective legislation for women and children, but later it moved away from this preoccupation. Instead it emphasized the principle of equal pay for equal work. In some respects the ILO had made more tangible progress during this period. Undoubtedly the most significant achievement came in 1951 in the form of the Convention No. 100 of June 29, 1951 concerning equal remuneration for men and women workers for work of equal value. Although the U.N. had taken some initiatives toward this goal, it came to play a somewhat subsidiary role. While the U.N. was adopting resolutions, the ILO proceeded to pass more conventions. In 1952 it was Convention No. 102 concerning the minimal norms for social security and Convention No. 103 on the pro-

---

[7]Commission on the Status of Women, op. cit., pp. 139-141.

tection of mothers. Other relevant conventions were passed in 1958 (No. 11), 1964 (No. 122) and 1967 (No. 128).

A change in approach to the basic issues of women's rights is more evident in a resolution adopted in June 1975 concerning equal opportunity and equal treatment. In Article 6 of this Resolution it is suggested that the existing protective provisions be either extended to men as well as women or abolished altogether. No examples were cited, but one is reminded of the protective legislation of the U.S.S.R. which forbids the employment of women in a large number of jobs which are considered too heavy or too hazardous for them. But on the basis of personal observation one is inclined to conclude that the protective legislation protects men from competition by women. The net effect has been to channel womanpower into lower paid and more menial labor.

There are other examples that come to mind, but the U.S.S.R. may be singled out because its legislation continues to reflect this protective if not overprotective character. In other European countries there are *de facto* conditions which the Council of Europe and the European Community consider to be directly or "indirectly" discriminatory.

The Council of Europe now consists of 21 European countries. In terms of the grouping used in this book, it includes all ten western European countries. Switzerland and Liechtenstein are members, as are all Scandinavian countries with the exception of Finland. Only the three ministates of Andorra, Monaco and San Marino are missing from the Southern and Mediterranean group. Ten of these countries are also members of the European Economic Community. Geopolitically, historically and economically, as well as culturally, they constitute a community of about 300 million people in which old conflicts are gradually being overcome. The Committee of Ministers is charged with the difficult task of harmonizing conflicting interests and establishing common standards. These may be stated in conventions which are binding on all members. Other, less generally acceptable principles may be stated in the form of resolutions and recommendations. The promotion of women's rights has been one of eight major areas of concern. The starting point in the Council of Europe, as in the United Nations, was the codification of human rights. Women's rights, from the very outset, were conceived as human rights. It was within this framework that the principle of equality between men and women was first recognized in the Convention for the Protection of Human Rights and Fundamental Freedoms of November 4, 1950. Article 14 states that

> the enjoyment of the rights and freedoms set forth in this Convention shall be secured without discrimination on any ground

such as sex, race, color, language, religion, political or other opinion, national or social origin, association with a national minority, property, birth or other status.

It should be emphasized that this provision is a part of a convention or a treaty, not merely another declaration or resolution.

Another great achievement, reached before the U.N. had accomplished anything comparable, was the *European Social Charter* which was signed on October 18, 1961.[8] This document is important, as far as definitions of specific women's rights are concerned and is included in the Appendix along with the other national and international documents.

Instead of generalities, Part I of the *European Social Charter* specifies 19 "rights and principles which are to be pursued by all appropriate means." Women's rights are not treated separately but within a comprehensive framework which applies to all workers.

On September 28, 1967 an important assessment was made by the Consultative Assembly of the Council of Europe in Resolution 356 (1967) on the political, social and civic position of women in Europe. It noted that while the participation by women in elections appeared to be satisfactory, women continued to be "underrepresented in most elective functions and posts of political responsibility."

On the same day the Consultative Assembly adopted the text of Recommendation 504 (1967) on the political, social and civic position of women in Europe. It noted that the principles of nondiscrimination, as laid down in a considerable number of international instruments "are not fully respected in reality, particularly in the matter of employment, promotion and pay." It recommended to the Committee of Ministers to "take immediately all appropriate actions to ensure that the provisions concerning non-discrimination contained in the conventions and treaties . . . are ratified and effectively applied." It also called for further study of specific problems and for an information campaign designed to bring about changes in traditional attitudes.

In the early 1970s the work of the Council of Europe on behalf of the rights of women continued to be more specific than that of the United Nations. It usually took the form of resolutions and recommendations to member states. Thus, on May 15, 1970 it made such recommendations concerning the social protection of single mothers and their children.[9]

[8]European Treaty Series, No. 35, 1978.
[9]Resolution (70) 15.

Because the legal codes of the various countries contained different concepts of "domicile" and "residence" the Committee of Ministers on January 18, 1972, made specific recommendations to the member states with a view to legal unification or standardization.[10]

In 1974 the Legal Affairs Committee submitted its Report on the legal position of women.[11] It confirmed that discrimination based on sex had not been completely eliminated and recommended that the member states be urged to sign and ratify the pertinent international conventions which prohibit discrimination.

The Council of Europe responded to Resolution 3010 (XXVII) of the General Assembly of the United Nations, which designated 1975 the "International Women's Year" by reviewing its own activities and outlining actions to be taken. The details were set forth in Recommendation 741 (1974) on the legal position of women, which was adopted by the Parliamentary Assembly of the Council of Europe on September 30, 1974. The text of this document is included in the Appendix.

On January 24, 1975 the Parliamentary Assembly of the Council of Europe adopted Recommendation 751 (1975) on the position and responsibility of parents in the modern family and their support by society. It recommended that the Committee of Ministers

> invite member governments to adopt policies in the areas of family law, social legislation, labor and education, etc. which promote and safeguard, as far as possible the equality of men and women, and a genuine partnership between them, in such a way as to enable parents to choose between remaining in the home and taking paid employment, without prejudice in either case to the upbringing of their small children or their own interest in terms of social security and other social benefits.

Appended to this recommendation were specific proposals concerning social security, organization of work, and child-care facilities.

On August 19, 1975 the Political Affairs Committee of the Parliamentary Assembly presented a Draft Resolution on the political rights of women, which was adopted in an amended form on October 9, 1975. An explanatory memorandum presented by Dr. Fletcher contained interesting comparative data on women's participation in the member states.[12]

[10]Conseil de l'Europe-Comité des Ministres Resolution (72) relative à l'unification des concepts juridiques de "domicile" et de "résidence".

[11]COE/Dec 3477 (16.9.74).

[12]Parliamentary Assembly of the Council of Europe, Report on the Political Rights and Position of Women (Rapporteur: Dr. Fletcher), Strasbourg, 1976.

Resolution 606 (1975) on the political rights and position of women noted that "reasons other than strictly legal ones, such as traditional ways of thinking and existing socio-economic structures are still obstacles which prevent women from taking up a number of posts in political bodies, including national parliaments, corresponding to the number of women in the community," and urged "political parties in the member states of the Council of Europe to take a more active part in political life." It also urged governments "to take appropriate steps to procure a wider participation of women in appointed bodies." Parliaments of member states were urged, when forming their delegations to the Parliamentary Assembly, "to recognize the talents of all their members, irrespective of sex." The full text is reproduced in the Appendix.

On October 15, 1975 the Council of Europe, meeting in Strasbourg, completed its work on the European Convention on the Legal Status of Children born out of wedlock. Article 6 states that "the father and mother of a child born out of wedlock shall have the same obligation to maintain the child as if it were born in wedlock." According to Article 9 "a child born out of wedlock shall have the same right of succession in the estate of its father and its mother and of a member of its father's and mother's family, as if it had been born in wedlock."[13]

On January 11, 1977, the Committee of Ministers adopted Resolution (77) concerning the employment of women. It did not break any new ground, but it reinforced the ongoing activities of the ILO as well as the Directives of the European Economic Community. It is concerned with the educational aspects of professional life, access to employment and the problems of reconciling family responsibilities with professional activities.[14]

A further step toward the legal equality between genders was taken on May 27, 1977 when the Committee of Ministers adopted Resolution (77) 12 On the Nationality of Spouses of Different Nationalities. It differs from the U.N. 1957 Resolution in that it goes further by recommending to the member states:

1. to move towards eliminating distinctions in the conditions under which their nationality may be acquired by the foreign husbands of their nationals, as compared with the foreign wives;
2. to proceed, from now on, to the arrangements necessary at the internal level to accord to the foreign husband of their

[13]European Treaty Series, No. 85, p. 13.
[14]Conseil de l'Europe-Comité des Ministres: Resolution (77)1.

nationals, for the acquisition of nationality, a treatment as close as possible to that granted to the foreign wives of their nationals;

3. not to require, for the acquisition of their nationality by the foreign spouse of a national, more than five years' residence on their territory including not more than three years of residence after the marriage;

4. to provide in any event that foreign spouses of their nationals may acquire their nationality on more favourable conditions than those generally required of other aliens.

Also on May 27, the Committee of Ministers adopted Resolution (77)13 On the Nationality of Children born in Wedlock.[15]

In the most recent period there have been several other resolutions which may appear to be tangential to the subject of women's rights, but such issues as access to family planning services have been declared to be "fundamental rights of men and women." This was done in Resolution (78)10 concerning programs for family planning, which was adopted by the Committee of Ministers on March 3, 1978. It took note of Resolution 2436(XXIII) of the General Assembly of the United Nations, which referred to the right of parents to determine freely and responsibly the number and the spacing of births.

The Committee of Ministers, noting that there existed great differences among the member states with respect to public health and legislation with regard to family planning, also made recommendations to the member states on guiding principles.

Another area of law, although not directly related to the subject of women's rights, has obvious implications for mothers whose children have encountered hardships because their fathers have failed to discharge their maintenance obligations. This matter had been discussed in Vienna in September 1977 at the European Conference on Family Law, which suggested that the Council of Europe should recommend to its member states to intervene by making advance payments in cases where either parent had failed to discharge maintenance obligations. The recommendation was linked with the efforts of the United Nations, which had declared 1979 the "International Year of the Child."

On June 28, 1979 the Standing Committee, acting on behalf of the Parliamentary Assembly, adopted the text of Recommendation 869 (1979) on payment by the state of advances on child maintenance. It suggested that the Committee of Ministers call on those member states

[15]While it concerns children rather than women, it is noted here as a further indication of the legal equality of fathers and mothers.

which had not already brought "their legislation into line with the principles approved by the Assembly." An approach to this recommendation outlined eight principles which might govern the advance payments.

One more international organization must be briefly mentioned here because the European Economic Community (EEC), now often called the Community, has significantly influenced the development of women's rights in the member states. The Community now consists of ten European states. Seven belong to the western group, one to the Scandinavian, and one to the Mediterranean and southern group.

As the name suggests, the European Economic Communities were created a quarter of a century ago to develop what was usually called a common market. Most qualified observers agree that, until a few years ago, the experiment was highly successful in achieving this objective. But it has accomplished more than that. Among some of the unexpected contributions have been the equalization of rights between men and women. What is even more surprising is the fact that these efforts have been increased during a time when all the countries of Europe, along with many others, are encountering great economic difficulties largely due to the staggering increases in the price of oil. As unemployment has increased rapidly, so has resistance to more employment opportunities for women. But the EEC has stuck to its principles and issued specific "Directives" to its members. Unlike the United Nations, it has not accepted reports by member states which failed to correspond to real conditions. Unfortunately, in its own personnel policies the Secretariat, like the United Nations, has failed to facilitate enough access for qualified women to the higher administrative positions. The original personnel was drawn from nationals of the six founding members: Belgium, France, Germany, Italy, Luxembourg and the Netherlands. Of these, only in the latter two countries did women have the right to vote by the end of World War II. All of them had it some twelve years later when the Treaty of Rome was signed and the Common Market was born. When Denmark, Great Britain and Ireland joined two decades later, only Denmark had an impressive record with respect to women's rights. On January 1, 1981, Greece became the tenth member of the EEC.

Around 1970 Norway was expected to become a member along with Denmark, Great Britain and Ireland, but in 1972 the people of Norway, in a national referendum, rejected membership. The only prospective members at the present time are Portugal and Spain.

Initially, the legal foundations on which community actions were taken on behalf of women's rights was the Treaty of Rome of March 25, 1957. More recently, three Council Directives have been adopted. They have constituted the basis for further action. The first Council Directive was dated February 10, 1975 and entitled On the approximation of the laws of the member states relating to the application of the principle of equal pay for men and women. (75/117/EEC)

The second Council Directive of February 9, 1976 was entitled On the implementation of the principle of equal treatment for men and women as regards access to employment, vocational training and promotion, and working conditions. (76/207/EEC)

The most recent Directive dates from December 19, 1978. It deals with social security and is called On the progressive implementation of the principle of equal treatment for men and women in matters of social security. (77/804/EEC)

All three Directives are reproduced in the Appendix.

CHAPTER 15

THE UNITED NATIONS DECADE FOR WOMEN INTERACTIONS OF NATIONAL AND INTERNATIONAL DEVELOPMENTS 1976-1985

In Chapter 14, reference was made to the important role of the United Nations and other international organizations in the movement for women's rights and political participation. There can be no doubt that without the United Nations this movement would not have progressed as rapidly as it did. An event of major importance was the International Women's Year Conference which met in Mexico City from June 19 to July 2, 1975.

One of the major documents adopted at that time was a *World Plan of Action* for the implementation of the objectives of the International Women's Year.[1] This lengthy document was subsequently summarized and issued by the Centre for Economic and Social Information of the United Nations. It was designed to provide guidelines for national and international actions.

Governments were urged to establish short-, medium- and long-term targets and priorities based on this plan of action and to adopt national strategies. They were also asked to undertake regular reviews and appraisals. The U.N. and all organizations within the U.N. system were expected to review and appraise the implementation of the world plan every two years. Particular emphasis was placed on the development of national commissions or "similar machinery" and on national legislation which would guarantee nondiscrimination. The plan also specified certain "minimum objectives to be achieved by 1980."

The General Assembly endorsed the World Plan at its thirteenth session on December 15, 1975. By Resolution 3520 (XXX) it proclaimed the period from 1976 to 1985 as the "United Nations Decade for Women: Equality, Development and Peace." It called for a conference in 1980 "to review and evaluate the progress" in mid-term of the decade.

---

[1]On December 18, 1972 the General Assembly adopted Resolution 3010 (XXVII) which proclaimed 1975 as "International Women's Year".

This conference was convened in Copenhagen from July 14 to July 30, 1980. Of the 34 countries of Europe, 30 attended. Only Andorra, Liechtenstein, Monaco and San Marino were not represented. In terms of gender representation 20 delegations were headed by women and 8 by men. (No information was available concerning the delegations from Cyprus and Malta.)

The delegations headed by men were the following: Belgium, Finland, German Federal Republic, Iceland, Ireland, Luxembourg, Norway and Turkey. Perhaps the only surprise was the fact that three of the five Scandinavian delegations were headed by men. The percentage of women who headed delegations from European countries was about the same as for the other countries of the world. The total for all the delegations was 110 to 23. The total includes the Byelorussian S.S.R. and the Ukrainian S.S.R. The United States was counted in both columns because it was the only delegation with two co-chairpersons, one of each gender.

As early as 1976 the Economic and Social Council had laid the groundwork for this conference. On May 12, 1977 by Resolution 2062 (LXII) it had created a preparatory Committee on which 23 member States with widely differing backgrounds were represented. The General Assembly endorsed these actions on December 16 by Resolution 32/140.

The Secretary-General appointed Mrs. Lucille M. Mair of Jamaica as Secretary-General of the Conference. In accordance with Economic Resolution 2060 (LXII) a questionnaire was prepared in 1979 which was designed to obtain the necessary information from individual governments for a comprehensive review of the progress made between 1975 and 1978.[2] The questionnaire was 53 pages long with several blank spaces for answers concerning six major topics: 1. National policies, planning and monitoring, 2. Legislation, 3. Political participation, international cooperation and the strengthening of international peace, 4. Education and training, 5. Employment and related economic roles, 6. Health and nutrition.

The first three topics are directly related to the subject of this book. It is regrettable, therefore, that the returned questionnaires were treated as confidential documents by the U.N. Secretariat. Apparently many governments failed to fill in the questionnaire. According to reliable informants the returned questionnaires reflected a widely differing quality and thoroughness.

---

[2]It was prepared and circulated by the Branch for the Advancement of Women in the Centre for the Social Development and Humanitarian Affairs, United Nations Secretariat.

In addition, individual governments responded to a request for information in the form of "national reports". Those that were received between May 29, 1980 and July 29, 1980, are listed in A/CONF. 94/35, The Report of the World Conference, which was published in October 1980. After reading as many as were available, one can fairly say that they are not as comprehensive as one might wish. Only 15 national reports were received from European countries.

On the basis of the replies received from these governments the U.N. Secretariat prepared a large number of topical reports, which are listed in the Report of the World Conference.[3] In addition to the topics listed in the questionnaires, there were many others on more ideological subjects which caused a certain amount of controversy at the Copenhagen meeting.

Students of comparative politics and law may be particularly interested in the Conference paper which deals with the National Machinery and Legislation. As stated in the introduction, it was based on the replies from 77 governments as well as specialized agencies of the U.N. and nongovernmental organizations.

The compilers of the report tried to classify the different types of machinery and provided no information on how they functioned. They cited the criticism and dissatisfaction expressed by Belgium, Denmark and Switzerland with respect to the "limited terms of reference and their lack of implementing and executive powers."[4] It appears that in the reports of the eastern European countries there were no such critical comments, and the report stated that these countries had made "significant progress" but did not provide any pertinent details.

An attempt was made to present women's organizations as "complementary to governmental efforts,"[5] but the report failed to develop this thesis. The comparative study of the organization and procedures of "national machinery" was not advanced by this section of the report.

The section on legislation is much better but not as detailed as one might have expected in view of all the material reports. It noted that "since 1975, several governments have established special bodies that deal with discrimination, in addition to the courts."[6] Of the countries of Europe mention is made of Great Britain, Iceland, Norway, Sweden

---

[3]A/Conf. 94/11. Report of the World Conference. Item 8 of the provisional agenda. Included were reports from 18 European countries: Austria, Belgium, Denmark, Finland, G.D.R., German Federal Republic, Great Britain, Hungary, Iceland, Ireland, Netherlands, Norway, Poland, Romania, Spain, Sweden, Turkey and Yugoslavia.

[4]Report on the World Conference, p. 12.

[5]Report on the World Conference, p. 13.

[6]Report on the World Conference, p. 19.

and the U.S.S.R. This was an incomplete list, as may be seen by referring to the English translations of pertinent legislation in the Appendix of this book.

One of the most important accomplishments of the Copenhagen World Conference of the United Nations was the adoption of the Programme of Action for the second half of the United Nations Decade for Women.

It is a lengthy document consisting of 287 paragraphs. The first part deals with the "background and framework." Part two contains "The Programme of Action at the National Level;" the third part concerns international and regional actions. It is the second part which refers to such topics as national machinery, legislative measures, political participation and related matters.

Another important accomplishment was the signing of the Convention on the Elimination of all Forms of Discrimination against Women. The way for this had been paved by General Assembly Resolution 34/180 of December 18, 1979.[7] This document differs from earlier declarations and resolutions in several significant ways. It is not only longer, but it also reflects a different ideological orientation.

The U.N. Convention on the Elimination of All Forms of Discrimination against Women consists of fifteen preambular paragraphs and thirty articles.[8] It is in many ways a most impressive document, which is likely to be the most important international instrument during the few remaining years of the U.N. Decade for Women.

The Convention does much to clarify and define the contemporary meaning of women's rights. Article 1 provides a very comprehensive definition of the term "discrimination against women." Article 2 calls upon the states parties to "condemn discrimination in all its forms" and to eliminate them "by all appropriate means and without delay." It specifies seven categories for action. The first requires the states not

---

[7]This resolution was preceded by a struggle which extended over a period of some sixteen years. As early as December 5, 1963 the General Assembly had asked for such a resolution. It was to be prepared by the Commission on the Status of Women. A Declaration on the Elimination of Discrimination Against Women was proclaimed by the General Assembly on November 7, 1967 by Resolution 2263 (XXII).

[8]The declaration of November 7, 1967 consists of 11 articles and eight preambular paragraphs which were devoid of ideology and rhetoric. General Assembly Resolution 3521 (XXX) of December 15, 1975, entitled Equality between Men and Women and Elimination of Discrimination against Women, is similar in its ideological tone to the language in some of the preambular paragraphs of the present declaration.

only "to embody the principle of equality of men and women in their national Constitutions or other appropriate legislation" but also "to ensure, through law and other appropriate means, the practical realization of this principle."

The first part of this obligation is easily fulfilled and has indeed been fulfilled in some 150 constitutions or about ninety percent of all the countries of the world. To date the U.N. has not been very critical or demanding on this score. All that has been required is one or more constitutional provisions which proclaim the equality of men and women before the law. Many of the more recent constitutions also contain provisions which prohibit discrimination on a variety of grounds, including sex. This would seem quite adequate if it were not for the fact that there are many constitutions, especially the older ones, which contain provisions which constitute indirect and even direct discrimination in that they associate the male gender with the chief officers in the state. As previously noted, this has not kept women, in a few instances, from becoming presidents, prime ministers and cabinet members, but the popular impression in many countries has been that those positions are reserved to men.

The other requirement of Article 2(a), which calls for legislation and "other appropriate means" to achieve the realization of the principle of equality and nondiscrimination, is quite a different and much less satisfactory matter. The U.N. has not been as strict as the EEC in monitoring this important directive.

Article 2(b) specifies the inclusion of "sanctions" on the part of "states parties" in cases of discrimination. Provisions for real sanctions are very rare, and where they do exist they are usually limited to the public sector.

Article 2(c) calls upon the states to establish "competent national tribunals and other public institutions" so as to ensure "the effective protection of women against any act of discrimination." Although many European countries have taken some measures toward the achievement of this objective, the overall situation is far from satisfactory.

Articles 2(d) and 2(e) are essentially elaborations of 2(b).

Most troublesome as far as implementation is concerned is Article 2(f) which asks states parties

> to take all appropriate measures, including legislation, to modify or abolish existing laws, regulations, customs and practices which constitute discrimination against women.

It is one thing to modify or abolish legislation, but experience has shown

309

that when it comes to customs, the pace is likely to be disappointingly slow.

Article 2(g) calls for the repeal of discriminatory penal provisions.

Article 3 is more general, if not vague, in calling for appropriate measures "to ensure the full development and advancement of women" by the guarantee of "human rights and fundamental freedoms on a basis of equality with men."

Article 4 makes provision for "temporary special measures aimed at accelerating de facto equality" and states that such measures shall not be considered discriminatory.

Article 5 elaborates the provisions of 2(f) in asking states parties to "take all appropriate measures: to modify the social and cultural patterns of conduct of men and women."

Article 6 is concerned with measures against prostitution and traffic in women.

These six articles make up Part I of the Convention. The second part consists of three articles which are concerned with distinctly political rights. They go beyond the scope defined by the Convention on the Political Rights of Women (1954) in that Article 7(b) asks states parties to ensure that women participate not only in the governments of their countries but also "in the formulation of government policy and the implementation thereof."

Article 8 also goes beyond the 1954 Convention in asking the states parties to ensure that women have

> the opportunity to represent their Governments at the international level and to participate in the work of international organizations.

As previously suggested, the U.N. could set a good example for the member states by taking all appropriate measures to increase the number of women in the higher echelon of the U.N. Civil Service.

Article 9 concerns the old problem of the nationality of women, especially married women.

Article 10 is focused on equal rights to education and equal opportunity within the educational system.

Article 11 is concerned with equal rights to and in employment. It carried forward the principles laid down in the International Convenant on Economic, Social and Cultural Rights and the previously mentioned Conventions of the International Labor Organization.

A new feature may be found in Article 11(3) which states that protective legislation "shall be reviewed periodically in the light of scientific and technological knowledge." In view of the fact that this protective legislation has been used in many instances not so much to protect women but rather men from women's competition, this review requirement could be potentially important.

Article 12 relates health care and family planning to the issue of discrimination.

Article 13 seeks to protect women against discrimination in the area of economic and social rights, especially with respect to family benefits, bank loans, mortgages and other forms of financial credits.

Article 14 is concerned with discrimination against rural women.

Article 15 seeks to strengthen the principle of equality before the law in relation to civil matters, to ensure that the legal capacity of women is "identical to that of men".

Article 16 extends the measures against discrimination into marriage and family relations. These provisions are somewhat patterned after the International Covenant on Civil and Political Rights. The object is to change from a patriarchal system to a parental one.

As has been noted, while there have been important efforts and accomplishments to change the legal framework, the de facto situation has not been greatly affected.

Part V of the Convention (Articles 17-22) is concerned with the implementation of the previous provisions. Article 17 provides for the establishment of a Committee on the Elimination of Discrimination against Women. It was to consist, initially, of 18 members. After the ratification of the Convention by the 35th State it was to be enlarged to include 23 members. It was expected that these members would be experts in this field. Although they were to be nominated by their governments, it was stated that they would serve in their personal capacity.

The concept of such a committee of experts is hardly new.[9] Nevertheless it was vehemently opposed by the Communist governments. They wanted the monitoring to be done by the Commission on the Status of Women.

The language of Article 17 was designed to accommodate the critics of the idea of an independent Committee. It stipulates that consideration shall be given

to equitable geographical distribution and to the representation

---

[9]It may be recalled that the International Covenant on Civil and Political Rights provides for such a committee. Another example would be the Committee on the Elimination of Racial Discrimination.

of the different forms of civilization as well as the principal legal systems.

There is no reason why one should object to these considerations. They are not only requirements of equity but of professionalism in a pluralistic society. There are cultural conditions and value systems which we cannot radically alter within a short period of time, and any attempt to do so is likely to stimulate over-reaction, as has often been shown in various parts of the world. Thus it is more a matter of professional prudence than equity.

If we are concerned about equity, as indeed we should be, then consideration should also be given to having women make up at least half of the representation on this and other committees which seek to end discrimination. To achieve this would not require an amendment of the convention. It would suffice if the General Assembly would pass an appropriate resolution or recommendation addressed to the Secretary-General of the United Nations.

It is the Secretary-General, who, according to Article 17(3) is required to prepare a list of all persons who have been nominated. The elections are to be held "at a meeting of States Parties convened by the Secretary-General at the United Nations Headquarters." (Article 17(4)) This list must be in alphabetical order with an indication of the states parties which have nominated them.

To have women placed on the list would not necessarily be advantageous to the immediate advancement of women's rights because some governments are likely to nominate women who will not exert themselves on behalf of their own gender. But it is important to establish the principle of women's representation as evidence of nondiscrimination on the part of the states parties.

The members of the Committee are to be elected by the states parties for a term of four years. "However, the terms of nine of the members elected at the first election shall expire at the end of two years; immediately after the first election the names of these nine shall be chosen by lot by the Chairman of the Committee." (Art. 17(5))
Article 18 requires that the

> States Parties undertake to submit to the Secretary-General of the United Nations, for consideration by the Committee, a report on the legislative, judicial, administrative or other measures which they have adopted to give effect to the provisions of the Convention and on the progress made in this respect:
> (a) within one year after the entry into force for the state concerned;

(b) thereafter at least every four years and further whenever the Committee so requests.

There is reason to believe that the requirement of having to report within one year after ratification was objected to by some states because their legal experts believe that some of the existing legislation and administrative regulations do not meet the standards established in this Convention. If this awareness should lead to appropriate remedial action the delay in ratifying the Convention would not be a misfortune. But at the present time the end of the Decade seems a long way off and there is not enough pressure to move decisively against discrimination.

The chances for ratification would have been enhanced if certain paragraphs in the preamble to the Convention had been omitted. Women in most countries have had to face so many obstacles on the long road to equality that they should not be confronted with new ones. Without passing judgment on the merits of the new international economic order, the issues of apartheid, racial discrimination, and general and complete disarmament, we may note that they are all readily exploited by ideologists for ideological purposes. They are best located separately on their own merits. If all these issues are lumped together and propounded under the women's rights banner they create an excessive burden which will not help the cause of women's rights.

As it turned out this Convention moved ahead more quickly than many other worthy international instruments. As previously noted, the General Assembly adopted it on December 18, 1979 and it was opened for signature on March 1, 1980.

On July 17, 1980, one of the highlights of the World Conference of the U.N. Decade for Women, held in Copenhagen, was the formal signing ceremony of the Convention.

At that time the representatives of 53 countries signed the Convention. Before the Conference adjourned 75 countries had signed and five had ratified the Convention.

The Convention came into force on September 3, 1981, in accordance with its Article 27 which states that it "shall enter into force on the thirtieth day after the date of deposit with the Secretary-General of the United Nations of the twentieth instrument of ratification or accession."

As of February 17, 1982, 37 states parties had ratified the Convention. The speedy ratification is one of the more encouraging events of the early 1980s. The Convention establishes definite international standards of equality and equity. It may also generate new vitality to the activities of the remaining part of the second half of the United Nations Decade for Women.[10]

The Second Half of *The United Nations Decade for Women*: Recent achievements and their impact on National Developments in Europe.

In a Report of the Secretary-General, dated January 14, 1982, which was prepared for the 29th Session of the Commission on the Status of Women, it was noted that information had been received by the governments of 41 states.[11] Sixteen belonged to what the U.N. has come to call "governments of developed market economies." Of the European countries, it included a total of eleven: Austria, Belgium, German Federal Republic, Ireland, Netherlands, Norway, Portugal, Spain, Sweden, Switzerland and the United Kingdom or Great Britain.

The five "governments of the centrally planned economies," which provided information included Hungary, Poland and the U.S.S.R.[12] None of the twenty "governments of the developing economies" were European. The sections of the Report which are of particular interest to anyone doing research on comparative women's rights and political participation are the following: C. Institutional arrangements (national machinery), D. Effective participation of women in decision-making, and E. Legislation.

Although this Report is in many respects more informative than most of the earlier reports, it is still not sufficiently specific to serve as a basis for comparative in-depth analyses.

It is understood, of course, that such a report cannot go beyond what information the governments send to the United Nations, but even this information seems to be too condensed to be very helpful. The report states that "several governments adopted new programs and plans."[13] It mentions Norway, the Netherlands, Switzerland and Ireland.

On the basis of research conducted for this book, several other countries could be listed. Of the ones which reported to the United Nations, Austria, Portugal and Switzerland come to mind. Whether or not they failed to provide this information cannot be ascertained because

[10]See Catherine Tinker, "Human Rights for Women: The U.N. Convention on the Elimination of All Forms of Discrimination against Women". *Human Rights Quarterly* 1981.

[11]E/CN. 6/1982/2, 14 January 1982, p. 3.

[12]A report was also received from the Byelorussian Soviet Socialist Republic and subsequently from the Ukrainian Soviet Socialist Republic, which were published as an addendum on February 4, 1982.

[13]E/CN. 6/1982/2, p. 6.

these country reports to the United Nations are treated as confidential documents.

With respect to progress made in developing national machinery, the Report is hardly more specific than those prepared for the Copenhagen Conference. Thus it states that each of the governments reported efforts to render more effective the institutional arrangements and procedures established to ensure that the advancement of women was integrated in policy-making and planning at national regional and local levels."[14] It contains only a few sentences referring to Austria, Belgium, Denmark, Great Britain, Netherlands, Norway, Portugal and Sweden. It is even less specific on the participation of women in decision-making.[15] Only Denmark and Norway are briefly mentioned.

The section of the Report on legislation and the "reformulation of legislation" deals with the implications of ratifying the Convention. It notes that some governments, including Austria, Belgium and Denmark, reported that "it would be necessary to reverse current legislation to bring it into conformity with the Convention."[16] This section is somewhat more specific, especially with respect to Great Britain. It also mentions recent efforts in Austria, Belgium, Denmark, Ireland, Portugal, Spain and Switzerland.[17]

Considerably less space is devoted to the "centrally planned economies." Barely five lines are given to the "institutional arrangements"[18] with respect to participation. It is noted that "the involvement of women in political and public life had grown in proportion to their participation in social production and their political and professional education."[19]

Under "E. Legislation", it is reported that "all the respondents from the centrally planned economies have ratified the Convention.

Recent Contributions by other International Organizations

The efforts of the United Nations toward the implementation of the

[14]*Ibid.*, p. 9.

[15]Several governments considered that improved participation of women in national political life and in decision-making at all levels within the system of government and public administration was of the greatest importance in effectively carrying out the Programme of Action and have taken various measures accordingly.

[16]E/CN. 6/1982/2, p. 12. By way of updating it might be added that Denmark completed this task in late May 1982.

[17]For examples of actual legislation not cited in the Report see the English translations in the Appendix of this book.

[18]On p. 22 of the Report this statement is made: "In the Centrally planned economies, efforts for the achievement of the goals of the Programme continued to be implemented and co-ordinated by the respective national machineries already set up for this purpose or within the related functional government departments in accordance with overall government policies integrating the concerns and interests of women."

[19]*Ibid.*, p. 22.

World Plan for Action on behalf of women's rights are being supported by many other international and nongovernmental organizations. It goes beyond the scope of this book to assess their accomplishments. But it is necessary to refer briefly to some of them because, as has been stated several times, without them the progress in individual countries would have proceeded much more slowly.

One of the organizations which must be mentioned again is the International Labor Organization. The ILO has continued to build on the foundations laid by Convention No. 100 concerning equal remuneration (1951) and Convention No. 111 concerning Discrimination (Employment and Occupation). On June 23, 1981 it adopted Convention 156 concerning equal opportunities and equal treatment for men and women: workers with family responsibilities.[20]

In addition to these Conventions a number of excellent research papers have been published, and the *International Labour Review* has recently published important articles on women workers in various countries from the point of view of equality of opportunity and treatment in employment.[21]

UNESCO has continued to be concerned with women's rights in terms of equalizing the opportunities of women in various fields of education. It is also interested in the curricular aspects and the status of teachers. In 1980 it financed a seminar on "Women and the Media" and a publication on "The Portrayal and Participation of Women in the Media."[22]

As stated in a recent report, The World Health Organization (WHO) has been concerned with women's problems in three major areas: (1) Health needs and problems specific to women, (2) Women as health care providers and (3) the interrelationship of women, health and development.[23] In the field of health care it has been conducting some multi-national studies.[24]

The Food and Agriculture Organization (FAO) has long been concerned with the role of women in rural development. In a recent report it noted that rural women in developing countries are responsible for

[20]See Appendix.
[21]See Bibliography.
[22]E/CN. 6/1982/5.
[23]E/CN. 6/1982/12. Report of the World Health Organization on its activities of special interest to women.
[24]Biei Dang Ha Doan: *The Participation of Women in the Health System: A Worldwide Panorama of the health Professions.* (HMD/80.6) Geneva: WHO 1980 *Multinational Study of Women as providers of health care: Annotated Bibliography.* (HMD 80.7) Geneva: WHO 1981 Report of a consultation on women as providers of health care. (HMD/81.2) Geneva: WHO 1981.

more than half of the food production for domestic consumption.[25] Many of its action programs are also important for the rural population in several European countries.

The Commission on the Status of Women is expected to play an important role as preparatory Committee for the 1985 World Conference. It is expected to meet for eight days in Vienna in 1983, 1984 and 1985 and will be mainly concerned with reviews and appraisals of recent activities. How well it can carry out this difficult assignment will depend on the quality and quantity of information which will be made available to it. There are lessons to be learned from the preparations for the Copenhagen Conference. One of these would call for a much more rigorous questionnaire which would make it impossible to evade specific questions. It should ask for more than descriptions of plans and programs and should call for specific documentation. As far as legislation is concerned, pertinent provisions should be translated into one of the official languages of the United Nations. Everything must be available for the processing of this information.

If this can be done the United Nations will be able to make another major contribution to the advancement of women's rights and political participation.

[25]E/CN. 6/1982/11. Report of the Food and Agriculture Organization of Special Interest to Women (Rome 1982). p. 16.

AN INTERIM ASSESSMENT OF ACHIEVEMENTS IN WOMEN'S RIGHTS AND POLITICAL PARTICIPATION

Concluding Comparative Notes

The last section of most scholarly books is usually entitled "Conclusions," but it seems premature to draw conclusions before the International Women's Decade comes to an end. One can only attempt an interim assessment of the achievements, to date, of 34 countries of Europe and of the roles of various international organizations. It is impossible to summarize the comparative developments which have been traced in this book. The most that can be attempted here is to state briefly on a comparative basis what the situations are in individual countries and what may reasonably be expected as a result of internal and external factors.

It is also necessary to explore whether or not there has been a clarification or greater consensus of what is meant by "women's rights" and "political participation." It would seem fair to say that nearly two centuries after Olympe de Gouges wrote her bold declaration on "The Rights of Woman " the concept of women's rights is still not clearly understood. In many European countries, as in the United States, the mere mention of the two words still generates controversies and disagreements. Liberals and socialists still disagree on the meaning and implications of such terms as feminism, emancipation and liberation. Clichés and stereotypes still abound. Ideological reactions are commonplace, but a comprehensive theory of women's rights has not yet been formulated. Nevertheless, progress has been made toward the formulation of a catalogue of women's rights, especially since the end of World War II. The worldwide concern over human rights has helped to strengthen the foundations of women's rights as integral elements of certain universal values. In 1948 the United Nations made one of its most significant contributions by formulating a Universal Declaration of Human Rights and by persisting in its often frustrating efforts to convert ethical norms into legal and thus enforceable standards. The international conventions which were subsequently concluded under the auspices of the United Nations paved the way for the recent Convention on the Elimination of all Forms of Discrimination against Women. It is this convention, more than any other, which will serve as the gauge by which we can measure or appraise contemporary national achievements. The seventh paragraph of the preamble introduces certain key concepts whose meaning must be clearly understood by anyone who ventures into this difficult area of political theory and comparative studies. It may be best to quote this paragraph before any attempt is made to use any of these concepts in a comparative critical analysis. The English text, which is equally authentic along with the Arabic, Chinese, French, Russian and Spanish versions, reads as follows:

> *Recalling* that discrimination against women violates the principles of equality of rights and respect for human dignity, is an obstacle to the participation of women, on equal terms with men, in the political, social, economic and cultural life of their countries, hampers the growth of the prosperity of society and the family, and makes more difficult the full development of the potentialities of women in the service of their countries and of humanity . . .[1]

Equality, human dignity, and participation are certainly key concepts, but they have been differently perceived by major political theorists and they have not been implemented in the same way in contemporary political systems. Furthermore, they need not be tied to the somewhat excessively collectivistic notion of "the full development of the potentialities of women in the service of their countries and of humanity." Feminists would probably say that women are individual human beings and thus entitled to individual rights whether or not they serve their countries or humanity. Others might say that the notion of equality is not necessarily equitable unless inequities have been removed by equalization. In other words, equality is status quo-oriented and thus does not go far enough.

No one is likely to quarrel with the idea of human dignity, but in terms of legal and political institutions it has, traditionally, not been linked with the idea of equality. In other words, the notion of "worthiness," when it comes to such fundamental equal rights as suffrage, was long denied to women. But, of course, it was also denied to the great majority of men, who were deemed to be good enough to fight but not

[1]United Nations Universal Declaration of Human Rights.

320

to vote. There was for a long time not only discrimination against women but against men also. It prevented them from political participation. When they were gradually allowed to participate, it was within a system that had been created a long time ago and which was not easily changed to be more in accord with their interests and aspirations. In our time, some European women feel the same way about the issue of political participation. They look at it as a system made by men and for men. Participation to them means being used to maintain a system which they did not create and in which they will not have sufficient power to effect major changes in terms of institutions and policies. The more one talks to women in different countries over a period of time, the more one is likely to conclude that we have exaggerated cross-national comparisons and contrasts. It appears that the importance of social stratification has not been sufficiently recognized.

Having disposed of these critical comments, we can now attempt to assess the prevailing situations in individual countries. As in the previous parts of the book, these assessments are made by means of looking at the four major areas.

The Scandinavian countries continue to lead the western and southern European countries in terms of legislation and political participation. Attitudes toward sex roles are also less traditional. Among the feminists of the Scandinavian countries there exist both cooperation and competition with respect to women's rights and related matters. They exchange information on a regular basis. The close links between government officials and leaders of the women's organizations have contributed much to progressive legislation and to the effective functioning of machinery for the protection of women's rights. In Denmark, the most recent legislative accomplishment is the Law on the taxation of married women (*Lov om ændring af forskellige skattelove*) which was passed on May 24, 1982. As shown in the Appendix, all the Scandinavian countries have enacted major laws concerning equal treatment of men and women. They have focused on the economic aspects of discrimination and provided for effective machinery to enforce equal treatment. Of all the industrialized market economy countries, Finland has had the highest number of women engaged in full-time employment. The percentage of working women is increasing in all of the Scandinavian countries. There is more concern over the growing number of women who are engaged in part-time work. The automation and computerization of many forms of work usually performed by women is a major current concern, which calls for new educational and retraining efforts. Consideration is being given to the possibility of flexible working hours which would facilitate greater compatibility between domestic and employment responsibilities.

Women leaders in the Scandinavian countries are convinced that while further legal and administrative reforms are indispensable, they must continue to organize and mobilize their forces so as to maximize their political effectiveness. Pressure must be exerted on government authorities, political parties, trade unions and organizations of employers. They are very clear in identifying their goals and they strive for partnership with men in achieving them.

It may best be left to the readers to judge which countries of western Europe have made the most important advances since the end of World War II in the field of women's rights. When it comes to overall economic advance, there can be no doubt that West Germany has outpaced all others. But the advances in the field of women's rights and political participation are not as impressive. If one were to judge by political participation alone, the German record is hardly outstanding. In the field of legislation there has been a somewhat exaggerated estimate of what one single Article (3) of the Basic Law has achieved. The key officials continue to feel that comprehensive legislation is not needed. But this view is not shared by scholars and activists in the women's rights movement. Helmut Schmidt, although sympathetic to the women's movement, thinks and has stated publicly that it may take generations to achieve gender equality.

By comparison, Austria has made more impressive gains. Considerable credit is due to Chancellor Bruno Kreisky and such energetic women as Johanna Dohnal who, as State Secretary on Women's Questions in the Chancellor's Office, has been very effective in fighting for equal rights. There remain regional differences even in a small country like Austria, but the old patriarchal order is slowly disintegrating. The new family legislation has been a major breakthrough.

Belgium has not been in the forefront of the struggle for equality. Suffrage was introduced only after World War II, and Belgian women who have competed for political offices have not been very successful. The fact that the EEC is located in Brussels may have a beneficial effect, at least as far as legislation is concerned.

France has produced some outstanding leaders of women's rights but, on the whole, its record is disappointing as far as representation is concerned. Under the presidency of Giscard d'Estaing, women were given strong support in their quest for a greater share in policy-making positions. Four women are now serving in the cabinet, but the prospects for further advances are still uncertain. The current legal provisions concerning the status of women have been criticized as insufficient to constitute a solid foundation for the equalization of rights. At the present time there is no comprehensive law which would guarantee equal treatment in all employment situations. President Mitterand announced on

March 8, 1982, on the occasion of a celebration of the International Women's Day, that discriminatory provisions of the Civil Service Code would be abolished in order to clear the way for more women seeking entry into the civil service. But, as was pointed out in the text, the Commission of the European Communities continues to believe that there are many other laws which will have to be amended before all the requirements of its Directives will have been complied with.

As previously indicated, the Federal Republic of Germany has not satisfied the expectations of leading feminists. But West German women may benefit from the competition with East Germany. Increasingly, comparative studies made by qualified individuals show that the German Democratic Republic has done more for women's rights than the Federal Republic of Germany.

The record of Great Britain is also disappointing. This may surprise some observers who have been impressed by the calm and competent conduct of Queen Elizabeth and the energetic efforts of Prime Minister Margaret Thatcher. The Queen is a constitutional monarch and her policy statements are written by the Prime Minister or in the Prime Minister's office. But Margaret Thatcher is not considered a feminist. In the House of Commons women continue to be woefully underrepresented and there have been no significant changes in the male-dominated higher echelons of the administration.

In Ireland the patriarchal tradition has remained intact. In spite of turbulent conditions, the political culture has not undergone major changes. The constitutional provisions (Art. 18) still make it difficult for women to be elected. But they have advanced in recent years. The 1973 Report of the Commission on the Status of Women provided a blueprint for a comprehensive strategy. Important legislation has been promulgated and Ireland's membership in the European Economic Community is likely to benefit women by opening up new opportunities.

As previously noted, Liechtenstein remains the only country in Europe in which women can vote only in local elections. However, women were encouraged by a speech from the throne on March 31, 1982. The Neue Zürcher Zeitung reported on April 30, 1982 that the State Court had rejected a claim by 25 women of Liechtenstein who contended that the denial of the right to vote was a violation of the constitutional principle of equality. The State rejected this claim, stating that national female suffrage could be established only by legislation and not by judicial interpretation. Some progress seems to have been made, however, because among the several new proposals presented on March 31, 1982 was a suggestion that legislation for women's suffrage might be introduced shortly.

In Luxembourg, the 1980 Draft Law on equal treatment has been revised so as to satisfy the criteria of the 1976 EEC Directive. It was published on December 8, 1981. (See Appendix for update)

During the past decade, progress has been made in the Netherlands, but it was more on the local level than in national politics. Law No. 86/1980 on the equality of treatment for men and women took a long time to hammer out in a form which satisfied the EEC. (Directive No. 76/207/EEC)

Switzerland has definitely made much progress since 1971. There are a few cantons in which the male voters refuse to allow women to vote in local elections, but on the federal level, important changes have been made, especially on June 14, 1981 with the amendment of Article 4 of the Federal Constitution which serves as a sound basis for further advances. The directions have been clearly outlined by the Federal Commission for Women's Questions in Bern. They have produced three excellent volumes on the Status of Women in Switzerland.

The progress made by women of the southern and Mediterranean countries has been uneven. In all of these ten countries, the roots of patriarchy are deep. Even in Turkey, where women's suffrage was enacted by Ataturk in 1934, the patriarchal culture has not been seriously challenged. But changes have taken place for a variety of reasons and in response to new circumstances.

In the case of Andorra, where women's suffrage was introduced or reintroduced in 1970, there were definite economic reasons, and this was candidly stated in the official explanations of the decrees of 1971 and 1973. The property rights of women had to be equalized so that the properties of Andorran women who married foreigners would not be lost to foreigners.

In Cyprus, whose activities for women's rights began too recently for this discussion, the Constitution of 1960 contains very satisfactory provisions which were designed to outlaw discrimination of all kinds, but it did not attempt to modify the traditional patriarchal system. Indeed, it created constitutional legitimacy for some of them. No empirical research of a comparative nature seems to have been done concerning the status of women in the Greek and Turkish communities. Such a study would be valuable if it could assess the relative importance of ethnic and religious factors along with the impact of urbanization and economic development.

It would also be interesting to have a comparative study of Greece and Cyprus which would evaluate these factors. The Greek Constitution provides a very solid foundation for the advancement of women. A new era for the women of Greece began on January 1, 1981 when Greece became a member of the EEC. The elections of October 1981, which resulted in the victory of Andreas Papandreou, were interpreted to mean that there would be more rapid progress toward gender equality. In any case, the status of women in Greece is likely to undergo significant changes before 1985.

In Italy major changes have already taken place since the Constitution of the Republic was promulgated in December 1947. Ten years later Italy was one of the founding members of the European Economic Community. In the Appendix a complete English translation of Law No. 903 of 1977 is included. As the analysis of this law concerning "equal treatment for men and women as regards employment" shows, it does incorporate all the essential elements of the EEC Council Directive 76/207.

No specific legislation was enacted in Malta to implement the provisions of the 1964 Constitution concerning the equal rights provisions. The Constitution was amended in 1974, but no changes were made in the wording of key provisions which seem to imply that all the major officeholders are expected to be males. As was noted previously, this did not prevent the election of a woman, Agatha Barbara, to the Office of President of the Republic by the House of Representatives on February 16, 1982.

With the exception of the late princess, the former Grace Kelly, women have not been prominent in the political life of the Mediterranean ministate of Monaco. The Constitution of 1962 proclaimed the principle of gender equality but there has been no further implementing legislation. There are some problems with respect to the property rights of women and also with the law concerning the nationality of married women.

Portugal has been given special attention in this book because it hopes to be admitted to membership in the European Economic Community, and it is desirable to have accurate and complete information on what has been accomplished in recent years in eradicating the authoritarian and anachronistic remnants of the Salazar regime. Readers will be able to judge for themselves. They will also get a better understanding of the magnitude and complexity of the process of democratization. The Constitution of 1976 is the foundation on which the legal and political framework is being constructed. The Commission on the Status of Women, established in 1977 under the Prime Minister, has done an outstanding job in analyzing needed reforms. In the Appendix, most of the important legislation is presented in English translation.

In San Marino, women's suffrage was introduced with the Electoral Law of December 23, 1958. Women voted for the first time in September

1964. They became eligible to run for political offices in 1974 and they have been quite active ever since. In 1978 a government commission was created to study ways and means of increasing the participation of women. While the political system is undergoing some changes, the traditional legal system is not. The patriarchal principle has not been challenged.

In Spain, as in Portugal, important changes have been made in the political and legal system. In the legal field they began well before the death of Franco, but they were piecemeal changes and were designed to satisfy moderate demands of Spanish feminists. The International Year of Woman, 1975, was a major milestone in the development of women's rights (*equiparacion*). The Civil Code was reformed in that year, along with the Commercial Code. As far as women's political rights and participation are concerned, the decisive change came with the promulgation of the new Constitution on December 26, 1978. Since that time, a process similar to Portugal's has taken place in that the Constitution made it necessary to enact certain implementing legislation. This process has not been completed and relatively few provisions are specifically concerned with the equalization of rights and equal treatment between men and women. There is likely to be more specific activity in this area in the near future as Spain seeks to be admitted to membership in the European Economic Community.

In Turkey, as previously indicated, progress has been somewhat disappointing as far as the advancement of women is concerned. There have always been great differences between the urban centers and the small towns and villages. In the 1950s, Prime Minister Menderes sought to strengthen his political base by catering to the devout Moslems. The Constitution of 1961 might have provided a suitable basis for renewed legislative activity on behalf of women, but the political climate was not favorable for such undertakings. At the present time the military regime maintains a tight grip over the entire political system. No real political opposition is allowed, and the regime has been quick and harsh with its critics. The atmosphere is not conducive to the development of women's rights or any political rights. It remains to be seen what kind of constitution the regime will produce and whether it can form a basis for a policy of liberalization.

It will be noted that the Appendix does not contain much legislation from the Eastern European countries. One can, of course, compile collections of laws, as has been done in the U.S.S.R. and in the G.D.R., concerning the status of women. What this would involve would be a compilation of constitutional provisions and excerpts from a variety of general legislation which concerns labor, family and social policy. A few examples of this type of legislation from the U.S.S.R. are included here. The constitutional provisions have been incorporated in the specific chapters.

There are, of course, other European countries which have enacted legislation to provide extra benefits for mothers with many children. Such legislation is intended to assist families in coping with severe economic hardships. The Catholic Church is against birth control, but it does not actively encourage families to produce more children than they can support. The situation in the U.S.S.R. is different because it actually encourages the families of Slavic origin to multiply so as to keep up with the rapidly growing Moslem population of the U.S.S.R. One can only wonder what Karl Marx would think about this state of affairs. He wanted to free women from being mere "instruments of production." Whether he would find that the U.S.S.R. has succeeded in this respect is doubtful, but he would probably be concerned that "women under socialism" have been induced to become Stakhanovites and instruments of reproduction. This may be harsh criticism, but the legislation speaks for itself.

Another characteristic of Eastern European legislation on behalf of women is its "protective" nature. Over a period of many years, the Council of Ministers of the U.S.S.R. and other bodies have produced long lists of jobs and work which are not to be performed by women. Whether or not these laws and regulations are actually observed everywhere in the U.S.S.R. is impossible to say with certainty because many areas are closed to outsiders. But even in the most western part of the Soviet Union one finds women performing arduous work. Obviously, women should be protected in certain respects, but they are more in need of access and opportunities for advancement. As has been shown, official statistics are often misleading because they fail to specify the number or percentage of women represented at different levels of the political and economic hierarchy. This criticism applies to all Eastern European countries. But women have advanced significantly in the Eastern European countries since the end of World War II. The advances in Albania and Bulgaria are both very impressive. In both countries the influence of women has been enhanced by entrusting the leadership of the women's organizations to the wives and close relatives of the communist leaders. In Albania it was Nexhmije Hoxha and Vito Kapo. Until her death, Ludmila Zhivkova, the daughter of Todor Zhivkov, veteran communist leader of Bulgaria, was the key person in the Bulgarian women's organization. In 1979 she was made a member of the Politburo.

The situation in Czechoslovakia after World War II has been quite different. Prior to 1938 Czechoslovakia had a very strong and effective women's movement. During the Nazi occupation its leaders either were eliminated or sought refuge abroad. When the Communists assumed full control in February 1948, they did not allow any independent women's organizations to function. They cultivated a new leadership and rewarded a few women with important posts. Already in late 1947, at a time when the U.S.S.R. had never had a woman cabinet member, Ludmila Jankovcova, a registered socialist, was made minister of industry. Although she was made deputy Prime Minister in 1954, the time had passed long ago when the regime tried to give special recognition to women. The percentage of women among the members of the Communist Party declined in the 1950s and 1960s and the Soviet intervention in 1968 caused deep disenchantment among men and women who had supported the Dubček regime. There are no women in the present cabinet.

The German Democratic Republic presents a contrasting case. Although there are the usual difficulties with official statistics which fail to mention how many women are in the higher echelons of the party and state apparatus, there can be no doubt that they have advanced much more than in the U.S.S.R. The legislation is also much more interesting. From the very beginning it was possible to deal effectively with problems of discrimination because the Constitution of 1949 declared in Article 7(2) not only that "men and women are equal before the law" but also that "all laws and provisions which are in conflict with the principle of equality are null and void."

Hungary may also be considered a relative success story not so much because it opened up many more opportunities for women, but mainly because after 1956 it perfected what Khrushchev called "Gulash Communism." A visitor coming from one of the neighboring Communist countries is immediately struck by a different atmosphere. Hungary has been much more successful than any of the other Communist states in developing its economy, and this has created more opportunities for men and women. The Hungarian Constitution goes further than most by not merely declaring equality before the law but by adding provisions for punishment in cases of violations. Article 50(2) states that "the law severely punishes any prejudicial discrimination of the citizen, by sex, religious affiliation or nationality."

As was noted, there are some close connections between government officials and women's organizations. The Speaker of the National Assembly is also President of the National Council of Hungarian Women.

At this time, it is difficult to make an assessment of the status of women in Poland. Women have been very active in the Solidarity movement. It is not known how many of them have been adversely affected by the repressive measures. At the present time there are no special issues involving women's rights apart from human rights. As for political participation, recent developments have been most discouraging.

In Romania, as in Albania and Bulgaria, the advancement of women has been facilitated by the family connections within the leadership group. Elena Ceausescu, the wife of the powerful leader of Romania, has been the President of the National Council of Women. In 1980 she was appointed one of eight deputy Prime Ministers. Another deputy Prime Minister, Cornelia Filipas, is the Vice-President of the National Council of Women.

As has been noted, the situation of women in Yugoslavia is different from those of women in other Eastern European countries because their participation started in World War II with struggle against foreign occupation. It is different also in that political participation, in comparison with economic activities, is considerably higher in all parts of Yugoslavia. The Associated Labor Act of 1976 has reinforced and increased the participation of women through the delegate and self-management systems. Increasingly, women have acquired experience in economic management of organizations of various size, and this has enabled them to participate in decision-making on equal terms with men. Last, though not least, it is important to note that the political atmosphere in Yugoslavia is more favorable than in most of the other Communist states of Eastern Europe, and this has greatly contributed to the advancement of women.

It is necessary to add some concluding remarks about the role of international organizations. During the inter-war period, it was the International Labor Organization rather than the League of Nations which contributed to the advancement of women's rights.

After World War II, the United Nations made some important contributions beginning in 1948 with the Universal Declaration of Human Rights and the various subsequent Conventions which have been discussed in Chapters 14 and 15. Its work has been particularly important during the current United Nations Decade for Women. While the 1975 World Conference in Mexico City has generally been viewed as highly successful, the 1980 Conference in Copenhagen received mixed reviews from participants and observers. The Danish hosts cannot be blamed for what happened and what did not happen. There is general agreement that they did all that could possibly have been done to make the Conference a real success. Judging by the enormous amount of paper generated before the Conference, it may be concluded that the quality did not match the quantity. At the Conference too many extraneous issues were presented as part of the official agenda. They reflected the changes which have taken place in the composition and interests of the United Nations.

The International Labor Organization has been more successful in avoiding bureaucratization and politicization. It has produced some important conventions, which are identified in Chapters 14 and 15. In these chapters reference is also made to the contributions made by the Food and Agriculture Organization (FAO), UNESCO, WHO and others.

Very constructive work has been done by certain regional organizations, such as the Council of Europe and the European Communities. The latter has been highly effective with the enforcement of three short directives. They may be compared and contrasted with the large if not excessive number of resolutions passed by the United Nations. The documentation and reports produced by these regional organizations are often much better than those prepared by the United Nations.

In 1980, one of the better U.N. reports (A/Conf. 94/11) prepared for the World Conference on the United Nations Decade for Women, stated on page 27 that "very few Governments indicated the creation of special legislation to rectify the effect of historical discrimination against women by allowing special treatment for women." There is no way of ascertaining whether or not this is a correct statement because the reports by the governments are treated as confidential documents. Actually, the above cited statement is contradicted elsewhere in the same report. On page 18 one may read:

> Several ECE countries had either passed or put into force new legislation or amended their constitutions regarding sexual discrimination. The Union of Soviet Socialist Republics in its Constitution of October 1977 strengthened previous measures to give equal rights to women and men and to grant special protection for the family. Romania amended its Constitution in 1975 to reinforce equality under the law without discrimination based on sex. The 1978 Spanish Constitution established the same principle in Spain. The United States of America, while having passed both state and federal legislation for equal rights, stated that the pending passage of the Equal Rights Amendment 'continues to be essential to the attainment of equal rights for women and men under the law.' In 1978, a draft proposal for a new Swiss Constitution was published by a group of experts; it stipulated the equality of men and women with respect to the family, education, job opportunities and salaries. The United Kingdom passed both the Sex Discrimination Act and the Equal Pay Act in 1975. The Canadian

Human Rights Act, effective in 1978, was designed in part to further improve the position of women. Norway's Act No. 45 of 1978 further improved the status of women. Austria passed three relevant laws: the Federal Act Reforming the Legal Effects of Marriage (1975), the Federal Act Amending the Law of Succession of Spouses, the Law of Property between Husband and Wife, and the Law of Divorce (1978) and the Federal Act Reforming the Law of Parent/Child Relations (1977). Iceland passed the Law on Equality of Women and Men in 1976. Both Sweden and Netherlands have legislation pending on equal employment opportunities.

n its "appraisal" of various types of national machinery the same report levoted particular attention to the Eastern European countries. It noted hat:

> ... the approach of the socialist countries differs from that of the market economies. Significant progress has been achieved in the socialist countries in increasing the participation of women in all aspects of national life and protection of their rights. Specifically, the involvement of women in social production through the advancement of their educational standards and occupational skills has become a distinctive feature of the socialist economies, where women constitute 42-51 per cent of the factory and office workers of the Council for Mutual Economic Assistance (CMEA) member countries. Women's political awareness has increased, enabling them to participate more fully in public life and the administration of government, while a comprehensive system of protection of female labour and mother and child care has significantly improved the health status of women. The experiences of the non-socialist countries have been different and merit a more detailed appraisal.[2]

The last sentence would appear to be the most important of the entire statement, but none of the U.N. documents provide such an appraisal. No information was provided on how these various systems actually function, but it was noted that "the significance of the location of the machinery in the over-all governmental structure is the degree of leverage they have on influencing and enforcing policy."[3] This is an area

[2]A/Conf 94/11. World Conference on the United Nations Decade for Women, p. 27.
[3]Ibid., p. 11.

in which more comparative research should be undertaken. The U.N. is not likely to be of much help, but many national governments are prepared to assist scholars.

It appears that the U.N. still does not have a collection of the actual legislation pertaining to women's rights and political participation. Considering the amount of money spent on these international conferences and the expenses for personnel and travel, this lack of documentation is distressing. Rather than merely hope for improvements in the preparation by the U.N. of such conferences, scholars and women's organizations should insist that more documentation be made available several weeks in advance.

The U.N., as has been noted, does not have a very good record with respect to the advancement of women. The percentage of women who have been able to advance into the upper echelons of the U.N. hierarchy has remained disappointingly low. It is thus not in a good position to tell member governments what they should do to implement their constitutional and legal provisions concerning gender equality. But the U.N. could, in its monitoring of the implementation of the Convention on the Elimination of all Forms of Discrimination against Women, be more insistent on obtaining documentary materials rather than merely accepting and reporting whatever various governments claim to be factual information. The Convention on the Elimination of all Forms of Discrimination against Women provides an excellent basis for critical and constructive comparative research and for the formulation of national action programs.

APPENDIX

DENMARK

THE EQUAL REMUNERATION (MEN AND WOMEN) ACT, No. 32, of 4th February 1976

1. Any employer who has engaged men and women to work in the same work-place shall pay them equal remuneration for the same work in pursuance of this Act, if he is not bound thereto in pursuance of a collective agreement.

2. An employee whose remuneration is lower than the remuneration of others in contravention of section 1 of the present Act shall have a claim to the difference.

3. Where an employee is dismissed for having put forward a claim for equal remuneration as prescribed by this Act the employer shall pay him a compensation.

4. Section 3 shall apply correspondingly to such agreement areas where employees are entitled to equal remuneration, but where there are no provisions applying to compensation for dismissal that is not reasonably justified by the circumstances of the employee or the undertaking. Such claim shall be treated by industrial procedure.

5. No employee may renounce the rights prescribed by this Act.

6. An employee who believes that his employer does not observe his obligation to pay equal remuneration as prescribed by this Act may take the matter into court for establishment of his claim.

7. The present Act may receive the Royal Assent immediately after its passage.

8. The present Act shall come into operation on 9th February 1976, with effect on remuneration for the period after the coming into operation of the Act.

9. This Act shall not apply to the Faroe Islands.

ACT NO 161 of April 1978

ACT ON EQUAL TREATMENT FOR MEN AND WOMEN AS REGARDS ACCESS TO EMPLOYMENT, ETC:

We, Margrethe II, Queen of the Kingdom of Denmark by the Grace of God, do hereby proclaim:

The *Folketing* has adopted and We have given our Royal Assent to the following Act:

1.—(1) For the purpose of this Act, the principle of equal treatment shall mean that there shall be no discrimination whatsoever on grounds of sex. This shall apply to both direct and indirect discrimination by reference in particular to pregnancy or to marital or family status.

(2) This Act shall be without prejudice to provisions concerning protection of women, particularly as regards pregnancy and maternity.

(3) The provisions of this Act shall not apply where a similar duty to observe the principle of equal treatment is laid down in a collective agreement.

2.—Any employer shall observe the principle of equal treatment of men and women in relation to access to employment. This shall also apply in relation to transfers and promotion.

3.—(1) Any employer who employs men and women at the same place of work shall observe the principle of equal treatment of men and women as regards access to vocational guidance, vocational training, advanced vocational training and retraining.

(2) The duty to observe the principle of equal treatment shall also apply to any person engaged in training or guidance activities as mentioned in subsection (1).

4.—Any employer who employs men and women at the same place of work shall observe the principle of equal treatment of men and women as regards working conditions. This shall also apply to conditions governing dismissal.

5.—The duty to observe the principle of equal treatment shall also apply to any person who controls entry to a profession. This shall also apply to any person who controls access to vocational training or lays down rules governing such training or the carrying on of a profession.

6.—No advertisement shall indicate that persons of a particular sex are wanted or preferred in connection with access to employment, training etc.

7.—Any provisions included in contracts or in the internal rules of undertakings, etc. which are contrary to the provisions laid down in Sections 2 to 5 shall be null and void. This shall also apply to provisions included in rules etc. governing independent professions.

8.—Any person whose rights under Sections 2 to 5 have been violated may be awarded compensation.

9.—(1) Where an employee is dismissed from his employment because he has claimed equal treatment under Sections 2 to 4 his employer shall be liable to pay compensation.

(2) The amount of the compensation under Subsection (1) shall be fixed having regard to the employee's length of service and to all the circumstances of the case, but shall not in any case exceed 26 weeks' remuneration.

(3) Subsections (1) and (2) shall be applied correspondingly where the duty to observe the principle of equal treatment is laid down in a collective agreement, but where the agreement does not include a provision to the effect that the employee shall be entitled to compensation on dismissal for reasons which cannot be reasonably justified by the employee's own conduct or the firm's requirements. Claims for compensation shall be subject to the normal rules for handling industrial disputes.

10.—Any agreement under which a person purports to waive his rights under this Act shall be null and void.

11.—(1) Where the sex of a person constitutes a determining factor in connection with the exercise of certain occupational activities and the training leading thereto the minister responsible for the activities in question may grant exemptions from the provisions laid down in Sections 2 to 6 after consultation with the Minister of Labour and the Council on Equality.

(2) The Minister of Labour may after consultation with the Council on Equality and the appropriate ministry sanction measures which are not in accordance with Sections 2 to 6 with a view to promoting equal opportunities for men and women, especially by redressing existing inequalities which influence the access to employment, vocational training, etc.

(3) The Minister of Labour may within certain specified fields delegate his power to make decisions under Subsection (2) to the Minister responsible for the occupational field concerned.

12.—(1) Any person who acts in contravention of the provisions laid down in Sections 2 to 6 shall be liable to a fine.

(2) In the case of contravention on the part of a limited liability company, cooperative society or a similar body the fine may be imposed on the company as such.

13.—(1) This Act shall come into operation on 1st July 1978.

(2) If an application for exemption under section 11(1) is sent in to the appropriate Minister before 1st August 1978, Sections 2 to 6 will not come into operation in the fields concerned until such exemption has been refused.

(3) Section 7 shall also apply to contracts, rules and regulations, etc. which have been concluded or laid down before the commencement of this Act.

14.—This Act shall not extend to the Faroe Islands.

Christiansborg, 12th April 1978

Under Our Royal Hand and Seal

Margrethe R.

Svend Auken.

FINLAND

Decree
on the Council for Equality
Given in Helsinki on the 8th of June 1972

On proposition of the Prime Minister is provided:

§ 1

For the purpose of promoting social equality between men and women and preparing reforms in order to increase the equality between men and women, there is in connection with the Cabinet Office a council for equality.

§ 2

The council:

1) coordinates research in different fields concerned with the equality between men and women;

2) prepares reforms in collaboration with the public authorities, national and municipal authorities, labour market organizations and other bodies for the purpose of promoting equality;

3) follows and promotes the realization of equality in community planning, and takes initiatives and makes proposals to promote research, education and information activities related to equality;

4) takes initiatives and makes proposals as to the development of legislation and administrative activities relating to equality;

5) follows the development in other countries in questions relating to equality between men and women; and

6) carries out research and planning, within the relevant field, as individually determined by the Cabinet Office.

§ 3

The council consists of a chairman, a vice chairman and a maximum of eleven other members, who together with the personal deputies of the members are appointed by the Cabinet for at most three years at a time.

If the chairman, vice chairman, a member or deputy member resigns before his period of appointment has elapsed, a new chairman, vice chairman, member or deputy member is appointed in his stead for the duration of the period.

§ 4

The authorities shall, on request of the council for equality provide information and render opinions on matters to be handled by the council.

§ 5

A quorum shall consist of the chairman or vice chairman and at least one-half of the other members. Voting shall be by simple majority. In case of a tied vote the chairman's vote is decisive.

§ 6

The Cabinet Office is the preparatory organ for the council for equality. The secretary general and the planners for the council shall be employed by the Cabinet Office under the terms of employment, within its budgetary limitations.

During vacations of the secretary general, or when he for some other reason temporarily is prevented to attend to his tasks, these will be carried out by one of the planners appointed by the Cabinet Office.

§ 7

Qualifications required of the secretary general and the planners include a university degree considered suitable for the task. The secretary general shall in addition have administrative experience and be familiar with questions related to the promotion of social equality between men and women.

§ 8

The council may appoint working committees and sections consisting of members of the council and, by permission of the Cabinet Office call permanent experts to the sections.

§ 9

Communications of the council are signed by the chairman or vice chairman together with the secretary general or one of the members.

§ 10

Otherwise the provisions enacted concerning committees are applicable to the council.

§ 11

More detailed instructions on the application of this decree will, as needed, be issued by the Cabinet Office.

Helsinki on the 8th of June 1972   The President of the Republic

Prime Minister

THE NATIONAL PROGRAMME OF FINLAND FOR PROMOTING EQUALITY BETWEEN WOMEN AND MEN DURING THE SECOND HALF OF THE UNITED NATIONS DECADE FOR WOMEN 1980—1985; EQUALITY, DEVELOPMENT AND PEACE (ADOPTED ON APRIL 29, 1980)

The Government regards the prevailing inequality between women and men in society as a serious shortcoming, which the public authorities, the labour market organizations and other associations as well as private citizens should strive to redress. In order to promote equality between women and men the Cabinet has adopted the following programme for the years 1980-1985. To the programme are attached the memorandum of the Council for Equality, the programmes of all the Ministries for the promotion of equality in the years 1980-1985, and the decision of the Cabinet on the implementation of the programme.

1. *Education and Culture*

1.1.   The promotion of equality between men and women will be included in the objectives and the practice of education at every level.

1.2.   In the comprehensive school and upper secondary level education equality between women and men will be promoted in the following ways:

It will be determined in which subjects equality education could be included, and the necessary measures will be taken.

Educational material will be further developed to promote equality between women and men.

Tutoring and vocational guidance will be developed with the aim of broadening the basis for occupational orientation and interest of girls and boys.

1.3. In upper secondary and higher education efforts will be made to decrease the segregation of fields of study on the basis of sex.

1.4. Education promoting equality will be included in teacher training.

1.5. In adult education attention will be paid to the improvement of study opportunities of women and men with family responsibilities.

1.6. Efforts will be made to achieve equality between women and men when safeguarding employment opportunities and awarding grants in the field of arts and cultural activities.

1.7. The problems caused by women by the interruption of their studies and scientific work brought about by child-bearing and child care will be looked into, and appropriate measures will be taken.

1.8. Measures will be taken to promote research into the status of women.

1.9. Efforts will be made to determine what measures could be taken to prevent the exploitation of women and, more generally, exploitation on the basis of sex in marketing and commercial mass entertainment.

2. *Working Life*

2.1. Women's equal right to work and to income maintenance in case of unemployment will be carried into effect irrespective of their marital status and the prevailing economic situation. Measures in the field of employment policy are aimed at the creation of permanent full-time jobs.

2.2. The segregation of the labour market by sex is being reduced as a part of the Government's employment policy. This aim is promoted i.e. by strengthening staff resources in local employment services.

2.3. The needs and obligations of male and female workers arising from child care and family life will be taken into particular consideration when determining the possibilities of shortening working-hours in general.

2.4. The adoption of flexible working hours in general, including the right of an employee to work part-time for personal reasons, will be aimed at.

2.5. Measures will be taken to secure the employment opportunities and vocational training of parents re-entering the labour market after caring for their children at home.

2.6. Finland will sign the Convention on the Elimination of All Forms of Discrimination against Women at the earliest opportunity and will take the necessary measures to ratify the Convention as soon as possible.

2.7. Legislation will be enacted to prohibit discrimination based on sex in working life and especially in hiring, job advertising, remuneration, promotion, in-service training and other comparable benefits, as well as to promote equal treatment of women in the labour market.

2.8. Employment security will be further strengthened in cases of pregnancy, maternity leave and parental leave so that dismissal or worsening of the terms of employment is made impossible.

2.9. Legislation to ensure a leave with compensation for the care of a sick child will be further developed.

2.10. Measures will be taken to make those employed in agriculture, in particular women, less tired by their work.

2.11. The above measures will also be applied, when appropriate, to self-employed persons.

3. *The Status of Women in State Administration*

3.1. In drawing up personnel policies and in developing personnel participation, special attention will be paid to the promotion of equality between women and men.

3.2. As a party on the labour market the State will work actively for bringing into force collective agreements prohibiting discrimination based on sex in working life.

3.3. The remuneration of female-dominated, low-income groups among state employees, will be contractually raised at a higher rate than the remuneration of other groups in order to diminish the relative differences.

3.4. Measures will be taken to improve the balance in certain male- or female dominated occupations, and the promotion of women to more demanding tasks will be encouraged.

3.5. Measures will be taken to achieve a considerable increase in the number of women in government committees, advisory bodies and commissions as well as in delegations to international conferences.

3.6. Work for equality between women and men in municipal and provincial administration will be encouraged.

4. *Family Law and Social Policy*

4.1. In further developing the social insurance scheme, the principle of individual benefits will be observed; the target will be to safeguard the subsistence of each individual citizen, irrespective of sex and marital status.

4.2. In further developing legislation on family policy and social policy women and men will be considered to have equal rights and obligations in regard to the care and maintenance of their children.

4.3. Legislation concerning family relations, in particular the provisions concerning family name, marriage, guardianship and citizenship, will be revised on the basis of equality between women and men.

4.4. Family education and co-operation will be promoted in the activities of the maternity and pediatric clinics, day care centres, schools and organizations with special emphasis on the importance of the father to the child. A part of the maternity leave will be converted into parental leave and the level of compensation will be raised.

4.5. In further developing employment security, social security of parents, and the benefits based on employment relationship, the care of small children shall rank equal with employment outside home and the right of parents to re-enter the labour market after a child care leave (maximum length 3 years) will be guaranteed.

4.6. The possibilities of renewing the system of survivors' pensions in such a way that the chief beneficiaries would be the dependent children, and the widow or widower, if she or he has been dependent on the income of the deceased, will be determined.

4.7. The principles of the division of the farm income, on which the farmer's pension is based, will be adjusted in such a way that the housewife's contribution will be recognized equitably. The provisions of the tax legislation concerning the determining of the income of a farmer and his wife for taxation purposes will be modified in such a way that a larger share of their income than at present will be assigned to the wife.

5. Regional Development and Community Planning Policies

5.1. Equality in vocational training and employment of women and men will be promoted by means of legislation concerning regional policy and by regional policy measures.
5.2. Efforts should be made to focus industrial policy in such a way that new jobs are created for women and men equally.
5.3. Experimental projects and research related to public transportation will be utilized to determine the possible significance of improvement in communications e.g. to unemployed women and men not officially registered as unemployed from the point of view of securing employment, use of cultural services and participation in public activities.
5.4. In developing the legislation and the measures relating to housing and environment, increasing attention will be paid to the wishes of the inhabitants, the needs of the children and the needs arising from child care and household duties. Special attention will be paid to increasing the opportunities of women to take part in the planning and decision-making concerning housing and environment.

6. Participation in Public Activities

The opportunities of women as well as of men with family responsibilities to participate in political, trade-union, cooperative and other public activities will be improved.

7. International Co–operation

Attempts will be made to increase the participation of women in international co-operation and in the promotion of peace and disarmament. In the Finnish participation in the activities of international organizations and in Finnish development co-operation special efforts will be made to bring up and resolve questions that are of special relevance from the point of view of equality between women and men.

THE IMPLEMENTATION OF THE NATIONAL PROGRAMME FOR THE SECOND HALF OF THE UNITED NATIONS DECADE FOR WOMEN (1980-1985) IN STATE ADMINISTRATION
(ADOPTED ON APRIL 29, 1980)

Having adopted the national programme of Finland for the promotion of equality between men and women during the second half of the United Nations Decade for Women (1980-1985) on April 29, 1980, the Cabinet has decided, on the proposal of the Prime Minister's Office, to issue the following instructions concerning the implementation of the national programme and of the programmes drawn up by the different Ministries for the years 1980-1985 in state administration:

1. *Responsibility for the Implementation of the National Programme*

   The responsibility for the implementation of the national programme rests with the Ministries in matters falling within their competence. It rests with those responsible for the different units of an administrative sector to ensure that the principles of the national programme are observed in the activities of their respective units.
   If the programme promoting equality drawn up by a Ministry for the years 1980-1985 is in conflict with the national programme, the Ministry concerned shall adjust its own programme so that it is in conformity with the national programme.
   For the planning and follow-up of the implementation of the programmes the Ministry concerned may appoint a working group.
   In each administrative sector the Ministry concerned guides and supervises the implementation of the programmes.

2. *Participation of the Personnel of an Administrative Unit in the Implementation of the Programmes*

   It rests with the management of each administrative unit to ensure that the programmes are implemented in its personnel administration, in-service training, planning and internal information.
   As far as personnel administration and personnel policy are concerned the implementation of the national programme is guided and supervised by the Ministry of Finance, which shall give detailed instructions and recommendations, and ensure suitable follow-up and reporting.
   As far as plans, decisions and annual adjustments concerning the implementation of the national programme and of the programmes drawn up by the administrative units are concerned, the co-operation

344

bodies of the personnel and management shall be consulted in matters falling within their competence.

3. *Annual Adjustment of the Programme of the Ministries*

For the implementation of the national programme and for the attainment of concrete and significant results the programmes drawn up by the Ministries shall be adjusted annually throughout the period of implementation on the basis of the reports received and experiences obtained. In the annual adjustments changes in the activities of an administrative sector shall be taken into account. The Ministry concerned shall approve the adjustments after consultation with the Prime Minister's Office.

4. *Reporting to the Prime Minister's Office*

For each calendar year of the period covered by the programme each Ministry shall, by the end of the following February, submit a report to the Prime Minister's Office on the implementation of the national programme and of the programme drawn up for its sector.
The Ministries shall submit their final reports on the implementation of the national programme and of the programmes drawn up for their respective administrative sectors to the Prime Minister's Office not later than March 1986.

5. *The Duties of the Prime Minister's Office*

The Prime Minister's Office, assisted by the Council for Equality, shall follow and guide the implementation of the national programme and the programmes drawn up by the Ministries.
By the end of May 1982 the Prime Minister's Office shall prepare a report to the Cabinet on the implementation of the national programme in 1980-1981.
On the basis of the final reports of the Ministries the Prime Minister's Office shall prepare a final report to the Cabinet on the implementation and effects of the national programme in state administration.

6. *Informing the Parliament*

The Cabinet shall give an account to the Parliament in 1986 on the basis of the final report on the implementation and effects of the national programme and the programmes of the ministries. The ac-

345

count shall, if possible, be given before reporting to the United Nations on the implementation of the programme.

7. *Additional Regulations*

In case the national programme has not been implemented within an administrative unit, the unit concerned shall give the respective Ministry an account of the reasons for this and of its plans for remedying the situation.

If the national programme has not been implemented in matters falling within the competence of a certain Ministry, the Ministry shall upon request give the Prime Minister's Office an account of the reasons for this and of its plans for remedying the situation.

Hereby the Prime Minister's Office brings the above to the Ministries' attention for observance. The Prime Minister's Office also wishes to inform the Ministries of the following:

In the Prime Minister's Office matters relating to the national programme are dealt with by the Council for Equality and its permanent secretariat in the Prime Minister's Office. The administrative units may refer to the secretariat for guidance with regard to the implementation of the programme. The address of the secretariat is Korkeavuorenkatu 47 B, 00130 HELSINKI 13. The members of the secretariat are: Ms. Leila Räsänen, Executive Secretary, tel. 160 4010, Ms. Anita Haataja, Consultant (education and training), tel. 160 4012, Ms. Pirkko Kiviaho, Consultant (social and family policies), tel 160 4011, and Ms. Eeva-Liisa Tuominen, Consultant (working life), tel. 160 4013.

It rests with the Ministries to bring the above to the attention of their subordinate administrative units for observance.

ICELAND

LAW
on
the Equality of Women and Men.
(No. 78 31 May 1976)

Art. 1.

The purpose of this Law is to promote the equality and equal position of women and men.

Art. 2.

Both women and men shall be provided with equal opportunity of employment and education and they shall receive equal wages for performing comparable work of equal value.

Art. 3.

It is unlawful for employers to discriminate between employees by sex, and this shall apply, *inter alia*, to recruitment and appointment to employment positions, promotions, employment titles, separation from employment, the provision of any type of employment benefits and general working conditions.

Art. 4.

An employment position, which has been advertised and for which applications are invited, shall be open equally to women and men. It is unlawful to indicate in such an advertisement, that an employee of one sex rather than another is being sought.

Art. 5.

In the event where an applicant for an employment position is a woman, and a man has been hired to fill that same position, then the Equality of Treatment Board shall, if the applicant so desires, require the employer concerned to provide in writing information as to what education, work experience and other particular qualifications the person who has been hired to fill the position may be endowed with.

A man, who has applied for such a position, shall enjoy the same right in the event that a woman has been hired to fill the position in question.

Art. 6.

Women and men who are employed by one and the same employer shall enjoy the same opportunity for continued work training and for participation in work training programmes organised to increase job qualifications, or in preparation for other types of work.

Art. 7.

Schools and other educational and pedagogical institutions shall provide instruction on equal rights for women and men. Textbooks and educational media used in such institutions shall be designed and con-

structed in such a manner that this does not indicate any discrimination of the sexes.
Art. 8.

Advertisers shall be prohibited to publish any type of advertisement, either by word or by illustrations which could be construed as being derogatory or humiliating for one or the other of the two sexes.
Art. 9.

The Equality of Treatment Board shall be in charge of the application of this Law. The Board shall consist of five members appointed for a term of three years at a time, and these shall, along with their alternates, be appointed in the following manner: One member appointed by the Supreme Court of Iceland, who shall also serve as the Chairman of the Board, and have a degree in law; one member appointed by the Minister of Social Affairs; one member appointed by the Federation of State and Municipal Employees; one member appointed by the Icelandic Federation of Labour and one member appointed by the Confederation of Icelandic Employers.

The Equality of Treatment Board has its own office and the Board hires its own Managing Director to be in charge of its functions. The expenditure incurred by the functions of the Board shall be paid by the State Treasury.
Art. 10.

The functions of the Equality of Treatment Board are as follows:

1. To make sure that the provision of Articles 2 to 8 of this Law pertaining to the equality of women and men are fulfilled.
2. To serve as an advisory body ontowards governmental authorities, institutions and societies in matters pertaining to the equal rights of women and men in respect of wages and working conditions, and in regard to the engagement or appointment of persons for positions of employment.
3. To follow social developments which, *inter alia*, are of concern to the subject matter of this legislation, and to make proposals for amendments in conformity with the purpose of this Law.
4. To promote good relations between the organisations of employers and wage earners, and those other individuals and institutions concerned with matters of equal rights of women and men in order that the objectives and purpose of this Law may be served in the most natural manner.
5. To initiate of its own accord the examination of the extent to which discrimination may occur in questions of

equal rights of women and men within the framework set by this Law. Public institutions and organisations operating in the labour market shall be required to provide the Equality of Treatment Board with any type of information that may be needed in respect of the pursuance of this objective.

6. To receive advice on the possible violation of the provisions of this Law, and to examine the nature of such information and, having completed its examination of the case in question, submit the documentary records pertaining thereto to the appropriate parties or authorities.

Art. 11.

In the event where the Equality of Treatment Board considers that the provisions of Articles 2 to 8 of this Law have been violated, then the Board shall submit substantiated proposals for specific action to the parties that may be concerned.

In case the party in question does not agree to accept the Board's proposals then it shall be authorized, in agreement with the employee concerned, to initiate a law suit on his/her behalf for the purpose of obtaining a recognition of his/her rights.

Art. 12.

Any person who premeditatedly or by negligence violates the provisions of this Law shall be subject to the payment of indemnities according to general provisions of law.

Such violations shall be subject to payment of fines, unless the law provides for a heavier penalty.

Art. 13.

Whenever a district judge conducts a trial arising from a violation of the provisions of this Law he/she shall call upon two other persons to sit on the bench with him/her as co-judges.

In selecting such co-judges preference shall be given, other things being equal, to persons with an extensive knowledge of matters pertaining to wages and working conditions of employees and their equality of treatment.

Art. 14.

The Minister of Social Affairs lays down further rules for the application of the provisions of this Law through the issuance of Regulations, having previously received the proposals of the Equality of Treatment Board.

Art. 15.

This Law supersedes and replaces Law No. 37 of April 24, 1973 on the Equality of Wages Board.

Art. 16.

This Law enters into force forthwith.

NORWAY

AN ACT RELATING TO EQUAL STATUS BETWEEN THE SEXES
June 9th. 1978, No. 45.

§ 1 (Purpose of the Act)

This Act shall promote equal status between the sexes and aims particularly at improving the position of women.

The public authorities shall facilitate equality of status between the sexes in all sectors of society. Women and men shall be given equal opportunities for education, employment and cultural and professional advancement.

§ 2 (The substantive scope of the Act)

The Act relates to discrimination between women and men in all areas, with the exception of internal conditions in religious communities.

The Act shall not be enforced by the authorities described in § 10 of the Act in respect of family life and purely personal relationships.

In special cases the King may determine that the Act shall not, in whole or in part, apply to certain specific sectors. Before any such decision is made, the opinion of the Board (cf. § 10) shall be obtained.

§ 3 (General clause)

Discrimination between women and men is not permitted. The term "discrimination" shall mean treatment differentiating between women and men because they are of different sexes. Discrimination furthermore includes treatment which in fact acts in such a manner that one sex is placed at an unreasonable disadvantage as compared with the other.

Different treatment which, in conformity with the purpose of the Act, promotes equal status between the sexes does not represent a contravention of the first paragraph. The same applies to women's special rights based on the existing difference in the situation of women and men.

§ 4 (Equal status in recruitment, etc.)

Except in cases where there is an obvious reason for doing so, a job must not be announced vacant for one sex only. Nor must the announcement give the impression that the employer expects or prefers one of the sexes for the position.

In recruitment, promotion, notice to leave or temporary lay-offs of employees, no difference must be made between women and men which is in contravention of § 3.

A job applicant who has not obtained an advertised job may demand that the employer state in writing the education, experience and other clearly demonstrable qualifications for the job possessed by a person of the opposite sex appointed to the job.

§ 5 (Equal pay for work of equal value)

Women and men employed by the same employer shall have equal pay for work of equal value.

The term "pay" shall mean ordinary remuneration for work together with other supplements or cash bonuses, or other benefits given by the employer.

The term "equal pay" shall mean that pay shall be determined in the same manner for women and men regardless of sex.

The King may prescribe by regulation specific rules as to who shall be considered to have the same employer in central and local government service.

§ 6 (Equal rights to education)

Women and men shall have the same rights to education. The employer shall consider women and men on equal terms in respect of training, further education and the granting of leave of absence in connection with education etc.

In respect of admission to courses, schools and studies, and of other efforts designed to promote recruitment to a particular trade or profession, when circumstances otherwise are approximately equal, it shall be possible to give priority to one sex if it is the case that this will help in the long term to regulate any imbalance between the sexes in the trade or profession in question.

§ 7 (Teaching aids)

In schools and in other educational institutions, the teaching aids used shall be based on equal status between the sexes.

§ 8 (Associations)

An association shall be open to women and men on equal terms when

1. membership of the association is of importance to the individual member in connection with possibilities for work or professional advancement, or
2. when the aims of the association are essentially to contribute towards a solution of general problems of a social nature.

The injunctions in the first paragraph shall not apply to an association where the main objective is to further the special interests of one sex.

§ 9 (Equal Status Council)

The King shall appoint an Equal Status Council having the authority and the number of members decided by the Storting at any one time.

§ 10 (Enforcement of the Act)

The King shall appoint an Equal Status Commissioner and a Board—the Equal Status Appeals Board—which are to collaborate in the implementation of this Act. The competence of the Commissioner and the Board shall comprise, with such limitations as follow from the second subsection of § 2, all private enterprise as well as all administrative and commercial activities in the public sector. The Commissioner is appointed by the King for six years at a time.

The Board shall consist of seven members with personal proxies. Two of the members, with proxies, shall be appointed at the recommendation of the Norwegian Federation of Trade Unions and the Norwegian Employers Confederation respectively. The King shall appoint the chairperson and the deputy chairperson, one of whom shall possess the qualifications specified for a judge.

The King may issue specific regulations regarding functions and organizations of the Commissioner and the Board. The opinion of the Board shall be obtained in advance.

§ 11 (The functions of the Commissioner and the Board)

The Commissioner shall, with respect to equal status between the sexes, verify that the provisions of this Act are not violated. The Commissioner shall, on his/her own initiative or on the basis of a request from others, seek to ensure that the provisions of this Act are observed. If a voluntary arrangement cannot be effectuated, the Commissioner may bring the case before the Board for a decision, pursuant to § 13.

If the Commissioner decides not to submit a case before the Board, it may be submitted by anyone who is a party in the case or who has brought action without being a party. Such cases may be decided by the Board unless the aggrieved party opposes this.

The Board may require the Commissioner to submit certain specific cases to the Board.

§ 12 (Decisions by the Commissioner)

If the Commissioner cannot effectuate a voluntary arrangement, and it must be assumed that waiting for the Board's decision will result in inconvenience or harmful effects, the Commissioner may render such decisions as provided for under § 13.

The Commissioner shall state the grounds for the decision at the time it is made. The Board shall be informed of the decision. The decision may be appealed to the Board.

§ 13 (Decisions by the Board)

The Board may prohibit an act which is in contravention of §§ 3 - 8 of this Act if the Board finds that intervention is required out of regard for equality of status between the sexes. The Board may impose measures which are necessary to ensure that the said act ceases and to prevent its repetition. If the Board is unable to make a decision, pursuant to the second paragraph, it shall state its opinion as to whether the circumstance brought before it contravenes this Act.

The Board may not repeal or alter administrative decisions made by others. Nor may the Board issue injunctions as to how the authority to adopt administrative decisions must be exercised in order not to contravene this Act. The term "administrative decision" shall mean such a decision as is covered by § 2, first subsection, litra (a) of the Public Administration Act. The Board may not make decisions binding on the King or any Ministry.

Ground shall be given for a decision of the Board at the time it is made.

The decision cannot be appealed to the King or to the Ministry but it may be brought before the courts for the full trial of the case within the framework of this Act.

§ 14 (The relationship of the Board to the Labour Disputes Court)

If a case under this Act which indirectly raises the question of the validity, interpretation, or continued existence of a collective wage agreement, is brought before the Board, each of the parties to the wage agreement may, with postponing effect, have this question decided by the Labour Disputes Court. The King shall issue rules for any such lawsuit.

The Board may in no case make any decisions which, in pursuance of the Act of 5 May 1927 relating to Labour Disputes and of the Act of 18 July 1958, No. 2, relating to Public Service Disputes, come under the competence of the Labour Disputes Court.

§ 15 (Duty to provide information)

Public authorities are required, regardless of their pledge of secrecy, to provide the Commissioner and the Board with such information as is necessary for the implementation of this Act. Such information may also be required of others who are under an obligation to give evidence in accordance with the Civil Disputes Act. § 211 of the Civil Disputes Act shall apply correspondingly. Decisions referred to in § 207, first subsection, second sentence, § 208, second subsection, and § 209, second subsection, cf. § 209, third paragraph, third sentence of the Civil Disputes Act, shall be rendered by the District or City Court.

The Board and the Commissioner may undertake such investigations and inspections as they find necessary in the execution of their duties pursuant to the Act. If necessary, they may demand the assistance of the police.

The Board or Commissioner may require that information shall be given to, or that investigations may be carried out by other official bodies which are enjoined to participate in the implementation of this Act.

§ 16 (Pledge of secrecy)

Anyone who serves or undertakes assignments for the Board or the Commissioner must not, without just and sufficient cause, allow others to acquire knowledge of information emerging in the course of such service or assignment concerning:

1. The personal affairs of any individual.
2. Technical devices, production methods, plans and prognoses etc., which other enterprises could exploit in their own operations to the detriment of the undertaking to which the information refers.

Nor may such information be exploited by the person in question in his own activities.

§ 17 (Liability for damages)

By wilfully or negligently violating the provisions of this Act, the tortfeasor shall be liable for damages according to the usual rules.

The court may modify liability under the first paragraph if the effect would be unreasonably burdensome or if other considerations so indicate.

§ 18 (Criminal liability)

Anyone who wilfully or negligently violates decisions made in pursuance of §§ 12 or 13, or who aids and abets therein, shall be punished by fines.

Violations committed by persons in subordinate positions shall not be punished if the violation is mainly due to the offender's subordinate relationship to the person for whom the act is carried out.

Enterprises, associations or foundations on whose behalf such violation has been committed or whose interests the said violation was intended to promote, or which have derived considerable benefit from the violation, may be sentenced to a fine. § 28 of the Penal Code does not apply to punishment by fines under this paragraph.

The wilful or negligent violation of injunctions issued pursuant to § 15 shall be punished by fines or by imprisonment up to 3 months, or both. Violations of § 16, first subsection, shall be punished pursuant to § 121 of the Penal Code, even if the guilty party is not a public servant. Violations of § 16, second subsection, shall be punished by fines or by imprisonment up to one year, or both.

§ 19 (Prosecution)

Violations of § 18, first to third subsection, shall not be subject to public prosecution, except at the request of the Board, unless so required in the public interest.

The prosecuting authorities may, in connection with the criminal case, request judgment in respect of measures to ensure that the unlawful act ceases and to prevent its repetition.

§ 20 (The geographical scope of the Act)

This Act shall apply in the Realm, in Svalbard and on board Norwegian vessels and aircraft in areas not subject to the sovereignty of any State. This Act shall also apply to activities on installations and devices on the Norwegian part of the continental shelf.

The King may make exceptions to the provisions of the first subsection and of the Act. Before such decisions are made, the opinion of the Board shall be obtained.

§ 21 (Entry into force etc.)

1. This Act shall enter into force at such time as the King decides.
2. From such date, the second subsection (new) of § 1 of Act No. 47 of 16 June 1972 relating to Marketing Control shall read:

"An advertiser and anyone who creates advertising matter shall ensure that the advertisement does not conflict with the inherent parity between the sexes and that it does not imply any derogatory judgement of either sex or portray a woman or man in an offensive manner."

SWEDEN

ACT CONCERNING EQUALITY BETWEEN WOMEN AND MEN AT WORK SFS 1980:412

Aim

Section 1
The aim of this Act is to promote equality between women and men in respect of employment, conditions of employment and opportunities for development in employment (equality at work).

Prohibition against discrimination on the ground of sex

Scection 2
An employer shall not discriminate against an employee or job applicant on the ground of her or his sex.

Section 3
Discrimination on the ground of sex shall be considered to exist where an employer, for purposes of recruitment, promotion or training for promotion, chooses one person in preference to another of the opposite sex despite the fact that the disadvantaged person is objectively better qualified for the job or training.

This does not apply, however, if the employer can show that the decision was not founded on the person's sex, that it constituted part of a conscious effort to promote equality at work or that it was justified having regard to some ideological or other special interest which would not be subordinated to that of equality at work.

Section 4
Discrimination on the grounds of sex shall also be considered to exist where an employer:

1. applies to an employee less favourable terms of employment than those applied by that employer to an employee of the opposite sex where the work they perform must be regarded as like work on the basis of a collective agreement or established practice within the branch of activity, or as equivalent according to an agreed job evaluation, unless the employer can show that any discrepancy in the terms of employment is due to differences in the employees' objective qualifications for the job or that such discrepancy is anyway not due to the employees' sex;
2. manages and distributes the work in such a way that one employee is manifestly disadvantaged compared with an employee of the opposite sex unless the employer can show that such treatment is not due to the employee's sex or that grounds of the nature specified in the second paragraph of Section 3 exist;

356

3. terminates a contract of employment, transfers, lays off, dismisses or takes any other comparable measure detrimental to an employee if the measure concerned is due to the employee's sex.

Section 5
Any contract or agreement providing for different treatment of women and men in respect of terms of employment or in any other way permitting discrimination on the ground of sex within the meaning of Sections 3 and 4 shall be null and void.

Active measures to promote equality

Section 6
Within the framework of the activity the employer shall consciously pursue active efforts to promote equality at work.

To this end the employer shall take such measures as may, having regard to the employer's resources and circumstances in general, be required to ensure that the working conditions are equally suited to women and men. The employer shall also seek to ensure that both sexes apply for job vacancies and promote, by means of training and other appropriate measures, an even distribution between women and men in different types of work and within different staff categories.

Where the distribution between women and men at a place of work is generally uneven in a certain type of work or within a certain staff category, the employer shall make special efforts when recruiting new staff to attract applications from the underrepresented sex and seek to ensure that the proportion of employees of that sex is gradually increased. The foregoing shall not, however, be applicable if there are special considerations making such measures undesirable or if they cannot reasonably be required having regard to the employer's resources and circumstances in general.

Section 7
In respect of the matters dealt with in Section 6, other rules may be laid down in a collective agreement concluded or approved by a central organisation of workers.

An employer bound by such a collective agreement may also apply that agreement in respect of an employee or job applicant who is not a member of the organisation of workers party to the agreement but is employed in a job covered by the agreement or is an applicant for such a job.

When assessing the obligations arising out of Section 6 for an employer who is not bound by a collective agreement under paragraph one above, account shall be taken of collective agreements in comparable conditions.

Compensation and other sanctions

Section 8
Where an employee suffers discrimination on the ground of her or his sex as

the result of a clause in a contract with the employer or of the employer terminating a contract or taking a similar legal act, that clause or legal act shall be declared invalid if the employee so requests.

Should discrimination consist of an employer appointing, as specified in Section 3, one or more persons in preference to one or more persons of the opposite sex, the employer shall pay compensation to the person or persons suffering discrimination for the moral injury caused by the discrimination. Where several persons have suffered discrimination and seek compensation in such a case, compensation shall be determined as if only one person had suffered discrimination and be divided equally among them.

Where an employee suffers discrimination as specified in Section 4, the employer shall pay her or him compensation for the loss sustained and for the moral injury caused by such discrimination.

Where reasonable, compensation may be reduced or disallowed entirely.

Section 9

An employer who fails to observe the provisions set out in Section 6 may be ordered, under penalty of a fine, to comply with his or her obligations.

In the event of an employer failing to comply with obligations under a collective agreement of the kind referred to in the first paragraph of Section 7, the relevant provisions on sanctions in the agreement or in the Co-determination at Work Act (1976:580) shall be applicable.

The Equal Opportunities Ombudsman and Equal Opportunities Commission

Section 10

The Government shall appoint an Ombudsman and a Commission for matters relating to equality between women and men at work (hereafter referred to as the Equal Opportunities Ombudsman and the Equal Opportunities Commission), whose task shall be to ensure compliance with this Act. The Equal Opportunities Ombudsman shall, in the exercise of his or her duties, seek firstly to persuade the employer to comply voluntarily with the provisions of the Act. The Ombudsman shall also participate generally in the efforts being made to promote equality at work.

The Equal Opportunities Commission shall consist of eleven members. The Chairman and a further four members shall be persons who represent the interests of neither employers nor employees. The Chairman shall have legal training and experience as a judge. Two of the four members shall have a specialised knowledge of labour market conditions and the other two experience of work with matters relating to equality between women and men. The Swedish Employers' Confederation, the Swedish Association of Local Authorities jointly with the Federation of the Swedish County Councils, the National Agency for Government Employers, the Swedish Trade Union Confederation, the Swedish Central Organisation of Salaried Employees and the Swedish Confederation of Professional Associations/Swedish Federation of Government Officers shall each nominate one of the remaining six members. Each member shall have a substitute. The provisions relating to members shall also be applicable to their substitutes. Where necessary, the Chairman may appoint temporary substitutes.

Procedure in disputes concerning discrimination

Section 11
Cases concerning the application of Sections 2 to 5 and 8 shall be dealt with in accordance with the Litigation in Labour Disputes Act (1974:371). Here job applicants shall be considered to be employees and any person or body to whom application has been made for a job to be an employer. The same shall apply in respect of implementation of the provisions governing settlement of disputes set out in the Co-determination at Work Act (1976:580) in a dispute concerning Sections 2 to 5 and 8.
In such disputes the Equal Opportunities Ombudsman may bring an action on behalf of an individual employee or job applicant with that person's consent if the Ombudsman considers that a decision in the dispute would constitute a valuable judicial precedent. Such actions shall be brought in the Labour Court. However, where an organisation of workers is entitled to bring an action on behalf of the person concerned by virtue of Chapter 4 Section 5 of the Litigation in Labour Disputes Act, the Equal Opportunities Ombudsman may bring an action only if the organisation does not do so. The provisions of the above Act regarding the individual's status in the proceedings shall also be applicable where the action is brought by the Ombudsman.
In cases concerning the application of Sections 2 to 5 and 8 the court may order, over and above what may be provided elsewhere, that the hearing be held *in camera* where the presence of the public can be expected to constitute a risk of significant prejudice to the parties involved or any other person through the disclosure of business, operational or other comparable conditions in the case of a firm or organisation or of economic or personal circumstances in the case of an individual.

Section 12
Where several employees or job applicants bring actions for compensation against the same employer and where the employer considers that any compensation should be divided among them as provided in the second paragraph of Section 8, the cases concerned shall, at the employers' request, be joined in the same proceedings.
Where actions have been brought in several courts, the Labour Court shall be competent to hear the cases if any of them fall within its jurisdiction. Should this not apply, the district court in which an action was first brought or, if actions have been brought simultaneously in several district courts, the district court chosen by the employer shall be competent. Cases brought before another court shall be transferred to the court which is to deal with all the cases. No appeal may be lodged against a decision to transfer a case.
In the event of several persons having brought actions before the same court, paragraph one above shall be applicable if the cases are not dealt with jointly anyway pursuant to some other legal provision.

Section 13
Proceedings in a case concerning compensation under the second paragraph of Section 8 shall be adjourned, at the employer's request, where this is necessary for the case to be dealt with jointly with any other such action for compensation which has already been or may be brought.

. . . .

AUSTRIA

STATEMENT OF PRIORITIES AND TARGETS
FOR THE SECOND HALF OF THE
DECADE FOR WOMEN
(1981–1985)
issued by the Federal Chancellor's Office

1. Family Care

1.1 Sexual Division of Tasks
- Campaigns should be organized to inform families, especially men, about the new Family Law, with a special emphasis on shared responsibilities and duties of husbands and fathers.
- Administrative measures should be reviewed as to their effectiveness in connection with the new Family Law.
- Legal measures should be taken to incorporate the basic principles of the new Family Law into social and labour-related legislation.
- Seminars should be initiated to increase the consciousness and self-confidence of housewives, in order to give them the opportunity to re-assess their value within society and to teach them to defend their interests in domestic and outside affairs.

1.2 Family Planning and Maternity Health Care
- To ensure that partners can freely decide whether they want a baby or not, the network of family planning facilities should be further increased. Information campaigns on contraceptive methods will be continued.
- The Mother and Child Health Care Passport, created to guarantee health care for pregnant women and for their children up to their first year, is linked to an allowance after completion of all checkups. This scheme should be extended by one more checkup of the pregnant mother and should cover the child's health care up to its second year. Information and counselling programmes for pregnant women should be improved and extended at the regional level.

1.3 Financial Support of Families
The main emphasis of the family support scheme should be on financial and material assistance to socially disadvantaged families and families with a large number of children. In 1981 child benefits will be scaled according to age to cover increased costs for older children.

1.4 Single-parent Families
The legal position of unmarried mothers should be made equal to that of married mothers.
The law on the advance of maintenance payments should be amended
- to enable children of convicts to benefit from advance payments provided by the State,

361

- to provide unmarried mothers with an interim aid, in case an affiliation takes too long.

As it is mostly single mothers earning low incomes who are the beneficiaries of direct financial and material assistance, this form of support should be continued.

2. Education

2.1 Equal Curricula for Boys and Girls at Secondary School Level
To ensure that boys and girls in grades 5–9 receive the same basic education, curricula reform activities should continue.

2.2 Information for Teachers

In order to make teachers more aware of women's questions, relevant topics should be included in their in-service-training.

2.3 Revision of School Books
- Inadequate presentation of men's and women's roles in schoolbooks should be analyzed and changed in a step-by-step-programme.
- The working situation of both sexes should be illustrated in a way corresponding to reality.

2.4 Improvement of Various School Types Primarily Attended by Girls
Curricula in secondary schools and girls' colleges should put more emphasis on aspects of future professional life. Training for kindergarten teachers and vocational teachers should be improved.

2.5 Measures to Diminish Sex-specific Training and Professional Choice
- Information programmes for girls, their parents, employers and vocational counsellors should be established to acquaint them with the system of equal training facilities.
- Vocational guidance programmes should be accelerated to inform girls about training possibilities in the technical professions.
- A campaign to invite "More Women to Technical Universities" should be initiated.

2.6 Admission to Universities
- Universities should be kept open and no quota system should be introduced.
- Activities to promote enrolment for students without college training should be supported.
- The number of available places at universities should be increased.

2.7 Adult Education
- Adult education centers should promote seminars especially designed to meet women's needs, i.e. by providing childcare and by opening at an appropriate time.

- Retraining activities should be intensified with a special view to women's needs.
- The system of university correspondence courses should be promoted so that women might get a chance to begin or continue their studies.

3. Labour Market

3.1 Equal Pay
- Any existing restrictive provisions—open or hidden—appearing in collective agreements that are contrary to the principle of equality should be discussed with the individual trade unions and possibly eliminated in pursuing meetings.
- Despite the fact that female wage scales only rarely show up in collective agreements, in practice, however, women are still to be found in the lower wage categories. In this respect a detailed dialogue between employers and the competent trade unions should be initiated.
- Promotion programmes should be set up to assist women in their efforts to increase their self-awareness and to defy any sex-specified discrimination.
- After a given time the Law on Equal Pay should be reviewed to assess whether intended results have been achieved or a possible amendment is needed. The principle of equal pay will also be included in the proposed Law on Remuneration Protection.

3.2 Segregation on the Labour Market
- To eliminate occupational segregation long-term solutions have to be found. To this end the Federal Ministry for Social Affairs will continue its work to advance the idea of equal opportunity and treatment of working women in concerted action with liaison officers especially established in the regional labour offices.

- To encourage women workers to choose non-traditional occupations so any restrictive measures that might exist should be continually reviewed for women of all age groups in the light of advances of scientific and technological knowledge.

3.3 Participation
- Special measures will be promoted to encourage women workers to participate in social and economic decision-making processes to increase the number of female representatives in the government commissions, the tripartite advisory boards, etc. dealing with questions of female employment, will be one of the prime goals of the second half of the UN Decade for Women.
- All appropriate measures should be taken to ensure that working women may participate in decisions concerning their working environment, i.e. when new types of work are developed, team work introduced, etc.
- To encourage working women to participate in internal company decisions, sex-specific job descriptions and titles should be eliminated from the relevant regulations.

363

3.4 Women in Management

- Promotion programmes for professional women will be initiated and support from bigger industries has to be obtained. On completion of these programmes some research will be done and the data obtained will be published in order to encourage other industries to apply these models in practice.

3.5 Public and Civil Service

- After completion of an intensive study a promotion programme for the public and civil services should be set up.
- Guidelines for job vacancy notices for the public and civil services have been laid down to ensure that neutral formulations are used applying to both sexes.
- Women employed with the public and civil services should be motivated to attend job training courses and other activities that might enhance their managerial skills and self-reliance.

4. Assistance to Peasant Women

- To assist peasant women in their economic, personal and social problems, promotion activities will be continued.
- Peasant women should be motivated to take over functions in their agricultural organizations' boards and co-operatives.
- The health care for peasant women should be actively improved.
- Activities should be intensified to change the public view of peasant women and their work to a more realistic one.

5. Health Care

- A special health programme for women will be incorporated into planned activities to accelerate health education and health care counselling in general. Research studies in this field, including health care during maternity, etc. will be undertaken.
- To identify possible health risks for women special screening programmes were included into a Preventive Health Care Programme, that has been carried out successfully for some years. The screening programme may be revised or extended in the light of new medical knowledge.
- Moreover, plans exist to gradually optimize the training of hospital staff, which primarily consists of women, i.e. 90 percent of the total hospital staff are women.

6. Legal Position

- In order to grant women the right to pass on the Austrian nationality to their children the Nationality Law should be amended accordingly.
- Difficulties that might arise in connection with the enforcement of new laws, i.e. the new Family Law concerned with the equal status of women, should

be removed in a step-by-step action. To this end special interdepartmental committees were set up initiated by the State Secretary for Women's Questions, who also co-ordinates the programme.

- Individual cases of discrimination, originating not in the law itself but in its application, are handled by the two State Secretaries dealing with women's problems, who compile them, bring them to the public's attention and try to find a positive solution.

- To assist women in their problems the following services were installed:
  1) Women's Advisory Board at the Federal Chancellery, which deals with general women's questions, e.g. divorce, alimony, discrimination in public services, etc.
  2) Telephone service "Hallo, colleague" for working women at the Federal Ministry for Social Affairs run by the State Secretary dealing with questions of the working women.
  These activities will be continued and intensified.
    - In order to encourage experts and decision-makers to review the legal status of women, a collection of papers concerned with this topic will be published.
- The formulation of an Anti-discrimination Act is under consideration.

7. Women and the Media
Women as Artists

- Increased attention should be paid to the ways the mass media depict women and their environment. Decision-makers in the media field should be made aware of the issue and a seminar should be held to this effect.
- A study on the role of women in children's books will be published. At the same time, authors of children's books will be asked to sensitize themselves to this question and to work out alternatives.
- The role of women in schoolbooks will be reviewed. A series of workshops on that topic will be organized for authors, editors, and advisory boards.
- Women journalists will receive first-hand information about ongoing activities. These meetings may also serve the purpose of strengthening the solidarity between women employed in the media.
- A workshop on the living and working situation of women artists will be organized.
- Efforts should be undertaken to eliminate discrimination in advertising using women's bodies for the promotion of products, e.g. cars, technical equipment, etc.

8. Participation in Political Life

- Women in political positions, female representatives of workers and employers' organizations and representatives of independent women's organizations should meet regularly to jointly discuss women's questions which may lead to a narrowing of views on some issues and may thus assist them to exert more pressure on political decision-makers.

- In particular women's meetings, organized by the State Secretariate, also women may participate in discussions on women's questions, who are not members of women's organizations. They may thus get in touch with women's organizations and obtain the necessary information on how to become politically involved and participate in policy-making.
- By means of polls investigating the degree of women's political interest the result of these efforts should be reviewed.

9. Research on Women

In the framework of national research promotion, research on issues related to women will be continued.

10. Development Aid

Development aid in areas indirectly related to women will be provided for health care and education.

11. Consumer Policy

- Women working in households are exceedingly prone to accidents. A detailed study on this topic is under consideration.
- To increase safety in households the following measures have been proposed:
— Improve safety of electrical equipment
— Appropriate labelling of inflammable textiles and clothes
— Protection against poisonous material e.g. by providing child-proof packing materials for medication and other dangerous substances.

AUSTRIA

EQUAL TREATMENT LAW

Equal Treatment Law

108. Federal Law of February 23, 1979 concerning the equal treatment of men and women in the determination of pay
The National Council has decided:

Part I
Area of effectiveness

Sec. 1. (1) The provisions of Part I apply to work relations of all kinds, which are based on private law contracts.

(2) Excluded are work relations

1. of the agricultural and forestry workers, to whom the agriculture law (Landarbeitsgesetz), BGB1. No. 140/1948 is to be applied.
2. to a Land, a communal association or a commune.
3. to the Federation.

(3) The provisions of Part I apply also to employment relations, to which the homework law (Heimarbeitsgesetz) 1960, BGB1. No. 105/1961 is to be applied.

Equal treatment order

Sec. 2. In the determination of pay no one may be discriminated against; discrimination is any disadvantaging differentiation, which is undertaken without any objective (sachliche) justification.

Equal treatment commission

Sec. 3. (1) In the Federal Ministry for social administration an Equal Treatment Commission is to be established.

(2) This Commission is to consist of eleven members. The presidency of the Commission is to be exercised by the Federal Minister for Social Administration or an official of the Federal Ministry for Social Administration entrusted by him.

(3) In addition to the Minister for Social Administration, the following are to be members of the Commission:

1. Two members who are proposed by the Federal Chamber of the industrial economy;
2. two members who are proposed by the Austrian Workers' Chamber (Arbeiterkammertag);
3. two members who are proposed by the Association of Austrian Industrialists;
4. two members of the Austrian Federation of Trade Unions;

5. one representative of the Federal Ministry for Social Administration and one from the Office of the Federal Chancellor.

(4) For each of the members mentioned in subparagraph 3, points 1 to 4 at least one alternate member is to be provided. These members (alternate members) must swear to the President (Vorsitzenden) that before assuming their functions they will carry out their activities conscientiously and in a non-partisan manner. They are to be appointed by the Federal Minister for Social Administration, on the proposal of the interest groups (Interessenvertretungen) mentioned in subparagraph 3, points 1 to 4, for a term of four years. If the right to propose is not exercised within a period of two months, after a request (is made), then the Federal Minister for Social Administration is not bound.

(5) The Federal Minister for Social Administration is to relieve a member (alternate Member) who was proposed by interest groups mentioned in subparagraph 3 (1 to 4), of his (seiner) functions in cases of resignation, recall of the proposal by the interest group which is entitled to make proposals, severe violation or continuing neglect of his (!) duties.

Tasks of the Equal Treatment Commission

Sec. 4. The Commission is to concern itself with all questions touching on discrimination in the determination of pay (Sec. 2).

Sec. 5. (1) On the request of one of the interest groups, named in Sec. 3 subparagraph 3 (1 - 4), or ex officio, the Commission is to produce expert opinions concerning discrimination in determination of pay.

(2) If an expert opinion, rendered in accordance with paragraph 1, involves discriminations in the regulations of collective legal construction, the Commission may form, for the preparation of its decision, a Work Committee, to which is to belong, in addition to the President, one member from each of those named in Sec. 3 subparagraph 3(1-4). The deliberations are to be joined by representatives by the parties of the actual collective agreement. Sec. 7 subparagraphs 2 to 4 and the first sentence of subparagraph 5 apply accordingly.

(3) Expert opinions of the Commission are to be published in the official notices of the Federal Ministry for Social Administration.

Sec. 6. (1) On a proposal of an employee, an employer, a management council of the interest groups named in Sec. 3 subparagraph 3(1-4) or ex officio, the Commission is to determine in (each) individual case, if a violation of the equal treatment order is involved.

(2) If the Commission is of the opinion that a violation of the equal treatment order does exist, it is to transmit to the employer in writing a proposal for the realization of equal treatment and to request that the discrimination be terminated.

(3) If the employer does not accept the proposal within one month, then each of the interest groups mentioned in Sec. 3 subparagraph 3(1-4) may sue before the competent labor court for the determination of a violation of the equal treatment order (Sec. 2). . . . .

BELGIUM

LAW OF AUGUST 4, 1978
ON ECONOMIC REORIENTATION
(M.B. of August 17, 1978)
TITLE V
promoting equal treatment of men and women in the workplace

(Selections translated from the French by G.H.F.)

Article 118
The principle of equal treatment in the sense of Title V of this law implies the absence of any discrimination based on sex, be it directly, or indirectly, with particular reference to marital or family status.

The special provisions relating to the protection of maternity shall not be deemed discriminatory.

Article 119
The provisions of Title V of the present law shall not impede the measures seeking to promote the equality of opportunities between men and women, in particular by removing actual inequalities which affect the opportunities of women in the areas referred to in Article 116(1).

The King, following consultations mentioned in Article 122, determines in which cases these measures shall be taken.

Article 121
Equal treatment must be assured in the provisions and practices relating to conditions of access, to the selection, including the criteria of selection for employment or work positions and to independent professions, of whatever sector and activity and to all levels of the professional hierarchy.

It is specifically forbidden:

1° to make reference to the gender (sexe) of the worker in the offers of employment and to professional promotion, or to use in such offers or advertisements (annonces) elements, which, though not referring explicitly, indicate or suggest the gender of the worker;

2° to make reference to the gender of the worker in the conditions of access, the selection and the criteria of selection for employment or work positions, of whatever sector or branch of activity, or to use in these conditions or criteria, elements, though not referring explicitly to the gender of the worker amount to discrimination (aboutissent à une discrimination);

3° to refuse or to hinder access to employment or professional promotion for explicit or implicit motives based directly or indirectly on the gender of the worker.

These prohibitions mentioned in paragraph 2 apply equally to the independent professions.

Article 122

The King may, by decree, after deliberation in the Council of Ministers, determine the cases in which mention may be made of the gender as a condition of access to employment or a professional activity, for which, by reason of its nature or conditions of its exercise, gender constitutes a determining condition.

For this effect, the King consults the "Commission on Women's Employment" (*Commission du Travail des femmes*). He consults also (*également*), for the private, the National Labor Council (*Conseil national du Travail*) and for the public sector, the General Consultative Committee of the Trade Union (*le Comité general de consultation syndicale*) or the General Common Committee of the public services, which is to be created by virtue of Article 3, paragraphs 1,3, of the Law of December 19, 1974, which organizes the relations between the public authorities and the syndicates of the agents relevant to these authorities.

The consulted organs give their advice within two months from the demand. Upon expiration of this interval, it can be passed.

SECTION 3
Conditions of work and dismissals

Article 126

The present section applies to employers and workers.

Article 127

Equal treatment must be assured to workers in all arrangements and practices relating to conditions of work and dismissals.

It is especially prohibited:

1° to make reference to the gender (*sexe*) of the worker in the conditions of work, criteria or motives for dismissal, or the use in these conditions, criteria or motives, elements which even without explicit reference to the gender of the worker amount to a discrimination;

2° to establish or apply conditions, criteria or motives in a discriminatory manner in relation to the gender of the worker.

Article 128

By conditions of work one understands the provisions and practices relating:

— to the contract of work, the statutory regimes of administrative law applicable to the teaching personnel of the state and of subsidized education;
— to the contract of apprenticeship;
— to collective agreements of work;
— to the duration of work and schedules;
— to holidays;
— to rest on Sunday;
— to night work;
— to work rules;

— to the health and security of the workers, as well as the healthfulness of the work and places of work;
— to the work of the young;
— to work councils, committees of safety, hygiene and the visual enhancement (*embellissement*) of the places of work, to the trade union delegations and to the existing councils and committees of the same nature in the public services;
— to the promotion of the work and the workers;
— to the remuneration and its protection;
— to the credits of hours and social promotion;
— to annual vacations;
— as well as generally to the practices relating to physical, moral and psychological conditions of work.

The King may complete the enumeration of matters listed in the first paragraph.

CHAPTER III
General Provisions

Article 130

Provisions contrary to the principle of equal treatment, as defined in Title V of this law, are void.

GERMAN FEDERAL REPUBLIC

LAW CONCERNING EQUAL TREATMENT OF MEN AND WOMEN AT THE WORKPLACE AND CONCERNING THE PRESERVATION OF CLAIMS IN TRANSFERS OF ENTERPRISES

(Labor law assimilation to that of the Economic Community of August 13, 1980)

(Translated by G.H.F. from *Bundesgesetzblatt*
Jahrgang 1980, Teil 1, pp. 1308–1309. No. 48,
Tag der Ausgabe: Bonn, den 20 August 1980.)

Introductory Note: As will be apparent the 1980 German Law concerning equal treatment is neither comprehensive nor easily comprehensible. It amounts to a piecemeal amendment of certain provisions of the Civil Code and the Law concerning the Labor Court. An English translation is included here to show why some observers have been somewhat critical of the West German approach toward gender equality.

G.H.F.

The Federal Parliament has decided this law:

Article 1
Modification of the Civil Code
The Civil Code . . . in the version of July 24, 1979 is amended as follows:
1. After Sec. 611 the following Sec. 611a is inserted:
Sec. 611a
(1) The employer must not discriminate on the basis of gender in a contract or a measure, especially in the establishment of the work relationship, in professional advancement, in a directive or in giving notice. However, a differential treatment on the basis of gender is permissible insofar as an agreement concerns the kind of activity of the employee and insofar as the gender of the employee constitutes an indispensable requirement for this activity. If, in a disputed case facts are presented which suggest discrimination on the basis of gender, the burden of proof rests with the employer that technical reasons justify the differential treatment (*sachliche*) and that gender constitutes an indispensable requirement of the activity to be carried out.
(Translator's summary: If the discriminatory treatment in the labor relationship has not been justified, the employers must provide compensation for damages.)
After Sec. 611a, Sec. 611b is inserted which reads:
(2) The employer must not advertise a work position, neither publicly nor within the enterprise as only for men or only for women, except in a case (defined) in the second sentence of Sec. 611a.
3. The following Subparagraph 3 is added to Sec. 612:
(3) In a work relationship no lesser wage (*vergütung*) may be agreed to for

equal work or for work of equal value on the basis of the gender of the employee. The agreement on a lesser wage is not justified by referring to protective provisions which apply to the employee.

4. After Sec. 612 the following Sec. 612a is inserted:

Sec. 612a

The employer must not discriminate against an employee in an agreement or a measure because the employee makes permissible use of his rights.

5. Sec. 613 is amended as follows:

a) In Subparagraph 1 the following sentences 2 to 4 are inserted:

If these rights and duties are regulated by legal norms of a wage agreement or work agreement, then they become the content of the work relationship between the new proprietor and the employee and must not be changed to the disadvantage of the employee before the expiration of one year from the time of the transfer. Sentence 2 does not apply, if the rights and duties of the new proprietor are regulated by legal norms of another wage agreement or work agreement. Before the expiration of the period in accordance with sentence 2, rights and duties can be changed, if the wage agreement or work agreement is no longer valid, or if, in the absence of a mutually binding wage agreement obligation, a new wage agreement is reached between the new proprietor and employee.

6. The following Subparagraph 4 is added:

(4) The notice of termination of the work relationship by the continuing employer or the new proprietor is void. The right to termination of the work relationship on the basis of other reasons remains untouched.

Article 2
Notice

The employer shall make available or post in a suitable location of the workplace for inspection a copy of Sections 611a, 611b, 612 subpar. 3 of the Civil Code in the version of this law.

Article 3
Change of the Law concerning the Labor Court

The Law concerning the Labor Court in the version in the publication of July 2, 1979 (BGB1. I S.853, 1036) amended by the Law of June 13, 1980 (BGB1. I S.677), is changed as follows:

Sec. 98 subpar. 2 is changed as follows:

1. The following new sentence 2 is inserted:

The complaint is to be filed within a period of two weeks with cause.

2. Sentences 2 and 3 become sentences 3 and 4.

Article 4
Berlin Clause

This Law also enters into effect in the Land Berlin in accordance with Sec. 13 subpar. 1 of the Third Transition Law (Überleitungsgesetz).

Article 5
Effectiveness
This law enters into force on the day of its publication.
Bonn, August 13, 1980.

GREAT BRITAIN

SEX DISCRIMINATION ACT 1975

An Act to render unlawful certain kinds of sex discrimination and discrimination on the ground of marriage, and establish a Commission with the function of working towards the elimination of such discrimination and promoting equality of opportunity between men and women generally; and for related purposes.

[12th November 1975]

PART I

DISCRIMINATION TO WHICH ACT APPLIES

1.—(1) A person discriminates against a woman in any circumstances relevant for the purposes of any provision of this Act if—

    (a) on the grounds of her sex he treats her less favourably than he treats or would treat a man, or

    (b) he applies to her a requirement or condition which he applies or would apply equally to a man but—

        (i) which is such that the proportion of women who can comply with it is considerably smaller than the proportion of men who can comply with it, and

        (ii) which he cannot show to be justifiable irrespective of the sex of the person to whom it is applied, and

        (iii) which is to her detriment because she cannot comply with it.

(2) If a person treats or would treat a man differently according to the man's marital status, his treatment of a woman is for the purposes of subsection (1)(a) to be compared to his treatment of a man having the like marital status.

2.—(1) Section 1, and the provisions of Parts II and III relating to sex discrimination against women, are to be read as applying equally to the treatment of men, and for that purpose shall have effect with such modifications as are requisite.

(2) In the application of subsection (1) no account shall be taken of special treatment afforded to women in connection with pregnancy or childbirth.

3.—(1) A person discriminates against a married person of either sex in any circumstances relevant for the purposes of any provision of Part II if—

    (a) on the ground of his or her marital status he treats that person less favourably than he treats or would treat an unmarried person of the same sex, or

(b) he applies to that person a requirement or condition which he applies or would apply equally to an unmarried person but—

(i)which is such that the proportion of married persons who can comply with it is considerably smaller than the proportion of unmarried persons of the same sex who can comply with it, and

(ii) which he cannot show to be justifiable irrespective of the marital status of the person to whom it is applied, and

(iii) which is to that person's detriment because he cannot comply with it.

(2) For the purposes of subsection (1), a provision of Part II framed with reference to discrimination against women shall be treated as applying equally to the treatment of men, and for that purpose shall have effect with such modifications as are requisite.

4.—(1) A person ("the discriminator") discriminates against another person ("the person victimised") in any circumstances relevant for the purposes of any provision of this Act if he treats the person victimised less favourably than in those circumstances he treats or would treat other persons, and do so by reason that the person victimised has—

(a) brought proceedings against the discriminator or any other person under this Act or the Equal Pay Act 1970, or

(b) given evidence or information in connection with proceedings brought by any person against the discriminator or any other person under this Act or the Equal Pay Act 1970, or

(c) otherwise done anything under or by reference to this Act or the Equal Pay Act 1970 in relation to the discriminator or any other person, or

(d) alleged that the discriminator or any other person has committed an act which (whether or not the allegation so states) would amount to a contravention of this Act or give rise to a claim under the Equal Pay Act 1970,

or by reason that the discriminator knows the person victimised intends to do any of those things, or suspects the person victimised has done, or intends to do, any of them.

(2) Subsection (1) does not apply to treatment of a person by reason of any allegation made by him if the allegation was false and not made in good faith.

(3) For the purposes of subsection (1), a provision of Part II or III framed with reference to discrimination against women shall be treated as applying equally to the treatment of men and for that purpose shall have effect with such modifications as are requisite.

5.—(1) In this Act—

(a) references to discrimination refer to any discrimination falling within sections 1 to 4; and

(b) references to sex discrimination refer to any discrimination falling within section 1 or 2,

and related expressions shall be construed accordingly.

. . . .

Part VI

Equal Opportunities Commission

53.—(1) There shall be a body of Commissioners named the Equal Opportunities Commission, consisting of at least eight but not more than fifteen individuals each appointed by the Secretary of State on a full-time or part-time basis, which shall have the following duties—

(a) to work towards the elimination of discrimination,

(b) to promote equality of opportunity between men and women generally, and

(c) to keep under review the working of this Act and the Equal Pay Act 1970 and, when they are so required by the Secretary of State or otherwise think it necessary, draw up and submit to the Secretary of State proposals for amending them.

(2) The Secretary of State shall appoint—

(a) one of the Commissioners to be chairman of the Commission, and

(b) either one or two of the Commissioners (as the Secretary of State thinks fit) to be deputy chairman or deputy chairmen of the Commission

(3) The Secretary of State may by order amend subsection (1) so far as it regulates the number of Commissioners.

(4) Schedule 3 shall have effect with respect to the Commission.

54.—(1) The Commisision may undertake or assist (financially or otherwise) the undertaking by other persons of any research, and any educational activities, which appear to the Commission necessary or expedient for the purposes of section 53(1).

(2) The Commission may make charges for educational or other facilities or services made available by them.

55.—(1) Without prejudice to the generality of section 53(1), the Commission, in pursuance of the duties imposed by paragraphs (a) and (b) of that subsection—

(a) shall keep under review the relevant statutory provisions in so far as they require men and women to be treated differently, and

(b) if so required by the Secretary of State, make to him a report on any matter specified by him which is connected with those duties and concerns the relevant statutory provisions.

Any such report shall be made within the time specified by the Secretary of State, and the Secretary of State shall cause the report to be published.

(2) Whenever the Commission think it necessary, they shall draw up and

submit to the Secretary of State proposals for amending the relevant statutory provisions.

(3) The Commission shall carry out their duties in relation to the relevant statutory provisions in consultation with the Health and Safety Commission.

(4) In this section "the relevant statutory provisions" has the meaning given by section 53 of the Health and Safety at Work etc. Act 1974.

56.—(1) As soon as practicable after the end of each calendar year the Commission shall make to the Secretary of State a report on their activities during the year (an "annual report").

(2) Each annual report shall include a general survey of developments, during the period to which it relates, in respect of matters falling within the scope of the Commission's duties.

(3) The Secretary of State shall lay a copy of every annual report before each House of Parliament, and shall cause the report to be published.

Codes of practice

[¹**56A.**—(1) The Commission may issue codes of practice containing such practical guidance as the Commission think fit for either or both of the following purposes, namely—

    (a) the elimination of discrimination in the field of employment;

    (b) the promotion of equality of opportunity in that field between men and women.

(2) When the Commission propose to issue a code of practice, they shall prepare and publish a draft of that code, shall consider any representations made to them about the draft and may modify the draft accordingly.

(3) In the course of preparing any draft code of practice for eventual publication under subsection (2) the Commission shall consult with—

    (a) such organisations or associations of organisations representative of employers or of workers; and

    (b) such other organisations, or bodies,

as appear to the Commission to be appropriate.

(4) If the Commission determine to proceed with the draft, they shall transmit the draft to the Secretary of State who shall—

    (a) if he approves of it, lay it before both Houses of Parliament; and

    (b) if he does not approve of it, publish details of his reasons for withholding approval.

(5) If, within the period of forty days beginning with the day on which a copy of a draft code of practice is laid before each House of Parliament, or, if such copies are laid on different days, with the later of the two days, either House so resolves, no further proceedings shall be taken thereon, but without prejudice to the laying before Parliament of a new draft.

(6) In reckoning the period of forty days referred to in subsection (5), no account shall be taken of any period during which Parliament is dissolved or prorogued or during which both Houses are adjourned for more than four days.

(7) If no such resolution is passed as is referred to in subsection (5), the

¹Cross-heading and s. 56A inserted by Race Relations Act 1976(c. 74). Sch. 4 para.1

Commission shall issue the code in the form of the draft and the code shall come into effect on such day as the Secretary of State may by order appoint.

(8) Without prejudice to section 81(4), an order under subsection (7) may contain such transitional provisions or savings as appear to the Secretary of State to be necessary or expedient in connection with the code of practice thereby brought into operation.

(9) The Commission may from time to time revise the whole or any part of a code of practice issued under this section and issue that revised code, and subsections (2) to (8) shall apply (with appropriate modifications) to such a revised code as they apply to the first issue of a code.

(10) A failure on the part of any person to observe any provision of a code of practice shall not of itself render him liable to any proceedings; but in any proceedings under this Act before an industrial tribunal any code of practice issued under this section shall be admissible in evidence, and if any provision of such a code appears to the tribunal to be relevant to any question arising in the proceedings it shall be taken into account in determining that question.

(11) Without prejudice to subsection (1), a code of practice issued under this section may include such practical guidance as the Commission think fit as to what steps it is reasonably practicable for employers to take for the purpose of preventing their employees from doing in the course of their employment acts made unlawful by this Act.]

Investigations

57.—(1) Without prejudice to their general power to do anything requisite for the performance of their duties under section 53(1), the Commission may if they think fit, and shall if required by the Secretary of State, conduct a formal investigation for any purpose connected with the carrying out of those duties.

(2) The Commission may, with the approval of the Secretary of State, appoint, on a full-time or part-time basis, one or more individuals as additional Commissioners for the purposes of a formal investigation.

(3) The Commission may nominate one or more Commissioners, with or without one or more additional Commissioners, to conduct a formal investigation on their behalf, and may delegate any of their functions in relation to the investigation to the persons so nominated.

58.—(1) The Commission shall not embark on a formal investigation unless the requirements of this section have been complied with.

(2) Terms of reference for the investigation shall be drawn up by the Commission or, if the Commission were required by the Secretary of State to conduct the investigation, by the Secretary of State after consulting the Commission.

(3) It shall be the duty of the Commission to give general notice of the holding of the investigation unless the terms of reference confine it to activities of persons named in them, but in such a case the Commission shall in the prescribed manner give those persons notice of the holding of the investigation.

[2(3A) Where the terms of reference of the investigation confine it to ac-

²S. 58 (3a) inserted by Race Relations Act 1976 (c. 74), Sch. 4 para. 2(1)

tivities of persons named in them and the Commission in the course of it propose to investigate any act made unlawful by this Act which they believe that a person so named may have done., the Commission shall—

    (a) inform that person of their belief and of their proposal to investigate the act in question; and

    (b) offer him an opportunity of making oral or written representations with regard to it (or both oral and written representations if he thinks fit);

and a person so named who avails himself of an opportunity under this subsection of making oral representations may be represented—

    (i) by counsel or a solicitor; or

    (ii) by some other person of his choice, not being a person to whom the Commission object on the ground that he is unsuitable.]

(4) The Commission or, if the Commission were required by the Secretary of State to conduct the investigation, the Secretary of State after consulting the Commission may from time to time revise the terms of reference; and subsections (1) [[3](3) and (3A)] shall apply to the revised investigation and terms of reference as they applied to the original.

59.—(1) For the purposes of a formal investigation the Commission, by a notice in the prescribed form served on him in the prescribed manner,—

    (a) may require any person to furnish such written information as may be described in the notice, and may specify the time at which, and the manner and form in which, the information is to be furnished;

    (b) may require any person to attend at such time and place as is specified in the notice and give oral information about, and produce all documents in his possession or control relating to, any matter specified in the notice.

(2) Except as provided by section 69, a notice shall be served under subsection (1) only where—

    (a) service of the notice was authorised by an order made by or on behalf of the Secretary of State, or

    (b) the terms of reference of the investigation state that the Commission believe that a person named in them may have done or may be doing acts of all or any of the following descriptions—

        (i) unlawful discriminatory acts,

        (ii) contraventions of section 37,

        (iii) contraventions of sections 38, 39 or 40, and

        (iv) acts in breach of a term modified or included by virtue of an equality clause,

    and confine the investigation to those acts.

(3) A notice under subsection (1) shall not require a person—

    (a) to give information, or produce any documents, which he could not be compelled to give in evidence, or produce, in civil proceedings before the High Court or the Court of Session, or

[3]Words substituted by Race Relations Act 1976 (c. 74), Sch. 4 para. 2(2)

(*b*) to attend at any place unless the necessary expenses of his journey to and from that place are paid or tendered to him.

(4) If a person fails to comply with a notice served on him under subsection (1) or the Commission has reasonable cause to believe that he intends not to comply with it, the Commission may apply to a county court for an order requiring him to comply with it or with such directions for the like purpose as may be contained in the order; and section 84 (penalty for neglecting witness summons) of the County Courts Act 1959 shall apply to failure without reasonable excuse to comply with any such order as it applies in the cases there provided.

(5) In the application of subsection (4) to Scotland—

(*a*) for the reference to a county court there shall be substituted a reference to a sheriff court, and

(*b*) for the words after "order; and" to the end of the subsection there shall be substituted the words "paragraph 73 of the First Schedule to the Sheriff Courts (Scotland) Act 1907 (power of sheriff to grant second diligence for compelling the attendances of witnesses or havers) shall apply to any such order as it applies in proceedings in the sheriff court".

(6) A person commits an offence if he—

(*a*) wilfully alters, suppresses, conceals or destroys a document which he has been required by a notice or order under this section to produce, or

(*b*) in complying with such a notice or order, knowingly or recklessly makes any statement which is false in a material particular,

and shall be liable on summary conviction to a fine not exceeding £400.

(7) Proceedings for an offence under subsection (6) may (without prejudice to any jurisdiction exercisable apart from this subsection) be instituted—

(*a*) against any person at any place at which he has an office or other place of business;

(*b*) against an individual at any place where he resides, or at which he is for the time being.

60.—(1) If in the light of any of their findings in a formal investigation it appears to the Commission necessary or expedient, whether during the course of the investigation or after its conclusion,—

(*a*) to make to any persons, with a view to promoting equality of opportunity between men and women who are affected by any of their activities, recommendations for changes in their policies or procedures, or as to any other matters, or

(*b*) to make to the Secretary of State any recommendations, whether for changes in the law or otherwise,

the Commission shall make those recommendations accordingly.

(2) The Commission shall prepare a report of their findings in any formal investigation conducted by them.

(3) If the formal investigation is one required by the Secretary of State—

(*a*) the Commission shall deliver the report to the Secretary of State,

381

and

(b) the Secretary of State shall cause the report to be published,

and unless required by the Secretary of State the Commission shall not publish the report.

(4) If the formal investigation is not one required by the Secretary of State, the Commission shall either publish the report, or make it available for inspection in accordance with subsection (5).

(5) Where under subsection (4) a report is to be made available for inspection, any person shall be entitled, on payment of such fee (if any) as may be determined by the Commission—

(a) to inspect the report during ordinary office hours and take copies of all or any part of the report, or

(b) to obtain from the Commission a copy, certified by the Commission to be correct, of the report.

(6) The Commission may if they think fit determine that the right conferred by subsection (5)(a) shall be exercisable in relation to a copy of the report instead of, or in addition to, the original.

(7) The Commission shall give general notice of the place or places where, and the times when, reports may be inspected under subsection (5).

61.—(1) No information given to the Commission by any person ("the informant") in connection with a formal investigation shall be disclosed by the Commission, or by any person who is or has been a Commissioner, additional Commissioner or employee of the Commission, except—

(a) on the order of any court, or

(b) with the informant's consent, or

(c) in the form of a summary or other general statement published by the Commission which does not identify the informant or any other person to whom the information relates, or

(d) in a report of the investigation published by the Commission or made available for inspection under section 60(5), or

(e) to the Commissioners, additional Commissioners or employees of the Commission, or, so far as may be necessary for the proper performance of the functions of the Commission, to other persons, or

(f) for the purpose of any civil proceedings under this Act to which the Commission are a party, or any criminal proceedings.

(2) Any person who discloses information in contravention of subsection (1) commits an offence and shall be liable on summary conviction to a fine not exceeding £400.

(3) In preparing any report for publication or for inspection the Commission shall exclude, so far as is consistent with their duties and the object of the report, any matter which relates to the private affairs of any individual or business interests of any person where the publication of that matter might, in the opinion of the Commission, prejudicially affect that individual or person.

. . . .

IRELAND

FINANCE ACT, 1980

provisions on Taxation of Married Persons

CHAPTER II

Taxation of Married Persons

18.—As respects assessments to income tax for the year 1980–81 and any subsequent year of assessment, Part IX of the Income Tax Act, 1967, is hereby amended by the substitution of the following chapter for Chapter I:

"CHAPTER I

Special Provisions as to Married Persons

192.—(1) A wife shall be treated for income tax purposes as living with her husband unless either—
  (a) they are separated under an order of a court of competent juris-diction or by deed of separation, or
  (b) they are in fact separated in such circumstances that the separation is likely to be permanent.
(2) (a) In this Chapter references to the income of a wife include references to any sum which, apart from this Chapter, would fall to be included in computing her total income, and the provisions of this Chapter shall have effect in relation to any such sum notwithstanding that some enactment (including, except so far as the contrary is expressly provided, an enactment passed after the passing of this Act) requires that that sum should not be treated as income of any person other than her.
  (b) In the Income Tax Acts a reference to a person who has duly elected to be assessed to tax in accordance with the provisions of a particular section includes a reference to a person who is deemed to have elected to be assessed to tax in accordance with the provisions of that section and any reference to a husband who is assessed to tax in accordance with the provisions of section 194 for a year of assessment includes a reference to a case where he and his wife are assessed to tax, for that year, in accordance with the provisions of section 197.
(3) In this Chapter 'the inspector' means, in relation to a notice, any inspector who might reasonably be considered by the person giving notice to be likely to be concerned with the subject-matter thereof or who declares himself ready to accept the notice.

(4) Any notice required to be served under any section in this Chapter may be served by post.

193.—In any case in which a wife is treated as living with her husband, income tax shall be assessed, charged and recovered, save as otherwise provided by the Income Tax Acts, on the income of the husband and on the income of the wife as if they were not married:

Provided that, where an election under section 195 has effect in relation to a husband and wife for a year of assessment, this section shall not have effect in relation to that husband and wife for that year of assessment.

194.—(1) Where, in the case of a husband and wife, an election under section 195 to be assessed to tax in accordance with the provisions of this section, has effect for a year of assessment—

(a) the husband shall be assessed and charged to tax, not only in respect of his total income (if any) for that year, but also in respect of his wife's total income (if any) for any part of that year of assessment during which she is living with him, and, for this purpose and for all the purposes of the Income Tax Acts, that last mentioned income shall be deemed to be income of his;

(b) the question whether there is any income of the wife chargeable to tax for any year of assessment and, if so, what is to be taken to be the amount thereof for tax purposes shall not be affected by the provisions of this section; and

(c) any tax falling to be assessed in respect of any income which, under this section, is deemed to be income of a woman's husband shall, instead of being assessed on her, or on her trustees, guardian or committee, or on her executors or administrators, be assessable on him or, in the appropriate cases, on his executors or administrators.

(2) Any relief from income tax which is authorised, by any provision of the Income Tax Acts, to be granted to a husband by reference to the income or profits or gains or losses of his wife or by reference to any payment made by her shall be granted to a husband for a year of assessment only if he is assessed to tax for that year in accordance with the provisions of this section.

195.—(1) A husband and his wife, where the wife is living with the husband, may, at any time during a year of assessment, by notice in writing given to the inspector, jointly elect to be assessed to tax for that year of assessment in accordance with the provisions of section 194, and where such election is made, the income of the husband and the income of the wife shall be assessed to tax for that year in accordance with those provisions.

(2) Where an election is made under subsection (1) in respect of a year of assessment, the election shall have effect for that year and for each subsequent year of assessment.

(3) Notwithstanding subsections (1) and (2), either the husband or the wife may, in relation to a year of assessment, by notice in writing given to the inspector before the end of the year, withdraw the election in respect of that year and, thereupon, the election shall not have effect for that year or for any subsequent year of assessment.

(4) (a) A husband and his wife, where the wife is living with the husband and where an election under subsection (1) has not been made by them for a year of assessment (or for any prior year of assessment) shall be deemed to have duly elected to be assessed to tax in accordance with the provisions of section 194 for that year unless, before the end of that year, either of them gives notice in writing to the inspector that he or she wishes to be assessed to tax for that year as a single person in accordance with the provisions of section 193.

(b) Where a husband or his wife has duly given notice under paragraph (a), that paragraph shall not have effect in relation to that husband and wife for the year of assessment for which the notice was given or for any subsequent year of assessment until the year of assessment in which the notice is withdrawn, by the person who gave it, by further notice in writing to the inspector.

196.—(1) Where—

(a) An assessment to income tax (in this section referred to as 'the original assessment') has been made for any year of assessment on a man, or on a man's trustee, guardian or committee, or on a man's executors or administrators,

(b) the Revenue Commissioners are of opinion that, if an application for separate assessment under section 197 had been in force with respect to that year of assessment, an assessment in respect of, or of part of, the same income would have fallen to be made on, or on the trustee, guardian or committee of, or on the executors or administrators of, a woman who is the said man's wife or was his wife in that year of assessment, and

(c) the whole or part of the amount payable under the original assessment has remained unpaid at the expiration of twenty-eight days from the time when it became due,

the Revenue Commissioners may give to her, or, if she is dead, to her executors or administrators, or, if such an assessment as is referred to in paragraph (b) could, in the circumstances therein referred to, have been made on her trustee, guardian or committee, to her or to her trustee, guardian or committee, a notice—

(i) stating particulars of the original assessment and of the amount remaining unpaid thereunder, and

(ii) stating particulars, to the best of their judgment, of the assessment which would have fallen to be made as aforesaid,

385

and requiring the person to whom the notice is given to pay the amount which would have been payable under the last-mentioned assessment if it conformed with those particulars, or the amount remaining unpaid under the original assessment, whichever is the less.

(2) The same consequences as respects—

    (a) the imposition of a liability to pay, and the recovery of, the tax with or without interest,

    (b) priority for the tax in bankruptcy or in the administration of the estate of a deceased person,

    (c) appeals to the Appeal Commissioners, the re-hearing of such appeals and the stating of cases for the opinion of the High Court, and

    (d) the ultimate incidence of the liability imposed,

shall follow on the giving of a notice under subsection (1) to a woman, or to her trustee, guardian or committee, or to her executors or administrators, as would have followed on the making on her, or on her trustee, guardian or committee, or on her executors or administrators, as the case may be, of such an assessment as is referred to in subsection (1) (b), being an assessment which—

    (i) was made on the day of the giving of the notice,

    (ii) charged the same amount of tax as is required to be paid by the notice,

    (iii) fell to be made and was made by the authority who made the original assessment, and

    (iv) was made by that authority to the best of his or their judgment,

and the provisions of this Act relating to the matters specified in paragraphs (a) to (d) shall, with the necessary adaptations, have effect accordingly.

(3) Where a notice is given under subsection (1), tax up to the amount required to be paid by the notice shall cease to be recoverable under the original assessment and, where the tax charged by the original assessment carried interest under section 550, such adjustment shall be made of the amount payable under that section in relation to that assessment and such repayment shall be made of any amounts previously paid under that section in relation thereto, as are necessary to secure that the total sum, if any, paid or payable under that section in relation to that assessment is the same as it would have been if the amount which ceases to be recoverable had never been charged.

(4) Where the amount payable under a notice under subsection (1) is reduced as the result of an appeal or of a case stated for the opinion of the High Court—

    (a) the Revenue Commissioners shall, if, having regard to that result, they are satisfied that the original assessment was excessive, cause such relief to be given by way of repayment or otherwise as appears to them to be just; but

    (b) subject to any relief so given, a sum equal to the reduction in the amount payable under the notice shall again become recoverable under the original assessment.

(5) The Revenue Commissioners and the inspector or other proper officer shall have the like powers of obtaining information with a view to the giving of, and otherwise in connection with, a notice under subsection (1) as they would have had with a view to the making of, and otherwise in connection with, such an assessment as is referred to in subsection (1) (b) if the necessary conditions had been fulfilled for the making of such an assessment.

(6) Where a woman dies who, at any time before her death, was a wife living with her husband, he or, if he is dead, his executors or administrators may, not later than two months from the date of the grant of probate or letters of administration in respect of her estate or, with the consent of her executors or administrators, at any later date, give to her executors or administrators and to the inspector a notice in writing declaring that, to the extent permitted by this section, he or they disclaims or disclaim responsibility for unpaid income tax in respect of all income of hers for any year of assessment or part of a year of assessment, being a year of assessment or part of a year of assessment for which any income of hers was deemed to be his income and in respect of which he was assessed to tax under section 194.

(7) A notice given pursuant to subsection (6) to the inspector shall be deemed not to be a valid notice unless it specifies the names and addresses of the woman's executors or administrators.

(8) Where a notice under subsection (6) has been given to a woman's executors or administrators and to the inspector—

    (a) it shall be the duty of the Revenue Commissioners and the Appeal Commissioners to exercise such powers as they may then or thereafter be entitled to exercise under subsections (1) to (5) in connection with any assessment made on or before the date when the giving of the said notice is completed, being an assessment in respect of any of the income to which the said notice relates, and

    (b) the assessments (if any), to tax, which may be made after that date shall, in all respects and in particular as respects the persons assessable and the tax payable, be the assessments which would have fallen to be made if—

        (i) an application for separate assessment under section 197 had been in force in respect of the year of assessment in question, and

        (ii) all assessments previously made had been made accordingly.

197.—(1) Where an election by a husband and wife to be assessed to tax in accordance with the provisions of section 194 has effect in relation to a year of assessment, and, in relation to that year of assessment, an application is made for the purpose under this section, in such manner and form as may be prescribed by the Revenue Commissioners, either by the husband or by the wife, income tax for that year shall be assessed, charged and recovered on the income of the husband and on the income of the wife as if they were not married and all the provisions of this Act with respect to the assessment, charge and recovery of tax shall, save as otherwise provided by this Act, apply as if they were not married except that—

    (a) the total deductions from total income allowed to the husband and wife by way of personal reliefs shall be the same as if the application had not had effect with respect to that year,

    (b) the total tax payable by the husband and wife for that year shall be the same as the total tax which would have been payable by them if the application had not had effect with respect to that year, and

    (c) the provisions set out in section 198 shall have effect.

(2) An application under this section in respect of a year of assessment may be made—

    (a) in the case of persons marrying during the course of that year, before the 6th day of July in the following year, and

    (b) in any other case, within 6 months before the 6th day of July in that year.

(3) Where an application is made under subsection (1), that subsection shall have effect not only for the year of assessment for which the application was made, but also for each subsequent year of assessment:

Provided that, in relation to a subsequent year of assessment, the person who made the application may, by notice in writing given to the inspector before the 6th day of July in that year, withdraw that election, and, thereupon, subsection (1) shall not have effect for the year of assessment in relation to which the notice was given or any subsequent year of assessment.

(4) A return of the total incomes of the husband and of the wife may be made for the purposes of this section either by the husband or by the wife but, if the Revenue Commissioners are not satisfied with any such return, they may require a return to be made by the wife or by the husband, as the case may be.

(5) The Revenue Commissioners may by notice require returns for the purposes of this section to be made at any time.

(6) In this section and in section 198 'personal reliefs' means relief under any of the following:

    (a) sections 138 to 145 and 151 and 152,

    (b) section 12 of the Finance Act, 1967,

    (c) section 3 of the Finance Act, 1969,

    (d) section 11 of the Finance Act, 1971,

    (e) section 8 of the Finance Act, 1974, and

    (f) section 7 of the Finance Act, 1979.

198.—(1) Where, pursuant to an application under section 197, a husband and wife are assessed to tax for a year of assessment in accordance with the provisions of that section—

(a) subject to subsection (2), the benefit flowing from the personal reliefs may be given either by way of reduction of the amount of the tax to be paid, or by repayment of any excess of tax which has been paid, or by both of those means, as the case requires, and shall be allocated to the husband and the wife—

    (i) so far as it flows from relief under sections 138 and 141 (other than subsection (2)), section 11 of the Finance Act, 1971, and section 8 of the Finance Act, 1974, in the proportions of one-half and one-half,

    (ii) so far as it flows from relief under section 138B, to the husband or to the wife according as the emoluments from which the deduction under that section is made are emoluments of the husband or of the wife,

    (iii) so far as it flows from relief in respect of a child under section 141 (2) or relief in respect of a dependent relative under section 142, to the husband or to the wife according as he or she maintains the child or relative,

    (iv) so far as it flows from relief under sections 143, 145, 151 and 152, to the husband or to the wife according as he or she made the payment giving rise to the relief,

    (v) so far as it flows from relief under section 12 of the Finance Act, 1967, in the proportions in which they bore the expenditure giving rise to relief,

    (vi) so far as it flows from relief under section 3 of the Finance Act, 1969, in the proportions in which they bear the cost of employing the person in respect of whom the relief is given,

    (vii) so far as it flows from relief under section 7 of the Finance Act, 1979, in the proportions in which they incurred the expenditure giving rise to the relief,

(b) subject to subsection (3), section 8 of the Finance Act, 1980, shall apply for that year, in relation to each of the spouses concerned, as if the part of taxable income specified in Part II of the Table to that section which is to be charged to tax at any of the rates specified therein (other than the rate expressed to be chargeable on the remainder of taxable income) were one-half of the part so specified.

(2) Where the amount of relief allocated to the husband under subsection (1) (a) exceeds the income tax chargeable on the income of the husband for the year of assessment, the balance shall be applied to reduce the income tax chargeable on the income of the wife for that year, and where the amount of relief allocated to the wife under that paragraph exceeds the income tax chargeable on her income for the year of assessment, the balance shall be applied to reduce the income tax chargeable on the income of the husband for that year.

(3) Where the part of taxable income of a spouse chargeable to tax in accordance with subsection (1) (b) at a particular rate specified in *Part II* of the Table to *section 8* of the *Finance Act, 1980*, is less than that of the other spouse and is less than the part of taxable income specified in *column* (1) of that Part (hereinafter referred to as 'the appropriate part') in respect of which the first-mentioned spouse is so chargeable to tax at that rate, the part of taxable income of the other spouse which, by virtue of that sub-section, is to be charged to tax at that rate shall be increased by the amount by which the taxable income of the first-mentioned spouse chargeable to tax at that rate is less than the appropriate part.".

19.—*Part III* of the *First Schedule* shall have effect, as respects the year 1980–81 and subsequent years of assessment, for the purpose of supplementing this Chapter.

20.—(1) In this section "relevant year" means the year 1979–80 or any earlier year of assessment.

(2) Notwithstanding anything contained in the Income Tax Acts, the regulations made thereunder or any assessment made (whether before or after the passing of this Act) in accordance with the said Acts or said regulations, no repayment of tax shall be made nor shall any credit be allowed to any person in respect of any overpayment of tax (whether paid by deduction or otherwise) suffered by him in respect of any relevant year, being an overpayment arising by virtue of the aggregation of the income of that person with the income of his spouse, unless, before the commencement of that relevant year, he had instituted legal proceedings to assert the unconstitutionality of the provisions of the Income Tax Acts purporting to authorise such aggregation.

21.—(1) In this section—

"assessment" includes an additional assessment;

"an assessment to which this section applies" means an assessment to tax made, on or after the passing of this Act, on an individual for a relevant year;

"relevant year" means the year 1979–80 or any earlier year of assessment;

"the relevant rate" means, as respects any of the years 1974–75 to 1979–80, the highest of the higher rates which applied for that year of assessment and, as respects any other relevant year, the rate equal to the aggregate of the standard rate of income tax for that year and the highest rate at which sur-tax was chargeable for that year;

"the relevant tax", in relation to an individual, means the amount of tax for a relevant year which—

(a) would have been payable by the individual for that year, or

(b) in a case where the individual is a wife who was treated as living with her husband for that year, would have been payable for that year by the husband of the individual,

if an assessment in respect of the total income of the individual and of his spouse for that year had been made on the 6th day of October in that year on the individual or on the husband of the individual, as the case may be, being an assessment made on the basis and in accordance with the practice prevailing at that time;

"tax" means income tax or sur-tax or income tax and sur-tax as the context requires.

(2) Where, for a relevant year, an assessment to which this section applies is to be made on an individual (being a husband whose wife was treated as living with him for the relevant year or being a wife who was treated as living with her husband for that year) and, in consequence thereof, the aggregate of the tax, which would be payable for that relevant year by the individual and the spouse of the individual, is less than the amount of the relevant tax in relation to the individual for that relevant year, the provisions of *subsection (3)* shall apply in relation to the said assessment.

(3) Where the provisions of this subsection apply in relation to an assessment for a relevant year, then, notwithstanding anything in the Income Tax Acts but subject to the provisions of *subsection (4)*—

    (a) the amount of income on which the individual is to be charged to tax shall be ascertained on the basis that section 138 of the Income Tax Act, 1967, had not been in force and had no effect for that year,

    (b) the assessment shall be made on the basis that the individual is to be charged to tax on his taxable income for the year at the relevant rate, and

    (c) where the individual on whom the assessment is to be made is a married person, the assessment shall be made on the basis that he is not married and such assessments or adjustments of assessments shall be made as are necessary to secure that the individual and his spouse shall be charged to tax for the relevant year in all respects as if they were not married:

Provided that any income contained in an assessment made on a husband which, before the 12th day of October, 1979, in accordance with the practice prevailing at the time the assessment was made, was deemed to be his income shall not be regarded as income of any other person.

(4) Where the provisions of *subsection (3)* apply in relation to any assessment on an individual for a relevant year, such relief, if any, from tax shall be given as is necessary to secure that the aggregate amount of tax payable by the individual and his spouse for that year shall not exceed the relevant tax for that year, and, in a case where assessments to which this section applies are made on the husband and on his spouse, the relief to be given under this subsection shall be apportioned between them in such manner as is just and reasonable.

. . . .

LUXEMBOURG

LAW OF DECEMBER 8, 1981 RELATIVE TO THE EQUALITY BETWEEN MEN AND WOMEN CONCERNING ACCESS TO EMPLOYMENT, VOCATIONAL TRAINING AND ADVANCEMENT AND TO WORKING CONDITIONS.

(Translated by G.H.F. from *Memorial Journal Officiel du Grand-Duche de Luxembourg, Recueil de Legislation* A, No. 91, 16 decembre 1981, pp. 2194–2196.)

Introductory Note: After this manuscript went to press, it was learned that the Draft Law had been replaced by the Law of December 8, 1981. The English translation of the Draft Law was therefore eliminated and in its place an English translation of the new law was inserted. Some of the criticism made in the text has been taken care of, but it appears that even the final text, especially the amended Article 2, makes allowances for too many derogations. Women are "temporarily" kept out of a variety of positions into which they have been accepted in several European countries.

G.H.F.

Article 1. The principle of equal treatment between men and women applies to access to employment, including advancement, advanced professional training, as well as to working conditions.

Article 2 (1) The principle of equal treatment in the sense of the provisions of this law, implies the absence of all discrimination based on gender (sexe), either directly or indirectly, with particular reference to marital or family status.

(2) Provisionally, the following are not considered to be contrary to the provisions of the present law:
1. the legal and regulatory provisions concerning night work by women in industry;
2. the legal and regulatory provisions concerning the employment of women in the mines;
3. the legal and regulatory provisions pertaining to the employment of female volunteers in the army . . .;
4. the legal, regulatory and administrative provisions pertaining to customs agents, postal agents, prison guards, forest guards, military musicians, bailiffs and clerics.

(3) Not considered contrary to the present law are: the legal, regulatory and administrative provisions relevant to the protection of pregnancy and maternity, and to the measures aiming to promote the equality of opportunities between men and women, in particular (those) remedying actual inequalities which affect the opportunities of women in the domains referred to in Article 1.

Article 3 (1) The equality of treatment in the matter of conditions to access, including the selection criteria to employment or positions of work, of whatever

392

sector or branch of activity, and to all levels of the professional hierarchy, must be assured in legislative, regulatory and administrative provisions, in the collective agreements and in individual work contracts, in the informal regulations of enterprises, and in the statutes of independent professions, as well as in practices.

It is specifically forbidden:

1° to make reference to the gender of the worker in offers of employment, or in the announcements relating to employment and to professional promotion, or to use in these offers or announcements relating to employment and to professional promotion, terms (elements) which, though not explicit, indicate or imply the gender of the worker;

2° to make reference to the gender of the salaried or independent worker in the conditions of access and selection criteria for employment or work positions, whatever the sector or branch of activity, or to use in these conditions or criteria terms (elements) which, though without explicit reference to the gender of the worker, amount to a discrimination;

3° to refuse or to hinder access to employment or to professional promotion for explicit or implicit motives, based directly or indirectly on the gender of the worker.

(2) The Government, after consulting the competent professional chambers and the committee of feminine work, which determines the organization, composition, attributions and functioning, may determine by "règlement grand-ducal," the cases in which mention may be made of gender (sexe) [because], by reason of the nature and conditions of the work, gender constitutes a determining condition for access to employment and professional activity.

Article 4. Equal treatment must be assured with respect to access to all types and to all levels of vocational guidance, training, advanced training and retraining, to every person in the legislative, regulatory and administrative provisions, in the collective agreements or in the individual work contracts, in the internal regulations of enterprises, as well as in the statutes of the independent professions.

It is specifically forbidden:

1° to make any mention of the gender of the person in the conditions or the criteria for access to vocational guidance, training, advanced training and professional retraining, or to use in the conditions or criteria, terms which though not explicitly referring to the gender of the person, amount to or imply a discrimination based on gender (sexe);

2° to present the training courses (formations), especially in the publicity and information provided by the establishments or organizations, which administer them, as being more particularly suitable to persons of one or the other gender;

3° to refuse access in one of the areas mentioned under 1, for motives linked directly or indirectly to the gender of the person;

4° to create, on the basis of gender, different conditions for the attainment or award of all types of diplomas or titles.

Article 5. Equal treatment, with regard to working conditions, including the conditions pertaining to dismissal, must be assured to workers in the legislative, regulatory, and administrative provisions, in the collective agreements and in the individual work contracts, in the internal regulations of enterprises, as well as in the statutes of the independent professions.

It is specifically forbidden:

1° to make reference to the gender of the worker in the working conditions, criteria or motives for dismissal, or to use in these conditions, criteria or motives of terms (elements) which, though without explicit reference to the gender of the worker, amount to a discrimination;

2° to establish or apply these conditions, criteria or motives in a discriminatory manner with regard to the gender of the worker.

Article 6. Any conventional, regulatory or statutory provision (stipulation), which is contrary to the principle of equal treatment, as defined in the present law, is null and void.

Article 7. Disputes arising from the application of the provisions of this law in the private sector are to be brought to the jurisdiction, which is competent in matters involving hiring and service contracts, and for the public sector to the *Comité du Contentieux* of the Council of State.

Article 8. It shall be considered abusive if the principal motive for dismissal (*licenciement*) is based on the reaction of the employer

— to a reasoned complaint, filed at the enterprise or the private or public service or the Inspectorate of Labor and the Mines,

— to an intervention by the Inspectorate of Labor and the Mines,

— to a legal action, aiming to achieve respect for the principle of equal treatment in the areas envisaged in this law.

Article 9. The employer, his representatives or agents or any person who distributes or publishes employment announcements or announcements relating to employment, which do not conform to the principle of equality of treatment between men and women, as provided in Article 3 of the present law, and who, in spite of the written injunction by the Employment Administration to conform to it, persists in maintaining these offers and announcements, are punishable by a fine of 2,501 to 20,000 francs. In the event of recidivism, this fine can be increased to the double of the maximum.

Article 10. To the extent that their competences concern the matters specified in Article 1, the Inspectorate of Labor and the Mines and the Employment Administration are charged, each within its concern, to watch over the application of the provisions of this law.

Chateau de Berg, December 8, 1981
(signed) Jean

NETHERLANDS

EQUAL TREATMENT LAW

Equal Treatment Law

As of May 1982 it appeared that the Commission of the European Communities was satisfied with the revisions which had been made in the Dutch legislation concerning equal treatment. The law which was signed by Queen Beatrice on July 2, 1980 contains very categorical provisions against discrimination.[1]

Article 1 states:

"In the civil public service (burgerlijke openbare dienst), the competent authority makes no distinction between men and women, neither directly nor indirectly, for instance by referring to the matrimonial or family status, in the appointment of the official or in the contractual work relationship according to civil law in the matter of remuneration on the basis of other work conditions, in the advancement and termination of the service contract. . . . "

Article 3 provides for the establishment of a "Commission for the equal treatment of men and women."

[1] Wet van 2 juli 1980, houdende aanpassing van de Nederlandse wetgeving op het terrein van het overheidspersoneelsbeleid met het oog op de richtlijn van de Raad van de Europese Gemeenschappen van 10 februari 1975 inzake de gelijke beloning van mannelijke en vrouwelijke werknemers en de richtlijn van 9 februari 1976 inzake de gelijke behandeling van mannen en vrouwen (Wet gelijke behandeling van mannen en vrouwen in de burgerlijke openbare dienst) published in *Staatsblad van Koninkrijk der Nederlanden*, Jaargang 1980, p. 384.

ANDORRA

English Translations of Relevant Parts of Andorran Decrees 1970-1973

1. Translated excerpts from a Decree of April 7, 1970.

Considering that Andorra has experienced a notable economic expansion in recent times, and that, due to the increasing tourist and commercial traffic, the transportation and communication facilities, and the volume of migratory currents, it is experiencing a considerable demographic growth;

Considering that a new situation has resulted from the above-mentioned facts, one which cannot be compared with the past, and which demands an adaptation of the traditional structures of the Valls to modern social conditions—an adaption that will be equitable, just, and useful to everyone, and that therefore, while respecting the traditions, uses, and customs of Andorra, it is necessary that the legislation respond to the country's current needs, so that a broader section of the populace may participate in public affairs;

Considering that the current legal norms applicable in matters of nationality are not in accord with the new situation and that, taking into account the general and higher interest of the country, it corresponds to the Co-Princes to gradually and prudently adapt the legal texts to each situation;

Considering that the obliged adaptation, referred to in the preceding paragraph, and which counsels the concession of the condition of Andorrans to certain persons born in the Valls, while carrying, by virtue of this our Decree, a special norm concerning the exercise of a right of option at the age of twenty, does not imply the modification of Andorran custom and law in that which concerns legal majority and other effects;

By common accord

WE DECREE

Article I.—The following persons will be able to acquire the condition of Andorrans with full political rights, which they may exercise when they reach the age required by Andorran Law:

1.—The children, born in the Valls, of a foreign father and an Andorran mother not an heiress, who has retained her original Andorran nationality, in accordance with Article IV of the Decree of June 17, 1939.

396

2.—The children, born in the Valls, of a father also born in Andorra, that is to say, second generation children born in Andorra.

Article II.—In those persons referred to in Article I, the following conditions must be verified:

1st: That parents and children have maintained and do maintain permanent residence in the Valls.

2nd: That in regard to the affairs of the country they satisfy the conditions established by Article V of the Decree of June, 1939, and by Article 1 of the Decree of December 26, 1941.

Article III.—Those persons referred to in the preceding articles may choose, within a period of six months after having reached the age of twenty-one, the father's nationality. This formality will be carried out, according to custom, by a statement signed before a notary and registered at the Syndicature, which will then communicate it to the Permanent Delegations.

Article IV.—The right of option envisaged in Article III does not belong to children of the 2nd generation born in Andorra, when the father has acquired by decree the condition of 1st generation Andorran.

Article V.—As a transitional concession, all persons who have passed the age indicated in Article III and who unite the conditions in Articles I and II are granted the space of one year, beginning with the publication of the present Decree, to request the granting of Andorran nationality with full political rights.

Article VI.—A foreign woman married to a 1st generation Andorran will have the right, if she requests it, to an Andorran passport, by the same right as her husband.

Article VII.—In all cases the rights created by the present Decree may not be acquired except by means of the procedure established by custom and by the above-mentioned texts.

2. Translated excerpts from "Explanation of Reasons" and Decree, dated April 14, 1970.

EXPLANATION OF THE REASONS FOR THE DECREE ON THE POLITICAL RIGHTS OF ANDORRAN WOMEN

Their Excellencies the Co-princes, attentive to the needs and to the legitimate aspirations of the Andorran people, consider that the moment has come to grant political rights to Andorran women, given that the constantly increasing role that women play in the Valls' social and economic life seems unfitted to their exclusion from public affairs.

The greater part of modern nations have granted the same political rights to citizens of both sexes, although in some cases access to public affairs has been accomplished in stages, in order to progressively prepare women for their new mission.

This wise prudence seems to be particularly called for in the Principality, where the customary institutions, such as "pubillatge" (female inheritance) have as their primary objective the safeguarding and preservation of the community, whose essential cell and basis is the "household."

These are the motives that have impelled us to dictate, in the name of and representing the Most Excellent Co-Princes, the current Decree, which represents a synthesis of the aspirations and views of a certain number of Andorran women of the Communes and the M.I. General Council of the Valls. By virtue of this document Andorran women are given the right to vote. In the future, and taking into account the results of the application of the present Decree, the question of their eligibility can be considered.

WE, the Permanent Delegates of Their Excellencies, the Co-Princes of the Valls of Andorra.

In view of the New Reform Plan adopted May 31, 1866 and subsequent documents regarding the electoral system of Andorra;

In view of the uses and customs of relevant application;

Considering that this affair is strictly within the competence of the Co-Princes, although we are happy to state that our decision accords with the majority view in the M.I. General Council and the Communes;

By common accord
WE DECREE:

SINGLE ARTICLE: All women in possession of full Andorran citizenship will have the right to vote. This right will be exercised in the same cases and under the same conditions as those postulated for men.

3. Translated excerpts from Decree dated July 19, 1971.

DECREE ON LEGAL AND POLITICAL MAJORITY: EXPLANATION OF REASONS (Exposicio de Motivs)

In the framework of the social, economic, and political evolution of the Valls of Andorra, and as a continuation of the measures already adopted in these matters, Their Excellencies the Co-Princes, attentive to the legitimate desires for progress evident in the country, have synthesized the views and desires of the people, of the M.I. General Council and the local Assemblies in regard to legal and political majority of age.

They have examined the plea transmitted, taking into account on the one hand modern public and private law, and on the other uses and customs, in order to ensure respect for the Andorran personality.

Their Excellencies, finally, have aspired to establish a better balance among the community established in the Valls, allowing a larger number of citizens to participate in public life. The coming generations will have to become conscious of their rights, but also of their duties as men and women responsible for the future of their country.

WE. THE PERMANENT DELEGATES OF THEIR EXCELLENCIES THE CO-PRINCES

In view of the request presented by a certain number of citizens of all parishes.

In view of the opinion formulated by the M.I. General Council and the plea which that council has sent to us;

In view of the New Reform adopted May 31, 1866 and subsequent texts regarding political rights, in particular our Decrees of April 7, and 14th, 1970;

In view of the personal rights of Andorrans of both sexes;

In view of the uses and customs concerning elections;

By common accord,

WE DECREE

FIRST ARTICLE: Legal majority for Andorrans of both sexes is fixed at twenty-one years of age.

The effects, in regard to acts of public life, will be the same ones that pertained until now with the majority of age at twenty-five years.

SECOND ARTICLE: All Andorrans who have reached the age of twenty-one by the day before the balloting and who enjoy political rights under the law currently in force in the Valls are electors.

THIRD ARTICLE: All Andorrans of male sex who enjoy political rights and who have reached the age of twenty-one may be elected to any elective position, with the exception of the Syndic and the Sub-Syndic, for whom the required age remains thirty.

FOURTH ARTICLE: This Decree will come into effect September 8, 1971, the Feast-Day of Our Lady of Meritxell, Patroness of Andorra.

Perpignan and the See of Urgel, the second of July of nineteen hundred seventy-one, Feast-Day of the Visitation of Our Lady.

4. Translation of excerpts from Explanations of Reasons and Decree, dated September 5, 1973.

EXPLANATION OF THE REASONS FOR—THE DECREE ON THE ELIGIBILITY OF ANDORRAN WOMEN

The M.I. General Council of the Valls, responding to the desire of Andorran public opinion, and with the purpose of welcoming the economic, social, and political evolution that has taken place in the majority of nations, has steadily carried out, in certain sectors, actions destined to accomplish these objectives.

To this purpose, the M.I. General Council of the Valls has asked Their Excellencies the Co-Princes to adopt measures tending to grant full political rights to Andorran women, with the same limitations for foreign women married to Andorrans of full citizenship as those applying to foreign men married to Andorran heiresses.

Their Excellencies the Co-Princes, wishing to efficaciously satisfy the legitimate and deep aspirations of the population, have responded, through the present Decree, to the proposal that the M.I. General Council of the Valls submitted to us.

WE, THE PERMANENT DELEGATES OF THEIR EXCELLENCIES THE CO-PRINCES

In view of the result of the deliberation of the M.I. General Council, dated May 24, 1973, which has been communicated to us by the

M.I. Syndic General Representative of the Valls, July 3, 1973; In view of the New Reform of 1866 and other subsequent dispositions relative to political rights and, above all, Our Decrees of June 17, 1939 (Article 6, paragraph 3), those of April 14, 1970, and that of July 2, 1971;

In view of the dispositions, uses, and customs in electoral matters;

By common accord,

WE DECREE

FIRST ARTICLE: Women in possession of Andorran citizenship are eligible, under the same conditions and with the same limitations as men.

SECOND ARTICLE: Foreign women, who have acquired full citizenship through marriage to an Andorran, remain submitted to the same conditions that prevail for foreign men married to Andorran heiresses.

THIRD ARTICLE: The present Decree will go into effect the 8th of September, 1973, the Feast-Day of Our Lady of Meritxell, Patroness of the Principality of Andorra.

Published at the See of Urgel and in Perpignan, September 5, 1973.

ITALY

EQUAL TREATMENT FOR MEN AND WOMEN AS REGARDS EMPLOYMENT *Law No. 903—December 1977*

The following Law has been approved by the Chamber of Deputies and the Senate of the Republic and promulgated by THE PRESIDENT OF THE REPUBLIC.

Article 1

No discrimination whatsoever shall be permitted on grounds of sex as regards access to employment, irrespective of the method of recruitment and whatever the sector or branch of activity, at all levels of the occupational hierarchy.

Discrimination within the meaning of the preceding paragraph shall include the following:

1) Discrimination by reference to marital or family status or to pregnancy;
2) Indirect discrimination exercised through selection criteria, or by printed advertisement or some other form of publicity, implying that membership of one sex or the other is a condition of employment.

Discrimination defined as above shall similarly be prohibited in all schemes for vocational guidance, training, advanced training and retraining as regards access and curriculum content.

Exemptions from the preceding provisions shall be permitted only in the case of especially heavy work specified as such under a collective agreement.

The fact that access to a job is made conditional upon membership of a particular sex shall not constitute discrimination where this is essential to the nature of the work or services rendered because the activity in question concerns fashion, art or spectacle.

Article 2

A female worker shall be entitled to the same remuneration as a male worker where the services required are equal or of equal value.

Common criteria for both men and women must be adopted in systems of job classification used in fixing remuneration.

Article 3

No discrimination between men and women shall be permitted as regards assessing qualifications, work allocation or career advancement.

402

Absences from work provided for under Articles 4 and 5 of Law 1204 of 30 December 1971 shall, for the purposes of career advancement, be deemed to be working periods, unless collective agreements lay down special conditions for this purpose.

Article 4

Female workers who satisfy the requirements entitling them to a retirement pension may, nevertheless, choose to continue working until they reach the age limits set for men by laws, regulations and contractual provisions; in which case they shall inform their employer at least three months before the date on which the right to a retirement pension accrues.

Female workers who on the date when this law comes into force are still in employment, although satisfying the requirements entitling them to a retirement pension, shall be exempted from notifying their employer in accordance with the preceding paragraph.

The provisions of the first paragraph shall, however, apply to female workers who first satisfy the aforesaid requirements within the three months following the date on which this law comes into force. In this latter case the employer must be notified not later than the date on which the aforesaid requirements are first satisfied.

In cases falling under the preceding paragraphs, the provisions of law No 604 of 15 July 1966 including subsequent amendments and supplements thereto, shall apply to female workers, in derogation of Article 11 of the said law.

Article 5

In manufacturing establishments, including small workshops, the employment of women shall not be permitted between midnight and six o'clock in the morning, with the exception of those engaged in management or employed in the establishment's medical services.

The prohibition imposed under the preceding paragraph may be modified or lifted by collective agreement, including an agreement made with the firm, regarding special production needs and taking account of the conditions under which the work is done and the way in which the services are organised. The parties to the agreement must jointly inform the Inspector of Work within fifteen days as to the rules to be observed specifying the number of female workers concerned.

The prohibition imposed under the preceding paragraph shall admit of no derogation for women, from the beginning of pregnancy until the time at which the child attains seven months of age.

403

Article 6

Female workers who have adopted children or who have undertaken the care of children with a view to adoption within the meaning of Article 314/20 of the Civil Code, provided that in each case the child is not more than six years old at the time of adoption or taking into care, may benefit from the mandatory absence from work provided for under Article 4 (c) of Law No 1204 of 30 December 1971 and the allowance payable in such cases for the three months immediately following the actual entry of the child into the adoptive family or the family taking it into care.

The above female workers may also, in addition to the right of absence from work provided for under Article 7 (2) of the above law, avail themselves of the right of absence from work provided for under Article 7 (1) of the said law for one year following the actual entry of the child into the family, provided always that the child is not more than three years old.

Article 7

The right to absence from work and the allowance, accorded under Articles 7 and 15 (2) respectively of Law No 1204 of 30 December 1971 shall similarly be granted to a working father, including an adoptive or foster father within the meaning of Article 314/20 of the Civil Code, instead of to the working mother, or in a case where the care of the children devolves upon a father alone.

For this purpose the working father shall serve a statement on his employer attesting the other parent's renunciation of all claims to the above rights and also, in cases falling under Article 7 (2) of Law No 1204 of 30 December 1971, the medical certificate proving the child's illness.

In cases falling under Article 7 (1) of Law No 1204 of 30 December 1971, the working father must serve his employer with a declaration from the employer of the other parent attesting the latter's renunciation.

The provisions contained in the preceding paragraphs shall apply to working fathers, including apprentices, whether employed in the service of private employers or of the public administration, including the autonomous organisations of the regions, the provinces, the districts and other public bodies, even those of a commercial nature, and also cooperatives even if the workers are members of the latter. Home workers shall be excluded and also domestic servants and family help.

Article 8

With effect from 1 January 1978, the sickness insurance fund with which a female worker is insured must pay an allowance equal to the whole amount of remuneration due in respect of the rest periods described under Article 10 of Law No 1204 of 30 December 1971.

The allowance shall be advanced by the employer who shall be compensated out of the contributions due to the insurance fund.

The burden imposed on the sickness funds as a result of the provision contained in the first paragraph shall be met by corresponding grants from the State. The sickness funds shall keep special accounts to provide evidence for this purpose.

Article 9

Family allowances, family supplements and increased pensions for family dependents may, in the alternative, be paid to a woman, who is working or in receipt of a pension, on the same terms and under the same conditions as those laid down for a man who is working or in receipt of a pension. In case of a claim by both parents, family allowances, family supplements and increased pensions for family dependents must be paid to the parent with whom the child is living.

All legislative provisions at variance with the rule contained in the preceding paragraph are hereby repealed.

Article 10

In Article 205 (b) of the consolidated text of the provisions covering insurance against industrial injury and occupational disease approved by Decree No 1124 of the President of the Republic on 30 June 1965 the words "their wives and children" are replaced by the words "their spouses and children".

Article 11

The pensions payable to surviving dependents by employees' pension funds under the general compulsory insurance for invalidity, retirement and surviving dependents shall be extended, on the same terms as are applicable to the wife of a male insured or pensioner, to the husband of a female insured or pensioner who dies after the date on which this law comes into force.

The provisions contained in the preceding paragraph shall similarly apply to employees of the State and other public bodies and to payments by way of pension replacing or supplementing the general compulsory insurance for invalidity, retirement and surviving dependents as well as to payments made by funds, associations and bodies instituted for the staff of employers excused or exempted from compulsory insurance and for self-employed workers and those exercising a profession.

Article 12

The payments to surviving dependents provided for in the consolidated text of the provisions for compulsory insurance against industrial injury and occupational diseases approved by Decree No 1124 of the President of the Republic on 30 July 1965 and by Law No 248 of 5 May 1976 shall be extended, on the same terms as are laid down for the wife of a male worker, to the husband of a female worker who dies after the date on which this law comes into force.

Article 13

The final paragraph of Article 15 of Law No 300 of 20 May 1970 is amended as follows:
"The provisions of the preceding paragraph shall equally apply to agreements or acts calculated to foster discrimination on grounds of politics, religion, race, language or sex".

Article 14

Independent female workers who are permanently employed on a permanent basis in a family enterprise shall be entitled to represent the enterprise on the statutory bodies of cooperatives, consortia or any other form of association.

Article 15

If an act or acts calculated to contravene the provisions contained in Articles 1 and 5 of this law have been committed, on appeal by the worker or by a delegate from his or her trade union organisation the pretore (judge of first instance) with jurisdiction for the area where the act complained of took place, acting as labour judge, shall, within the two days following, summon the parties for summary proceeding and, if he finds the alleged contravention established, shall issue a reasoned decree which shall have immediate effect, ordering the originator of the act complained of to cease his unlawful conduct and to remedy its effects.

No stay of execution shall be granted until the pretore has given final judgment in any proceedings which may be brought under the rule contained in the following paragraph.

Proceedings to set the decree aside may be brought before the pretore, within fifteen days of the parties being notified thereof, and the pretore shall then deliver a judgment for immediate execution. The provisions of Articles 413 and following of the Code of Civil Procedures shall be observed.

Failure to comply with the decree described in the first paragraph or with the judgment given in the proceedings to set it aside shall be punishable under Article 650 of the Penal Code.

Where contraventions falling under the first paragraph concern public employees, the rules regarding suspension of execution contained in the last paragraph of Article 21 of Law No 1034 of 6 December 1971 shall apply.

Article 16

Failure to observe the provisions contained in Articles 1 (1, 2 and 3), 2.3 and 4 of this law shall be punishable by a fine of 200.000 to 1.000.000 lire.

Failure to observe the provisions contained in Article 5 shall be punishable by a fine of 200.000 to 1.000.000 lire in respect of each female worker and each working day, with a minimum of 400.000 lire.

In case of failure to observe the provisions of Articles 6 and 7 the penalties incurred shall be those laid down by Article 31 of Law No 1204 of 30 December 1971.

Article 17

The expenses incurred in implementing Articles 9 and 10 of this law, estimated at 10 and 18 thousand million per year respectively shall, for the financial year 1977, be met by a levy on the increased receipts under Decree Law No 691 of 8 October 1976, now consolidated as Law No 786 of 30 November 1976, altering the tax system for certain petroleum products and methane gas for automobile traction.

The Minister for the Treasury is hereby authorized to issue decrees introducing the relevant adjustments into the budget.

Article 18

The government shall present an annual report to Parliament showing the degree to which this law has been implemented.

Article 19

All legislative provisions at variance with the rules of this law are repealed. Internal rules and administrative acts by the State and other public bodies which conflict with the provisions of this law shall consequently cease to have effect.

Provisions contained in collective or individual employment contracts or in firms' internal rules or in vocational codes of practice, which conflict with the rules contained in this law, shall similarly be null and void.

This law shall come into force on the day following that on which it is published in the Official Gazette (Gazzetta Ufficiale).

This law shall be confirmed by the seal of the State and entered in the official collection of laws and decrees of the Italian Republic. It is the duty of all concerned to observe it and to ensure its observance as the law of the State.

Done at Rome, 9 December 1977

LEONE
Andreotti—Anselmi—Stammati

PORTUGAL

MAJOR LEGISLATION PERTAINING TO WOMEN'S RIGHTS
an analysis by Maria Leonor Beleza

1 - Before April 25, 1974, the juridical situation of women underwent a slow evolution. It was inevitable, but not without errors. The profound changes which have taken place since then, in particular the access to democracy, could not fail to be reflected in considerable alterations to the laws; these alterations were initially consolidated in the new 1976 Constitution, and subsequently in the laws required after the entry into force of this Consitution.

The principle of equality of rights between citizens is established in Article 13 of the Constitution, number 2, which prohibits discrimination on the grounds of sex, among other factors, and does not expressly admit any restriction. Indeed, when the Constitution was being drawn up, a special provision on equality between men and women in general was refused.

The constitutional text refers also expressly to questions of equality of individuals of both sexes with regard to two areas: the family and work; but it is clear that all others are covered by the principle of Article 13.

As to the family, number 3 of Article 36 establishes a status of equality of the spouses. As the Constitution determined the cessation of the validity of previous law contrary to itself (Article 293-1) and the direct application of the constitutional precepts regarding rights, freedom and guarantees (Article 18-1), family law was immediately and profoundly modified; practical difficulties were created, which were only resolved by the introduction of Decree-Law no. 496/77, of November 25.

Mention should also be made of number 4 of Article 36, which ends discrimination against children born out of wedlock, given the importance of this provision for the mothers of such children.

As regards work, the Constitution imposes equality of access (Article 52-c) and prohibits the application of sex factors for determining wages and working conditions in general. (Article 53)

It should also be noted that, with all clarity, this Constitution is not concerned with the simple imposition of formal equality. Its context—and provisions such as subparagraph c) of Article 52—give rise to the need for a policy directed toward equality of opportunity, legitimizing the taking, if need be, of so-called "positive discrimination" measures. It is worth pointing out that the Constitution itself determines special treatment for women only as regards maternity, affirmed as an "outstanding social value" in provision 1 of Article 68; this provision, on referring to the "irreplaceable role (of the mother) in the upbringing of children," introduces an unsettling element in the constitutional system of equality. The same provision aims to ensure the mother's professional fulfillment and her participation in the country's civic life.

Subparagraph c) of Article 54 and provision 2 of Article 68 are important within the context of protection for maternity.

It should also be mentioned that access to family planning is constitutionally guaranteed.

2 - In 1977, the Revision of the Civil Code was published. (Decree-law no.

409

496/77, of November 25) Its main objective was to adapt the Civil Code to the Constitution, and it dealt mainly with family law. The principle of equality of the spouses entailed many modifications, as it was in the field of family relations that women were previously most discriminated against.

According to family law in force, the minimum marrying age is sixteen, for both men and women. (Article 1601-a) Until reaching majority, i.e. eighteen years, neither boys nor girls can marry without their parents' consent. (Article 1604-a)

Marriage is based on the equality and freedom of both spouses.

The alterations were designed to establish a statute of absolute equality between husband and wife. This statute means that an end was put to the predominance of either of them with respect to the other, and to the assignment of certain family tasks to either partner in particular.

Family affairs are managed by both partners. (Article 1671-2) For more important matters, such as the choice of the family residence (Article 1673-1), their agreement is required. But for everyday matters, either of them can make the decisions.

Husband and wife must be jointly responsible for the life of the family they have established, while the division of tasks between them will correspond not to stereotyped images but rather to the division which they both establish at each moment, based on the possibilities of each one. (Article 1676-1) The law implicitly recognizes the economic value of work done in the home and in the upbringing of children, considered equivalent to professional work.

Equal status between husband and wife implied new regulations concerning the choice of family residence (Article 1673), the name of the spouses (Articles 1677 to 1677-c), the exercising of a profession and other activities (Article 1677-D), the management of property (Article 1678), parental authority (Article 1901, 1902), etc.

Community of acquired property is, since 1967, the legal supportive system. But a prenuptial agreement is possible for the adoption of any other system.

Husband and wife manage each one their own property. (Article 1678-1) The management of common property is entrusted to both partners, except for property particularly connected to one of them, in which case the latter only shall have powers of management. (Article 1678-2 and 3)

Under one system of community of property, the disposal of real estate requires the agreement of both parties. (Article 1682-A-1) The disposal of the family home and furniture, under whatever property ownership system, requires the agreement of the husband and the wife. (Articles 1682-3, 1682-A-2 and 1682-B)

Either partner is free to exercise any occupation or other activity, without the agreement of the other. (Article 1677-D)

There is divorce by mutual agreement and by litigation. The latter recognizes causes of guilt and objective causes, such as "de facto" separation for six consecutive years.

As regards the establishment of filiation, it should be mentioned that there has been a clear opening to the biological truth, in an approximation to the Germanic filiation system.

Parents, married to each other, exercise joint parental authority. (Articles 1901 and 1902) In the event of divorce or judicial separation of persons and property, only the parent to whom the care of the child is given, exercises parental authority in personal matters. (Article 1906-1)

If the parents are not married, parental authority is exercised by the parent who has care of the child. The law presumes that the care of the child is given to the mother, but permits the judicial refutation of presumption. If the parents live together, they shall exercise joint parental authority, if they so declare. (Article 1911)

According to the new law, as regards succession, the position of the surviving spouse is now that of a son in principle, in a clear recognition of the relevance of the conjugal family—and of revaluation of marriage.

It is of interest to concentrate, for a few moments, on the situation of "de facto" union, which, in Portuguese law, does not constitute a family relationship. But the law recognizes, in certain circumstances, the right to maintenance of the person who has lived with another in a situation similar to that of husband and wife; the maintenance is to be paid out of the estate of the pre-deceased. The law requires that the latter was not married, that the cohabitation lasted for at least two years, and that the surviving party is unable to obtain maintenance from his/her family. (Article 2020) Social legislation gives a certain amount of protection to the situation of "de facto" union (medical and medicinal assistance, widowhood pension).

3 - In 1979, Decree-law no. 392/79, of September 20, was published, assuring women equality with men as regards access to and conditions in work and employment. It is in line with Conventions no.'s 100 and 111 of the International Labour Organization, and enables Portugal essentially to comply with, when necessary, the directives of the European Community Council of 10 February 1975 and 9 February 1976, on equality of remuneration and equality of access and conditions, respectively.

That decree-law covers three basic areas: firstly, it prohibits discrimination, which it defines (Article 2-a), whether in access to employment (Articles 4 and 12-1), in vocational training (Articles 5 and 6), in the offer of employment and recruitment (Article 7), in remuneration (Articles 9 and 12-2), or in promotion (Article 10); secondly, it assures access to the courts for those who feel themselves the victims of prejudice (Article 16); thirdly, it prohibits the application of sanctions against those who make a complaint of discrimination (Article 11).

Under the terms of this law, only the genetic function can justify limitations to women's access to employment; it admits so-called "positive discrimination" (Article 3-2), which, indeed, is immediately used (Article 5).

The same decree-law sets up a Commission for Equality in Work and Employment, of tripartite composition, the purpose of which is to promote the application of the law. (Articles 14 and 15)

4 - Even before the entry into force of the Constitution, decree-law no. 112/76 of February 7, established the right of working women to 90-days leave of absence for childbirth, without the loss of benefits. The Constitution, indeed, confirmed this right, giving it constitutional status. (Article 68-2) According

to the decree-law, it is compulsory to take sixty of the ninety days, and these must be taken immediately following childbirth. (Article 2-1) This illustrates in particular the thinking behind the law, to the effect that it is a right granted to the exclusive benefit of the child. The woman has a right to an allowance corresponding to her wages. (Articles 4 and 5)

Maternity protection in work also consists of the prohibition and limitation of activities harmful to the genetic function (Article 8 of decree-law no. 392/79 of 20 September). The sector subject to the Individual Labour Contract system is covered, in this matter, by Order no. 186/73 of 13 March; State employees are covered by Normative Ruling ("Despacho Normativo") no. 205/80 of 30 June, published in the Government Gazette ("Diario da Republica") I Series of 15 July 1980.

Working women subject to the Individual Labour Contract system have the right to interrupt their daily work for two half-hour periods, to nurse their children. (Article 118-1 of Decree-law no. 49408 of 24 November 1969)

Decree-law no. 503/80 of 20 October, which contains general rules protecting the family and maternity, recognizes that maternity and paternity are outstanding social values (Article 2), and that the upbringing of the children is the co-responsibility of both parents. It states a series of principles of family policy, and principles to make professional work compatible with family responsibilities. Thus it mentions that the State should introduce family planning (Article 4), a national network of mother and child care (Article 5), and structures suitable for looking after children and young people (Article 6); it creates leave for either of the parents who wishes to interrupt his/her professional work, in order to look after the children (Article 9), and an allowance for them (Article 11); it also establishes the principle of the generalization of part-time work and of flexible working hours, so as to reconcile working and family tasks. (Article 10)

The possibility of part-time work and of flexible working hours already exists for those in state employment (Decree-law no. 167/80 of 29 May, and Resolution no. 142/79 of 11 May, respectively).

The law also allows workers of both sexes to miss work, in order to look after ill members of their family (Decree-law no. 165/80 of 29 May, for state employees,and Article 23-2-e of Decree-law no. 874/76 of 28 December, for workers covered by the Individual Labour Contract system).

5 - The new Nationality Law (Law no. 37/81, of 3 October), which adopts as its fundamental criterion that of "jus sanguinis," puts an end to discrimination on the grounds of sex and of birth in or out of wedlock; this was indispensable, in the light of the Constitution. Both Portuguese fathers and mothers can acquire Portuguese nationality for their children; this acquisition is regulated under the same conditions, in both cases. (Article 1) As regards the effects of marriage, the foreign man or woman, married to a Portuguese woman or man, can acquire Portuguese nationality by declaration and in equality of conditions; acquisition is no longer automatic. (Article 3) Marriage with a foreign man or woman has no special effects in this matter. (Article 8)

6 - The Advertising Code (Decree-law no. 421/80, of 30 September) is of great

interest for the status of women, to the extent that it prohibits advertising which favors sexual discrimination or is contrary to morality and good custom. (Article 8-2) It also prohibits advertisements carrying the idea that women are inferior or subordinate to men, or which reduce them to their traditional domestic role. (Article 23-1) Neither can the female image be used as a mere object for promoting goods or services, of which she is not the sole consumer. (Article 23-2)

It is important to note that this Code aims not only to safeguard woman's dignity, which is not compatible with the unreasonable exhibition of her image, but also to prevent advertising being yet another vehicle for preserving the traditional social roles of both sexes.

7 - The Code of Complementary Tax, which is levied on the incomes of the family, contained serious discriminations against a married woman, considered a dependent of the husband—the sole taxpayer—like a child; the nature of the progressive tax on accumulated income strongly discouraged the woman from working.

Decree-law no. 183-F/80 of 9 June, which altered the Complementary Tax Code, placed both spouses on an equal footing, considering them both as taxpayers; both must sign the tax declaration form. It also attenuated the prejudicial effects of income accumulation by bringing in lower tax rates for married individuals.

8 - It is also worth referring briefly to other legislation aimed at ending sex discrimination.

As regards public law, even before the Constitution, several laws had given women access to certain positions of public employment: to the magistrature (Decree-law no. 251/74 of 12 June), to the diplomatic service (Decree-law no. 308/74 of 6 July) and to positions of local administration which were previously closed to them (Decree-law no. 492/74 of 27 September).

As for local government elections, the only ones where discrimination still persisted in 1974, elections came to be held through the suffrage of citizens resident in the area. (Articles 48-2, 241-2, 246-1, 251 and 252 of the Constitution, Decree-law no. 701-B/76 of 29 September, and Law no. 79/77 of 25 October)

From the Penal Code, the remaining discriminatory provisions were revoked: Article 372, on extraordinary attenuation in the case of homicide or corporal offenses provoked by adultery (Decree-law no. 262/75 of 27 May), provision 1 of Article 405, on the crime of the husband's procurement in relation to the wife, and that part of provision 1 of Article 461 which allowed the husband to open his wife's correspondence. (Decree-law no. 474/76 of 16 June)

9 - Some legislation in the field of social security, concerning working women covered by the Individual Labour Contract system, was not adapted to the principle of equality: thus, retirement age for men is 65 years, and for women 62 years; the terms for granting the widowhood pension are different for men and women. The prohibition of night work for women in industry (Decree-law no. 409/71 of 27 September) raises constitutional problems, which would be best solved in the negative sense.

413

10 - It should also be mentioned that Portugal ratified the Convention on the Elimination of all Forms of Discrimination against Women, with the norms contained in international conventions having validity in internal Portuguese law. (Article 8-2 of the Constitution).

11 - Finally, it should be pointed out that Decree-law no. 485/77 of 17 November, institutionalized in Portugal a Commission on the Status of Women. Its objective is "to contribute, in every way possible, towards a change of attitudes of Portuguese women, and towards the elimination of the discrimination practiced against them." (Article 2) The Commission is attached to the Prime Minister's Office (Article 1), which reflects the realization that the problems in question are of a general nature, and which facilitates intersectorial action. The Commission's competence, established in Article 3, includes the possibility of intervening in the definition and application of policies related to the status of women.

The Commission on the Status of Women has, in fact, played a very active role in promoting this status, having, in particular, collaborated on the most important legislative modifications.

DECREE-LAW N° 392/79 of 20 September
on equality between men and women in work and employment

DECREE-LAW N° 485/77
institutionalizing the Commission on the Status of Women

DECREE-LAW N° 421/80 of 30 September
regulating advertising activity

THE PORTUGUESE CONSTITUTION
of 1976
(Selection of articles)

ARTICLE 13
Principle of equality

1. All citizens shall have the same social status and shall be equal before the law.
2. No one shall be privileged, favoured, prejudiced, deprived of any right or exempt from any duty because of his ancestry, sex, race, language, territory of origin, religion, political or ideological convictions, education, economic situation or social condition.

ARTICLE 36
Family, marriage and filiation

1. Everyone shall have the right to establish a family and marry on terms of complete equality.
2. The conditions for and effects of marriage and its dissolution by death or divorce shall be regulated by law without regard to the form of solemnisation.
3. Husbands and wives shall have equal rights and duties with regard to civil and political capacity and the maintenance and education of their children.
4. Children born out of wedlock shall not for that reason be subject to discrimination; discriminatory designations of filiation shall not be used by the law or by government departments.
5. Parents shall have the right and duty to bring up their children.

6. Children shall not be separated from their parents unless the latter fail to perform their fundamental duties towards the former, and then only by judicial decision.

ARTICLE 48
Participation in public life

1. All citizens shall have the right to take part in the country's political life and in the running of its public affairs, either directly or through freely-elected representatives.
2. There shall be universal, secret and equal suffrage for all citizens over the age of 18 years, subject to the incapacities as provided for in general law. Its exercise shall be personal and constitute a civic duty.
3. Every citizen shall have the right to objective information about acts of state and other public bodies and to be informed by the Government and other authorities about the management of public affairs.
4. All citizens shall have the right of access to public functions under conditions of equality and freedom.

ARTICLE 52

Duties of the State with regard to the right to work
It shall be the duty of the State, by implementing plans for economic and social policy, to safeguard the right to work, ensuring:

a. the implementation of policies of full employment and the right to material assistance for persons involuntarily unemployed.
b. security of employment, dismissals without just cause or for political or ideological motives being prohibited;
c. equality of opportunity in the choice of occupation or type of work and conditions preventing access to any post, work or professional category being prohibited or restricted by reason of a person's sex;
d. cultural, technical and vocational training for workers, combining manual and intellectual work.

ARTICLE 53
Rights of workers

All workers shall be entitled, regardless of age, sex, race, nationality, religion or ideology, to:
a. remuneration for their work according to its quantity, nature and quality, on the principle of equal pay for equal work so as to ensure an appropriate livelihood;
b. the organization of work in dignifying conditions, so as to permit personal fulfilment;

c. safe and healthy working conditions;
d. rest and recreation, a limit to the length of the working day, a weekly rest day and paid holidays.

ARTICLE 54

Duties of the State with regard to the rights of workers
It shall be the duty of the State to secure the conditions of work, remuneration and rest to which workers are entitled, in particular by;

a. fixing and updating a national minimum wage and maximum wage, having regard among other factors to workers' needs, the increase in the cost of living, the requirements of economic and financial stability and the formation of capital for development;
b. fixing a national work time-table;
c. special protection at work for women during pregnancy and after childbirth, for minors, for disabled persons and for those engaged in activities requiring particular effort or working in unhealthy, poisonous or dangerous conditions;
d. systematic development of a network of rest and holiday centres, in cooperation with welfare organizations;

ARTICLE 67
Family

The State shall recognize the establishment of the family and ensure its protection, in particular by:
a. promoting the social and economic independence of family units;
b. developing a national network of mother and child care and carrying out a policy for the aged;
c. cooperating with parents in the education of their children;
d. promoting by all necessary means the wider knowledge of family planning methods and setting up legal and technical structures to further the exercise of responsible parenthood;
e. adjusting taxes and social security benefits in line with family responsibilities.

ARTICLE 68
Maternity

1. The State shall recognize the outstanding social importance of maternity by protecting the mother in her irreplaceable role in the upbringing of children and by guaranteeing her professional status and her participation in the civic life of the country.

2. Women at work shall be entitled to a period of leave before and after giving birth without loss of remuneration or other privileges.

ARTICLE 74
Education

1. The State shall recognize and safeguard the right of all citizens to education and to equality of opportunity in schooling.
2. The State shall reform education so as to eliminate its function of perpetuating the social division of labour.
3. In the implementation of its education policy, it shall be the duty of the State to:
a. ensure compulsory, free, and universal basic education;
b. institute a public system of pre-school education;
c. ensure permanent education and abolish illiteracy;
d. secure that all citizens, in accordance with their ability, have access to the highest levels of education, scientific research and artistic creation;
e. institute by stages free education at all levels;
f. coordinate education with productive and social activities;
g. promote the training of scientific and technical staff of working-class origins.

Decree-Law n° 392/79, of 20 September

The Constitution of the Portuguese Republic recognizes and guarantees, in Article 13, the equality of all citizens, with the consequent refusal of privileges or discriminations, based, namely, on sex.

However, various forms of discrimination persist in Portuguese society. These affect women at various levels, and indeed prevent them from attaining full citizenship.

This discrimination is reflected also in the world of labour. Here it continues, in spite of the fact that the right to equal pay for equal work is constitutionally guaranteed—Article 53, sub-paragraph a)—and that the State is entrusted with the task of ensuring that sex does not function as a limitation to access to any positions, work or professional category—Article 52, sub-paragraph a).

This law aims to create, on the one hand, norms defining the legal framework that can translate the constitutional principles to the reality of the labour world and of labour legislation, and, on the other, action mechanisms to make viable the practical application of these laws and principles.

The fact is not ignored that effective equality of remuneration will considerably alter the structure of enterprises in many sectors. This is what happened in countries where the average disparity between men's and women's remuneration was lower than that presently existing in Portugal. Indeed international practice points to the gradual application, in phases, of provisions aimed at ensuring effective equality. As the Constitution makes it impossible to follow along this path, it is the task of the Commission for Equality in Work and Employment to continually improve the concepts of equal work and equal value, so as to avoid negative effects on the economy, without ever losing sight of the final objective of real, "de facto", equality between men and women, with respect to all the material conditions that are a part of the act of working.

The regime now created also represents an approximation of Portuguese labour legislation to other legal orders, in particular to those of international organizations of which Portugal is, or is soon to be, a member, and the utilization of lessons learnt from the rich foreign experience in this field.

The public discussion of this present law revealed that the labour unions which, under the terms of Law n° 16/79, of 26th May, gave an opinion on it, approved, in general, the contents of its provisions, along the lines contained in the Constitution. However, they put forward numerous suggestions and criticisms for alterations in detail. These, representing a valuable contribution to the improvement of the text's form and substance, were incorporated, totally or partially, in large numbers, with particular emphasis on the alteration of the composition of the Commission for Equality in Work and Employment, which came to include employers' and workers' representatives, and on the immediate, rather than deferred, application of this law.

Conscious that the equality enshrined in the Constitution will not be achieved merely through the law, so deep are the social, economic and political roots of discrimination against women, we are confident, nevertheless, that this law will contribute significantly and decisively to the non-discrimination of women at work.

Under these terms:

Using the faculty conferred by sub-paragraph a) of n° 1 of Article 201 of the Constitution, the Government decrees the following:

Article 1 - 1. This present law aims to guarantee women equality with men as regards opportunities and status in work and employment, as a consequence of the right to work, enshrined in the Constitution of the Portuguese Republic.

2 - The provisions of this law will be equally applicable, with the necessary adaptations, to any discriminatory situations or practices against men.

Article 2 - For the purposes of the application of the present law:

a) Discrimination is understood to be: any distinction, exclusion, restriction or preference based on sex, the purpose or consequence of which is to jeopardize or to refuse the recognition, enjoyment or the exercise of the rights assured by labour legislation;

b) Employer is understood to be: any person, single or collective, with capacity, as employer, to make individual labour contracts;

c) Remuneration is understood to be: every and any payment to which the worker has a right through his individual labour contract, whether as recompense or not, made in money or in kind, in particular basic remuneration, service ratings, seniority premiums, holiday and Christmas allowances, productivity premiums, sales commissions, expense allowance, transport allowance, accounts adjustment allowance, payment for nightwork, overtime, work on rest days and on holidays, shift allowances, meal allowances, the supply of lodging, housing or goods;

d) Equal work is understood to be: work done for the same employer where the tasks carried out are equal or objectively similar;

e) Work of equal value is understood to be: work done for the same employer where the tasks carried out, although of a different nature, are considered equivalent as the result of the application of objective task evaluation criteria.

Article 3 - 1. The right to work implies the absence of any discrimination based on sex, either direct or indirect, namely through reference to civil status or to family situation.

2 - Provisions are not considered discriminatory which are of a temporary nature, establishing a preference of sex, imposed by the need to correct an inequality held as a social value.

Article 4 - 1. The access of women to any job, profession or post, is guaranteed.

2 - With the exception of that laid down in n° 8, legal and regulatory provisions, as well as the provisions of collective labour regulation instruments, of individual labour contracts, of company regulations, of the articles of association of labour unions or of independent professions, and of professional licence regulations, which limit in any way the access of women to any job, profession or post, are considered null and void.

Article 5 - 1. It is incumbent upon the State to promote, encourage and coordinate actions of vocational guidance and training for women, in accordance with their motivations and with employment trends.

2 - In the carrying out of these actions, preference will be given to the age groups of 14–19 years and 20–24 years, having no minimum schooling qualification or certificate, and to single mothers.

3 - The access is guaranteed of women, in accordance with the preferences established in the previous number, to professional training courses, at a percentage to be fixed annually by a Ministry of Labour order.

4 - The employment reintegration of women who interrupted their professional activity, both in the aspects of guidance, and in the carrying out of special refresher programmes, will be the object of suitable measures.

Article 6 - Employers must assure female workers equality of opportunity and status with men, as regards professional training of all levels and types.

Article 7 - 1. Employment offer advertisements and other forms of advertising connected with pre-selection and recruitment cannot contain, directly or indirectly, any restriction, specification or preference based on sex.

2 - Recruitment for any employment post will be done exclusively on the basis of objective criteria. It is not permitted to make physical requirements which are not related to the occupation or the conditions of its exercise.

3 - It is not considered discrimination to condition recruitment to one or other sex in fashion, art or show activities, when this is essential to the nature of the task to be performed, there being a qualitative difference whether it is performed by a man or a woman.

Article 8 - 1. Work which by law is considered to represent an effective or potential risk for the genetic function, is prohibited or must be subject to conditions.

2 - The legal, regulatory or administrative provisions envisaged in the previous number must be periodically reviewed in the light of scientific and technical knowledge. In accordance with this knowledge, they must be updated, revoked or made extensive to all workers.

Article 9 - 1. Equal pay to male and female workers for equal work or work of equal value, done for the same employer, is assured.

2 - Variations in effective remuneration will not be considered discrimination if based on objective criteria, common to both men and women.

3 - Systems of job description and evaluation of tasks must be based on objective criteria common to both men and women, so as to exclude any discrimination based on sex.

4 - The female worker who alleges discrimination must base this allegation with reference to the worker or workers in relation to whom she considers herself discriminated. It is incumbent upon the employer to prove that effective remuneration differences are based on factors other than sex.

Article 10 - 1. Female workers are guaranteed, in the same conditions as men, the development of a professional career which enables them to reach the highest level of their profession.

2 - The right, recognized in the previous number, is extended to the occupying of positions of responsibility and to the changing of professional career.

Article 11 - 1. The employer is forbidden to dismiss, apply sanctions or in any way prejudice the female worker because of her having lodged a complaint of discrimination.

2 - Until proof to the contrary, the application of any sanction on the female worker, up to a year after the complaint of discrimination, is presumed abusive.

3 - The violation of the provisions of n° 1 of this article gives the female worker a right to compensation, within the general terms of law, which will be added to any others envisaged in law.

Article 12 - 1. This law considers null and void the provisions of any collective labour regulations which establish professions and professional categories specifically for female or male personnel; these provisions are considered substituted by others covering both sexes.

2 - Equally, this law considers null and void the provisions of collective labour regulations which establish, for the same professional categories or for equivalent professional categories, lower remuneration for women; this is considered substituted, by full right, by the remuneration awarded to men.

3 - For the purposes of that laid down in the previous number, the professional category is considered to be the same or equivalent when the respective job description corresponds to equal work or to work of equal value respectively.

4 - Collective labour agreements should include, whenever possible, provisions for the effective application of the norms of this law, in particular through the participation of labour unions in job recruitment, selection and training.

Article 13 - 1. Those provisions of collective labour agreements are null and void which establish different remuneration for female apprentices at the same level of apprenticeship, measured by the time served.

2 - In the cases envisaged in the final part of the previous number, the corresponding remuneration for male apprentices substitutes, by full right, that established by the annulled provision.

Article 14 - 1. The Commission for Equality in Work and Employment is set up, attached to the Ministry of Labour. Its objective is to promote the application of the provisions of this law.

2 - The Commission will consist of three qualified persons of recognized competence, appointed by the Minister of Labour, one of whom shall preside, two representatives of the Commission on the Status of Women, three representatives of labour unions and three representatives of employer associations.

3 - The Commission shall be advised by employment experts, designated by the Secretary of State for Population and Employment.

4 - The Commission shall have a Secretariat composed of two Ministry of Labour representatives and one representative of the Commission on the Status of Women.

5 - The Minister of Labour must regulate the installation and operating conditions of the Commission, and endow it with the human and material means necessary for it to fulfill its appointed duties.

Article 15 - 1. The Commission for Equality in Work and Employment must:

a) Recommend to the Minister of Labour the adoption of regulatory and administrative provisions for improving the application of the norms contained in this law;

b) Promote the carrying out of studies and research with the aim of eliminating discrimination against women in work and employment;

c) Encourage and give dynamism to actions aimed at making known the objectives of this law;

d) Approve options, relating to equality in work and employment, which are submitted to it by the secretariat;

e) Make public, through all the means at its disposal, cases of proven violation of the norms of this law, as long as the decision is taken unanimously by its members or receives the agreement of the Minister of Labour.

2 - The secretariat must:

a) Advise the bodies responsible for the drawing up of collective labour regulations, with a view to correctly establishing the correlations between the various professional categories and their corresponding remunerations;

b) Issue opinions, regarding equality in work and employment, whenever so requested by the Labour Inspectorate, by the judge of the case, by unions and employer organizations, by the entity charged with attempting conciliation in individual labour conflicts, or by any interested party;

c) Visit places of work or request these visits from the Labour Inspectorate, with the purpose of proving any discriminatory practices;

d) Manage the Commission's daily business, superintend the respective departments, represent the Commission, and, in general, ensure the conditions necessary for the development of its activity.

3 - The competence given by sub-paragraph a) of the previous number must be exercised with regard to the commissions charged with drawing up labour regulation orders.

4 - In the exercise of its competence, the secretariat shall be able to request information and opinions from any entity, public or private, as well as the collaboration of the advisers it needs.

5 - As regards employment, the Commission must coordinate its actions with the National Plan Council.

Article 16 - 1. Actions can be brought before the competent courts for the application of the norms of this law.

2 - The right to bring an action, referred to in the previous number, shall be exercised by the worker who considers himself/herself discriminated against or, if he/she so wishes, by the labour union which represents him/her.

Article 17 - 1. The Work Inspectorate must supervise the application of this law.

2 - The entities referred to in Article 43 of Decree-Law n° 47/78, of 21st March, which violate the provisions of Articles 4, 6, 7, 8, 9, 10, 11, 12 and 13 shall be punished by a fine of 5,000 to 10,000 escudos for each female worker in relation to whom the infraction occurs.

3 - In cases of recurrence, the minimum limit shall be raised to double.

4 - When the violation results in a credit to the female worker, the amount of the fine shall be scaled between the value of the remuneration due and double this amount. It can never be less than the minimums fixed in n°'s 2 and 3.

5 - The proceeds of the fines revert to the Unemployment Fund.

Article 18 - When, in the application of the provisions of Articles 4, 6, 7, 9 and 10, the Labour Inspectorate has well-founded doubts as to the possible existence of a discriminatory situation or practice, it shall only start to open the respective case after a prior opinion from the Commission for Equality in Work and Employment.

Article 19 - 1. The provisions of Article 12 and 13 shall only be applicable to collective labour regulations, the making or drawing up of which begins after the third month of the validity of this present law.

2 - For the purposes of the previous number, the process is considered to begin with the presentation of the proposal, in the case of collective labour agreements, or with the issue of the ministerial order setting up the technical commission, in the case of labour regulation orders.

Article 20 - 1. Domestic service and domiciliary work relations will be the subject of an independent regulatory law, which may introduce alterations to the regime of this law, if found necessary by the specific nature of the sector.

2 - This law should be made applicable, as soon as possible, to the State, local Government, municipalized services and social security institutions, and to the workers in their service.

3 - For the purposes of that laid down in the previous number, the Commission for Equality in Work and Employment shall, in collaboration with the Ombudsman and the Secretary of State for Public Administration, study and propose suitable legislative measures.

Article 21 - It is incumbent upon the government of the autonomous regions to proceed with the creation, at a regional level, of the structures necessary for achieving the objectives of this law, as well as to propose the forms of coordination with the Commission envisaged in Article 14 and with Work Inspectorate delegations.

Article 22 - This law must be reviewed within two years.

Article 23 - 1. All legal, regulatory and administrative provisions are revoked which are contrary to the free access of women to any job, profession or post, as are those which refer to selection criteria, in whatever branch or sector of activity, at all levels of the professional hierarchy.

2 - N° 2 of Article 2 of Decree-Law n° 47 500, of 18 January 1967 is revoked.

Seen and approved by the Council of Ministers of 31 July 1979. Signed by: Carlos Alberto da Mota Pinto, Manuel Jacinto Nunes, Eusébio Marques de Carvalho, António Jorge de Figueiredo Lopes.

Promulgated on 31 August 1979.

Let it be published

The President of the Republic, António Ramalho Eanes.

Decree-Law n° 485/77
which institutionalizes the Commission on the Status of Women

The Constitution requires that the Status of Women in Portuguese Society should be redefined. This is an imperative which derives from the principles set down with regard to the equality of all citizens.

To women, just as to men, the Constitution guarantees social dignity and equality before the law. Amongst other principles, all people have equal rights and duties in both civic and political spheres, in the family, in employment and in all sectors of social life.

The Constitution further recognises the social importance of maternity, considered as a responsibility to be assumed by society itself. Hence the fact that women should be protected in their maternal role, particularly at the time of pregnancy and childbirth and the State's obligation to ensure the necessary supporting infrastructures.

The picture which the Constitution reflects of the position of women in Portuguese Society is, however, far from the real situation.

Victims of discrimination to a greater or lesser extent in the family, in employment, in education and in professional training and far as they still are from civic and political life, there is still a long way to go before women attain full equality of rights and duties and the same social status as men.

In the chapter dealing with the Organization of the Democratic State, the Programme of the Constitutional Government includes measures concerning the situation of women. The government has pledged itself to assume its responsibilities in the light of the constitutional imperatives to improve the status of women in Portuguese Society, in order to rapidly eliminate all sex discrimination which still exists in the law and in social life.

Further to this pledge and in harmony with the recommendations of the United Nations Organization, the already existing Comissão da Condição Feminina (Commission on the Status of Women) is hereby institutionalised by the present decree-law, and is provided with adequate means and the working conditions required for its task.

Given the intersectorial character of its activities, collaboration between the Comissão da Condição Feminina and the different official departments wil' necessarily be very close as only coordinated and concerted action will allow for the desired goals to be attained.

The Comissão da Condição Feminina, under the guidance of the Government, will give its contribution to the fulfillment in Portugal of the World Plan of Action for the 1976–1985 Decade approved at the International Women's Year Conference, organised by the United Nations Organization, a stage which is considered fundamental in order that women and men assume co-responsibility for all the roles of citizens at every level of society.

Thus:

The Government decrees, in the terms of paragraph a) of n° 1, Article n° 201 of the Constitution, the following:

CHAPTER I

Nature and Attributions

Article 1

The Comissão da Condição Feminina, hereinafter referred to as the Commission, is attached to the Prime Minister's Office and will be responsible to the Prime Minister or to the Member of the Government delegated for the purpose.

Article 2

The Commission is set up to support every form of awareness-development of Portuguese Women and the elimination of discrimination against them, in order to gain their participation in the process of change of Portuguese Society in accordance with the principles set down in the Constitution.

Article 3

1—The attributions of the Commission are:
   a) To promote activities which lead women to gain an awareness of the situation of discrimination in which they find themselves and to play an active part in the improvement of their status;
   b) To promote individual and collective awareness of the need for a new concept of the role of women in society;
   c) To play an active role in concrete cases in which women are involved with a view to improve their living conditions;
   d) To participate in the drawing up of a general policy on the status of women;
   e) To give recommendations on proposed sectorial policies affecting the situation of women and to participate in the discussion of such policies;

425

f) To propose suitable legislative measures which will enable maternity to be considered as a social function;

g) To propose measures which will eliminate sex-discrimination in existing legislation;

h) To give recommendations on proposed legal measures which affect, direct or indirectly, the status of women and participate in the drawing up of such legal measures;

i) To propose the creation of the dispositions which may prove necessary, at any time, for effective compliance with new legislation;

J) To carry out, support and publicise research on the situation of women, particularly through studies, the creation of a Documentation Centre, the publication of a bulletin and the supply of information;

l) To cooperate with official departments and non-government organizations in joint projects and activities;

m) To cooperate with government and non-government organizations of an international nature and with foreign organizations with similar aims, to establish solidarity with the women of all countries in every field of social, cultural and political life.

2—Government departments with activities particularly concerning the situation of women will submit to the Commission, for prior appraisal, any and all legislative proposals and drafts referred to in e) and h) in Number 1.

CHAPTER II
Organization, Competence and Mode of Functioning
Article 4

1—The Commission is endowed with the following organs:
   a) The President
   b) The Coordinating Committee
   c) The Consultative Council

2—The Consultative Council is divided into two sections:
   - The Interministerial Section
   - The Section of Non-Governmental Organizations

Article 5

1—The Commission will be provided with the following departments
   a) Research department
   b) Documentation and Information department
   c) Regional activities and international relations department
   d) Administrative department

2—The President may determine the setting-up of temporary working-groups charged with the carrying-out of specific tasks.

Article 6

1—The President is equivalent in category to director-general and is appointed by the Prime Minister.

2—If the President is absent a member of the staff previously indicated to the Prime Minister, will act in replacement.

3—The President is responsible for the supervision and coordination of the Commission's activities and the calling of and presiding over meetings of the Coordinating Committee and of the Consultative Council with a deciding vote.

Article 7

The Coordinating Committee is comprised of the specialists who are in charge of the departments referred to in a), b) and c) of Article 5 and two members of the staff designated annually by the President.

Article 8

The Coordinating Committee is responsible for:
a) The appraisal of priorities of action.
b) The definition of positions to be taken in important matters concerning the situation of women.
c) The drawing-up of an annual programme of activities and the coordination of the carrying-out of such programmes.
d) The appraisal of the Commission's annual budget proposal.

Article 9

1—The interministerial section of the Consultative Council will be made up by representatives from the following Government departments.
a) The Ministry of Home Administration
b) The Ministry of Justice
c) The Ministry of Finance
d) The Ministry of Foreign Affairs
e) The Ministry of Agriculture and Fisheries
f) The Ministry of Industry and Technology
g) The Ministry of Trade and Tourism
h) The Ministry of Labour
i) The Ministry of Education and Scientific Research
j) The Ministry of Social Affairs
k) The Ministry of Housing, Development and Building
l) The Secretariat of State for Public Administration
m) The Secretariat of State for Social Communication
n) The Secretariat of State for the Environment
o) The Secretariat of State for Population and Employment.
2—Nominations are made by the respective Ministers or Secretaries-of-State.
3—The Section of Non-Governmental Organizations is made up of representatives of women's organizations whose aims are included within the dispositions of Article 2, namely those which are established in different parts of the country and which have fields of action and programmes which are concerned with the improvement of women's conditions or their standard of life and status.
4—For the effects of the previous Number, each non-governmental organization shall nominate two representatives annually, one of which shall be an effective member and the other a substitute.

5—The organizations covered by Number 3 of this article will be designated by an order of the Prime-Minister, in accordance with the President's proposal.

6—Persons of recognised competence in the matter of the status of women may be invited by the President to take part in the meetings of the Consultative Council or of the sections, without the right to take part in voting.

Article 10

1—The Interministerial Section is responsible for:
   a) Guaranteeing the cooperation of all sectors of the Administration whose activities affect the status of women;
   b) Coordinating their respective intervention in the scope of the implementation and definition of the overall policy on the status of women;
   c) The recommendation of action to be taken;
   d) Deciding upon projects which are presented and the annual plan of action of the Commission;

2—The Section of Non-Governmental Organizations is responsible for:
   a) Contributing to the drawing-up of the policy on the status of women by informing on the opinion of the women represented by the different organizations;
   b) Collaborating in the implementation of the above-mentioned policy, namely through the mobilisation of the women which the organizations represent;
   c) Expressing opinions on the projects submitted to it and on the Commission's annual programme of activities;
   d) Recommending of action to be taken.

3—The Consultative Council may meet at a general meeting or by sections, the latter being able to operate as restricted groups.

Article 11

The Research Department is responsible for the carrying out, promotion and support of research or studies required for the performance of the attributions of the Commission set down in article 3.

Article 12

The Documentation and Information Department is responsible for the gathering and diffusion of documentation and information concerning the status of women, on a national and international scale, within the scope of attributions defined in Article 3.

Article 13

The Regional Activities and International Relations Department is responsible for the support and coordination of action to be taken by the Commission at regional level as well as the contacts to be established with international organizations and foreign organizations with similiar goals.

Article 14

The Administrative department is responsible for the general administrative work and the carrying-out of the administrative tasks which are essential for the running of the organs of Commission and its departments.

Article 15

The Commission will be provided with the regional structures it requires for the fulfillment of its attributions; such regional structure will cooperate with central and local official departments and with non-governmental organizations established in the respective regions.

CHAPTER III
Staff
Article 16

The Commission is staffed according to the table adjoining the present decree-law, of which it is an integral part.

Article 17

1—The appointment of staff, as per the table, will be carried out by nomination, except in cases where appointment is by contract in accordance with current norms;

2—Nominations will be of a provisional nature for the period of one year at the end of which the staff members in question will be definitively appointed if they have shown the required capability or will otherwise be dismissed.

Article 18

1—If a civil servant of another official department is nominated to any position on the staff of the Commission, this nomination is considered a transfer, which will last for a period of one year but which will be subject to extension for equal periods of time; this nomination may be confirmed as permanent after a year's service if the said civil servant has shown capability for the post and the Ministry where the civil servant previously worked so authorises.

2—The posts of the said civil servant in original table will be temporarily filled, a vacancy being made available only when and if the nomination is confirmed as permanent in the Commission.

Article 19

1—The President of the Commission is appointed for an indefinite period of time and will be chosen from amongst persons of recognised competence in matters concerning the status of women.

2—The remaining posts will be filled by order of the Prime Minister, in accordance with the proposals of the President, in harmony with the following rules:

a) Specialists, by promotion of Principal Officers, based on appreciation of curriculum;

b) Principal Officers and First-Class Officers by promotion, based on presentation of qualifications, of First-Class Officers and Second-Class Officers, respectively, with at least three years of satisfactory and effective service in the post;

c) Second-Class Officers, selected from amongst master's or bachelor's degree holders with suitable university courses accepted on the basis of presentation of qualifications;

d) First-Class Auxiliary Officer, by promotion from 2nd Class Auxiliary Officer with at least 3 years of satisfactory and effective service;

e) Second-Class Auxiliary Officer selected from amongst persons having completed the general high-school course or having equivalent qualifications;

f) Secretary, accepted on the basis of presentation of qualifications selected from candidates holding a suitable degree;

g) Head of Administrative Department selected from candidates holding a suitable degree or alternatively a First-Class Official with at least 6 years of satisfactory service in the post and holding the classification "good";

h) First and Second-Class Officials on the basis of an examination; selected from amongst civil servants of the category immediately below, with at least 3 years of satisfactory and effective service at that level and the qualifications as required by current administrative regulations;

i) Third-Class Officials, in accordance with the current administrative regulations;

j) Clerk-Typists, on the basis of an examination; selected from candidates having completed compulsory schooling;

Telephonist, driver and attendants by selection from amongst candidates having completed at least compulsory schooling.

Article 20

1—Personnel considered indispensable for the carrying-out of functions which cannot be performed by permanent staff may be contracted in addition to the permanent staff.

2—The carrying-out of studies, surveys and other tasks of an occasional nature, including training, may be entrusted to national or foreign bodies not related to the departments, on the basis of a contract for services rendered.

3—The contract for services rendered must be in writing with details of the period of execution, remuneration, severing conditions and mention of the fact that in no circumstances is the qualification of civil servant granted.

Article 21

1—By means of an order of the Prime Minister and with the agreement of the Minister concerned, the Commission may requisition staff from other ministerial departments, paid from a special sum for the effect which is part of the Commission's budget.

2—Any requisitions effected, in the terms of the previous Number, will depend on the agreement of the civil servant in question and during the period of requisition, the respective post may be filled temporarily.

3—Civil servants requisitioned according to the terms of this Article may opt for the salaries corresponding to their original posts.

CHAPTER IV
Final and Transitory Dispositions
Article 22

1—The officers, auxiliary-officers, administrative and auxiliary staff who, at the date of coming into force of the present decree-law are employed in any position by the Commission, will be definitely appointed as per the adjoining table, in accordance with a list of appointments to be approved by the Prime Minister; to be published in the "Diário da República" (Government Gazette) without any further formality except for the approval of the Auditing Office.

2—Staff included in the same category will not lose the accumulated service obtained in that category.

3—Staff referred to in Number 1 who have already been appointed as permanent Members of the Civil Service will have this situation safeguarded as regards the staff-post to which they are appointed.

4—Staff referred to in Number 1 will remain in office with the corresponding rights they are entitled to until the publication of the list of appointments.

Article 23

Until the definition and organization of the regions is established, the Commission may avail itself of delegates provided with the necessary support, wherever this is possible and convenient.

Article 24

Any doubts which arise regarding the application of this decree-law will be solved by order of the Prime-Minister.

Article 25

Decree n° 482/73 of September 27, 1973, and Decree n° 47/75 of February 1, 1975, are hereby revoked.

DECREE-LAW N° 421/80 OF 30 SEPTEMBER

(We have translated below some of the articles having greatest bearing on the concerns of the Commission on the Status of Women, taken from Decree-Law n° 421/80 which regulates advertising activity.

Thus, Article 8 prohibits advertising implying any racial, sexual, political or religious discrimination or offense, as well as against morality or customs; Art. 22 refers to the protection and participation of children and young people; Art. 23 bears exclusively on women; Art. 26, on study-courses, prohibits their being restricted on the basis of sex.)

ARTICLE 8
(Illicit Purposes)
1.—It is illicit to use advertising which, by its form, object or purpose, offends the fundamental institutions of the Nation, democracy and liberty.
2.—Neither will advertising be allowed which favours or stimulates any type of racial, sexual, political or religious discrimination or offense, or which goes against morality or custom.

ARTICLE 22
(Protection and Participation of Children and Young People)
1.—Advertising messages directed at young people or children must always bear in mind their psychological vulnerability, and may not, in particular:
   a) Cause them moral, mental or physical harm;
   b) Entice them to organized meetings for predominantly advertising purposes, or incite them to talk with strangers;
   c) Lead them to seriously importune those directly in charge of them or third parties, or, also, lead them into obviously condemnable positions;
   d) Transmit an implied inferiority of the minor who does not consume the product advertised.
2.—Children and young people can only be the principal actors in advertising messages in which there is a fundamental link between them and the product or service being promoted. Under no circumstances can they recommend these products or services.

ARTICLE 23
(Women)
1.—Advertising must not transmit the idea of women being inferior or subordinate to men, or reduce them to their traditional domestic role, at the expense of other functions and aspirations.
2.—Neither is advertising allowed which uses woman's image as a mere promotional object of goods or services, of which she is not the exclusive consumer.

ARTICLE 26
(Courses)
1.—Advertising messages on courses must obey the following rules:
   a) They must contain an indication on the nature of the course, in accordance with the designation officially accepted by the competent services;
   b) They cannot offer academic titles or degrees;
   c) They cannot contain promises of future employment or benefits that are manifestly exaggerated, which result from the courses;
   d) They cannot refer to fraudulent courses;
   e) They must state the time of duration of the course and the name of the person conducting it;
   f) They must indicate the total price of the course, and not simply the cost of a fraction;
   g) They cannot contain indications limiting the course on the basis of sex.

EASTERN EUROPEAN COUNTRIES

Eastern European Countries

In most of the Eastern European countries there are no comprehensive laws which seek to equalize the rights of women. Leading authorities in these countries have taken the position that there is no need for such legislation because the problem of gender discrimination or the exploitation of women by men has ceased long ago. They point to their constitutional provisions as fully guaranteeing gender equality. Most of these provisions have been cited in the preceding chapters and the full texts are readily available.[1]

As far as the U.S.S.R. is concerned, there are many laws which have been collected and translated.[2] During the war and for many years after 1945, women in the Soviet Union were called upon to perform very heavy manual labor which was limited to men in most countries. To compensate for these demands some special measures were taken to protect their health. As manpower increased during the early 1950s, more and more legislation was enacted to improve the working conditions of women. In many areas men now replaced women. It was emphasized that this was done to protect women and was not to be viewed as discriminatory. However, women were excluded from many kinds of industrial work which were neither particularly strenuous nor hazardous. Indeed, some of the work which was increasingly assigned to them in agriculture was no less demanding. During the Khrushchev era many decrees were promulgated which restricted the employment of women in hazardous and excessively strenuous work. Some of these regulations were enacted by "decisions" of the Council of Ministers of the U.S.S.R. An example of this type was Decision No. 839 of July 13, 1957 which stated that it was necessary for a further improvement of the protection of women workers to discontinue the employment of women on underground projects in the ore-mining industry. Many of these regulations were codified in Labor Code of the U.S.S.R. of July 15, 1970 and the labor codes of the Republics which were enacted during the following year. Thus, Article 160 of the Labor Code of the Russian Soviet Federative Socialist Republic of December 9, 1971 defined the jobs in which female labor is prohibited. Specific lists were published from time to time.

The new constitutional provisions have not changed the basic character of the legislation pertaining to women. Even the most recent legislation reflects the earlier protectionist approach.

The following 1978 document is the most recent in a long series of decrees and decisions. It was obtained for our use by Dr. Blanka Kudej and translated from Russian by the author with the assistance of Eva Radvan.

---

[1] *Constitutions of the Countries of the World.* ed., Albert P. Blaustein and Gisbert H. Flanz, Oceana Publications, Inc., Dobbs Ferry, NY, 1971 + .

[2] *Soviet Legislation on Women's Rights, Collection of Normative Acts.* compiled by A.M. Belyakova and others. Moscow: Progress Publishers, 1978.

433

Decree of the Council of Ministers of the U.S.S.R.
and the All-Union Central Council of
Trade Unions

ON SUPPLEMENTARY MEASURES FOR THE IMPROVEMENT OF
CONDITIONS OF LABOR FOR WOMEN EMPLOYED IN THE NATIONAL
ECONOMY

With the aims of further improving the conditions of labor of women employed in the national economy and the protection of their health, the Council of Ministers of the U.S.S.R. and the All-Union Central Council of Trade Unions decree:

1.   To delegate to the State Committee of the Council of Ministers of the U.S.S.R. on Labor and Social Questions together with the All-Union Central Council of Trade Unions and by Agreement with the U.S.S.R. Ministry of Health, to establish, by July 1, 1978, a new List of production operations, occupations, and jobs with difficult and dangerous working conditions in which the employment of women's labor is forbidden, and also to establish the procedure and conditions for the application of this List.

2.   For ministries and departments of the U.S.S.R., councils of ministers of union and autonomous republics, provinces, regions, areas, city and district executive committees of soviets of people's deputies, for leaders of enterprises and organizations, to ensure the job placement of women released from heavy work and work with dangerous conditions of labor, and where job placement is impossible in their occupations (or specialties), to ensure their retraining (perekvalikacija) or training in new professions.

3.   To protect for women, released from difficult work and work with dangerous conditions of labor, in accordance with this decree:

a) an uninterrupted period of work, if the interruption between the date of release from doing difficult work and work with dangerous conditions of labor and the date of starting other work or study does not exceed six months;

b) the average monthly wage at the previous place of work for the period of study or retraining, but not over six months;

c) the right to use departmental housing as well as children's preschool institutions at the previous place of work.

4. For the State Committee of the Council of Ministers of the U.S.S.R. for professional and technical education, and the ministries and departments engaged in preparation of cadres for the national economy, to cease, starting in 1978, the acceptance of women for training in the professions provided in the List indicated in item 1 of the present decree.

5.   For the ministries and departments of the U.S.S.R. and the councils of ministers of the union republics together with the central committees and republic councils of trade unions, to work out and to approve, by January 1, 1979, plans of measures for 1979-85 for the mechanization of manual work and the further improvement of the health conditions of the work of women.

6. To establish that changes in and additions to the List of production operations, occupations, and jobs with difficult and dangerous working conditions at which application of the labor of women is prohibited may be introduced by ministries, heads of departments of the U.S.S.R., and by the councils of ministers of the union republics in accord with the State Committee of the Council of Ministers of the U.S.S.R. on Labor and Social Questions, the Ministry of Health of the U.S.S.R, and the All-Union Central Council of Trade Unions.

7. Control over the fulfillment of the measures provided in the present decree shall be carried out by the State Committee of the Council of Ministers of the U.S.S.R. on Labor and Social Questions and the All-Union Central Council of Trade Unions.

8. The Central Statistical Administration of the U.S.S.R. shall supplement statistical reporting on labor with indicators of the number of women released from difficult work and work with damaging conditions by branches of industry and the national economy.

9. To repeal, in connection with the present decree, as of July 1, 1978, decisions of the Government of the U.S.S.R. in accordance with the attached List.

President of the Council
of Ministers U.S.S.R.

A. Kosygin

Moscow, April 25, 1978, No. 320.

President of the All-
Union Central Council
of Trade Unions.

A. Shibaev

The list of jobs which are considered difficult and dangerous is very long and diverse. In an appendix to Decree No. 240 of July 25, 1978, they are arranged by such categories as metalworking, construction work, mining work, well-drilling, drilling and processing of oil and gas, ferrous metallurgy, non-ferrous metallurgy, chemical production, rubber processing, paper production, cement production, stoneworking, and railroad and subway operators. Also included are certain food production workers (fish processing). Some of the prohibited activities appear excessively protective. Thus the above mentioned decree bars women from driving vehicles and buses with more than 14 seats.

There' is no comparable legislation in most of the other Eastern European countries. This reflects the fact that women were usually not called upon to perform excessively strenuous physical labor. One could compile laws concerning labor, social security and related fields which apply to men and women alike. Such a compilation would show that there are similar discrepancies with respect to the age of retirement and retirement benefits. There exists, as has

435

already been noted, extensive legislation concerning maternity leaves and job security. The tone of legislation from most of the other Eastern European countries is less protective, but the benefits are very similar.

One could also compile provisions on educational benefits. However, this book is not concerned with benefits for women but with women's rights. Not only in practice but in law as well there has been discrimination against the children whose parents have been regarded as opponents of communism. The unfair practices are easily documented but the discriminatory legal regulations are not publicized.

It might also be interesting to compare recent laws pertaining to military service.

The most recent example of this type is the following law concerning military service in the German Democratic Republic of March 25, 1982. ("Gesetz uber den Wehrdienst in der Deutschen Demokratischen Republik" *Gesetzblatt der DDR*, 1982, I, p. 221.)

The Defense Law was recently amended to extend the military obligations of women. Section 3 (1-5) now provides that "female citizens of the GDR may be included in mobilization during a state of defense from the age of 18 to the end of 50 years." Furthermore, according to Sec. 6(3) "female citizens may be drafted (erfasst) anytime for the preparation of mobilization and the state of defense."

In Yugoslavia, as in the other Eastern European countries, the Constitution of 1974 provides the basic framework for women's rights. But there are also laws concerning women's rights in the republics and autonomous provinces. As has been noted, many legal aspects are covered in the so-called Little Constitution or the *Associated Labor Act* of 1976. A complete compilation of the pertinent provisions would take up many pages. The most important provisions have been identified in the preceding analysis. The text may be found in *Constitutions of the Countries of the World*.

436

UNITED NATIONS

CONVENTION ON THE ELIMINATION
OF ALL FORMS OF
DISCRIMINATION AGAINST WOMEN

The States Parties to the present Convention,

Noting that the Charter of the United Nations reaffirms faith in fundamental human rights, in the dignity and worth of the human person and in the equal rights of men and women,

Noting that the Universal Declaration of Human Rights affirms the principle of the inadmissibility of discrimination and proclaims that all human beings are born free and equal in dignity and rights and that everyone is entitled to all the rights and freedoms set forth therein, without distinction of any kind including distinction based on sex,

Noting that States Parties to the International Covenant on Human Rights have the obligation to secure the equal rights of men and women to enjoy all economic, social, cultural, civil and political rights,

Considering the international conventions concluded under the auspices of the United Nations and the specialized agencies promoting equality of rights of men and women,

Noting also the resolutions, declarations and recommendations adopted by the United Nations and the specialized agencies promoting equality of rights of men and women,

Concerned, however, that despite these various instruments extensive discrimination against women continues to exist,

Recalling that discrimination against women violates the principles of equality of rights and respect for human dignity, is an obstacle to the participation of women, on equal terms with men, in the political, social, economic and cultural life of their countries, hampers the growth of the prosperity of society and the family, and makes more difficult the full development of the potentialities of women in the service of their countries and of humanity,

Concerned that in situations of poverty women have the least access to food, health, education, training and opportunities for employment and other needs,

Convinced that the establishment of the new international economic order based on equity and justice will contribute significantly towards the promotion of equality between men and women,

Emphasizing that the eradication of *apartheid,* of all forms of racism, racial discrimination, colonialism, neo-colonialism, aggression, foreign occupation and domination and interference in the internal affairs of States is essential to the full enjoyment of the rights of men and women,

Affirming that the strengthening of international peace and security, relaxation of international tension, mutual co-operation among all States irrespective of their social and economic systems, general and complete disarmament and in particular nuclear disarmament under strict and effective international control, the affirmation of the principles of justice, equality and mutual benefit in relations among countries, and the realization of the right of peoples under alien and colonial domination and foreign occupation to self-determination and independence as well as respect for national sovereignty and territorial integrity will promote social progress and development and as a consequence will contribute to the attainment of full equality between men and women,

Convinced that the full and complete development of a country, the welfare of the world and the cause of peace require the maximum participation of women on equal terms with men in all fields,

Bearing in mind the great contribution of women to the welfare of the family and to the development of society, so far not fully recognized, the social significance of maternity and the role of both parents in the family and in the upbringing of children, and aware that the role of women in procreation should not be a basis for discrimination but that the upbringing of children requires a sharing of responsibility between men and women and society as a whole,

Aware that a change in the traditional role of men as well as the role of women in society and in the family is needed to achieve full equality between men and women,

Determined to implement the principles set forth in the Declaration on the Elimination of Discrimination against Women and, for that purpose, to adopt the measures required for the elimination of such discrimination in all its forms and manifestations,

Have agreed on the following:

PART I
Article 1

For the purposes of the present Convention, the term "discrimination against women shall mean any distinction, exclusion or restriction made on the basis of sex which has the effect or purpose of impairing or nullifying the recognition, enjoyment or exercise by women, irrespective of their marital status, on a basis of equality of men and women, of human rights and fundamental freedoms in the political, economic, social, cultural, civil or any other field.

Article 2

States Parties condemn discrimination against women in all its forms, agree to pursue, by all appropriate means and without delay, a policy of eliminating discrimination against women and, to this end, undertake:

(a) To embody the principle of the equality of men and women in their national Constitutions or other appropriate legislation if not yet incorporated therein, and to ensure, through law and other appropriate means, the practical realization of this principle;

(b) To adopt appropriate legislative and other measures, including sanctions where appropriate, prohibiting all discrimination against women;

(c) To establish legal protection of the rights of women on an equal basis with men and to ensure through competent national tribunals and other public institutions the effective protection of women against any act of discrimination;

(d) To refrain from engaging in any act or practice of discrimination against women and to ensure that public authorities and institutions shall act in conformity with this obligation;

(e) To take all appropriate measures to eliminate discrimination against women by any person, organization or enterprise;

(f) To take all appropriate measures, including legislation, to modify or abolish existing laws, regulations, customs and practices which constitute discrimination against women;

(g) To repeal all national penal provisions which constitute discrimination against women.

Article 3

States Parties shall take in all fields, in particular in the political, social, economic and cultural fields, all appropriate measures, including legislation, to ensure the full development and advancement of women, for the purpose of guaranteeing them the exercise and enjoyment of human rights and fundamental freedoms on a basis of equality with men.

Article 4

1. Adoption by States Parties of temporary special measures aimed at accelerating *de facto* equality between men and women shall not be considered discrimination as defined in this Convention, but shall in no way entail, as a consequence, the maintenance of unequal or separate standards; these measures shall be discontinued when the objectives of equality of opportunity and treatment have been achieved.

2. Adoption by States Parties of special measures, including those measures contained in the present Convention, aimed at protecting maternity, shall not be considered discriminatory.

Article 5

States Parties shall take all appropriate measures:

(a) To modify the social and cultural patterns of conduct of men and women, with a view to achieving the elimination of prejudices and customary and all other practices which are based on the idea of the inferiority or the superiority of either of the sexes or on stereotyped roles for men and women;

(b) To ensure that family education includes a proper understanding of maternity as a social function and the recognition of the common responsibility of men and women in the upbringing and development of their children, it being understood that the interest of the children is the primordial consideration in all cases.

Article 6

States Parties shall take all appropriate measures, including legislation, to suppress all forms of traffic in women and exploitation of prostitution of women.

PART II
Article 7

States Parties shall take all appropriate measures to eliminate discrimination against women in the political and public life of the country and, in particular, shall ensure, on equal terms with men, the right:

(a) To vote in all elections and public referenda and to be eligible for election to all publicly elected bodies;

(b) To participate in the formulation of government policy and the implementation thereof and to hold public office and perform all public functions at all levels of government;

(c) To participate in non-governmental organizations and associations concerned with the public and political life of the country.

Article 8

States Parties shall take all appropriate measures to ensure to women on equal terms with men and, without any discrimination, the opportunity to represent their Governments at the international level and to participate in the work of international organizations.

Article 9

1.   States Parties shall grant women equal rights with men to acquire, change or retain their nationality. They shall ensure in particular that neither marriage to an alien nor change of nationality by the husband during marriage shall automatically change the nationality of the wife, render her stateless or force upon her the nationality of the husband.

2.   States Parties shall grant women equal rights with men with respect to the nationality of their children.

PART III
Article 10

States Parties shall take all appropriate measures to eliminate discrimination against women in order to ensure to them equal rights with men in the field of education and in particular to ensure, on a basis of equality of men and women:

(a) The same conditions for career and vocational guidance, for access to studies and for the achievement of diplomas in educational establishments of all categories in rural as well as in urban areas; this equality shall be ensured in pre-school, general, technical, professional and higher technical education, as well as in all types of vocational training;

(b) Access to the same curricula, the same examinations, teaching staff with qualifications of the same standard and school premises and equipment of the same quality;

(c) The elimination of any stereotyped concept of the roles of men and women at all levels and in all forms of education by encouraging coeducation and other types of education which will help to achieve this aim and, in particular, by the revision of textbooks and school programmes and the adaptation of teaching methods;

(d) The same opportunities to benefit from scholarships and other study grants;

(e) The same opportunities for access to programmes of continuing education, including adult and functional literacy programmes, particularly those aimed at reducing, at the earliest possible time, any gap in education existing between men and women;

(f) The reduction of female student drop-out rates and the organization of programmes for girls and women who have left school prematurely;

(g) The same opportunities to participate actively in sports and physical education;

(h) Access to specific educational information to help to ensure the health and well-being of families, including information and advice on family planning.

Article 11

1.   States Parties shall take all appropriate measures to eliminate discrimination against women in the field of employment in order to ensure, on a basis of equality of men and women, the same rights, in particular:

(a) The right to work as an inalienable right of all human beings;

(b) The right to the same employment opportunities, including the application of the same criteria for selection in matters of employment;

(c) The right to free choice of profession and employment, the right to promotion, job security and all benefits and conditions of service and the right to receive vocational training and retraining, including apprenticeships, advanced vocational training and recurrent training;

(d) The right to equal remuneration, including benefits, and to equal treatment in respect of work of equal value, as well as equality of treatment in the evaluation of the quality of work;

(e) The right to social security, particularly in cases of retirement, unemployment, sickness, invalidity and old age and other incapacity to work, as well as the right to paid leave;

(f) The right to protection of health and to safety in working conditions, including the safeguarding of the function of reproduction.

2.   In order to prevent discrimination against women on the grounds of marriage or maternity and to ensure their effective right to work, States Parties shall take appropriate measures:

(a) To prohibit, subject to the imposition of sanctions, dismissal on the grounds of pregnancy or of maternity leave and discrimination in dismissals on the basis of marital status;

(b) To introduce maternity leave with pay or with comparable social benefits without loss of former employment, seniority or social allowances;

(c) To encourage the provision of the necessary supporting social services to enable parents to combine family obligations with work responsibilities and participation in public life, in particular through promoting the establishment and development of a network of child-care facilities

(d) To provide special protection to women during pregnancy in types of work proved to be harmful to them.

3.   Protective legislation relating to matters covered in this article shall be reviewed periodically in the light of scientific and technological knowledge and shall be revised, repealed or extended as necessary.   -

Article 12

1.   States Parties shall take all appropriate measures to eliminate discrimination against women in the field of health care in order to ensure, on a basis of equality of men and women, access to health care services, including those related to family planning.

2.   Notwithstanding the provisions of paragraph 1 above, States Parties shall ensure to women appropriate services in connexion with pregnancy, confinement and the post-natal period, granting free services where necessary, as well as adequate nutrition during pregnancy and lactation.

Article 13

States Parties shall take all appropriate measures to eliminate discrimination against women in other areas of economic and social life in order to ensure, on a basis of equality of men and women, the same rights, in particular:

(a) The right to family benefits;

(b) The right to bank loans, mortgages and other forms of financial credit;

(c) The right to participate in recreational activities, sports and in all aspects of cultural life.

Article 14

1.   States Parties shall take into account the particular problems faced by rural women and the significant roles which they play in the economic survival of their families, including their work in the non-monetized sectors of the economy, and shall take all appropriate measures to ensure the application of the provisions of this Convention to women in rural areas.

2.   States Parties shall take all appropriate measures to eliminate discrimination against women in rural areas in order to ensure, on a basis of equality of men and women, that they participate in and benefit from rural development and, in particular, shall ensure to such women the right:

(a) To participate in the elaboration and implementation of development planning at all levels

(b) To have access to adequate health care facilities, including information, counselling and services in family planning;

(c) To benefit directly from social security programmes;

(d) To obtain all types of training and education, formal and non-formal, including that relating to functional literacy, as well as the benefit of all community and extension services, *inter alia*, in order to increase their technical proficiency;

(e) To organize self-help groups and co-operatives in order to obtain equal access to economic opportunities through employment or self-employment;

(f) To participate in all community activities;

(g) To have access to agricultural credit and loans, marketing facilities, appropriate technology and equal treatment in land and agrarian reform as well as in land resettlement schemes;

(h) To enjoy adequate living conditions, particularly in relation to housing, sanitation, electricity and water supply, transport and communications.

PART IV
Article 15

1.   States Parties shall accord to women equality with men before the law.

2.   States Parties shall accord to women, in civil matters, a legal capacity identical to that of men and the same opportunities to exercise that capacity. They shall in particular give women equal rights to conclude contracts and to administer property and treat them equally in all stages of procedure in courts and tribunals.

3.   States Parties agree that all contract and all other private instruments of any kind with a legal effect which is directed at restricting the legal capacity of women shall be deemed null and void.

4.   States Parties shall accord to men and women the same rights with regard to the law relating to the movement of persons and the freedom to choose their residence and domicile.

Article 16

1.   States Parties shall take all appropriate measures to eliminate discrimination against women in all matters relating to marriage and family relations and in particular shall ensure, on a basis of equality of men and women:

(a) The same right to enter into marriage;

(b) The same right freely to choose a spouse and to enter into marriage only with their free and full consent;

(c) The same rights and responsibilities during marriage and at its dissolution;

(d) The same rights and responsibilities as parents, irrespective of their marital status, in matters relating to their children. In all cases the interests of the children shall be paramount;

(e) The same rights to decide freely and responsibly on the number and spacing of their children and to have access to the information, education and means to enable them to exercise these rights;

(f) The same rights and responsibilities with regard to guardianship, wardship, trusteeship and adoption of children, or similar institutions where these concepts exist in national legislation. In all cases the interest of the children shall be paramount;

(g) The same personal rights as husband and wife, including the right to choose a family name, a profession and an occupation;

(h) The same rights for both spouses in respect of the ownership, acquisition, management, administration, enjoyment and disposition of property, whether free of charge or for a valuable consideration.

2.   The betrothal and the marriage of a child shall have no legal effect and all necessary action, including legislation, shall be taken to specify a minimum age for marriage and to make the registration of marriages in an official registry compulsory.

PART V
Article 17

1.   For the purpose of considering the progress made in the implementation of the present Convention, there shall be established a Committee on the Elimination of Discrimination against Women (hereinafter referred to as the Committee) consisting, at the time of entry into force of the Convention, of 18 and, after its ratification or accession by the thirty-fifth State Party, of 23 experts of high moral standing and competence in the field covered by the Convention. The experts shall be elected by States Parties from among their nationals and shall serve in their personal capacity, consideration being given to equitable geographical distribution and to the representation of the different forms of civilization as well as the principal legal systems.

2.   The members of the Committee shall be elected by secret ballot from a list of persons nominated by States Parties. Each State Party may nominate one person from among its own nationals.

3.   The initial election shall be held six months after the date of the entry into force of the present Convention. At least three months before the date of each election the Secretary-General of the United Nations shall address a letter to the States Parties inviting them to submit their nominations within two months. The Secretary-General shall prepare a list in alphabetical order

of all persons thus nominated, indicating the States Parties which have nominated them, and shall submit it to the States Parties.

4.   Elections of the members of the Committee shall be held at a meeting of States Parties convened by the Secretary-General at United Nations Headquarters. At that meeting, for which two thirds of the States Parties shall constitute a quorum, the persons elected to the Committee shall be those nominees who obtain the largest number of votes and an absolute majority of the votes of the representatives of States Parties present and voting.

5.   The members of the Committee shall be elected for a term of four years. However, the terms of nine of the members elected at the first election shall expire at the end of two years; immediately after the first election the names of these nine members shall be chosen by lot by the Chairman of the Committee.

6.   The election of the five additional members of the Committee shall be held in accordance with the provisions of paragraphs 2, 3 and 4 of the present article following the thirty-fifth ratification or accession. The terms of two of the additional members elected on this occasion shall expire at the end of two years, the names of these two members having been chosen by lot by the Chairman of the Committee.

7.   For the filling of casual vacancies, the State Party whose expert has ceased to function as a member of the Committee shall appoint another expert from among its nationals, subject to the approval of the Committee.

8.   The members of the Committee shall, with the approval of the General Assembly, receive emoluments from United Nations resources on such terms and conditions as the General Assembly may decide, having regard to the importance of the Committee's responsibilities.

9.   The Secretary-General of the United Nations shall provide the necessary staff and facilities for the effective performance of the functions of the Committee under the present Convention.

Article 18

1.   States Parties undertake to submit to the Secretary-General of the United Nations, for consideration by the Committee, a report on the legislative, judicial, administrative or other measures which they have adopted to give effect to the provisions of the Convention and on the progress made in this respect:

(a) Within one year after the entry into force for the State concerned;

(b) Thereafter at least every four years and further whenever the Committee so requests.

2. · Reports may indicate factors and difficulties affecting the degree of fulfilment of obligations under the present Convention.

Article 19

1.   The Committee shall adopt its own rules of procedure.

2. The Committee shall elect its officers for a term of two years.

Article 20

1. The Committee shall normally meet for a period of not more than two weeks annually in order to consider the reports submitted in accordance with article 18 of the present Convention.
2. The meetings of the Committee shall normally be held at United Nations Headquarters or at any other convenient place as determined by the Committee.

Article 21

1. The Committee shall, through the Economic and Social Council, report annually to the General Assembly on its activities and may make suggestions and general recommendations based on the examination of reports and information received from the States Parties. Such suggestions and general recommendations shall be included in the report of the Committee together with comments, if any, from States Parties.
2. The Secretary-General shall transmit the reports of the Committee to the Commission on the Status of Women for its information.

Article 22

Specialized agencies shall be entitled to be represented at the consideration of the implementation of such provisions of the present Convention as fall within the scope of their activities. The Committee may invite the specialized agencies to submit reports on the implementation of the Convention in areas falling within the scope of their activities.

PART VI
Article 23

Nothing in this Convention shall affect any provisions that are more conducive to the achievement of equality between men and women which may be contained
(a) in the legislation of a State Party; or
(b) in any other international convention, treaty or agreement in force for that State.

Article 24

States Parties undertake to adopt all necessary measures at the national level aimed at achieving the full realization of the rights recognized in the present Convention.

Article 25

1.   The present Convention shall be open for signature by all States.

2.   The Secretary-General of the United Nations is designated as the depositary of the present Convention.

3.   The present Convention is subject to ratification. Instruments of ratification shall be deposited with the Secretary-General of the United Nations.

4.   The present Convention shall be open to accession by all States. Accession shall be effected by the deposit of an instrument of accession with the Secretary-General of the United Nations.

Article 26

1.   A request for the revision of the present Convention may be made at any time by any State Party by means of a notification in writing addressed to the Secretary-General of the United Nations.

2.   The General Assembly of the United Nations shall decide upon the steps, if any, to be taken in respect of such a request.

Article 27

1.   The present Convention shall enter into force on the thirtieth day after the date of deposit with the Secretary-General of the United Nations of the twentieth instrument of ratification or accession.

2.   For each State ratifying the present Convention or acceding to it after the deposit of the twentieth instrument of ratification or accession, the Convention shall enter into force on the thirtieth day after the date of the deposit of its own instrument of ratification or accession.

Article 28

1.   The Secretary-General of the United Nations shall receive and circulate to all States the text of reservations made by States at the time of ratification or accession.

2.   A reservation incompatible with the object and purpose of the present Convention shall not be permitted.

3.   Reservations may be withdrawn at any time by notification to this effect addressed to the Secretary-General of the United Nations who shall then inform all States thereof. Such notification shall take effect on the date on which it is received.

Article 29

1.   Any dispute between two or more States Parties concerning the interpretation or application of the present Convention which is not settled by negotiation shall, at the request of one of them, be submitted to arbitration. If

within six months from the date of the request for arbitration the parties are unable to agree on the organization of the arbitration, any one of those parties may refer the dispute to the International Court of Justice by request in conformity with the Statute of the Court.

2.　　　Each State Party may at the time of signature or ratification of this Convention or accession thereto declare that it does not consider itself bound by paragraph 1 of this article. The other States Parties shall not be bound by paragraph 1 of this article with respect to any State Party which has made such a reservation.

3.　　　Any State Party which has made a reservation in accordance with paragraph 2 of this article may at any time withdraw that reservation by notification to the Secretary-General of the United Nations.

Article 30

The present Convention, the Arabic, Chinese, English, French, Russian and Spanish texts of which are equally authentic, shall be deposited with the Secretary-General of the United Nations.

IN WITNESS WHEREOF the undersigned, duly authorized, have signed the present Convention.

INTERNATIONAL LABOR ORGANIZATION

CONVENTION 156
concerning equal opportunities and equal
treatment for men and women workers
1981

The General Conference of the International Labour Organisation,

Having been convened at Geneva by the Governing Body of the International Labour Office and having met in its Sixty-seventh Session on 3 June 1981, and

Noting the Declaration of Philadelphia concerning the Aims and Purposes of the International Labour Organisation which recognises that "all human beings, irrespective of race, creed or sex, have the right to pursue their material well-being and their spiritual development in conditions of freedom and dignity, of economic security and equal opportunity", and

Noting the terms of the Declaration on Equality of Opportunity and Treatment for Women Workers and of the resolution concerning a plan of action with a view to promoting equality of opportunity and treatment for women workers, adopted by the International Labour Conference in 1975, and

Noting the provisions of international labour Conventions and Recommendations aimed at ensuring equality of opportunity and treatment for men and women workers, namely the Equal Remuneration Convention and Recommendation, 1951, the Discrimination (Employment and Occupation) Convention and Recommendation, 1958, and Part VIII of the Human Resources Development Recommendation, 1975, and

Recalling that the Discrimination (Employment and Occupation) Convention, 1958, does not expressly cover distinctions made on the basis of family responsibilities, and considering that supplementary standards are necessary in this respect, and

Noting the terms of the Employment (Women with Family Responsibilities) Recommendation, 1965, and considering the changes which have taken place since its adoption, and

Noting that instruments on equality of opportunity and treatment for men and women have also been adopted by the United Nations and other specialised agencies, and recalling, in particular, the fourteenth paragraph of the Preamble of the United Nations Convention on the Elimination of all Forms of Discrimination against Women, 1979, to the effect that States Parties are "aware that a change in the traditional role of men as well as the role of women in society and in the family is needed to achieve full equality between men and women", and

Recognising that the problems of workers with family responsibilities are aspects of wider issues regarding the family and society which should be taken into account in national policies, and

Recognising the need to create effective equality of opportunity and treatment as between men and women workers with family responsibilities and be-

449

tween such workers and other workers, and

Considering that many of the problems facing all workers are aggravated in the case of workers with family responsibilities and recognising the need to improve the conditions of the latter both by measures responding to their special needs and by measures designed to improve the conditions of workers in general, and

Having decided upon the adoption of certain proposals with regard to equal opportunities and equal treatment for men and women workers: workers with family responsibilities, which is the fifth item on the agenda of the session, and

Having determined that these proposals shall take the form of an international Convention,

adopts this twenty-third day of June of the year one thousand nine hundred and eighty-one the following Convention, which may be cited as the Workers with Family Responsibilities Convention, 1981:

Article 1

1. This Convention applies to men and women workers with responsibilities in relation to their dependent children, where such responsibilities restrict their possibilities of preparing for, entering, participating in or advancing in economic activity.

2. The provisions of this Convention shall also be applied to men and women workers with responsibilities in relation to other members of their immediate family who clearly need their care or support, where such responsibilities restrict their possibilities of preparing for, entering, participating in or advancing in economic activity.

3. For the purposes of this Convention, the terms "dependent child" and "other member of the immediate family who clearly needs care or support" mean persons defined as such in each country by one of the means referred to in Article 9 of this Convention.

4. The workers covered by virtue of paragraphs 1 and 2 of this Article are hereinafter referred to as "workers with family responsibilities"

Article 2

This Convention applies to all branches of economic activity and all categories of workers.

Article 3

1. With a view to creating effective equality of opportunity and treatment for men and women workers, each Member shall make it an aim of national policy to enable persons with family responsibilities who are engaged or wish to engage in employment to exercise their right to do so without being subject to discrimination and, to the extent possible, without conflict between their employment and family responsibilities.

2. For the purposes of paragraph 1 of this Article, the term "discrimination" means discrimination in employment and occupation as defined by Articles 1 and 5 of the Discrimination (Employment and Occupation) Convention, 1958.

Article 4

With a view to creating effective equality of opportunity and treatment for men and women workers, all measures compatible with national conditions and possibilities shall be taken—
(a) to enable workers with family responsibilities to exercise their right to free choice of employment; and
(b) to take account of their needs in terms and conditions of employment and in social security.

Article 5

All measures compatible with national conditions and possibilities shall further be taken—
(a) to take account of the needs of workers with family responsibilities in community planning; and
(b) to develop or promote community services, public or private, such as child-care and family services and facilities.

Article 6

The competent authorities and bodies in each country shall take appropriate measures to promote information and education which engender broader public understanding of the principle of equality of opportunity and treatment for men and women workers and of the problems of workers with family responsibilities, as well as a climate of opinion conducive to overcoming these problems.

Article 7

All measures compatible with national conditions and possibilities, including measures in the field of vocational guidance and training, shall be taken to enable workers with family responsibilities to become and remain integrated in the labour force, as well as to re-enter the labour force after an absence due to those responsibilities.

Article 8

Family responsibilities shall not, as such, constitute a valid reason for termination of employment.

Article 9

The provisions of this Convention may be applied by laws or regulations, collective agreements, works rules, arbitration awards, court decisions or a combination of these methods, or in any other manner consistent with national practice which may be appropriate, account being taken of national conditions.

Article 10

1. The provisions of this Convention may be applied by stages if necessary, account being taken of national conditions: Provided that such measures of implementation as are taken shall apply in any case to all the workers covered by Article 1, paragraph 1.

2. Each Member which ratifies this Convention shall indicate in the first report on the application of the Convention submitted under article 22 of the Constitution of the International Labour Organisation in what respect, if any, it intends to make use of the faculty given by paragraph 1 of this Article, and shall state in subsequent reports the extent to which effect has been given or is proposed to be given to the Convention in that respect.

Article 11

Employers' and workers' organisations shall have the right to participate, in a manner appropriate to national conditions and practice, in devising and applying measures designed to give effect to the provisions of this Convention.

Article 12

The formal ratifications of this Convention shall be communicated to the Director-General of the International Labour Office for registration.

Article 13

1. This Convention shall be binding only upon those Members of the International Labour Organisation whose ratifications have been registered with the Director-General.

2. It shall come into force twelve months after the date on which the ratifications of two Members have been registered with the Director-General.

3. Thereafter, this Convention shall come into force for any Member twelve months after the date on which its ratification has been registered.

Article 14

1. A Member which has ratified this Convention may denounce it after the expiration of ten years from the date on which the Convention first comes into force, by an act communicated to the Director-General of the International

Labour Office for registration. Such denunciation shall not take effect until one year after the date on which it is registered.

2. Each Member which has ratified this Convention and which does not, within the year following the expiration of the period of ten years mentioned in the preceding paragraph, exercise the right of denunciation provided for in this Article, will be bound for another period of ten years and, thereafter, may denounce this Convention at the expiration of each period of ten years under the terms provided for in this Article.

Article 15

1. The Director-General of the International Labour Office shall notify all Members of the International Labour Organisation of the registration of all ratifications and denunciations communicated to him by the Members of the Organisation.

2. When notifying the Members of the Organisation of the registration of the second ratification communicated to him, the Director-General shall draw the attention of the Members of the Organisation to the date upon which the Convention will come into force.

Article 16

The Director-General of the International Labour Office shall communicate to the Secretary-General of the United Nations for registration in accordance with Article 102 of the Charter of the United Nations full particulars of all ratifications and acts of denunciation registered by him in accordance with the provisions of the preceding Articles.

Article 17

At such times as it may consider necessary the Governing Body of the International Labour Office shall present to the General Conference a report on the working of this Convention and shall examine the desirability of placing on the agenda of the Conference the question of its revision in whole or in part.

Article 18

1. Should the Conference adopt a new Convention revising this Convention in whole or in part, then, unless the new Convention otherwise provides—
(a) the ratification by a Member of the new revising Convention shall *ipso jure* involve the immediate denunciation of this Convention, notwithstanding the provisions of Article 14 above, if and when the new revising Convention shall have come into force;
(b) as from the date when the new revising Convention comes into force this Convention shall cease to be open to ratification by the Members.

2. This Convention shall in any case remain in force in its actual form

and content for those Members which have ratified it but have not ratified the revising Convention.

Article 19

The English and French versions of the text of this Convention are equally authoritative.

COMMISSION
OF THE
EUROPEAN COMMUNITIES

COUNCIL DIRECTIVE 75/117/EEC
on the application of the principle of
equal pay for men and women

COUNCIL DIRECTIVE 76/207/EEC
on the implementation of the principle of
equal treatment of men and women
in the labor market

COUNCIL DIRECTIVE 77/804/EEC
on action by the European Social Fund for women

Council Directive 75/117/EEC

A.1. Council Directive of 10 February 1975 on the approximation of the laws of the Member States relating to the application of the principle of equal pay for men and women (75/117/EEC)

The Council of the European Communities

Having regard to the Treaty establishing the Euorpean Economic Community, and in particular Article 100 thereof.
Having regard to the proposal from the Commission;
Having regard to the Opinion of the European Parliament;
Having regard to the Opinion of the Economic and Social Committee;
Whereas implementation of the principle that men and women should receive equal pay contained in Article 119 of the Treaty is an integral part of the establishment and functioning of the common market;
Whereas it is primarily the responsibility of the Member States to ensure the application of this principle by means of appropriate laws, regulations and administrative provisions;
Whereas the Council resolution of 21 January 1974 concerning a social action programme, aimed at making it possible to harmonize living and working conditions while the improvement is being maintained and at achieving a balanced social and economic development of the Community, recognized that priority should be given to action taken on behalf of women as regards access to employment and vocational training and advancement, and as regards working conditions, including pay;
Whereas it is desirable to reinforce the basic laws by standards aimed at facilitating the practical application of the principle of equality in such a way that all employees in the Community can be protected in these matters;
Whereas differences continue to exist in the various Member States despite the

efforts made to apply the resolution of the conference of the Member States of 30 December 1961 on equal pay for men and women and whereas, therefore, the national provisions should be approximated as regards application of the principle of equal pay,

has adopted this directive:

Article 1—The principle of equal pay for men and women outlined in Article 119 of the Treaty, hereinafter called 'principle of equal pay', means, for the same work or for work to which equal value is attributed, the elimination of all discrimination on grounds of sex with regard to all aspects and conditions of remuneration.

In particular, where a job classification system is used for determining pay, it must be based on the same criteria for both men and women and so drawn up as to include any discrimination on grounds of sex.

Article 2—Member States shall introduce into their national legal systems such measures as are necessary to enable all employees who consider themselves wronged by failure to apply the principle of equal pay to pursue their claims by judicial process after possible recourse to other competent authorities.

Article 3—Member States shall abolish all discrimination between men and women arising from laws, regulations or administrative provisions which is contrary to the principle of equal pay.

Article 4—Member States shall take the necessary measures to ensure that provisions appearing in collective agreements, wage scales, wage agreements or individual contracts of employment which are contrary to the principle of equal pay shall be, or may be declared, null and void or may be amended.

Article 5—Member States shall take the necessary measures to protect employees against dismissal by the employer as a reaction to a complaint within the undertaking or to any legal proceedings aimed at enforcing compliance with the principle of equal pay.

Article 6—Member States shall, in accordance with their national circumstances and legal systems, take the measures necessary to ensure that the principle of equal pay is applied. They shall see that effective means are available to take care that this principle is observed.

Article 7—Member States shall take care that the provisions adopted pursuant to this Directive, together with the relevant provisions already in force, are brought to the attention of employees by all appropriate means, for example at their place of employment.

Article 8—1. Member States shall put into force the laws, regulations and administrative provisions necessary in order to comply with this Directive within one year of its notification and shall immediately inform the Commission thereof.

2. Member States shall communicate to the Commission the texts of the laws, regulations and administrative provisions which they adopt in the field covered by this Directive.

Article 9—Within two years of the expiry of the one-year period referred to in Article 8, Member States shall forward all necessary information to the Commission to enable it to draw up a report on the application of this Directive for submission to the Council.

Article 10—This Directive is addressed to the Member States.

Council Directive 76/207/EEC

A.2. Council Directive of 9 February 1976 on the implementation of the principle of equal treatment for men and women as regards access to employment, vocational training and promotion, and working conditions (76/207/EEC)

The Council of the European Communities

Having regard to the Treaty establishing the European Economic Community, and in particular Article 235 thereof,
Having regard to the proposal from the Commission,
Having regard to the opinion of the European Parliament,
Having regard to the opinion of the Economic and Social Committee,
Whereas, the Council, in its resolution of 21 January 1974 concerning a social action programme, included among the priorities action for the purpose of achieving equality between men and women as regards access to employment and vocational training and promotion and as regards working conditions, including pay;
Whereas, with regard to pay, the Council adopted on 10 February 1975 Directive 75/117/EEC on the approximation of the laws of the Member States relating to the application of the principle of equal pay for men and women;
Whereas Community action to achieve the principle of equal treatment for men and women in respect of access to employment and vocational training and promotion and in respect of other working conditions also appears to be necessary; whereas, equal treatment for male and female workers constitutes one of the objectives of the Community, in so far as the harmonization of living and working conditions while maintaining their improvement are *inter alia* to be furthered;
whereas the Treaty does not confer the necessary specific powers for this purpose;

Whereas the definition and progressive implementation of the principle of equal treatment in matters of social security should be ensured by means of subsequent instruments,

has adopted this directive:

Article 1—1. The purpose of this Directive is to put into effect in the Member States the principle of equal treatment for men and women as regards access to employment, including promotion, and to vocational training and as regards working conditions and, on the conditions referred to in paragraph 2, social security. This principle is hereinafter referred to as 'the principle of equal treatment.'

2. With a view to ensuring the progressive implementation of the principle of equal treatment in matters of social security, the Council, acting on a proposal from the Commission, will adopt provisions defining its substance, its scope and the arrangements for its application.

Article 2—1. For the purposes of the following provisions, the principle of equal treatment shall mean that there shall be no discrimination whatsoever on grounds of sex either directly or indirectly by reference in particular to marital or family status.

2. This Directive shall be without prejudice to the right of Member States to exclude from its field of application those occupational activities and, where appropriate, the training leading thereto, for which, by reason of their nature or the context in which they are carried out, the sex of the worker constitutes a determining factor.

3. This Directive shall be without prejudice to provisions concerning the protection of women, particularly as regards pregnancy and maternity.

4. This Directive shall be without prejudice to measures to promote equal opportunity for men and women, in particular by removing existing inequalities which affect women's opportunities in the areas referred to in Article 1.(1).

Article 3—1. Application of the principle of equal treatment means that there shall be no discrimination whatsoever on grounds of sex in the conditions, including selection criteria, for access to all jobs or posts, whatever the sector or branch of activity, and to all levels of the occupational hierarchy.

2. To this end, Member States shall take the measures necessary to ensure that:

a) any laws, regulations and administrative provisions contrary to the principle of equal treatment shall be abolished;

b) any provisions contrary to the principle of equal treatment which are included in collective agreements, individual contracts of employment, internal rules of undertakings or in rules governing the independent occupations and professions shall be, or may be declared, null and void or may be amended;

c) those laws, regulations and administrative provisions contrary to the principle of equal treatment when the concern for protection which originally inspired them is no longer well founded shall be revised; and that where similar provisions are included in collective agreements labour and management shall be requested to undertake the desired revision.

Article 4—Application of the principle of equal treatment with regard to access to all types and to all levels, of vocational guidance, vocational training, advanced vocational training and re-training, means that Member States shall take all necessary measures to ensure that:

a) any laws, regulations and administrative provisions contrary to the principle of equal treatment shall be abolished;

b) any provisions contrary to the principle of equal treatment which are included in collective agreements, individual contracts of employment, internal rules of undertakings or in rules governing the independent occupations and professions shall be, or may be declared, null and void or may be amended;

c) without prejudice to the freedom granted in certain Member States to certain private training establishments, vocational guidance, vocational training, advanced vocational training and retraining shall be accessible on the basis of the same criteria and at the same levels without any discrimination on grounds of sex.

Article 5—1. Application of the principle of equal treatment with regard to working conditions, including the conditions governing dismissal, means that men and women shall be guaranteed the same conditions without discrimination on grounds of sex.

2. To this end, Member States shall take the measures necessary to ensure that:

a) any laws, regulations and administrative provisions contrary to the principle of equal treatment shall be abolished;

b) any provisions contrary to the principle of equal treatment which are included in collective agreements, individual contracts of employment, internal rules of undertakings or in rules governing the independent occupations and professions shall be, or may be declared, null and void or may be amended;

c) those laws, regulations and administrative provisions contrary to the principle of equal treatment when the concern for protection which originally inspired them is no longer well founded shall be revised; and that where similar provisions are included in collective agreements labour and management shall be requested to undertake the desired revision.

Article 6—Member States shall introduce into their national legal systems such measures as are necessary to enable all persons who consider themselves wronged by failure to apply to them the principle of equal treatment within the meaning of Articles 3, 4 and 5 to pursue their claims by judicial process after possible recourse to other competent authorities.

Article 7—Member States shall take the necessary measures to protect employees against dismissal by the employer as a reaction to a complaint within the undertaking or to any legal proceedings aimed at enforcing compliance with the principle of equal treatment.

Article 8—Member States shall take care that the provisions adopted pursuant to this Directive, together with the relevant provisions already in force, are brought to the attention of employees by all appropriate means, for example at their place of employment.

Article 9—1. Member States shall put into force the laws, regulations and administrative provisions necessary in order to comply with this Directive within 30 months of its notification and shall immediately inform the Commission thereof.

However, as regards the first part of Article 3(2)(c) and the first part of Article 5(2)(c), Member States shall carry out a first examination and if necessary a first revision of the laws, regulations and administrative provisions referred to therein within four years of notification of this Directive.

2. Member States shall periodically assess the occupational activities referred

to in Article 2(2) in order to decide, in the light of social developments, whether there is justification for maintaining the exclusions concerned. They shall notify the Commission of the results of this assessment.

3. Member States shall also communicate to the Commission the texts of laws, regulations and administrative provisions which they adopt in the field covered by this Directive.

Article 10—Within two years following expiry of the 30-month period laid down in the first subparagraph of Article 9(1), Member States shall forward all necessary information to the Commission to enable it to draw up a report on the application of this Directive for submission to the Council.

Article 11—This Directive is addressed to the Member States.

Council Directive 77/804/EEC

A.3. Council Directive of 20 December 1977 on action by the European Social Fund for women (77/804/EEC)

The Council of the European Communities,

Having regard to the Treaty establishing the European Economic Community,
Having regard to Council Decision 71/66/EEC of 1 February 1971 on the reform of the European Social Fund, as amended by Council Decision 77/801/EEC, and in particular Article 4 thereof,
Having regard to the proposal from the Commission,
Having regard to the opinion of the European Parliament,
Having regard to the opinion of the Economic and Social Committee,
Whereas the Heads of State or of Government, meeting in Rome on 25 and 26 March 1977, agreed on the need to undertake action to resolve certain specific labour market problems, especially as regards the training and employment of women;
Whereas, the situation as regards women who are unemployed or seeking employment shows the need for specific joint action aimed at improving the balance between supply and demand on the Community labour market;
Whereas, in order to overcome specific obstacles to the entry or re-entry of women into working life, vocational training for women must be accompanied by complementary measures; whereas it is also essential to encourage the vocational adaptation of instructors;
Whereas the procedures of the Fund have been defined in Council Regulation (EEC) No 2396/71 of 8 November 1971 implementing the Council Decision of 1 February 1971 on the reform of the European Social Fund, as amended by Regulation (EEC) No 2893/77,

has decided as follows:

Article 1—1. Assistance may be granted from the Fund, pursuant to Article 4 of Decision 71/66/EEC, for operations to encourage the employment of women

of or over 25 years of age with no vocational qualifications or with insufficient vocational qualifications where the entry or re-entry of these persons into working life proves particularly difficult, provided that these operations are for:
— women who wish to exercise an occupation for the first time or after a long break, or
— women who have lost their employment.

Such operations must include vocational training measures in the framework of measures aimed, on the one hand, at preparing for working life or at motivating new choices of occupation and, on the other, at facilitating entry into occupations where there are job prospects.

2. Assistance may also be granted from the Fund pursuant to Article 4 of Decision 71/66/EEC for vocational adaptation operations for instructors where these persons pursue their activities in connection with the operations referred to in paragraph 1.

Article 2—The aids eligible for assistance from the Fund pursuant to this Decision shall be those laid down in Article 3(1) of Regulation (EEC) No 2396/71.

Article 3—This Decision shall be published in the *Official Journal of the European Communities* and shall enter into force on 1 January 1978.

It shall apply to operations covered by applications for assistance which have received the approval of the Commission before 1 January 1981.

A4. Council Directive of 19 December 1978 on the progressive implementation of the principle of equal treatment for men and women in matters of social security (79/7/EEC)

The Council of the European Communities

Having regard to the Treaty establishing the European Economic Community, and in particular Article 235 thereof,
Having regard to the proposal from the Commission,
Having regard to the opinion of the European Parliament,
Having regard to the opinion of the Economic and Social Committee,
Whereas Article 1 (2) of Council Directive 76/207/EEC of 9 February 1976 on the implementation of the principle of equal treatment for men and women as regards access to employment, vocational training and promotion, and working conditions provides that, with a view to ensuring the progressive implementation of the principle of equal treatment in matters of social security, the Council, acting on a proposal from the Commission, will adopt provisions defining its substance, its scope and the arrangements for its application; whereas the Treaty does not confer the specific powers required for this prupose;
Whereas the principle of equal treatment in matters of social security should be implemented in the first place in the statutory schemes which provide protection against the risks of sickness, invalidity, old age, accidents at work, occupational diseases and unemployment, and in social assistance in so far as it is intended to supplement or replace the above mentioned schemes;

461

Whereas the implementation of the principle of equal treatment in matters of social security does not prejudice the provisions relating to the protection of women on the ground of maternity; whereas, in this respect, Member States may adopt specific provisions for women to remove existing instances of in-equal treatment.

has adopted this directive:

Article 1—The purpose of this Directive is the progressive implementation in the field of social security and other elements of social protection provided for in Article 3, of the principle of equal treatment for men and women in matters of social security, hereinafter referred to as 'the principle of equal treatment'.

Article 2—This Directive shall apply to the working population—including self-employed persons, workers and self-employed persons whose activity is interrupted by illness, accident or involuntary unemployment and persons seeking employment—and to retired or invalided workers and self-employed persons.

Article 3—1. This Directive shall apply to:

a)   statutory schemes which provide protection against the following risks:
— sickness,
— invalidity,
— old age,
— accidents at work and occupational diseases,
— unemployment;

b)   social assistance, in so far as it is intended to supplement or replace the schemes referred to in (a).

2. This Directive shall not apply to the provisions concerning survivors' benefits nor to those concerning family benefits, except in the case of family benefits granted by way of increases of benefits due in respect of the risks referred to in paragraph 1 (a).

3. With a view to ensuring implementation of the principle of equal treatment in occupational schemes, the Council, acting on a proposal from the Commission, will adopt provisions defining its substances, its scope and the arrangements for its application.

Article 4—1. The principle of equal treatment means that there shall be no discrimination whatsoever on ground of sex either directly, or indirectly by reference in particular to marital or family status, in particular as concerns:
— the scope of the schemes and the conditions of access thereto.
— the obligation to contribute and the calculation of contributions,
— The calculation of benefits including increases due in respect of a spouse and for dependants and the conditions governing the duration and retention of entitlement to benefits.

2. The principle of equal treatment shall be without prejudice to the provisions relating to the protection of women on the grounds of maternity.

Article 5—Member States shall take the measures necessary to ensure that any laws, regulations and administrative provisions contrary to the principle of

462

equal treatment are abolished.

Article 6—Member States shall introduce into their national legal systems such measures as are necessary to enable all persons who consider themselves wronged by failure to apply the principle of equal treatment to pursue their claims by judicial process, possibly after recourse to other competent authorities.

Article 7—1. This Directive shall be without prejudice to the right of Member States to exclude from its scope:

a)   the determination of pensionable age for the purposes of granting old-age and retirement pensions and the possible consequences thereof for other benefits;

b)   advantages in respect of old-age pension schemes granted to persons who have brought up children; the acquisition of benefit entitlements following periods of interruption of employment due to the bringing up of children;

c)   the granting of old-age or invalidity benefit entitlements by virtue of the derived entitlements of a wife;

d)   the granting of increases of long-term invalidity, old-age, accidents at work and occupational disease benefits for a dependent wife;

e)   the consequences of the exercise, before the adoption of this Directive, of a right of option not to acquire rights or incur obligations under a statutory scheme.

2. Member States shall periodically examine matters excluded under paragraph 1 in order to ascertain, in the light of social developments in the matter concerned, whether there is justification for maintaining the exclusions concerned.

Article 8—1. Member States shall bring into force the laws, regulations and administrative provisions necessary to comply with this Directive within six years of its notification. They shall immediately inform the Commission thereof.

2. Member States shall communicate to the Commission the text of laws, regulations and administrative provisions which they adopt in the field covered by this Directive, including measures adopted pursuant to Article 7(2).

They shall inform the Commission of their reasons for maintaining any existing provisions on the matters referred to in Article 7(1) and of the possibilities for reviewing them at a later date.

Article 9—Within seven years of notification of this Directive, Member States shall forward all information necessary to the Commission to enable it to draw up a report on the application of this Directive for submission to the Council and to propose such further measures as may be required for the implementation of the principle of equal treatment.

Article 10—This Directive is addressed to the Member States.

Done at Brussels, 19 December 1978.

PARLIAMENTARY ASSEMBLY OF THE COUNCIL OF EUROPE

TWENTY-SIXTH ORDINARY SESSION
RECOMMENDATION 741 (1974)
on the legal position of women

TWENTY-SEVENTH ORDINARY SESSION
RECOMMENDATION 606 (1975)
on the political rights and
position of women

Recommendation 741

The Assembly,

1.   Considering that Resolution 3010 (XXVII) of the General Assembly of the United Nations proclaimed 1975 "International Women's Year";

2.   Recalling its Recommendation 504 (1967) on the political, social and civic position of women in Europe;

3.   Welcoming the existence, in domestic and international law, of rules prohibiting discrimination on the basis of sex, in particular Article 14 of the European Convention on Human Rights;

4.   Noting, however, that discrimination based on sex still subsists in certain aspects of our societies, and that, while it is often based on psychological, social and economic factors, it is also sanctioned by many legal provisions;

5.   Considering that questions relative to the implementation of the principle of non-discrimination in such fields as the nationality of married women and of children of mixed marriages, family law, social security for non-gainfully employed women and labour law must be solved at European level;

6.   Welcoming the numerous initiatives and projects for reform which have been undertaken in these fields by the Council of Europe and its member states, and by the European Communities;

7.   Noting with satisfaction that the theme selected for the 14th Conference of European Ministers responsible for Family Affairs to be held in 1975, is "The equality of man and woman; its implications for family life and governmental action";

8.   Stressing at the same time the importance it attaches to having these various projects and initiatives implemented with maximum efficiency and co-ordination;

9.   Recalling, in respect of the nationality of married women and of children of mixed marriages, the solutions advocated in Recommendations 519 (1968), on the nationality of married women, and 696 (1973), on certain aspects of the acquisition of nationality;

10.   Considering, in respect of parental law, that both parents must have equal rights and obligations towards their under-age children, and that they must exercise these rights and perform their obligations jointly and exclusively in the interests of the child;

464

11.   Recalling, with regard to social security for non-gainfully-employed women, that work in the home must be considered as an economic activity giving immediate entitlement to social security benefits;

12.   Considering that much has still to be done to implement the principle of equal pay for men and women, not only for equal work but also for work of equal value;

13.   Recalling also that the provisions intended to protect the special needs of women or abolish discrimination relative thereto must not result in discrimination against men,

14.   Recommends that the Committee of Ministers of the Council of Europe:

i. invite the member states which have not yet done so to sign and ratify the international conventions containing provisions prohibiting discrimination based on sex, in particular:

— the 1957 United Nations Convention on the Nationality of Married Women, and

— the European Social Charter;

ii. pursue with determination the various activities relative to the position of women which are included in the Work Programme 1973-74 and in the draft Work Proggramme 1975-76, and see to it that the aim is achieved with efficacity and co-ordination;

iii. see to it that the various legislative reforms planned in the member states are based on common principles and lead to substantial harmonisation of legislation;

iv. bear the principle of non-discrimination in mind when asked to adopt the draft recommendation on social security for non-gainfully-employed women, which is not being prepared by the Committee of Experts on Social Security;

v. study, when the time comes, the possibility of extending to all member states of the Council of Europe the provisions of the Community directive now being drafted on harmonisation of the legislations of the member states on application of the principle of equality of remuneration for men and women workers.

Recommendation 606

The Assembly,

1.   Considering that 1975 has been proclaimed "International Women's Year" by the General Assembly of the United Nations;

2.   Recalling Recommendation 741 (1974), on the legal position of women, and Recommendation 751 (1975), on the position and responsibility of parents in the modern family and their support by society;

3.   Considering that the solution of problems affecting women is in the interest of society as a whole, and that women's liberation is truly the liberation of all people;

4.   Considering that reasons other than strictly legal ones, such as traditional ways of thinking and existing socio-economic structures, still are obstacles which prevent women from taking up a number of posts in political bodies,

including national parliaments, corresponding to the number of women in the community;

5.   Convinced that an increased participation of women in political life at all levels will undoubtedly allow politicians of both sexes to gain a more thorough and objective understanding of all the problems with which modern democratic societies are confronted;

6.   Considering that discrimination against women can be eradicated only by means of special efforts in education and increased public expenditure for social reforms, particularly in the fields of health services, professional training and baby-care facilities;

7.   Concerned that in 1975, as in all periods of economic difficulties, women are the first victims of recession,

8.   i. Shares the three objectives of International Women's Year—equality, development, peace—convinced as it is that only through equality can development and peace be ensured;

    ii. Supports all policies and programmes designed to combat sexual discrimination undertaken by the United Nations, the Council of Europe, EEC and the eighteen member states, whether in conjunction with International Women's Year or not;

    iii. Urges political parties in the member states of the Council of Europe to encourage women to take a more active part in political life, to make more room for women in party executives and definitely to select more women as candidates to public offices and to support actively their election;

    iv. Urges the governments of the member states to take appropriate steps to ensure a wider participation of women in appointed bodies, the individual's intellectual and professional qualifications being the only prerequisite for such appointments;

    v. Urges the parliaments of the member states to recognise the talents of all their members, irrespective of sex, when forming their delegations to the Parliamentary Assembly;

    vi. Urges the Committee of Ministers and the Secretary General of the Council of Europe to see to it that internal regulations and practice concerning staff do not result in discrimination on the grounds of sex, including unintentional discrimination.

COUNCIL OF EUROPE

EUROPEAN SOCIAL CHARTER
European Treaty Series No. 35
September 1978

Introductory Note: The European Social Charter, which was signed in Turin On October 18, 1961, established a broad legal framework for the development of social rights and policies of the member states of the Council of Europe.

It states in its preamble that "the enjoyment of social rights should be secured without discrimination on grounds of race, color, sex, religion, political opinion, national extraction and social origin."

The excerpts which follow are those which contribute most significantly to the establishment of gender equality in the labor market.

G.H.F.

ARTICLE 4
THE RIGHT TO A FAIR REMUNERATION

With a view to ensuring the effective exercise of the right to a fair remuneration, the Contracting Parties undertake:

1. to recognise the right of workers to a remuneration such as will give them and their families a decent standard of living;
2. to recognise the right of workers to an increased rate of remuneration for overtime work, subject to exceptions in particular cases;
3. to recognise the right of men and women workers to equal pay for work of equal value;
4. to recognise the right of all workers to a reasonable period of notice for termination of employment;
5. to permit deductions from wages only under conditions and to the extent prescribed by national laws or regulations or fixed by collective agreements or arbitration awards.

The exercise of these rights shall be achieved by freely concluded collective agreements, by statutory wage-fixing machinery, or by other means appropriate to national conditions.

. . . .

ARTICLE 8
THE RIGHT OF EMPLOYED WOMEN TO PROTECTION

With a view to ensuring the effective exercise of the right of employed women to protection, the Contracting Parties undertake:

1. to provide either by paid leave, by adequate social security benefits or by benefits from public funds for women to take leave before and after childbirth up to a total of at least 12 weeks;

2. to consider it as unlawful for an employer to give a woman notice of dismissal during her absence on maternity leave or to to give her notice of dismissal at such a time that the notice would expire during such absence;

3. to provide that mothers who are nursing their infants shall be entitled to sufficient time off for this purpose;

4. (a) to regulate the employment of women workers on night work in industrial employment;

(b) to prohibit the employment of women workers in underground mining, and, as appropriate, on all other work which is unsuitable for them by reason of its dangerous, unhealthy, or arduous nature.

. . . .

Selective Bibliography

Compiled by Blanka Kudej

Selective Bibliography

Books and articles are listed here under four categories: General and historical studies; Comparative Studies; Studies and reports of international organizations or with international scope; and Studies on individual countries, listed alphabetically by country. In each category, works are grouped as either English-language or other-language publications.

GENERAL AND HISTORICAL STUDIES

A) Books and articles in English

Bernard, Jessie Shirley. *The female world*. New York: Free Press, c 1981.

Bokorne-Szego, H. "Influence of social development on treaties relating to the rights of women". (Summ. in French & Russian). 18 *Acta Juridica Academiae Scientiarium Hungaricae* (Hun.), 315-340, 1976.

Branca, Patricia. *Women in Europe since 1750*. New York, N.Y., Saint Martin's Press, 1978.

Bridenthal, Renate & Koonz, Claudia (editors), *Becoming visible: Women in European history*. Boston, Mass., Houghton Mifflin, 1977.

Daube, David. "Biblical landmarks in the struggle for women's rights". *Juridical Review* 177-197, 1978.

European Women: *A documentary history, 1789-1945*. Ed. by Eleanor S. Riemer and John C. Fout. New York: Schocken Books, 1980.

Gelber, S.M. "Social Security and Women: A partisan view". 112 *International Labour Review* (Swi), 431-444, 1975.

Gies, Frances. *Women in the Middle Ages*. New York, Crowell, 1978.

Hamilton, Roberta. *The liberation of women: A study of patriarchy and capitalism*. London/Boston: G. Allen & Unwin, 1978.

Hammond, Dorothy. *Women in cultures of the world*. Menlo Park, California, Cummings Pub., Co., 1976.

Janjic, M. "Diversifying women's employment: The only road to genuine equality of opportunity." 120 *International Labour Review* (Swi) 149-163, 1981.

Khushalami, Yougindra. *Dignity and Honour of Women as Basic and Fundamental Human Rights*. Hague, The Netherlands, M. Nijhoff, 1982.

Morgenstern, F. "Women workers and the courts". 112 *International Labour Review* (Swi), 15-27, 1975.

Newland, Kathleen. *The sisterhood of man*. New York: Norton, 1979.

Power, Eileen Edna. *Medieval Women*. Cambridge (England), New York, Cambridge University Press, 1975.

Raming, Ida. *The exclusion of women from priesthood: Divine law or sex discrimination? A historical investigation of the juridical and doctrinal foundations of the code of canon law*, Canon § 968.1, Metuchen, N.J. : Scarecrow Press, 1976.

Reed, Evelyn. *Woman's evolution from matriarchal clan to patriarchal family*. New York, Pathfinder Press, 1975.

Rowbotham, Sheila. *Hidden from history; 300 years of women's oppression and the fight against it.* London, Pluto Press, 1973.

Rowbotham, Sheila. *Women, resistance and revolution, a history of women and revolution in the modern world.* New York, Pantheon Books, 1972.

Rowbotham, Sheila. *Women's liberation & the new politics.* Nottingham, Bertrand Russell Peace Foundation, 1971.

Shelton, D.L. "Women and the right to education". 8 *Revue des droits del'homme (Human Rights Journal)* (Fra) 51-70, 1975.

Socialist women: European Socialist feminism in the nineteenth and early twentieth centuries. Ed. by Marilyn J. Boxer & Jean H. Quataert. New York: Elsevier North-Holland, 1978.

Unesco. *Unequal opportunities: The case of Women and the Media.* Paris, UNESCO, 1981.

Women, Power and Political Systems. Edited by Margherita Rendel. New York, St. Martin's Press, Inc., c 1981.

B)   Books and articles in other languages

Bensadon, Ney. *Les droits de la femme des origines à nos jours.* Paris, Presses Universitaires de France, 1980.

Berenstein, A. Egalité des sexes en droit du travail. 17 *Rivista di Diritto Internationale e Comparato del Lavoro* (Ita), 3-30, 1977.

Charzat, Gisèle. *Femmes, violence, pouvoir.* Paris, J.C. Simoën, c 1979.

Dessai, Elizabeth. *Hat der Mann versagt? Streitschrift für eine weltsichere Gesellschaft.* Ungekürzte Ausg., Reinbek bei Hamburg: Rowohlt, 1972.

Engels, W. "Problematiek rond de vrijmaking van de vrouw". 37 *Rechtskunding Weekblad* (Bel), 785-800, 1973.

Frick, Inge, et al. *Frauen befreien sich: Bilder zur Geschichte d. Frauenarbeit u. Frauenbewegung/.* Munchen: Frauenbuchverlag, 1976.

Hanquet, Huberte. *Travail professionel des femmes et mutations sociales.* Bruxelles, Editions Vie Ouvriere, 1972.

Klole jomfruers ?: Om kirke, kristendom og kvinnernfrigjoring. Oslo: H. Aschehoug (W. Nygaard), 1978.

Kunstmann, Antje. *Frauenbefreiung- Privileg einer Klasse ?* Starnberg, Raith, 1971.

May, G. "Zu der Frage der Weihefähigkeit der Frau". 91 *Zeit - schrift der Savigny - Stiftung für Rechtsgeschichte, Romanistische Abteitung* (Ger), 375-393, 1974.

Piettre, Monique A. *La condition feminine à travers les âges.* Paris, Editions France- Empire, 1974.

COMPARATIVE STUDIES

A) Books and articles in English

Allendorf, Marlies. *Women in Socialist Society/* English version by Ruth Michaelis- Jena and Patrick Murrary. Leipzig, East Germany, London, England, distributed by G. Prior, 1976.

Berent, Jerzy. "Some demographic aspects of female employment in Eastern Europe and the USSR".101 *International Labour Review* (Swi), 175-192, 1970.

Bouten, Jacob. *Mary Wollstonecraft and the beginnings of female emancipation in France and England.* Philadelphia: Porcupine Pess, 1975.

Chao, Paul. *Women under Communism: Family in Russia and China.* Bayside, New York: General Hall, 1977.

Conference on Women in Eastern Europe and the Soviet Union, University of Alberta, 1978. New York, Praeger, 1980.

European Population Seminar, 2d, Hague and Brussels, 1976. *Demographic Aspects of the changing status of women in Europe.* Edited by Marry Niphuis-Nell. Leiden: Boston, Martinus Nijhoff Social Science Division.

Galenson, Marjorie. *Women and work, an international comparison.* N.Y., State School of Industrial and Labor Relations, Cornell University, 1973.

Haavio- Manila, Elina. "Convergences between East and West; tradition and modernity in sex roles in Sweden, Finland and the Soviet Union". 14 *Acta Sociologica* (Den) 114-125, 1971.

Heitlinger, Alena. *Women and state socialism: Sex, inequality in the Soviet Union and Czechoslovakia.* London, Macmillan Press, 1979.

Jancar, Barbara Wolfe. *Women under Communism.* Baltimore: John Hopkins University Press, 1978.

Jenness, Linda (comp). *Feminism and socialism.* New York, Pathfinder Press, 1975, c 1972.

Leijon, A.G. "Sexual equality in the labor market. Some experiences and views of the Nordic countries". 112 *International Labour Review* (Swi) 109-123, 1975.

Mies, Maria. "Class struggle or emancipation? Women's emancipation movements in Europe and the U.S." 8 *Economic and Political Weekly* (Bombay), 2221-2230, 1973.

Paoli, Chantal. "Women workers and maternity: Some examples from Western Europe". 121 *International Labour Review* (Swi) 1-16, 1982.

Quataert, Jean H. *Reluctant feminists in German social democracy, 1885-1917.* Princeton, New Jersey, Princeton University Press, 1979.

Sachs, Albert Louis. *Sexism and the law: A study of male beliefs and legal bias in Britain and the United States.* Albert Sachs & Joan Hoff Wilson. Oxford [England]: M. Robertson, 1978.

Scott, Hilda. *Does socialism liberate women? Experiences from Eastern Europe.* Boston, Beacon Press, 1974.

Shaffer, Harry G. *Women in the two Germanies; a comparative study in a*

473

socialist and non- socialist society. Elmsford, New York, Pergamon Press, 1981.

Small, Rosemary. *Women: The road to equality and socialism.* London, Communist Party of Great Britain, 1972.

Socialist women: European Socialist feminism in the 19th and early twentieth centuries. Ed. by Marilyn J. Boxer & Jean H. Quataert. New York: Elsevier North-Holland, 1978.

Thompson, Roger. *Women in Stuart England and America.* London, Boston, Routledge and K. Paul, 1974.

Tilly, Louise. *Women, work and family.* New York: Holt, Rinehart and Winston, 1978.

Weinbaum, Batya. *The curious courtship of women's liberation and socialism.* Boston, MA, South End Press, c 1978.

Wilson, Elizabeth. *Women and the welfare state.* London: Tavistock Publications, 1977.

Women in the world: A comparative study. Lynn B. Iglitzin, Ruth Ross, editors. Santa Barbara, California: Clio Books, c 1976.

B) Books and articles in other languages

Arbeiterinnen kämpfen um ihr Recht: Autobiographische Texte zum Kampf rechtloser und entrechterer "Frauenspersonen" in Deutschland, Ostereich und Schweiz d. 19 u. 20. Wuppertal: Hammer, 1975.

Bensandon, Ney. *Les droits de la femme: des origines a nos jours.* Paris, Presses Universitaires de France, c 1980.

Camparini, Aurelia. *Questione femminile e Terza Internazionale.* Bari: De Donato, 1978.

Dahlerup, Drude. *Socialisme og kvindefrigrelse i det 19. arhundere-de.* En analyse af Charles Fourier, Karl Marx, Fr. Engels, August Bebel og Clara Zetkin, m.fl. Kobenhavn Folaget GMTM, 1973.

Diglio, C. "Condizione della donna del lavoro subordinato in Francia e in Italia". 36 *Diritto e Giurisprudencia* (Ita) 1-22, 1980.

Eberhardt, K.H. "Gondolatok a szocialista jog hatékonyságának noveléséröl a nö további felszabaditasában". 29 *Jogtudomanyi Kozlony* (Hun) 209-214, 1974.

Halgash, R. "Familienrechtsprinzipien und die Regelung der ehelichen Vermögensbeziehungen in den Familienrechtsordnungen socialistischer Staaten". 27 *Neue Juztiz* (Ger. E.) 201-205, 1973.

Kuhrig. H. "Gleichberechtigung von Mann und Frau-unveräusserliches Prinzip der sozialistischen Gesellschaft". 29 *Neue Juztiz* (Ger.E.) 527-532, 1975.

Merfeld, Mechthild. *Die Emanzipation der Frau-in der sozialistischen Theorie und Praxis.* Reinbek bei Hamburg, Rowohlt, 1972.

Meulenbelt, Anja. *Feminisme en socialisme: een inleiding.* Amsterdam: Van Gennep, 1976.

Outshoorn, Joyce. *Vrouwenemancipatie en socialisme. Een onderzoek naar de* houding van de SDAP ten opzichte van hit vrouwenvraa gstuk tussen 1894 en 1919. Nijmegen, Socialistische Uitgeveeij Nijmegen, 1973.

Randzio-Plath, Christa. *Europa eine Chance fur Frauen: der Kampf um die Gleichstellung ist nicht verloren.* Baden-Baden: Nomos-Verlagsgesellschaft, 1978.

Tolkunova, V.N. "Okhrana truda zhenschin v evropeískikh sotsialisticheskikh stranakh". 44 *Sovetskoe Gosudarstvo i Pravo* No. 3: 96-101, 1974.

Wassner-Blum, Gaby- Sophie. *Die Mitarbeit der Ehefrau in Deutschland, Frankreich und der Schweiz.* Bern, Frankfurt, 1976.

STUDIES AND REPORTS OF INTERNATIONAL ORGANIZATIONS OR WITH INTERNATIONAL SCOPE.

A) In English

Boals, K. "Women's transnational privileges and disabilities". 69 *American Society of International Law, Proceedings* 107-113, 1975.

Byrne, Eileen M. *Equality of education and training for girls (10-18).* Commission of the European Communities, Collection Studies, Education Series No. 9, Brussels, July 1978.

Burrows, N. "Promotion of women's rights by the European Economic Community". 17 *Common Market Law Review* (U.K.) 191-209, 1980.

Commission of the European Communities. *A new Community Action Programme on the promotion of equal opportunities for women, 1982-85.* Supplement 1 1982, to the Bulletin of European Communities, 1982.

Commission of the European Communities. *Equality of treatment between men and women workers.* Communication of the Commission to the Council. Brussels: Commission of the European Communities, 1975.

Commission of the European Communities. *European Women in Paid Employment, their perception of discrimination at work.* Brussels, Commission of the European Communities, 1980.

Commission of the European Communities. *Men and women of Europe. Comparative attitudes to a number of problems of our society.* Brussels: Commission of the European Communities, 1975.

Commission of the European Communities. *Report of the Commission to the Council on the application as of 12 February 1978 of the principle of equal pay for men and women.* Brussels: Commission of the European Communities, 1978.

Commission of the European Communities. *Report of the Commission to the Council on the application of the Principle of equal pay for men and women, situation on the 31 December 1972.* Brussels: Commission of the European Communities, 1973.

Commission of the European Communities. *Report of the Commission to the Council on the application of the principle of equal pay for men and women in Denmark, Ireland and the United Kingdom situation on the 31 December, 1973.* Brussels: Commission of the European Communities, 1974.

Commission of the European Communities. *The European Community and work for women.* Brussels: Commission of the European Communities, 1977.

Commission of the European Communities. *Vocational Guidance and training for women workers. European Seminar 24-25 November 1975, Paris.* Luxembourg: Commission of the European Communities, 1976.

Commission of the European Communities. *Women of Europe.* No. 1- 1980—. Published bi-monthly by the Commission of the European Communities.

Commission of the European Communities. *Women of Europe: Equal Opportunities* (Supplement # 9) Commission of the European Communities, 1981.

Commission of the European Communities. *Women of Europe : European*

Women in Paid Employment. (Suppl. # 5). Brussels. Commission of the European Communities, 1980.

Commission of the European Communities: Women of Europe: Women and Men of Europe in 1978 (Supplement # 3). Brussels, Commission of the European Communities, 1980.

Commission of the European Communities. Women of Europe: Women and the European Social Fund. (Supplement # 6). Brussels. Commission of the European Communities, 1981.

Commission of the European Communities. Women of Europe: Women at work in the European Community, 50 questions, 50 answers. (Supplement # 7). Brussels. Commission of the European Communities, 1981.

Commission of the European Communities. Women of Europe: Women in the European Parliament. (Supplement # 4). Brussels, Commission of the European Communities, 1980.

Cornu, Robert B. Women and employment in the United Kingdom, Ireland and Denmark. Brussels: Commission of the European Communities, 1974.

Council of Europe. Directorate of Information. Council of Europe activities to further women's interests. Strasbourg, Directorate of Press and Information, Council of Europe, 1975.

European Trade Union Confederation. Women at work. White paper on working women in Europe. Brussels: European Trade Union Confederation, 1976.

Food and Agriculture Organization of the United Nations. European Commission of Agriculture. The changing role of women in European agriculture. Rome, Food and Agriculture Organization, 1972.

Guggenheim, M.H. "Implementation of human rights by the U.N. Commission on the status of women: A brief comment". 12 Texas International Law Journal 239-249, 1977.

Haimbaugh, G.D., et al. International women's year: Focus on transnational needs and initiatives for women". 69 American Society of International Law, Proceedings 1-39, 1975.

Hosken, Fran P. "Toward a definition of women's rights". 3 Human Rights Quarterly, 1- , 1981.

International Labor Office. Employment of women with family responsibilities: Summary of reports on recommendation # 123 (article 19 of the constitution). Geneva: International Labour Office, 1978.

International Labor Office. Equality of Opportunity and Treatment for women workers: eighth item on the agenda. Geneva: International Labour Office, 1974.

International Labor Office. General Survey of the reports relating to the employment (women with family responsibilities) recommendation, 1968 (no. 123): Report of Conventions and Recommendations (articles 19, 22 and 35 of the constitution). Volume B. International Labour Office, Geneva: The Office, 1978.

Ireland, P. "International advancement and protection of human rights for women". 10 Lawyer of the Americas 87-98, 1978.

McCallum, I.M. & I. Snaith. "EEC law and United Kingdom occupational pen-

477

sions schemes". 2 *European Law Review* (UK) 266-273, 1977.

McDougal, M.S. & et al. "Human Rights for women and world public order: The outlawing of sex-based discrimination". 69 *American Journal of International Law* 497-533, 1975.

Organization for Economic Cooperation and Development. *Women and Employment.* Paris, Organization for Economic Cooperation and Development, 1980.

OECD Working Party on the role of Women in the economy. Equal opportunities for women. Paris, Organization for Economic Co-operation and Development (Washington, D.C.: sold by OECD Publication and Information Center, 1979).

Paoli, Chantal. "Women workers and maternity: Some examples from Western Europe". *121 International Labour Review* (Swi) 1-16, 1982.

Polson, T.E. "Rights of working women: An international perspective". 14 *Virginia Journal of International Law* 729-746, 1974.

Rabier, Jacques Rene. *European men and women in 1978: A comparative study of socio-political attitudes in the European community.* Brussels. Commission of the European Communities, 1979.

Rabier, Jacques Rene. *European men and women: May 1975.* Principal investigators, Jacques-Rene Rabier, Ronald Inglehart. 1st ICPSR ed., Ann Arbor, Michigan: Inter-University Consortium for Political and Social Research, 1979.

Reanda, Laura. "Human Rights and Women's Rights: The United Nations Approach". 3 *Human Rights Quarterly,* No. 2:11- , 1981.

Ricafrente, C.L.S. "International labor standards for working women". 50 *Philippine Law Journal* (Phi) 55-79, 1975.

Sullerot, E. "Equality of remuneration for men and women in the member states of the E.E.C.". 112 *International Labour Review* (Swi) 87-108, 1975.

Thomson, V.M. & F. Wooldridge. "Equal pay, sex discrimination and European community law". *Legal Issues of European Integration* (Net), No. 2:1-45, 1980.

Tinker, Catherine. "Human Rights for Women: The U.N. Convention on the elimination of all forms of discrimination against women". 3 *Human Rights Quarterly,* No. 2, : 32- , 1981.

United Nations. General Assembly. *Equal Rights for women, a call for action: The United Nations declaration on the elimination of discrimination against women.* New York: United Nations Office of Public Information, 1975.

United Nations. *Reports of the World Conference of the United Nations Decade for Women: Equality Development and Peace.* Conference Background papers. (Copenhagen, 14- 30, July 1980). New York, United Nations, 1980. Docs. Nos. A/Conf. 94/BP. . . .

United Nations. Secretary General, 1961 - (Thant). *United Nations assistance for the advancement of women; report of the Secretary General.* New York: United Nations, 1967. Doc. No. E/CN.6/467.

U.S. Women's Bureau. *Political rights of women in member nations of the United Nations.* Washington, Government Printing Office, 1963.

Woman and the law: Round Table Conference. Achieving for women full equality before the law/ edited by Yolanda Q. Tavellana. Quezon City, Philippines: U.P. Law Center, 1975. Reprinted from Philippine Law Journal, Vol. 50, No. 1, February, 1975. Jointly sponsored by the Federacion International de Abogados and the U.P. Law Center at the Malcolm Hall, U.P. Diliman, on March 1, 8, and 15, 1975.

B) In other languages

Annoussamy, D. "Jurisprudence internationale en matière de travail feminin". *Droit Social* (Fra) 42-50, 1976.

Commissie van de Europese Gemeenschappen. *De vrouwenarbeid en de daarmede verbonden problematiek in de lid-staten van de Europese Gemeenschap.* Brussels: Commissie van de Europese Gemeenschappen, 1970.

Commissione della Comunita Europea. *L'occupazione delle donne i suoi problemi negli stati membri della Comunita Europea.* Bruxelles: Commissione della Comunita Europea, 1970.

Communautés Européennes. Commission. *L' emploi des femmes et ses problèmes dans les Etat membres de la Communaute; abrégé du rapport de E. Sullerot.* Luxembourg, Communautés Européennes, 1971?

Cristini, R. "Jurisprudence sur l'égalité des sexes dans la fonction publique internationale". 19 *Annuaire Francais de Droit International* (Fra) 505-527, 1973.

Degeller, Lies. *De arbeidsomstandigheden en voorwaarden van vrouwen in Loondienst in de zes lid-staten van de Europese Gemeenschap,* Nederland. Brussels: Commissie van de Europese Gemeenschappen, 1972.

Dmitrieva, G.K. "Mezhdunarodnyi god zhenschin [Summ. in English]". 45 *Sovetskoe Gosudarstovo i Pravo* (USSR) No. 3:3-10, 1975.

Dmitrieva, G.K. "O mezhdunarodnoi zashite prav zhenshchin". 19 *Pravovedenie* (USSR) No. 6:7-13, 1975.

Federici, Nora. *Le condizione di Lavoro delle donne salariate nei sei stati membri della Comunita Europea, Italia.* Con la collaborazione di Carla Bielli e Antonella Pinnelli. Bruxelles: Commissione della Comunita Europea, 1972.

Frandsen, Dorothea & Daldrup, Ursula. *Frauenfragen in internationalen Organisationen.* [Hannover] Niedersächsische Landeszentrale für Politische Bildung, 1970.

Kommission der Europäischen Germeinschaften. *Die Erwerbstätigkeit der Frauen und ihre Probleme in den Mitgliedstaaten der Europaischen Gemeinschaft.* Brüssel: Kommission der Europäischen Gemeinschaften, 1970.

Lulling, Astrid. *Les conditions de travail des femmes salariées dans les six Etats membres de la Communauté Européenne, Grand-Duché de Luxembourg.* Bruxelles. Commission des Communautés Europeennés, 1972.

Mrŭchkov, V. "Mezhdunarodnopravna zashita na truda na zhenata". 19 *Pravna Misul* (Bul) No. 3:29-44, 1975.

Podbierowa, Eugenia. *Pozycja kobiet w dokumentach prawa miedzynarodowego.* Poznan, UAM, 1975.

Pross, Helge. *Die Arbeitsbedingungen der erwerbstätigen Frauen der sechs Mitgliedstaaten der Europaischen Gemeinschaft, Deutschland.* Brüssel: Kommission der Europäischen Gemeinschaften, 1972.

Pross, Helge. *Gleichberechtigung im Beruf.* Eine Untersuchung mit 7000 Arbeitnehmerinen in der EWG. Frankfurt, M. Athenäum, 1973.

Sgrosso, Catalano G. "Principio della parità di trattamento tra lavoratrice e lavoratrici del diritto comunitario". 19 *Rivista di Diritto Europeo* (Ita) 245-259, 1979.

Shibaeva, E.A. "Mezhdunarodnyi god zhenschiny". 30 *Vestnik Moskovskogo Universiteta, Seriia Pravo* (USSR) 6:3-7, 1975.

Sipilä, H. "Über die Tätigkeit der Vereinten Nationen zur Förderung der Gleichberechtigung der Geschlechter-das internationale Jahr der Frau. 73 *Lakimies* (Fin) 763-773, 1975.

Strážnická, V. & Z. Valentovič. K niektorym otázkám medzinarodnoprávnej ochrany žien. [Summ. In Russian & English]. 58 *Právný Obzor* 881-895, 1975.

Sullerot, Evelyn. *L'emploi des femmes et ses problèmes dans les Etats membres de la Communauté Européenne.* Bruxelles. Commission des Communautes Europeennes, 1970.

Sullerot, Evelyn. *Les conditions de travail des femmes dans les six Etats Membres de la Communauté Européenne, France.* Bruxelles, Commission des Communautés Européennes, 1972.

Tomšič V. "United Nations and the Status of Women". [In Serbo-Croatian, Summary in English]. 23 *Jugoslovenska Revija za Medunarodno Pravo* 31-46, 1976.

Traikova, L.D. "Mezhdunarodnopravni aktove v zashtita na pravata na zhenite" 22 *Pravina Misal,* (Bul) 6:86-94, 1978.

Vogel-Polsky, Eliane. *Les conditions de travail des femmes' salarieés dans les six Etats Membres de la Communauté Européenne, Belgique.* Bruxelles, Commission des Communautés Européennes, 1972.

STUDIES BY COUNTRY

ALBANIA

A) Books and articles in English

An Outline of the People's Socialist Republic of Albania, Tirana: The "8 Nentori" Publishing House, 1978.

Bardhoshi, Besim and Kareco, Theodor. *The Economic and Social Development of the People's Republic of Albania During Thirty Years of People's Power.* Tirana, Albania, "8 Nentori" Publishing House, 1974.

Constitution of the People's Republic of Albania, Tirana: The "8 Nentori" Publishing House, 1977.

Hoxha, Enver. *Speeches, 1967-1968,* Tirana: The "8 Nentori" Publishing House, 1969.

Hoxha, Enver. *Speeches, 1971-1973,* Tirana: The "8 Nentori" Publishing House, 1974.

Hoxha, Enver and Ramiz Alia. *On some aspects of the problem of the Albanian woman; speeches delivered at the 2nd Plenum of the CC of the Party of Labor of Albania on June 15, 1967.* Tirana, Naim Frasheri Pub. House, 1967. 105 pp.

Leka, Laudie. "The Revolutionary Road to Emancipation of the Women in Albania". 53 *Albania Today* (Al) 22-27, 1980,

Logoreci, Anton. *The Albanians.* London, England, Victor Gollanz, Ltd., 1977.

The 8th Congress of the Women's Union of Albania, Tirana: The "8 Nentori" Publishing House, 1978.

Tirana, State University of. *Problems of the Struggle for the Complete Emancipation of Women.* Tirana, Albania, Political Book Publishing House, 1973.

B) Books and articles in other languages

Begaja, Ksanthipi. *Les Droits et le role des femmes dans la Republique Populaire d'Albanie.* Tirana: Naim Frasheri, 1967.

Hoxha, Enver. *L'emancipation de la femme Albanese, grande victoire de la Revolution Socialiste.* Tirana: Editiones "8 Nentori", 1978.

Miske, Annick. *Des Albanaises.* Paris, France, Editions des femmes, 1976.

Naddeo, I. "Femme et politique en Albanie". *Revue française d'Etudes Politiques Méditerranéenes,* vol. 24, 50-64, 1976.

AUSTRIA

A)Books and articles in English

Bundeskanzleramt. *U.N. Decade for Women 1976-1985. Mid-Decade 1980, Re-*

view and Evaluation of Progress. Wien, Osterreichische Staatsdruckerei, (1980).

The Status of Women in Austria. Gaudart, Dorothea, ed., Vienna, Austria, Austrian Federal Ministry of Social Affairs, 1976.

B) Books and articles in other languages

Aicher, J. "Reform des Rechts der Ehescheidung und der unterhalstrechtlichen Scheidungsfolgen in Österreich".
27 Zeitschrift für das gesamte Familienrecht: Ehe und Familie im privaten und öffentlichen Recht (Ger. W.) 426-434, 1980. (Part I)
27 Zeitschrift für das gesamte Familienrecht: Ehe und Familie im privaten und öffentlichen Recht (Ger. W.) 637-646, 1980, (Part II)

Beirat für Wirtschafts-und Sozialfragen. Frauenbeschäftigung in Österreich. Wien, Austria, C. Ueberreuter, 1974.

Bericht über die Situation der Frau in Österreich. Wien, Austria, Bundeskanzleramt, 1975.

Firnberg, Hertha and Ludwig S. Rutschka. Die Frau in Österreich. Wien, Österreichischer Gewerkschaftsbund, 1967.

Hoyer, H. "Neues Scheidungsrecht". 103 Juristische Blätter (Aus) 11-15, (1981).

Kerschner, F. "Zum Unterhalt nach Scheidung nach neuem Recht". 101 Juristische Blätter (Aus) 561-575, 1979.

Palten, G. "Regelung der Rechtsverhältnisse der Ehewohnung und an anderen Wohnungen nach dem neuen Scheidungsfolgenrecht". 34 Osterreichische Juristen-Zeitung (Aus) 375-385, 1979.

Pichler, H. "Einige Probleme des neuen Eherechts". 103 Juristische Blätter (Aus) 281-289, 1981.

Rigler, Edith. Frauenleitbild und Frauenarbeit in Österreich vom ausgehenden 19. Jh. bis zum Zweiten Weltkrieg. Wien: Verl. f. Geschichte u. Politik, 1976.

Schueringer, Brunhilde. Die Berufsmobilität von Frauen. Linz, Österr. Inst. f. Arbeitsmarktpolitik, 1972.

Schwind, F. "Reform des österreichischen Eherechts." 26 Zeitschrift für das gesamte Familienrecht: Ehe und Familie im privaten und offentlichen Recht (Ger. W.) 649-655, 1979.

Traxler, Gabrielle. Zwischen Tradition und Emanzipation. Probleme der Frauenarbeit in Österreich. Wien, W. Braumüller, 1973.

BELGIUM

A) Books and articles in English

Pichault, C. "Belgian Commission on the Employment of woman". 115 International Labour Review (Swi) 157-191, 1977.

B) Books and articles in other languages

Bawin-Legros, B. "A propos du vote des femmes ... l'isoloir isole-t-til?" 19 *Annales de la Faculté de Droit de Liège*, (Bel) 205-225, 1974.

Hanquet, Huberte. *Travail professionel des femmes et mutations sociales.* Bruxelles, Éditions "Vie Ouvrière", (1972).

Lambotte, C. "Femme salariée en droit belge". 28 *Revue Juridique et Politique, Indépendence et Coopération* (Fra) 1098-1112, 1974.

Martens, F. "Influence des dispositions legislatives de protection des femmes au travail sur l'attitude des employeurs". 15 *Annales de la Faculté de Droit de Liège* (Bel) 295- , 1970.

Rigaux, F. "Exercice, par un époux, de la liberté de changer de religion ou de conviction". 34 *Revue Critique de Jurisprudence Belge* (Bel) 195-209, 1980.

Rouard, P. "Proposition de loi créant les tribunaux de la famille". 88 *Journal des tribunaux* (Bel) 701-710, 1973.

Schoonbroodt, Joseph. *Les Femmes et le Travail. Mille travailleuses parlent sur une enquête d' Étienne Rohaert et du service feminin de la CSC.*, Brussels, Belgium, Editions "Vie Ouvriere", 1973.

Slachmuylder, L. "Pour un tribunal de la famille?" 86 *Journal des tribunaux* (Bel) 229- , 1971.

Waeler, D. van de. *Vrouw en arbeid.* Brual, Rijksinstituut voor ziekte-en invaliditeitsverzekering, 1971.

BULGARIA

A) Books and articles in English

The Bulgarian Woman. D. Mihailov, ed. Sofia, Bulgaria, Sofia Press, 1971.

Dinkova, Mariia. *The Social progress of the Bulgarian Woman.* Sofia, Sofia Press, 1972.

Ilieva, Nikolina. *The Bulgarian Woman.* Sofia, Bulgaria, Sofia Press, 1970.

The Status of women in the People's Republic of Bulgaria. Sofia, Committee of Bulgarian Women, 1972.

Turlakova, Eleonora. *Bulgarian Women.* Sofia, Sofia Press, 1976.

Women in the People's Republic of Bulgaria. Sofia, Sofia Press, 1972.

B) Books and articles in other languages

Bogatinova, Dona. *Trudno i slavno minalo.* Sofia, Partizdat, 1973.

Bradinska, Radka N. *Vuznikvane i oformiavane na zhenskoto sotsialdemokratichesko dvizhenie v Bulgariia.* Sofia, Bulgaria, NS OF, 1969.

Ilieva, Nikolina. *Ikonomicheski i sotsialni problemi na trudovata zaetost na zhenite.* Sofia: Nauka i izkustvo, 1970.

Ilieva, Nikolina. *Izpolzvane na zhenskite trudovi resursi vi NRB.* Sofia, Partizdat, 1973.

Ilieva, Nikolina. *Kvalifikatsiiata na rabotnichkite i tekhnicheskiiat progres.* Sofia: Profizdat, 1973.

Khristova, E. "Usŭvŭshenstvuvane na garantsiite za trudovite i osiguritelnite prava na zhenata v Narodna republika Bŭlgariia." 25 *Pravna Misul* (Bul) 51-59, 1976.

Lekova, S. "Mezhdunarodnata godina na zhenata i bŭlgarskite iuristki". 24 *Sotsialisticbesko Pravo,* (Bul) 6-10, 1975, No. 6.

Liutov, At., et al. *Zhenata-trud u bit.* Sb. Statii; red. kolegia. Sofia: BAN, 1977.

Poliata na profsiuzite za reshavane na socialnite problemi na trudeshtite se zheniv socialiticheshite strani: (materiali ot) mezhdunar sreshta za obmiana na opit, 2-5 iuni 1975 g., Sofia (s- stav. Natalia Velichkova). Vedemstveno izd. Sofia: Profizdat, 1975.

Sukmandzhieva, Mariia Teneva. *Zhenite sa ogromna sila.* Sofia, NS OF, 1969.

Vodenicharova, Zdravka. *Revoliucionnoto Zhensko dvizhenie v Bulgaria.* Sofia, OF, 1972.

Zhenata- maĭka, truzhenichka, obshchestvenichka. Sofia, Partizdat, 1974.

Zhenata- trud i bit: (sb. statii/ red. kolegia At Lintov, et al). Sofia, BAN, 1977.

Zheni v obshestvenite nauki: iubileen sb. (posveten na) mezdunar. g. na zenata 1975: nauchii trudove. Sofia: AONSU pri CK na BKP, 1976.

CZECHOSLOVAKIA

A) Books and articles in English

Heitlinger, Alena. *Women and state socialism: Sex inequality in the Soviet Union and Czechoslovakia.* London, England, Macmillan Press, 1979.

Jancar, Barbara Wolfe. *Women under communism.* Baltimore: John Hopkins University Press, 1978.

Scott, Hilda. *Does Socialism liberate women?* Experiences from Eastern Europe. Boston, Beacon Press, 1974.

Wolchik, Sharon L. "Demography, Political Reform and Women's Issues in Czechoslovakia". In: *Women, Power and Political Systems.* Ed. by Margherita Rendel. New York, St. Martin's Press, Inc., c 1981, pp. 135-150.

B) Books and articles in other languages

Bauerová, Jaroslava. *Zaměstnaná žena a rodina.* Praha: Práce, 1974.

Glos, J. "Lze právo rodinné zdokonalit?" 110 *Právnik* (Cze) 291-302, 1971.

Glos, J. "ZáKon o rodině pod drobnohledem". 109 *Právnik* (Cze) 1094-1105, 1970.

Güttler, V. "Poznámka k pracím zakázaným těhotným ženám". 57 *Pravny Obzor* (Cze) 459-468, 1974.

Haderka, J. "K problematice institutu rodičovské moci." 110 *Právnik* (Cze) 183-192, 1971.

Němcová, Jarmila. "Postoje k ekonomické činnosti žen". 13 *Demografie* (Cze) 11-18, 1971.

Tomková, Vlasta. "Problematika práce ženy v zaměstnáni a v rodině". 15 *Demografie* (Cze) 146-151, 1973.

Žena a právo. Zprac. kol. pod ved. Senty Radvanové. Praha, Orbis, 1971.

DENMARK

A) Books and articles in English

Pedersen, Inger Margrete. "Recent trends in Danish Family law and their historical background". 20 *International and Comparative Law Quarterly* (UK) 332-334, 1971.

B) Books and articles in other languages

Christensen, Lilli. *Kvinder og politik.* København, Hans Reitzel, 1973.

Due, Jesper. Thyra Nielse, Hurup. *Beretningen om, hvordan arbejdsformialing og orbejdsgivere i et egnsudviklingsområde bekaemper faglig aktivitet,* København, Demos, 1974.

Giese, Suzanne. *Derfor kvindekamp. En bog om kvinders undertrykkelse* København, Tiderne Skifter, Eksp: Istedgade 54, 1973.

Hansen, Eva Hemmer. *Kvinderne og Faellesmarkedet en samling oplysninger og et depatoplaeg.* Aarhus, Frit Norden, 1972.

Hasselbalch, O. "Barselsorlovsloven". 63 *Juristen og Økonomen* (Den) 150-156, 1981.

Heltberg, Bettina. *Kvindesag.* Copenhagen, Munksgaard, 1976.

Højgaard, Lis. *Bidrag til den danske kvindebevaegelses historie, 1870-1900.* København, Akademisk Forlag, 1977.

Høyrup, Else. *Kvinder: arbejde og intellektuel udvikling. En blandet samling betragtninger.* København, RUC Boghandel & Forlag, 1974.

Kommissionen vedrørende kvindernes stilling i samfundet. *Betaenkning vedrørende kvindernes stilling i samfundet sluttrapport.* København: Statens Trykningskontor, Eksp.: DBK, 1974.

Kommissionen vedrorende kvindernes stilling i samfundet. *Betaekning vedrørende ligestilling Afgivet af et udvalg under kommissionen vedrørende kvindernes stilling i samfundet.* København, Statens Trykningskontori, Eksp.: DBK, 1972.

Kvindeundertrykkelsen under kapitalismen. København, SIL: Distribueres af forlaget GMT, 1975.

Reintoft, Hanne. *Kvinden i klassesamfundet.* København, Stig Vendelkaer, 1972.

Rex, Jytte. *Kvindernes bog.* København, Rhodos, 1972.

485

Sørensen, Lise. *Den nødvendige nedtur besyv om Mathilde Fibiger og kvindernes gamle sag.* København: Gyldendal, 1977.

Terp, Anna Marie. *Kvindelbevaegelsernes historie nyere tid.* København: Attika, 1973.

FINLAND

A) Books and articles in English

Haavio-Manila, Elina. "Convergences between East and West; tradition and modernity in sex roles in Sweden, Finland and the Soviet Union". 14 *Acta Sociologia* (Nor) 114-125, 1971, No. 1-2.

Naisten Asemaa Tutkiva Komitea. *Report of the Committee on the Position of Women in Finnish Society.* Helsinki, 1973.

B) Books and articles in other languages

Aro, Pirkko. *Eipas vaieta seurakunnassa: liberaalin ajatuksia.* Helsinki, Weilin and Goos, 1970.

FRANCE

A) Books and articles in English

Alexandre, Danièle. "The status of women in France." 20 *American Journal of Comparative Law,* 647-661, 1972.

Bouteiller, Jacques. *Male and female wage differentials in France: Theory and measurement.* Hull: Emmasglen Ltd. for the International Institute of Economics, 1975.

Bouten, Jacob. *Mary Wollstonecraft and the beginnings of female emancipation in France and England.* Philadelphia, Pennsylvania, Porcupine Press, 1975.

Devaud, M. & M. Levy. "Women's employment in France: protection or equality. 6 *International Labour Review,* (Swi) 739-754, 1980.

Silver, Catherine Bodard. "Salon, foyer, bureau; women and the professions in France". 78 *American Journal of Sociology,* 836-851, 1973.

Strumingher, Laura S. *Women and the making of the working class, Lyon 1830-1970,* St. Alban's, Vt., Eden Press, 1979.

Women in Revolutionary Paris, 1789-1795: Selected documents translated with notes and commentary by Darline Gay Levy, Harriet Branson Apple-White, Mary Durham Johnson. Urbana: University of Illinois Press, 1979.

B) Books and articles in other languages

Abitol, E. Essai sur la nouvelle séparation judiciaire instituée par l'article 258 du code civil. 79 *Revue Trimestrielle de Droit Civil* (Fra) 37-96, 1981.

Albistur, Maité. *Histoire du fèminisme français du Moyen Age à nos jours.* Paris: Des Femmes, 1977.

Ayoub, Eliane. "La femme dans la fonction publique". *Droit Social* (Fra) 153-164, 1971.

Bécane- Pascaud, Geneviève M. *Les femmes dans la fonction publique,* Paris, Direction de la Documentation, 1974.

Bénabent, A. "Bilan de cinq ans d'application de la réforme du divorce". *Recueil Dalloz Sirey* (Fra) 33-40, 1981.

Bergerès, M.C. "Vers une égalité des conjoints en droit fiscal?" *Recueil Dalloz Sirey,* (Fra) 25-30, 1980.

Bersani, C. "Femme et la fonction publique". *Droit Social* (Fra) 51-55, 1976.

Boyer, Y. "Révision de la prestation compensatoire". *Recueil Dalloz Sirey,* (Fra) 263-272, 1980.

Brimo, Albert. *Les femmes françaises face au pouvoir politique.* Paris, Montchrestien, 1975.

Budiner, M. Le Droit de la femme à l'égalité de salaire, Paris, Librarie Générale de Droit et de Jurisprudence, 1975.

Champion, Jean. *Les problèmes juridiques des femmes seules.* Paris, J. Delmas, 1969.

Chanet, C. "Femme et le divorce". *Droit Social* (Fra) 78-81, 1976.

Chartier, Y. "Domicile conjugal et vie familiale". 69 *Revue Trimestrielle de droit Civil* (Fra) 510- , 1971.

Charzat, Gisèle. *Les françaises sont-elles des citoyennes?* Paris, Denoëp, 1972.

Chemithe, P. "Femmes détenues à Fleury-Medogis". *Revue de Science Criminelle et de Droit Pénal Comparé,* (Fra) 395-405, 1978.

Colin, Madeleine. *Ce n'est pas d'aujourd' hui. Les femmes en lutte.* Paris, Ed. Sociales, 1975.

Combette, M.J. "Vers une nouvelle condition de la femme au travail", *Droit Social* (Fra) 23-38, 1976.

Congrès des notaires de France. 52d. Biarritz, 1953. *Status juridique de la femme mariée; la maison familiale,* Biarritz, 1953.

Cornu, G. "Traduction concrète de la vocation de la femme en droit civil français". 28 *Revue Juridique et Politique, Indépendence et Coopération,* (Fra) 1157-1175, 1974.

Cresson, Edith. *Avec le soleil.* Paris: J.C. Lattès, 1976.

Decaux, Alain. *Histoire des Françaises,* Paris Librarie Académique Perrin, 1972.

Dechezelles, A. "Condition de la femme salarieé en France". 28 *Revue Juridique et Politique, Indépendence et Coopération* (Fra) 1195-1216, 1974.

Delatour, Yvonne. *Le travail des femmes pendant la Première Guerre mondiale et ses conséquences sur l'evolution de leur rôle dans la société.* (In: Francia: Forschungen zur westeuropäischen Geschichte, Bd 2) München, W. Fink Verlag, 1975.

Deltaglia, Liliane; *La mère au travail, son bonheur et celui des siens.* Paris, Livre Clé, S.P.E.R., 1971.

Demars-Sion, V. "Liberalisation du divorce: l'apport veritable de la loi du 11 juillet 1975 à la lumière de celle du 20 Septembre 1972." 78 *Revue Trimes-*

trielle de Droit Civil (Fra) 231-265, 1980.

Devaud, M. "Obstacles à l'application de la loi sur l'égalité de rémunérations entre les hommes et les femmes". *Droit Social* (Fra), 39-41, 1976.

Diglio, C. "Condizione della donna del lavoro subordinato in Francia e in Italia". 36 *Diritto e Giurisprudenzia* (Ita) 1-22, Jan-Mr, 1980.

Droulers, Marie Françoise. *Travail à temps partiel, élasticité de la durée du travail temporaire.* Préf. de Georges Lasserre. Valenciennes, 1972.

Duhet, Paule Marie. (comp). *Les femmes et la Révolution, 1789-1794.* Paris, Julliard, 1971.

Les femmes aujourd'hui, demain. Semaines de la pensée marxiste, 29 janvier-4 fevrier 1975. Paris, Editions Sociales, 1975.

Garnier, Christine. *A chances égales, des femmes qui ont résolu d'étonner.* Pref. de Pierre Lazareff. Paris, Hachette, 1971.

Gaspard, Françoise. Madame le . . . . Paris, B. Grasset, 1979.

Giffard, J. "Françaises et la politique". 28 *Revue Juridique et Politique, Indépendence et Coopération* (Fra) 1113-1125, 1974.

Gisserot, F. "Nouveau domicile de la femme mariée". 77 *Revue Trimestrielle de Droit Civil* (Fra) 724-746, 1979.

Gobert, M. "Femme en droit civil français". 28 *Revue Juridique et Politique, Indépendence et Coopération* (Fra) 1146-1155, 1974.

Granrut du, C. "Comité du Travail Féminin et les réalités du travail des femmes.". *Droit Social* (Fra) 18-22, 1976.

Groult, Benoîte. *Ainsi soit-elle.* Paris, B. Grasset, 1975.

Guilbert, Madeleine. *Les fonctions des femmes dans l'industrie.* Paris, Manton, 1966.

Halimi, Gisèle. *La cause des femmes. Propos recueillis par Marie Cardinal.* Paris, B. Grasset, 1973.

Hardouin, M. "Grossesse et liberté de la femme". *Droit Social* (Fra) 287-310, 1977, No. 9-10.

Journet-Durca, Isabelle. *La femme et ses nouveaux droits: Guide pratique.* Paris, A. Michel, 1975.

Labourie-Racapé, Annie. *L'activité féminine: enquête sur la discontinuité de la vie professionelle.* Paris: Presses universitaires de France, 1977.

Ladhari, M. "Epoux et l'exercice de la fonction publique". Recueil Dalloz Sirey (Fra) 9-16, 1980.

Laot, Jeannette. *Stratégie pour les femmes.* Paris, Stock, 1977.

Leclereq, Jacques. *La femme aujoud'hui et demain.* Paris, Casterman, 1968.

Leduc, G. "Participation féminine au dévelopement économique". 28 *Revue Juridique et Politique, Indépendence et Coopération* (Fra) 1243-1256, 1974.

Levasseur, G. "Droit Pénal et la condition de la femme". 28 *Revue Juridique et Politique, Indépendence et Coopération* (Fra) 1217-1242, 1974.

Libération des femmes, année zéro. . . . Paris. F. Maspero, 1972.

Ligue du Droit des Femmes. "Quelques réflexions sur l'action du secretariat d'État à la condition féminine". *Droit Social* (Fra) 86-95, 1976.

Mayaud, Y. "Adultère cause de divorce, depuis la loi du juillet 1975." 78 *Revue Trimestrielle de Droit Civil* (Fra) 494-523, 1980.

Maruani, Margaret. *Les syndicats a l'épreuve du féminisme*. Paris, Syros, 1979.

Michel, Andrée. *Le féminisme*. Paris, Presses Universitaires de France, 1979.

Michel, Jacques. *Les Nouveaux droits de la femme*. Paris, Dunod, 1970.

Monsallier, B. Divorce pour rupture de la vie commune (loi du 11 juillet, 1975).
Part I 78 *Revue Trimestrielle de Droit Civil* (Fra) 266-290, 1980.
Part II 78 *Revue Trimestrielle de Droit Civil* (Fra) 468-493, 1980.

Nerson, R. "Personnes et droit de famille". 70 *Revue trimestrielle de droit civil* (Fra) 582-594, 1972.

Pelletier, Madeleine. *L'education féministe des filles, suivi de Le droit à l'avortement; La femme en lutte pour ses droits, la tactique féministe; Le droit au travail pour la femme*. Paris, Syros, 1978.

Plantey, A. "Femme et la fonction publique". 28 *Revue Juridique et Politique, Indépendence et Coopération* (Fra) 1127-1145, 1974.

Plantey, Alain. *Prospective de l'Etat*. Paris, Editions du Centre National de la Recherche Scientifique, 1975.

Porteau-Bitker, A. "Criminalité et délinquance féminines dans le droit pénal des XIIIᵉ et XIVᵉ siècles". 58 *Revue Historique de Droit Français et Etranger*, (Fra) 13-56, 1980.

Le Programme commun des femmes: présenté par Gisèle Halimi. Paris: B. Grasset, 1978.

Rigaux, F. "Notions de famille et de mariage en droit civil contemporain.". 87 *Journal des tribunaux* (Bel) 669-674, 1972.

Rollier, Anne-Marie Dourlen. "Law and the status of women in France". 8 *Columbia Human Rights Law Review* 51-68, 1976.

Roqueplo, J.C. "Condition militaire et condition féminine". 32 *Revue Administrative*, (Fra) 595-599, 1979.

Ruellan, R. "Femme et la sécurité sociale". *Droit Social* (Fra) 56-73, 1976.

Sartin, Pierrete. *Aujourd'hui, la femme; pour une politique pratique de la femme*. Paris, Stock, 1974.

Secretariat d'Etat à la condition féminine. *Cent mesures pour les femmes*. Presentées par Françoise Giroud. Paris: Documentation Française, 1976.

Sousi-Roubi, B. "Réflexions sur les discriminations sexistes dans l'emploi. *Droit Social* (Fra) 31-38, 1980.

Sutton, G. "Conflicts familiaux et dialogue avec les justiciables." 46 *Scientia juridica, revista bimestral portuguesa e brasileira* (Por), 2472-, 1972.

Wassner-Blum, Gaby-Sofie. *Die Mitarbeit der Ehefrau im Deutschland, Frankreich und der Schweiz: Eherecht, Steuerrecht, Socialrecht*. Bern: Herbert Lang, 1976.

GERMANY

A) Books and articles in English

Rupp, Leila J. *Mobilizing women for war: German and American Propaganda, 1939-1945*. Princeton, N.J., Princeton University Press, 1978.

Stephenson, Jill. *Women in Nazi society*. London, Croom Helm, 1975.

B) Books and articles in other languages

Elling, Hanna. *Frauen im deutschen Widerstand: 1933-45.* Frankfurt am Main, Röderberg- Verlag, 1978.

Geller, Luise. "Probleme der Frauenarbeit". 27 *Arbeit und Leistung* (Ger) 272-273, 1973.

McRae, Verena. *Frauen, eine Mehrheit als Minderheit: Materialen zum Thema: Sexismus.* Gelnhausen, Berlin: Burckhardthaus-Verlag, 1975.

Ottmüller, Uta. *Die Dienstbotenfrage zur Sozialgeschichte d. doppelten Ausnützung von Dienstmädchen im deutschen Kaiserreich.* Münster: Verlag Frauenpolitik, 1978.

Reuter, Angelika, *Seit 1848 Frauen im Widerstand Frauen im Faschismus, 1933-1945.* Münster, Verlag Frauenpolitik, 1977.

Scholtz-Klink, Gertrud. *Die Frau im Dritten Reich,* Tübingen, Grabert, 1978.

EAST GERMANY

A) Books and articles in English

Kuhrig, Herta. *Equal rights for women in the German Democratic Republic.* Berlin, GDR. Com. for Human Rights, 1973.

Scholze, Siegfried. "GDR women struggle for peace and security". 12 *German Foreign Policy* (Ger.E.) 205-216, 1973.

Shaffer, Harry G. *Women in the two Germanies; a comparative study in a socialist and non-socialist society.* Elmsford, N.Y., Pergamon Press, 1981.

Statkowa, Susanne. *Women and socialism: facts, figures and information on equality for women in the GDR.* Berlin, Panorama DDR, 1977.

B) Books and articles in other languages

Arendt, Ingrid. *Bibliographie zur Geschichte des Kampfes der deutchen Arbeiterklasse für die Befreiung der Frau und zur Rolle der Frau in der deuthschen Arbeiterbewegung.* Leipzig, Hrsg. von der Pädagogischen Hochschule "Clara Zetkin", 1974.

Baumgart, A. & E. Hein. "Arbeitisrechtliche Regelungen zur Gewährleistung der Gleichberechtigung der Frau". 30 *Neue Justiz,* (Ger.E.) 174-178, 1976.

Bechthold, I. "Familienrecht der BRD aus der Sicht der DDR Juristen". 15 *Recht in Ost und West* (Ger.W.), März, 1971.

Bongardt, Ilse. *Eins zu Null für mein Gegenüber. Frauenporträts.* Berlin: Union Verlag, 1975.

Die Frau und die Gesellschaft: aus der Geschichte des Kampfes um die Gleichberechtigung der Frau. Hrsg. von der Forschungsgemeinschaft Geschichte des Kampfes der Arbeiterklasse um die Befreiung der Frau an der Pädagogischen Hochschule Clara Zetkin. Leipzig: Verlag für die Frau, 1974.

Dücker, K. and R. Kreissl. "Sozialistische Familienpolitik; Bestandteil staatlicher Leitungstätigkeit". 22 *Staat und Recht*, (Ger.E.) 575-583, 1973.

Eisenreich, Helmut. *Der Frauenausschuss*. Berlin, Verlag Tribune, 1975.

Fuhrmann, R. "Sozialistische Familienbeziehungen- ein Element der entwickten sozialistischen Gesellschaft". 20 *Staat und Recht*, (Ger. E) 1437-1443, 1971.

Gast, Gabriele. *Die politische Rolle der Frau in der DDR*. Dusseldorf, Bertelsmann Universitätsverlag, 1973.

Helwig, Gisela. *Frau '75 Bundesrepublik Deutschland, DDR*. Köln: Verlag Wissenschaft und Politik, 1975.

Helwig, Gisela. *Zwischen Familie und Beruf: die Stellung der Frau in beiden deutschen Staaten*. Köln: Verlag Wissenschaft und Politik, 1974.

Kuhrig, Herta. *Die Gleichberechtigung der Frauen in der Deutschen Demokratischen Republik*. Berlin, 1973.

Kuhrig, Herta & Wulfram Speigner. *Wie emanzipiert sind die Frauen in der DDR? Beruf, Bildung, Familie*. Köln: Pahel- Rugenstein, 1979.

Mühlmann, J. "Bemerkungen zur 4. Auflage des FGB- Kommentars". 28 *Neue Justiz*, (Ger. E.) 261-264, 1974.

Oeser, E. "Völkerrechtliche Konventionen zum Schutze der Frau und ihre Verwirklichung in der DDR". 29 *Neue Justiz*, (Ger.E.) 435-439, 1975.

Plat, Wolfgang. *Die Familie in der DDR*. Frankfurt am Main, S. Fischer, 1972.

Staatliche Zentralverwaltung für Statistik. *Die Frau in der DDR. Fakten und Zahlen*. Berlin: Staatsverlag der Deutschen Demokratischen Republik, 1975.

Statkowa, Susanne. *Die Frau im Sozialismus: Informationen, Fakten über die Gleichberechtigung in der DDR*. Berlin: Panorama, 1974.

Stern, Katja. *Das schöne Geschlecht und die Gleichberechtigung in der DDR*. Berlin, Aus erster Hand, 1972.

Strasberg, W. "Aufgaben der Gerichte zur Erhaltung und Festigung von Ehe und Familie". 24 *Neue Justiz*, (Ger.E.) 445- , 1970.

Strasberg, W. "Beitrag der Gerichte zur Entwicklung sozialistischer Familienbeziehungen". 27 *Neue Justiz*, (Ger.E.) 42-45, 1973.

Thiel, W. "Gleichberechtigung der Frau im Arbeitprozess und Aufgaben des Arbeitsrechts". 29 *Neue Justiz*, (Ger. E.) 559-562, 1975.

Walther, R. "Rolle der Familie im Bildungs-und Erziehungsprozess der Jugend". 26 *Neue Justiz*, (Ger. E.) 473- , 1972.

Wander, Maxie. *Guten Morgen, du Schöne: Frauen in der DDR*. Darmstadt, Luchterhand, 1978.

Zur gesellschaftlichen stellung der Frau in der DDR: Sammelband. Hrsg. vom Wissenschaftlichen Beirat Die Frau in der Sozialistischen Gesellschaft bei der Akademie der Wissenschaften der DDR unter Leitung von Herta Kuhrig und Wulfram Speigner. Leipzig: Verlag für die Frau, 1978.

WEST GERMANY

A) Books and articles in English

Agassi, Judith B. *Women on the job: the attitudes of women to their work.* Lexington, Mass, Lexington Books, 1979.

Hippel, Theodore Gottlieb von. *On improving the status of women.* Trans. and ed. with an introduction by Timothy F. Sellner. Detroit: Wayne State University Press, 1979.

Jessel, Penelope. *The ascent of women.* London, Liberal Publication Department, 1975.

Shaffer, Harry G. *Women in the two Germanies: A comparative study in a socialist and non-socialist society.* Elmsford, N.Y., Pergamon Press, 1981.

B) Books and articles in other languages

Arbeiterinnen kampfen um ihr Recht: Autobiographisele texte zum kampf rechtlosen und entiechterer frauenspersonen in Deutschland, Österreich und Schweiz. Wuppertal, West Germany, Hammer, 1975.

Beitzke, G. "Causas de divorcio en el nuevo derecho alemán". 29 *Revista de la Facultad de Derecho de México* (Mex) 39-52, 1979.

Berg, M.L., Kettig, A., Proft, H., and Steinmam, E. "Festtellungen und Forderungen der demokratischen Frauenbewegung in der Bundes-republik". 21 *Blätter für deutsche und internationale Politik* (Ger) 1018-1028, 1976.

Bechthold, I. "Familienrecht der BRD aus der Sicht der DDR Juristen". 15 *Recht in Ost und West* (Ger.) 64- , Marz, 1971.

Blum, Sigrid. "Probleme der Diskriminierung der berufstätigen Frau". 12 *Marxistische Blätter,* (Ger) 56-62, 1974.

Bosch, F.W. "Aktuelle Probleme des Familien-und Erbrechts". 17 Zeitschrift für das gesamte Familienrecht: *Ehe und Familie im privaten und öffentlichen Recht,* 497- , 1970.

Boschan, S. "Derecho de familia en la República Federal de Alemania". 57 *Revista de Derecho Privado* (Spa) 497-518, 1973.

Brandt, Gisela. *Zur Frauenfrage im Kapitalismus.* Frankfurt, Suhrkamp, 1973.

Chassard, Jean. *Die deutsche Frau.* Paris, A. Colin, 1969.

Cielak, Werner, et al. "Gewerkschaften im Kampf um die Rechte der berufstätigen Frau". 10 *Marxistische Blätter* (Ger) 60-68, 1972.

Deinhardt, K. "Neuere Stimmen und Vorschläge zur Eherechsreform". 19 *Zeitschrift für das gesamte Familienrecht: Ehe und Familie im privaten und öffentlichen Recht* (Ger.) 236- , 1972.

Dertinger, Autje. *Die bessere Hälfte kämpft um ihr Recht: über den Amspruch der Frauen auf Erwerb und auf Selbstverständlichkeit.* Köln: Bund-Verlag, 1980.

Dieckman, A. & P. Drause. "Zum Urteil des Bundesverfassungsgerichts vom 28.2.1980 (Fam RZ 1980, 326 ff) betreffend den Versorgungsausgleich." 27 *Zeitschrift für das gesamte, Familienrecht: Ehe und Familie im privaten und öffentlichen Recht* (Ger) 965-971, 1980.

Doorman, Lottemi. *Keiner Schiebt uns weg: Zwischenbilanz d. Frauenbewegung in der Bundesrepublik.* Weinheim, Basil: Beltz, 1979.

492

Eckart, Christel. *Frauenarbeit in Familie und Fabrik.* Frankfurt am Main: Campus-Verlag, 1979.

Fehmel, H.W. "Ist das Verbot des gemeinsamen elterlichen Sorgerechts nach der Scheidung (1671 Abs. IV S.1 BGB) verfassungswidrig?" 27 *Zeitschrift für das gesamte Familienrecht: Ehe und familie im privaten und öffentlichen Recht* (Ger) 758-761, 1980.

Finger, P. "Eheufhebung und das neue Scheidungrecht". 34 *Neue Juristische Wochenschrift* (Ger) 1534-1541, 1981.

Frauenhandbuch. Lore Breuer, ed. Koblenz, West Germany, Frauen Verlag, 1974.

Frick, Inge. *Frauen befreien sich: Bilder zur Geschichte der Frauenarbeit und Frauenbewegung.* Munchen: Frauenbuchverlag, 1976.

Frischauer, Paul. *Moral und Unmoral der deutschen Frau.* München, Zurich. Droemer/Knaur, 1970.

Gersdorff, Ursula von. *Frauenarbeit und Frauenemanzipation im Ersten Weltkrieg.* (In: Francia; Forschungen zur westeuropäischen Geschichte. Bd. 2 , Munchen, W. Fink Verlag, 1975.

Giesen, D. "Neues Scheidungsrecht auf dem Prufstand der Rechtprechung". *Juristische Rundschau* (Ger) 177-184, 1980.
Juristische Rundschau (Ger) 316-325, 1980.

Gitter, W. "Soziale Sicherung der "Nur-Hausfrau". 21 *Zeitschrift für das gesamte familienrecht: Ehe und Familie im privaten und öffentlichen Recht* (Ger.) 233-237, 1974.

Groot de, G.R. "Nationaliteisrecht en emancipatie van de vrouw in de Bondsrepubliek". 50 *Nederlands Juristenblad* (Net.) 782-787, 1975.

Heinz, Margarete. *Über das politische Bewusstsein von Frauen in der Bundesrepublik: eine Sekundäranalyse empirischer Materialien.* München, Goldmann, 1971.

Held, P. "Stellungsnahme des Bundesrates zur Reform des Eherechts." 18 *Zeitschrift für das gesamte Familienrecht: Ehe und Familie im privaten und öffentlichen Recht* (Ger.) 481- , 1971.

Helwig, Gisela. *Frau '75: Bundesrepublik Deutschland, DDR.* Köln; Verlag Wissenschaft und Politik, 1975.

Herbst, L. "Lautlose Diskriminierung der Frau im Beamtenrecht". 27 *Die Offentliche Verwaltung* (Ger) 547-551, 1974.

Hofbauer, Hans. "Ausbildungs-und Qualifikationsstruktur der erwerbstätigen Frauen in der Bundesrepublik Deutschland. 23 *Gewerkschafliche Monatshefte,* (Ger) 700 707, 1972.

Institut für Angewandte Sozialwissenschaft *Die Rolle des Mannes und ihr Einfluss auf die Wahlmöglichkeiten der Frau: eine empirische untersuchung des Instituts für Angewandte Sozialwissenschaft.* Bonn-Bad Godesberg, bearb. von Wolfgang Burkhardt und Heiner Meulemann. Stuttgart: W. Kohlhammer, 1976.

Jurczyk, Karin. *Frauenarbeit und Frauenrolle zum Zusammenhang von Familienpolitik w. Frauenerwerbstätigkeit in Deutschland von 1918-1975.* Frankfurt (Main), Munchen: Aspekte-Verlag, 1976.

Kluzinger, E. "Mitarbeit im Familienverband." 19 *Zeitschrift für das gesamte privaten und öffentliche Recht* (Ger), 70- , 1972.

Kollenberg, Udo. *-Partnerschaft im Rentenrecht zur eigenständigen sozialen Sicherung der Frau.* 2 erw. Aufl. Köln: Deutscher Instituts Verlag, 1978.

Krause, P. "Zum Urteil des Bundesverfassungsgerichts vom 28.2.1980. (FamRZ 1980, 326 ff) betr. den Versorgungsausgleich." 27 *Zeitschrift für das gesamte Familienrecht: Ehe und Familie im privaten und öffentlichen Recht,* (Ger) 534-540, 1980.

Krenzler, M. " 'Zum Vorsorgeunterhalt' " und seiner Bemessung". 26 *Zeitschrift für das gesamte Familienrecht: Ehe und Familie im privaten und öffentlichen Recht,* (Ger) 877-881, 1979.

Lantzke, U. "Unterhalt und Getrenntleben: eine Bilanz der Eherechtsreform". 32 *Neue Juristische Wochenschrift* (Ger) 1483-1487, 1979.

Limbach, J. "Unterhaltsverlust wegen grober Unbilligkeit bei Getrenntleben". 33 *Neue Jursitische Wochenschrift,* (Ger) 871-875, 1980.

Lischke-Arbert, Herta. "Frauen im Betriebstrat nur ein Alibi?" 23 *Gewerkschaftliche Monatshefte,* (Ger) 740-744, 1972.

Löffler, F. & C. Theurer. "Zur Bewertung teildynamischer Versorgungen im Versorgungsausgleich: eine (vermeidbare?) Lücke der Barwertverordnung." 28 *Zeitschrift für das gesamte Familienrecht: Ehe und Familie im privaten und öffentlichen Recht,* (Ger) 8-12, 1981.

Losseff-Tillmans, Gisela. *Frauenemanzipation und Gewerkschaften.* Wuppertal, Hammer, 1978.

Maeder, Paula. *Die Gesellschaftliche Situation der Frau, ein Politikum unserer Zeit.* Hannover: Niedersachsischen Landeszentrale für Politische Bildung, 1968.

Maier, I. "Gleichberechtigung der Frau im Arbeitsleben". 27 *Neue Juristische Wochenschrift* (Ger) 1685-1689, 1974.

Maydell von, B. "Überblick über die bisherige Rechtsprechung zum Versorgungsausgleich. 28 *Zeitschrift für das gesamte Familienrecht: Ehe und Familie im privaten und öffentlichen Recht* (Ger) 623-632, 1981.

Menschik, Jutta. *Feminismus: Geschichte, Theorie, Praxis.* Köln: Pahl- Rugenstein, 1977.

Menschik, Jutta. *Gleichberechtigung order Emanzipation? Die Frau im Erwerbsleben der Bundesrepublik.* Frankfurt a. M.: Fischer-Taschenbuch Verlag, 1971.

Menschik, Jutta. "Zur Lage erwerbstätiger Frauen in der Bundesrepublik Deutschland. 13 *Zeitschrift fur Philosophie und Sozialwissenschaften* (Ger) 645-673, 1971.

Meyer-Harter, Renate. *Die Stellung der Frau in der Frau in der Sozialversicherung Lageanalyse und Reformmöglichkeit.* Berlin: Duncker & Humboldt, 1974.

Mikat, P. "Zum Regierungsentwurf eines Ersten Gesetzes zur Reform des Ehe- und Familienrechts. 19 *Zeitschrift für das gesamte Familienrecht: Ehe und Familie im privaten und öffentlichen Recht,* (Ger) 1- , 1972.

Mollwo, Ingrid. *Frauen und Arbeitsmarkt: ausgewählte Aspekte der Frau-*

enerwerbstätigkeit. Nürnberg, Bundesamt für Arbeit Geschäftsstelle für Veröffentlichungen, 1976.

Paulus, J. "Anspruch des getrennt legenden oder geschiedenen Ehegatten auf Ausbildungsunterhalt im Verhältnis zur Ausbildungsforderung nach dem Bundesausbildungsforderunsgesetz (BAfoG)". 28 *Zeitschrift für das gesamte Familienrecht: Ehe und Familie im privaten und öffentlichen Recht* (Ger) 640-645, 1981.

Pieper, Ingrid. *Wünsche und Möglichkeiten für aussenbetriebliche Teilzeitbestandigung von in der Landwirtschaft lebenden Frauen* Erstellet von der Agrarsozialen Gesellschaft. Göttingen, 1976.

Pinl, Claudia. *Das Arbeitnehmer-Patriarchat der Frauenpolitik der Gewerkschaften*. Köln: Kiepenheuer und Witsch, 1977.

Reitz, Gertraud. *Die Rolle der Frau und die Lebensplanung der Mädchen*. Munchen, Juventud Verlag, 1974.

Ruland, F. "Stellung der Frau in der Sozialversicherung". 22 *Zeitschrift für das gesamte Familienrecht: Ehe und Familie im privaten und öffentlichen Recht* (Ger) 144-155, 1975.

Scheffler, Erna. *Die Stellung der Frau in Familie und Gesellschaft in Wandel der Rechtsordnung zeit 1918*. Frankfurt am Main, A. Metzner, 1970.

Scheffler, Sabine. *Wiederaufnahme einer Berufstätigkeit bei Frauen, ein Beitrag zur Berufstätigkeit der Frau aus psychologischer Sicht*. Bonn, 1971.

Scheuringer, Brunhilde. "Berufsweg und Derufswirklichkeit von Arbeitnehmerinnen". 27 *Arbeit und Leistung* (Ger) 41-43, 1973.

Schnapp, F.E. "Zur Gleichstellung der Frau im Arbeits-und Sozialrecht, *Juristische Rundschau* (Ger) 316-320, 1974.

Schneider-Canwitz, Anneliese. "Der Bericht der Bundersregierung über die Massnahmen zur Verbesserung der Situation der Frau". 26 *Recht der Arbeit* (Ger) 243-247, 1973.

Schröeder, Hannelore. *Die Rechtlosigkeit der Frau im Rechstaat*. Frankfurt/Main; New York: Campus Verlag, 1979.

Schwarzer, Alice. *Frauenarbeit, Frauenbefreiung: Praxis Beispiele und Analysen*. Frankfurt am Main: Suhrkamp, 1973.

Schwerdtner, P. "Welche gesetzlichen Massnahmen sind vordringlich, un die Gleichstellung der Frauen mit den Männern im Beruf zu gewährleisten?" 29 *Juristenzeitung* (Ger) 476-483, 1974.

Shevchuk, V.D. "Zhenskii trud i ego oplata v FRG". 29 *Vestnik Moskovskogo Universiteta, Seriia Pravo,* (USSR) 65-70, 1974, No. 6.

Skiba, Rainer. "Volkswirtschaftliche Dimensionen der Frauenarbeit". 23 *Gewerkeschaftliche Monatshefte*, 693-700, 1972.

Stiegler, Barbara. *Die Mitsbestimmung der Arbeiterin: Frauen zwischen traditioneller Familienbindung und gewerkschaftlichen Engagement im Betrieb: ein Bitrag zur Psychologie der Arbeiterin*. Bonn-BadGodesberg: Verlag Neue Gesselschaft, 1976.

Strecker, Gabriele. *Der Weg der Frau in die Politik*. 4, erw. und uberarb. Aufl. Melle: Knoth, 1980.

Strehhuber, J. "Probleme des Versorgungsusgleichs in der Zusatzversorgung des öffentlichen Dienstes". 25 *Zeitschrift für das gesamte Familienrecht: Ehe und Familie im privaten und öffentlichen Recht* (Ger) 764-771, 1979.

Twellman, Margrit. *Die deutsche Frauenbewegung im Spiegel repräsentativer Frauenzeitschriften; ihre Anfange und erste Entwicklung, 1843-1899*. Neisenheim am Glan, A. Hain, 1972.

Walter, G. "Schuldprinzip kraft Ehevertrags?" 34 *Neue Juristische Wochenschrift* (Ger) 1409-1414, 1981.

Wassner-Blum, Gaby-Sophie. *Die Mitarbeit der Ehefran in Deutschland, Frankreich und der Schweiz: Eherecht, Steuerrecht, Sozialrecht*. Bern: Herbert Lang, 1976.

Wilkens, E. "Zur verfassungsrechtichen Prufung der Scheidungsgründe im 1. Ehe RG. 27 *Zeitschrift für das gesamte familienrecht: Ehe und familie im privaten und öffentlichen Recht* Ger) 527- , 1980.

GREECE

Books and articles in other languages

Agallopoulos-Zervoyannis, P. "Reflexions sur la loi hellénique transitoire no. 8681979 concernant le divorce pour rupture prolongée de la vie conjugale", 32 *Revue Internationale de Droit Compare* (Fra) 363-372, 1980.

HUNGARY

A) Books and articles in English

Hagalmayer, I. "Labor Law protection of working women" (Summ. in Russian & German). 22 *Annales Universitates Scientiarium Budapestinensis de Rolando Eötvös, Section Juridica,* (Hun) 37-60, 1980.

B) Books and articles in other languages

Racz, I. "A gyermekkel való érintkezés (láthatás) mint szülöi alanyi jog". 27 *Jogtudomanyi közlöny* (Hun) 92- , 1972.

Szabady, Egon. *Tanulmányok a nök hlevzetéröl*. Budapest, Magyar Nök Orszâgos Tanácsa, 1972.

Szegrávi, K. "Formation des femmes aux universités et aux écoles superieures" (Summ. in Russian & German). 16 *Annales Universitatis Scientiarium Budapestinensis de Rolando Eötvös, Sectio Juridica* (Hun) 99-116, 1974.

Szegvari, K. "Richtungen der Frauenbewegung in Ungarn während der Revolutionen von 1918-19 und zur Zeit der Machtübernahme der Konterrevolution". 19 *Annales Universitatis Scientiarium Budapestinensis de Rolando Eötvös, Sectio Juridica* (Hun) 197-213, 1977.

Vorozheïkin, E.N. "A felelósség ismérvei a családi jogban". 27 *Jogtudományi közlony,* (Hun) 499- , 1972.

IRELAND

Books and articles in English

MacCurtain, Margaret. "The Vote and Revolution" in: *Women in Irish Society-The Historical Dimension*, Margaret MacCurtain and Donneha O'Corrain, eds., Westport, Conn: Greenwood Press, 1979.

O'Connell, Thomas. "Women and private life in the Republic of Ireland", (from IADL Conference on Women-1979). 37 *National Lawyers Guide Practitioner*, 13-22, 1980.

ITALY

A) Books and articles in English

"Italian women, 1982". 32 *Swiss Review of World Affairs*, (Swi) 12-13, 1982.

B) Books and articles in other languages

Abbiate-Fubini, Anna. *I complessi della casalinga*. Firenze, La Nuova Italia, 1974.

Alfieri, Paola & Giangiulio Ambrosini. *La condizione economica, sociale e giuridica della donna in Italia*. Torino, Paravia, 1975.

Alloisio, Mirella. *La donna nel socialismo italiano tra cronaca e storia, 1892-1978*. Cosenza, Lerici, 1978.

Aspesi, Natalia. *La Donna Immobile*. Milano, Fratelli Fabbri Editori, 1973.

Baratta, V. "In tema di ordinamento della famiglia nel diritto italiano; le nozione di famiglia e di matrimonio." 29 *Diritto e giurisprudenza* (Ita) 333-342, 1973.

Bellenzier-Garutti, Maria Teresa. *Idea e realtà della donna*. Roma: Città Nuova, 1978.

Bellomo, Manlio. *La condizione giuridica della donna in Italia; vicende antiche e moderne*. Torino, 1970.

Bielli, Carla. *Fecondità e lavoro della donna in ambiente urbano*. Roma, Universita di Roma, Istituto di demografia, 1975.

Bielli, Carla, A. Pinnelli (and) A. Russo. *Fecondità e lavoro della donna; un'indagine in quattro zone tipiche italiane*. Roma, Istituto di Demografia, 1973.

Blinova, Elena Petrovna. *Sotsial'no-ekonomicheskoe polozhenie trudiashchikhsia zhenshchin Italii*. Moskva, Nauka, 1972.

Boggio, Maricla. *Ragazza madre*. Venezia, Ed. Venezia Padova: Marsilio, 1975.

Boneschi, Marta, et al. *Donne in liquidazione: storie di operaie della Unidal*. Milano, 1978.

Bove, L. "Appunti sul progetto di reforma del diritto di famiglia; I. costituzione e nullità del matrimonio. 29 *Diritto e giurisprudenza* (Ita) 16-32, 1973.

497

Branca, G. "Autoritarismo, spirito punitivo e diritto di famiglia. 96 *Foro italiano*" (Ita) 197-205, 1973.

Busnelli, F. Donato. "Libertà e responsabilità dei coniuginella vita famil." 29 *Rivista di diritto civile* (Ita) 333-342, 1973.

Carrion, S. "Notas en sede doctrinal sobre el régimen jurídico de la separación conyugal en el ordenamiento italiano".

   I. No. 429   *Revista General de Derecho, (Spa)* 650-659, 1980, No. 429.

   II. No. 430   *Revista General de Derecho (Spa)* 826-834, 1980, No. 430.

Cottrau, Giorgio. *La tutela della donna lavoratrice* . . . . Torino, G. Giappichelli, 1971.

Crespi, Franco, et al. *Il Lavoro a domicilio.* Bari, De Donato, 1975.

Cutrufelli, Maria Rosa. *Disoccupata con onore.* Milano; G. Mazzota, 1975.

Cutrufelli, Maria Rosa. *L'invenzione della donna: miti e techniche di uno sfruttamento.* Milano: G. Mazzotta, 1974.

De Cupis, A. "Debilitazione legislativa della famiglia legittima." 18 *Rivista di diritto civile* (Ita) 317-329, 1972, 18(I).

Delitala, C. "Brevi osservazioni critiche sulla riforma del diritto di famiglia". 17 *Rivista di diritto civile,* (Ita) 639- , 1971, 17(11).

De Marco, Clara & Manlio Talamo. *Lavoro Nero.* Milano, G. Mazzotta, 1977.

De Vita, A. "Protección de los derechos del hombre y la prohibición de la discriminación fundada en el sexo, en derecho italiano". 40 *Revista de Derecho y Ciencias Sociales,* (Chile) 8-18, 1973.

Dighlio, C. "Condizione della donna del lavoro subordinato in Francia e in Italia". 36 *Diritto e Giurisprudencia,* (Ita) 1-

Donne e diritto.—Milano, Gulliver, 1978.

Faccio, Adele. *Le mie ragioni: conversazioni con 70 donne.* Milano, Feltrinelli, 1975.

Frey, Luigi. *Occupazione e sottoccupazione femminile in Italia.* Milano: F. Angeli, 1976.

Gaiotti de Biase, Paola. *Sulla questione femminile.* Roma, Cedis, 1978.

Giampietro, F. "Tutela delle lavoratrici-madri e adozione speciale". 98 *Foro Italiano* (Ita) 85-97, 1975.

I movimenti femministi in Italia. Rosabla Spagnoletti, comp. La Nuova Sinistra, Roma, 1972?

Lavoro femminile e minorile, adolescenti, apprendiste, donne, lavoratrice spose, lavoratrici madri. Legislazione vigente, giurisprudenza circolari ministeriali. Falcucci, Giancarlo, comp., Milano: L. di G. Pirola, 1972.

Mori, Anna Maria. *Il silenzio donne e il caso Moro.* Cosenza, Lerici, 1978.

Padoa Schioppa, Fiorella. *La forza lavoro femminile.* Bologna, Il Mulino, 1977.

Pera, G. et al. "Procedimiento sommario a tutela della parita della lavoratrice". 100 *Foro Italiano* (Ita) 326-339, 1977.

Perlingieri, P. "Riflessione sull" "unita della famiglia". 26 *Diritto e giurisprudenza* (Ita) 7- , 1970.

Pessi, R. "Orientamenti legislativi per la tutela del lavoro femminile." 125 *Giurisprudenza Italiana* (Ita) 199-224, 1973.

Piepoli, G. "Realtà sociale e modello normativo nella tutela della famiglia di fatto". 26 *Rivista trimestrale di diritto e procedura civile* (Ita) 1433-1456, 1972.

Pieroni Bortolotti, Franca. *Socialismo e questione femminile in Italia*. Milano, G. Mazzotta, 1974.

Pistoso, Giuliana, *Donne*. Firenze, Nardini editore- Centro internationale del libro, 1973.

Pompei, A. "Parità fra uomini e donne nel mondo del lavoro". 18 *Rivista di Diritto Internazionale Privato e Processuale* (Ita) 201-210, 1978.

Ricciardi- Ruocco, Maria. *La donna fra utopia e realtà: educazione e vita femminile*. Firenze: Bulgarini, 1974.

Sabattini, Gianfranco. *L'occupazione femminile, Il caso Sardegna*, Milano, F. Angeli, 1979.

Sepe, O. "Considerazione sulla posizione della donna nell'administrazione statale in Italia". 25 *Rivista Trimestrale di Diritto Publico* (Ita) 2077-2111, 1975.

Tiso, Aida. *I communisti e la questione femminile*. Roma, Editori Riuniti, 1976.

Treu, T. "Lavoro femminile e principio di uguaglianza". 31 *Rivista Trimestrale di Diritto e Procedura Civile* (Ita), 1-73, 1977.

Vidiri, G. "Sul divieto di licenziamento delle lavoratrici che contraggono matrimonio, gestanti e puerpere". 31 *Diritto e Giurisprudenza* (Ita) 321-332, 1975.

Zaccaria, Roberto. *Emancipazione femminile e Constituzione*. Firenze, Palazzo Medici Riccardi, 1971.

Zatti, P. "Diritto di famiglia nei progetti de riforma". *Rivista di diritto civile*, (Ita) 365- , 1970. 16 (II).

LUXEMBOURG

Books and articles in other languages

Goerens, F. "Condition politique et sociale de la femme au grand-duché de Luxembourg". 28 *Revue Juridique et Politique, Indépendence et Coopération*, (Fra) 1257-1263, 1974.

NETHERLANDS

A) Books and articles in English

Haardt, W.L. "Changes in Dutch family law". 108 *Tidskrift, utgiven av juridiska foreningen* (Fin) 425-436, 1972.

B) Books and articles in other languages

Angenent, H. "I winkeldiefstal een vrouwendelict?" 11 *Delikt en Delinkwent*

(Voortzetting van het Tijschrift voor Strafrecht) (Net) 337-344, 1981.

Angenent, H. "Winkeldiefstal door vrouwen". 11 *Delikt en Delinkwent* (Voortzetting van het tijdschrift voor Strafrecht) (Net) 441-445, 1981.

Bergamin, R.J.B. & A.M. Gerritsma. "Wet ter bestrijding van discriminatie wegens sexe of huwelijkse staat?" 52 *Neon Dikaion* (Gre) 473-478, 1977.

Brenninkmeijer, A.F.M. "Onglijke behandeling van vrouwen en mannen in de AAw". 56 *Nederlands Juristenblad,* (Net) 613-620, 1981.

Commissie opvoering Produktiviteit van de Sociaal- Economische Raad. *Het bedrif en de Werkende gehuwde vrow.* Verslag van een anderzoek uitgevoerd door het Gemeenschappelick Instituut voor Toegepacte Psychologie, Afdeling Research, 1968.

Drion, H. "Een parlementaire enquete over discriminatie van de vrouw?" 30 *Socialisme en démocratie,* (Net) 448-452, 1973.

Jaeger de, D.M. "Vrouw in het arbeidsproces: een aparte situatie". 42 *Rechtskundig Weekblad,* (Bel) 1329-1360, 1979.

Klasse en emancipatie. Nijmegen, Sociologisch Instituut, Katholieke Universiteit, 1972?

Leydesdorff, Selma. *Verborgen arbeid, vergeten arbeid: een verkenning in de geschiedenis van de vrouwenarbeid rond negentienhonderd.* Assen: Van Gorcum, 1977.

Maarseven, van H. "Wrouw en Recht", 55 *Netherland Juristenblad,* (Net) 1170-1182, 1980.

Pessers, J.M. "Congres Vrouw en Recht". 55 *Nederlands Juristenblad* (Net) 1182-1185, 1980.

Schoonenboom, I.J. *De emancipatie van de vrouw.* Gravenhage, Staatsuit geverij, 1976.

Sloot, B.B. "Officiële vitsluiting van vrouwen in juridische beroepen". 55 *Nederlands Juristenblad, (Net)* 1186-1195, 1980.

Tan, M.L. "Namenrecht in het licht van de emancipatie van de vrouw". 50 *Nederlands Juristenblad,* (Net) 108-112, 1975.

Tromp, Ferry. *Een vrouw als jij.* Leiden, Meander, 1979.

Van binnen uit: vrouwen over welzijnswerk en zelforganisatie. Femsoc Schrijfcollectief Vlijtig Liesje. Amsterdam: Feministische Uitgeverij Sara, 1978.

Vrowenarbeid: bevrijdend of onderdrukkend? Amsterdam: Stichting Vorming en Scholing PSP, 1978.

Westerhoek, Coby, *Vrouwen en maatschappelijk werk.* Amsterdam: Feministische Uitgeverij Sara, 1978.

NORWAY

A) Books and articles in English

Heffemehl, Karin Bruzelius. "The status of women in Norway". 20 *American Journal of Comparative Law,* 630-646, 1972.

Means, Ingunn Norderval. "Political recruitment of women in Norway". 25 *Western Political Quarterly*, 491-521, 1972.

Vangsnes, Kari. "Equal pay in Norway". 103 *International Labour Review*, (Swi) 379-392, 1971.

B) Books and articles in other languages

Boe, E. "Nye sider ved markedsforing slovens $1 kjonnsdiskriminerende reklame". 49 *Nordisk Immateriell Rättsskydd* (Swe) 306-324, 1980.

Bratelli, Randi. *Veien de gikk*. Oslo: Tiden, 1978.

Evju, S. "Retten til á amme". *Lovog Rett, Norsk Juridisk Tidsskrift* (Nor) 423-428, 1975.

Halsaa Albrektsen, Beatrice. *Kvinner og politisk deltakelse*. Oslo, Pax, 1977.

Kvinnens lille røde Red. Komité: Berit Ås, Oslo, Gyldendal, 1971.

Skogheim, Dag. *Kvinner i nordnorsk arbeiderbevegelse*. Oslo, Tiden, 1978.

Wiborg, Ingrid Segerstedt. *Kvinnorna i Nordiska rådet*. Stockholm, LiberFörlag, 1978.

POLAND

A) Books and articles in English

Lewicka Halina. "The professional woman in modern Poland". 25 *Impact of Science on Society*, (Fra) 155-158, 1975.

Sokolowska, Magdalena. "All or nothing". *World Health*, (Swi) 26-29, 1975.

Wrochno, Krystyna. *Women in Poland*. Warsaw: Interpress Publishers, 1969.

B) Books and articles in other languages

Eberhardt, K.H. "Role of socialist law in the endeavor for the full liberation of women" [in Polish]. 31 *Nowe Prawo*, (Pol) 97-105, 1975.

Gwiazdomorski, J. "Die Verfassungsrechtliche Grundlagen und die leitenden Grudsätze des neuen polnischen Familiengesetzbuches". 17 *Osteuropa-Recht*, (Ger) 89-102, 1971.

Korecki, J. "Further step towards making punishment of imprisonment of women fit the individual woman" [in Polish]. 32 *Nowe Prawo* (Pol) 407-413, 1976.

Korolec, R. "Intensified protection of working women" [In Polish, Summ. in English]. 28 *Pánstwo i Prawo*, (Pol) 37-51, 1973.

Kukolowiczowa, Teresa. "Loisir de la femme mariée, ses activités professionelle et ses devoirs de famille". 3 *Slaskie studia historycznoteologiczne*, (Pol) 105-119, 1973.

Palecki, Krysztof. "Spoleczny i ustawowy wzorzec wybranych stosunków majatkowych w rodzinie". 27 *Pánstwo i prawo*, (Pol) 57-69, 1972.

Proba oceny ekonomicznej efektywnósci prácy zawodowej kobiet. 28 *Gospodarke planowa*, (Pol) 756-761, 1973.

PORTUGAL

Compiled by Maria Regina Tavares da Silva

ALMEIDA, Jayme d' - *A Questão Feminista (esboço crítico).* Porto, Livraria Portuguesa Editora, 1909 - ("The Feminist Question")

ALVES, Maria Clara Correia - *Féminisme (Toujours et encore).* Lisboa, Imp. Manuel Lucas Torres, s.d.

ANTUNES, Albertino; AMORIM, Lolanda - *Guia Jurídico da Mulher.* Lisboa, Edicão Heptágono Estudos e Publicaçoes SCARL, (s.d.) - ("Woman's Legal Guide")

BARRENO, Maria Isabel; HORTA, Maria Teresa; COSTA, Maria Velho da - *Novas Cartas Portuguesas.* Lisboa, Estúdio Cor, 1972 - ("New Portuguese Letters")

BARROS, Teresa Leitão de - *Escritoras de Portugal.* 2 vol. Lisboa, Tip. Artur, Imp. Lucas e Pap. Fernandes, 1924 - ("Women Writers of Portugal")

BELEZA, Maria Leonor - "A Reforma do Código Civil e a situação legal das mulheres" in *Boletim da Comissão da Condição Feminina.* Lisboa (10) 1980. ("The Reform of the Civil Code and the situation of women")

BELEZA, Maria Leonor - "Os Efeitos do Casamento" in *Reforma do Código Civil.* Lisboa, Ordem dos Advogados, 1981.- ("Effects of Marriage")

BELEZA, Maria Leonor - "O Estatuto das Mulheres na Constituição" in *Estudos sobre a Constituição.* Lisboa, Livraria Petrony, 1977. - ("The Status of Women in the Constitution")

BRAZÃO, Arnaldo - *O primeiro Congresso Feminista e de educação"* Lisboa, Ediçoes Spartacus, 1925.- ("The First Feminist Convention")

CAIEL - *Comentários à vida.* Lisboa António Maria Pereira, 1900.- ("Comments on Life")

CAIEL - *La femme et la paix. Appel aux mères portugaises.* Lisboa, Imprensa Nacional, 1898.

CARVALHO, Maria Amália Vaz de - *As nossas filhas. Cartas às mães.* Lisboa, António Maria Pereira, 1904. ("Our daughters. Letters to mothers").

CASTRO E GOUVEIA, Aurora de - *Reivindicaçoes sociais e politicas da mulher portuguesa na Republica.* Lisboa, Tipografia da Cooperativa Militar, 1921. ("Social and political demands of portuguese women in the Republic")

CASTRO E GOUVEIA, Aurora de - *I Reivindicações políticas da mulher portuguesa. II Situação da mulher casada nas relaçoes matrimoniais dos bens do casal.* Lisboa, Tip. da Casa Garret, 1924. - ("Political demands of portuguese women" and "The situation of married women in what regards common property in marriage")

COELHO, Mariana - *Evolução do Feminismo: Subsídios para a sua história.* Rio de Janeiro, Imprensa Moderna, 1933. ("Evolution of Feminism")

COSTA, D. António da - *A Mulher em Portugal* - Lisboa, Typ. de Companhia Nacional Editora, 1892- ("Woman in Portugal")

COSTA, Emilia de Sousa - *A Mulher. Educação Infantil.* Rio de Janeiro, Tip. do Anuário de Brasil, 1923.- ("Woman" and "Children's Education")

COSTA, Emilia de Sousa - *Olha a maldade e a malicia das Mulheres* - Lisboa-Empresa do Anuário Comercial, 1932. ("See the wrongs and malice of women")

COSTA, Emilio - *As Mulheres e o Feminismo* - Lisboa, Tip. da Seara Nova, 1929.- ("Women and Feminism")

DUARTE, Innocêncio de Sousa - *A Mulher na Sociedade Civil: compêndio dos seus direitos, obrigações e privilégios segundo as leis em Portugal.* Lisboa, Imprensa Nacional, 1870. - ("Woman in civil society: a compilation of her rights, duties and privileges according to portuguese laws")

GERSÃO, Eliana - "A igualdade juridica dos cônjuges a propósito do Projecto do Código Civil" in *Revista de Direito e de Estudos Sociais.* Coimbra 13 (1-2) 1966.

GONÇALVES, Ruy - *Dos privilégios & prerrogativas q̃ ho genero feminino tẽ por dereito comu & ordenações do Reyno mais q̃ ho genero masculino.* s.l., Joannes Barrerius, 1557 ("Of the privileges and prerrogatives that women have by common law and regulations of the Kingdom more than men")

GUIMARAÉS, Elina - *Coisas de Mulheres.* Porto, Editorial Promoção, 1975.- ("Women's things")

GUIMARAÉS, Elina - *A Lei em que vivemos (Noções de direito usual relativo à vida feminina).* Lisboa, Editorial O Século, 1936 ("The Law in which we live")

GUIMARAÉS, Elina - *Femmes Portugaises: hier et aujour'dui.* (Lisboa), Comissão da Condição Feminina, 1978.

GUIMARAÉS, Elina - *O Poder Maternal.* Lisboa, Livraria Morais, 1933- ("The Power of the Mother")

GUIMARAÉS, Elina; **KOKL,** Marcelle - *La condition de la Femme au Portugal.-* Paris, Librairie du Recueil Sirey, 1938.

LAMAS, Maria - *A Mulher no Mundo* - 2 vol. Lisboa, Livraria Editora da Casa do Estudante do Brasil, 1952.- ("Women in the World")

LAMAS, Maria - *As Mulheres do meu país.* Lisboa, Actualis Ltd., 1948.- ("Women of my country")

LOPES, Laura - *A mulher, a família e a lei.* Lisboa, Seara Nova, 1977.- ("Women, family and law")

MELLO, Carlos de - *O Escândalo do Feminismo.* Lisboa, A Editora, 1910. - ("The Scandal of Feminism")

MIGUEL, Angela - *A Mulher na sociedade contemporâneai cielo de cológuios organizado pela Secão cultural da Associaçao Académica da Faculdade de Direito de Lisboa.* Lisboa, Prelo, 1969.

MIRANDA, Jorge- *A igualdade de sufrágio político da Mulher.* Braga, Livraria Cruz, 1970.- ("Equality for women in political suffrage")

MOURA, Carneiro de - *A Mulher e a Civilização: estudo historico, economico* e jurídico da evoluçao parallela dos sexos. Lisboa, Companhia Nacional Editora, 1900.

A Mulher na sociedade contemporânea. Lisboa, Prelo, 1969. - ("Woman in Contemporary Society")

NEVES, Helena - O problema feminino e a questão social. Lisboa, Prelo, 1973. - ("The feminine problem and the social question")

OLIM, Ivone & MARQUES, Margarida - Luta de Mulheres pelo Voto. Lisboa, Editora das Mulheres, 1979.- ("Women's struggle for the right to vote")

OSÓRIO, Ana de Castro - A educação civica da mulher. Lisboa, Grupo Português de Estudos Feministas, 1908. - ("Civic education of women")

OSÓRIO, Ana de Castro - A Mulher no casamento e no divórcio. Lisboa, Guimarães e Ca., 1911.- ("Woman in marriage and divorce")

OSÓRIO, Ana de Castro - As Mulheres Portuguesas. Lisboa, Livraria Editora Viúva Tavares Cardoso, 1905.- ("Address to Portuguese Women")

PEREIRA, João Manuel Esteves - O Feminismo na Indústria Portugueza. Lisboa, Secção Editorial da Companhia Nacional Editora, 1897.- ("Feminism in Portuguese Industry")

PORTUGAL - Comissão da Condição Feminina - Discriminações contra a Mulher no Direito de Familia. Lisboa, Comissão da Condição Feminina, 1976.- ("Discriminations against Women in Family Law")

PORTUGAL - Comissão da Condição Feminina - Participação das Mulheres na vida sindical, civica e política. Lisboa, Comissão da Condição Feminina, 1976.- ("The participation of women in civic and political life and in trade unions")

PRAÇA, José Joaquim Lopes - A Mulher e a vida ou a Mulher considerada debaixo dos seus principais aspectos. Coimbra, Imprensa da Universidade, 1872. - ("Women and Life")

SALGADO, Abilio José - A situação da mulher na sociedade portuguesa actual. Lisboa, Iniciativas Editoriais, 1978.

SANCHES de FRIAS, David Correia - A Mulher, sua infância, educação e influência na sociedade. Pará, Tavares Cardoso e Ca., 1880.- ("Woman—her childhood, education and influence in society")

SILVA, Maria Regina Tavares da - Feminismo em Portugal na voz de mulheres escritoras no inicio do sec. XX (paper presented to the Conference "The Formation of Contemporary Portugal" in December 1981) - to be published shortly.- ("Feminism in Portugal in the voice of women-writers of the beginning of the XX century")

SILVA, Maria Regina Tavares da - "Mulheres Portuguesas - Vidas e obras celebradas e vidas e obras ignoradas: alguns marcos importantes para o estudo da História da Mulher em Portugal" in Boletim da Comissão da Condição Feminina. Lisboa, 7(4) 1981. - ("Some important sources for the study of the History of Women in Portugal")

SILVEIRA, Olga Moraes Sarmento da - Problema Feminista. Lisboa, Typographia de Francisco Luiz Conçalves, 1906.- ("Feminist problem")

SOUSA, Mide C.H. de C. - Condicão feminina. 25 Scientia Juridica, Rivista Bimestral Portuguesa e Brasileira 344- ,

Tractado sobre a Igualdade dos sexos ou Elogio do Merecimento das Mulheres, offerecido e dedicado ás Senhoras Illustres de Portugal por hum amigo da razão. Lisboa, Offic. Patriarch. de Francisco Luiz Ameno, 1790.- ("Treaty on Sex Equality or the Praise of Women's Merit")

VASCONCELLOS, Carolina Michelis de - "O Movimento Feminista em Portugal" in *O Primeiro de Janeiro.* Lisboa, 11, 12, 13, 14, 16 & 18 Setembro 1902.- ("The Feminist Movement in Portugal")

VIEGAS, Lia - *A Constituição e a Condição da Mulher.* Lisboa, Diabril, 1977.- ("The Constitution and the Status of Women")

Selected Periodicals

Voz Feminina. Lisboa, 1868
- ("Feminine Voice")
Progresso. Lisboa, 1869
- ("Progress")
A Mulher e a Criança. Lisboa, 1909
Prop.—Liga Republicana das Mulheres Portuguesas
- ("Woman and Child")
A Madrugada. Lisboa, 1911
Prop.—Liga Republicana d-s Mulheres Portuguesas
- ("Dawn")
A Mulher Portuguesa. Lisboa, 1912
Prop.—Associação de Propaganda Feminista
-("The Portuguese Woman")
Boletim do Conselho Nacional das Mulheres Portuguesas. Lisboa, 1914
Prop.—Conselho Nacional das Mulheres Portuguesas
-("Bulletin of the National Council of Portuguese Women")
Alma Feminina. Lisboa, 1917
Prop.—Conselho Nacional das Mulheres Portuguesas
-("Feminine Soul")
Portugal Feminino. Lisboa, 1930
- ("Feminine Portugal")
Mulher, modas e bordados. Lisboa, 1975
- ("Woman, fashion and embroidery"—formerly "Modas e Bordados")
Boletim da Comissão da Condição Feminina. Lisboa, 1975
Prop.—Comissão da Condição Feminina
-("Bulletin of the National Commission on the Status of Women")
Mulheres. Lisboa, 1978
- ("Women")
Lua, revista feminista - Boletim do IDM. Lisboa, 1980
Prop.—Informação, Documentação Mulheres
- ("Moon, feminist magazine - IDM Bulletin")

ROMANIA

Books and articles in other languages

Cădere, Victor G. *L' économie planifiée et la famille en droit socialiste roumain.* Paris, Presses Universitaires de France, 1972.

Dan- Spânoiu, Georgeta. *Factori objectivi si subjectivi în integrarea profesională a femeii.* Bucureşti, Editura Academiei, 1974.

Deliman, Ecaterina. *Femeia, personalitate politică in societatea noastra socialistă* Bucureşti, Editura Politică, 1977.

Dumitrescu, Clara & Stella Fomino. *Activitatea comisiilor femeilor din întrepreinderi si institutii.* Bucureşti, Editura Politică, 1974.

Eminescu, Y. & M. Strãonu. "Condition de la femme en Roumanie et les objectifs de l' Année Internationale de la Femme." 19 *Revue Roumaine de Sciences Sociales, Série de Sciences Juridiques,* (Rou) 137-151, 1975.

Florescu, M. "Propuneri privindîmbunătătirea statutului social-juridic al femeii încadrate în muncă". 21 *Studii si Cercetări Juridice,* (Rou) 259-266, 1976.

Florescu, M. "Protection de la femme dans le droit du travail de la République Socialiste de Roumaine". 17 *Revue Roumaine des Sciences Sociales; série de Sciences Juridiques,* (Rou) 47-54, 1973.

Georgescu Elena and Jitu Georgescu. *Miscarea democratică si revolutionară a femeilor din România/* Craiova, Scrisul Românesc, 1975.

Ocretirea, Minorilor. "Copil aflat in plasament familial. Dreptul femeii încadrate in muncă la concediu plătit in cazul îmbolnăvirii acestuia (Jud. Drobeta Turnu Severin, sent. civ. nr. 6050/ 1980, cu nota de Cecilia Ciocoiu si Sever Ciocoiu)". 37 *Revista Română de Drept,* (Rou) 36- , 1981.

Perfectionarea regimului de ocrotire al minorilor prin modificarea unor texte din Codul familiei. 18 *Studii si cercetári juridice,* (Rou) 125- , 1973.

Rolul femeii in viata economică, politică si socială a României socialiste. Bucureşti, Editura politică, 1973.

Statutul Social al femeilor Salariate. Referate si Comunicări prezentate la Simpozionul. "Statutul Social al femeilor Salariate din Republica Socialista România si Contributia lor la operate edificare a Socialismului", organizat de Uniunea Generală a Sindicatelor din România în Colaborare cu Consiliul National al Femeilor. Iulie 1969. Bucureşti, Editura Politică, 1971.

SPAIN

A) Books and articles in English

Commission of the European Communities. *Women of Europe: Women in Spain.* (Suppl. No. 8). Brussels, Commission of the European Communities, 1981.

Jimenez Butrageno, María de los Angeles. "Protective legislation and equal opportunity treatment for women in Spain". 121 *International Labour Re-*

view, (Swi) 185-198, 1982.

Organization for Economic Cooperation. High Level Conference on Women's Employment. *The Integration of Spanish Women into the World of Work.* National Report Spain. Paris, Organization for Economic Cooperation and Development, 1980.

B) Books and articles in other languages

Arenal de García Carrasco, Concepción. *1820-1893. La emancipación de la mujer en España*. Madrid, Jucar, 1974.

Asociación Española de Mujeres Juristas. *Derechos que no tiene la mujer.* Madrid. Editorial Reus, (Real Sociedad Economica Matritense de Amigos del País. Publicaciones), 1973.

Capel, Rosa María. *El sufragio femenino en la 2a república española.* Granada, Universidad de Granada, 1975.

Carrasco Belinchón, Julia. *Presencia y ausencia de la mujer en la vida local española: análisis de su problemática, según el pensamiento de 694 mujeres y 262 hombres.* Madrid: Instituto de Estudios de Administración Local, 1975.

Casten-Vazquez, J.M. & M. Luz Albacar. "Nouveau statut juridique de la femme marieé en droit espagnol selon la loi du Mai 1975". 28 *Revue Internationale de Droit Comparé* (Fra) 793-798, 1976.

Congreso Internacional de la Mujer, Madrid, 1970. *Congreso Internacional de la mujer*, Madrid, 7 al 14 de Junio de 1970. Memoria. Madrid, Almena, 1972.

Derechos que no tine la mujer, por la Asociación Española de Mujeres Juristas. Madrid: Editorial Reus, 1973.

Dominquez, Lalaguna E. "Nulidad del matrimonio después de la constitución". 79 *Revista General de Legislación y Jurisprudencia*, (Spa) 3-24, 1979 and 177-230, 1979.

Durán, Maria Angeles. *El trabajo de la mujer en España, un estudio sociológico.* Madrid, Editorial Tecnos, 1972.

García Mendez, E. *La actuación de la mujer en las Cortes de la Segunda República.* Madrid, Ministerio de Cultura, 1979.

Gonzalez, Anabel. *El Feminismo en España hoy: Apéndices, bibliografía completa y documentos.* Madrid, Distribuidor Exclusivo, ZYX, 1979.

Maria Luz del Socorro, Mother. *Mujer, liberación y destino: un nuevo enfoque sobre la liberación femenina.* Madrid, Studium, 1974.

Miguel, Amando de. *El miedo a la igualdad: Varones y mujeres en una sociedad machista.* Barcelona, ediciones Grijalbo, 1975.

Miguel, Amando de. *Sexo, mujer y natalidad en España.* Madrid, Edicusa, 1974.

Mitchell, Juliet. *La liberación de la mujer: la larga lucha.* Barcelona, Editorial Anagrama, 1975, c. 1966.

Morenilla- Rodríguez, J.M. "Igualdad Jurídica de la mujer en España: 1975-1980." 81 *Revista General de Legislación y Jurisprudencia*, (Spa) 443-458, 1980.

Mujer y entorno social. Madrid, Fundación General Mediterránea, Patronato José Ferrer, 1976?

Mujer y trabajo. Jornadas sindicales nacionales: ponencias y conclusiones. Madrid, Organización Sindical, Consejo Nacional de Trabajores, 1975 ?

López, Marín A. "Nacionalidad de la mujer casada en derecho español". 29 *Revista Española de Derecho Internacional*, (Spa) 397-417, 1976.

Peña, María del Pilar de la. *La condición jurídica y social de la mujer.* Madrid, Editorial Cuadernos para el Diálogo, 1974.

Ramirez López, José Antonio. *Cartas de un abogado a las mujeres de España.* Navarra, Slavat, 1973.

Rico-Perez, F. "Nouveaux droits de la femme et de la famille en Espagne". 102 *Foro Italiano*, (Ita) 94-100, 1979.

Sau, Victoria. *Manifiesto para la liberación de la mujer.* Barcelona, Editorial Bruguera, 1975.

Scanlon, Geraldine. *La Polémica Feminista en la España Contemporánea, (1868-1974).* Madrid, Siglo Veintiuno de España Editores, S.A., 1976.

SWEDEN

A) Books and articles in English

The Changing roles of men and women. Ed. by Edmund Dahlström. Trans. by Gunilla and Steven Anderman. Boston, Beacon Press, 1971.

Haavio-Manila, Elina. "Convergences between East and West; tradition and modernity in sex roles in Sweden, Finland and the Soviet Union". 14 *Acta Sociologica*, (Nor) 114-125, 1971.

Herman, Sondra R. The liberated women of Sweden. 7 Center for the study of Democratic Institutions magazine, 76-78, 1974.

Linnér, Birgitta. "Status of Women in Sweden". 8 *Columbia Human Rights Law Review*, 263-294, 1976.

Sandberg, Elisabeth. *Equality is the goal: a Swedish report:* International Women's year, 1975. Advisory Council to the Prime Minister on Equality between Men and Women. Stockholm: Swedish Institute, 1975.

Scott, Hilda. *Sweden's right to be human sex role equality: the goal and the reality.* Armonk, N.Y., M.E. Sharpe, 1982.

Wallin, Gunvor. "The status of women in Sweden". 20 *American Journal of Comparative Law*, 622-629, 1972.

Woman in Sweden in the light of Statistics. Stockholm, Arbetsmarknadens kvinnonamnd, 1973.

B) Books and articles in other languages

Kellgren, Ragna. (comp). Kvinnor i politiken. Artiklar ur den politiska, radikala veckotidningen Tidevarvet (1923-1936) i urval av Ragna Kellgren. Stockholm,

LT: (Solna, Seelig), 1971.

Kvinnan i politiken. Hedvall, Barbro, ed. Stockholm, Trevi, Solna: Seeling, 1975.

Östnäs, Anna. *Bostadsplaneringen och kvinnornas politiska representation.* Göteborg, Institutionen, 1971.

Widerberg, Karin. *Kvinnor klasse och lagar, 1750-1980.* Stockholm: Liber Forlag, 1980.

SWITZERLAND

A) Books and articles in English

Thalmann-Antenen, Helene. "Equal pay; the position in Switzerland". 104 *International Labour Review,* (Swi) 275-288, 1971.

B) Books and articles in other languages

Bernard, Jean François. *Le problème de l'égalité des salaires masculins et feminins en Suisse.* Fribourg, Office Multigraphe Renggli, 1971.

Bigler-Eggenberger, Margrith. *Sociale Sicherung der Frau.* Bern, Verlag Peter Lang, 1979.

Bührig, Marga. *Die Frau in der Schweiz.* Bern, Haupt, 1969.

Geser, Guido. *Die Frau als Vorgesetzte; eine Untersuchung der die Karriere weblicher Personen beeinflussenden Faktoren.* Zurich, Schulthess Polygraphischer Verlag, 1973.

Haller-Zimmermann, Margareta. *Die UNO -Menschenrechtskonventionen und die rechtliche Stellung der Frau in der Schweiz.* Zurich, Schulthess Polygraphischer, 1973.

Held, Thomas and Rene, Levy. *Die Stellung der Frau in Familie und Gesellschaft/Eine Soziologische Analyse am Beispiel der Schweiz.* Frauenfeld, Stuttgart, Huber, 1974.

Institut für Meinungsforschung AG. *Frauen in der Politik.* Baden-Verlag, Buchdruckerei AG, Baden, 1975.

Krähenbühl, Hans-Ulrich. "Diskrimierung der Frauenarbeit in der Schweitz." 41 *Industrielle Organisation,* 37-42, 1972.

Ligue Marxiste révolutionnaire. *Femmes: de l' oppression à la révolution.* Lausanne: CEDIPS, 1975.

Ligue Marxiste révolutionnaire. *Opprimées, exploitées, licenciées: Les femmes luttent pour leur liberation.* Lausanne: CEDIPS, 1975.

Mirocha, L. Gleichberechtigung der Geschlechter und personenrechtliche Wirkungen der Ehe. 73 *Schweizerische Juristen- Zeitung* (Swi) 213-221, 1977.

Ries-Schlapfer, Marie Louise. *Die zweite Berufswahl der Frau: 100 neue Berufe und Betätigungsfelder für Frauen über dreissig.* Zurich: Benziger, 1974.

Wassner-Blum, Gaby-Sofie. *Die Mitarbeit der Ehefrau in Deutschland, Frank-*

reich und der Schweiz: Eherecht, Steuerucht, Socialrecht, Bern: Herbert Lang, 1976.

Woodtli, Susanna. Gleichberechtigung: der Kampf um die politischen Rechte der Frau in der Schweiz. Frauenfeld, Huber, 1975.

TURKEY

A) Books and articles in English

Abadan-Unat, Nermin. "Women in Government as Policy-makers and Bureaucrats: The Turkish case". In: Women, Power and Political Systems. Ed. by Margherita Rendel. New York, St. Martin's Press, Inc., c. 1981.

Inan, Afet. The emancipation of the Turkish Woman. Paris, UNESCO, 1962.

Taskiran, Tezer. Women in Turkey. Translated by Nida Tekta's, edited by Anna G. Edmonds. Istanbul, Redhouse Yayineri, 1976.

B) Books and articles in other languages

Afetinan, A. Atatürk ve Turk kadin haklarinin kazanilmasi; tarih boyunen Türk Kadininin hak ve görevleri, yazan. Istanbul, M.E.B., Devlet Kitaplari Müdürlügü, 1968.

Fisek, S. "Aperçu de la situation juridique et sociale de la femme en Turquie. 28 Revue Juridique et Politique, Indépendence et Coopération (Fra) 1306-1314, 1974.

Uctum, N.R. "Evolução da muhler na Turquia". 21 Scientia juridica, revista bi-mestral portuguesa e brasileira (Por) 121- , 1972.

UNITED KINGDOM

A) Books and articles in English

Adam, Ruth. A Woman's place, 1910-1975. London, Chatto & Windus, 1975.

Anden, Andrew. "Cohabitation and the Housing Act 1980". 131 New Law Journal, (U.K.) 165-166, 1981.

Barr, N.A. "Taxation of Married Women's Incomes. British Tax Review (UK), 398-412, 1980.

Bates, Frank. "Duress as Grounds for Nullity: a new perspective". 130 New Law Journal, (U.K.) 1035-1036, 1980.

Berkovits, Bernard. "The Matrimonial Home Yet Again". 43 Modern Law Review, (U.K.) 225-228, 1980.

Boston, Sarah. Women Workers and the Trade Union Movement. London, Davis-Poynter, 1980.

Bouten, Jacob. Mary Wollstonecraft and the beginnings of female emancipation *in France and England.* Philadelphia, Pennsylvania, Porcupine Press, 1975.

Bowers, John and Andrew Clarke. "Four Years of the Equal Pay Act". 130 *New Law Journal,* (U.K.) 3048- , 1980.

Chiplin, Brian. *Sex Discrimination in the Labour Market.* London, Macmillan, 1976.

Coote, Anna. *Equal at work?: Women in men's jobs.* Glasgow, Collins, 1979.

Coussins, Jean. *The equality report: one year of the Equal Pay Act, the sex discrimination Act, The equal opportunities Commission.* London, National Council for Civil Liberties, Rights for Women Unit, 1976.

Creighton, William Breen. *Working Women and the law.* London, Mansell, 1979.

Crow, Duncan. *The Edwardian Woman.* London, Allen & Unwin, 1978.

Currell, Melville. *Political woman.* London, Groom Helm, 1974.

Davies, Ross. *Women and work.* London, Hutchinson, 1975.

Dyer, Barbara. *Implementing equal pay.* London, Industrial Society, 1976.

Fogarty, Michael Patrick. *Sex, career and family: Including an international review of women's roles.* London, Allen & Unwin, 1971.

Freeman, M.O.A. "Violence against women: Does the legal system provide solutions or itself constitute the problem?" 7 *British Journal of Law and Society* (U.K.) 215-241, 1980.

Freeman, Stephen. "Wives, conveyancers and justice: Notes and cases". 43 *Modern Law Review* (U.K.) 692-696, 1980.

Glover, Graham. "Matrimonial Home: Widow's claim or husband's intestacy." 10 *Family Law* (U.K.) 239- , 1980.

Great Britain. Central Office of Information. Reference Division. *Women in Britain.* London, H.M. Stationery Office, 1972.

Great Britain, Dept. of Employment. *Women and work: A statistical Survey.* London, H.M. Stationery Office, 1974.

Great Britain. Labour Party. Study Group on Discrimination Against Women. *Discrimination against women; report of a Labour party study group.* London, Labour Party, 1972.

Hays, Mary. *Appeal to the men of Great Britain on behalf of women.* New York, Garland Pub., 1974.

Hogrefe, Pearl. *Women of action in Tudor England: Nine bibliographical sketches.* Ames: Iowa State University Press, 1977.

Lang, Beverly. "Equal Pay, Job evaluation, & the EEC". *L.A.G. Bulletin,* (U.K.) 242-43, 1980.

Lang, Beverly. "Sex Discrimination: Application of the Act to Public Servants. 9 *Industrial Law Journal* (Canada) 118-120, 1980.

Larsen, C.A. "Equal pay for women in the United Kingdom". 103 *International Labour Review* (Swi) 1- , 1971.

Lasok, Dominik. *Equality of the sexes as a problem of law reform:* An inaugural lecture delivered in the University of Exeter on 14 February, 1969. England University of Exeter, 1979.

Luba, Jan. "Domestic Violence and the Housing Act of 1980". *L.A.G. Bulletin,* (U.K.) 82-87, 1981.

McCallum, I.M. and Snait, I. "EEC law and United Kingdom occupational pensions schemes". 2 *European Law Review,* (U.K.) 266- , 1977.

The measurement of sex and marital status- Discrimination at the workplace- 1981. 48 Economica (U.K.) 125-141, 1981.

Murphy, W.T. & R.W. Rawlings. "The matrimonial Homes (Co-Ownership) Bill: The right way forward?" 10 *Family Law* (U.K.) 136-140, 1980.

Pearson, Rose & Albie Sachs. "Barristers and Gentlemen: A Critical look at Sexism in the legal profession". 43 *Modern Law Review* (U.K.) 400-414, 1980.

Sachs, Albert L. and Joan Hoff Wilson. *Sexism and the law: A study of male beliefs and legal bias in Britain and the United States.* Oxford, England, J.M. Robertson, 1978.

Schofield, Peter. "Recent Cases: Equal Pay; Requirements of Community Law". 9 *Industrial Law Journal* (Canada) 173-177, 1980.

Scott, Kevin. "The domestic Violence and Matrimonial Proceedings Act of 1976". 4 *Trent Law Journal,* (U.K.) 29-35, 1980.

Sedley, Ann. "Discrimination round-up (British cases)". *L.A.G. Bulletin* (U.K.) 69-71, 1980.

Smith, R.J. "Overriding interests, wives, and the House of Lords". 97 *Law Quarterly Review* (U.K.) 12-15, 1981.

The sociology of law. Issue editor Pat Carlen; managing editors W.M. Williams and R.G. Frakenberg. [Keele, Eng], University of Keele, 1976.

Stapely, Sue. "Judicial Attitudes towards Domestic Violence". 10 *Kingston Law Review* (U.K.) 156-184, 1980.

Stassinopoulos, Arianna. *The female women.* London, Davis-Poynter, 1973.

Stobaugh, Beverly Parker. *Women and Parliament.* Hicksville, New York, Exposition Press, 1978.

Stone, Olive M. "The status of women in Great Britain." 20 *American Journal of Comparative Law* 592-621, 1972.

Sydenham, Colin. "Overreaching and the ratio of Boland's case". *Conveyancer and Property Lawyer* (Canada) 427-432, 1980.

Thompson, J.M. "Equal Pay & EEC Law". 97 *Law Quarterly Review* (U.K.) 5-7, 1981.

Thompson, J.M. "Dismissal for pregnancy, not sex discrimination". 96 *Law Quarterly Review* (U.K.) 330-331, 1980.

Thompson, J.M. "Sex Discrimination and Redundancy". 96 *Law Quarterly Review,* (U.K.) 488- , 1980.

Thompson, Roger. *Women in Stuart England and America.* London, England, Routlege and Kegan Paul, 1974.

Tiley, J. "Finance Act Notes: Widowhood Anomalies". *British Tax Review* (U.K.) 216-218, 1980.

Vallance, Elizabeth. "Equality for women; a note on the White paper." 46 *Political Quarterly* (U.K.) 201- , 1975.

Vallance, Elizabeth M. *Women in the House: A study of members of Parliament.* London: Athlone Press, Atlantic Highlands, 1979.

Women in the Labour movement: The British experience. Lucy Middleton, ed. London, Croom Helm, Totowa, N.J., Rowman and Littlefield, 1977.

Women in public: Documents of the Victorian women's movement, 1850-1900.
  Compiled by Patricia Hollis. London; Boston, G. Allen & Unwin, 1979.
The women of England: From Anglo-Saxon times to the present: Interpretive
  bibliographical essays. Barbara Kanner, ed. Hamden, Conn., Archon Books,
  1979.

B) Books and articles in other languages

Kerst, Henri. *La femme dans la société anglaise: Étude et témoignages*
  littéraires. Paris, Masson et Cie., 1971.
Martiny, D. "Gleichberechtigung im Arbeitsleben in Grossbritannien, [Summ.
  in English]. 42 *Rabels Zeitschrift fur Ausländisches und Internationales Pri-*
  vatrecht (Ger) 116-169, 1978.

U.S.S.R.

A) Books and articles in English

Berent, Jerzy. "Some demographic aspects of female employment in Eastern
  Europe and the USSR". 101 *International Labour Review* (Swi) 175-192,
  1970.
Chao, Paul. *Women under Communism: Family in Russia and China.* Bayside,
  New York, General Hall, 1977.
Conference on Women in Eastern Europe and the Soviet Union, University of
  Alberta, 1978. New York, N.Y., Prager Publishers, 1980.
Dodge, Norton T. *Women in the Soviet Economy, their role in economic, sci-*
  entific and technical development. Baltimore, Johns Hopkins Press, 1966.
Fidell, Linda S., comp. *Women in the professions: What's all the fuss about?*
  Ed. by Linda S. Fidell and John De Lamoter. Beverly Hills, California, Sage
  Publications, 1971.
Golugniuk, M.N. "Questions of prevention of crime by women". 19 *Law and*
  Government 41-53, 1980.
Haavio-Manila, Elina. "Convergences between East and West; tradition and
  modernity in sex roles in Sweden, Finland and the Soviet Union". 14 *Acta*
  Sociologica (Nor) 114-125, 1971.
Heitlinger, Alena. *Women and state socialism: Sex Inequality in the Soviet*
  Union and Czechoslovakia. London, England, Macmillan Press, 1979.
Kohn, Jeffrey. "The population policy of the Soviet Union: A study of working
  women and the birthrate. 15 *Industrial and Labor Relations* 3-26, 1981.
Kurganov, Ivan Alekseevich. *Women in the U.S.S.R.* Translated from Russian
  by R.R. Piontkovsky. London, Ont. S.B.O.N.R. Publishing House, 1971.
Lapidus, Gail Warshofsky. *Women in Soviet Society: Equality, Development*
  and Social Change. Los Angeles, University of California Press, 1978.
Mandel, William. *Soviet Women.* Garden City, N.Y., Anchor Books, 1975.

Nejinskaya, Larissa. "Women and work in the Soviet Union (from IADL Conference on Women- 1979)." 37 *National Lawyers Guild Practitioner* 32-, 1980.

Porter, Cathy. *Fathers and daughters: Russian Women in revolution.* London: Virago, Quartet Books, 1976.

The role and status of women in the Soviet Union. Ed. by Donald R. Brown. New York, Teachers College Press, 1968.

Sacks, Michael Paul. *Women's work in Soviet Russia: continuity in the midst of change:* New York, Praeger, 1976.

Salaff, Janet Weitzner and Judith Merkle. Women in revolution; the lessons of the Soviet Union and China. 15 *Berkeley Journal of Sociology* 166-191, 1970.

Schwartz, J.S. "Women under Socialism: role definitions of Soviet women". 58 *Social forces* 67-88, 1979.

Sheptulina, N. "Improving guarantees of women's labor rights under the conditions of developed socialist society". *Soviet Law and government* No. 3: 74-78, 1974-75.

Sheptulina, N. "USSR constitution and the further development of legislation on female labor". *Soviet law and government* No. 3: 36-43, 1980-81.

Soviet legislation on Women's Rights. Collection of Normative Acts. Belyakova, A.M., Beliayeva, Z.S., Sheptulina, N.N., and Tolkunova, V.N. comps. Moscow, Progress Publishers, 1978.

Stites, Richard. *The women's liberation movement in Russia: feminism, nihilism and bolshevism, 1860-1930.* Princeton, New Jersey, Princeton University Press, 1978.

Tatarinova, Nadezhda Ivanovna. *Women in the USSR: at home, at work, in society.* Moscow: Novosti Press Agency Pub. House, 1969 ?

Tay, A.E.S. "Status of women in the Soviet Union". 52 *Philippine Law Journal* (Phi) 123-153, 1977.

B) Books and articles in other languages

Abramova, Aleksandra Afanasévna. *Okhrana truda zhenshchin: Spravochnik po zakonodatel'stvu.* Moskva, Profizdat, 1972.

Aiueva, E.I. Ukreplenie zakonnosti v oblasti okhrany brachno- semeinykh otnoshenii. 41 *Sovetskoe gosudarstvo i pravo,* (USSR) 30- , 1971.

Aminova, R. Kh. Zhenshchiny Uzbekistana v avangarde stroitelei kommunizma. *Obshcestvennye nauki i Uzbekistane* (USSR) No.3: 3-8, 1974.

Belyakova, A.M. Zakonodatelstvo o pravach zhen zhenscin v SSSR. Sbornik normat. dktov. Moskva: Iurid. lit., 1975.

Belogorskaia, E.M. Osnovaniia vosnikoveniia roditel'skikh prav i obiazannostei. 26 *Vestnik Moskovskogo Universiteta,* seriia pravo (USSR) 23- , 1971.

Chumakova, Tamara Efimovna. Trud i byt zhenscin: Social pravovye aspekty. Nauc. red V.N. Artemova. Minsk: Nauka i technika, 1978.

Davydenko, H. "Prava zhinok za radianskym zakonodavstvom". *Radians'ke Pravo* (USSR) No. 3: 18-22, 1973.

Ermolenkova, T.D. "I'meneniia sotsial'nogo polozheniia zhenshchiny-krest'ianki v protsesse stroistel'stva sotsializma. *Vestnik Belorusskovo Universiteta;* ser-

iia 3, Istoria, filosofia, nauchnyi kommunizm, ekonomika, pravo (USSR) No. 1: 51-57, 1973.

Golodniuk, M.N. "Nekotorye voprosy zhenskoi prestupnosti" 33 *Vestnik Moskovskogo Universiteta, Seriia Pravo* (USSR) 23-30, 1978.

Iushina, L.N. "Marksizm-Leninizm o ravenstve i ravnopravii zhenshchin s muzhchinami v sfere obshchestvennoi organizatsii truda". 28 *Vestnik Moskovskogo Universiteta, Seriia Pravo* (USSR) 54- , 1973.

Korol, T. "Mistsevi Radyi pytannia pratsi ta pobuty Zhinok". *Radians'ke Pravo* (USSR) No. 10: 26-30, 1978.

Nabieva, Rohat. *Zhenshchiny Tadzhikistana v borbe za sotsializm.* Dushanbe, Efron, 1973.

Nazarenko, I.N. "Slavni dochky Radians'koi Bat'kivshchyny." *Radians'ke Pravo (USSR)* No. 3: 6-10, 1981.

Nikonchuck, I. "Rozhliad sudamy sprav pro rozirvannia shliubu". *Radians'ke Pravo* (USSR) No. 9: 40-44, 1979.

Pankin, N.E. *Lgoty rabochin i sluzhashchim.* 2nd ed. Moscow, Profizdat, 1979.

Pavshukova, O. Radians'ki zhinky-aktyvni budivnyky Komunistychnovo suspil'stva. *Radians'ke Pravo* (USSR) No. 3: 3-8, 1977.

Pavshukova, O. "Vilni rivnopravni radians'ki zhinkv—aktyvna tvorcha syla suspil'stva". *Radians'ke Pravo* (USSR) No.3: 3-7, 1975.

Remizova, E.V. "Nekotorye pravoye voprosy obespecheniia zhenskovo ravnopraviia v SSSR"/ 30 *Vestnik Moskovskovo Universiteta, Seriia Pravo* (USSR) 3-13, 1975.

Sheptulina, N.N. "Konstitutsiia SSSR i razvitie zakonodatelstva o trude zhenshchin [Summ. in English]". 48 *Sovetskoe Gosudarstvo i Pravo* (USSR) 27-31, 1978.

Shevchenko, V.S. "Nova Konstytutsia-Zhinkam krainy Rad". *Radians'ke Pravo* (USSR) No. 3: 3-12, 1978.

Starodub, Valentina Illarionovna. *Zhenschina: Obshchestvennyĭ trud.* Leningrad, Lenizdat, 1975.

Syvolob, V.I. "Radians'ki zhinky-aktivini uchasnytsi kommunistychnovo budivir.ytstva". *Radians'ke Pravo* (USSR) No. 3:3-7, 1979.

Vitruk, Liudmyla Dmytrivna. *ZHinky-trudivnystsi v period sotsialistychnoi industrializatsii: Na materialakh promyslovosti Ukrainskoi RSR.* Kyiv, Nauk. dumka, 1973.

YUGOSLAVIA

Books and articles in English

Alincic, Mira. "Law and the status of Women in Yugoslavia". 8 *Columbia Human Rights Law Review*, 345-371, 1976.

Chloros, A.G. *Yugoslav Civil Law: history, family, property.* Oxford, Clarendon Press, 1970.

Tomšič, Vida: *Woman in the Development of Socialist Self-managing Yugoslavia*. Belgrade: Yugoslovenska stvarmost, 1980. Original title: *Žena u razvoj u samoupravne Yugoslavije*.

Index